CW01064904

The Great Boer War

The Great Boer War
The Final Edition Covering the Entire Conflict 1899–1902

Arthur Conan Doyle

LEONAUR

*The Great Boer War: t he Final Edition Covering the
Entire Conflict 1899-1902*
by Arthur Conan Doyle

Leonaur is an imprint of Oakpast Ltd

Material original to this edition and
presentation of text in this form
copyright © 2010 Oakpast Ltd

ISBN: 978-0-85706-361-8 (hardcover)
ISBN: 978-0-85706-362-5 (softcover)

http://www.leonaur.com

Publisher's Notes

Contents

Preface to the Final Edition 7

The Boer Nations 9

The Cause of Quarrel 24

The Negotiations 36

The Eve of War 45

Talana Hill 60

Elandslaagte and Rietfontein 70

The Battle of Ladysmith 78

Lord Methuen's Advance 89

Battle of Magersfontein 104

The Battle of Stormberg 114

Battle of Colenso 120

The Dark Hour 134

The Siege of Ladysmith 141

The Colesberg Operations 158

Spion Kop 168

Vaalkranz 181

Buller's Final Advance 188

The Siege and Relief of Kimberley 202

Paardeberg 215

Roberts's Advance on Bloemfontein 231

Strategic Effects of Lord Roberts's March 238

The Halt at Bloemfontein 248

The Clearing of the South-East 261

The Siege of Mafeking 271

The March on Pretoria 284

Diamond Hill—Rundle's Operations 297

The Lines of Communication 306

The Halt at Pretoria 318

The Advance to Komatipoort   329
The Campaign of De Wet   342
The Guerilla Warfare in the Transvaal: Nooitgedacht   356
The Second Invasion of Cape Colony   373
The Northern Operations   386
The Winter Campaign   401
The Guerilla Operations in Cape Colony   418
The Spring Campaign   431
The Campaign of January to April, 1902   454
De La Rey's Campaign of 1902   467
The End   479
Appendix   485
Maps   491

Preface to the Final Edition

During the course of the war some sixteen Editions of this work have appeared, each of which was, I hope, a little more full and accurate than that which preceded it. I may fairly claim, however, that the absolute mistakes made have been few in number, and that I have never had occasion to reverse, and seldom to modify, the judgments which I have formed. In this final edition the early text has been carefully revised and all fresh available knowledge has been added within the limits of a single volume narrative. Of the various episodes in the latter half of the war it is impossible to say that the material is available for a complete and final chronicle. By the aid, however, of the official dispatches, of the newspapers, and of many private letters, I have done my best to give an intelligible and accurate account of the matter. The treatment may occasionally seem too brief but some proportion must be observed between the battles of 1899-1900 and the skirmishes of 1901-1902.

My private informants are so numerous that it would be hardly possible, even if it were desirable, that I should quote their names. Of the correspondents upon whose work I have drawn for my materials, I would acknowledge my obligations to Messrs. Burleigh, Nevinson, Battersby, Stuart, Amery, Atkins, Baillie, Kinneir, Churchill, James, Ralph, Barnes, Maxwell, Pearce, Hamilton, and others. Especially I would mention the gentleman who represented the 'Standard' in the last year of the war, whose accounts of Vlakfontein, Von Donop's Convoy, and Tweebosch were the only reliable ones which reached the public.

Arthur Conan Doyle
Undershaw
Hindhead
September 1902

CHAPTER 1
The Boer Nations

Take a community of Dutchmen of the type of those who defended themselves for fifty years against all the power of Spain at a time when Spain was the greatest power in the world. Intermix with them a strain of those inflexible French Huguenots who gave up home and fortune and left their country for ever at the time of the revocation of the Edict of Nantes. The product must obviously be one of the most rugged, virile, unconquerable races ever seen upon earth. Take this formidable people and train them for seven generations in constant warfare against savage men and ferocious beasts, in circumstances under which no weakling could survive, place them so that they acquire exceptional skill with weapons and in horsemanship, give them a country which is eminently suited to the tactics of the huntsman, the marksman, and the rider. Then, finally, put a finer temper upon their military qualities by a dour fatalistic Old Testament religion and an ardent and consuming patriotism. Combine all these qualities and all these impulses in one individual, and you have the modern Boer—the most formidable antagonist who ever crossed the path of Imperial Britain. Our military history has largely consisted in our conflicts with France, but Napoleon and all his veterans have never treated us so roughly as these hard-bitten farmers with their ancient theology and their inconveniently modern rifles.

Look at the map of South Africa, and there, in the very centre of the British possessions, like the stone in a peach, lies the great stretch of the two republics, a mighty domain for so small a people. How came they there? Who are these Teutonic folk who have burrowed so deeply into Africa? It is a twice-told tale, and yet it must be told once again if this story is to have even the most superficial of introductions. No one can know or appreciate the Boer who does not know his past, for he is what his past has made him.

It was about the time when Oliver Cromwell was at his zenith—in 1652, to be pedantically accurate—that the Dutch made their first lodgement at the Cape of Good Hope. The Portuguese had been there before them, but, repelled by the evil weather, and lured forwards by rumours of gold, they had passed the true seat of empire and had voyaged further to settle along the eastern coast. Some gold there was, but not much, and the Portuguese settlements have never been sources of wealth to the mother country, and never will be until the day when Great Britain signs her huge cheque for Delagoa Bay. The coast upon which they settled reeked with malaria. A hundred miles of poisonous marsh separated it from the healthy inland plateau. For centuries these pioneers of South African colonisation strove to obtain some further footing, but save along the courses of the rivers they made little progress. Fierce natives and an enervating climate barred their way.

But it was different with the Dutch. That very rudeness of climate which had so impressed the Portuguese adventurer was the source of their success. Cold and poverty and storm are the nurses of the qualities which make for empire. It is the men from the bleak and barren lands who master the children of the light and the heat. And so the Dutchmen at the Cape prospered and grew stronger in that robust climate. They did not penetrate far inland, for they were few in number and all they wanted was to be found close at hand. But they built themselves houses, and they supplied the Dutch East India Company with food and water, gradually budding off little townlets, Wynberg, Stellenbosch, and pushing their settlements up the long slopes which lead to that great central plateau which extends for fifteen hundred miles from the edge of the Karoo to the Valley of the Zambezi. Then came the additional Huguenot emigrants—the best blood of France three hundred of them, a handful of the choicest seed thrown in to give a touch of grace and soul to the solid Teutonic strain. Again and again in the course of history, with the Normans, the Huguenots, the emigres, one can see the great hand dipping into that storehouse and sprinkling the nations with the same splendid seed. France has not founded other countries, like her great rival, but she has made every other country the richer by the mixture with her choicest and best. The Rouxs, Du Toits, Jouberts, Du Plessis, Villiers, and a score of other French names are among the most familiar in South Africa.

For a hundred more years the history of the colony was a record of the gradual spreading of the Afrikaners over the huge expanse of *veldt* which lay to the north of them. Cattle raising became an industry, but in a country where six acres can hardly support a sheep, large farms are necessary for even small herds. Six thousand acres was the usual size, and five pounds a year the rent payable to Government. The diseases which follow the white man had in Africa, as in America and Australia, been fatal to the natives, and an epidemic of smallpox cleared the country for the newcomers. Further and further north they pushed, founding little towns here and there, such as Graaf-Reinet and Swellendam, where a Dutch Reformed Church and a store for the sale of the bare necessaries of life formed a nucleus for a few scattered dwellings. Already the settlers were showing that independence of control and that detachment from Europe which has been their most prominent characteristic. Even the sway of the Dutch Company (an older but weaker brother of John Company in India) had caused them to revolt. The local rising, however, was hardly noticed in the universal cataclysm which followed the French Revolution. After twenty years, during which the world was shaken by the Titanic struggle between England and France in the final counting up of the game and paying of the stakes, the Cape Colony was added in 1814 to the British Empire.

In all our vast collection of States there is probably not one the title-deeds to which are more incontestable than to this one. We had it by two rights, the right of conquest and the right of purchase. In 1806 our troops landed, defeated the local forces, and took possession of Cape Town. In 1814 we paid the large sum of six million pounds to the Stadholder for the transference of this and some South American land. It was a bargain which was probably made rapidly and carelessly in that general redistribution which was going on. As a house of call upon the way to India the place was seen to be of value, but the country itself was looked upon as unprofitable and desert. What would Castlereagh or Liverpool have thought could they have seen the items which we were buying for our six million pounds? The inventory would have been a mixed one of good and of evil; nine fierce Kaffir wars, the greatest diamond mines in the world, the wealthiest gold mines, two costly and humiliating campaigns with men whom we respected even when we fought with them, and now at last, we hope, a South Africa of peace and prosperity, with equal rights and equal duties for all men. The future should hold something very good for us in that land, for if we merely count the past we should be compelled to say that we should have been stronger, richer, and higher in the world's esteem had our possessions there never passed beyond the range of the guns of our men-of-war. But surely the most arduous is the most honourable, and, looking back from the end of their journey, our descendants may see that our long record of struggle, with its mixture of disaster and success, its outpouring of blood and of treasure, has always tended to some great and enduring goal.

The title-deeds to the estate are, as I have said, good ones, but there is one singular and ominous flaw in their provisions. The ocean has marked three boundaries to it, but the fourth is undefined. There is no word of the 'Hinterland;' for neither the term nor the idea had then been thought of.

Had Great Britain bought those vast regions which extended beyond the settlements? Or were the discontented Dutch at liberty to pass onwards and found fresh nations to bar the path of the Anglo-Celtic colonists? In that question lay the germ of all the trouble to come. An American would realise the point at issue if he could conceive that after the founding of the United States the Dutch inhabitants of the State of New York had trekked to the westward and established fresh communities under a new flag. Then, when the American population overtook these western States, they would be face to face with the problem which this country has had to solve. If they found these new States fiercely anti-American and extremely unprogressive, they would experience that aggravation of their difficulties with which our statesmen have had to deal.

At the time of their transference to the British flag the colonists— Dutch, French, and German—numbered some thirty thousand. They were slaveholders, and the slaves were about as numerous as themselves. The prospect of complete amalgamation between the British and the original settlers would have seemed to be a good one, since they were of much the same stock, and their creeds could only be distinguished by their varying degrees of bigotry and intolerance. Five thousand British emigrants were landed in 1820, settling on the Eastern borders of the colony, and from that time onwards there was a slow but steady influx of English speaking colonists. The Government had the historical faults and the historical virtues of British rule. It was mild, clean, honest, tactless, and inconsistent. On the whole, it might have done very well had it been content to leave things as it found them. But to change the habits of the most conservative of Teutonic races was a dangerous venture, and one which has led to a long series of complications, making up the troubled history of South Africa. The Imperial Government has always taken an honourable and philanthropic view of the rights of the native and the claim which he has to the protection of the law. We hold and rightly, that British justice, if not blind, should at least be colour-blind. The view is irreproachable in theory and incontestable in argument, but it is apt to be irritating when urged by a Boston moralist or a London philanthropist upon men whose whole society has been built upon the assumption that the black is the inferior race. Such a people like to find the higher morality for themselves, not to have it imposed upon them by those who live under entirely different conditions. They feel—and with some reason— that it is a cheap form of virtue which, from the serenity of a well-ordered household in Beacon Street or Belgrave Square, prescribes what the relation shall be between a white employer and his half-savage, half-childish retainers. Both branches of the Anglo-Celtic race have grappled with the question, and in each it has led to trouble.

12

The British Government in South Africa has always played the unpopular part of the friend and protector of the native servants. It was upon this very point that the first friction appeared between the old settlers and the new administration. A rising with bloodshed followed the arrest of a Dutch farmer who had maltreated his slave. It was suppressed, and five of the participants were hanged. This punishment was unduly severe and exceedingly injudicious. A brave race can forget the victims of the field of battle, but never those of the scaffold. The making of political martyrs is the last insanity of statesmanship. It is true that both the man who arrested and the judge who condemned the prisoners were Dutch, and that the British Governor interfered on the side of mercy; but all this was forgotten afterwards in the desire to make racial capital out of the incident. It is typical of the enduring resentment which was left behind that when, after the Jameson raid, it seemed that the leaders of that ill-fated venture might be hanged, the beam was actually brought from a farmhouse at Cookhouse Drift to Pretoria, that the Englishmen might die as the Dutchmen had died in 1816. Slagter's Nek marked the dividing of the ways between the British Government and the Afrikaners.

And the separation soon became more marked. There were injudicious tamperings with the local government and the local ways, with a substitution of English for Dutch in the law courts. With vicarious generosity, the English Government gave very lenient terms to the Kaffir tribes who in 1834 had raided the border farmers. And then, finally, in this same year there came the emancipation of the slaves throughout the British Empire, which fanned all smouldering discontents into an active flame.

It must be confessed that on this occasion the British philanthropist was willing to pay for what he thought was right. It was a noble national action, and one the morality of which was in advance of its time, that the British Parliament should vote the enormous sum of twenty million pounds to pay compensation to the slaveholders, and so to remove an evil with which the mother country had no immediate connection. It was as well that the thing should have been done when it was, for had we waited till the colonies affected had governments of their own it could never have been done by constitutional methods. With many a grumble the good British householder drew his purse from his fob, and he paid for what he thought to be right. If any special grace attends the virtuous action which brings nothing but tribulation in this world, then we may hope for it over this emancipation. We spent our money, we ruined our West Indian colonies, and we started a disaffection in South Africa, the end of which we have not seen. Yet if it were to be done again we should doubtless do it. The highest morality may prove also to be the highest wisdom when the half-told story comes to be finished.

But the details of the measure were less honourable than the principle. It was carried out suddenly, so that the country had no time to adjust itself to the new conditions. Three million pounds were ear-marked for South Africa, which gives a price per slave of from sixty to seventy pounds, a sum considerably below the current local rates. Finally, the compensation was made payable in London, so that the farmers sold their claims at reduced prices to middlemen. Indignation meetings were held in every little townlet and cattle camp on the Karoo. The old Dutch spirit was up—the spirit of the men who cut the dykes. Rebellion was useless. But a vast untenanted land stretched to the north of them. The nomad life was congenial to them, and in their huge ox-drawn wagons—like those bullock-carts in which some of their old kinsmen came to Gaul—they had vehicles and homes and forts all in one. One by one they were loaded up, the huge teams were inspanned, the women were seated inside, the men, with their long-barrelled guns, walked alongside, and the great exodus was begun. Their herds and flocks accompanied the migration, and the children helped to round them in and drive them. One tattered little boy of ten cracked his *sjambok* whip behind the bullocks. He was a small item in that singular crowd, but he was of interest to us, for his name was Paul Stephanus Kruger.

It was a strange exodus, only comparable in modern times to the sallying forth of the Mormons from Nauvoo upon their search for the promised laud of Utah. The country was known and sparsely settled as far north as the Orange River, but beyond there was a great region which had never been penetrated save by some daring hunter or adventurous pioneer. It chanced—if there be indeed such an element as chance in the graver affairs of man—that a Zulu conqueror had swept over this land and left it untenanted, save by the dwarf bushmen, the hideous aborigines, lowest of the human race. There were fine grazing and good soil for the emigrants. They travelled in small detached parties, but their total numbers were considerable, from six to ten thousand according to their historian, or nearly a quarter of the whole population of the colony. Some of the early bands perished miserably. A large number made a trysting-place at a high peak to the east of Bloemfontein in what was lately the Orange Free State. One party of the emigrants was cut off by the formidable Matabeli, a branch of the great Zulu nation. The survivors declared war upon them, and showed in this, their first campaign, the extraordinary ingenuity in adapting their tactics to their adversary which has been their greatest military characteristic. The commando which rode out to do battle with the Matabeli numbered, it is said, a hundred and thirty-five farmers. Their adversaries were twelve thousand spearmen. They met at the Marico River, near Mafeking. The Boers combined the use of their horses and of their rifles so cleverly that they slaughtered a third of their antagonists without any loss to themselves. Their tactics were to gallop up within range of the enemy, to fire a volley, and then to ride away again before the spearmen could reach them. When the savages pursued the Boers fled. When the pursuit halted the Boers halted and the rifle fire began anew. The strategy was simple but most effective. When one remembers how often since then our own horsemen have been pitted against savages in all parts of the world, one deplores that ignorance of all military traditions save our own which is characteristic of our service.

This victory of the *voortrekkers* cleared all the country between the Orange River and the Limpopo, the sites of what has been known as the Transvaal and the Orange Free State. In the meantime another body of the emigrants had descended into what is now known as Natal, and had defeated Dingaan, the great Chief of the Zulus. Being unable, owing to the presence of their families, to employ the cavalry tactics which had been so effective against the Matabeli, they again used their ingenuity to meet this new situation, and received the Zulu warriors in a square of *laagered* wagons, the men firing while the women loaded. Six burghers were killed and three thousand Zulus. Had such a formation been used forty years afterwards against these very Zulus, we should not have had to mourn the disaster of Isandhlwana.

And now at the end of their great journey, after overcoming the difficulties of distance, of nature, and of savage enemies, the Boers saw at the end of their travels the very thing which they desired least—that which they had come so far to avoid—the flag of Great Britain. The Boers had occupied Natal from within, but England had previously done the same by sea, and a small colony of Englishmen had settled at Port Natal, now known as Durban. The home Government, however, had acted in a vacillating way, and it was only the conquest of Natal by the Boers which caused them to claim it as a British colony. At the same time they asserted the unwelcome doctrine that a British subject could not at will throw off his allegiance, and that, go where they might, the wandering farmers were still only the pioneers of British colonies. To emphasise the fact three companies of soldiers were sent in 1842 to what is now Durban—the usual Corporal's guard with which Great Britain starts a new empire. This handful of men was waylaid by the Boers and cut up, as their successors have been so often since. The survivors, however, fortified themselves, and held a defensive position—as also their successors have done so many times since—until reinforcements arrived and the farmers dispersed. It is singular how in history the same factors will always give the same result. Here in this first skirmish is an epitome of all our military relations with these people. The blundering headstrong attack, the defeat, the powerlessness of the farmer against the weakest fortifications—it is the same tale over and over again in different scales of importance. Natal from this time onward became a British colony, and the majority of the Boers trekked north and east with bitter hearts to tell their wrongs to their brethren of the Orange Free State and of the Transvaal.

Had they any wrongs to tell? It is difficult to reach that height of philosophic detachment which enables the historian to deal absolutely impartially where his own country is a party to the quarrel. But at least we may allow that there is a case for our adversary. Our annexation of Natal had been by no means definite, and it was they and not we who first broke that bloodthirsty Zulu power which threw its shadow across the country. It was hard after such trials and such exploits to turn their back upon the fertile land which they had conquered, and to return to the bare pastures of the upland *veldt*. They carried out of Natal a heavy sense of injury, which has helped to poison our relations with them ever since. It was, in a way, a momentous episode, this little skirmish of soldiers and emigrants, for it was the heading off of the Boer from the sea and the confinement of his ambition to the land. Had it gone the other way, a new and possibly formidable flag would have been added to the maritime nations.

The emigrants who had settled in the huge tract of country between the Orange River in the south and the Limpopo in the north had been recruited by newcomers from the Cape Colony until they numbered some fifteen thousand souls. This population was scattered over a space as large as Germany, and larger than Pennsylvania, New York, and New England. Their form of government was individualistic and democratic to the last degree compatible with any sort of cohesion. Their wars with the Kaffirs and their fear and dislike of the British Government appear to have been the only ties which held them together. They divided and subdivided within their own borders, like a germinating egg. The Transvaal was full of lusty little high-mettled communities, who quarrelled among themselves as fiercely as they had done with the authorities at the Cape. Lydenburg, Zoutpansberg, and Potchefstroom were on the point of turning their rifles against each other. In the south, between the Orange River and the Vaal, there was no form of government at all, but a welter of Dutch farmers, Basutos, Hottentots, and half-breeds living in a chronic state of turbulence, recognising neither the British authority to the south of them nor the Transvaal republics to the north. The chaos became at last unendurable, and in 1848 a garrison was placed in Bloemfontein and the district incorporated in the British Empire. The emigrants made a futile resistance at Boomplaats, and after a single defeat allowed themselves to be drawn into the settled order of civilised rule.

At this period the Transvaal, where most of the Boers had settled, desired a formal acknowledgment of their independence, which the British authorities determined once and for all to give them. The great barren country, which produced little save marksmen, had no attractions for a Colonial Office which was bent upon the limitation of its liabilities. A Convention was concluded between the two parties, known as the Sand River Convention, which is one of the fixed points in South African history. By it the British Government guaranteed to the Boer farmers the right to manage their own affairs, and to govern themselves by their own laws without any interference upon the part of the British. It stipulated that there should be no slavery, and with that single reservation washed its hands finally, as it imagined, of the whole question. So the South African Republic came formally into existence.

In the very year after the Sand River Convention a second republic, the Orange Free State, was created by the deliberate withdrawal of Great Britain from the territory which she had for eight years occupied. The Eastern Question was already becoming acute, and the cloud of a great war was drifting up, visible to all men. British statesmen felt that their commitments were very heavy in every part of the world, and the South African annexations had always been a doubtful value and an undoubted trouble. Against the will of a large part of the inhabitants, whether a majority or not it is impossible to say, we withdrew our troops as amicably as the Romans withdrew from Britain, and the new republic was left with absolute and unfettered independence. On a petition being presented against the withdrawal, the Home Government actually voted forty-eight thousand pounds to compensate those who had suffered from the change. Whatever historical grievance the Transvaal may have against Great Britain, we can at least, save perhaps in one matter, claim to have a very clear conscience concerning our dealings with the Orange Free State. Thus in 1852 and in 1854 were born those sturdy States who were able for a time to hold at bay the united forces of the empire.

In the meantime Cape Colony, in spite of these secessions, had prospered exceedingly, and her population—English, German, and Dutch—had grown by 1870 to over two hundred thousand souls, the Dutch still slightly predominating. According to the Liberal colonial policy of Great Britain, the time had come to cut the cord and let the young nation conduct its own affairs. In 1872 complete self-government was given to it, the Governor, as the representative of the Queen, retaining a nominal unexercised veto upon legislation. According to this system the Dutch majority of the colony could, and did, put their own representatives into power and run the government upon Dutch lines. Already Dutch law had been restored, and Dutch put on the same footing as English as the official language of the country. The extreme liberality of such measures, and the uncompromising way in which they have been carried out, however distasteful the legislation might seem to English ideas, are among the chief reasons which made the illiberal treatment of British settlers in the Transvaal so keenly resented at the Cape. A Dutch Government was ruling the British in a British colony, at a moment when the Boers would not give an Englishman a vote upon a municipal council in a city which he had built himself. Unfortunately, however, 'the evil that men do lives after them,' and the ignorant Boer farmer continued to imagine that his southern relatives were in bondage, just as the descendant of the Irish emigrant still pictures an Ireland of penal laws and an alien Church.

For twenty-five years after the Sand River Convention the burghers of the South African Republic had pursued a strenuous and violent existence, fighting incessantly with the natives and sometimes with each other, with an occasional fling at the little Dutch republic to the south. The semi-tropical sun was waking strange ferments in the placid Friesland blood, and producing a race who added the turbulence and restlessness of the south to the formidable tenacity of the north. Strong vitality and violent ambitions produced feuds and rivalries worthy of medieval Italy, and the story of the factious little communities is like a chapter out of Guicciardini. Disorganisation ensued. The burghers would not pay taxes and the treasury was empty. One fierce Kaffir tribe threatened them from the north, and the Zulus on the east. It is an exaggeration of English partisans to pretend that our intervention saved the Boers, for no one can read their military history without seeing that they were a match for Zulus and Sekukuni combined. But certainly a formidable invasion was pending, and the scattered farmhouses were as open to the Kaffirs as our farmers' homesteads were in the American colonies when the Indians were on the warpath. Sir Theophilus Shepstone, the British Commissioner, after an inquiry of three months, solved all questions by the formal annexation of the country. The fact that he took possession of it with a force of some twenty-five men showed the honesty of his belief that no armed resistance was to be feared. This, then, in 1877 was a complete reversal of the Sand River Convention and the opening of a new chapter in the history of South Africa.

There did not appear to be any strong feeling at the time against the annexation. The people were depressed with their troubles and weary of contention. Burgers, the President, put in a formal protest, and took up his abode in Cape Colony, where he had a pension from the British Government. A memorial against the measure received the signatures of a majority of the Boer inhabitants, but there was a fair minority who took the other view. Kruger himself accepted a paid office under Government.

There was every sign that the people, if judiciously handled, would settle down under the British flag. It is even asserted that they would themselves have petitioned for annexation had it been longer withheld. With immediate constitutional government it is possible that even the most recalcitrant of them might have been induced to lodge their protests in the ballot boxes rather than in the bodies of our soldiers.

But the empire has always had poor luck in South Africa, and never worse than on that occasion. Through no bad faith, but simply through preoccupation and delay, the promises made were not instantly fulfilled. Simple primitive men do not understand the ways of our circumlocution offices, and they ascribe to duplicity what is really red tape and stupidity. If the Transvaalers had waited they would have had their Volksraad and all that they wanted. But the British Government had some other local matters to set right, the rooting out of Sekukuni and the breaking of the Zulus, before they would fulfil their pledges. The delay was keenly resented. And we were unfortunate in our choice of Governor. The burghers are a homely folk, and they like an occasional cup of coffee with the anxious man who tries to rule them. The three hundred pounds a year of coffee money allowed by the Transvaal to its President is by no means a mere form. A wise administrator would fall into the sociable and democratic habits of the people. Sir Theophilus Shepstone did so. Sir Owen Lanyon did not. There was no Volksraad and no coffee, and the popular discontent grew rapidly. In three years the British had broken up the two savage hordes which had been threatening the land. The finances, too, had been restored. The reasons which had made so many favour the annexation were weakened by the very power which had every interest in preserving them.

It cannot be too often pointed out that in this annexation, the starting-point of our troubles, Great Britain, however mistaken she may have been, had no obvious selfish interest in view. There were no Rand mines in those days, nor was there anything in the country to tempt the most covetous. An empty treasury and two native wars were the reversion which we took over. It was honestly considered that the country was in too distracted a state to govern itself, and had, by its weakness, become a scandal and a danger to its neighbours. There was nothing sordid in our action, though it may have been both injudicious and high-handed.

In December 1880 the Boers rose. Every farmhouse sent out its riflemen, and the trysting-place was the outside of the nearest British fort. All through the country small detachments were surrounded and besieged by the farmers. Standerton, Pretoria, Potchefstroom, Lydenburg, Wakkerstroom, Rustenberg, and Marabastad were all invested and all held out until the end of the war. In the open country we were less fortunate. At

Bronkhorst Spruit a small British force was taken by surprise and shot down without harm to their antagonists. The surgeon who treated them has left it on record that the average number of wounds was five per man. At Laing's Nek an inferior force of British endeavoured to rush a hill which was held by Boer riflemen. Half of our men were killed and wounded. Ingogo may be called a drawn battle, though our loss was more heavy than that of the enemy. Finally came the defeat of Majuba Hill, where four hundred infantry upon a mountain were defeated and driven off by a swarm of sharpshooters who advanced under the cover of boulders. Of all these actions there was not one which was more than a skirmish, and had they been followed by a final British victory they would now be hardly remembered. It is the fact that they were skirmishes which succeeded in their object which has given them an importance which is exaggerated. At the same time they may mark the beginning of a new military era, for they drove home the fact—only too badly learned by us—that it is the rifle and not the drill which makes the soldier. It is bewildering that after such an experience the British military authorities continued to serve out only three hundred cartridges a year for rifle practice, and that they still encouraged that mechanical volley firing which destroys all individual aim. With the experience of the first Boer war behind them, little was done, either in tactics or in musketry, to prepare the soldier for the second. The value of the mounted rifleman, the shooting with accuracy at unknown ranges, the art of taking cover—all were equally neglected.

The defeat at Majuba Hill was followed by the complete surrender of the Gladstonian Government, an act which was either the most pusillanimous or the most magnanimous in recent history. It is hard for the big man to draw away from the small before blows are struck but when the big man has been knocked down three times it is harder still. An overwhelming British force was in the field, and the General declared that he held the enemy in the hollow of his hand. Our military calculations have been falsified before now by these farmers, and it may be that the task of Wood and Roberts would have been harder than they imagined; but on paper, at least, it looked as if the enemy could be crushed without difficulty. So the public thought, and yet they consented to the upraised sword being stayed. With them, as apart from the politicians, the motive was undoubtedly a moral and Christian one. They considered that the annexation of the Transvaal had evidently been an injustice, that the farmers had a right to the freedom for which they fought, and that it was an unworthy thing for a great nation to continue an unjust war for the sake of a military revenge. It was the height of idealism, and the result has not been such as to encourage its repetition.

An armistice was concluded on March 5th, 1881, which led up to a peace on the 23rd of the same month. The Government, after yielding to force what it had repeatedly refused to friendly representations, made a clumsy compromise in their settlement. A policy of idealism and Christian morality should have been thorough if it were to be tried at all. It was obvious that if the annexation were unjust, then the Transvaal should have reverted to the condition in which it was before the annexation, as defined by the Sand River Convention. But the Government for some reason would not go so far as this. They niggled and quibbled and bargained until the State was left as a curious hybrid thing such as the world has never seen. It was a republic which was part of the system of a monarchy, dealt with by the Colonial Office, and included under the heading of 'Colonies' in the news columns of the 'Times.' It was autonomous, and yet subject to some vague suzerainty, the limits of which no one has ever been able to define. Altogether, in its provisions and in its omissions, the Convention of Pretoria appears to prove that our political affairs were as badly conducted as our military in this unfortunate year of 1881.

It was evident from the first that so illogical and contentious an agreement could not possibly prove to be a final settlement, and indeed the ink of the signatures was hardly dry before an agitation was on foot for its revision. The Boers considered, and with justice, that if they were to be left as undisputed victors in the war then they should have the full fruits of victory. On the other hand, the English-speaking colonies had their allegiance tested to the uttermost. The proud Anglo-Celtic stock is not accustomed to be humbled, and yet they found themselves through the action of the home Government converted into members of a beaten race. It was very well for the citizen of London to console his wounded pride by the thought that he had done a magnanimous action, but it was different with the British colonist of Durban or Cape Town, who by no act of his own, and without any voice in the settlement, found himself humiliated before his Dutch neighbour. An ugly feeling of resentment was left behind, which might perhaps have passed away had the Transvaal accepted the settlement in the spirit in which it was meant, but which grew more and more dangerous as during eighteen years our people saw, or thought that they saw, that one concession led always to a fresh demand, and that the Dutch republics aimed not merely at equality, but at dominance in South Africa. Professor Bryce, a friendly critic, after a personal examination of the country and the question, has left it upon record that the Boers saw neither generosity nor humanity in our conduct, but only fear. An outspoken race, they conveyed their feelings to their neighbours. Can it be wondered at that South Africa has been in a ferment ever since, and that the British Africander has yearned with an intensity of feeling unknown in England for the hour of revenge?

21

The Government of the Transvaal after the war was left in the hands of a triumvirate, but after one year Kruger became President, an office which he continued to hold for eighteen years. His career as ruler vindicates the wisdom of that wise but unwritten provision of the American Constitution by which there is a limit to the tenure of this office. Continued rule for half a generation must turn a man into an autocrat. The old President has said himself, in his homely but shrewd way, that when one gets a good ox to lead the team it is a pity to change him. If a good ox, however, is left to choose his own direction without guidance, he may draw his wagon into trouble.

During three years the little State showed signs of a tumultuous activity. Considering that it was as large as France and that the population could not have been more than 50,000, one would have thought that they might have found room without any inconvenient crowding. But the burghers passed beyond their borders in every direction. The President cried aloud that he had been shut up in a *kraal*, and he proceeded to find ways out of it. A great trek was projected for the north, but fortunately it miscarried. To the east they raided Zululand, and succeeded, in defiance of the British settlement of that country, in tearing away one third of it and adding it to the Transvaal. To the west, with no regard to the three-year-old treaty, they invaded Bechuanaland, and set up the two new republics of Goshen and Stellaland. So outrageous were these proceedings that Great Britain was forced to fit out in 1884 a new expedition under Sir Charles Warren for the purpose of turning these freebooters out of the country. It may be asked, why should these men be called freebooters if the founders of Rhodesia were pioneers? The answer is that the Transvaal was limited by treaty to certain boundaries which these men transgressed, while no pledges were broken when the British power expanded to the north. The upshot of these trespasses was the scene upon which every drama of South Africa rings down. Once more the purse was drawn from the pocket of the unhappy taxpayer, and a million or so was paid out to defray the expenses of the police force necessary to keep these treaty-breakers in order. Let this be borne in mind when we assess the moral and material damage done to the Transvaal by that ill-conceived and foolish enterprise, the Jameson Raid.

In 1884 a deputation from the Transvaal visited England, and at their solicitation the clumsy Treaty of Pretoria was altered into the still more clumsy Convention of London. The changes in the provisions were all in favour of the Boers, and a second successful war could hardly have given them more than Lord Derby handed them in time of peace. Their style was altered from the Transvaal to the South African Republic, a change which was ominously suggestive of expansion in the future. The control of Great Britain over their foreign policy was also relaxed, though a power of veto was retained. But the most important thing of all, and the fruitful cause of future trouble, lay in an omission. A suzerainty is a vague term, but in politics, as in theology, the more nebulous a thing is the more does it excite the imagination and the passions of men. This suzerainty was declared in the preamble of the first treaty, and no mention of it was made in the second. Was it thereby abrogated or was it not? The British contention was that only the articles were changed, and that the preamble continued to hold good for both treaties. They pointed out that not only the suzerainty, but also the independence, of the Transvaal was proclaimed in that preamble, and that if one lapsed the other must do so also. On the other hand, the Boers pointed to the fact that there was actually a preamble to the second Convention, which would seem, therefore, to have taken the place of the first. The point is so technical that it appears to be eminently one of those questions which might with propriety have been submitted to the decision of a board of foreign jurists—or possibly to the Supreme Court of the United States. If the decision had been given against Great Britain, we might have accepted it in a chastened spirit as a fitting punishment for the carelessness of the representative who failed to make our meaning intelligible. Carlyle has said that a political mistake always ends in a broken head for somebody. Unfortunately the somebody is usually somebody else. We have read the story of the political mistakes. Only too soon we shall come to the broken heads.

This, then, is a synopsis of what had occurred up to the signing of the Convention, which finally established, or failed to establish, the position of the South African Republic. We must now leave the larger questions, and descend to the internal affairs of that small State, and especially to that train of events which has stirred the mind of our people more than anything since the Indian Mutiny.

CHAPTER 2

The Cause of Quarrel

There might almost seem to be some subtle connection between the barrenness and worthlessness of a surface and the value of the minerals which lie beneath it. The craggy mountains of Western America, the arid plains of West Australia, the ice-bound gorges of the Klondyke, and the bare slopes of the Witwatersrand *veldt*—these are the lids which cover the great treasure chests of the world.

Gold had been known to exist in the Transvaal before, but it was only in 1886 that it was realised that the deposits which lie some thirty miles south of the capital are of a very extraordinary and valuable nature. The proportion of gold in the quartz is not particularly high, nor are the veins of a remarkable thickness, but the peculiarity of the Rand mines lies in the fact that throughout this 'blanket' formation the metal is so uniformly distributed that the enterprise can claim a certainty which is not usually associated with the industry. It is quarrying rather than mining. Add to this that the reefs which were originally worked as outcrops have now been traced to enormous depths, and present the same features as those at the surface. A conservative estimate of the value of the gold has placed it at seven hundred millions of pounds.

Such a discovery produced the inevitable effect. A great number of adventurers flocked into the country, some desirable and some very much the reverse. There were circumstances, however, which kept away the rowdy and desperado element who usually make for a newly opened goldfield. It was not a class of mining which encouraged the individual adventurer. There were none of those nuggets which gleamed through the mud of the dollies at Ballarat, or recompensed the forty-niners in California for all their travels and their toils. It was a field for elaborate machinery, which could only be provided by capital. Managers, engineers, miners, technical experts, and the tradesmen and middlemen who live upon them, these were the Uitlanders, drawn from all the races under the sun, but with the Anglo-Celtic vastly predominant. The best engineers were American, the best miners were Cornish, the best managers were English, the money to run the mines was largely subscribed in England. As time went on, however, the German and French interests became more extensive, until their joint holdings are now probably as heavy as those of the British. Soon the population of the mining centres became greater than that of the whole Boer community, and consisted mainly of men in the prime of life—men, too, of exceptional intelligence and energy.

The situation was an extraordinary one. I have already attempted to bring the problem home to an American by suggesting that the Dutch of New York had trekked west and founded an anti-American and highly unprogressive State. To carry out the analogy we will now suppose that that State was California, that the gold of that State attracted a large in-rush of American citizens, who came to outnumber the original inhabitants, that these citizens were heavily taxed and badly used, and that they deafened Washington with their outcry about their injuries. That would be a fair parallel to the relations between the Transvaal, the Uitlanders, and the British Government.

That these Uitlanders had very real and pressing grievances no one could possibly deny. To recount them all would be a formidable task, for their whole lives were darkened by injustice. There was not a wrong which had driven the Boer from Cape Colony which he did not now practise himself upon others—and a wrong may be excusable in 1885 which is monstrous in 1895. The primitive virtue which had characterised the farmers broke down in the face of temptation. The country Boers were little affected, some of them not at all, but the Pretoria Government became a most corrupt oligarchy, venal and incompetent to the last degree. Officials and imported Hollanders handled the stream of gold which came in from the mines, while the unfortunate Uitlander who paid nine-tenths of the taxation was fleeced at every turn, and met with laughter and taunts when he endeavoured to win the franchise by which he might peaceably set right the wrongs from which he suffered. He was not an unreasonable person. On the contrary, he was patient to the verge of meekness, as capital is likely to be when it is surrounded by rifles. But his situation was intolerable, and after successive attempts at peaceful agitation, and numerous humble petitions to the Volksraad, he began at last to realise that he would never obtain redress unless he could find some way of winning it for himself.

Without attempting to enumerate all the wrongs which embittered the Uitlanders, the more serious of them may be summed up in this way.

1. That they were heavily taxed and provided about seven-eighths of the revenue of the country. The revenue of the South African Republic—which had been 154,000 pounds in 1886, when the gold fields were

opened—had grown in 1899 to four million pounds, and the country through the industry of the newcomers had changed from one of the poorest to the richest in the whole world (per head of population).

2. That in spite of this prosperity which they had brought, they, the majority of the inhabitants of the country, were left without a vote, and could by no means influence the disposal of the great sums which they were providing. Such a case of taxation without representation has never been known.

3. That they had no voice in the choice or payment of officials. Men of the worst private character might be placed with complete authority over valuable interests. Upon one occasion the Minister of Mines attempted himself to jump a mine, having officially learned some flaw in its title. The total official salaries had risen in 1899 to a sum sufficient to pay 40 pounds per head to the entire male Boer population.

4. That they had no control over education. Mr. John Robinson, the Director General of the Johannesburg Educational Council, has reckoned the sum spent on Uitlander schools as 650 pounds out of 63,000 pounds allotted for education, making one shilling and tenpence per head *per annum* on Uitlander children, and eight pounds six shillings per head on Boer children—the Uitlander, as always, paying seven-eighths of the original sum.

5. No power of municipal government. Water carts instead of pipes, filthy buckets instead of drains, a corrupt and violent police, a high death-rate in what should be a health resort—all this in a city which they had built themselves.

6. Despotic government in the matter of the press and of the right of public meeting.

7. Disability from service upon a jury.

8. Continual harassing of the mining interest by vexatious legislation. Under this head came many grievances, some special to the mines and some affecting all Uitlanders. The dynamite monopoly, by which the miners had to pay 600,000 pounds extra *per annum* in order to get a worse quality of dynamite; the liquor laws, by which one-third of the Kaffirs were allowed to be habitually drunk; the incompetence and extortions of the State-owned railway; the granting of concessions for numerous articles of ordinary consumption to individuals, by which high prices were maintained; the surrounding of Johannesburg by tolls from which the town had no profit—these were among the economical grievances, some large, some petty, which ramified through every transaction of life.

And outside and beyond all these definite wrongs imagine to a free born progressive man, an American or a Briton, the constant irritation of being absolutely ruled by a body of twenty-five men, twenty-one of whom had in the case of the Selati Railway Company been publicly and circumstantially accused of bribery, with full details of the bribes received, while to their corruption they added such crass ignorance that they argue in the published reports of the Volksraad debates that using dynamite bombs to bring down rain was firing at God, that it is impious to destroy locusts, that the word 'participate' should not be used because it is not in the Bible, and that postal pillar boxes are extravagant and effeminate. Such *obiter dicta* may be amusing at a distance, but they are less entertaining when they come from an autocrat who has complete power over the conditions of your life.

From the fact that they were a community extremely preoccupied by their own business, it followed that the Uitlanders were not ardent politicians, and that they desired to have a share in the government of the State for the purpose of making the conditions of their own industry and of their own daily lives more endurable. How far there was need of such an interference may be judged by any fair-minded man who reads the list of their complaints. A superficial view may recognise the Boers as the champions of liberty, but a deeper insight must see that they (as represented by their elected rulers) have in truth stood for all that history has shown to be odious in the form of exclusiveness and oppression. Their conception of liberty has been a selfish one, and they have consistently inflicted upon others far heavier wrongs than those against which they had themselves rebelled.

As the mines increased in importance and the miners in numbers, it was found that these political disabilities affected some of that cosmopolitan crowd far more than others, in proportion to the amount of freedom to which their home institutions had made them accustomed. The continental Uitlanders were more patient of that which was unendurable to the American and the Briton. The Americans, however, were in so great a minority that it was upon the British that the brunt of the struggle for freedom fell. Apart from the fact that the British were more numerous than all the other Uitlanders combined, there were special reasons why they should feel their humiliating position more than the members of any other race. In the first place, many of the British were British South Africans, who knew that in the neighbouring countries which gave them birth the most liberal possible institutions had been given to the kinsmen of these very Boers who were refusing them the management of their own drains and water supply. And again, every Briton knew that Great Britain claimed to be the paramount power in South Africa, and so he felt as if his own land, to which he might have looked for protection, was conniving at and acquiescing in his ill treatment. As citizens of the paramount power, it was peculiarly galling that they should be held in political subjection. The British, therefore, were the most persistent and energetic of the agitators.

But it is a poor cause which cannot bear to fairly state and honestly consider the case of its opponents. The Boers had made, as has been briefly shown, great efforts to establish a country of their own. They had travelled far, worked hard, and fought bravely. After all their efforts they were fated to see an influx of strangers into their country, some of them men of questionable character, who outnumbered the original inhabitants. If the franchise were granted to these, there could be no doubt that though at first the Boers might control a majority of the votes, it was only a question of time before the newcomers would dominate the Raad and elect their own President, who might adopt a policy abhorrent to the original owners of the land. Were the Boers to lose by the ballot-box the victory which they had won by their rifles? Was it fair to expect it? These newcomers came for gold. They got their gold. Their companies paid a hundred per cent. Was not that enough to satisfy them? If they did not like the country why did they not leave it? No one compelled them to stay there. But if they stayed, let them be thankful that they were tolerated at all, and not presume to interfere with the laws of those by whose courtesy they were allowed to enter the country.

That is a fair statement of the Boer position, and at first sight an impartial man might say that there was a good deal to say for it; but a closer examination would show that, though it might be tenable in theory, it is unjust and impossible in practice.

In the present crowded state of the world a policy of Thibet may be carried out in some obscure corner, but it cannot be done in a great tract of country which lies right across the main line of industrial progress. The position is too absolutely artificial. A handful of people by the right of conquest take possession of an enormous country over which they are dotted at such intervals that it is their boast that one farmhouse cannot see the smoke of another, and yet, though their numbers are so disproportionate to the area which they cover, they refuse to admit any other people upon equal terms, but claim to be a privileged class who shall dominate the newcomers completely. They are outnumbered in their own land by immigrants who are far more highly educated and progressive, and yet they hold them down in a way which exists nowhere else upon earth. What is their right? The right of conquest. Then the same right may be justly invoked to reverse so intolerable a situation. This they would themselves acknowledge. 'Come on and fight! Come on!' cried a member of the Volksraad when the franchise petition of the Uitlanders was presented. 'Protest! Protest! What is the good of protesting?' said

Kruger to Mr. W. Y. Campbell; 'you have not got the guns, I have.' There was always the final court of appeal. Judge Creusot and Judge Mauser were always behind the President.

Again, the argument of the Boers would be more valid had they received no benefit from these immigrants. If they had ignored them they might fairly have stated that they did not desire their presence. But even while they protested they grew rich at the Uitlander's expense. They could not have it both ways. It would be consistent to discourage him and not profit by him, or to make him comfortable and build the State upon his money; but to ill-treat him and at the same time to grow strong by his taxation must surely be an injustice.

And again, the whole argument is based upon the narrow racial supposition that every naturalised citizen not of Boer extraction must necessarily be unpatriotic. This is not borne out by the examples of history. The newcomer soon becomes as proud of his country and as jealous of her liberty as the old. Had President Kruger given the franchise generously to the Uitlander, his pyramid would have been firm upon its base and not balanced upon its apex. It is true that the corrupt oligarchy would have vanished, and the spirit of a broader more tolerant freedom influenced the counsels of the State. But the republic would have become stronger and more permanent, with a population who, if they differed in details, were united in essentials. Whether such a solution would have been to the advantage of British interests in South Africa is quite another question. In more ways than one President Kruger has been a good friend to the empire.

So much upon the general question of the reason why the Uitlander should agitate and why the Boer was obdurate. The details of the long struggle between the seekers for the franchise and the refusers of it may be quickly sketched, but they cannot be entirely ignored by any one who desires to understand the inception of that great contest which was the outcome of the dispute.

At the time of the Convention of Pretoria (1881) the rights of burghership might be obtained by one year's residence. In 1882 it was raised to five years, the reasonable limit which obtains both in Great Britain and in the United States. Had it remained so, it is safe to say that there would never have been either an Uitlander question or a great Boer war. Grievances would have been righted from the inside without external interference.

In 1890 the inrush of outsiders alarmed the Boers, and the franchise was raised so as to be only attainable by those who had lived fourteen years in the country. The Uitlanders, who were increasing rapidly in numbers and were suffering from the formidable list of grievances already enumerated, perceived that their wrongs were so numerous that it was hopeless to have them set right *seriatim*, and that only by obtaining the leverage of the franchise could they hope to move the heavy burden which weighed them down. In 1893 a petition of 13,000 Uitlanders, couched in most respectful terms, was submitted to the Raad, but met with contemptuous neglect. Undeterred, however, by this failure, the National Reform Union, an association which organised the agitation, came back to the attack in 1894. They drew up a petition which was signed by 35,000 adult male Uitlanders, a greater number than the total Boer male population of the country. A small liberal body in the Raad supported this memorial and endeavoured in vain to obtain some justice for the newcomers. Mr. Jeppe was the mouthpiece of this select band. 'They own half the soil, they pay at least three quarters of the taxes,' said he. 'They are men who in capital, energy, and education are at least our equals.

What will become of us or our children on that day when we may find ourselves in a minority of one in twenty without a single friend among the other nineteen, among those who will then tell us that they wished to be brothers, but that we by our own act have made them strangers to the republic?' Such reasonable and liberal sentiments were combated by members who asserted that the signatures could not belong to law-abiding citizens, since they were actually agitating against the law of the franchise, and others whose intolerance was expressed by the defiance of the member already quoted, who challenged the Uitlanders to come out and fight. The champions of exclusiveness and racial hatred won the day. The memorial was rejected by sixteen votes to eight, and the franchise law was, on the initiative of the President, actually made more stringent than ever, being framed in such a way that during the fourteen years of probation the applicant should give up his previous nationality, so that for that period he would really belong to no country at all. No hopes were held out that any possible attitude upon the part of the Uitlanders would soften the determination of the President and his burghers. One who remonstrated was led outside the State buildings by the President, who pointed up at the national flag. 'You see that flag?' said he. 'If I grant the franchise, I may as well pull it down.' His animosity against the immigrants was bitter. 'Burghers, friends, thieves, murderers, newcomers, and others,' is the conciliatory opening of one of his public addresses. Though Johannesburg is only thirty-two miles from Pretoria, and though the State of which he was the head depended for its revenue upon the gold fields, he paid it only three visits in nine years.

This settled animosity was deplorable, but not unnatural. A man imbued with the idea of a chosen people, and unread in any book save the one which cultivates this very idea, could not be expected to have learned the historical lessons of the advantages which a State reaps from a liberal policy. To him it was as if the Ammonites and Moabites had demanded admission into the twelve tribes. He mistook an agitation against the exclusive policy of the State for one against the existence of the State itself. A wide franchise would have made his republic firm-based and permanent. It was a small minority of the Uitlanders who had any desire to come into the British system. They were a cosmopolitan crowd, only united by the bond of a common injustice. But when every other method had failed, and their petition for the rights of freemen had been flung back at them, it was natural that their eyes should turn to that flag which waved to the north, the west, and the south of them—the flag which means purity of government with equal rights and equal duties for all men. Constitutional agitation was laid aside, arms were smuggled in, and everything prepared for an organised rising.

The events which followed at the beginning of 1896 have been so thrashed out that there is, perhaps, nothing left to tell—except the truth. So far as the Uitlanders themselves are concerned, their action was most natural and justifiable, and they have no reason to exculpate themselves for rising against such oppression as no men of our race have ever been submitted to. Had they trusted only to themselves and the justice of their cause, their moral and even their material position would have been infinitely stronger. But unfortunately there were forces behind them which were more questionable, the nature and extent of which have never yet, in spite of two commissions of investigation, been properly revealed. That there should have been any attempt at misleading inquiry, or suppressing documents in order to shelter individuals, is deplorable, for the impression left—I believe an entirely false one—must be that the British Government connived at an expedition which was as immoral as it was disastrous.

It had been arranged that the town was to rise upon a certain night, that Pretoria should be attacked, the fort seized, and the rifles and ammunition used to arm the Uitlanders. It was a feasible device, though it must seem to us, who have had such an experience of the military virtues of the burghers, a very desperate one. But it is conceivable that the rebels might have held Johannesburg until the universal sympathy which their cause excited throughout South Africa would have caused Great Britain to intervene. Unfortunately they had complicated matters by asking for outside help. Mr. Cecil Rhodes was Premier of the Cape, a man of immense energy, and one who had rendered great services to the empire. The motives of his action are obscure—certainly, we may say that they were not sordid, for he has always been a man whose thoughts were large and whose habits were simple. But whatever they may have been—whether an ill-regulated desire to consolidate South

Africa under British rule, or a burning sympathy with the Uitlanders in their fight against injustice—it is certain that he allowed his lieutenant, Dr. Jameson, to assemble the mounted police of the Chartered Company, of which Rhodes was founder and director, for the purpose of co-operating with the rebels at Johannesburg. Moreover, when the revolt at Johannesburg was postponed, on account of a disagreement as to which flag they were to rise under, it appears that Jameson (with or without the orders of Rhodes) forced the hand of the conspirators by invading the country with a force absurdly inadequate to the work which he had taken in hand. Five hundred policemen and three field guns made up the forlorn hope who started from near Mafeking and crossed the Transvaal border upon December 29th, 1895. On January 2nd they were surrounded by the Boers amid the broken country near Dornkop, and after losing many of their number killed and wounded, without food and with spent horses, they were compelled to lay down their arms. Six burghers lost their lives in the skirmish.

The Uitlanders have been severely criticised for not having sent out a force to help Jameson in his difficulties, but it is impossible to see how they could have acted in any other manner. They had done all they could to prevent Jameson coming to their relief, and now it was rather unreasonable to suppose that they should relieve their reliever. Indeed, they had an entirely exaggerated idea of the strength of the force which he was bringing, and received the news of his capture with incredulity. When it became confirmed they rose, but in a half-hearted fashion which was not due to want of courage, but to the difficulties of their position. On the one hand, the British Government disowned Jameson entirely, and did all it could to discourage the rising; on the other, the President had the raiders in his keeping at Pretoria, and let it be understood that their fate depended upon the behaviour of the Uitlanders. They were led to believe that Jameson would be shot unless they laid down their arms, though, as a matter of fact, Jameson and his people had surrendered upon a promise of quarter. So skilfully did Kruger use his hostages that he succeeded, with the help of the British Commissioner, in getting the thousands of excited Johannesburgers to lay down their arms without bloodshed. Completely out-manoeuvred by the astute old President, the leaders of the reform movement used all their influence in the direction of peace, thinking that a general amnesty would follow; but the moment that they and their people were helpless the detectives and armed burghers occupied the town, and sixty of their number were hurried to Pretoria Gaol.

To the raiders themselves the President behaved with great generosity. Perhaps he could not find it in his heart to be harsh to the men who had managed to put him in the right and won for him the sympathy of the world. His own illiberal and oppressive treatment of the newcomers was forgotten in the face of this illegal inroad of filibusters. The true issues were so obscured by this intrusion that it has taken years to clear them, and perhaps they will never be wholly cleared. It was forgotten that it was the bad government of the country which was the real cause of the unfortunate raid. From then onwards the government might grow worse and worse, but it was always possible to point to the raid as justifying everything. Were the Uitlanders to have the franchise? How could they expect it after the raid? Would Britain object to the enormous importation of arms and obvious preparations for war? They were only precautions against a second raid. For years the raid stood in the way, not only of all progress, but of all remonstrance. Through an action over which they had no control, and which they had done their best to prevent, the British Government was left with a bad case and a weakened moral authority.

The raiders were sent home, where the rank and file were very properly released, and the chief officers were condemned to terms of imprisonment which certainly did not err upon the side of severity. Cecil Rhodes was left unpunished, he retained his place in the Privy Council, and his Chartered Company continued to have a corporate existence. This was illogical and inconclusive. As Kruger said, 'It is not the dog which should be beaten, but the man who set him on to me.' Public opinion—in spite of, or on account of, a crowd of witnesses—was ill informed upon the exact bearings of the question, and it was obvious that as Dutch sentiment at the Cape appeared already to be thoroughly hostile to us, it would be dangerous to alienate the British Africanders also by making a martyr of their favourite leader. But whatever arguments may be founded upon expediency, it is clear that the Boers bitterly resented, and with justice, the immunity of Rhodes.

In the meantime, both President Kruger and his burghers had shown a greater severity to the political prisoners from Johannesburg than to the armed followers of Jameson. The nationality of these prisoners is interesting and suggestive. There were twenty-three Englishmen, sixteen South Africans, nine Scotchmen, six Americans, two Welshmen, one Irishman, one Australian, one Hollander, one Bavarian, one Canadian, one Swiss, and one Turk. The prisoners were arrested in January, but the trial did not take place until the end of April. All were found guilty of high treason. Mr. Lionel Phillips, Colonel Rhodes (brother of Mr. Cecil Rhodes), George Farrar, and Mr. Hammond, the American engineer, were condemned to death, a sentence which was afterwards commuted to the payment of an enormous fine. The other prisoners were condemned to two years' imprisonment, with a fine of 2000 pounds each. The imprisonment was of the most arduous and trying sort, and was embittered by the harshness of the gaoler, Du Plessis. One of the unfortunate men cut his throat, and several fell seriously ill, the diet and the sanitary conditions being equally unhealthy. At last at the end of May all the prisoners but six were released. Four of the six soon followed, two stalwarts, Sampson and Davies, refusing to sign any petition and remaining in prison until they were set free in 1897. Altogether the Transvaal Government received in fines from the reform prisoners the enormous sum of 212,000 pounds. A certain comic relief was immediately afterwards given to so grave an episode by the presentation of a bill to Great Britain for 1,677, 938 pounds 3 shillings and 3 pence—the greater part of which was under the heading of moral and intellectual damage.

The raid was past and the reform movement was past, but the causes which produced them both remained. It is hardly conceivable that a statesman who loved his country would have refrained from making some effort to remove a state of things which had already caused such grave dangers, and which must obviously become more serious with every year that passed. But Paul Kruger had hardened his heart, and was not to be moved. The grievances of the Uitlanders became heavier than ever. The one power in the land to which they had been able to appeal for some sort of redress amid their grievances was the law courts. Now it was decreed that the courts should be dependent on the Volksraad. The Chief Justice protested against such a degradation of his high office, and he was dismissed in consequence without a pension. The judge who had condemned the reformers was chosen to fill the vacancy, and the protection of a fixed law was withdrawn from the Uitlanders.

A commission appointed by the State was sent to examine into the condition of the mining industry and the grievances from which the newcomers suffered. The chairman was Mr. Schalk Burger, one of the most liberal of the Boers, and the proceedings were thorough and impartial. The result was a report which amply vindicated the reformers, and suggested remedies which would have gone a long way towards satisfying the Uitlanders. With such enlightened legislation their motives for seeking the franchise would have been less pressing. But the President and his Raad would have none of the recommendations of the commission. The rugged old autocrat declared that Schalk Burger was a traitor to his country for having signed such a document, and a new reactionary committee was chosen to report upon the report. Words and papers were the only outcome of the affair. No amelioration came to the newcomers. But at least they had again put their case publicly upon record, and it had been endorsed by the most respected of the burghers. Gradually in the press of the English-speaking countries the raid was ceasing to obscure the issue. More and more clearly it was coming out that no permanent settlement was possible where the majority of the population was oppressed by the minority. They had tried peaceful means and failed. They had tried warlike means and failed. What was there left for them to do? Their own country, the paramount power of South Africa, had never helped them. Perhaps if it were directly appealed to it might do so. It could not, if only for the sake of its own imperial prestige, leave its children for ever in a state of subjection. The Uitlanders determined upon a petition to the Queen, and in doing so they brought their grievances out of the limits of a local controversy into the broader field of international politics. Great Britain must either protect them or acknowledge that their protection was beyond her power. A direct petition to the Queen praying for protection was signed in April 1899 by twenty-one thousand Uitlanders. From that time events moved inevitably towards the one end. Sometimes the surface was troubled and sometimes smooth, but the stream always ran swiftly and the roar of the fall sounded ever louder in the ears.

CHAPTER 3

The Negotiations

The British Government and the British people do not desire any direct authority in South Africa. Their one supreme interest is that the various States there should live in concord and prosperity, and that there should be no need for the presence of a British redcoat within the whole great peninsula. Our foreign critics, with their misapprehension of the British colonial system, can never realise that whether the four-coloured flag of the Transvaal or the Union Jack of a self-governing colony waved over the gold mines would not make the difference of one shilling to the revenue of Great Britain. The Transvaal as a British province would have its own legislature, its own revenue, its own expenditure, and its own tariff against the mother country, as well as against the rest of the world, and England be none the richer for the change. This is so obvious to a Briton that he has ceased to insist upon it, and it is for that reason perhaps that it is so universally misunderstood abroad. On the other hand, while she is no gainer by the change, most of the expense of it in blood and in money falls upon the home country. On the face of it, therefore, Great Britain had every reason to avoid so formidable a task as the conquest of the South African Republic. At the best she had nothing to gain, and at the worst she had an immense deal to lose. There was no room for ambition or aggression. It was a case of shirking or fulfilling a most arduous duty.

There could be no question of a plot for the annexation of the Transvaal. In a free country the Government cannot move in advance of public opinion, and public opinion is influenced by and reflected in the newspapers. One may examine the files of the press during all the months of negotiations and never find one reputable opinion in favour of such a course, nor did one in society ever meet an advocate of such a measure. But a great wrong was being done, and all that was asked was the minimum change which would set it right, and restore equality between the white races in Africa. 'Let Kruger only be liberal in the extension of the franchise,' said the paper which is most representative of the sanest British opinion, 'and he will find that the power of the republic will become not weaker, but infinitely more secure. Let him once give the majority of the resident males of full age the full vote, and he will have given the republic a stability and power which nothing else can. If he rejects all pleas of this kind, and persists in his present policy, he may possibly stave off the evil day, and preserve his cherished oligarchy for another few years; but the end will be the same.' The extract reflects the tone of all of the British press, with the exception of one or two papers which considered that even the persistent ill usage of our people, and the fact that we were peculiarly responsible for them in this State, did not justify us in interfering in the internal affairs of the republic. It cannot be denied that the Jameson raid and the incomplete manner in which the circumstances connected with it had been investigated had weakened the force of those who wished to interfere energetically on behalf of British subjects. There was a vague but widespread feeling that perhaps the capitalists were engineering the situation for their own ends. It is difficult to imagine how a state of unrest and insecurity, to say nothing of a state of war, can ever be to the advantage of capital, and surely it is obvious that if some arch-schemer were using the grievances of the Uitlanders for his own ends the best way to checkmate him would be to remove those grievances. The suspicion, however, did exist among those who like to ignore the obvious and magnify the remote, and throughout the negotiations the hand of Great Britain was weakened, as her adversary had doubtless calculated that it would be, by an earnest but fussy and faddy minority. Idealism and a morbid, restless conscientiousness are two of the most dangerous evils from which a modern progressive State has to suffer.

It was in April 1899 that the British Uitlanders sent their petition praying for protection to their native country. Since the April previous a correspondence had been going on between Dr. Leyds, Secretary of State for the South African Republic, and Mr. Chamberlain, Colonial Secretary, upon the existence or non-existence of the suzerainty. On the one hand, it was contended that the substitution of a second convention had entirely annulled the first; on the other, that the preamble of the first applied also to the second. If the Transvaal contention were correct it is clear that Great Britain had been tricked and jockeyed into such a position, since she had received no *quid pro quo* in the second convention, and even the most careless of Colonial Secretaries could hardly have been expected to give away a very substantial something for nothing. But the contention throws us back upon the academic question of what a suzerainty is. The Transvaal admitted a power of veto over their foreign policy, and this admission in itself, unless they openly tore up the convention, must deprive them of the position of a sovereign State. On the whole, the question must be acknowledged to have been one which might very well have been referred to trustworthy arbitration.

But now to this debate, which had so little of urgency in it that seven months intervened between statement and reply, there came the bitterly vital question of the wrongs and appeal of the Uitlanders. Sir Alfred Milner, the British Commissioner in South Africa, a man of liberal views who had been appointed by a Conservative Government, commanded the respect and confidence of all parties. His record was that of an able, clear-headed man, too just to be either guilty of or tolerant of injustice. To him the matter was referred, and a conference was arranged between President Kruger and him at Bloemfontein, the capital of the Orange Free State. They met on May 30th. Kruger had declared that all questions might be discussed except the independence of the Transvaal. 'All, all, all!' he cried emphatically. But in practice it was found that the parties could not agree as to what did or what did not threaten this independence. What was essential to one was inadmissible to the other. Milner contended for a five years' retroactive franchise, with provisions to secure adequate representation for the mining districts. Kruger offered a seven years' franchise, coupled with numerous conditions which whittled down its value very much, promised five members out of thirty-one to represent a majority of the male population, and added a provision that all differences should be subject to arbitration by foreign powers, a condition which is incompatible with any claim to suzerainty. The proposals of each were impossible to the other, and early in June Sir Alfred Milner was back in Cape Town and President Kruger in Pretoria, with nothing settled except the extreme difficulty of a settlement. The current was running swift, and the roar of the fall was already sounding louder in the ear.

On June 12th Sir Alfred Milner received a deputation at Cape Town and reviewed the situation. 'The principle of equality of races was,' he said, essential for South Africa. The one State where inequality existed kept all the others in a fever. Our policy was one not of aggression, but of singular patience, which could not, however, lapse into indifference.' Two days later Kruger addressed the Raad. 'The other side had not conceded one tittle, and I could not give more. God has always stood by us. I do not want war, but I will not give more away. Although our independence has once been taken away, God has restored it.' He spoke with sincerity no doubt, but it is hard to hear God invoked with such confidence for the system which encouraged the liquor traffic to the natives, and bred the most corrupt set of officials that the modern world has seen.

A dispatch from Sir Alfred Milner, giving his views upon the situation, made the British public recognise, as nothing else had done, how serious the position was, and how essential it was that an earnest national effort should be made to set it right. In it he said:

'The case for intervention is overwhelming. The only attempted answer is that things will right themselves if left alone. But, in fact, the policy of leaving things alone has been tried for years, and it has led to their going from bad to worse. It is not true that this is owing to the raid. They were going from bad to worse before the raid. We were on the verge of war before the raid, and the Transvaal was on the verge of revolution. The effect of the raid has been to give the policy of leaving things alone a new lease of life, and with the old consequences.

'The spectacle of thousands of British subjects kept permanently in the position of helots, constantly chafing under undoubted grievances, and calling vainly to her Majesty's Government for redress, does steadily undermine the influence and reputation of Great Britain within the Queen's dominions. A section of the press, not in the Transvaal only, preaches openly and constantly the doctrine of a republic embracing all South Africa, and supports it by menacing references to the armaments of the Transvaal, its alliance with the Orange Free State, and the active sympathy which, in case of war, it would receive from a section of her Majesty's subjects. I regret to say that this doctrine, supported as it is by a ceaseless stream of malignant lies about the intentions of her Majesty's Government, is producing a great effect on a large number of our Dutch fellow colonists. Language is frequently used which seems to imply that the Dutch have some superior right, even in this colony, to their fellow-citizens of British birth. Thousands of men peaceably disposed, and if left alone perfectly satisfied with their position as British subjects, are being drawn into disaffection, and there is a corresponding exasperation upon the part of the British.

'I can see nothing which will put a stop to this mischievous propaganda but some striking proof of the intention of her Majesty's Government not to be ousted from its position in South Africa.'

Such were the grave and measured words with which the British pro-consul warned his countrymen of what was to come. He saw the storm-cloud piling in the north, but even his eyes had not yet discerned how near and how terrible was the tempest.

Throughout the end of June and the early part of July much was hoped from the mediation of the heads of the Afrikander Bond, the political union of the Dutch Cape colonists. On the one hand, they were the kinsmen of the Boers; on the other, they were British subjects, and were enjoying the blessings of those liberal institutions which we were anxious to see extended to the Transvaal. 'Only treat our folk as we treat yours! Our whole contention was compressed into that prayer. But nothing came of the mission, though a scheme endorsed by Mr. Hofmeyer and Mr. Herholdt, of the Bond, with Mr. Fischer of the Free State, was introduced into the Raad and applauded by Mr. Schreiner, the Africander Premier of Cape Colony. In its original form the provisions were obscure and complicated, the franchise varying from nine years to seven under different conditions. In debate, however, the terms were amended until the time was reduced to seven years, and the proposed representation of the gold fields placed at five. The concession was not a great one, nor could the representation, five out of thirty-one, be considered a generous provision for the majority of the population; but the reduction of the years of residence was eagerly hailed in England as a sign that a compromise might be effected. A sigh of relief went up from the country. 'If,' said the Colonial Secretary, 'this report is confirmed, this important change in the proposals of President Kruger, coupled with previous amendments, leads Government to hope that the new law may prove to be the basis of a settlement on the lines laid down by Sir Alfred Milner in the Bloemfontein Conference.' He added that there were some vexatious conditions attached, but concluded, 'Her Majesty's Government feel assured that the President, having accepted the principle for which they have contended, will be prepared to reconsider any detail of his scheme which can be shown to be a possible hindrance to the full accomplishment of the object in view, and that he will not allow them to be nullified or reduced in value by any subsequent alterations of the law or acts of administration.' At the same time, the *Times* declared the crisis to be at an end. 'If the Dutch statesmen of the Cape have induced their brethren in the Transvaal to carry such a Bill, they will have deserved the lasting gratitude, not only of their own countrymen and of the English colonists in South Africa, but of the British Empire and of the civilised world.'

But this fair prospect was soon destined to be overcast. Questions of detail arose which, when closely examined, proved to be matters of very essential importance. The Uitlanders and British South Africans, who had experienced in the past how illusory the promises of the President might be, insisted upon guarantees. The seven years offered were two years more than that which Sir Alfred Milner had declared to be an irreducible minimum. The difference of two years would not have hindered their acceptance, even at the expense of some humiliation to our representative. But there were conditions which excited distrust when drawn up by so wily a diplomatist. One was that the alien who aspired to burghership had to produce a certificate of continuous registration for a certain time. But the law of registration had fallen into disuse in the Transvaal, and consequently this provision might render the whole Bill valueless. Since it was carefully retained, it was certainly meant for use. The door had been opened, but a stone was placed to block it. Again, the continued burgher-ship of the newcomers was made to depend upon the resolution of the first Raad, so that should the mining members propose any measure of reform, not only their Bill but they also might be swept out of the house by a Boer majority. What could an Opposition do if a vote of the Government might at any moment unseat them all? It was clear that a measure which contained such provisions must be very carefully sifted before a British Government could accept it as a final settlement and a complete concession of justice to its subjects. On the other hand, it naturally felt loth to refuse those clauses which offered some prospect of an amelioration in their condition. It took the course, therefore, of suggesting that each Government should appoint delegates to form a joint commission which should inquire into the working of the proposed Bill before it was put into a final form. The proposal was submitted to the Raad upon August 7th, with the addition that when this was done Sir Alfred Milner was prepared to discuss anything else, including arbitration without the interference of foreign powers.

The suggestion of this joint commission has been criticised as an unwarrantable intrusion into the internal affairs of another country. But then the whole question from the beginning was about the internal affairs of another country, since the internal equality of the white inhabitants was the condition upon which self-government was restored to the Transvaal. It is futile to suggest analogies, and to imagine what France would do if Germany were to interfere in a question of French franchise. Supposing that France contained as many Germans as Frenchmen, and that they were ill-treated, Germany would interfere quickly enough and continue to do so until some fair *modus vivendi* was established. The fact is that the case of the Transvaal stands alone, that such a condition of things has never been known, and that no previous precedent can apply to it, save the general rule that a minority of white men cannot continue indefinitely to tax and govern a majority. Sentiment inclines to the smaller nation, but reason and justice are all on the side of England.

A long delay followed upon the proposal of the Secretary of the Colonies. No reply was forthcoming from Pretoria. But on all sides there came evidence that those preparations for war which had been quietly going on even before the Jameson raid were now being hurriedly perfected. For so small a State enormous sums were being spent upon military equipment. Cases of rifles and boxes of cartridges streamed into the arsenal, not only from Delagoa Bay, but even, to the indignation of the English colonists, through Cape Town and Port Elizabeth. Huge packing-cases, marked 'Agricultural Instruments' and 'Mining Machinery,' arrived from Germany and France, to find their places in the forts of Johannesburg or Pretoria. Men of many nations but of a similar type showed their martial faces in the Boer towns. The *condottieri* of Europe were as ready as ever to sell their blood for gold, and nobly in the end did they fulfil their share of the bargain. For three weeks and more during which Mr. Kruger was silent these eloquent preparations went on. But beyond them, and of infinitely more importance, there was one fact which dominated the situation. A burgher cannot go to war without his horse, his horse cannot move without grass, grass will not come until after rain, and it was still some weeks before the rain would be due. Negotiations, then, must not be unduly hurried while the *veldt* was a bare russet-coloured dust-swept plain. Mr. Chamberlain and the British public waited week after week for their answer. But there was a limit to their patience, and it was reached on August 26th, when the Colonial Secretary showed, with a plainness of speech which is as unusual as it is welcome in diplomacy, that the question could not be hung up for ever. 'The sands are running down in the glass,' said he. 'If they run out, we shall not hold ourselves limited by that which we have already offered, but, having taken the matter in hand, we will not let it go until we have secured conditions which once for all shall establish which is the paramount power in South Africa, and shall secure for our fellow-subjects there those equal rights and equal privileges which were promised them by President Kruger when the independence of the Transvaal was granted by the Queen, and which is the least that in justice ought to be accorded them.' Lord Salisbury, a little time before, had been equally emphatic. 'No one in this country wishes to disturb the conventions so long as it is recognised that while they guarantee the independence of the Transvaal on the one side, they guarantee equal political and civil rights for settlers of all nationalities upon the other. But these conventions are not like the laws of the Medes and the Persians. They are mortal, they can be destroyed...and once destroyed they can never be reconstructed in the same shape.' The long-enduring patience of Great Britain was beginning to show signs of giving way.

In the meantime a fresh dispatch had arrived from the Transvaal which offered as an alternative proposal to the joint commission that the Boer Government should grant the franchise proposals of Sir Alfred Milner on condition that Great Britain withdrew or dropped her claim to a suzerainty, agreed to arbitration, and promised never again to interfere in the internal affairs of the republic. To this Great Britain answered that she would agree to arbitration, that she hoped never again to have occasion to interfere for the protection of her own subjects, but that with the grant of the franchise all occasion for such interference would pass away, and, finally, that she would never consent to abandon her position as suzerain power. Mr. Chamberlain's dispatch ended by reminding the Government of the Transvaal that there were other matters of dispute open between the two Governments apart from the franchise, and that it would be as well to have them settled at the same time. By these he meant such questions as the position of the native races and the treatment of Anglo-Indians.

On September 2nd the answer of the Transvaal Government was returned. It was short and uncompromising. They withdrew their offer of the franchise. They re-asserted the non-existence of the suzerainty. The negotiations were at a deadlock. It was difficult to see how they could be re-opened. In view of the arming of the burghers, the small garrison of Natal had been taking up positions to cover the frontier. The Transvaal asked for an explanation of their presence. Sir Alfred Milner answered that they were guarding British interests, and preparing against contingencies. The roar of the fall was sounding loud and near.

On September 8th there was held a Cabinet Council—one of the most important in recent years. A message was sent to Pretoria, which even the opponents of the Government have acknowledged to be temperate, and offering the basis for a peaceful settlement. It begins by repudiating emphatically the claim of the Transvaal to be a sovereign international State in the same sense in which the Orange Free State is one. Any proposal made conditional upon such an acknowledgment could not be entertained.

The British Government, however, was prepared to accept the five years' 'franchise' as stated in the note of August 19th, assuming at the same time that in the Raad each member might talk his own language.

'Acceptance of these terms by the South African Republic would at once remove tension between the two Governments, and would in all probability render unnecessary any future intervention to secure redress for grievances which the Uitlanders themselves would be able to bring to the notice of the Executive Council and the Volksraad.

'Her Majesty's Government are increasingly impressed with the danger of further delay in relieving the strain which has already caused so much injury to the interests of South Africa, and they earnestly press for an immediate and definite reply to the present proposal. If it is acceded to they will be ready to make immediate arrangements...to settle all details of the proposed tribunal of arbitration...If, however, as they most anxiously hope will not be the case, the reply of the South African Republic should be negative or inconclusive, I am to state that her Majesty's Government must reserve to themselves the right to reconsider the situation de novo, and to formulate their own proposals for a final settlement.'

Such was the message, and Great Britain waited with strained attention for the answer. But again there was a delay, while the rain came and the grass grew, and the *veldt* was as a mounted rifleman would have it. The burghers were in no humour for concessions. They knew their own power, and they concluded with justice that they were for the time far the strongest military power in South Africa. 'We have beaten England before, but it is nothing to the licking we shall give her now,' cried a prominent citizen, and he spoke for his country as he said it. So the empire waited and debated, but the sounds of the bugle were already breaking through the wrangles of the politicians, and calling the nation to be tested once more by that hammer of war and adversity by which Providence still fashions us to some nobler and higher end.

CHAPTER 4

The Eve of War

The message sent from the Cabinet Council of September 8th was evidently the precursor either of peace or of war. The cloud must burst or blow over. As the nation waited in hushed expectancy for a reply it spent some portion of its time in examining and speculating upon those military preparations which might be needed. The War Office had for some months been arranging for every contingency, and had made certain dispositions which appeared to them to be adequate, but which our future experience was to demonstrate to be far too small for the very serious matter in hand.

It is curious in turning over the files of such a paper as the *Times* to observe how at first one or two small paragraphs of military significance might appear in the endless columns of diplomatic and political reports, how gradually they grew and grew, until at last the eclipse was complete, and the diplomacy had been thrust into the tiny paragraphs while the war filled the journal. Under July 7th comes the first glint of arms amid the drab monotony of the state papers. On that date it was announced that two companies of Royal Engineers and departmental corps with reserves of supplies and ammunition were being dispatched. Two companies of engineers! Who could have foreseen that they were the vanguard of the greatest army which ever at any time of the world's history has crossed an ocean, and far the greatest which a British general has commanded in the field?

On August 15th, at a time when the negotiations had already assumed a very serious phase, after the failure of the Bloemfontein conference and the dispatch of Sir Alfred Milner, the British forces in South Africa were absolutely and absurdly inadequate for the purpose of the defence of our own frontier. Surely such a fact must open the eyes of those who, in spite of all the evidence, persist that the war was forced on by the British. A statesman who forces on a war usually prepares for a war, and this is exactly what Mr. Kruger did and the British authorities did not. The overbearing suzerain power had at that date, scattered over a huge frontier, two cavalry regiments, three field batteries, and six and a half infantry battalions—say six thousand men. The innocent pastoral States could put in the field forty or fifty thousand mounted riflemen, whose mobility doubled their numbers, and a most excellent artillery, including the heaviest guns which have ever been seen upon a battlefield. At this time it is most certain that the Boers could have made their way easily either to Durban or to Cape Town. The British force, condemned to act upon the defensive, could have been masked and afterwards destroyed, while the main body of the invaders would have encountered nothing but an irregular local resistance, which would have been neutralised by the apathy or hostility of the Dutch colonists. It is extraordinary that our authorities seem never to have contemplated the possibility of the Boers taking the initiative, or to have understood that in that case our belated reinforcements would certainly have had to land under the fire of the republican guns.

In July Natal had taken alarm, and a strong representation had been sent from the prime minister of the colony to the Governor, Sir W. Hely Hutchinson, and so to the Colonial Office. It was notorious that the Transvaal was armed to the teeth, that the Orange Free State was likely to join her, and that there had been strong attempts made, both privately and through the press, to alienate the loyalty of the Dutch citizens of both the British colonies. Many sinister signs were observed by those upon the spot. The *veldt* had been burned unusually early to ensure a speedy grass-crop after the first rains, there had been a collecting of horses, a distribution of rifles and ammunition. The Free State farmers, who graze their sheep and cattle upon Natal soil during the winter, had driven them off to places of safety behind the line of the Drakensberg. Everything pointed to approaching war, and Natal refused to be satisfied even by the dispatch of another regiment. On September 6th a second message was received at the Colonial Office, which states the case with great clearness and precision.

'The Prime Minister desires me to urge upon you by the unanimous advice of the Ministers that sufficient troops should be dispatched to Natal immediately to enable the colony to be placed in a state of defence against an attack from the Transvaal and the Orange Free State. I am informed by the General Officer Commanding, Natal, that he will not have enough troops, even when the Manchester Regiment arrives, to do more than occupy Newcastle and at the same time protect the colony south of it from raids, while Laing's Nek, Ingogo River and Zululand must be left undefended. My Ministers know that every preparation has been made, both in the Transvaal and the Orange Free State, which would enable an attack to be made on Natal at short notice. My Ministers believe that the Boers have made up their minds that war will take place almost certainly, and their best chance will be, when it seems unavoidable, to deliver a blow before reinforcements have time to arrive. Information has been received that raids in force will be made by way of Middle Drift and Greytown and by way of Bond's Drift and Stangar, with a view to striking the railway between Pietermaritzburg and Durban and cutting off communications of troops and supplies. Nearly all the Orange Free State farmers in the Klip River division, who stay in the colony usually till October at least, have trekked, at great loss to themselves; their sheep are lambing on the road, and the lambs die or are destroyed. Two at least of the Entonjanani district farmers have trekked with all their belongings into the Transvaal, in the first case attempting to take as hostages the children of the natives on the farm. Reliable reports have been received of attempts to tamper with loyal natives, and to set tribe against tribe in order to create confusion and detail the defensive forces of the colony. Both food and warlike stores in large quantities have been accumulated at Volksrust, Vryheid and Standerton. Persons who are believed to be spies have been seen examining the bridges on the Natal Railway, and it is known that there are spies in all the principal centres of the colony. In the opinion of Ministers, such a catastrophe as the seizure of Laing's Nek and the destruction of the northern portion of the railway, or a successful raid or invasion such as they have reason to believe is contemplated, would produce a most demoralising effect on the natives and on the loyal Europeans in the colony, and would afford great encouragement to the Boers and to their sympathisers in the colonies, who, although armed and prepared, will probably keep quiet unless they receive some encouragement of the sort. They concur in the policy of her Majesty's Government of exhausting all peaceful means to obtain redress of the grievances of the Uitlanders and authoritatively assert the supremacy of Great Britain before resorting to war; but they state that this is a question of defensive precaution, not of making war.'

In answer to these and other remonstrances the garrison of Natal was gradually increased, partly by troops from Europe, and partly by the dispatch of five thousand British troops from India. The 2nd Berkshires, the 1st Royal Munster Fusiliers, the 1st Manchesters, and the 2nd Dublin Fusiliers arrived in succession with reinforcements of artillery. The 5th Dragoon Guards, 9th Lancers, and 19th Hussars came from India, with the 1st Devonshires, 1st Gloucesters, 2nd King's Royal Rifles and 2nd Gordon Highlanders. These with the 21st, 42nd, and 53rd batteries of Field Artillery made up the Indian Contingent. Their arrival late in September raised the number of troops in South Africa to 22,000, a force which was inadequate to a contest in the open field with the numerous, mobile, and gallant enemy to whom they were to be opposed, but which proved to be strong enough to stave off that overwhelming disaster which, with our fuller knowledge, we can now see to have been impending.

As to the disposition of these troops a difference of opinion broke out between the ruling powers in Natal and the military chiefs at the spot. Prince Kraft has said, 'Both strategy and tactics may have to yield to politics;' but the political necessity should be very grave and very clear when it is the blood of soldiers which has to pay for it. Whether it arose from our defective intelligence, or from that caste feeling which makes it hard for the professional soldier to recognise (in spite of deplorable past experiences) a serious adversary in the mounted farmer, it is certain that even while our papers were proclaiming that this time, at least, we would not underrate our enemy, we were most seriously underrating him. The northern third of Natal is as vulnerable a military position as a player of *kriegspiel* could wish to have submitted to him. It runs up into a thin angle, culminating at the apex in a difficult pass, the ill-omened Laing's Nek, dominated by the even more sinister bulk of Majuba. Each side of this angle is open to invasion, the one from the Transvaal and the other from the Orange Free State. A force up at the apex is in a perfect trap, for the mobile enemy can flood into the country to the south of them, cut the line of supplies, and throw up a series of entrenchments which would make retreat a very difficult matter. Further down the country, at such positions as Ladysmith or Dundee, the danger, though not so imminent, is still an obvious one, unless the defending force is strong enough to hold its own in the open field and mobile enough to prevent a mounted enemy from getting round its flanks. To us, who are endowed with that profound military wisdom which only comes with a knowledge of the event, it is obvious that with a defending force which could not place more than 12,000 men in the fighting line, the true defensible frontier was the line of the Tugela. As a matter of fact, Ladysmith was chosen, a place almost indefensible itself, as it is dominated by high hills in at least two directions.

Such an event as the siege of the town appears never to have been contemplated, as no guns of position were asked for or sent. In spite of this, an amount of stores, which is said to have been valued at more than a million of pounds, was dumped down at this small railway junction, so that the position could not be evacuated without a crippling loss. The place was the point of bifurcation of the main line, which divides at this little town into one branch running to Harrismith in the Orange Free State, and the other leading through the Dundee coal fields and Newcastle to the Laing's Nek tunnel and the Transvaal. An importance, which appears now to have been an exaggerated one, was attached by the Government of Natal to the possession of the coal fields, and it was at their strong suggestion, but with the concurrence of General Penn Symons, that the defending force was divided, and a detachment of between three and four thousand sent to Dundee, about forty miles from the main body, which remained under General Sir George White at Ladysmith. General Symons underrated the power of the invaders, but it is hard to criticise an error of judgment which has been so nobly atoned and so tragically paid for. At the time, then, which our political narrative has reached, the time of suspense which followed the dispatch of the Cabinet message of September 8th, the military situation had ceased to be desperate, but was still precarious. Twenty-two thousand regular troops were on the spot who might hope to be reinforced by some ten thousand colonials, but these forces had to cover a great frontier, the attitude of Cape Colony was by no means whole-hearted and might become hostile, while the black population might conceivably throw in its weight against us. Only half the regulars could be spared to defend Natal, and no reinforcements could reach them in less than a month from the outbreak of hostilities. If Mr. Chamberlain was really playing a game of bluff, it must be confessed that he was bluffing from a very weak hand.

For purposes of comparison we may give some idea of the forces which Mr. Kruger and Mr. Steyn could put in the field, for by this time it was evident that the Orange Free State, with which we had had no shadow of a dispute, was going, in a way which some would call wanton and some chivalrous, to throw in its weight against us. The general press estimate of the forces of the two republics varied from 25,000 to 35,000 men. Mr. J. B. Robinson, a personal friend of President Kruger's and a man who had spent much of his life among the Boers, considered the latter estimate to be too high. The calculation had no assured basis to start from. A very scattered and isolated population, among whom large families were the rule, is a most difficult thing to estimate. Some reckoned from the supposed natural increase during eighteen years, but the figure given at that date was itself an assumption. Others took their calculation from the number of voters in the last presidential election: but no one could tell how many abstentions there had been, and the fighting age is five years earlier than the voting age in the republics. We recognise now that all calculations were far below the true figure. It is probable, however, that the information of the British Intelligence Department was not far wrong. According to this the fighting strength of the Transvaal alone was 32,000 men, and of the Orange Free State 22,000. With mercenaries and rebels from the colonies they would amount to 60, 000, while a considerable rising of the Cape Dutch would bring them up to 100,000. In artillery they were known to have about a hundred guns, many of them (and the fact will need much explaining) more modern and powerful than any which we could bring against them. Of the quality of this large force there is no need to speak. The men were brave, hardy, and fired with a strange religious enthusiasm. They were all of the seventeenth century, except their rifles. Mounted upon their hardy little ponies, they possessed a mobility which practically doubled their numbers and made it an impossibility ever to outflank them. As marksmen they were supreme. Add to this that they had the advantage of acting upon internal lines with shorter and safer communications, and one gathers how formidable a task lay before the soldiers of the empire. When we turn from such an enumeration of their strength to contemplate the 12,000 men, split into two detachments, who awaited them in Natal, we may recognise that, far from bewailing our disasters, we should rather congratulate ourselves upon our escape from losing that great province which, situated as it is between Britain, India, and Australia, must be regarded as the very keystone of the imperial arch.

At the risk of a tedious but very essential digression, something must be said here as to the motives with which the Boers had for many years been quietly preparing for war. That the Jameson raid was not the cause is certain, though it probably, by putting the Boer Government into a strong position, had a great effect in accelerating matters. What had been done secretly and slowly could be done more swiftly and openly when so plausible an excuse could be given for it. As a matter of fact, the preparations were long antecedent to the raid. The building of the forts at Pretoria and Johannesburg was begun nearly two years before that wretched incursion, and the importation of arms was going on apace. In that very year, 1895, a considerable sum was spent in military equipment.

But if it was not the raid, and if the Boers had no reason to fear the British Government, with whom the Transvaal might have been as friendly as the Orange Free State had been for forty years, why then should they arm? It was a difficult question, and one in answering which we find ourselves in a region of conjecture and suspicion rather than of ascertained fact. But the fairest and most unbiased of historians must confess that there is a large body of evidence to show that into the heads of some of the Dutch leaders, both in the northern republics and in the Cape, there had entered the conception of a single Dutch commonwealth, extending from Cape Town to the Zambezi, in which flag, speech, and law should all be Dutch. It is in this aspiration that many shrewd and well-informed judges see the true inner meaning of this persistent arming, of the constant hostility, of the forming of ties between the two republics (one of whom had been reconstituted and made a sovereign independent State by our own act), and finally of that intriguing which endeavoured to poison the affection and allegiance of our own Dutch colonists, who had no political grievances whatever. They all aimed at one end, and that end was the final expulsion of British power from South Africa and the formation of a single great Dutch republic. The large sum spent by the Transvaal in secret service money—a larger sum, I believe, than that which is spent by the whole British Empire—would give some idea of the subterranean influences at work. An army of emissaries, agents, and spies, whatever their mission, were certainly spread over the British colonies. Newspapers were subsidised also, and considerable sums spent upon the press in France and Germany.

In the very nature of things a huge conspiracy of this sort to substitute Dutch for British rule in South Africa is not a matter which can be easily and definitely proved. Such questions are not discussed in public documents, and men are sounded before being taken into the confidence of the conspirators. But there is plenty of evidence of the individual ambition of prominent and representative men in this direction, and it is hard to believe that what many wanted individually was not striven for collectively, especially when we see how the course of events did actually work towards the end which they indicated. Mr. J.P. FitzPatrick, in 'The Transvaal from Within'—a book to which all subsequent writers upon the subject must acknowledge their obligations—narrates how in 1896 he was approached by Mr. D.P. Graaff, formerly a member of the Cape Legislative Council and a very prominent Afrikander Bondsman, with the proposition that Great Britain should be pushed out of South Africa. The same politician made the same proposal to Mr. Beit. Compare with this the following statement of Mr. Theodore Schreiner, the brother of the Prime Minister of the Cape:

> I met Mr. Reitz, then a judge of the Orange Free State, in Bloemfontein between seventeen and eighteen years ago, shortly after the retrocession of the Transvaal, and when he was busy establishing the Afrikander Bond. It must be patent to every one that at that time, at all events, England and its Government had no intention of taking away the independence of the Transvaal, for she had just "magnanimously" granted the same; no intention of making war on the republics, for she had just made peace; no intention to seize the Rand gold fields, for they were not yet discovered. At that time, then, I met Mr. Reitz, and he did his best to get me to become a member of his Afrikander Bond, but, after studying its

constitution and programme, I refused to do so, whereupon the following colloquy in substance took place between us, which has been indelibly imprinted on my mind ever since:

Reitz: Why do you refuse? Is the object of getting the people to take an interest in political matters not a good one?

Myself: Yes, it is; but I seem to see plainly here between the lines of this constitution much more ultimately aimed at than that.

Reitz: What?

Myself: I see quite clearly that the ultimate object aimed at is the overthrow of the British power and the expulsion of the British flag from South Africa.

Reitz (with his pleasant conscious smile, as of one whose secret thought and purpose had been discovered, and who was not altogether displeased that such was the case): Well, what if it is so?

Myself: You don't suppose, do you, that that flag is going to disappear from South Africa without a tremendous struggle and fight?

Reitz (with the same pleasant self-conscious, self satisfied, and yet semi-apologetic smile): Well, I suppose not; but even so, what of that?

Myself: Only this, that when that struggle takes place you and I will be on opposite sides; and what is more, the God who was on the side of the Transvaal in the late war, because it had right on its side will be on the side of England, because He must view with abhorrence any plotting and scheming to overthrow her power and position in South Africa, which have been ordained by Him.

Reitz: We'll see.

Thus the conversation ended, but during the seventeen years that have elapsed I have watched the propaganda for the overthrow of British power in South Africa being ceaselessly spread by every possible means—the press, the pulpit, the platform, the schools, the colleges, the Legislature—until it has culminated in the present war, of which Mr. Reitz and his co-workers are the origin and the cause. Believe me, the day on which F.W. Reitz sat down to pen his ultimatum to Great Britain was the proudest and happiest moment of his life, and one which had for long years been looked forward to by him with eager longing and expectation.

Compare with these utterances of a Dutch politician of the Cape, and of a Dutch politician of the Orange Free State, the following passage from a speech delivered by Kruger at Bloemfontein in the year 1887:

I think it too soon to speak of a United South Africa under one flag. Which flag was it to be? The Queen of England would object to having her flag hauled down, and we, the burghers of the Transvaal, object to hauling ours down. What is to be done? We are now small and of little importance, but we are growing, and are preparing the way to take our place among the great nations of the world.

'The dream of our life,' said another, 'is a union of the States of South Africa, and this has to come from within, not from without. When that is accomplished, South Africa will be great.' Always the same theory from all quarters of Dutch thought, to be followed by many signs that the idea was being prepared for in practice. I repeat that the fairest and most unbiased historian cannot dismiss the conspiracy as a myth.

And to this one may retort, why should they not conspire? Why should they not have their own views as to the future of South Africa? Why should they not endeavour to have one universal flag and one common speech? Why should they not win over our colonists, if they can, and push us into the sea? I see no reason why they should not. Let them try if they will. And let us try to prevent them. But let us have an end of talk about British aggression, of capitalist designs upon the gold fields, of the wrongs of a pastoral people, and all the other veils which have been used to cover the issue. Let those who talk about British designs upon the republics turn their attention for a moment to the evidence which there is for republican designs upon the colonies. Let them reflect that in the one system all white men are equal, and that on the other the minority of one race has persecuted the majority of the other, and let them consider under which the truest freedom lies, which stands for universal liberty and which for reaction and racial hatred. Let them ponder and answer all this before they determine where their sympathies lie.

Leaving these wider questions of politics, and dismissing for the time those military considerations which were soon to be of such vital moment, we may now return to the course of events in the diplomatic struggle between the Government of the Transvaal and the Colonial Office. On September 8th, as already narrated, a final message was sent to Pretoria, which stated the minimum terms which the British Government could accept as being a fair concession to her subjects in the Transvaal. A definite answer was demanded, and the nation waited with sombre patience for the reply.

There were few illusions in this country as to the difficulties of a Transvaal war. It was clearly seen that little honour and immense vexation were in store for us. The first Boer war still smarted in our minds, and we knew the prowess of the indomitable burghers. But our people, if gloomy, were none the less resolute, for that national instinct which is beyond the wisdom of statesmen had borne it in upon them that this was no local quarrel, but one upon which the whole existence of the empire hung. The cohesion of that empire was to be tested. Men had emptied their glasses to it in time of peace. Was it a meaningless pouring of wine, or were they ready to pour their hearts' blood also in time of war? Had we really founded a series of disconnected nations, with no common senti-ment or interest, or was the empire an organic whole, as ready to thrill with one emotion or to harden into one resolve as are the several States of the Union? That was the question at issue, and much of the future history of the world was at stake upon the answer.

Already there were indications that the colonies appreciated the fact that the contention was no affair of the mother country alone, but that she was upholding the rights of the empire as a whole, and might fairly look to them to support her in any quarrel which might arise from it. As early as July 11th, Queensland, the fiery and semitropical, had offered a contingent of mounted infantry with machine guns; New Zealand, Western Australia, Tasmania, Victoria, New South Wales, and South Australia followed in the order named. Canada, with the strong but more deliberate spirit of the north, was the last to speak, but spoke the more firmly for the delay. Her citizens were the least concerned of any, for Australians were many in South Africa but Canadians few. None the less, she cheerfully took her share of the common burden, and grew the readier and the cheerier as that burden came to weigh more heavily. From all the men of many hues who make up the British Empire, from Hindoo Rajahs, from West African Houssas, from Malay police, from Western Indians, there came offers of service. But this was to be a white man's war, and if the British could not work out their own salvation then it were well that empire should pass from such a race. The magnifi-cent Indian army of 150,000 soldiers, many of them seasoned veterans, was for the same reason left untouched. England has claimed no credit or consideration for such abstention, but an irresponsible writer may well ask how many of those foreign critics whose respect for our public morality appears to be as limited as their knowledge of our principles and history would have advocated such self denial had their own coun-tries been placed in the same position.

On September 18th the official reply of the Boer Government to the message sent from the Cabinet Council was published in London. In manner it was unbending and unconciliatory; in substance, it was a complete rejection of all the British demands. It refused to recommend or propose to the Raad the five years' franchise and the other measures which had been defined as the minimum which the Home Government could accept as a fair measure of justice towards the Uitlanders. The suggestion that the debates of the Raad should be bilingual, as they have been in the Cape Colony and in Canada, was absolutely waived aside. The British Government had stated in their last dispatch that if the reply should be negative or inconclusive they reserved to themselves the right to 'reconsider the situation *de novo* and to formulate their own proposals for a final settlement.' The reply had been both negative and inconclusive, and on September 22nd a council met to determine what the next message should be. It was short and firm, but so planned as not to shut the door upon peace. Its purport was that the British Government expressed deep regret at the rejection of the moderate proposals which had been submitted in their last dispatch, and that now, in accordance with their promise, they would shortly put forward their own plans for a settlement. The message was not an ultimatum, but it foreshadowed an ultimatum in the future.

In the meantime, upon September 21st the Raad of the Orange Free State had met, and it became more and more evident that this republic, with whom we had no possible quarrel, but, on the contrary, for whom we had a great deal of friendship and admiration, intended to throw in its weight against Great Britain. Some time before, an offensive and defensive alliance had been concluded between the two States, which must, until the secret history of these events comes to be written, appear to have been a singularly rash and unprofitable bargain for the smaller one. She had nothing to fear from Great Britain, since she had been voluntarily turned into an independent republic by her and had lived in peace with her for forty years. Her laws were as liberal as our own. But by this suicidal treaty she agreed to share the fortunes of a State which was deliberately courting war by its persistently unfriendly attitude, and whose reactionary and narrow legislation would, one might imagine, have alienated the sympathy of her progressive neighbour. There may have been ambitions like those already quoted from the report of Dr. Reitz's conversation, or there may have been a complete hallucination as to the comparative strength of the two combatants and the probable future of South Africa; but however that may be, the treaty was made, and the time had come to test how far it would hold.

The tone of President Steyn at the meeting of the Raad, and the support which he received from the majority of his burghers, showed unmistakably that the two republics would act as one. In his opening speech Steyn declared uncompromisingly against the British contention, and declared that his State was bound to the Transvaal by everything which was near and dear. Among the obvious military precautions which could no longer be neglected by the British Government was the sending of some small force to protect the long and exposed line of railway which lies just outside the Transvaal border from Kimberley to Rhodesia. Sir Alfred Milner communicated with President Steyn as to this movement of troops, pointing out that it was in no way directed against the Free State. Sir Alfred Milner added that the Imperial Government was still hopeful of a friendly settlement with the Transvaal, but if this hope were disappointed they looked to the Orange Free State to preserve strict neutrality and to prevent military intervention by any of its citizens. They undertook that in that case the integrity of the Free State frontier would be strictly preserved. Finally, he stated that there was absolutely no cause to disturb the good relations between the Free State and Great Britain, since we were animated by the most friendly intentions towards them. To this the President returned a somewhat ungracious answer, to the effect that he disapproved of our action towards the Transvaal, and that he regretted the movement of troops, which would be considered a menace by the burghers. A subsequent resolution of the Free State Raad, ending with the words, 'Come what may, the Free State will honestly and faithfully fulfil its obligations towards the Transvaal by virtue of the political alliance existing between the two republics,' showed how impossible it was that this country, formed by ourselves and without a shadow of a cause of quarrel with us, could be saved from being drawn into the whirlpool. Everywhere, from over both borders, came the news of martial preparations. Already at the end of September troops and armed burghers were gathering upon the frontier, and the most incredulous were beginning at last to understand that the shadow of a great war was really falling across them. Artillery, war munitions, and stores were being accumulated at Volksrust upon the Natal border, showing where the storm might be expected to break. On the last day of September, twenty-six military trains were reported to have left Pretoria and Johannesburg for that point. At the same time news came of a concentration at Malmani, upon the Bechuanaland border, threatening the railway line and the British town of Mafeking, a name destined before long to be familiar to the world.

On October 3rd there occurred what was in truth an act of war, although the British Government, patient to the verge of weakness, refused to regard it as such, and continued to draw up their final state paper. The mail train from the Transvaal to Cape Town was stopped at Vereeniging, and the week's shipment of gold for England, amounting to about half a million pounds, was taken by the Boer Government. In a debate at Cape Town upon the same day the Africander Minister of the Interior admitted that as many as 404 trucks had passed from the

Government line over the frontier and had not been returned. Taken in conjunction with the passage of arms and cartridges through the Cape to Pretoria and Bloemfontein, this incident aroused the deepest indignation among the Colonial English and the British public, which was increased by the reports of the difficulty which border towns, such as Kimberley and Vryburg, had had in getting cannon for their own defence. The Raads had been dissolved, and the old President's last words had been a statement that war was certain, and a stern invocation of the Lord as final arbiter. England was ready less obtrusively but no less heartily to refer the quarrel to the same dread Judge.

On October 2nd President Steyn informed Sir Alfred Milner that he had deemed it necessary to call out the Free State burghers—that is, to mobilise his forces. Sir A. Milner wrote regretting these preparations, and declaring that he did not yet despair of peace, for he was sure that any reasonable proposal would be favourably considered by her Majesty's Government. Steyn's reply was that there was no use in negotiating unless the stream of British reinforcements ceased coming into South Africa. As our forces were still in a great minority, it was impossible to stop the reinforcements, so the correspondence led to nothing. On October 7th the army reserves for the First Army Corps were called out in Great Britain and other signs shown that it had been determined to send a considerable force to South Africa. Parliament was also summoned that the formal national assent might be gained for those grave measures which were evidently pending.

It was on October 9th that the somewhat leisurely proceedings of the British Colonial Office were brought to a head by the arrival of an unexpected and audacious ultimatum from the Boer Government. In contests of wit, as of arms, it must be confessed that the laugh has been usually upon the side of our simple and pastoral South African neighbours. The present instance was no exception to the rule. While our Government was cautiously and patiently leading up to an ultimatum, our opponent suddenly played the very card which we were preparing to lay upon the table. The document was very firm and explicit, but the terms in which it was drawn were so impossible that it was evidently framed with the deliberate purpose of forcing an immediate war. It demanded that the troops upon the borders of the republic should be instantly withdrawn, that all reinforcements which had arrived within the last year should leave South Africa, and that those who were now upon the sea should be sent back without being landed. Failing a satisfactory answer within forty-eight hours, 'the Transvaal Government will with great regret be compelled to regard the action of her Majesty's Government as a formal declaration of war, for the consequences of which it will not hold itself responsible.' The audacious message was received throughout the empire with a mixture of derision and anger. The answer was dispatched next day through Sir Alfred Milner.

> 10th October.—Her Majesty's Government have received with great regret the peremptory demands of the Government of the South African Republic, conveyed in your telegram of the 9th October. You will inform the Government of the South African Republic in reply that the conditions demanded by the Government of the South African Republic are such as her Majesty's Government deem it impossible to discuss.

And so we have come to the end of the long road, past the battle of the pens and the wrangling of tongues, to the arbitration of the Lee-Metford and the Mauser. It was pitiable that it should come to this. These people were as near akin to us as any race which is not our own. They were of the same Frisian stock which peopled our own shores. In habit of mind, in religion, in respect for law, they were as ourselves. Brave, too, they were, and hospitable, with those sporting instincts which are dear to the Anglo-Celtic race. There was no people in the world who had more qualities which we might admire, and not the least of them was that love of independence which it is our proudest boast that we have encouraged in others as well as exercised ourselves. And yet we had come to this pass, that there was no room in all vast South Africa for both of us. We cannot hold ourselves blameless in the matter. 'The evil that men do lives after them,' and it has been told in this small superficial sketch where we have erred in the past in South Africa. On our hands, too, is the Jameson raid, carried out by Englishmen and led by officers who held the Queen's Commission; to us, also, the blame of the shuffling, half-hearted inquiry into that most unjustifiable business. These are matches which helped to set the great blaze alight, and it is we who held them. But the fagots which proved to be so inflammable, they were not of our setting. They were the wrongs done to half the community, the settled resolution of the minority to tax and vex the majority, the determination of a people who had lived two generations in a country to claim that country entirely for themselves. Behind them all there may have been the Dutch ambition to dominate South Africa. It was no petty object for which Britain fought. When a nation struggles uncomplainingly through months of disaster she may claim to have proved her conviction of the justice and necessity of the struggle. Should Dutch ideas or English ideas of government prevail throughout that huge country? The one means freedom for a single race, the other means equal rights to all white men beneath one common law. What each means to the coloured races let history declare. This was the main issue to be determined from the instant that the clock struck five upon the afternoon of Wednesday, October the eleventh, eighteen hundred and ninety-nine. That moment marked the opening of a war destined to determine the fate of South Africa, to work great changes in the British Empire, to seriously affect the future history of the world, and incidentally to alter many of our views as to the art of war. It is the story of this war which, with limited material but with much aspiration to care and candour, I shall now endeavour to tell.

CHAPTER 5

Talana Hill

It was on the morning of October 12th, amid cold and mist, that the Boer camps at Sandspruit and Volksrust broke up, and the burghers rode to the war. Some twelve thousand of them, all mounted, with two batteries of eight Krupp guns each, were the invading force from the north, which hoped later to be joined by the Freestaters and by a contingent of Germans and Transvaalers who were to cross the Free State border. It was an hour before dawn that the guns started, and the riflemen followed close behind the last limber, so that the first light of day fell upon the black sinuous line winding down between the hills. A spectator upon the occasion says of them: 'Their faces were a study. For the most part the expression worn was one of determination and bulldog pertinacity. No sign of fear there, nor of wavering. Whatever else may be laid to the charge of the Boer, it may never truthfully be said that he is a coward or a man unworthy of the Briton's steel.' The words were written early in the campaign, and the whole empire will endorse them today. Could we have such men as willing fellow-citizens, they are worth more than all the gold mines of their country.

This main Transvaal body consisted of the commando of Pretoria, which comprised 1800 men, and those of Heidelberg, Middelburg, Krugersdorp, Standerton, Wakkerstroom, and Ermelo, with the State Artillery, an excellent and highly organised body who were provided with the best guns that have ever been brought on to a battlefield. Besides their sixteen Krupps, they dragged with them two heavy six-inch Creusot guns, which were destined to have a very important effect in the earlier part of the campaign. In addition to these native forces there were a certain number of European auxiliaries. The greater part of the German corps were with the Free State forces, but a few hundred came down from the north. There was a Hollander corps of about two hundred and fifty and an Irish—or perhaps more properly an Irish-American-corps of the same number, who rode under the green flag and the harp.

The men might, by all accounts, be divided into two very different types. There were the town Boers, smartened and perhaps a little enervated by prosperity and civilisation, men of business and professional men, more alert and quicker than their rustic comrades. These men spoke English rather than Dutch, and indeed there were many men of English descent among them. But the others, the most formidable both in their numbers and in their primitive qualities, were the back-*veldt* Boers, the sunburned, tangle-haired, full-bearded farmers, the men of the Bible and the rifle, imbued with the traditions of their own guerrilla warfare. These were perhaps the finest natural warriors upon earth, marksmen, hunters, accustomed to hard fare and a harder couch. They were rough in their ways and speech, but, in spite of many calumnies and some few unpleasant truths, they might compare with most disciplined armies in their humanity and their desire to observe the usages of war.

A few words here as to the man who led this singular host. Piet Joubert was a Cape Colonist by birth—a fellow countryman, like Kruger himself, of those whom the narrow laws of his new country persisted in regarding as outside the pale. He came from that French Huguenot blood which has strengthened and refined every race which it has touched, and from it he derived a chivalry and generosity which made him respected and liked even by his opponents. In many native broils and in the British campaign of 1881 he had shown himself a capable leader. His record in standing out for the independence of the Transvaal was a very consistent one, for he had not accepted office under the British, as Kruger had done, but had remained always an irreconcilable. Tall and burly, with hard grey eyes and a grim mouth half hidden by his bushy beard, he was a fine type of the men whom he led. He was now in his sixty-fifth year, and the fire of his youth had, as some of the burghers urged, died down within him; but he was experienced, crafty, and war wise, never dashing and never brilliant, but slow, steady, solid, and inexorable.

Besides this northern army there were two other bodies of burghers converging upon Natal. One, consisting of the commandoes from Utrecht and the Swaziland districts, had gathered at Vryheid on the flank of the British position at Dundee. The other, much larger, not less probably than six or seven thousand men, were the contingent from the Free State and a Transvaal corps, together with Schiel's Germans, who were making their way through the various passes, the Tintwa Pass, and Van Reenen's Pass, which lead through the grim range of the Drakensberg and open out upon the more fertile plains of Western Natal. The total force may have been something between twenty and thirty thousand men. By all accounts they were of an astonishingly high heart, convinced that a path of easy victory lay before them, and that nothing could bar their way to the sea. If the British commanders underrated their opponents, there is ample evidence that the mistake was reciprocal.

A few words now as to the disposition of the British forces, concerning which it must be borne in mind that Sir George White, though in actual command, had only been a few days in the country before war was declared, so that the arrangements fell to General Penn Symons, aided or hampered by the advice of the local political authorities. The main position was at Ladysmith, but an advance post was strongly held at Glencoe, which is five miles from the station of Dundee and forty from Ladysmith. The reason for this dangerous division of force was to secure each end of the Biggarsberg section of the railway, and also to cover the important collieries of that district. The positions chosen seem in each case to show that the British commander was not aware of the number and power of the Boer guns, for each was equally defensible against rifle fire and vulnerable to an artillery attack. In the case of Glencoe it was particularly evident that guns upon the hills above would, as they did, render the position untenable. This outlying post was held by the 1st Leicester Regiment, the 2nd Dublin Fusiliers, and the first battalion of Rifles, with the 18th Hussars, three companies of mounted infantry, and three batteries of field artillery, the 13th, 67th, and 69th. The 1st Royal Irish Fusiliers were on their way to reinforce it, and arrived before the first action. Altogether the Glencoe camp contained some four thousand men.

The main body of the army remained at Ladysmith. These consisted of the 1st Devons, the 1st Liverpools, and the 2nd Gordon Highlanders, with the 1st Gloucesters, the 2nd King's Royal Rifles, and the 2nd Rifle Brigade, reinforced later by the Manchesters. The cavalry included the 5th Dragoon Guards, the 5th Lancers, a detachment of 19th Hussars, the Natal Carabineers, the Natal Mounted Police, and the Border Mounted Rifles, reinforced later by the Imperial Light Horse, a fine body of men raised principally among the refugees from the Rand. For artillery there were the 21st, 42nd, and 53rd batteries of field artillery, and No. 10 Mountain Battery, with the Natal Field Artillery, the guns of which were too light to be of service, and the 23rd Company of Royal Engineers. The whole force, some eight or nine thousand strong, was under the immediate command of Sir George White, with Sir Archibald Hunter, fresh from the Soudan, General French, and General Ian Hamilton as his lieutenants.

The first shock of the Boers, then, must fall upon 4000 men. If these could be overwhelmed, there were 8000 more to be defeated or masked. Then what was there between them and the sea? Some detachments of local volunteers, the Durban Light Infantry at Colenso, and the Natal Royal Rifles, with some naval volunteers at Estcourt. With the power of the Boers and their mobility it is inexplicable how the colony was saved. We are of the same blood, the Boers and we, and we show it in our failings. Over-confidence on our part gave them the chance, and over-confidence on theirs prevented them from instantly availing themselves of it. It passed, never to come again.

The outbreak of war was upon October 11th. On the 12th the Boer forces crossed the frontier both on the north and on the west. On the 13th they occupied Charlestown at the top angle of Natal. On the 15th they had reached Newcastle, a larger town some fifteen miles inside the border. Watchers from the houses saw six miles of canvas-tilted bullock wagons winding down the passes, and learned that this was not a raid but an invasion. At the same date news reached the British headquarters of an advance from the western passes, and of a movement from the Buffalo River on the east. On the 13th Sir George White had made a reconnaissance in force, but had not come in touch with the enemy. On the 15th six of the Natal Police were surrounded and captured at one of the drifts of the Buffalo River. On the 18th our cavalry patrols came into touch with the Boer scouts at Acton Homes and Besters Station, these being the *voortrekkers* of the Orange Free State force. On the 18th also a detachment was reported from Hadders Spruit, seven miles north of Glencoe Camp. The cloud was drifting up, and it could not be long before it would burst.

Two days later, on the early morning of October 20th, the forces came at last into collision. At half-past three in the morning, well before daylight, the mounted infantry picket at the junction of the roads from Landmans and Vants Drifts was fired into by the Doornberg commando, and retired upon its supports. Two companies of the Dublin Fusiliers were sent out, and at five o'clock on a fine but misty morning the whole of Symons's force was under arms with the knowledge that the Boers were pushing boldly towards them. The khaki-clad lines of fighting men stood in their long thin ranks staring up at the curves of the saddle-back hills to the north and east of them, and straining their eyes to catch a glimpse of the enemy. Why these same saddle-back hills were not occupied by our own people is, it must be confessed, an insoluble mystery. In a hollow on one flank were the 18th Hussars and the mounted infantry. On the other were the eighteen motionless guns, limbered up and ready, the horses fidgeting and stamping in the raw morning air.

And then suddenly—could that be they? An officer with a telescope stared intently and pointed. Another and another turned a steady field glass towards the same place. And then the men could see also, and a little murmur of interest ran down the ranks.

A long sloping hill—Talana Hill—olive-green in hue, was stretching away in front of them. At the summit it rose into a rounded crest. The mist was clearing, and the curve was hard-outlined against the limpid blue of the morning sky. On this, some two and a half miles or three miles off, a little group of black dots had appeared. The clear edge of the skyline had become serrated with moving figures. They clustered into a knot, then opened again, and then—

There had been no smoke, but there came a long crescendo hoot, rising into a shrill wail. The shell hummed over the soldiers like a great bee, and sloshed into soft earth behind them. Then another—and yet another—and yet another. But there was no time to heed them, for there was the hillside and there the enemy. So at it again with the good old murderous obsolete heroic tactics of the British tradition! There are times when, in spite of science and book-lore, the best plan is the boldest plan, and it is well to fly straight at your enemy's throat, facing the chance that your strength may fail before you can grasp it. The cavalry moved off round the enemy's left flank. The guns dashed to the front, unlimbered, and opened fire. The infantry were moved round in the direction of Sandspruit, passing through the little town of Dundee, where the women and children came to the doors and windows to cheer them. It was thought that the hill was more accessible from that side. The Leicesters and one field battery—the 67th—were left behind to protect the camp and to watch the Newcastle Road upon the west. At seven in the morning all was ready for the assault.

Two military facts of importance had already been disclosed. One was that the Boer percussion-shells were useless in soft ground, as hardly any of them exploded; the other that the Boer guns could outrange our ordinary fifteen-pounder field gun, which had been the one thing perhaps in the whole British equipment upon which we were prepared to pin our faith. The two batteries, the 13th and the 69th, were moved nearer, first to 3000, and then at last to 2300 yards, at which range they quickly dominated the guns upon the hill. Other guns had opened from another crest to the east of Talana, but these also were mastered by the fire of the 13th Battery. At 7.30 the infantry were ordered to advance, which they did in open order, extended to ten paces. The Dublin Fusiliers formed the first line, the Rifles the second, and the Irish Fusiliers the third.

The first thousand yards of the advance were over open grassland, where the range was long, and the yellow brown of the khaki blended with the withered *veldt*. There were few casualties until the wood was reached, which lay halfway up the long slope of the hill. It was a plantation of larches, some hundreds of yards across and nearly as many deep. On the left side of this wood—that is, the left side to the advancing troops—there stretched a long *nullah* or hollow, which ran perpendicularly to the hill, and served rather as a conductor of bullets than as a cover.

So severe was the fire at this point that both in the wood and in the *nullah* the troops lay down to avoid it. An officer of Irish Fusiliers has narrated how in trying to cut the straps from a fallen private a razor lent him for that purpose by a wounded sergeant was instantly shot out of his hand. The gallant Symons, who had refused to dismount, was shot through the stomach and fell from his horse mortally wounded. With an excessive gallantry, he had not only attracted the enemy's fire by retaining his horse, but he had been accompanied throughout the action by an orderly bearing a red pennon. 'Have they got the hill? Have they got the hill?' was his one eternal question as they carried him dripping to the rear. It was at the edge of the wood that Colonel Sherston met his end.

From now onwards it was as much a soldiers' battle as Inkermann. In the shelter of the wood the more eager of the three battalions had pressed to the front until the fringe of the trees was lined by men from all of them. The difficulty of distinguishing particular regiments where all were clad alike made it impossible in the heat of action to keep any sort of formation. So hot was the fire that for the time the advance was brought to a standstill, but the 69th battery, firing shrapnel at a range of 1400 yards, subdued the rifle fire, and about half-past eleven the infantry were able to push on once more.

Above the wood there was an open space some hundreds of yards across, bounded by a rough stone wall built for herding cattle. A second wall ran at right angles to this down towards the wood. An enfilading rifle fire had been sweeping across this open space, but the wall in front does not appear to have been occupied by the enemy, who held the *kopje* above it. To avoid the cross fire the soldiers ran in single file under the shelter of the wall, which covered them to the right, and so reached the other wall across their front. Here there was a second long delay, the men dribbling up from below, and firing over the top of the wall and between the chinks of the stones. The Dublin Fusiliers, through being in a more difficult position, had been unable to get up as quickly as the others, and most of the hard-breathing excited men who crowded under the wall were of the Rifles and of the Irish Fusiliers. The air was so full of bullets that it seemed impossible to live upon the other side of this shelter. Two hundred yards intervened between the wall and the crest of the *kopje*. And yet the *kopje* had to be cleared if the battle were to be won.

Out of the huddled line of crouching men an officer sprang shouting, and a score of soldiers vaulted over the wall and followed at his heels. It was Captain Connor, of the Irish Fusiliers, but his personal magnetism carried up with him some of the Rifles as well as men of his own command. He and half his little forlorn hope were struck down—he, alas! to die the same night—but there were other leaders as brave to take his place. 'Forrard away, men, forrard away!' cried Nugent, of the Rifles. Three bullets struck him, but he continued to drag himself up the boulder-studded hill. Others followed, and others, from all sides they came running, the crouching, yelling, khaki-clad figures, and the supports rushed up from the rear. For a time they were beaten down by their own shrapnel striking into them from behind, which is an amazing thing when one considers that the range was under 2000 yards. It was here, between the wall and the summit, that Colonel Gunning, of the Rifles, and many other brave men met their end, some by our own bullets and some by those of the enemy; but the Boers thinned away in front of them, and the anxious onlookers from the plain below saw the waving helmets on the crest, and learned at last that all was well.

But it was, it must be confessed, a Pyrrhic victory. We had our hill, but what else had we? The guns which had been silenced by our fire had been removed from the *kopje*. The commando which seized the hill was that of Lucas Meyer, and it is computed that he had with him about 4000 men. This figure includes those under the command of Erasmus, who made half-hearted demonstrations against the British flank. If the shirkers be eliminated, it is probable that there were not more than a thousand actual combatants upon the hill. Of this number about fifty were killed and a hundred wounded. The British loss at Talana Hill itself was 41 killed and 180 wounded, but among the killed were many whom the army could ill spare. The gallant but optimistic Symons, Gunning of the Rifles, Sherston, Connor, Hambro, and many other brave men died that day. The loss of officers was out of all proportion to that of the men.

An incident which occurred immediately after the action did much to rob the British of the fruits of the victory. Artillery had pushed up the moment that the hill was carried, and had unlimbered on Smith's Nek between the two hills, from which the enemy, in broken groups of 50 and 100, could be seen streaming away. A fairer chance for the use of shrapnel has never been. But at this instant there ran from an old iron church on the reverse side of the hill, which had been used all day as a Boer hospital, a man with a white flag. It is probable that the action was in good faith, and that it was simply intended to claim a protection for the ambulance party which followed him. But the too confiding gunner in command appears to have thought that an armistice had been declared, and held his hand during those precious minutes which might have turned a defeat into a rout. The chance passed, never to return. The double error of firing into our own advance and of failing to fire into the enemy's retreat makes the battle one which cannot be looked back to with satisfaction by our gunners.

In the meantime some miles away another train of events had led to a complete disaster to our small cavalry force—a disaster which robbed our dearly bought infantry victory of much of its importance. That action alone was undoubtedly a victorious one, but the net result of the day's fighting cannot be said to have been certainly in our favour. It was Wellington who asserted that his cavalry always got him into scrapes, and the whole of British military history might furnish examples of what he meant. Here again our cavalry got into trouble. Suffice it for the civilian to chronicle the fact, and leave it to the military critic to portion out the blame.

One company of mounted infantry (that of the Rifles) had been told off to form an escort for the guns. The rest of the mounted infantry with part of the 18th Hussars (Colonel Moller) had moved round the right flank until they reached the right rear of the enemy. Such a movement, had Lucas Meyer been the only opponent, would have been above criticism; but knowing, as we did, that there were several commandoes converging upon Glencoe it was obviously taking a very grave and certain risk to allow the cavalry to wander too far from support. They were soon entangled in broken country and attacked by superior numbers of the Boers. There was a time when they might have exerted an important influence upon the action by attacking the Boer ponies behind the hills, but the opportunity was allowed to pass. An attempt was made to get back to the army, and a series of defensive positions were held to cover the retreat, but the enemy's fire became too hot to allow them to be retained. Every route save one appeared to be blocked, so the horsemen took this, which led them into the heart of a second commando of the enemy. Finding no way through, the force took up a defensive position, part of them in a farm and part on a *kopje* which overlooked it.

The party consisted of two troops of Hussars, one company of mounted infantry of the Dublin Fusiliers, and one section of the mounted infantry of the Rifles—about two hundred men in all. They were subjected to a hot fire for some hours, many being killed and wounded. Guns were brought up, and fired shell into the farmhouse. At 4.30 the force, being in a perfectly hopeless position, laid down their arms. Their ammunition was gone, many of their horses had stampeded, and they were hemmed in by very superior numbers, so that no slightest slur can rest upon the survivors for their decision to surrender, though the movements which brought them to such a pass are more open to criticism. They were the vanguard of that considerable body of humiliated and bitter-hearted men who were to assemble at the capital of our brave and crafty enemy. The remainder of the 18th Hussars, who under Major Knox had been detached from the main force and sent across the

Boer rear, underwent a somewhat similar experience, but succeeded in extricating themselves with a loss of six killed and ten wounded. Their efforts were by no means lost, as they engaged the attention of a considerable body of Boers during the day and were able to bring some prisoners back with them.

The battle of Talana Hill was a tactical victory but a strategic defeat. It was a crude frontal attack without any attempt at even a feint of flanking, but the valour of the troops, from general to private, carried it through. The force was in a position so radically false that the only use which they could make of a victory was to cover their own retreat. From all points Boer commandoes were converging upon it, and already it was understood that the guns at their command were heavier than any which could be placed against them. This was made more clear on October 21st, the day after the battle, when the force, having withdrawn overnight from the useless hill which they had captured, moved across to a fresh position on the far side of the railway. At four in the afternoon a very heavy gun opened from a distant hill, altogether beyond the extreme range of our artillery, and plumped shell after shell into our camp. It was the first appearance of the great Creusot. An officer with several men of the Leicesters, and some of our few remaining cavalry, were hit. The position was clearly impossible, so at two in the morning of the 22nd the whole force was moved to a point to the south of the town of Dundee. On the same day a reconnaissance was made in the direction of Glencoe Station, but the passes were found to be strongly occupied, and the little army marched back again to its original position. The command had fallen to Colonel Yule, who justly considered that his men were dangerously and uselessly exposed, and that his correct strategy was to fall back, if it were still possible, and join the main body at Ladysmith, even at the cost of abandoning the two hundred sick and wounded who lay with General Symons in the hospital at Dundee. It was a painful necessity, but no one who studies the situation can have any doubt of its wisdom. The retreat was no easy task, a march by road of some sixty or seventy miles through a very rough country with an enemy pressing on every side. Its successful completion without any loss or any demoralisation of the troops is perhaps as fine a military exploit as any of our early victories. Through the energetic and loyal cooperation of Sir George White, who fought the actions of Elandslaagte and of Rietfontein in order to keep the way open for them, and owing mainly to the skilful guidance of Colonel Dartnell, of the Natal Police, they succeeded in their critical manoeuvre. On October 23rd they were at Beith, on the 24th at Waselibank Spruit, on the 25th at Sunday River, and next morning they marched, sodden with rain, plastered with mud, dog-tired, but in the best of spirits, into Ladysmith amid the cheers of their comrades. A battle, six days without settled sleep, four days without a proper meal, winding up with a single march of thirty-two miles over heavy ground and through a pelting rain storm—that was the record of the Dundee column. They had fought and won, they had striven and toiled to the utmost capacity of manhood, and the end of it all was that they had reached the spot which they should never have left. But their endurance could not be lost—no worthy deed is ever lost. Like the light division, when they marched their fifty odd unbroken miles to be present at Talavera, they leave a memory and a standard behind them which is more important than success. It is by the tradition of such sufferings and such endurance that others in other days are nerved to do the like.

CHAPTER 6

Elandslaagte and Rietfontein

While the Glencoe force had struck furiously at the army of Lucas Meyer, and had afterwards by hard marching disengaged itself from the numerous dangers which threatened it, its comrades at Ladysmith had loyally co-operated in drawing off the attention of the enemy and keeping the line of retreat open.

On October 20th—the same day as the Battle of Talana Hill—the line was cut by the Boers at a point nearly midway between Dundee and Ladysmith. A small body of horsemen were the forerunners of a considerable commando, composed of Freestaters, Transvaalers, and Germans, who had advanced into Natal through Botha's Pass under the command of General Koch. They had with them the two Maxim-Nordenfelds which had been captured from the Jameson raiders, and were now destined to return once more to British hands. Colonel Schiel, the German artillerist, had charge of these guns.

On the evening of that day General French, with a strong reconnoitring party, including the Natal Carabineers, the 5th Lancers, and the 21st battery, had defined the enemy's position. Next morning (the 21st) he returned, but either the enemy had been reinforced during the night or he had underrated them the day before, for the force which he took with him was too weak for any serious attack. He had one battery of the Natal artillery, with their little seven-pounder popguns, five squadrons of the Imperial Horse, and, in the train which slowly accompanied his advance, half a battalion of the Manchester Regiment. Elated by the news of Talana Hill, and anxious to emulate their brothers of Dundee, the little force moved out of Ladysmith in the early morning.

Some at least of the men were animated by feelings such as seldom find a place in the breast of the British soldier as he marches into battle. A sense of duty, a belief in the justice of his cause, a love for his regiment and for his country, these are the common incentives of every soldier. But to the men of the Imperial Light Horse, recruited as they were from among the British refugees of the Rand, there was added a burning sense of injustice, and in many cases a bitter hatred against the men whose rule had weighed so heavily upon them. In this singular corps the ranks were full of wealthy men and men of education, who, driven from their peaceful vocations in Johannesburg, were bent upon fighting their way back to them again. A most unmerited slur had been cast upon their courage in connection with the Jameson raid—a slur which they and other similar corps have washed out for ever in their own blood and that of their enemy. Chisholm, a fiery little Lancer, was in command, with Karri Davis and Wools-Sampson, the two stalwarts who had preferred Pretoria Gaol to the favours of Kruger, as his majors. The troopers were on fire at the news that a cartel had arrived in Ladysmith the night before, purporting to come from the Johannesburg Boers and Hollanders, asking what uniform the Light Horse wore, as they were anxious to meet them in battle. These men were fellow townsmen and knew each other well. They need not have troubled about the uniform, for before evening the Light Horse were near enough for them to know their faces.

It was about eight o'clock on a bright summer morning that the small force came in contact with a few scattered Boer outposts, who retired, firing, before the advance of the Imperial Light Horse. As they fell back the green and white tents of the invaders came into view upon the russet-coloured hillside of Elandslaagte. Down at the red brick railway station the Boers could be seen swarming out of the buildings in which they had spent the night. The little Natal guns, firing with obsolete black powder, threw a few shells into the station, one of which, it is said, penetrated a Boer ambulance which could not be seen by the gunners. The accident was to be regretted, but as no patients could have been in the ambulance the mischance was not a serious one.

But the busy, smoky little seven-pounder guns were soon to meet their master. Away up on the distant hillside, a long thousand yards beyond their own furthest range, there was a sudden bright flash. No smoke, only the throb of flame, and then the long sibilant scream of the shell, and the thud as it buried itself in the ground under a limber. Such judgment of range would have delighted the most martinet of inspectors at Oakhampton. Bang came another, and another, and another, right into the heart of the battery. The six little guns lay back at their extremest angle, and all barked together in impotent fury. Another shell pitched over them, and the officer in command lowered his field-glass in despair as he saw his own shells bursting far short upon the hillside. Jameson's defeat does not seem to have been due to any defect in his artillery. French, peering and pondering, soon came to the conclusion that there were too many Boers for him, and that if those fifteen-pounders desired target practice they should find some other mark than the Natal Field Artillery. A few curt orders, and his whole force was making its way to the rear. There, out of range of those perilous guns, they halted, the telegraph wire was cut, a telephone attachment was made, and French whispered his troubles into the sympathetic ear of Ladysmith. He did not whisper in vain. What he had to say was that where he had expected a few hundred riflemen he found something like two thousand, and that where he expected no guns he found two very excellent ones. The reply was that by road and by rail as many men as could be spared were on their way to join him.

Soon they began to drop in, those useful reinforcements—first the Devons, quiet, business-like, reliable; then the Gordons, dashing, fiery, brilliant. Two squadrons of the 5th Lancers, the 42nd R.F.A., the 21st R.F.A., another squadron of Lancers, a squadron of the 5th Dragoon Guards—French began to feel that he was strong enough for the task in front of him. He had a decided superiority of numbers and of guns. But the others were on their favourite defensive on a hill. It would be a fair fight and a deadly one.

It was late after noon before the advance began. It was hard, among those billowing hills, to make out the exact limits of the enemy's position. All that was certain was that they were there, and that we meant having them out if it were humanly possible. 'The enemy are there,' said Ian Hamilton to his infantry; 'I hope you will shift them out before sunset—in fact I know you will.' The men cheered and laughed. In long open lines they advanced across the *veldt*, while the thunder of the two batteries behind them told the Boer gunners that it was their turn now to know what it was to be outmatched.

The idea was to take the position by a front and a flank attack, but there seems to have been some difficulty in determining which was the front and which the flank. In fact, it was only by trying that one could know. General White with his staff had arrived from Ladysmith, but refused to take the command out of French's hands. It is typical of White's chivalrous spirit that within ten days he refused to identify himself with a victory when it was within his right to do so, and took the whole responsibility for a disaster at which he was not present. Now he rode amid the shells and watched the able dispositions of his lieutenant.

About half-past three the action had fairly begun. In front of the advancing British there lay a rolling hill, topped by a further one. The lower hill was not defended, and the infantry, breaking from column of companies into open order, advanced over it. Beyond was a broad grassy valley which led up to the main position, a long *kopje* flanked by a small sugar-loaf one Behind the green slope which led to the ridge of death an ominous and terrible cloud was driving up, casting its black shadow over the combatants. There was the stillness which goes before some great convulsion of nature. The men pressed on in silence, the soft thudding of their feet and the rattle of their sidearms filling the air with a low and continuous murmur. An additional solemnity was given to the attack by that huge black cloud which hung before them.

The British guns had opened at a range of 4400 yards, and now against the swarthy background there came the quick smokeless twinkle of the Boer reply. It was an unequal fight, but gallantly sustained. A shot and another to find the range; then a wreath of smoke from a bursting shell exactly where the guns had been, followed by another and another. Overmatched, the two Boer pieces relapsed into a sulky silence, broken now and again by short spurts of frenzied activity. The British batteries turned their attention away from them, and began to search the ridge with shrapnel and prepare the way for the advancing infantry.

The scheme was that the Devonshires should hold the enemy in front while the main attack from the left flank was carried out by the Gordons, the Manchesters, and the Imperial Light Horse. The words 'front' and 'flank,' however, cease to have any meaning with so mobile and elastic a force, and the attack which was intended to come from the left became really a frontal one, while the Devons found themselves upon the right flank of the Boers. At the moment of the final advance the great black cloud had burst, and a torrent of rain lashed into the faces of the men. Slipping and sliding upon the wet grass, they advanced to the assault.

And now amid the hissing of the rain there came the fuller, more menacing whine of the Mauser bullets, and the ridge rattled from end to end with the rifle fire. Men fell fast, but their comrades pressed hotly on. There was a long way to go, for the summit of the position was nearly 800 feet above the level of the railway. The hillside, which had appeared to be one slope, was really a succession of undulations, so that the advancing infantry alternately dipped into shelter and emerged into a hail of bullets. The line of advance was dotted with khaki-clad figures, some still in death, some writhing in their agony. Amid the litter of bodies a major of the Gordons, shot through the leg, sat philosophically smoking his pipe. Plucky little Chisholm, Colonel of the Imperials, had fallen with two mortal wounds as he dashed forward waving a coloured sash in the air. So long was the advance and so trying the hill that the men sank panting upon the ground, and took their breath before making another rush. As at Talana Hill, regimental formation was largely gone, and men of the Manchesters, Gordons, and Imperial Light Horse surged upwards in one long ragged fringe, Scotchman, Englishman, and British Africander keeping pace in that race of death. And now at last they began to see their enemy. Here and there among the boulders in front of them there was the glimpse of a slouched hat, or a peep at a flushed bearded face which drooped over a rifle barrel. There was a pause, and then with a fresh impulse the wave of men gathered themselves together and flung themselves forward. Dark figures sprang up from the rocks in front. Some held up their rifles in token of surrender. Some ran with heads sunk between their shoulders, jumping and ducking among the rocks. The panting breathless climbers were on the edge of the plateau. There were the two guns which had flashed so brightly, silenced now, with a litter of dead gunners around them and one wounded officer standing by a trail. A small body of the Boers still resisted. Their appearance horrified some of our men. 'They were dressed in black frock coats and looked like a lot of rather seedy business men,' said a spectator. 'It seemed like murder to kill them.' Some surrendered, and some fought to the death where they stood. Their leader Koch, an old gentleman with a white beard, lay amidst the rocks, wounded in three places. He was treated with all courtesy and attention, but died in Ladysmith Hospital some days afterwards.

In the meanwhile the Devonshire Regiment had waited until the attack had developed and had then charged the hill upon the flank, while the artillery moved up until it was within 2000 yards of the enemy's position. The Devons met with a less fierce resistance than the others, and swept up to the summit in time to head off some of the fugitives. The whole of our infantry were now upon the ridge.

But even so these dour fighters were not beaten. They clung desperately to the further edges of the plateau, firing from behind the rocks. There had been a race for the nearest gun between an officer of the Manchesters and a drummer sergeant of the Gordons. The officer won, and sprang in triumph on to the piece. Men of all regiments swarmed round yelling and cheering, when upon their astonished ears there sounded the 'Cease fire' and then the 'Retire.' It was incredible, and yet it pealed out again, unmistakable in its urgency. With the instinct of discipline the men were slowly falling back. And then the truth of it came upon the minds of some of them. The crafty enemy had learned our bugle calls. 'Retire be damned! shrieked a little bugler, and blew the 'Advance' with all the breath that the hillside had left him. The men, who had retired a hundred yards and uncovered the guns, flooded back over the plateau, and in the Boer camp which lay beneath it a white flag showed that the game was up. A squadron of the 5th Lancers and of the 5th Dragoon Guards, under Colonel Gore of the latter regiment, had prowled round the base of the hill, and in the fading light they charged through and through the retreating Boers, killing several, and making from twenty to thirty prisoners. It was one of the very few occasions in the war where the mounted Briton overtook the mounted Boer.

'What price Majuba?' was the cry raised by some of the infantry as they dashed up to the enemy's position, and the action may indeed be said to have been in some respects the converse of that famous fight. It is true that there were many more British at Elandslaagte than Boers at Majuba, but then the defending force was much more numerous also, and the British had no guns there. It is true, also, that Majuba is very much more precipitous than Elandslaagte, but then every practical soldier knows that it is easier to defend a moderate glacis than an abrupt slope, which gives cover under its boulders to the attacker while the defender has to crane his head over the edge to look down. On the whole, this brilliant little action may be said to have restored things to their true proportion, and to have shown that, brave as the Boers undoubtedly are, there is no military feat within their power which is not equally possible to the British soldier. Talana Hill and Elandslaagte, fought on successive days, were each of them as gallant an exploit as Majuba.

We had more to show for our victory than for the previous one at Dundee. Two Maxim-Nordenfeld guns, whose efficiency had been painfully evident during the action, were a welcome addition to our artillery. Two hundred and fifty Boers were killed and wounded and about two hundred taken prisoners, the loss falling most heavily upon the Johannesburgers, the Germans, and the Hollanders. General Koch, Dr. Coster, Colonel Schiel, Pretorius, and other well-known Transvaalers fell into our hands. Our own casualty list consisted of 41 killed and 220 wounded, much the same number as at Talana Hill, the heaviest losses falling upon the Gordon Highlanders and the Imperial Light Horse.

In the hollow where the Boer tents had stood, amid the *laagered* wagons of the vanquished, under a murky sky and a constant drizzle of rain, the victors spent the night. Sleep was out of the question, for all night the fatigue parties were searching the hillside and the wounded were being carried in. Camp-fires were lit and soldiers and prisoners crowded round them, and it is pleasant to recall that the warmest corner and the best of their rude fare were always reserved for the downcast Dutchmen, while words of rude praise and sympathy softened the pain of defeat. It is the memory of such things which may in happier days be more potent than all the wisdom of statesmen in welding our two races into one.

Having cleared the Boer force from the line of the railway, it is evident that General White could not continue to garrison the point, as he was aware that considerable forces were moving from the north, and his first duty was the security of Ladysmith. Early next morning (October 22nd), therefore, his weary but victorious troops returned to the town. Once there he learned, no doubt, that General Yule had no intention of using the broken railway for his retreat, but that he intended to come in a circuitous fashion by road. White's problem was to hold tight to the town and at the same time to strike hard at any northern force so as to prevent them from interfering with Yule's retreat. It was in the furtherance of this scheme that he fought upon October 24th the action of Rietfontein, an engagement slight in itself, but important on account of the clear road which was secured for the weary forces retiring from Dundee.

The army from the Free State, of which the commando vanquished at Elandslaagte was the vanguard, had been slowly and steadily debouching from the passes, and working south and eastwards to cut the line between Dundee and Ladysmith. It was White's intention to prevent them from crossing the Newcastle Road, and for this purpose he sallied out of Ladysmith on Tuesday the 24th, having with him two regiments of cavalry, the 5th Lancers and the 19th Hussars, the 42nd and 53rd field batteries with the 10th mountain battery, four infantry regiments, the Devons, Liverpools, Gloucesters, and 2nd King's Royal Rifles, the Imperial Light Horse, and the Natal Volunteers—some four thousand men in all.

The enemy were found to be in possession of a line of hills within seven miles of Ladysmith, the most conspicuous of which is called Tinta Inyoni. It was no part of General White's plan to attempt to drive him from this position—it is not wise generalship to fight always upon ground of the enemy's choosing—but it was important to hold him where he was, and to engage his attention during this last day of the march of the retreating column. For this purpose, since no direct attack was intended, the guns were of more importance than the infantry—and indeed the infantry should, one might imagine, have been used solely as an escort for the artillery. A desultory and inconclusive action ensued which continued from nine in the morning until half-past one in the afternoon. A well-directed fire of the Boer guns from the hills was dominated and controlled by our field artillery, while the advance of their riflemen was restrained by shrapnel. The enemy's guns were more easily marked down than at Elandslaagte, as they used black powder. The ranges varied from three to four thousand yards. Our losses in the whole action would have been insignificant had it not happened that the Gloucester Regiment advanced somewhat incautiously into the open and was caught in a cross fire of musketry which struck down Colonel Wilford and fifty of his officers and men. Within four days Colonel Dick-Cunyngham, of the Gordons, Colonel Chisholm, of the Light Horse, Colonel Gunning, of the Rifles, and now Colonel Wilford, of the Gloucesters, had all fallen at the head of their regiments. In the afternoon General White, having accomplished his purpose and secured the safety of the Dundee column while traversing the dangerous Biggarsberg passes, withdrew his force to Ladysmith. We have no means of ascertaining the losses of the Boers, but they were probably slight. On our side we lost 109 killed and wounded, of which only 13 cases were fatal. Of this total 64 belonged to the Gloucesters and 25 to the troops raised in Natal. Next day, as already narrated, the whole British army was re-assembled once more at Ladysmith, and the campaign was to enter upon a new phase.

At the end of this first vigorous week of hostilities it is interesting to sum up the net result. The strategical advantage had lain with the Boers. They had made our position at Dundee untenable and had driven us back to Ladysmith. They had the country and the railway for the northern quarter of the colony in their possession. They had killed and wounded between six and seven hundred of our men, and they had captured some two hundred of our cavalry, while we had been compelled at Dundee to leave considerable stores and our wounded, including General Penn Symons, who actually died while a prisoner in their hands. On the other hand, the tactical advantages lay with us. We had twice driven them from their positions, and captured two of their guns. We had taken two hundred prisoners, and had probably killed and wounded as many as we had lost. On the whole, the honours of that week's fighting in Natal may be said to have been fairly equal—which is more than we could claim for many a weary week to come.

CHAPTER 7

The Battle of Ladysmith

Sir George White had now reunited his force, and found himself in command of a formidable little army some twelve thousand in number. His cavalry included the 5th Lancers, the 5th Dragoons, part of the 18th and the whole of the 19th Hussars, the Natal Carabineers, the Border Rifles, some mounted infantry, and the Imperial Light Horse. Among his infantry were the Royal Irish Fusiliers, the Dublin Fusiliers, and the King's Royal Rifles, fresh from the ascent of Talana Hill, the Gordons, the Manchesters, and the Devons who had been blooded at Elandslaagte, the Leicesters, the Liverpools, the 2nd battalion of the King's Royal Rifles, the 2nd Rifle Brigade, and the Gloucesters, who had been so roughly treated at Rietfontein. He had six batteries of excellent field artillery—the 13th, 21st, 42nd, 53rd, 67th, 69th, and No. 10 Mountain Battery of screw guns. No general could have asked for a more compact and workmanlike little force.

It had been recognised by the British General from the beginning that his tactics must be defensive, since he was largely outnumbered and since also any considerable mishap to his force would expose the whole colony of Natal to destruction. The actions of Elandslaagte and Rietfontein were forced upon him in order to disengage his compromised detachment, but now there was no longer any reason why he should assume the offensive. He knew that away out on the Atlantic a trail of transports which already extended from the Channel to Cape de Verde were hourly drawing nearer to him with the army corps from England. In a fortnight or less the first of them would be at Durban. It was his game, therefore, to keep his army intact, and to let those throbbing engines and whirling propellers do the work of the empire. Had he entrenched himself up to his nose and waited, it would have paid him best in the end.

But so tame and inglorious a policy is impossible to a fighting soldier. He could not with his splendid force permit himself to be shut in without an action. What policy demands honour may forbid. On October

27th there were already Boers and rumours of Boers on every side of him. Joubert with his main body was moving across from Dundee. The Freestaters were to the north and west. Their combined numbers were uncertain, but at least it was already proved that they were far more numerous and also more formidable than had been anticipated. We had had a taste of their artillery also, and the pleasant delusion that it would be a mere useless encumbrance to a Boer force had vanished for ever. It was a grave thing to leave the town in order to give battle, for the mobile enemy might swing round and seize it behind us. Nevertheless White determined to make the venture.

On the 29th the enemy were visibly converging upon the town. From a high hill within rifle-shot of the houses a watcher could see no fewer than six Boer camps to the east and north. French, with his cavalry, pushed out feelers, and coasted along the edge of the advancing host. His report warned White that if he would strike before all the scattered bands were united he must do so at once. The wounded were sent down to Pietermaritzburg, and it would bear explanation why the non-combatants did not accompany them. On the evening of the same day Joubert in person was said to be only six miles off, and a party of his men cut the water supply of the town. The Klip, however, a fair-sized river, runs through Ladysmith, so that there was no danger of thirst. The British had inflated and sent up a balloon, to the amazement of the back-*veldt* Boers; its report confirmed the fact that the enemy was in force in front of and around them.

On the night of the 29th General White detached two of his best regiments, the Irish Fusiliers and the Gloucesters, with No. 10 Mountain Battery, to advance under cover of the darkness and to seize and hold a long ridge called Nicholson's Nek, which lay about six miles to the north of Ladysmith. Having determined to give battle on the next day, his object was to protect his left wing against those Freestaters who were still moving from the north and west, and also to keep a pass open by which his cavalry might pursue the Boer fugitives in case of a British victory. This small detached column numbered about a thousand men—whose fate will be afterwards narrated.

At five o'clock on the morning of the 30th the Boers, who had already developed a perfect genius for hauling heavy cannon up the most difficult heights, opened fire from one of the hills which lie to the north of the town. Before the shot was fired, the forces of the British had already streamed out of Ladysmith to test the strength of the invaders.

White's army was divided into three columns. On the extreme left, quite isolated from the others, was the small Nicholson's Nek detachment under the command of Colonel Carleton of the Fusiliers (one of three gallant brothers each of whom commands a British regiment). With him was Major Adye of the staff. On the right British flank Colonel Grim-wood commanded a brigade composed of the 1st and 2nd battalions of the King's Royal Rifles, the Leicesters, the Liverpools, and the Royal Dublin Fusiliers. In the centre Colonel Ian Hamilton commanded the Devons, the Gordons, the Manchesters, and the 2nd battalion of the Rifle Brigade, which marched direct into the battle from the train which had brought them from Durban. Six batteries of artillery were massed in the centre under Colonel Downing. French with the cavalry and mounted infantry was on the extreme right, but found little opportunity for the use of the mounted arm that day.

The Boer position, so far as it could be seen, was a formidable one. Their centre lay upon one of the spurs of Signal Hill, about three miles from the town. Here they had two forty-pounders and three other light-er guns, but their artillery strength developed both in numbers and in weight of metal as the day wore on. Of their dispositions little could be seen. An observer looking westward might discern with his glass sprays of mounted riflemen galloping here and there over the downs, and pos-sibly small groups where the gunners stood by their guns, or the leaders gazed down at that town which they were destined to have in view for such a weary while. On the dun-coloured plains before the town, the long thin lines, with an occasional shifting sparkle of steel, showed where Hamilton's and Grimwood's infantry were advancing. In the clear cold air of an African morning every detail could be seen, down to the distant smoke of a train toiling up the heavy grades which lead from Frere over the Colenso Bridge to Ladysmith.

The scrambling, inconsequential, unsatisfactory action which en-sued is as difficult to describe as it must have been to direct. The Boer front covered some seven or eight miles, with *kopjes*, like chains of for-tresses, between. They formed a huge semicircle of which our advance was the chord, and they were able from this position to pour in a con-verging artillery fire which grew steadily hotter as the day advanced. In the early part of the day our forty-two guns, working furiously, though with a want of accuracy which may be due to those errors of refraction which are said to be common in the limpid air of the *veldt*, preserved their superiority. There appears to have been a want of concentration about our fire, and at some periods of the action each particular battery was firing at some different point of the Boer half-circle. Sometimes for an hour on end the Boer reply would die away altogether, only to break out with augmented violence, and with an accuracy which increased our respect for their training. Huge shells—the largest that ever burst upon a battlefield—hurled from distances which were unattainable by our fifteen-pounders, enveloped our batteries in smoke and flame. One enormous Creusot gun on Pepworth Hill threw a 96-pound shell a distance of four miles, and several 40-pound howitzers out-weighed our field guns. And on the same day on which we were so roughly taught how large the guns were which labour and good will could haul on to the field of battle, we learned also that our enemy—to the disgrace of our Board of Ordnance be it recorded—was more in touch with modern invention than we were, and could show us not only the largest, but also the smallest, shell which had yet been used. Would that it had been our officials instead of our gunners who heard the devilish little one-pound shells of the Vickers-Maxim automatic gun, exploding with a continuous string of crackings and bangings, like a huge cracker, in their faces and about their ears!

Up to seven o'clock our infantry had shown no disposition to press the attack, for with so huge a position in front of them, and so many hills which were held by the enemy, it was difficult to know what line of advance should be taken, or whether the attack should not be converted into a mere reconnaissance. Shortly after that hour, however, the Boers decided the question by themselves developing a vigorous movement upon Grimwood and the right flank. With field guns, Maxims, and rifle fire, they closed rapidly in upon him. The centre column was drafted off, regiment by regiment, to reinforce the right. The Gordons, Devons, Manchesters, and three batteries were sent over to Grimwood's relief, and the 5th Lancers, acting as infantry, assisted him to hold on.

At nine o'clock there was a lull, but it was evident that fresh commandoes and fresh guns were continually streaming into the firing line. The engagement opened again with redoubled violence, and Grimwood's three advanced battalions fell back, abandoning the ridge which they had held for five hours. The reason for this withdrawal was not that they could not continue to hold their position, but it was that a message had just reached Sir George White from Colonel Knox, commanding in Ladysmith, to the effect that it looked as if the enemy was about to rush the town from the other side. Crossing the open in some disorder, they lost heavily, and would have done so more had not the 13th Field Battery, followed after an interval by the 53rd, dashed forward, firing shrapnel at short ranges, in order to cover the retreat of the infantry. Amid the bursting of the huge 96-pound shells, and the snapping of the vicious little automatic one-pounders, with a cross-fire of rifles as well, Abdy's and Dawkins' gallant batteries swung round their muzzles, and hit back right and left, flashing and blazing, amid their litter of dead horses and men. So severe was the fire that the guns were obscured by the dust knocked up by the little shells of the automatic gun. Then, when their work was done and the retiring infantry had straggled over the ridge, the covering guns whirled and bounded after them. So many horses had fallen that two pieces were left until the teams could be brought back for them, which was successfully done through the gallantry of Captain Thwaites. The action of these batteries was one of the few gleams of light in a not too brilliant day's work. With splendid coolness and courage they helped each other by alternate retirements after the retreating infantry had passed them. The 21st Battery (Blewitt's) also distinguished itself by its staunchness in covering the retirement of the cavalry, while the 42nd (Goulburn's) suffered the heaviest losses of any. On the whole, such honours as fell to our lot were mainly with the gunners.

White must have been now uneasy for his position, and it had become apparent that his only course was to fall back and concentrate upon the town. His left flank was up in the air, and the sound of distant firing, wafted over five miles of broken country, was the only message which arrived from them. His right had been pushed back, and, most dangerous of all, his centre had ceased to exist, for only the 2nd Rifle Brigade remained there. What would happen if the enemy burst rudely through and pushed straight for the town? It was the more possible, as the Boer artillery had now proved itself to be far heavier than ours. That terrible 96-pounder, serenely safe and out of range, was plumping its great projectiles into the masses of retiring troops. The men had had little sleep and little food, and this unanswerable fire was an ordeal for a force which is retreating. A retirement may very rapidly become a rout under such circumstances. It was with some misgivings that the officers saw their men quicken their pace and glance back over their shoulders at the whine and screech of the shell. They were still some miles from home, and the plain was open. What could be done to give them some relief?

And at that very moment there came the opportune and unexpected answer. That plume of engine smoke which the watcher had observed in the morning had drawn nearer and nearer, as the heavy train came puffing and creaking up the steep inclines. Then, almost before it had drawn up at the Ladysmith siding, there had sprung from it a crowd of merry bearded fellows, with ready hands and strange sea cries, pulling and hauling, with rope and purchase to get out the long slim guns which they had lashed on the trucks. Singular carriages were there, specially invented by Captain Percy Scott, and labouring and straining, they worked furiously to get the 12-pounder quick-firers into action. Then at last it was done, and the long tubes swept upwards to the angle at which they might hope to reach that monster on the hill at the horizon. Two of them craned their long inquisitive necks up and exchanged repartees with the big Creusot. And so it was that the weary and dispirited British troops heard a crash which was louder and sharper than that of their field guns, and saw far away upon the distant hill a great spurt of smoke and flame to show where the shell had struck. Another and another and another—and then they were troubled no more. Captain Hedworth Lambton and his men had saved the situation. The masterful gun had met its own master and sank into silence, while the somewhat bedraggled field force came trailing back into Ladysmith, leaving three hundred of their number behind them. It was a high price to pay, but other misfortunes were in store for us which made the retirement of the morning seem insignificant.

In the meantime we may follow the unhappy fortunes of the small column which had, as already described, been sent out by Sir George White in order, if possible, to prevent the junction of the two Boer armies, and at the same time to threaten the right wing of the main force, which was advancing from the direction of Dundee, Sir George White throughout the campaign consistently displayed one quality which is a charming one in an individual, but may be dangerous in a commander. He was a confirmed optimist. Perhaps his heart might have failed him in the dark days to come had he not been so. But whether one considers the non-destruction of the Newcastle Railway, the acquiescence in the occupation of Dundee, the retention of the non combatants in Ladysmith until it was too late to get rid of their useless mouths, or the failure to make any serious preparations for the defence of the town until his troops were beaten back into it, we see always the same evidence of a man who habitually hopes that all will go well, and is in consequence remiss in making preparations for their going ill. But unhappily in every one of these instances they did go ill, though the slowness of the Boers enabled us, both at Dundee and at Ladysmith, to escape what might have been disaster.

Sir George White has so nobly and frankly taken upon himself the blame of Nicholson's Nek that an impartial historian must rather regard his self-condemnation as having been excessive. The immediate causes of the failure were undoubtedly the results of pure ill-fortune, and depended on things outside his control. But it is evident that the strategic plan which would justify the presence of this column at Nicholson's Nek was based upon the supposition that the main army won their action at Lombard's Kop. In that case White might swing round his right and pin the Boers between himself and Nicholson's Nek. In any case he could then re-unite with his isolated wing. But if he should lose his battle—what then? What was to become of this detachment five miles up in the air? How was it to be extricated? The gallant Irishman seems to have waved aside the very idea of defeat. An assurance was, it is reported, given to the leaders of the column that by eleven o'clock next morning they would be relieved. So they would if White had won his action. But—

The force chosen to operate independently consisted of four and a half companies of the Gloucester regiment, six companies of the Royal Irish Fusiliers, and No. 10 Mountain Battery of six seven-pounder screwguns. They were both old soldier regiments from India, and the Fusiliers had shown only ten days before at Talana Hill the stuff of which they were made. Colonel Carleton, of the Fusiliers, to whose exertions much of the success of the retreat from Dundee was due, commanded the column, with Major Adye as staff officer. On the night of Sunday, October 29th, they tramped out of Ladysmith, a thousand men, none better in the army. Little they thought, as they exchanged a jest or two with the outlying pickets, that they were seeing the last of their own armed countrymen for many a weary month.

The road was irregular and the night was moonless. On either side the black loom of the hills bulked vaguely through the darkness. The column tramped stolidly along, the Fusiliers in front, the guns and Gloucesters behind. Several times a short halt was called to make sure of the bearings. At last, in the black cold hours which come between midnight and morning, the column swung to the left out of the road. In front of them, hardly visible, stretched a long black *kopje*. It was the very Nicholson's Nek which they had come to occupy. Carleton and Adye must have heaved a sigh of relief as they realised that they had actually struck it. The force was but two hundred yards from the position, and all had gone without a hitch. And yet in those two hundred yards there came an incident which decided the fate both of their enterprise and of themselves.

Out of the darkness there blundered and rattled five horsemen, their horses galloping, the loose stones flying around them. In the dim light they were gone as soon as seen. Whence coming, whither going, no one knows, nor is it certain whether it was design or ignorance or panic which sent them riding so wildly through the darkness. Somebody fired. A sergeant of the Fusiliers took the bullet through his hand. Some one else shouted to fix bayonets. The mules which carried the spare ammunition kicked and reared. There was no question of treachery, for they were led by our own men, but to hold two frightened mules, one with either hand, is a feat for a Hercules. They lashed and tossed and bucked themselves loose, and an instant afterwards were flying helter-skelter through the column. Nearly all the mules caught the panic. In vain the men held on to their heads. In the mad rush they were galloped over and knocked down by the torrent of frightened creatures. In the gloom of that early hour the men must have thought that they were charged by cavalry. The column was dashed out of all military order as effectively as if a regiment of dragoons had ridden over them. When the cyclone had passed, and the men had with many a muttered curse gathered themselves into their ranks once more, they realised how grave was the misfortune which had befallen them. There, where those mad hoofs still rattled in the distance, were their spare cartridges, their shells, and their cannon. A mountain gun is not drawn upon wheels, but is carried in adjustable parts upon mule-back. A wheel had gone south, a trail east, a chase west. Some of the cartridges were strewn upon the road. Most were on their way back to Ladysmith. There was nothing for it but to face this new situation and to determine what should be done.

It has been often and naturally asked, why did not Colonel Carleton make his way back at once upon the loss of his guns and ammunition, while it was still dark? One or two considerations are evident. In the first place, it is natural to a good soldier to endeavour to retrieve a situation rather than to abandon his enterprise. His prudence, did he not do so, might become the subject of public commendation, but might also provoke some private comment. A soldier's training is to take chances, and to do the best he can with the material at his disposal. Again, Colonel Carleton and Major Adye knew the general plan of the battle which would be raging within a very few hours, and they quite understood that by withdrawing they would expose General White's left flank to attack from the forces (consisting, as we know now, of the Orange Freestaters and of the Johannesburg Police) who were coming from the north and west. He hoped to be relieved by eleven, and he believed that, come what might, he could hold out until then. These are the most obvious of the considerations which induced Colonel Carleton to determine to carry out so far as he could the programme which had been laid down for him and his command. He marched up the hill and occupied the position.

His heart, however, must have sunk when he examined it. It was very large—too large to be effectively occupied by the force which he commanded. The length was about a mile and the breadth four hundred yards. Shaped roughly like the sole of a boot, it was only the heel end which he could hope to hold. Other hills all round offered cover for Boer riflemen. Nothing daunted, however, he set his men to work at once building sangars with the loose stones. With the full dawn and the first snapping of Boer Mausers from the hills around they had thrown up some sort of rude defences which they might hope to hold until help should come.

But how could help come when there was no means by which they could let White know the plight in which they found themselves? They had brought a heliograph with them, but it was on the back of one of those accursed mules. The Boers were thick around them, and they could not send a messenger. An attempt was made to convert a polished biscuit tin into a heliograph, but with poor success. A Kaffir was dispatched with promises of a heavy bribe, but he passed out of history. And there in the clear cold morning air the balloon hung to the south of them where the first distant thunder of White's guns was beginning to sound. If only they could attract the attention of that balloon! Vainly they wagged flags at it. Serene and unresponsive it brooded over the distant battle.

And now the Boers were thickening round them on every side. Christian de Wet, a name soon to be a household word, marshalled the Boer attack, which was soon strengthened by the arrival of Van Dam and his Police. At five o'clock the fire began, at six it was warm, at seven warmer still. Two companies of the Gloucesters lined a sangar on the tread of the sole, to prevent any one getting too near to the heel. A fresh detachment of Boers, firing from a range of nearly one thousand yards, took this defence in the rear. Bullets fell among the men, and smacked up against the stone breastwork. The two companies were withdrawn, and lost heavily in the open as they crossed it. An incessant rattle and crackle of rifle fire came from all round, drawing very slowly but steadily nearer. Now and then the whisk of a dark figure from one boulder to another was all that ever was seen of the attackers. The British fired slowly and steadily, for every cartridge counted, but the cover of the Boers was so cleverly taken that it was seldom that there was much to aim at. 'All you could ever see,' says one who was present, 'were the barrels of the rifles.' There was time for thought in that long morning, and to some of the men it may have occurred what preparation for such fighting had they ever had in the mechanical exercises of the parade ground, or the shooting of an annual bagful of cartridges at exposed targets at a measured range. It is the warfare of Nicholson's Nek, not that of Laffan's Plain, which has to be learned in the future.

During those weary hours lying on the bullet-swept hill and listening to the eternal hissing in the air and clicking on the rocks, the British soldiers could see the fight which raged to the south of them. It was not a cheering sight, and Carleton and Adye with their gallant comrades must have felt their hearts grow heavier as they watched. The Boers' shells bursting among the British batteries, the British shells bursting short of their opponents. The Long Toms laid at an angle of forty-five plumped their huge shells into the British guns at a range where the latter would not dream of unlimbering. And then gradually the rifle fire died away also, crackling more faintly as White withdrew to Ladysmith. At eleven o'clock Carleton's column recognised that it had been left to its fate. As early as nine a heliogram had been sent to them to retire as the opportunity served, but to leave the hill was certainly to court annihilation.

The men had then been under fire for six hours, and with their losses mounting and their cartridges dwindling, all hope had faded from their minds. But still for another hour, and yet another, and yet another, they held doggedly on. Nine and a half hours they clung to that pile of stones. The Fusiliers were still exhausted from the effect of their march from Glencoe and their incessant work since. Many fell asleep behind the boulders. Some sat doggedly with their useless rifles and empty pouches beside them. Some picked cartridges off their dead comrades. What were they fighting for? It was hopeless, and they knew it. But always there was the honour of the flag, the glory of the regiment, the hatred of a proud and brave man to acknowledge defeat. And yet it had to come. There were some in that force who were ready for the reputation of the British army, and for the sake of an example of military virtue, to die stolidly where they stood, or to lead the 'Faugh-a-ballagh' boys, or the gallant 28th, in one last death-charge with empty rifles against the unseen enemy. They may have been right, these stalwarts. Leonidas and his three hundred did more for the Spartan cause by their memory than by their living valour. Man passes like the brown leaves, but the tradition of a nation lives on like the oak that sheds them—and the passing of the leaves is nothing if the bole be the sounder for it. But a counsel of perfection is easy at a study table. There are other things to be said—the responsibility of officers for the lives of their men, the hope that they may yet be of service to their country. All was weighed, all was thought of, and so at last the white flag went up. The officer who hoisted it could see no one unhurt save himself, for all in his sangar were hit, and the others were so placed that he was under the impression that they had withdrawn altogether. Whether this hoisting of the flag necessarily compromised the whole force is a difficult question, but the Boers instantly left their cover, and the men in the sangars behind, some of whom had not been so seriously engaged, were ordered by their officers to desist from firing. In an instant the victorious Boers were among them.

It was not, as I have been told by those who were there, a sight which one would wish to have seen or care now to dwell upon. Haggard officers cracked their sword-blades and cursed the day that they had been born. Privates sobbed with their stained faces buried in their hands. Of all tests of discipline that ever they had stood, the hardest to many was to conform to all that the cursed flapping handkerchief meant to them. 'Father, father, we had rather have died,' cried the Fusiliers to their priest. Gallant hearts, ill paid, ill thanked, how poorly do the successful of the world compare with their unselfish loyalty and devotion!

But the sting of contumely or insult was not added to their misfortunes. There is a fellowship of brave men which rises above the feuds of nations, and may at last go far, we hope, to heal them. From every rock there rose a Boer—strange, grotesque figures many of them— walnut-brown and shaggy-bearded, and swarmed on to the hill. No term of triumph or reproach came from their lips. 'You will not say now that the young Boer cannot shoot,' was the harshest word which the least restrained of them made use of. Between one and two hundred dead and wounded were scattered over the hill. Those who were within reach of human help received all that could be given. Captain Rice, of the Fusiliers, was carried wounded down the hill on the back of one giant, and he has narrated how the man refused the gold piece which was offered him. Some asked the soldiers for their embroidered waist-belts as souvenirs of the day. They will for generations remain as the most precious ornaments of some colonial farmhouse. Then the victors gathered together and sang psalms, not jubilant but sad and quavering. The prisoners, in a downcast column, weary, spent, and unkempt, filed off to the Boer *laager* at Waschbank, there to take train for Pretoria. And at Ladysmith a bugler of Fusiliers, his arm bound, the marks of battle on his dress and person, burst in upon the camp with the news that two veteran regiments had covered the flank of White's retreating army, but at the cost of their own annihilation.

CHAPTER 8

Lord Methuen's Advance

At the end of a fortnight of actual hostilities in Natal the situation of the Boer army was such as to seriously alarm the public at home, and to cause an almost universal chorus of ill-natured delight from the press of all European nations. Whether the reason was hatred of ourselves, or the sporting instinct which backs the smaller against the larger, or the influence of the ubiquitous Dr. Leyds and his secret service fund, it is certain that the continental papers have never been so unanimous as in their premature rejoicings over what, with an extraordinary want of proportion, and ignorance of our national character, they imagined to be a damaging blow to the British Empire. France, Russia, Austria, and Germany were equally venomous against us, nor can the visit of the German Emperor, though a courteous and timely action in itself, entirely atone for the senseless bitterness of the press of the Fatherland. Great Britain was roused out of her habitual apathy and disregard for foreign opinion by this chorus of execration, and braced herself for a greater effort in consequence. She was cheered by the sympathy of her friends in the United States, and by the good wishes of the smaller nations of Europe, notably of Italy, Denmark, Greece, Turkey, and Hungary.

The exact position at the end of this fortnight of hard slogging was that a quarter of the colony of Natal and a hundred miles of railway were in the hands of the enemy. Five distinct actions had been fought, none of them perhaps coming within the fair meaning of a battle. Of these one had been a distinct British victory, two had been indecisive, one had been unfortunate, and one had been a positive disaster. We had lost about twelve hundred prisoners and a battery of small guns. The Boers had lost two fine guns and three hundred prisoners. Twelve thousand British troops had been shut up in Ladysmith, and there was no serious force between the invaders and the sea. Only in those distant transports, where the grimy stokers shovelled and strove, were there hopes for the safety of Natal and the honour of the Empire. In Cape

Colony the loyalists waited with bated breath, knowing well that there was nothing to check a Free State invasion, and that if it came no bounds could be placed upon how far it might advance, or what effect it might have upon the Dutch population.

Leaving Ladysmith now apparently within the grasp of the Boers, who had settled down deliberately to the work of throttling it, the narrative must pass to the western side of the seat of war, and give a consecutive account of the events which began with the siege of Kimberley and led to the ineffectual efforts of Lord Methuen's column to relieve it.

On the declaration of war two important movements had been made by the Boers upon the west. One was the advance of a considerable body under the formidable Cronje to attack Mafeking, an enterprise which demands a chapter of its own. The other was the investment of Kimberley by a force which consisted principally of Freestaters under the command of Wessels and Botha. The place was defended by Colonel Kekewich, aided by the advice and help of Mr. Cecil Rhodes, who had gallantly thrown himself into the town by one of the last trains which reached it. As the founder and director of the great De Beers diamond mines he desired to be with his people in the hour of their need, and it was through his initiative that the town had been provided with the rifles and cannon with which to sustain the siege.

The troops which Colonel Kekewich had at his disposal consisted of four companies of the Loyal North Lancashire Regiment (his own regiment), with some Royal Engineers, a mountain battery, and two machine guns. In addition there were the extremely spirited and capable local forces, a hundred and twenty men of the Cape Police, two thousand Volunteers, a body of Kimberley Light Horse, and a battery of light seven-pounder guns. There were also eight Maxims which were mounted upon the huge mounds of debris which surrounded the mines and formed most efficient fortresses.

A small reinforcement of police had, under tragic circumstances, reached the town. Vryburg, the capital of British Bechuanaland, lies 145 miles to the north of Kimberley. The town has strong Dutch sympathies, and on the news of the approach of a Boer force with artillery it was evident that it could not be held. Scott, the commandant of police, made some attempt to organise a defence, but having no artillery and finding little sympathy, he was compelled to abandon his charge to the invaders. The gallant Scott rode south with his troopers, and in his humiliation and grief at his inability to preserve his post he blew out his brains upon the journey. Vryburg was immediately occupied by the Boers, and British Bechuanaland was formally annexed to the South African Republic. This policy of the instant annexation of all territories invaded was habitually carried out by the enemy, with the idea that British subjects who joined them would in this way be shielded from the consequences of treason. Meanwhile several thousand Freestaters and Transvaalers with artillery had assembled round Kimberley, and all news of the town was cut off. Its relief was one of the first tasks which presented itself to the inpouring army corps. The obvious base of such a movement must be Orange River, and there and at De Aar the stores for the advance began to be accumulated. At the latter place especially, which is the chief railway junction in the north of the colony, enormous masses of provisions, ammunition, and fodder were collected, with thousands of mules which the long arm of the British Government had rounded up from many parts of the world. The guard over these costly and essential supplies seems to have been a dangerously weak one. Between Orange River and De Aar, which are sixty miles apart, there were the 9th Lancers, the Royal Munsters, the 2nd King's Own Yorkshire Light Infantry, and the 1st Northumberland Fusiliers, under three thousand men in all, with two million pounds' worth of stores and the Free State frontier within a ride of them. Verily if we have something to deplore in this war we have much also to be thankful for.

Up to the end of October the situation was so dangerous that it is really inexplicable that no advantage was taken of it by the enemy. Our main force was concentrated to defend the Orange River railway bridge, which was so essential for our advance upon Kimberley. This left only a single regiment without guns for the defence of De Aar and the valuable stores. A fairer mark for a dashing leader and a raid of mounted riflemen was never seen. The chance passed, however, as so many others of the Boers' had done. Early in November Colesberg and Naauwpoort were abandoned by our small detachments, who concentrated at De Aar. The Berkshires joined the Yorkshire Light Infantry, and nine field guns arrived also. General Wood worked hard at the fortifying of the surrounding *kopjes*, until within a week the place had been made tolerably secure.

The first collision between the opposing forces at this part of the seat of war was upon November 10th, when Colonel Gough of the 9th Lancers made a reconnaissance from Orange River to the north with two squadrons of his own regiment, the mounted infantry of the Northumberland Fusiliers, the Royal Munsters, and the North Lancashires, with a battery of field artillery. To the east of Belmont, about fifteen miles off, he came on a detachment of the enemy with a gun. To make out the Boer position the mounted infantry galloped round one of their flanks, and in doing so passed close to a *kopje* which was occupied by sharpshooters. A deadly fire crackled suddenly out from among the boulders. Of six men hit four were officers, showing how cool were the marksmen and how dangerous those dress distinctions which will probably disappear hence forwards upon the field of battle. Colonel Keith-Falconer of the North-umberlands, who had earned distinction in the Soudan, was shot dead. So was Wood of the North Lancashires. Hall and Bevan of the North-umberlands were wounded. An advance by train of the troops in camp drove back the Boers and extricated our small force from what might have proved a serious position, for the enemy in superior numbers were working round their wings. The troops returned to camp without any good object having been attained, but that must be the necessary fate of many a cavalry reconnaissance.

On November 12th Lord Methuen arrived at Orange River and proceeded to organise the column which was to advance to the relief of Kimberley. General Methuen had had some previous South African experience when in 1885 he had commanded a large body of irregular horse in Bechuanaland. His reputation was that of a gallant fearless soldier. He was not yet fifty-five years of age.

The force which gradually assembled at Orange River was formidable rather from its quality than from its numbers. It included a brigade of Guards (the 1st Scots Guards, 3rd Grenadiers, and 1st and 2nd Cold-streams), the 2nd Yorkshire Light Infantry, the 2nd Northamptons, the 1st Northumberlands, and a wing of the North Lancashires whose comrades were holding out at Kimberley, with a naval brigade of seamen gunners and marines. For cavalry he had the 9th Lancers, with detachments of mounted infantry, and for artillery the 75th and 18th Batteries R.F.A.

Extreme mobility was aimed at in the column, and neither tents nor comforts of any sort were permitted to officers or men—no light matter in a climate where a tropical day is followed by an arctic night. At daybreak on November 22nd the force, numbering about eight thousand men, set off upon its eventful journey. The distance to Kimberley was not more than sixty miles, and it is probable that there was not one man in the force who imagined how long that march would take or how grim the experiences would be which awaited them on the way. At the dawn of Wednesday, November 22nd, Lord Methuen moved forward until he came into touch with the Boer position at Belmont. It was surveyed that evening by Colonel Willoughby Verner, and every disposition made to attack it in the morning.

The force of the Boers was much inferior to our own, some two or three thousand in all, but the natural strength of their position made it a difficult one to carry, while it could not be left behind us as a menace to our line of communications. A double row of steep hills lay across the road to Kimberley, and it was along the ridges, snuggling closely among the boulders, that our enemy was waiting for us. In their weeks of preparation they had constructed elaborate shelter pits in which they could lie in comparative safety while they swept all the level ground around with their rifle fire. Mr. Ralph, the American correspondent, whose letters were among the most vivid of the war, has described these lairs, littered with straw and the debris of food, isolated from each other, and each containing its grim and formidable occupant. 'The eyries of birds of prey' is the phrase with which he brings them home to us. In these, with nothing visible but their peering eyes and the barrels of their rifles, the Boer marksmen crouched, and munched their biltong and their mealies as the day broke upon the morning of the 23rd. With the light their enemy was upon them.

It was a soldiers' battle in the good old primeval British style, an Alma on a small scale and against deadlier weapons. The troops advanced in grim silence against the savage-looking, rock-sprinkled, crag-topped position which confronted them. They were in a fierce humour, for they had not breakfasted, and military history from Agincourt to Talavera shows that want of food wakens a dangerous spirit among British troops. A Northumberland Fusilier exploded into words which expressed the gruffness of his comrades. As a too energetic staff officer pranced before their line he roared in his rough North-country tongue, 'Domn thee! Get thee to hell, and let's fire!' In the golden light of the rising sun the men set their teeth and dashed up the hills, scrambling, falling, cheering, swearing, gallant men, gallantly led, their one thought to close with that grim bristle of rifle-barrels which fringed the rocks above them.

Lord Methuen's intention had been an attack from front and from flank, but whether from the Grenadiers losing their bearings, or from the mobility of the Boers, which made a flank attack an impossibility, it is certain that all became frontal. The battle resolved itself into a number of isolated actions in which the various *kopjes* were rushed by different British regiments, always with success and always with loss. The honours of the fight, as tested by the grim record of the casualty returns, lay with the Grenadiers, the Coldstreams, the Northumberlands, and the Scots Guards. The brave Guardsmen lay thickly on the slopes, but their comrades crowned the heights. The Boers held on desperately and fired their rifles in the very faces of the stormers. One young officer had his jaw blown to pieces by a rifle which almost touched him. Another, Blundell of the Guards, was shot dead by a wounded desperado to whom he was offering his water-bottle. At one point a white flag was waved by the defenders, on which the British left cover, only to be met by a volley. It was there that Mr. E. F. Knight, of the *Morning Post*, became the victim of a double abuse of the usages of war, since his wound, from which he lost his right arm, was from an explosive bullet. The man who raised the flag was captured, and it says much for the humanity of British soldiers that he was not bayoneted upon the spot. Yet it is not fair to blame a whole people for the misdeeds of a few, and it is probable that the men who descended to such devices, or who deliberately fired upon our ambulances, were as much execrated by their own comrades as by ourselves.

The victory was an expensive one, for fifty killed and two hundred wounded lay upon the hillside, and, like so many of our skirmishes with the Boers, it led to small material results. Their losses appear to have been much about the same as ours, and we captured some fifty prisoners, whom the soldiers regarded with the utmost interest. They were a sullen slouching crowd rudely clad, and they represented probably the poorest of the burghers, who now, as in the middle ages, suffer most in battle, since a long purse means a good horse. Most of the enemy galloped very comfortably away after the action, leaving a fringe of sharpshooters among the *kopjes* to hold back our pursuing cavalry. The want of horsemen and the want of horse artillery are the two reasons which Lord Methuen gives why the defeat was not converted into a rout. As it was, the feelings of the retreating Boers were exemplified by one of their number, who turned in his saddle in order to place his outstretched fingers to his nose in derision of the victors. He exposed himself to the fire of half a battalion while doing so, but he probably was aware that with our present musketry instruction the fire of a British half-battalion against an individual is not a very serious matter.

The remainder of the 23rd was spent at Belmont Camp, and next morning an advance was made to Enslin, some ten miles further on. Here lay the plain of Enslin, bounded by a formidable line of *kopjes* as dangerous as those of Belmont. Lancers and Rimington's Scouts, the feeble but very capable cavalry of the Army, came in with the report that the hills were strongly held. Some more hard slogging was in front of the relievers of Kimberley.

The advance had been on the line of the Cape Town to Kimberley Railway, and the damage done to it by the Boers had been repaired to the extent of permitting an armoured train with a naval gun to accompany the troops. It was six o'clock upon the morning of Saturday the 25th that this gun came into action against the *kopjes*, closely followed by the guns of the field artillery. One of the lessons of the war has been to disillusion us as to the effect of shrapnel fire. Positions which had been made theoretically untenable have again and again been found to be most inconveniently tenanted. Among the troops actually engaged the confidence in the effect of shrapnel fire has steadily declined with their experience. Some other method of artillery fire than the curving bullet from an exploding shrapnel shell must be devised for dealing with men who lie close among boulders and behind cover.

These remarks upon shrapnel might be included in the account of half the battles of the war, but they are particularly apposite to the action at Enslin. Here a single large *kopje* formed the key to the position, and a considerable time was expended upon preparing it for the British assault, by directing upon it a fire which swept the face of it and searched, as was hoped, every corner in which a rifleman might lurk. One of the two batteries engaged fired no fewer than five hundred rounds. Then the infantry advance was ordered, the Guards being held in reserve on account of their exertions at Belmont. The Northumberlands, Northamptons, North Lancashires, and Yorkshires worked round upon the right, and, aided by the artillery fire, cleared the trenches in their front. The honours of the assault, however, must be awarded to the sailors and marines of the Naval Brigade, who underwent such an ordeal as men have seldom faced and yet come out as victors. To them fell the task of carrying that formidable hill which had been so scourged by our artillery. With a grand rush they swept up the slope, but were met by a horrible fire. Every rock spurted flame, and the front ranks withered away before the storm of the Mauser. An eye-witness has recorded that the brigade was hardly visible amid the sand knocked up by the bullets. For an instant they fell back into cover, and then, having taken their breath, up they went again, with a deep-chested sailor roar. There were but four hundred in all, two hundred seamen and two hundred marines, and the losses in that rapid rush were terrible. Yet they swarmed up, their gallant officers, some of them little boy-middies, cheering them on. Ethelston, the commander of the 'Powerful,' was struck down. Plumbe and Senior of the Marines were killed. Captain Prothero of the 'Doris' dropped while still yelling to his seamen to 'take that *kopje* and be hanged to it!' Little Huddart, the middy, died a death which is worth many inglorious years. Jones of the Marines fell wounded, but rose again and rushed on with his men. It was on these gallant marines, the men who are ready to fight anywhere and anyhow, moist or dry, that the heaviest loss fell. When at last they made good their foothold upon the crest of that murderous hill they had left behind them three officers and eighty-eight men out of a total of 206—a loss within a few minutes of nearly 50 per cent. The bluejackets, helped by the curve of the hill, got off with a toll of eighteen of their number. Half the total British losses of the action fell upon this little body of men, who upheld most gloriously the honour and reputation of the service from which they were drawn. With such men under the white ensign we leave our island homes in safety behind us.

The battle of Enslin had cost us some two hundred of killed and wounded, and beyond the mere fact that we had cleared our way by another stage towards Kimberley it is difficult to say what advantage we had from it. We won the *kopjes*, but we lost our men. The Boer killed and wounded were probably less than half of our own, and the exhaustion and weakness of our cavalry forbade us to pursue and prevented us from capturing their guns. In three days the men had fought two exhausting actions in a waterless country and under a tropical sun. Their exertions had been great and yet were barren of result. Why this should be so was naturally the subject of keen discussion both in the camp and among the public at home. It always came back to Lord Methuen's own complaint about the absence of cavalry and of horse artillery. Many very unjust charges have been hurled against our War Office—a department which in some matters has done extraordinarily and unexpectedly well—but in this question of the delay in the despatch of our cavalry and artillery, knowing as we did the extreme mobility of our enemy, there is certainly ground for an inquiry.

The Boers who had fought these two actions had been drawn mainly from the Jacobsdal and Fauresmith commandoes, with some of the burghers from Boshof. The famous Cronje, however, had been descending from Mafeking with his old guard of Transvaalers, and keen disappointment was expressed by the prisoners at Belmont and at Enslin that he had not arrived in time to take command of them. There were evidences, however, at this latter action, that reinforcements for the enemy were coming up and that the labours of the Kimberley relief force were by no means at an end. In the height of the engagement the Lancer patrols thrown out upon our right flank reported the approach of a considerable body of Boer horsemen, who took up a position upon a hill on our right rear. Their position there was distinctly menacing, and Colonel Willoughby Verner was despatched by Lord Methuen to order up the brigade of Guards. The gallant officer had the misfortune in his return to injure himself seriously through a blunder of his horse. His mission, however, succeeded in its effect, for the Guards moving across the plain intervened in such a way that the reinforcements, without an open attack, which would have been opposed to all Boer traditions, could not help the defenders, and were compelled to witness their defeat. This body of horsemen returned north next day and were no doubt among those whom we encountered at the following action of the Modder River.

The march from Orange River had begun on the Wednesday. On Thursday was fought the action of Belmont, on Saturday that of Enslin. There was no protection against the sun by day nor against the cold at night. Water was not plentiful, and the quality of it was occasionally vile. The troops were in need of a rest, so on Saturday night and Sunday they remained at Enslin. On the Monday morning (November 27th) the weary march to Kimberley was resumed.

On Monday, November 27th, at early dawn, the little British army, a dust-coloured column upon the dusty *veldt*, moved forwards again towards their objective. That night they halted at the pools of Klipfontein, having for once made a whole day's march without coming in touch with the enemy. Hopes rose that possibly the two successive defeats had taken the heart out of them and that there would be no further resistance to the advance. Some, however, who were aware of the presence of Cronje, and of his formidable character, took a juster view of the situation. And this perhaps is where a few words might be said about the celebrated leader who played upon the western side of the seat of war the same part which Joubert did upon the east.

Commandant Cronje was at the time of the war sixty-five years of age, a hard, swarthy man, quiet of manner, fierce of soul, with a reputation among a nation of resolute men for unsurpassed resolution. His dark face was bearded and virile, but sedate and gentle in expression. He spoke little, but what he said was to the point, and he had the gift of those fire-words which brace and strengthen weaker men. In hunting expeditions and in native wars he had first won the admiration of his countrymen by his courage and his fertility of resource. In the war of 1880 he had led the Boers who besieged Potchefstroom, and he had pushed the attack with a relentless vigour which was not hampered by the chivalrous usages of war. Eventually he compelled the surrender of the place by concealing from the garrison that a general armistice had been signed, an act which was afterwards disowned by his own government. In the succeeding years he lived as an autocrat and a patriarch amid his farms and his herds, respected by many and feared by all. For a time he was Native Commissioner and left a reputation for hard dealing behind him. Called into the field again by the Jameson raid, he grimly herded his enemies into an impossible position and desired, as it is stated, that the hardest measure should be dealt out to the captives. This was the man, capable, crafty, iron-hard, magnetic, who lay with a reinforced and formidable army across the path of Lord Methuen's tired soldiers. It was a fair match. On the one side the hardy men, the trained shots, a good artillery, and the defensive; on the other the historical British infantry, duty, discipline, and a fiery courage. With a high heart the dust-coloured column moved on over the dusty *veldt*.

So entirely had hills and Boer fighting become associated in the minds of our leaders, that when it was known that Modder River wound over a plain, the idea of a resistance there appears to have passed away from their minds. So great was the confidence or so lax the scouting that a force equalling their own in numbers had assembled with many guns within seven miles of them, and yet the advance appears to have been conducted without any expectation of impending battle. The supposition, obvious even to a civilian, that a river would be a likely place to meet with an obstinate resistance, seems to have been ignored. It is perhaps not fair to blame the General for a fact which must have vexed his spirit more than ours—one's sympathies go out to the gentle and brave man, who was heard calling out in his sleep that he 'should have had those two guns'— but it is repugnant to common sense to suppose that no one, neither the cavalry nor the Intelligence Department, is at fault for so extraordinary a state of ignorance.[1] On the morning of Tuesday, November 28th, the British troops were told that they would march at once, and have their breakfast when they reached the Modder River—a grim joke to those who lived to appreciate it.

The army had been reinforced the night before by the welcome addition of the Argyll and Sutherland Highlanders, which made up for the losses of the week. It was a cloudless morning, and a dazzling sun rose in a deep blue sky. The men, though hungry, marched cheerily, the reek of their tobacco-pipes floating up from their ranks. It cheered them to see that the murderous *kopjes* had, for the time, been left behind, and that the great plain inclined slightly downwards to where a line of green showed the course of the river. On the further bank were a few scattered buildings, with one considerable hotel, used as a week-end resort by the businessmen of Kimberley. It lay now calm and innocent, with its open windows looking out upon a smiling garden; but death lurked at the windows and death in the garden, and the little dark man who stood by the door, peering through his glass at the approaching column, was the minister of death, the dangerous Cronje. In consultation with him was one who was to prove even more formidable, and for a longer time. Semitic in face, high-nosed, bushy-bearded, and eagle-eyed, with skin burned brown by a life of the *veldt*—it was De la Rey, one of the trio of fighting chiefs whose name will always be associated with the gallant resistance of the Boers. He was there as adviser, but Cronje was in supreme command.

His dispositions had been both masterly and original. Contrary to the usual military practice in the defence of rivers, he had concealed his men upon both banks, placing, as it is stated, those in whose staunchness he had least confidence upon the British side of the river, so that they could only retreat under the rifles of their inexorable companions. The trenches had been so dug with such a regard for the slopes of the ground that in some places a triple line of fire was secured. His artillery, consisting of several heavy pieces and a number of machine guns (including one of the diabolical 'pompoms'), was cleverly placed upon the further side of the stream, and was not only provided with shelter pits but had rows of

1. Later information makes it certain that the cavalry did report the presence of the enemy to Lord Methuen.

reserve pits, so that the guns could be readily shifted when their range was found. Rows of trenches, a broadish river, fresh rows of trenches, fortified houses, and a good artillery well worked and well placed, it was a serious task which lay in front of the gallant little army. The whole position covered between four and five miles.

An obvious question must here occur to the mind of every non-military reader—Why should this position be attacked at all? Why should we not cross higher up where there were no such formidable obstacles?' The answer, so far as one can answer it, must be that so little was known of the dispositions of our enemy that we were hopelessly involved in the action before we knew of it, and that then it was more dangerous to extricate the army than to push the attack. A retirement over that open plain at a range of under a thousand yards would have been a dangerous and disastrous movement. Having once got there, it was wisest and best to see it through.

The dark Cronje still waited reflective in the hotel garden. Across the *veldt* streamed the lines of infantry, the poor fellows eager, after seven miles of that upland air, for the breakfast which had been promised them. It was a quarter to seven when our patrols of Lancers were fired upon. There were Boers, then, between them and their meal! The artillery was ordered up, the Guards were sent forward on the right, the 9th Brigade under Pole-Carew on the left, including the newly arrived Argyll and Sutherland Highlanders. They swept onwards into the fatal fire zone—and then, and only then, there blazed out upon them four miles of rifles, cannon, and machine guns, and they realised, from general to private, that they had walked unwittingly into the fiercest battle yet fought in the war.

Before the position was understood the Guards were within seven hundred yards of the Boer trenches, and the other troops about nine hundred, on the side of a very gentle slope which made it most difficult to find any cover. In front of them lay a serene landscape, the river, the houses, the hotel, no movement of men, no smoke—everything peaceful and deserted save for an occasional quick flash and sparkle of flame. But the noise was horrible and appalling. Men whose nerves had been steeled to the crash of the big guns, or the monotonous roar of Maxims and the rattle of Mauser fire, found a new terror in the malignant *ploop-plooping* of the automatic quick-firer. The Maxim of the Scots Guards was caught in the hell-blizzard from this thing—each shell no bigger than a large walnut, but flying in strings of a score—and men and gun were destroyed in an instant. As to the rifle bullets the air was humming and throbbing with them, and the sand was mottled like a pond in a shower. To advance was impossible, to retire was hateful. The men fell upon their faces and huddled close to the earth, too happy if some friendly ant-heap gave them a precarious shelter.

And always, tier above tier, the lines of rifle fire rippled and palpitated in front of them. The infantry fired also, and fired, and fired—but what was there to fire at? An occasional eye and hand over the edge of a trench or behind a stone is no mark at seven hundred yards. It would be instructive to know how many British bullets found a billet that day.

The cavalry was useless, the infantry was powerless—there only remained the guns. When any arm is helpless and harried it always casts an imploring eye upon the guns, and rarely indeed is it that the gallant guns do not respond. Now the 75th and 18th Field Batteries came rattling and dashing to the front, and unlimbered at one thousand yards. The naval guns were working at four thousand, but the two combined were insufficient to master the fire of the pieces of large calibre which were opposed to them. Lord Methuen must have prayed for guns as Wellington did for night, and never was a prayer answered more dramatically. A strange battery came lurching up from the British rear, unheralded, unknown, the weary gasping horses panting at the traces, the men, caked with sweat and dirt, urging them on into a last spasmodic trot. The bodies of horses which had died of pure fatigue marked their course, the sergeants' horses tugged in the gun-teams, and the sergeants staggered along by the limbers. It was the 62nd Field Battery, which had marched thirty-two miles in eight hours, and now, hearing the crash of battle in front of them, had with one last desperate effort thrown itself into the firing line. Great credit is due to Major Granet and his men. Not even those gallant German batteries who saved the infantry at Spicheren could boast of a finer feat.

Now it was guns against guns, and let the best gunners win! We had eighteen field-guns and the naval pieces against the concealed cannon of the enemy. Back and forward flew the shells, howling past each other in mid-air. The weary men of the 62nd Battery forgot their labours and fatigues as they stooped and strained at their clay-coloured 15-pounders. Half of them were within rifle range, and the limber horses were the centre of a hot fire, as they were destined to be at a shorter range and with more disastrous effect at the Tugela. That the same tactics should have been adopted at two widely sundered points shows with what care the details of the war had been pre-arranged by the Boer leaders. 'Before I got my horses out,' says an officer, 'they shot one of my drivers and two horses and brought down my own horse. When we got the gun round one of the gunners was shot through the brain and fell at my feet. Another was shot while bringing up shell. Then we got a look in.' The roar of the cannon was deafening, but gradually the British were gaining the upper hand. Here and there the little knolls upon the further side which had erupted into constant flame lay cold and silent.

One of the heavier guns was put out of action, and the other had been withdrawn for five hundred yards. But the infantry fire still crackled and rippled along the trenches, and the guns could come no nearer with living men and horses. It was long past midday, and that unhappy breakfast seemed further off than ever.

As the afternoon wore on, a curious condition of things was established. The guns could not advance, and, indeed, it was found necessary to withdraw them from a 1200 to a 2800-yard range, so heavy were the losses. At the time of the change the 75th Battery had lost three officers out of five, nineteen men, and twenty-two horses. The infantry could not advance and would not retire. The Guards on the right were prevented from opening out on the flank and getting round the enemy's line, by the presence of the Riet River, which joins the Modder almost at a right angle. All day they lay under a blistering sun, the sleet of bullets whizzing over their heads. 'It came in solid streaks like telegraph wires,' said a graphic correspondent. The men gossiped, smoked, and many of them slept. They lay on the barrels of their rifles to keep them cool enough for use. Now and again there came the dull thud of a bullet which had found its mark, and a man gasped, or drummed with his feet; but the casualties at this point were not numerous, for there was some little cover, and the piping bullets passed for the most part overhead.

But in the meantime there had been a development upon the left which was to turn the action into a British victory. At this side there was ample room to extend, and the 9th Brigade spread out, feeling its way down the enemy's line, until it came to a point where the fire was less murderous and the approach to the river more in favour of the attack. Here the Yorkshires, a party of whom under Lieutenant Fox had stormed a farmhouse, obtained the command of a drift, over which a mixed force of Highlanders and Fusiliers forced their way, led by their Brigadier in person. This body of infantry, which does not appear to have exceeded five hundred in number, were assailed both by the Boer riflemen and by the guns of both parties, our own gunners being unaware that the Modder had been successfully crossed. A small hamlet called Rosmead formed, however, a *point d'appui*, and to this the infantry clung tenaciously, while reinforcements dribbled across to them from the farther side. 'Now, boys, who's for otter hunting?' cried Major Coleridge, of the North Lancashires, as he sprang into the water. How gladly on that baking, scorching day did the men jump into the river and splash over, to climb the opposite bank with their wet khaki clinging to their figures! Some blundered into holes and were rescued by grasping the unwound putties of their comrades. And so between three and four o'clock a strong party of the British had established their position upon the right flank of the Boers, and were holding on like grim death with an intelligent appreciation that the fortunes of the day depended upon their retaining their grip.

'Hollo, here is a river!' cried Codrington when he led his forlorn hope to the right and found that the Riet had to be crossed. 'I was given to understand that the Modder was fordable everywhere,' says Lord Methuen in his official despatch. One cannot read the account of the operations without being struck by the casual, sketchy knowledge which cost us so dearly. The soldiers slogged their way through, as they have slogged it before; but the task might have been made much lighter for them had we but clearly known what it was that we were trying to do. On the other hand, it is but fair to Lord Methuen to say that his own personal gallantry and unflinching resolution set the most stimulating example to his troops. No General could have done more to put heart into his men.

And now, as the long weary scorching hungry day came to an end, the Boers began at last to flinch from their trenches. The shrapnel was finding them out and this force upon their flank filled them with vague alarm and with fears for their precious guns. And so as night fell they stole across the river, the cannon were withdrawn, the trenches evacuated, and next morning, when the weary British and their anxious General turned themselves to their grim task once more, they found a deserted village, a line of empty houses, and a litter of empty Mauser cartridge-cases to show where their tenacious enemy had stood.

Lord Methuen, in congratulating the troops upon their achievement, spoke of 'the hardest-won victory in our annals of war,' and some such phrase was used in his official despatch. It is hypercritical, no doubt, to look too closely at a term used by a wounded man with the flush of battle still upon him, but still a student of military history must smile at such a comparison between this action and such others as Albuera or Inkerman, where the numbers of British engaged were not dissimilar. A fight in which five hundred men are killed and wounded cannot be classed in the same category as those stern and desperate encounters where more of the victors were carried than walked from the field of battle. And yet there were some special features which will differentiate the fight at Modder River from any of the hundred actions which adorn the standards of our regiments. It was the third battle which the troops had fought within the week, they were under fire for ten or twelve hours, were waterless under a tropical sun, and weak from want of food. For the first time they were called upon to face modern rifle fire and modern machine guns in the open. The result tends to prove that those who hold that it will from now onwards be impossible ever to make such frontal attacks as those which the English made at the Alma or the French at Waterloo, are justified in their belief. It is beyond human hardihood to face the pitiless beat of bullet and shell which comes from modern quick-firing weapons. Had our flank not made a lodgement across the river, it is impossible that we could have carried the position. Once more, too, it was demonstrated how powerless the best artillery is to disperse resolute and well-placed riflemen. Of the minor points of interest there will always remain the record of the forced march of the 62nd Battery, and artillerymen will note the use of gun-pits by the Boers, which ensured that the range of their positions should never be permanently obtained.

The honours of the day upon the side of the British rested with the Argyll and Sutherland Highlanders, the Yorkshire Light Infantry, the 2nd Coldstreams, and the artillery. Out of a total casualty list of about 450, no fewer than 112 came from the gallant Argylls and 69 from the Coldstreams. The loss of the Boers is exceedingly difficult to gauge, as they throughout the war took the utmost pains to conceal it. The number of desperate and long-drawn actions which have ended, according to the official Pretorian account, in a loss of one wounded burgher may in some way be better policy, but does not imply a higher standard of public virtue, than those long lists which have saddened our hearts in the halls of the War Office. What is certain is that the loss at Modder River could not·have been far inferior to our own, and that it arose almost entirely from artillery fire, since at no time of the action were any large number of their riflemen visible. So it ended, this long pelting match, Cronje sullenly withdrawing under the cover of darkness with his resolute heart filled with fierce determination for the future, while the British soldiers threw themselves down on the ground which they occupied and slept the sleep of exhaustion.

CHAPTER 9
Battle of Magersfontein

Lord Methuen's force had now fought three actions in the space of a single week, losing in killed and wounded about a thousand men, or rather more than one-tenth of its total numbers. Had there been evidence that the enemy were seriously demoralised, the General would no doubt have pushed on at once to Kimberley, which was some twenty miles distant. The information which reached him was, however, that the Boers had fallen back upon the very strong position of Spytfontein, that they were full of fight, and that they had been strongly reinforced by a commando from Mafeking. Under these circumstances Lord Methuen had no choice but to give his men a well-earned rest, and to await reinforcements. There was no use in reaching Kimberley unless he had completely defeated the investing force. With the history of the first relief of Lucknow in his memory he was on his guard against a repetition of such an experience.

It was the more necessary that Methuen should strengthen his position, since with every mile which he advanced the more exposed did his line of communications become to a raid from Fauresmith and the southern districts of the Orange Free State. Any serious danger to the railway behind them would leave the British Army in a very critical position, and precautions were taken for the protection of the more vulnerable portions of the line. It was well that this was so, for on the 8th of December Commandant Prinsloo, of the Orange Free State, with a thousand horsemen and two light seven-pounder guns, appeared suddenly at Enslin and vigorously attacked the two companies of the Northampton Regiment who held the station. At the same time they destroyed a couple of culverts and tore up three hundred yards of the permanent way. For some hours the Northamptons under Captain Godley were closely pressed, but a telegram had been despatched to Modder Camp, and the 12th Lancers with the ubiquitous 62nd Battery were sent to their assistance. The Boers retired with their usual mobility, and in ten hours the line was completely restored.

Reinforcements were now reaching the Modder River force, which made it more formidable than when it had started. A very essential addition was that of the 12th Lancers and of G battery of Horse Artillery, which would increase the mobility of the force and make it possible for the General to follow up a blow after he had struck it. The magnificent regiments which formed the Highland Brigade—the 2nd Black Watch, the 1st Gordons, the 2nd Seaforths, and the 1st Highland Light Infantry had arrived under the gallant and ill-fated Wauchope. Four five-inch howitzers had also come to strengthen the artillery. At the same time the Canadians, the Australians, and several line regiments were moved up on the line from De Aar to Belmont. It appeared to the public at home that there was the material for an overwhelming advance; but the ordinary observer, and even perhaps the military critic, had not yet appreciated how great is the advantage which is given by modern weapons to the force which acts upon the defensive. With enormous pains Cronje and De la Rey were entrenching a most formidable position in front of our advance, with a confidence, which proved to be justified that it would be on their own ground and under their own conditions that in this, as in the three preceding actions, we should engage them.

On the morning of Saturday, December 9th, the British General made an attempt to find out what lay in front of him amid that semi-circle of forbidding hills. To this end he sent out a reconnaissance in the early morning, which included G Battery Horse Artillery, the 9th Lancers, and the ponderous 4.7 naval gun, which, preceded by the majestic march of thirty-two bullocks and attended by eighty seamen gunners, creaked forwards over the plain. What was there to shoot at in those sunlit boulder-strewn hills in front? They lay silent and untenanted in the glare of the African day. In vain the great gun exploded its huge shell with its fifty pounds of Lyddite over the ridges, in vain the smaller pieces searched every cleft and hollow with their shrapnel. No answer came from the far-stretching hills. Not a flash or twinkle betrayed the fierce bands who lurked among the boulders. The force returned to camp no wiser than when it left.

There was one sight visible every night to all men which might well nerve the rescuers in their enterprise. Over the northern horizon, behind those hills of danger, there quivered up in the darkness one long, flashing, quivering beam, which swung up and down, and up again like a seraphic sword-blade. It was Kimberley praying for help, Kimberley solicitous for news. Anxiously, distractedly, the great De Beers searchlight dipped and rose. And back across the twenty miles of darkness, over the hills where Cronje lurked, there came that other southern column of light which answered, and promised, and soothed. 'Be of good heart, Kimberley. We are here! The Empire is behind us. We have not forgotten you. It may be days, or it may be weeks, but rest assured that we are coming.'

About three in the afternoon of Sunday, December 10th, the force which was intended to clear a path for the army through the lines of Magersfontein moved out upon what proved to be its desperate enterprise. The 3rd or Highland Brigade included the Black Watch, the Seaforths, the Argyll and Sutherlands, and the Highland Light Infantry. The Gordons had only arrived in camp that day, and did not advance until next morning. Besides the infantry, the 9th Lancers, the mounted infantry, and all the artillery moved to the front. It was raining hard, and the men with one blanket between two soldiers bivouacked upon the cold damp ground, about three miles from the enemy's position. At one o'clock, without food, and drenched, they moved forwards through the drizzle and the darkness to attack those terrible lines. Major Benson, R.A., with two of Rimington's scouts, led them on their difficult way.

Clouds drifted low in the heavens, and the falling rain made the darkness more impenetrable. The Highland Brigade was formed into a column—the Black Watch in front, then the Seaforths, and the other two behind. To prevent the men from straggling in the night the four regiments were packed into a mass of quarter column as densely as was possible, and the left guides held a rope in order to preserve the formation. With many a trip and stumble the ill-fated detachment wandered on, uncertain where they were going and what it was that they were meant to do. Not only among the rank and file, but among the principal officers also, there was the same absolute ignorance. Brigadier Wauchope knew, no doubt, but his voice was soon to be stilled in death. The others were aware, of course, that they were advancing either to turn the enemy's trenches or to attack them, but they may well have argued from their own formation that they could not be near the riflemen yet. Why they should be still advancing in that dense clump we do not now know, nor can we surmise what thoughts were passing through the mind of the gallant and experienced chieftain who walked beside them. There are some who claim on the night before to have seen upon his strangely ascetic face that shadow of doom which is summed up in the one word 'fey.' The hand of coming death may already have lain cold upon his soul. Out there, close beside him, stretched the long trench, fringed with its line of fierce, staring, eager faces, and its bristle of gun-barrels. They knew he was coming. They were ready. They were waiting. But still, with the dull murmur of many feet, the dense column, nearly four thousand strong, wandered onwards through the rain and the darkness, death and mutilation crouching upon their path.

It matters not what gave the signal, whether it was the flashing of a lantern by a Boer scout, or the tripping of a soldier over wire, or the firing of a gun in the ranks. It may have been any, or it may have been none, of these things. As a matter of fact I have been assured by a Boer who was present that it was the sound of the tins attached to the alarm wires which disturbed them. However this may be, in an instant there crashed out of the darkness into their faces and ears a roar of point-blank fire, and the night was slashed across with the throbbing flame of the rifles. At the moment before this outflame some doubt as to their whereabouts seems to have flashed across the mind of their leaders. The order to extend had just been given, but the men had not had time to act upon it. The storm of lead burst upon the head and right flank of the column, which broke to pieces under the murderous volley. Wauchope was shot, struggled up, and fell once more for ever. Rumour has placed words of reproach upon his dying lips, but his nature, both gentle and soldierly, forbids the supposition. 'What a pity!' was the only utterance which a brother Highlander ascribes to him. Men went down in swathes, and a howl of rage and agony, heard afar over the *veldt*, swelled up from the frantic and struggling crowd. By the hundred they dropped—some dead, some wounded, some knocked down by the rush and sway of the broken ranks. It was a horrible business. At such a range and in such a formation a single Mauser bullet may well pass through many men. A few dashed forwards, and were found dead at the very edges of the trench. The few survivors of companies A, B, and C of the Black Watch appear to have never actually retired, but to have clung on to the immediate front of the Boer trenches, while the remains of the other five companies tried to turn the Boer flank. Of the former body only six got away unhurt in the evening after lying all day within two hundred yards of the enemy. The rest of the brigade broke and, disentangling themselves with difficulty from the dead and the dying, fled back out of that accursed place. Some, the most unfortunate of all, became caught in the darkness in the wire defences, and were found in the morning hung up 'like crows,' as one spectator describes it, and riddled with bullets.

Who shall blame the Highlanders for retiring when they did? Viewed, not by desperate and surprised men, but in all calmness and sanity, it may well seem to have been the very best thing which they could do. Dashed into chaos, separated from their officers, with no one who knew what was to be done, the first necessity was to gain shelter from this deadly fire, which had already stretched six hundred of their number upon the ground. The danger was that men so shaken would be stricken with panic, scatter in the darkness over the face of the country, and cease to exist as a military unit. But the Highlanders were true to their character and their traditions. There was shouting in the darkness, hoarse voices calling for the Seaforths, for the Argylls, for Company C, for Company H, and everywhere in the gloom there came the answer of the clansmen. Within half an hour with the break of day the Highland regiments had re-formed, and, shattered and weakened, but undaunted, prepared to renew the contest. Some attempt at an advance was made upon the right, ebbing and flowing, one little band even reaching the trenches and coming back with prisoners and reddened bayonets. For the most part the men lay upon their faces, and fired when they could at the enemy; but the cover which the latter kept was so excellent that an officer who expended 120 rounds has left it upon record that he never once had seen anything positive at which to aim. Lieutenant Lindsay brought the Seaforths' Maxim into the firing-line, and, though all her crew except two were hit, it continued to do good service during the day. The Lancers' Maxim was equally staunch, though it also was left finally with only the lieutenant in charge and one trooper to work it.

Fortunately the guns were at hand, and, as usual, they were quick to come to the aid of the distressed. The sun was hardly up before the howitzers were throwing Lyddite at 4000 yards, the three field batteries (18th, 62nd, 75th) were working with shrapnel at a mile, and the troop of Horse Artillery was up at the right front trying to enfilade the trenches. The guns kept down the rifle-fire, and gave the wearied Highlanders some respite from their troubles. The whole situation had resolved itself now into another Battle of Modder River. The infantry, under a fire at from six hundred to eight hundred paces, could not advance and would not retire. The artillery only kept the battle going, and the huge naval gun from behind was joining with its deep bark in the deafening uproar. But the Boers had already learned—and it is one of their most valuable military qualities that they assimilate their experience so quickly—that shell fire is less dangerous in a trench than among rocks. These trenches, very elaborate in character, had been dug some hundreds of yards from the foot of the hills, so that there was hardly any guide to our artillery fire. Yet it is to the artillery fire that all the losses of the Boers that day were due. The cleverness of Cronje's disposition of his trenches some hundred yards ahead of the *kopjes* is accentuated by the fascination which any rising object has for a gunner. Prince Kraft tells the story of how at Sadowa he unlimbered his guns two hundred yards in front of the church of Chlum, and how the Austrian reply fire almost invariably pitched upon the steeple. So our own gunners, even at a two thousand-yard mark, found it difficult to avoid overshooting the invisible line, and hitting the obvious mark behind.

As the day wore on reinforcements of infantry came up from the force which had been left to guard the camp. The Gordons arrived with the first and second battalions of the Coldstream Guards, and all the artillery was moved nearer to the enemy's position. At the same time, as there were some indications of an attack upon our right flank, the Grenadier Guards with five companies of the Yorkshire Light Infantry were moved up in that direction, while the three remaining companies of Barter's Yorkshiremen secured a drift over which the enemy might cross the Modder. This threatening movement upon our right flank, which would have put the Highlanders into an impossible position had it succeeded, was most gallantly held back all morning, before the arrival of the Guards and the Yorkshires, by the mounted infantry and the 12th Lancers, skirmishing on foot. It was in this long and successful struggle to cover the flank of the 3rd Brigade that Major Milton, Major Ray, and many another brave man met his end. The Coldstreams and Grenadiers relieved the pressure upon this side, and the Lancers retired to their horses, having shown, not for the first time, that the cavalryman with a modern carbine can at a pinch very quickly turn himself into a useful infantry soldier. Lord Airlie deserves all praise for his unconventional use of his men, and for the gallantry with which he threw both himself and them into the most critical corner of the fight.

While the Coldstreams, the Grenadiers, and the Yorkshire Light Infantry were holding back the Boer attack upon our right flank the indomitable Gordons, the men of Dargai, furious with the desire to avenge their comrades of the Highland Brigade, had advanced straight against the trenches and succeeded without any very great loss in getting within four hundred yards of them. But a single regiment could not carry the position, and anything like a general advance upon it was out of the question in broad daylight after the punishment which we had received. Any plans of the sort which may have passed through Lord Methuen's mind were driven away for ever by the sudden unordered retreat of the stricken brigade. They had been very roughly handled in this, which was to most of them their baptism of fire, and they had been without food and water under a burning sun all day. They fell back rapidly for a mile, and the guns were for a time left partially exposed. Fortunately the lack of initiative on the part of the Boers which has stood our friend so often came in to save us from disaster and humiliation. It is due to the brave unshaken face which the Guards presented to the enemy that our repulse did not deepen into something still more serious.

The Gordons and the Scots Guards were still in attendance upon the guns, but they had been advanced very close to the enemy's trenches, and there were no other troops in support. Under these circumstances it was imperative that the Highlanders should rally, and Major Ewart with other surviving officers rushed among the scattered ranks and strove hard to gather and to stiffen them. The men were dazed by what they had undergone, and Nature shrank back from that deadly zone where the bullets fell so thickly. But the pipes blew, and the bugles sang, and the poor tired fellows, the backs of their legs so flayed and blistered by lying in the sun that they could hardly bend them, hobbled back to their duty. They worked up to the guns once more, and the moment of danger passed.

But as the evening wore on it became evident that no attack could succeed, and that therefore there was no use in holding the men in front of the enemy's position. The dark Cronje, lurking among his ditches and his barbed wire, was not to be approached, far less defeated. There are some who think that, had we held on there as we did at the Modder River, the enemy would again have been accommodating enough to make way for us during the night, and the morning would have found the road clear to Kimberley. I know no grounds for such an opinion— but several against it. At Modder Cronje abandoned his lines, knowing that he had other and stronger ones behind him. At Magersfontein a level plain lay behind the Boer position, and to abandon it was to give up the game altogether. Besides, why should he abandon it? He knew that he had hit us hard. We had made absolutely no impression upon his defences. Is it likely that he would have tamely given up all his advantages and surrendered the fruits of his victory without a struggle? It is enough to mourn a defeat without the additional agony of thinking that a little more perseverance might have turned it into a victory. The Boer position could only be taken by outflanking it, and we were not numerous enough nor mobile enough to outflank it. There lay the whole secret of our troubles, and no conjectures as to what might under other circumstances have happened can alter it.

About half-past five the Boer guns, which had for some unexplained reason been silent all day, opened upon the cavalry. Their appearance was a signal for the general falling back of the centre, and the last attempt to retrieve the day was abandoned. The Highlanders were deadbeat; the Coldstreams had had enough; the mounted infantry was badly mauled. There remained the Grenadiers, the Scots Guards, and two or three line regiments who were available for a new attack. There are occasions, such as Sadowa, where a General must play his last card. There are others where with reinforcements in his rear, he can do better by saving his force and trying once again. General Grant had an axiom that the best time for an advance was when you were utterly exhausted, for that was the moment when your enemy was probably utterly exhausted too, and of two such forces the attacker has the moral advantage. Lord Methuen determined—and no doubt wisely—that it was no occasion for counsels of desperation. His men were withdrawn—in some cases withdrew themselves—outside the range of the Boer guns, and next morning saw the whole force with bitter and humiliated hearts on their way back to their camp at Modder River.

The repulse of Magersfontein cost the British nearly a thousand men, killed, wounded, and missing, of which over seven hundred belonged to the Highlanders. Fifty-seven officers had fallen in that brigade alone, including their Brigadier and Colonel Downman of the Gordons. Colonel Codrington of the Coldstreams was wounded early, fought through the action, and came back in the evening on a Maxim gun. Lord Winchester of the same battalion was killed, after injudiciously but heroically exposing himself all day. The Black Watch alone had lost nineteen officers and over three hundred men killed and wounded, a catastrophe which can only be matched in all the bloody and glorious annals of that splendid regiment by their slaughter at Ticonderoga in 1757, when no fewer than five hundred fell before Montcalm's muskets. Never has Scotland had a more grievous day than this of Magersfontein. She has always given her best blood with lavish generosity for the Empire, but it may be doubted if any single battle has ever put so many families of high and low into mourning from the Tweed to the Caithness shore. There is a legend that when sorrow comes upon Scotland the old Edinburgh Castle is lit by ghostly lights and gleams white at every window in the murk of midnight. If ever the watcher could have seen so sinister a sight, it should have been on this, the fatal night of December 11, 1899. As to the Boer loss it is impossible to determine it. Their official returns stated it to be seventy killed and two hundred and fifty wounded, but the reports of prisoners and deserters placed it at a very much higher figure. One unit, the Scandinavian corps, was placed in an advanced position at Spytfontein, and was overwhelmed by the Seaforths, who killed, wounded, or took the eighty men of whom it was composed. The stories of prisoners and of deserters all speak of losses very much higher than those which have been officially acknowledged.

In his comments upon the battle next day Lord Methuen was said to have given offence to the Highland Brigade, and the report was allowed to go uncontradicted until it became generally accepted. It arose, however, from a complete misunderstanding of the purport of Lord Methuen's remarks, in which he praised them, as he well might, for their bravery, and condoled with them over the wreck of their splendid regiments. The way in which officers and men hung on under conditions to which no troops have ever been exposed was worthy of the highest traditions of the British army. From the death of Wauchope in the early morning, until the assumption of the command of the brigade by Hughes-Hallett in the late afternoon, no one seems to have taken the direction. 'My lieutenant was wounded and my captain was killed,' says a private. 'The General was dead, but we stayed where we were, for there was no order to retire.' That was the story of the whole brigade, until the flanking movement of the Boers compelled them to fall back.

The most striking lesson of the engagement is the extreme bloodiness of modern warfare under some conditions, and its bloodlessness under others. Here, out of a total of something under a thousand casualties seven hundred were incurred in about five minutes, and the whole day of shell, machine-gun, and rifle fire only furnished the odd three hundred. So also at Ladysmith the British forces (White's column) were under heavy fire from 5.30 to 11.30, and the loss again was something under three hundred. With conservative generalship the losses of the battles of the future will be much less than those of the past, and as a consequence the battles themselves will last much longer, and it will be the most enduring rather than the most fiery which will win. The supply of food and water to the combatants will become of extreme importance to keep them up during the prolonged trials of endurance, which will last for weeks rather than days. On the other hand, when a General's force is badly compromised, it will be so punished that a quick surrender will be the only alternative to annihilation.

On the subject of the quarter-column formation which proved so fatal to us, it must be remembered that any other form of advance is hardly possible during a night attack, though at Tel-el-Kebir the exceptional circumstance of the march being over an open desert allowed the troops to move for the last mile or two in a more extended formation. A line of battalion double-company columns is most difficult to preserve in the darkness, and any confusion may lead to disaster. The whole mistake lay in a miscalculation of a few hundred yards in the position of the trenches. Had the regiments deployed five minutes earlier it is probable (though by no means certain) that the position would have been carried.

The action was not without those examples of military virtue which soften a disaster, and hold out a brighter promise for the future. The Guards withdrew from the field as if on parade, with the Boer shells bursting over their ranks. Fine, too, was the restraint of G Battery of Horse Artillery on the morning after the battle. An armistice was understood to exist, but the naval gun, in ignorance of it, opened on our extreme left. The Boers at once opened fire upon the Horse Artillery, who, recognising the mistake, remained motionless and unlimbered in a line, with every horse, and gunner and driver in his place, without taking any notice of the fire, which presently slackened and stopped as the enemy came to understand the situation. It is worthy of remark that in this battle the three field batteries engaged, as well as G Battery, R.H.A., each fired over 1000 rounds and remained for 30 consecutive hours within 1500 yards of the Boer position.

But of all the corps who deserve praise, there was none more gallant than the brave surgeons and ambulance bearers, who encounter all the dangers and enjoy none of the thrills of warfare. All day under fire these men worked and toiled among the wounded. Beevor, Ensor, Douglas, Probyn—all were equally devoted. It is almost incredible, and yet it is true, that by ten o'clock on the morning after the battle, before the troops had returned to camp, no fewer than five hundred wounded were in the train and on their way to Cape Town.

CHAPTER 10

The Battle of Stormberg

Some attempt has now been made to sketch the succession of events which had ended in the investment of Ladysmith in northern Natal, and also to show the fortunes of the force which on the western side of the seat of war attempted to advance to the relief of Kimberley. The distance between these forces may be expressed in terms familiar to the European reader by saying that it was that which separates Paris from Frankfort, or to the American by suggesting that Ladysmith was at Boston and that Methuen was trying to relieve Philadelphia. Waterless deserts and rugged mountain ranges divided the two scenes of action. In the case of the British there could be no connection between the two movements, but the Boers by a land journey of something over a hundred miles had a double choice of a route by which Cronje and Joubert might join hands, either by the Bloemfontein-Johannesburg-Laing's Nek Railway, or by the direct line from Harrismith to Lady-smith. The possession of these internal lines should have been of enormous benefit to the Boers, enabling them to throw the weight of their forces unexpectedly from the one flank to the other.

In a future chapter it will be recorded how the Army Corps arriving from England was largely diverted into Natal in order in the first instance to prevent the colony from being overrun, and in the second to rescue the beleaguered garrison. In the meantime it is necessary to deal with the military operations in the broad space between the eastern and western armies.

After the declaration of war there was a period of some weeks during which the position of the British over the whole of the northern part of Cape Colony was full of danger. Immense supplies had been gathered at De Aar which were at the mercy of a Free State raid, and the burghers, had they possessed a cavalry leader with the dash of a Stuart or a Sheridan, might have dealt a blow which would have cost us a million pounds' worth of stores and dislocated the whole plan of campaign. However, the chance was allowed to pass, and when, on November 1st, the burghers at last in a leisurely fashion sauntered over the frontier, arrangements had been made by reinforcement and by concentration to guard the vital points. The objects of the British leaders, until the time for a general advance should come, were to hold the Orange River Bridge (which opened the way to Kimberley), to cover De Aar Junction, where the stores were, to protect at all costs the line of railway which led from Cape Town to Kimberley, and to hold on to as much as possible of those other two lines of railway which led, the one through Colesberg and the other through Stormberg, into the Free State. The two bodies of invaders who entered the colony moved along the line of these two railways, the one crossing the Orange River at Norval's Pont and the other at Bethulie. They enlisted many recruits among the Cape Colony Dutch as they advanced, and the scanty British forces fell back in front of them, abandoning Colesberg on the one line and Stormberg on the other. We have, then, to deal with the movements of two British detachments. The one which operated on the Colesberg line—which was the more vital of the two, as a rapid advance of the Boers upon that line would have threatened the precious Cape Town to Kimberley connection—consisted almost entirely of mounted troops, and was under the command of the same General French who had won the battle of Elandslaagte. By an act of foresight which was only too rare upon the British side in the earlier stages of this war, French, who had in the recent large manoeuvres on Salisbury Plain shown great ability as a cavalry leader, was sent out of Ladysmith in the very last train which made its way through. His operations, with his instructive use of cavalry and horse artillery, may be treated separately.

The other British force which faced the Boers who were advancing through Stormberg was commanded by General Gatacre, a man who bore a high reputation for fearlessness and tireless energy, though he had been criticised, notably during the Soudan campaign, for having called upon his men for undue and unnecessary exertion. 'General Back-acher' they called him, with rough soldierly chaff. A glance at his long thin figure, his gaunt Don Quixote face, and his aggressive jaw would show his personal energy, but might not satisfy the observer that he possessed those intellectual gifts which qualify for high command. At the action of the Atbara he, the brigadier in command, was the first to reach and to tear down with his own hands the *zareeba* of the enemy—a gallant exploit of the soldier, but a questionable position for the General. The man's strength and his weakness lay in the incident.

General Gatacre was nominally in command of a division, but so cruelly had his men been diverted from him, some to Buller in Natal and some to Methuen, that he could not assemble more than a brigade.

Falling back before the Boer advance, he found himself early in December at Sterkstroom, while the Boers occupied the very strong position of Stormberg, some thirty miles to the north of him. With the enemy so near him it was Gatacre's nature to attack, and the moment that he thought himself strong enough he did so. No doubt he had private information as to the dangerous hold which the Boers were getting upon the colonial Dutch, and it is possible that while Buller and Methuen were attacking east and west they urged Gatacre to do something to hold the enemy in the centre. On the night of December 9th he advanced.

The fact that he was about to do so, and even the hour of the start, appear to have been the common property of the camp some days before the actual move. The *Times'* correspondent under the date December 7th details all that it is intended to do. It is to the credit of our Generals as men, but to their detriment as soldiers, that they seem throughout the campaign to have shown extraordinarily little power of dissimulation. They did the obvious, and usually allowed it to be obvious what they were about to do. One thinks of Napoleon striking at Egypt; how he gave it abroad that the real object of the expedition was Ireland, but breathed into the ears of one or two intimates that in very truth it was bound for Genoa. The leading official at Toulon had no more idea where the fleet and army of France had gone than the humblest caulker in the yard. However, it is not fair to expect the subtlety of the Corsican from the downright Saxon, but it remains strange and deplorable that in a country filled with spies any one should have known in advance that a so-called 'surprise' was about to be attempted.

The force with which General Gatacre advanced consisted of the 2nd Northumberland Fusiliers, 960 strong, with one Maxim; the 2nd Irish Rifles, 840 strong, with one Maxim, and 250 Mounted Infantry. There were two batteries of Field Artillery, the 74th and 77th. The total force was well under 3000 men. About three in the afternoon the men were entrained in open trucks under a burning sun, and for some reason, at which the impetuous spirit of the General must have chafed, were kept waiting for three hours. At eight o'clock they detrained at Molteno, and thence after a short rest and a meal they started upon the night march which was intended to end at the break of day at the Boer trenches. One feels as if one were describing the operations of Magersfontein once again and the parallel continues to be painfully exact.

It was nine o'clock and pitch dark when the column moved out of Molteno and struck across the black gloom of the *veldt*, the wheels of the guns being wrapped in hide to deaden the rattle. It was known that the distance was not more than ten miles, and so when hour followed hour and the guides were still unable to say that they had reached their point it must have become perfectly evident that they had missed their way. The men were dog-tired, a long day's work had been followed by a long night's march, and they plodded along drowsily through the darkness. The ground was broken and irregular. The weary soldiers stumbled as they marched. Daylight came and revealed the column still looking for its objective, the fiery General walking in front and leading his horse behind him. It was evident that his plans had miscarried, but his energetic and hardy temperament would not permit him to turn back without a blow being struck. However one may commend his energy, one cannot but stand aghast at his dispositions. The country was wild and rocky, the very places for those tactics of the surprise and the ambuscade in which the Boers excelled. And yet the column still plodded aimlessly on in its dense formation, and if there were any attempt at scouting ahead and on the flanks the result showed how ineffectively it was carried out. It was at a quarter past four in the clear light of a South African morning that a shot, and then another, and then a rolling crash of musketry, told that we were to have one more rough lesson of the result of neglecting the usual precautions of warfare. High up on the face of a steep line of hill the Boer riflemen lay hid, and from a short range their fire scourged our exposed flank. The men appear to have been chiefly colonial rebels, and not Boers of the back-*veldt*, and to that happy chance it may be that the comparative harmlessness of their fire was due. Even now, in spite of the surprise, the situation might have been saved had the bewildered troops and their harried officers known exactly what to do. It is easy to be wise after the event, but it appears now that the only course that could commend itself would be to extricate the troops from their position, and then, if thought feasible, to plan an attack. Instead of this a rush was made at the hillside, and the infantry made their way some distance up it only to find that there were positive ledges in front of them which could not be climbed. The advance was at a dead stop, and the men lay down under the boulders for cover from the hot fire which came from inaccessible marksmen above them. Meanwhile the artillery had opened behind them, and their fire (not for the first time in this campaign) was more deadly to their friends than to their foes. At least one prominent officer fell among his men, torn by British shrapnel bullets. Talana Hill and Modder River have shown also, though perhaps in a less tragic degree, that what with the long range of modern artillery fire, and what with the difficulty of locating infantry who are using smokeless powder, it is necessary that officers commanding batteries should be provided with the coolest heads and the most powerful glasses of any men in the service, for a responsibility which will become more and more terrific rests upon their judgment.

The question now, since the assault had failed, was how to extricate the men from their position. Many withdrew down the hill, running the gauntlet of the enemy's fire as they emerged from the boulders on to the open ground, while others clung to their positions, some from a soldierly hope that victory might finally incline to them, others because it was clearly safer to lie among the rocks than to cross the bullet-swept spaces beyond. Those portions of the force who extricated themselves do not appear to have realised how many of their comrades had remained behind, and so as the gap gradually increased between the men who were stationary and the men who fell back all hope of the two bodies reuniting became impossible. All the infantry who remained upon the hillside were captured. The rest rallied at a point fifteen hundred yards from the scene of the surprise, and began an orderly retreat to Molteno.

In the meanwhile three powerful Boer guns upon the ridge had opened fire with great accuracy, but fortunately with defective shells. Had the enemy's contractors been as trustworthy as their gunners in this campaign, our losses would have been very much heavier, and it is possible that here we catch a glimpse of some consequences of that corruption which was one of the curses of the country. The guns were moved with great smartness along the ridge, and opened fire again and again, but never with great result. Our own batteries, the 74th and 77th, with our handful of mounted men, worked hard in covering the retreat and holding back the enemy's pursuit.

It is a sad subject to discuss, but it is the one instance in a campaign containing many reverses which amounts to demoralisation among the troops engaged. The Guards marching with the steadiness of Hyde Park off the field of Magersfontein, or the men of Nicholson's Nek chafing because they were not led in a last hopeless charge, are, even in defeat, object lessons of military virtue. But here fatigue and sleeplessness had taken all fire and spirit out of the men. They dropped asleep by the roadside and had to be prodded up by their exhausted officers. Many were taken prisoners in their slumber by the enemy who gleaned behind them. Units broke into small straggling bodies, and it was a sorry and bedraggled force which about ten o'clock came wandering into Molteno. The place of honour in the rear was kept throughout by the Irish Rifles, who preserved some military formation to the end. Our losses in killed and wounded were not severe—military honour would have been less sore had they been more so. Twenty-six killed, sixty-eight wounded—that is all. But between the men on the hillside and the somnambulists of the column, six hundred, about equally divided between the Irish Rifles and the Northumberland Fusiliers, had been left as prisoners. Two guns, too, had been lost in the hurried retreat.

It is not for the historian—especially for a civilian historian—to say a word unnecessarily to aggravate the pain of that brave man who, having done all that personal courage could do, was seen afterwards sobbing on the table of the waiting-room at Molteno, and bewailing his 'poor men.' He had a disaster, but Nelson had one at Teneriffe and Napoleon at Acre, and built their great reputations in spite of it. But the one good thing of a disaster is that by examining it we may learn to do better in the future, and so it would indeed be a perilous thing if we agreed that our reverses were not a fit subject for open and frank discussion.

It is not to the detriment of an enterprise that it should be daring and call for considerable physical effort on the part of those who are engaged in it. On the contrary, the conception of such plans is one of the signs of a great military mind. But in the arranging of the details the same military mind should assiduously occupy itself in foreseeing and preventing every unnecessary thing which may make the execution of such a plan more difficult. The idea of a swift sudden attack upon Stormberg was excellent—the details of the operation are continually open to criticism.

How far the Boers suffered at Stormberg is unknown to us, but there seems in this instance no reason to doubt their own statement that their losses were very slight. At no time was any body of them exposed to our fire, while we, as usual, fought in the open. Their numbers were probably less than ours, and the quality of their shooting and want of energy in pursuit make the defeat the more galling. On the other hand, their guns were served with skill and audacity. They consisted of commandos from Bethulie, Rouxville, and Smithfield, under the orders of Olivier, with those colonials whom they had seduced from their allegiance.

This defeat of General Gatacre's, occurring, as it did, in a disaffected district and one of great strategic importance, might have produced the worst consequences.

Fortunately no very evil result followed. No doubt the recruiting of rebels was helped, but there was no forward movement and Molteno remained in our hands. In the meanwhile Gatacre's force was reinforced by a fresh battery, the 79th, and by a strong regiment, the Derbyshires, so that with the 1st Royal Scots and the wing of the Berkshires he was strong enough to hold his own until the time for a general advance should come. So in the Stormberg district, as at the Modder River, the same humiliating and absurd position of stalemate was established.

CHAPTER 11

Battle of Colenso

Two serious defeats had within the week been inflicted upon the British forces in South Africa. Cronje, lurking behind his trenches and his barbed wire entanglements barred Methuen's road to Kimberley, while in the northern part of Cape Colony Gatacre's wearied troops had been defeated and driven by a force which consisted largely of British subjects. But the public at home steeled their hearts and fixed their eyes steadily upon Natal. There was their senior General and there the main body of their troops. As brigade after brigade and battery after battery touched at Cape Town, and were sent on instantly to Durban, it was evident that it was in this quarter that the supreme effort was to be made, and that there the light might at last break. In club, and dining room, and railway car—wherever men met and talked—the same words might be heard: 'Wait until Buller moves.' The hopes of a great empire lay in the phrase.

It was upon October 30th that Sir George White had been thrust back into Ladysmith. On November 2nd telegraphic communication with the town was interrupted. On November 3rd the railway line was cut. On November 10th the Boers held Colenso and the line of the Tugela. On the 14th was the affair of the armoured train. On the 18th the enemy were near Estcourt. On the 21st they had reached the Mooi River. On the 23rd Hildyard attacked them at Willow Grange. All these actions will be treated elsewhere. This last one marks the turn of the tide. From then onwards Sir Redvers Buller was massing his troops at Chieveley in preparation for a great effort to cross the river and to relieve Ladysmith, the guns of which, calling from behind the line of northern hills, told their constant tale of restless attack and stubborn defence.

But the task was as severe a one as the most fighting General could ask for. On the southern side the banks formed a long slope which could be shaved as with a razor by the rifle fire of the enemy. How to advance across that broad open zone was indeed a problem. It was one of many occasions in this war in which one wondered why, if a bullet-proof shield capable of sheltering a lying man could be constructed, a trial should not be given to it. Alternate rushes of companies with a safe rest after each rush would save the troops from the continued tension of that deadly never ending fire. However, it is idle to discuss what might have been done to mitigate their trials. The open ground had to be passed, and then they came to—not the enemy, but a broad and deep river, with a single bridge, probably undermined, and a single ford, which was found not to exist in practice. Beyond the river was tier after tier of hills, crowned with stone walls and seamed with trenches, defended by thousands of the best marksmen in the world, supported by an admirable artillery. If, in spite of the advance over the open and in spite of the passage of the river, a ridge could still be carried, it was only to be commanded by the next; and so, one behind the other, like the billows of the ocean, a series of hills and hollows rolled northwards to Ladysmith. All attacks must be in the open. All defence was from under cover. Add to this, that the young and energetic Louis Botha was in command of the Boers. It was a desperate task, and yet honour forbade that the garrison should be left to its fate. The venture must be made.

The most obvious criticism upon the operation is that if the attack must be made it should not be made under the enemy's conditions. We seem almost to have gone out of our way to make every obstacle— the glacis-like approach, the river, the trenches—as difficult as possible. Future operations were to prove that it was not so difficult to deceive Boer vigilance and by rapid movements to cross the Tugela. A military authority has stated, I know not with what truth, that there is no instance in history of a determined army being stopped by the line of a river, and from Wellington at the Douro to the Russians on the Danube many examples of the ease with which they may be passed will occur to the reader. But Buller had some exceptional difficulties with which to contend. He was weak in mounted troops, and was opposed to an enemy of exceptional mobility who might attack his flank and rear if he exposed them. He had not that great preponderance of numbers which came to him later, and which enabled him to attempt a wide turning movement. One advantage he had, the possession of a more powerful artillery, but his heaviest guns were naturally his least mobile, and the more direct his advance the more effective would his guns be. For these or other reasons he determined upon a frontal attack on the formidable Boer position, and he moved out of Chieveley Camp for that purpose at daybreak on Friday, December 15th.

The force which General Buller led into action was the finest which any British general had handled since the battle of the Alma. Of infantry he had four strong brigades: the 2nd (Hildyard's) consisting of the 2nd

Devons, the 2nd Queen's or West Surrey, the 2nd West Yorkshire, and the 2nd East Surrey; the 4th Brigade (Lyttelton's) comprising the 2nd Cameronians, the 3rd Rifles, the 1st Durhams, and the 1st Rifle Brigade; the 5th Brigade (Hart's) with the 1st Inniskilling Fusiliers, the 1st Connaught Rangers, 2nd Dublin Fusiliers, and the Border Regiment, this last taking the place of the 2nd Irish Rifles, who were with Gatacre. There remained the 6th Brigade (Barton's), which included the 2nd Royal Fusiliers, the 2nd Scots Fusiliers, the 1st Welsh Fusiliers, and the 2nd Irish Fusiliers—in all about 16,000 infantry. The mounted men, who were commanded by Lord Dundonald, included the 13th Hussars, the 1st Royals, Bethune's Mounted Infantry, Thorneycroft's Mounted Infantry, three squadrons of South African Horse, with a composite regiment formed from the mounted infantry of the Rifles and of the Dublin Fusiliers with squadrons of the Natal Carabineers and the Imperial Light Horse. These irregular troops of horse might be criticised by martinets and pedants, but they contained some of the finest fighting material in the army, some urged on by personal hatred of the Boers and some by mere lust of adventure. As an example of the latter one squadron of the South African Horse was composed almost entirely of Texan muleteers, who, having come over with their animals, had been drawn by their own gallant spirit into the fighting line of their kinsmen.

Cavalry was General Buller's weakest arm, but his artillery was strong both in its quality and its number of guns. There were five batteries (30 guns) of the Field Artillery, the 7th, 14th, 63rd, 64th, and 66th. Besides these there were no fewer than sixteen naval guns from H.M.S. 'Terrible'—fourteen of which were 12-pounders, and the other two of the 4.7 type which had done such good service both at Ladysmith and with Methuen. The whole force which moved out from Chieveley Camp numbered about 21,000 men.

The work which was allotted to the army was simple in conception, however terrible it might prove in execution. There were two points at which the river might be crossed, one three miles off on the left, named Bridle Drift, the other straight ahead at the Bridge of Colenso. The 5th or Irish Brigade was to endeavour to cross at Bridle Drift, and then to work down the river bank on the far side so as to support the 2nd or English Brigade,—which was to cross at Colenso. The 4th Brigade was to advance between these, so as to help either which should be in difficulties. Meanwhile on the extreme right the mounted troops under Dundonald were to cover the flank and to attack Hlangwane Hill, a formidable position held strongly by the enemy upon the south bank of the Tugela. The remaining Fusilier brigade of infantry was to support this movement on the right. The guns were to cover the various attacks, and if possible gain a position from which the trenches might be enfiladed. This, simply stated, was the work which lay before the British army. In the bright clear morning sunshine, under a cloudless blue sky, they advanced with high hopes to the assault. Before them lay the long level plain, then the curve of the river, and beyond, silent and serene, like some peaceful dream landscape, stretched the lines and lines of gently curving hills. It was just five o'clock in the morning when the naval guns began to bay, and huge red dust clouds from the distant foothills showed where the Lyddite was bursting. No answer came back, nor was there any movement upon the sunlit hills. It was almost brutal, this furious violence to so gentle and unresponsive a countryside. In no place could the keenest eye detect a sign of guns or men, and yet death lurked in every hollow and crouched by every rock.

It is so difficult to make a modern battle intelligible when fought, as this was, over a front of seven or eight miles, that it is best perhaps to take the doings of each column in turn, beginning with the left flank, where Hart's Irish Brigade had advanced to the assault of Bridle Drift.

Under an unanswered and therefore an unaimed fire from the heavy guns the Irish infantry moved forward upon the points which they had been ordered to attack. The Dublins led, then the Connaughts, the Inniskillings, and the Borderers. Incredible as it may appear after the recent experiences of Magersfontein and of Stormberg, the men in the two rear regiments appear to have been advanced in quarter column, and not to have deployed until after the enemy's fire had opened. Had shrapnel struck this close formation, as it was within an ace of doing, the loss of life must have been as severe as it was unnecessary.

On approaching the Drift—the position or even the existence of which does not seem to have been very clearly defined—it was found that the troops had to advance into a loop formed by the river, so that they were exposed to a very heavy cross-fire upon their right flank, while they were rained on by shrapnel from in front. No sign of the enemy could be seen, though the men were dropping fast. It is a weird and soul-shaking experience to advance over a sunlit and apparently a lonely countryside, with no slightest movement upon its broad face, while the path which you take is marked behind you by sobbing, gasping, writhing men, who can only guess by the position of their wounds whence the shots came which struck them down. All round, like the hissing of fat in the pan, is the monotonous crackle and rattle of the Mausers; but the air is full of it, and no one can define exactly whence it comes. Far away on some hill upon the skyline there hangs the least gauzy veil of thin smoke to indicate whence the six men who have just all fallen together, as if it were some grim drill, met their death. Into such a hell-storm as this it was that the soldiers have again and again advanced in the course of this war, but it may be questioned whether they will not prove to be among the last of mortals to be asked to endure such an ordeal. Other methods of attack must be found or attacks must be abandoned, for smokeless powder, quick-firing guns, and modern rifles make it all odds on the defence!

The gallant Irishmen pushed on, flushed with battle and careless for their losses, the four regiments clubbed into one, with all military organisation rapidly disappearing, and nothing left but their gallant spirit and their furious desire to come to hand-grips with the enemy. Rolling on in a broad wave of shouting angry men, they never winced from the fire until they had swept up to the bank of the river. Northern Inniskilling and Southern man of Connaught, orange and green, Protestant and Catholic, Celt and Saxon, their only rivalry now was who could shed his blood most freely for the common cause. How hateful seem those provincial politics and narrow sectarian creeds which can hold such men apart!

The bank of the river had been gained, but where was the ford? The water swept broad and unruffled in front of them, with no indication of shallows. A few dashing fellows sprang in, but their cartridges and rifles dragged them to the bottom. One or two may even have struggled through to the further side, but on this there is a conflict of evidence. It may be, though it seems incredible, that the river had been partly dammed to deepen the Drift, or, as is more probable, that in the rapid advance and attack the position of the Drift was lost. However this may be, the troops could find no ford, and they lay down, as had been done in so many previous actions, unwilling to retreat and unable to advance, with the same merciless pelting from front and flank. In every fold and behind every anthill the Irishmen lay thick and waited for better times. There are many instances of their cheery and uncomplaining humour. Colonel Brooke, of the Connaughts, fell at the head of his men. Private Livingstone helped to carry him into safety, and then, his task done, he confessed to having 'a bit of a rap meself,' and sank fainting with a bullet through his throat. Another sat with a bullet through both legs. 'Bring me a tin whistle and I'll blow ye any tune ye like,' he cried, mindful of the Dargai piper. Another with his arm hanging by a tendon puffed morosely at his short black pipe. Every now and then, in face of the impossible, the fiery Celtic valour flamed furiously upwards. 'Fix bayonets, men, and let us make a name for ourselves,' cried a colour sergeant, and he never spoke again. For five hours, under the tropical sun, the grimy parched men held on to the ground they had occupied. British shells pitched short and fell among them. A regiment in support fired at them, not knowing that any of the line were so far advanced. Shot at from the front, the flank, and the rear, the 5th Brigade held grimly on.

But fortunately their orders to retire were at hand, and it is certain that had they not reached them the regiments would have been uselessly destroyed where they lay. It seems to have been Buller himself, who showed extraordinary and ubiquitous personal energy during the day, that ordered them to fall back. As they retreated there was an entire absence of haste and panic, but officers and men were hopelessly jumbled up, and General Hart—whose judgment may occasionally be questioned, but whose cool courage was beyond praise—had hard work to reform the splendid brigade which six hours before had tramped out of Chieveley Camp. Between five and six hundred of them had fallen—a loss which approximates to that of the Highland Brigade at Magersfontein. The Dublins and the Connaughts were the heaviest sufferers.

So much for the mishap of the 5th Brigade. It is superfluous to point out that the same old omissions were responsible for the same old results. Why were the men in quarter column when advancing against an unseen foe? Why had no scouts gone forward to be certain of the position of the ford? Where were the clouds of skirmishers which should precede such an advance? The recent examples in the field and the teachings of the text-books were equally set at naught, as they had been, and were to be, so often in this campaign. There may be a science of war in the lecture-rooms at Camberley, but very little of it found its way to the *veldt*. The slogging valour of the private, the careless dash of the regimental officer—these were our military assets—but seldom the care and foresight of our commanders. It is a thankless task to make such comments, but the one great lesson of the war has been that the army is too vital a thing to fall into the hands of a caste, and that it is a national duty for every man to speak fearlessly and freely what he believes to be the truth.

Passing from the misadventure of the 5th Brigade we come as we move from left to right upon the 4th, or Lyttelton's Brigade, which was instructed not to attack itself but to support the attack on either side of it. With the help of the naval guns it did what it could to extricate and cover the retreat of the Irishmen, but it could play no very important part in the action, and its losses were insignificant. On its right in turn Hildyard's English Brigade had developed its attack upon Colenso and the bridge. The regiments under Hildyard's lead were the 2nd West Surrey, the 2nd Devons (whose first battalion was doing so well with the Ladysmith force), the East Surreys, and the West Yorkshires. The enemy had evidently anticipated the main attack on this position, and not only were the trenches upon the other side exceptionally strong, but their artillery converged upon the bridge, at least a dozen heavy pieces, besides a number of quick-firers, bearing upon it. The Devons and the Queens, in open order (an extended line of khaki dots, blending so admirably with the plain that they were hardly visible when they halted), led the attack, being supported by the East Surrey and the West Yorkshires. Advancing under a very heavy fire the brigade experienced much the same ordeal as their comrades of Hart's brigade, which was mitigated by the fact that from the first they preserved their open order in columns of half-companies extended to six paces, and that the river in front of them did not permit that right flank fire which was so fatal to the Irishmen. With a loss of some two hundred men the leading regiments succeeded in reaching Colenso, and the West Surrey, advancing by rushes of fifty yards at a time, had established itself in the station, but a catastrophe had occurred at an earlier hour to the artillery which was supporting it which rendered all further advance impossible. For the reason of this we must follow the fortunes of the next unit upon their right.

This consisted of the important body of artillery who had been told off to support the main attack. It comprised two field batteries, the 14th and the 66th, under the command of Colonel Long, and six naval guns (two of 4.7, and four 12-pounders) under Lieutenant Ogilvy of the 'Terrible.' Long has the record of being a most zealous and dashing officer, whose handling of the Egyptian artillery at the battle of the Atbara had much to do with the success of the action. Unfortunately, these barbarian campaigns, in which liberties may be taken with impunity, leave an evil tradition, as the French have found with their Algerians. Our own close formations, our adherence to volley firing, and in this instance the use of our artillery all seem to be legacies of our savage wars. Be the cause what it may, at an early stage of the action Long's guns whirled forwards, outstripped the infantry brigades upon their flanks, left the slow-moving naval guns with their ox-teams behind them, and unlimbered within a thousand yards of the enemy's trenches. From this position he opened fire upon Fort Wylie, which was the centre of that portion of the Boer position which faced him.

But his two unhappy batteries were destined not to turn the tide of battle, as he had hoped, but rather to furnish the classic example of the helplessness of artillery against modern rifle fire. Not even Mercer's famous description of the effect of a flank fire upon his troop of horse artillery at Waterloo could do justice to the blizzard of lead which broke over the two doomed batteries. The teams fell in heaps, some dead, some mutilated, and mutilating others in their frantic struggles. One driver, crazed with horror, sprang on a leader, cut the traces and tore madly off the field. But a perfect discipline reigned among the vast majority of the gunners, and the words of command and the laying and working of the guns were all as methodical as at Oakhampton. Not only was there a most deadly rifle fire, partly from the lines in front and partly from the village of Colenso upon their left flank, but the Boer automatic quick-firers found the range to a nicety, and the little shells were crackling and banging continually over the batteries. Already every gun had its litter of dead around it, but each was still fringed by its own group of furious officers and sweating desperate gunners. Poor Long was down, with a bullet through his arm and another through his liver. 'Abandon be damned! We don't abandon guns!' was his last cry as they dragged him into the shelter of a little *donga* hard by. Captain Goldie dropped dead. So did Lieutenant Schreiber. Colonel Hunt fell, shot in two places. Officers and men were falling fast. The guns could not be worked, and yet they could not be removed, for every effort to bring up teams from the shelter where the limbers lay ended in the death of the horses. The survivors took refuge from the murderous fire in that small hollow to which Long had been carried, a hundred yards or so from the line of bullet-splashed cannon. One gun on the right was still served by four men who refused to leave it. They seemed to bear charmed lives, these four, as they strained and wrestled with their beloved 15-pounder, amid the spurting sand and the blue wreaths of the bursting shells. Then one gasped and fell against the trail, and his comrade sank beside the wheel with his chin upon his breast. The third threw up his hands and pitched forward upon his face; while the survivor, a grim powder-stained figure, stood at attention looking death in the eyes until he too was struck down. A useless sacrifice, you may say; but while the men who saw them die can tell such a story round the camp fire the example of such deaths as these does more than clang of bugle or roll of drum to stir the warrior spirit of our race.

For two hours the little knot of heart-sick humiliated officers and men lay in the precarious shelter of the *donga* and looked out at the bullet-swept plain and the line of silent guns. Many of them were wounded. Their chief lay among them, still calling out in his delirium for his guns. They had been joined by the gallant Baptie, a brave surgeon, who rode across to the *donga* amid a murderous fire, and did what he could for the injured men. Now and then a rush was made into the open, sometimes in the hope of firing another round, sometimes to bring a wounded comrade in from the pitiless pelt of the bullets. How fearful was that lead-storm may be gathered from the fact that one gunner was found with sixty-four wounds in his body. Several men dropped in these sorties, and the disheartened survivors settled down once more in the *donga*.

The hope to which they clung was that their guns were not really lost, but that the arrival of infantry would enable them to work them once more. Infantry did at last arrive, but in such small numbers that it made the situation more difficult instead of easing it. Colonel Bullock had brought up two companies of the Devons to join the two companies (A and B) of Scots Fusiliers who had been the original escort of the guns, but such a handful could not turn the tide. They also took refuge in the *donga*, and waited for better times.

In the meanwhile the attention of Generals Buller and Clery had been called to the desperate position of the guns, and they had made their way to that further *nullah* in the rear where the remaining limber horses and drivers were. This was some distance behind that other *donga* in which Long, Bullock, and their Devons and gunners were crouching. 'Will any of you volunteer to save the guns?' cried Buller. Corporal Nurse, Gunner Young, and a few others responded. The desperate venture was led by three *aides-de-camp* of the Generals, Congreve, Schofield, and Roberts, the only son of the famous soldier. Two gun teams were taken down; the horses galloping frantically through an infernal fire, and each team succeeded in getting back with a gun. But the loss was fearful. Roberts was mortally wounded. Congreve has left an account which shows what a modern rifle fire at a thousand yards is like. 'My first bullet went through my left sleeve and made the joint of my elbow bleed, next a clod of earth caught me smack on the right arm, then my horse got one, then my right leg one, then my horse another, and that settled us.' The gallant fellow managed to crawl to the group of castaways in the *donga*. Roberts insisted on being left where he fell, for fear he should hamper the others.

In the meanwhile Captain Reed, of the 7th Battery, had arrived with two spare teams of horses, and another determined effort was made under his leadership to save some of the guns. But the fire was too murderous. Two-thirds of his horses and half his men, including himself, were struck down, and General Buller commanded that all further attempts to reach the abandoned batteries should be given up. Both he and General Clery had been slightly wounded, and there were many operations over the whole field of action to engage their attention. But making every allowance for the pressure of many duties and for the confusion and turmoil of a great action, it does seem one of the most inexplicable incidents in British military history that the guns should ever have been permitted to fall into the hands of the enemy. It is evident that if our gunners could not live under the fire of the enemy it would be equally impossible for the enemy to remove the guns under a fire from a couple of battalions of our infantry. There were many regiments which had hardly been engaged, and which could have been advanced for such a purpose. The men of the Mounted Infantry actually volunteered for this work, and none could have been more capable of carrying it out. There was plenty of time also, for the guns were abandoned about eleven and the Boers did not venture to seize them until four. Not only could the guns have been saved, but they might, one would think, have been transformed into an excellent bait for a trap to tempt the Boers out of their trenches. It must have been with fear and trembling that Cherry Emmett and his men first approached them, for how could they believe that such incredible good fortune had come to them? However, the fact, humiliating and inexplicable, is that the guns were so left, that the whole force was withdrawn, and that not only the ten cannon, but also the handful of Devons, with their Colonel, and the Fusiliers were taken prisoners in the *donga* which had sheltered them all day.

We have now, working from left to right, considered the operations of Hart's Brigade at Bridle Drift, of Lyttelton's Brigade in support, of Hildyard's which attacked Colenso, and of the luckless batteries which were to have helped him. There remain two bodies of troops upon the right, the further consisting of Dundonald's mounted men who were to attack Hlangwane Hill, a fortified Boer position upon the south of the river, while Barton's Brigade was to support it and to connect this attack with the central operations.

Dundonald's force was entirely too weak for such an operation as the capture of the formidable entrenched hill, and it is probable that the movement was meant rather as a reconnaissance than as an assault. He had not more than a thousand men in all, mostly irregulars, and the position which faced him was precipitous and entrenched, with barbed-wire entanglements and automatic guns. But the gallant colonials were out on their first action, and their fiery courage pushed the attack home. Leaving their horses, they advanced a mile and a half on foot before they came within easy range of the hidden riflemen, and learned the lesson which had been taught to their comrades all along the line, that given approximately equal numbers the attack in the open has no possible chance against the concealed defence, and that the more bravely it is pushed the more heavy is the repulse. The irregulars carried themselves like old soldiers, they did all that mortal man could do, and they retired coolly and slowly with the loss of 130 of the brave troopers. The 7th Field Battery did all that was possible to support the advance and cover the retirement. In no single place, on this day of disaster, did one least gleam of success come to warm the hearts and reward the exertions of our much-enduring men.

Of Barton's Brigade there is nothing to be recorded, for they appear neither to have supported the attack upon Hlangwane Hill on the one side nor to have helped to cover the ill-fated guns on the other. Barton was applied to for help by Dundonald, but refused to detach any of his troops. If General Buller's real idea was a reconnaissance in force in order to determine the position and strength of the Boer lines, then of course his brigadiers must have felt a reluctance to entangle their brigades in a battle which was really the result of a misunderstanding. On the other hand, if, as the orders of the day seem to show, a serious engagement was always intended, it is strange that two brigades out of four should have played so insignificant a part. To Barton's Brigade was given the responsibility of seeing that no right flank attack was carried out by the Boers, and this held it back until it was clear that no such attack was contemplated. After that one would have thought that, had the situation been appreciated, at least two battalions might have been spared to cover the abandoned guns with their rifle fire. Two companies of the Scots Fusiliers did share the fortunes of the guns. Two others, and one of the Irish Fusiliers, acted in support, but the brigade as a whole, together with the 1st Royals and the 13th Hussars, might as well have been at Aldershot for any bearing which their work had upon the fortunes of the day.

And so the first attempt at the relief of Ladysmith came to an end. At twelve o'clock all the troops upon the ground were retreating for the camp. There was nothing in the shape of rout or panic, and the withdrawal was as orderly as the advance; but the fact remained that we had just 1200 men in killed, wounded, and missing, and had gained absolutely nothing. We had not even the satisfaction of knowing that we had inflicted as well as endured punishment, for the enemy remained throughout the day so cleverly concealed that it is doubtful whether more than a hundred casualties occurred in their ranks. Once more it was shown how weak an arm is artillery against an enemy who lies in shelter.

Our wounded fortunately bore a high proportion to our killed, as they always will do when it is rifle fire rather than shell fire which is effective. Roughly we had 150 killed and about 720 wounded. A more humiliating item is the 250 or so who were missing. These men were the gunners, the Devons, and the Scots Fusiliers, who were taken in the *donga* together with small bodies from the Connaughts, the Dublins, and other regiments who, having found some shelter, were unable to leave it, and clung on until the retirement of their regiments left them in a hopeless position. Some of these small knots of men were allowed to retire in the evening by the Boers, who seemed by no means anxious to increase the number of their prisoners. Colonel Thackeray, of the Inniskilling Fusiliers, found himself with a handful of his men surrounded by the enemy, but owing to their good humour and his own tact he succeeded in withdrawing them in safety. The losses fell chiefly on Hart's Brigade, Hildyard's Brigade, and the colonial irregulars, who bore off the honours of the fight.

In his official report General Buller states that were it not for the action of Colonel Long and the subsequent disaster to the artillery he thought that the battle might have been a successful one. This is a hard saying, and throws perhaps too much responsibility upon the gallant but unfortunate gunner. There have been occasions in the war when greater dash upon the part of our artillery might have changed the fate of the day, and it is bad policy to be too severe upon the man who has taken a risk and failed. The whole operation, with its advance over the open against a concealed enemy with a river in his front, was so absolutely desperate that Long may have seen that only desperate measures could save the situation. To bring guns into action in front of the infantry without having clearly defined the position of the opposing infantry must always remain one of the most hazardous ventures of war. 'It would certainly be mere folly,' says Prince Kraft, 'to advance artillery to within 600 or 800 yards of a position held by infantry unless the latter were under the fire of infantry from an even shorter range.' This 'mere folly' is exactly what Colonel Long did, but it must be remembered in extenuation that he shared with others the idea that the Boers were up on the hills, and had no inkling that their front trenches were down at the river. With the imperfect means at his disposal he did such scouting as he could, and if his fiery and impetuous spirit led him into a position which cost him so dearly it is certainly more easy for the critic to extenuate his fault than that subsequent one which allowed the abandoned guns to fall into the hands of the enemy. Nor is there any evidence that the loss of these guns did seriously affect the fate of the action, for at those other parts of the field where the infantry had the full and unceasing support of the artillery the result was not more favourable than at the centre.

So much for Colenso. A more unsatisfactory and in some ways inexplicable action is not to be found in the range of British military history. And the fuller the light which has been poured upon it, the more extraordinary does the battle appear. There are a preface and a sequel to the action which have put a severe strain upon the charity which the British public has always shown that it is prepared to extend to a defeated General. The preface is that General Buller sent word to General White that he proposed to attack upon the 17th, while the actual attack was delivered upon the 15th, so that the garrison was not prepared to make that demonstration which might have prevented the besiegers from sending important reinforcements to Botha, had he needed them. The sequel is more serious. Losing all heart at his defeat, General Buller, although he had been officially informed that White had provisions for seventy days, sent a heliogram advising the surrender of the garrison. White's first reply, which deserves to live with the anecdote of Nelson's telescope at his blind eye, was to the effect that he believed the enemy had been tampering with Buller's messages. To this Buller despatched an amended message, which with Sir George White's reply, is here appended:

Message of December 16th, as altered by that of December 17th, 1899.

I tried Colenso yesterday, but failed; the enemy is too strong for my force except with siege operations, and these will take one full month to prepare. Can you last so long?

How many days can you hold out? I suggest you firing away as much ammunition as you can, and making best terms you can. I can remain here if you have alternative suggestion, but unaided I cannot break in. I find my infantry cannot fight more than ten miles from camp, and then only if water can be got, and it is scarce here. Whatever happens, recollect to burn your cipher, decipher, and code books, and all deciphered messages.

From Sir G. White to Sir R. Buller. December 16th, 1899.

Yours of today received and understood. My suggestion is that you take up strongest available position that will enable you to keep touch of the enemy and harass him constantly with artillery fire, and in other ways as much as possible. I can make food last for much longer than a month, and will not think of making terms till I am forced to. You may have hit enemy harder than you think. All our native spies report that your artillery fire made considerable impression on enemy. Have your losses been very heavy? If you lose touch of enemy, it will immensely increase his opportunities of crushing me, and have worst effect elsewhere. While you are in touch with him and in communication with me, he has both of our forces to reckon with. Make every effort to get reinforcements as early as possible, including India, and enlist every man in both colonies who will serve and can ride. Things may look brighter. The loss of 12,000 men here would be a heavy blow to England. We must not yet think of it. I fear I could not cut my way to you. Enteric fever is increasing alarmingly here. There are now 180 cases, all within last month. Answer fully. I am keeping everything secret for the present till I know your plans.

Much allowance is to be made for a man who is staggering under the mental shock of defeat and the physical exertions which Buller had endured. That the Government made such allowance is clear from the fact that he was not instantly recalled. And yet the cold facts are that we have a British General, at the head of 25,000 men, recommending another General, at the head of 12,000 men only twelve miles off, to lay down his arms to an army which was certainly very inferior in numbers to the total British force; and this because he had once been defeated, although he knew that there was still time for the whole resources of the Empire to be poured into Natal in order to prevent so shocking a disaster. Such is a plain statement of the advice which Buller gave and which White rejected. For the instant the fate not only of South Africa but even, as I believe, of the Empire hung upon the decision of the old soldier in Ladysmith, who had to resist the proposals of his own General as sternly as the attacks of the enemy. He who sorely needed help and encouragement became, as his message shows, the helper and the encourager. It was a tremendous test, and Sir George White came through it with a staunchness and a loyalty which saved us not only from overwhelming present disaster, but from a hideous memory which must have haunted British military annals for centuries to come.

CHAPTER 12

The Dark Hour

The week which extended from December 10th to December 17th, 1899, was the blackest one known during our generation, and the most disastrous for British arms during the century. We had in the short space of seven days lost, beyond all extenuation or excuse, three separate actions. No single defeat was of vital importance in itself, but the cumulative effect, occurring as they did to each of the main British forces in South Africa, was very great. The total loss amounted to about three thousand men and twelve guns, while the indirect effects in the way of loss of prestige to ourselves and increased confidence and more numerous recruits to our enemy were incalculable.

It is singular to glance at the extracts from the European press at that time and to observe the delight and foolish exultation with which our reverses were received. That this should occur in the French journals is not unnatural, since our history has been largely a contest with that Power, and we can regard with complacency an enmity which is the tribute to our success. Russia, too, as the least progressive of European States, has a natural antagonism of thought, if not of interests, to the Power which stands most prominently for individual freedom and liberal institutions. The same poor excuse may be made for the organs of the Vatican. But what are we to say of the insensate railing of Germany, a country whose ally we have been for centuries? In the days of Marlborough, in the darkest hours of Frederick the Great, in the great world struggle of Napoleon, we have been the brothers-in-arms of these people. So with the Austrians also. If both these countries were not finally swept from the map by Napoleon, it is largely to British subsidies and British tenacity that they owe it. And yet these are the folk who turned most bitterly against us at the only time in modern history when we had a chance of distinguishing our friends from our foes. Never again, I trust, on any pretext will a British guinea be spent or a British soldier or sailor shed his blood for such allies. The political lesson of this writer has been that we should make ourselves strong within the empire, and let all outside it, save only our kinsmen of America, go their own way and meet their own fate without let or hindrance from us. It is amazing to find that even the Americans could understand the stock from which they are themselves sprung so little that such papers as the *New York Herald* should imagine that our defeat at Colenso was a good opportunity for us to terminate the war. The other leading American journals, however, took a more sane view of the situation, and realised that ten years of such defeats would not find the end either of our resolution or of our resources.

In the British Islands and in the empire at large our misfortunes were met by a sombre but unalterable determination to carry the war to a successful conclusion and to spare no sacrifices which could lead to that end. Amid the humiliation of our reverses there was a certain undercurrent of satisfaction that the deeds of our foemen should at least have made the contention that the strong was wantonly attacking the weak an absurd one. Under the stimulus of defeat the opposition to the war sensibly decreased. It had become too absurd even for the most unreasonable platform orator to contend that a struggle had been forced upon the Boers when every fresh detail showed how thoroughly they had prepared for such a contingency and how much we had to make up. Many who had opposed the war simply on that sporting instinct which backs the smaller against the larger began to realise that what with the geographical position of these people, what with the nature of their country, and what with the mobility, number, and hardihood of their forces, we had undertaken a task which would necessitate such a military effort as we had never before been called upon to make. When Kipling at the dawn of the war had sung of *'fifty thousand horse and foot going to Table Bay,'* the statement had seemed extreme. Now it was growing upon the public mind that four times this number would not be an excessive estimate. But the nation rose grandly to the effort. Their only fear, often and loudly expressed, was that Parliament would deal too tamely with the situation and fail to demand sufficient sacrifices. Such was the wave of feeling over the country that it was impossible to hold a peace meeting anywhere without a certainty of riot. The only London daily which had opposed the war, though very ably edited, was overborne by the general sentiment and compelled to change its line. In the provinces also opposition was almost silent, and the great colonies were even more unanimous than the mother country. Misfortune had solidified us where success might have caused a sentimental opposition.

On the whole, the energetic mood of the nation was reflected by the decided measures of the Government. Before the deep-sea cables had told us the lists of our dead, steps had been taken to prove to the world how great were our latent resources and how determined our spirit. On December 18th, two days after Colenso, the following provisions were made for carrying on the campaign.

1. That as General Buller's hands were full in Natal the supervision and direction of the whole campaign should be placed in the hands of Lord Roberts, with Lord Kitchener as his chief of staff. Thus the famous old soldier and the famous young one were called together to the assistance of the country.

2. That all the remaining army reserves should be called out.

3. That the 7th Division (10,000 men) should be despatched to Africa, and that an 8th Division should be formed ready for service.

4. That considerable artillery reinforcements, including a howitzer brigade, should go out.

5. That eleven Militia battalions be sent abroad.

6. That a strong contingent of Volunteers be sent out.

7. That a Yeomanry mounted force be despatched.

8. That mounted corps be raised at the discretion of the commander-in-chief in South Africa.

9. That the patriotic offers of further contingents from the colonies be gratefully accepted.

By these measures it was calculated that from seventy to a hundred thousand men would be added to our South African armies, the numbers of which were already not short of a hundred thousand.

It is one thing, however, to draw up paper reinforcements, and it is another, in a free country where no compulsion would be tolerated, to turn these plans into actual regiments and squadrons. But if there were any who doubted that this ancient nation still glowed with the spirit of its youth his fears must soon have passed away. For this far-distant war, a war of the unseen foe and of the murderous ambuscade, there were so many volunteers that the authorities were embarrassed by their numbers and their pertinacity. It was a stimulating sight to see those long queues of top-hatted, frock-coated young men who waited their turn for the orderly room with as much desperate anxiety as if hard fare, a *veldt* bed, and Boer bullets were all that life had that was worth the holding. Especially the Imperial Yeomanry, a corps of riders and shots, appealed to the sporting instincts of our race. Many could ride and not shoot, many could shoot and not ride, more candidates were rejected than were accepted, and yet in a very short time eight thousand men from every class were wearing the grey coats and bandoliers. This singular and formidable force was drawn from every part of England and Scotland, with a contingent of hard-riding Irish fox-hunters. Noblemen and grooms rode knee to knee in the ranks, and the officers included many well-known country gentlemen and masters of hounds. Well horsed and well armed, a better force for the work in hand could not be imagined. So high did the patriotism run that corps were formed in which the men not only found their own equipment but contributed their pay to the war fund. Many young men about town justified their existence for the first time. In a single club, which is peculiarly consecrated to the *jeunesse dorée*, three hundred members rode to the wars.

Without waiting for these distant but necessary reinforcements, the Generals in Africa had two divisions to look to, one of which was actually arriving while the other was on the sea. These formed the 5th Division under Sir Charles Warren, and the 6th Division under General Kelly-Kenny. Until these forces should arrive it was obviously best that the three armies should wait, for, unless there should be pressing need of help on the part of the besieged garrisons or imminent prospects of European complications, every week which passed was in our favour. There was therefore a long lull in the war, during which Methuen strengthened his position at Modder River, Gatacre held his own at Sterkstroom, and Buller built up his strength for another attempt at the relief of Ladysmith. The only connected series of operations during that time were those of General French in the neighbourhood of Colesberg, an account of which will be found in their entirety elsewhere. A short narrative may be given here of the doings of each of these forces until the period of inaction came to an end.

Methuen after the repulse at Magersfontein had fallen back upon the lines of Modder River, and had fortified them in such a way that he felt himself secure against assault. Cronje, on the other hand, had extended his position both to the right and to the left, and had strengthened the works which we had already found so formidable. In this way a condition of inaction was established which was really very much to our advantage, since Methuen retained his communications by rail, while all supplies to Cronje had to come a hundred miles by road. The British troops, and especially the Highland Brigade, were badly in need of a rest after the very severe ordeal which they had undergone. General Hector Macdonald, whose military record had earned the soldierly name of 'Fighting Mac,' was sent for from India to take the place of the ill-fated Wauchope. Pending his arrival and that of reinforcements, Methuen remained quiet, and the Boers fortunately followed his example. From over the northern horizon those silver flashes of light told that Kimberley was dauntless in the present and hopeful of the future. On January 1st the British post of Kuruman fell, by which twelve officers and 120 police were captured.

The town was isolated, and its capture could have no effect upon the general operations, but it is remarkable as the only capture of a fortified post up to this point made by the Boers.

The monotony of the long wait was broken by one dashing raid carried out by a detachment from Methuen's line of communications. This force consisted of 200 Queenslanders, 100 Canadians (Toronto Company), 40 mounted Munster Fusiliers, a New South Wales Ambulance, and 200 of the Duke of Cornwall's Light Infantry with one horse battery. This singular force, so small in numbers and yet raked from the ends of the earth, was under the command of Colonel Pilcher. Moving out suddenly and rapidly from Belmont, it struck at the extreme right of the Boer line, which consisted of a *laager* occupied by the colonial rebels of that part of the country. Nothing could exceed the enthusiasm of the colonists at the prospect of action. 'At last!' was the cry which went up from the Canadians when they were ordered to advance. The result was an absolute success. The rebels broke and fled, their camp was taken, and forty of them fell into our hands. Our own loss was slight, three killed and a few wounded. The flying column occupied the town of Douglas and hoisted the British flag there; but it was decided that the time had not yet come when it could be held, and the force fell back upon Belmont. The rebel prisoners were sent down to Cape Town for trial. The movement was covered by the advance of a force under Babington from Methuen's force. This detachment, consisting of the 9th and 12th Lancers, with some mounted infantry and G troop of Horse Artillery, prevented any interference with Pilcher's force from the north. It is worthy of record that though the two bodies of troops were operating at a distance of thirty miles, they succeeded in preserving a telephonic connection, seventeen minutes being the average time taken over question and reply.

Encouraged by this small success, Methuen's cavalry on January 9th made another raid over the Free State border, which is remarkable for the fact that, save in the case of Colonel Plumer's Rhodesian Force, it was the first time that the enemy's frontier had been violated. The expedition under Babington consisted of the same regiments and the same battery which had covered Pilcher's advance. The line taken was a south-easterly one, so as to get far round the left flank of the Boer position. With the aid of a party of the Victorian Mounted Rifles a considerable tract of country was overrun, and some farmhouses destroyed. The latter extreme measure may have been taken as a warning to the Boers that such depredations as they had carried out in parts of Natal could not pass with impunity, but both the policy and the humanity of such a course appear to be open to question, and there was some cause for the remonstrance which President Kruger shortly after addressed to us upon the subject. The expedition returned to Modder Camp at the end of two days without having seen the enemy. Save for one or two similar cavalry reconnaissances, an occasional interchange of long-range shells, a little sniping, and one or two false alarms at night, which broke the whole front of Magersfontein into yellow lines of angry light, nothing happened to Methuen's force which is worthy of record up to the time of that movement of General Hector Macdonald to Koodoosberg which may be considered in connection with Lord Roberts's decisive operations, of which it was really a part.

The doings of General Gatacre's force during the long interval which passed between his disaster at Stormberg and the final general advance may be rapidly chronicled. Although nominally in command of a division, Gatacre's troops were continually drafted off to east and to west, so that it was seldom that he had more than a brigade under his orders. During the weeks of waiting, his force consisted of three field batteries, the 74th, 77th, and 79th, some mounted police and irregular horse, the remains of the Royal Irish Rifles and the 2nd Northumberland Fusiliers, the 1st Royal Scots, the Derbyshire regiment, and the Berkshires, the whole amounting to about 5500 men, who had to hold the whole district from Sterkstroom to East London on the coast, with a victorious enemy in front and a disaffected population around. Under these circumstances he could not attempt to do more than to hold his ground at Sterkstroom, and this he did unflinchingly until the line of the Boer defence broke down. Scouting and raiding expeditions, chiefly organised by Captain De Montmorency—whose early death cut short the career of one who possessed every quality of a partisan leader—broke the monotony of inaction. During the week which ended the year a succession of small skirmishes, of which the town of Dordrecht was the centre, exercised the troops in irregular warfare.

On January 3rd the Boer forces advanced and attacked the camp of the Cape Mounted Police, which was some eight miles in advance of Gatacre's main position. The movement, however, was a half-hearted one, and was beaten off with small loss upon their part and less upon ours. From then onwards no movement of importance took place in Gatacre's column until the general advance along the whole line had cleared his difficulties from in front of him.

In the meantime General Buller had also been playing a waiting game, and, secure in the knowledge that Ladysmith could still hold out, he had been building up his strength for a second attempt to relieve the hard-pressed and much-enduring garrison. After the repulse at Colenso, Hildyard's and Barton's brigades had remained at Chieveley with the mounted infantry, the naval guns, and two field batteries. The rest of the force retired to Frere, some miles in the rear. Emboldened by their success, the

Boers sent raiding parties over the Tugela on either flank, which were only checked by our patrols being extended from Springfield on the west to Weenen on the east. A few plundered farmhouses and a small list of killed and wounded horsemen on either side were the sole result of these spasmodic and half-hearted operations.

Time here as elsewhere was working for the British, for reinforcements were steadily coming to Buller's army. By the new year Sir Charles Warren's division (the 5th) was nearly complete at Estcourt, whence it could reach the front at any moment. This division included the 10th brigade, consisting of the Imperial Light Infantry, 2nd Somersets, the 2nd Dorsets, and the 2nd Middlesex; also the 11th, called the Lancashire Brigade, formed by the 2nd Royal Lancaster, the 2nd Lancashire Fusiliers, the 1st South Lancashire, and the York and Lancaster. The division also included the 14th Hussars and the 19th, 20th, and 28th batteries of Field Artillery. Other batteries of artillery, including one howitzer battery, came to strengthen Buller's force, which amounted now to more than 30,000 men. Immense transport preparations had to be made, however, before the force could have the mobility necessary for a flank march, and it was not until January 11th that General Buller's new plans for advance could be set into action. Before describing what these plans were and the disappointing fate which awaited them, we will return to the story of the siege of Ladysmith, and show how narrowly the relieving force escaped the humiliation—some would say the disgrace—of seeing the town which looked to them for help fall beneath their very eyes. That this did not occur is entirely due to the fierce tenacity and savage endurance of the disease-ridden and half-starved men who held on to the frail lines which covered it.

CHAPTER 13

The Siege of Ladysmith

Monday, October 30th, 1899, is not a date which can be looked back to with satisfaction by any Briton. In a scrambling and ill-managed action we had lost our detached left wing almost to a man, while our right had been hustled with no great loss but with some ignominy into Ladysmith. Our guns had been outshot, our infantry checked, and our cavalry paralysed. Eight hundred prisoners may seem no great loss when compared with a Sedan, or even with an Ulm; but such matters are comparative, and the force which laid down its arms at Nicholson's Nek is the largest British force which has surrendered since the days of our great grandfathers, when the egregious Duke of York commanded in Flanders.

Sir George White was now confronted with the certainty of an investment, an event for which apparently no preparation had been made, since with an open railway behind him so many useless mouths had been permitted to remain in the town. Ladysmith lies in a hollow and is dominated by a ring of hills, some near and some distant. The near ones were in our hands, but no attempt had been made in the early days of the war to fortify and hold Bulwana, Lombard's Kop, and the other positions from which the town might be shelled. Whether these might or might not have been successfully held has been much disputed by military men, the balance of opinion being that Bulwana, at least, which has a water-supply of its own, might have been retained. This question, however, was already academic, as the outer hills were in the hands of the enemy. As it was, the inner line—Caesar's Camp, Wagon Hill, Rifleman's Post, and round to Helpmakaar Hill—made a perimeter of fourteen miles, and the difficulty of retaining so extensive a line goes far to exonerate General White, not only for abandoning the outer hills, but also for retaining his cavalry in the town.

After the battle of Ladysmith and the retreat of the British, the Boers in their deliberate but effective fashion set about the investment of the town, while the British commander accepted the same as inevitable,

141

content if he could stem and hold back from the colony the threatened flood of invasion. On Tuesday, Wednesday, Thursday, and Friday the commandoes gradually closed in upon the south and east, harassed by some cavalry operations and reconnaissances upon our part, the effect of which was much exaggerated by the press. On Thursday, November 2nd, the last train escaped under a brisk fire, the passengers upon the wrong side of the seats. At 2 p.m. on the same day the telegraph line was cut, and the lonely town settled herself sombrely down to the task of holding off the exultant Boers until the day—supposed to be imminent—when the relieving army should appear from among the labyrinth of mountains which lay to the south of them. Some there were who, knowing both the enemy and the mountains, felt a cold chill within their hearts as they asked themselves how an army was to come through, but the greater number, from General to private, trusted implicitly in the valour of their comrades and in the luck of the British Army.

One example of that historical luck was ever before their eyes in the shape of those invaluable naval guns which had arrived so dramatically at the very crisis of the fight, in time to check the monster on Pepworth Hill and to cover the retreat of the army. But for them the besieged must have lain impotent under the muzzles of the huge Creusots. But in spite of the naive claims put forward by the Boers to some special Providence—a process which a friendly German critic described as 'commandeering the Almighty'—it is certain that in a very peculiar degree, in the early months of this war there came again and again a happy chance, or a merciful interposition, which saved the British from disaster. Now in this first week of November, when every hill, north and south and east and west, flashed and smoked, and the great 96-pound shells groaned and screamed over the town, it was to the long thin 4.7's and to the hearty bearded men who worked them, that soldiers and townsfolk looked for help. These guns of Lambton's, supplemented by two old-fashioned 6.3 howitzers manned by survivors from No. 10 Mountain Battery, did all that was possible to keep down the fire of the heavy Boer guns. If they could not save, they could at least hit back, and punishment is not so bad to bear when one is giving as well as receiving.

By the end of the first week of November the Boers had established their circle of fire. On the east of the town, broken by the loops of the Klip River, is a broad green plain, some miles in extent, which furnished grazing ground for the horses and cattle of the besieged. Beyond it rises into a long flat-topped hill the famous Bulwana, upon which lay one great Creusot and several smaller guns. To the north, on Pepworth Hill, was another Creusot, and between the two were the Boer batteries upon Lombard's Kop. The British naval guns were placed upon this side, for, as the open loop formed by the river lies at this end, it is the part of the defences which is most liable to assault. From thence all round the west down to Besters in the south was a continuous series of hills, each crowned with Boer guns, which, if they could not harm the distant town, were at least effective in holding the garrison to its lines. So formidable were these positions that, amid much outspoken criticism, it has never been suggested that White would have been justified with a limited garrison in incurring the heavy loss of life which must have followed an attempt to force them.

The first few days of the siege were clouded by the death of Lieutenant Egerton of the 'Powerful,' one of the most promising officers in the Navy. One leg and the other foot were carried off, as he lay upon the sandbag parapet watching the effect of our fire. 'There's an end of my cricket,' said the gallant sportsman, and he was carried to the rear with a cigar between his clenched teeth.

On November 3rd a strong cavalry reconnaissance was pushed down the Colenso road to ascertain the force which the enemy had in that direction. Colonel Brocklehurst took with him the 18th and 19th Hussars, the 5th Lancers and the 5th Dragoon Guards, with the Light Horse and the Natal Volunteers. Some desultory fighting ensued which achieved no end, and was chiefly remarkable for the excellent behaviour of the Colonials, who showed that they were the equals of the Regulars in gallantry and their superiors in the tactics which such a country requires. The death of Major Taunton, Captain Knapp, and young Brabant, the son of the General who did such good service at a later stage of the war, was a heavy price to pay for the knowledge that the Boers were in considerable strength to the south.

By the end of this week the town had already settled down to the routine of the siege. General Joubert, with the chivalry which had always distinguished him, had permitted the garrison to send out the non-combatants to a place called Intombi Camp (promptly named Funkersdorp by the facetious) where they were safe from the shells, though the burden of their support still fell of course upon the much-tried commissariat. The hale and male of the townsfolk refused for the most part to avoid the common danger, and clung tenaciously to their shot-torn village. Fortunately the river has worn down its banks until it runs through a deep channel, in the sides of which it was found to be possible to hollow out caves which were practically bomb-proof. Here for some months the townsfolk led a troglodytic existence, returning to their homes upon that much appreciated seventh day of rest which was granted to them by their Sabbatarian besiegers.

The perimeter of the defence had been divided off so that each corps

143

might be responsible for its own section. To the south was the Manchester Regiment upon the hill called Caesar's Camp. Between Lombard's Kop and the town, on the north-east, were the Devons. To the north, at what seemed the vulnerable point, were the Rifle Brigade, the Rifles, and the remains of the 18th Hussars. To the west were the 5th Lancers, 19th Hussars, and 5th Dragoon Guards. The rest of the force was encamped round the outskirts of the town.

There appears to have been some idea in the Boer mind that the mere fact that they held a dominant position over the town would soon necessitate the surrender of the army. At the end of a week they had realised, however, just as the British had, that a siege lay before both. Their fire upon the town was heavy but not deadly, though it became more effective as the weeks went on. Their practice at a range of five miles was exceedingly accurate. At the same time their riflemen became more venturesome, and on Tuesday, November 7th, they made a half-hearted attack upon the Manchesters' position on the south, which was driven back without difficulty. On the 9th, however, their attempt was of a more serious and sustained character. It began with a heavy shell-fire and with a demonstration of rifle-fire from every side, which had for its object the prevention of reinforcements for the true point of danger, which again was Caesar's Camp at the south. It is evident that the Boers had from the beginning made up their minds that here lay the key of the position, as the two serious attacks—that of November 9th and that of January 6th—were directed upon this point.

The Manchesters at Caesar's Camp had been reinforced by the 1st battalion 60th Rifles, who held the prolongation of the same ridge, which is called Wagon Hill. With the dawn it was found that the Boer riflemen were within eight hundred yards, and from then till evening a constant fire was maintained upon the hill. The Boer, however, save when the odds are all in his favour, is not, in spite of his considerable personal bravery, at his best in attack. His racial traditions, depending upon the necessity for economy of human life, are all opposed to it. As a consequence two regiments well posted were able to hold them off all day with a loss which did not exceed thirty killed and wounded, while the enemy, exposed to the shrapnel of the 42nd battery, as well as the rifle-fire of the infantry, must have suffered very much more severely. The result of the action was a well-grounded belief that in daylight there was very little chance of the Boers being able to carry the lines. As the date was that of the Prince of Wales's birthday, a salute of twenty-one shotted naval guns wound up a successful day.

The failure of the attempt upon Ladysmith seems to have convinced the enemy that a waiting game, in which hunger, shell-fire, and disease

144

were their allies, would be surer and less expensive than an open assault. From their distant hilltops they continued to plague the town, while garrison and citizens sat grimly patient, and learned to endure if not to enjoy the crash of the 96-pound shells, and the patter of shrapnel upon their corrugated-iron roofs. The supplies were adequate, and the besieged were fortunate in the presence of a first-class organiser, Colonel Ward of Islington fame, who with the assistance of Colonel Stoneman systematised the collection and issue of all the food, civil and military, so as to stretch it to its utmost. With rain overhead and mud underfoot, chafing at their own idleness and humiliated by their own position, the soldiers waited through the weary weeks for the relief which never came. On some days there was more shell-fire, on some less; on some there was sniping, on some none; on some they sent a little feeler of cavalry and guns out of the town, on most they lay still—such were the ups and downs of life in Ladysmith. The inevitable siege paper, *The Ladysmith Lyre*, appeared, and did something to relieve the monotony by the exasperation of its jokes. Night, morning, and noon the shells rained upon the town until the most timid learned fatalism if not bravery. The crash of the percussion, and the strange musical tang of the shrapnel sounded ever in their ears. With their glasses the garrison could see the gay frocks and parasols of the Boer ladies who had come down by train to see the torture of the doomed town.

The Boers were sufficiently numerous, aided by their strong positions and excellent artillery, to mask the Ladysmith force and to sweep on at once to the conquest of Natal. Had they done so it is hard to see what could have prevented them from riding their horses down to salt water. A few odds and ends, half battalions and local volunteers, stood between them and Durban. But here, as on the Orange River, a singular paralysis seems to have struck them. When the road lay clear before them the first transports of the army corps were hardly past St. Vincent, but before they had made up their mind to take that road the harbour of Durban was packed with our shipping and ten thousand men had thrown themselves across their path.

For a moment we may leave the fortunes of Ladysmith to follow this southerly movement of the Boers. Within two days of the investment of the town they had swung round their left flank and attacked Colenso, twelve miles south, shelling the Durban Light Infantry out of their post with a long-range fire. The British fell back twenty-seven miles and concentrated at Estcourt, leaving the all-important Colenso railway-bridge in the hands of the enemy. From this onwards they held the north of the Tugela, and many a widow wore crepe before we got our grip upon it once more. Never was there a more critical week in the war, but having got Colenso the Boers did little more. They formally annexed the whole of Northern Natal to the Orange Free State—a dangerous precedent when the tables should be turned. With amazing assurance the burghers pegged out farms for themselves and sent for their people to occupy these newly won estates.

On November 5th the Boers had remained so inert that the British returned in small force to Colenso and removed some stores—which seems to suggest that the original retirement was premature. Four days passed in inactivity—four precious days for us—and on the evening of the fourth, November 9th, the watchers on the signal station at Table Mountain saw the smoke of a great steamer coming past Robben Island. It was the *Roslin Castle* with the first of the reinforcements. Within the week the *Moor, Yorkshire, Aurania, Hawarden Castle, Gascon, Armenian, Oriental,* and a fleet of others had passed for Durban with 15,000 men. Once again the command of the sea had saved the Empire.

But, now that it was too late, the Boers suddenly took the initiative, and in dramatic fashion. North of Estcourt, where General Hildyard was being daily reinforced from the sea, there are two small townlets, or at least geographical (and railway) points. Frere is about ten miles north of Estcourt, and Chieveley is five miles north of that and about as far to the south of Colenso. On November 15th an armoured train was despatched from Estcourt to see what was going on up the line. Already one disaster had befallen us in this campaign on account of these clumsy contrivances, and a heavier one was now to confirm the opinion that, acting alone, they are totally inadmissible. As a means of carrying artillery for a force operating upon either flank of them, with an assured retreat behind, there may be a place for them in modern war, but as a method of scouting they appear to be the most inefficient and also the most expensive that has ever been invented. An intelligent horseman would gather more information, be less visible, and retain some freedom as to route. After our experience the armoured train may steam out of military history.

The train contained ninety Dublin Fusiliers, eighty Durban Volunteers, and ten sailors, with a naval 7-pounder gun. Captain Haldane of the Gordons, Lieutenant Frankland (Dublin Fusiliers), and Winston Churchill, the well-known correspondent, accompanied the expedition. What might have been foreseen occurred. The train steamed into the advancing Boer army, was fired upon, tried to escape, found the rails blocked behind it, and upset. Dublins and Durbans were shot helplessly out of their trucks, under a heavy fire. A railway accident is a nervous thing, and so is an ambuscade, but the combination of the two must be appalling. Yet there were brave hearts which rose to the occasion. Haldane and Frankland rallied the troops, and Churchill the engine-driver. The engine was disentangled and sent on with its cab full of wounded. Churchill, who had escaped upon it, came gallantly back to share the fate of his comrades. The dazed shaken soldiers continued a futile resistance for some time, but there was neither help nor escape and nothing for them but surrender. The most Spartan military critic cannot blame them. A few slipped away besides those who escaped upon the engine. Our losses were two killed, twenty wounded, and about eighty taken. It is remarkable that of the three leaders both Haldane and Churchill succeeded in escaping from Pretoria.

A double tide of armed men was now pouring into Southern Natal. From below, trainload after trainload of British regulars were coming up to the danger point, feted and cheered at every station. Lonely farmhouses near the line hung out their Union Jacks, and the folk on the *stoep* heard the roar of the choruses as the great trains swung upon their way. From above the Boers were flooding down, as Churchill saw them, dour, resolute, riding silently through the rain, or chanting hymns round their camp fires—brave honest farmers, but standing unconsciously for medievalism and corruption, even as our rough-tongued Tommies stood for civilisation, progress, and equal rights for all men.

The invading force, the numbers of which could not have exceeded some few thousands, formidable only for their mobility, lapped round the more powerful but less active force at Estcourt, and struck behind it at its communications. There was for a day or two some discussion as to a further retreat, but Hildyard, strengthened by the advice and presence of Colonel Long, determined to hold his ground. On November 21st the raiding Boers were as far south as Nottingham Road, a point thirty miles south of Estcourt and only forty miles north of the considerable city of Pietermaritzburg. The situation was serious. Either the invaders must be stopped, or the second largest town in the colony would be in their hands. From all sides came tales of plundered farms and broken households. Some at least of the raiders behaved with wanton brutality. Smashed pianos, shattered pictures, slaughtered stock, and vile inscriptions, all exhibit a predatory and violent side to the paradoxical Boer character.[1]

The next British post behind Hildyard's at Estcourt was Barton's upon the Mooi River, thirty miles to the south. Upon this the Boers made a half-hearted attempt, but Joubert had begun to realise the strength of the British reinforcements and the impossibility with the numbers at his disposal of investing a succession of British posts. He ordered Botha to withdraw from Mooi River and begin his northerly trek.

The turning-point of the Boer invasion of Natal was marked, though

---

1. More than once I have heard the farmers in the Free State acknowledge that the ruin which had come upon them was a just retribution for the excesses of Natal.

we cannot claim that it was caused, by the action of Willow Grange. This was fought by Hildyard and Walter Kitchener in command of the Estcourt garrison, against about 2000 of the invaders under Louis Botha. The troops engaged were the East and West Surreys (four companies of the latter), the West Yorkshires, the Durban Light Infantry, No. 7 battery R.F.A., two naval guns, and some hundreds of Colonial Horse.

The enemy being observed to have a gun upon a hill within striking distance of Estcourt, this force set out on November 22nd to make a night attack and to endeavour to capture it. The hill was taken without difficulty, but it was found that the gun had been removed. A severe counter-attack was made at daylight by the Boers, and the troops were compelled with no great loss and less glory to return to the town. The Surreys and the Yorkshires behaved very well, but were placed in a difficult position and were badly supported by the artillery. Martyn's Mounted Infantry covered the retirement with great gallantry, but the skirmish ended in a British loss of fourteen killed and fifty wounded or missing, which was certainly more than that of the Boers. From this indecisive action of Willow Grange the Boer invasion receded until General Buller, coming to the front on November 27th, found that the enemy was once more occupying the line of the Tugela. He himself moved up to Frere, where he devoted his time and energies to the collection of that force with which he was destined, after three failures, to make his way into Ladysmith.

One unexpected and little known result of the Boer expedition into Southern Natal was that their leader, the chivalrous Joubert, injured himself through his horse stumbling, and was physically incapacitated for the remainder of the campaign. He returned almost immediately to Pretoria, leaving the command of the Tugela in the hands of Louis Botha.

Leaving Buller to organise his army at Frere, and the Boer commanders to draw their screen of formidable defences along the Tugela, we will return once more to the fortunes of the unhappy town round which the interest of the world, and possibly the destiny of the Empire, were centring. It is very certain that had Ladysmith fallen, and twelve thousand British soldiers with a million pounds' worth of stores fallen into the hands of the invaders, we should have been faced with the alternative of abandoning the struggle, or of reconquering South Africa from Cape Town northwards. South Africa is the keystone of the Empire, and for the instant Ladysmith was the keystone of South Africa. But the courage of the troops who held the shell-torn townlet, and the confidence of the public who watched them, never faltered for an instant.

December 8th was marked by a gallant exploit on the part of the beleaguered garrison. Not a whisper had transpired of the coming sortie, and a quarter of an hour before the start officers engaged had no idea of it. *O si sic omnia!* At ten o'clock a band of men slipped out of the town. There were six hundred of them, all irregulars, drawn from the Imperial Light Horse, the Natal Carabineers, and the Border Mounted Rifles, under the command of Hunter, youngest and most dashing of British Generals. Edwardes and Boyston were the subcommanders. The men had no knowledge of where they were going or what they had to do, but they crept silently along under a drifting sky, with peeps of a quarter moon, over a mimosa-shadowed plain. At last in front of them there loomed a dark mass—it was Gun Hill, from which one of the great Creusots had plagued them. A strong support (four hundred men) was left at the base of the hill, and the others, one hundred Imperials, one hundred Borders and Carabineers, ten Sappers, crept upwards with Major Henderson as guide. A Dutch outpost challenged, but was satisfied by a Dutch-speaking Carabineer. Higher and higher the men crept, the silence broken only by the occasional slip of a stone or the rustle of their own breathing. Most of them had left their boots below. Even in the darkness they kept some formation, and the right wing curved forward to outflank the defence. Suddenly a Mauser crack and a spurt of flame—then another and another! 'Come on, boys! Fix bayonets!' yelled Karri Davies. There were no bayonets, but that was a detail. At the word the gunners were off, and there in the darkness in front of the storming party loomed the enormous gun, gigantic in that uncertain light. Out with the huge breech-block! Wrap the long lean muzzle round with a collar of gun-cotton! Keep the guard upon the run until the work is done! Hunter stood by with a night light in his hand until the charge was in position, and then, with a crash which brought both armies from their tents, the huge tube reared up on its mountings and toppled backwards into the pit. A howitzer lurked beside it, and this also was blown into ruin. The attendant Maxim was dragged back by the exultant captors, who reached the town amid shoutings and laughter with the first break of day. One man wounded, the gallant Henderson, is the cheap price for the best-planned and most dashing exploit of the war. Secrecy in conception, vigour in execution—they are the root ideas of the soldier's craft. So easily was the enterprise carried out, and so defective the Boer watch, that it is probable that if all the guns had been simultaneously attacked the Boers might have found themselves without a single piece of ordnance in the morning.[2]

---

2. The destruction of the Creusot was not as complete as was hoped. It was taken back to Pretoria, three feet were sawn off the muzzle, and a new breech-block provided. The gun was then sent to Kimberley, and it was the heavy cannon which arrived late in the history of that siege and caused considerable consternation among the inhabitants.

On the same morning (December 9th) a cavalry reconnaissance was pushed in the direction of Pepworth Hill. The object no doubt was to ascertain whether the enemy were still present in force, and the terrific roll of the Mausers answered it in the affirmative. Two killed and twenty wounded was the price which we paid for the information. There had been three such reconnaissances in the five weeks of the siege, and it is difficult to see what advantage they gave or how they are to be justified. Far be it for the civilian to dogmatise upon such matters, but one can repeat, and to the best of one's judgment endorse, the opinion of the vast majority of officers.

There were heart burnings among the Regulars that the colonial troops should have gone in front of them, so their martial jealousy was allayed three nights later by the same task being given to them. Four companies of the 2nd Rifle Brigade were the troops chosen, with a few sappers and gunners, the whole under the command of Colonel Metcalfe of the same battalion. A single gun, the 4.7 howitzer upon Surprise Hill, was the objective. Again there was the stealthy advance through the darkness, again the support was left at the bottom of the hill, again the two companies carefully ascended, again there was the challenge, the rush, the flight, and the gun was in the hands of the stormers.

Here and only here the story varies. For some reason the fuse used for the guncotton was defective, and half an hour elapsed before the explosion destroyed the howitzer. When it came it came very thoroughly, but it was a weary time in coming. Then our men descended the hill, but the Boers were already crowding in upon them from either side. The English cries of the soldiers were answered in English by the Boers, and slouch hat or helmet dimly seen in the murk was the only badge of friend or foe. A singular letter is extant from young Reitz (the son of the Transvaal secretary), who was present. According to his account there were but eight Boers present, but assertion or contradiction equally valueless in the darkness of such a night, and there are some obvious discrepancies in his statement. 'We fired among them,' says Reitz. 'They stopped and all cried out "Rifle Brigade." Then one of them said "Charge!" One officer, Captain Paley, advanced, though he had two bullet wounds already. Joubert gave him another shot and he fell on the top of us. Four Englishmen got hold of Jan Luttig and struck him on the head with their rifles and stabbed him in the stomach with a bayonet. He seized two of them by the throat and shouted "Help, boys!" His two nearest comrades shot two of them, and the other two bolted. Then the English came up in numbers, about eight hundred, along the footpath' (there were two hundred on the hill, but the exaggeration is pardonable in the darkness), 'and we lay as quiet as mice along the bank. Farther on the English killed three of our men with bayonets and wounded two. In the morning we found Captain Paley and twenty-two of them killed and wounded.' It seems evident that Reitz means that his own little party were eight men, and not that that represented the force which intercepted the retiring riflemen. Within his own knowledge five of his countrymen were killed in the scuffle, so the total loss was probably considerable. Our own casualties were eleven dead, forty-three wounded, and six prisoners, but the price was not excessive for the howitzer and for the morale which arises from such exploits. Had it not been for that unfortunate fuse, the second success might have been as bloodless as the first. 'I am sorry,' said a sympathetic correspondent to the stricken Paley. 'But we got the gun,' Paley whispered, and he spoke for the Brigade.

Amid the shell-fire, the scanty rations, the enteric and the dysentery, one ray of comfort had always brightened the garrison. Buller was only twelve miles away—they could hear his guns—and when his advance came in earnest their sufferings would be at an end. But now in an instant this single light was shut off and the true nature of their situation was revealed to them. Buller had indeed moved...but backwards. He had been defeated at Colenso, and the siege was not ending but beginning. With heavier hearts but undiminished resolution the army and the townsfolk settled down to the long, dour struggle. The exultant enemy replaced their shattered guns and drew their lines closer still round the stricken town.

A record of the siege onwards until the break of the New Year centres upon the sordid details of the sick returns and of the price of food. Fifty on one day, seventy on the next, passed under the hands of the overworked and devoted doctors. Fifteen hundred, and later two thousand, of the garrison were down. The air was poisoned by foul sewage and dark with obscene flies. They speckled the scanty food. Eggs were already a shilling each, cigarettes sixpence, whisky five pounds a bottle: a city more free from gluttony and drunkenness has never been seen.

Shell-fire has shown itself in this war to be an excellent ordeal for those who desire martial excitement with a minimum of danger. But now and again some black chance guides a bomb—one in five thousand perhaps—to a most tragic issue. Such a deadly missile falling among Boers near Kimberley is said to have slain nine and wounded seventeen. In Ladysmith too there are days to be marked in red when the gunner shot better than he knew. One shell on December 17th killed six men (Natal Carabineers), wounded three, and destroyed fourteen horses. The grisly fact has been recorded that five separate human legs lay upon the ground. On December 22nd another tragic shot killed five and wounded twelve of the Devons. On the same day four officers of the 5th Lancers (including the Colonel) and one sergeant were wounded—a most disastrous day. A little later it was again the turn of the Devons, who lost one officer killed and ten wounded. Christmas set in amid misery, hunger, and disease, the more piteous for the grim attempts to amuse the children and live up to the joyous season, when the present of Santa Claus was too often a 96-pound shell. On the top of all other troubles it was now known that the heavy ammunition was running short and must be husbanded for emergencies. There was no surcease, however, in the constant hail which fell upon the town. Two or three hundred shells were a not unusual daily allowance. The monotonous bombardment with which the New Year had commenced was soon to be varied by a most gallant and spirit-stirring clash of arms. On January 6th the Boers delivered their great assault upon Ladysmith—an onfall so gallantly made and gallantly met that it deserves to rank among the classic fights of British military history. It is a tale which neither side need be ashamed to tell. Honour to the sturdy infantry who held their grip so long, and honour also to the rough men of the *veldt*, who, led by untrained civilians, stretched us to the utmost capacity of our endurance.

It may be that the Boers wished once for all to have done at all costs with the constant menace to their rear, or it may be that the deliberate preparations of Buller for his second advance had alarmed them, and that they realised that they must act quickly if they were to act at all. At any rate, early in the New Year a most determined attack was decided upon. The storming party consisted of some hundreds of picked volunteers from the Heidelberg (Transvaal) and Harrismith (Free State) contingents, led by de Villiers. They were supported by several thousand riflemen, who might secure their success or cover their retreat. Eighteen heavy guns had been trained upon the long ridge, one end of which has been called Caesar's Camp and the other Wagon Hill. This hill, three miles long, lay to the south of the town, and the Boers had early recognised it as being the most vulnerable point, for it was against it that their attack of November 9th had been directed. Now, after two months, they were about to renew the attempt with greater resolution against less robust opponents. At twelve o'clock our scouts heard the sounds of the chanting of hymns in the Boer camps. At two in the morning crowds of barefooted men were clustering round the base of the ridge, and threading their way, rifle in hand, among the mimosa-bushes and scattered boulders which cover the slope of the hill. Some working parties were moving guns into position, and the noise of their labour helped to drown the sound of the Boer advance. Both at Caesar's Camp, the east end of the ridge, and at Wagon Hill, the west end (the points being, I repeat, three miles apart), the attack came as a complete surprise. The outposts were shot or driven in, and the stormers were on the ridge almost as soon as their presence was detected. The line of rocks blazed with the flash of their guns.

Caesar's Camp was garrisoned by one sturdy regiment, the Manchesters, aided by a Colt automatic gun. The defence had been arranged in the form of small sangars, each held by from ten to twenty men. Some few of these were rushed in the darkness, but the Lancashire men pulled themselves together and held on strenuously to those which remained. The crash of musketry woke the sleeping town, and the streets resounded with the shouting of the officers and the rattling of arms as the men mustered in the darkness and hurried to the points of danger.

Three companies of the Gordons had been left near Caesar's Camp, and these, under Captain Carnegie, threw themselves into the struggle. Four other companies of Gordons came up in support from the town, losing upon the way their splendid colonel, Dick-Cunyngham, who was killed by a chance shot at three thousand yards, on this his first appearance since he had recovered from his wounds at Elandslaagte. Later four companies of the Rifle Brigade were thrown into the firing line, and a total of two and a half infantry battalions held that end of the position. It was not a man too much. With the dawn of day it could be seen that the Boers held the southern and we the northern slopes, while the narrow plateau between formed a bloody debatable ground. Along a front of a quarter of a mile fierce eyes glared and rifle barrels flashed from behind every rock, and the long fight swayed a little back or a little forward with each upward heave of the stormers or rally of the soldiers. For hours the combatants were so near that a stone or a taunt could be thrown from one to the other. Some scattered sangars still held their own, though the Boers had passed them. One such, manned by fourteen privates of the Manchester Regiment, remained untaken, but had only two defenders left at the end of the bloody day.

With the coming of the light the 53rd Field Battery, the one which had already done so admirably at Lombard's Kop, again deserved well of its country. It was impossible to get behind the Boers and fire straight at their position, so every shell fired had to skim over the heads of our own men upon the ridge and so pitch upon the reverse slope. Yet so accurate was the fire, carried on under an incessant rain of shells from the big Dutch gun on Bulwana, that not one shot miscarried and that Major Abdy and his men succeeded in sweeping the further slope without loss to our own fighting line. Exactly the same feat was equally well performed at the other end of the position by Major Blewitt's 21st Battery, which was exposed to an even more searching fire than the 53rd. Any one who has seen the iron endurance of British gunners and marvelled at the answering shot which flashes out through the very dust of the enemy's exploding shell, will understand how fine must have been the spectacle of these two batteries working in the open, with the ground round them sharded with splinters. Eye-witnesses have left it upon record that the sight of Major Blewitt strolling up and down among his guns, and turning over with his toe the last fallen section of iron, was one of the most vivid and stirring impressions which they carried from the fight. Here also it was that the gallant Sergeant Bosley, his arm and his leg stricken off by a Boer shell, cried to his comrades to roll his body off the trail and go on working the gun.

At the same time as—or rather earlier than—the onslaught upon Caesar's Camp a similar attack had been made with secrecy and determination upon the western end of the position called Wagon Hill. The barefooted Boers burst suddenly with a roll of rifle-fire into the little garrison of Imperial Light Horse and Sappers who held the position. Mathias of the former, Digby-Jones and Dennis of the latter, showed that 'two in the morning' courage which Napoleon rated as the highest of military virtues. They and their men were surprised but not disconcerted, and stood desperately to a slogging match at the closest quarters. Seventeen Sappers were down out of thirty, and more than half the little body of irregulars. This end of the position was feebly fortified, and it is surprising that so experienced and sound a soldier as Ian Hamilton should have left it so. The defence had no marked advantage as compared with the attack, neither trench, sangar, nor wire entanglement, and in numbers they were immensely inferior. Two companies of the 60th Rifles and a small body of the ubiquitous Gordons happened to be upon the hill and threw themselves into the fray, but they were unable to turn the tide. Of thirty-three Gordons under Lieutenant MacNaughten thirty were wounded.[3] As our men retired under the shelter of the northern slope they were reinforced by another hundred and fifty Gordons under the stalwart Miller-Wallnutt, a man cast in the mould of a Berserk Viking. To their aid also came two hundred of the Imperial Light Horse, burning to assist their comrades. Another half-battalion of Rifles came with them. At each end of the long ridge the situation at the dawn of day was almost identical. In each the stormers had seized one side, but were brought to a stand by the defenders upon the other, while the British guns fired over the heads of their own infantry to rake the further slope.

It was on the Wagon Hill side, however, that the Boer exertions were most continuous and strenuous and our own resistance most desperate.

3. The Gordons and the Sappers were there that morning to re-escort one of Lambton's 4.7 guns, which was to be mounted there. Ten seamen were with the gun, and lost three of their number in the defence.

There fought the gallant de Villiers, while Ian Hamilton rallied the defenders and led them in repeated rushes against the enemy's line. Continually reinforced from below, the Boers fought with extraordinary resolution. Never will any one who witnessed that Homeric contest question the valour of our foes. It was a murderous business on both sides. Edwardes of the Light Horse was struck down. In a gun-emplacement a strange encounter took place at point-blank range between a group of Boers and of Britons. De Villiers of the Free State shot Miller-Wallnut dead, Ian Hamilton fired at de Villiers with his revolver and missed him. Young Albrecht of the Light Horse shot de Villiers. A Boer named de Jaeger shot Albrecht. Digby-Jones of the Sappers shot de Jaeger. Only a few minutes later the gallant lad, who had already won fame enough for a veteran, was himself mortally wounded, and Dennis, his comrade in arms and in glory, fell by his side.

There has been no better fighting in our time than that upon Wagon Hill on that January morning, and no better fighters than the Imperial Light Horsemen who formed the centre of the defence. Here, as at Elandslaagte, they proved themselves worthy to stand in line with the crack regiments of the British army.

Through the long day the fight maintained its equilibrium along the summit of the ridge, swaying a little that way or this, but never amounting to a repulse of the stormers or to a rout of the defenders. So intermixed were the combatants that a wounded man more than once found himself a rest for the rifles of his enemies. One unfortunate soldier in this position received six more bullets from his own comrades in their efforts to reach the deadly rifleman behind him. At four o'clock a huge bank of clouds which had towered upwards unheeded by the struggling men burst suddenly into a terrific thunderstorm with vivid lightnings and lashing rain. It is curious that the British victory at Elandslaagte was heralded by just such another storm. Up on the bullet-swept hill the long fringes of fighting men took no more heed of the elements than would two bulldogs who have each other by the throat. Up the greasy hillside, foul with mud and with blood, came the Boer reserves, and up the northern slope came our own reserve, the Devon Regiment, fit representatives of that virile county. Admirably led by Park, their gallant Colonel, the Devons swept the Boers before them, and the Rifles, Gordons, and Light Horse joined in the wild charge which finally cleared the ridge.

But the end was not yet. The Boer had taken a risk over this venture, and now he had to pay the stakes. Down the hill he passed, crouching, darting, but the *spruits* behind him were turned into swirling streams, and as he hesitated for an instant upon the brink the relentless sleet of bullets came from behind. Many were swept away down the gorges and into

155

the Klip River, never again to be accounted for in the lists of their field-cornet. The majority splashed through, found their horses in their shelter, and galloped off across the great Bulwana Plain, as fairly beaten in as fair a fight as ever brave men were yet.

The cheers of victory as the Devons swept the ridge had heartened the weary men upon Caesar's Camp to a similar effort. Manchesters, Gordons, and Rifles, aided by the fire of two batteries, cleared the long-debated position. Wet, cold, weary, and without food for twenty-six hours, the bedraggled Tommies stood yelling and waving, amid the litter of dead and of dying.

It was a near thing. Had the ridge fallen the town must have followed, and history perhaps have been changed. In the old stiff-rank Majuba days we should have been swept in an hour from the position. But the wily man behind the rock was now to find an equally wily man in front of him. The soldier had at last learned something of the craft of the hunter. He clung to his shelter, he dwelled on his aim, he ignored his dressings, he laid aside the eighteenth-century traditions of his pigtailed ancestor, and he hit the Boers harder than they had been hit yet. No return may ever come to us of their losses on that occasion; 80 dead bodies were returned to them from the ridge alone, while the slopes, the *dongas*, and the river each had its own separate tale. No possible estimate can make it less than three hundred killed and wounded, while many place it at a much higher figure. Our own casualties were very serious and the proportion of dead to wounded unusually high, owing to the fact that the greater part of the wounds were necessarily of the head. In killed we lost 13 officers, 135 men. In wounded 28 officers, 244 men—a total of 420, Lord Ava, the honoured Son of an honoured father, the fiery Dick-Cunyngham, stalwart Miller-Wallnutt, the brave boy sappers Digby-Jones and Dennis, Adams and Packman of the Light Horse, the chivalrous Lafone—we had to mourn quality as well as numbers. The grim test of the casualty returns shows that it was to the Imperial Light Horse (ten officers down, and the regiment commanded by a junior captain), the Manchesters, the Gordons, the Devons, and the 2nd Rifle Brigade that the honours of the day are due.

In the course of the day two attacks had been made upon other points of the British position, the one on Observation Hill on the north, the other on the Helpmakaar position on the east. Of these the latter was never pushed home and was an obvious feint, but in the case of the other it was not until Schutte, their commander, and forty or fifty men had been killed and wounded, that the stormers abandoned their attempt. At every point the assailants found the same scattered but impenetrable fringe of riflemen, and the same energetic batteries waiting for them.

Throughout the Empire the course of this great struggle was watched with the keenest solicitude and with all that painful emotion which springs from impotent sympathy. By heliogram to Buller, and so to the farthest ends of that great body whose nerves are the telegraphic wires, there came the announcement of the attack. Then after an interval of hours came 'everywhere repulsed, but fighting continues.' Then, 'Attack continues. Enemy reinforced from the south.' Then 'Attack renewed. Very hard pressed.' There the messages ended for the day, leaving the Empire black with apprehension. The darkest forecasts and most dreary anticipations were indulged by the most temperate and best-informed London papers. For the first time the very suggestion that the campaign might be above our strength was made to the public. And then at last there came the official news of the repulse of the assault. Far away at Ladysmith, the weary men and their sorely tried officers gathered to return thanks to God for His manifold mercies, but in London also hearts were stricken solemn by the greatness of the crisis, and lips long unused to prayer joined in the devotions of the absent warriors.

CHAPTER 14

The Colesberg Operations

Of the four British armies in the field I have attempted to tell the story of the western one which advanced to help Kimberley, of the eastern one which was repulsed at Colenso, and of the central one which was checked at Stormberg. There remains one other central one, some account of which must now be given.

It was, as has already been pointed out, a long three weeks after the declaration of war before the forces of the Orange Free State began to invade Cape Colony. But for this most providential delay it is probable that the ultimate fighting would have been, not among the mountains and *kopjes* of Stormberg and Colesberg, but amid those formidable passes which lie in the Hex Valley, immediately to the north of Cape Town, and that the armies of the invader would have been doubled by their kinsmen of the Colony. The ultimate result of the war must have been the same, but the sight of all South Africa in flames might have brought about those Continental complications which have always been so grave a menace.

The invasion of the Colony was at two points along the line of the two railways which connect the countries, the one passing over the Orange River at Norval's Pont and the other at Bethulie, about forty miles to the eastward. There were no British troops available (a fact to be considered by those, if any remain, who imagine that the British entertained any design against the Republics), and the Boers jogged slowly southward amid a Dutch population who hesitated between their unity of race and speech and their knowledge of just and generous treatment by the Empire. A large number were won over by the invaders, and, like all apostates, distinguished themselves by their virulence and harshness towards their loyal neighbours. Here and there in towns which were off the railway line, in Barkly East or Ladygrey, the farmers met together with rifle and bandolier, tied orange *puggarees* round their hats, and rode off to join the enemy. Possibly these ignorant and isolated men hardly recognised what it was that they were doing. They have found out since. In some of the border districts the rebels numbered ninety per cent of the Dutch population.

In the meanwhile, the British leaders had been strenuously endeavouring to scrape together a few troops with which to make some stand against the enemy. For this purpose two small forces were necessary—the one to oppose the advance through Bethulie and Stormberg, the other to meet the invaders, who, having passed the river at Norval's Pont, had now occupied Colesberg. The former task was, as already shown, committed to General Gatacre. The latter was allotted to General French, the victor of Elandslaagte, who had escaped in the very last train from Ladysmith, and had taken over this new and important duty. French's force assembled at Arundel and Gatacre's at Sterkstroom. It is with the operations of the former that we have now to deal.

General French, for whom South Africa has for once proved not the grave but the cradle of a reputation, had before the war gained some name as a smart and energetic cavalry officer. There were some who, watching his handling of a considerable body of horse at the great Salisbury manoeuvres in 1898, conceived the highest opinion of his capacity, and it was due to the strong support of General Buller, who had commanded in these peaceful operations, that French received his appointment for South Africa. In person he is short and thick, with a pugnacious jaw. In character he is a man of cold persistence and of fiery energy, cautious and yet audacious, weighing his actions well, but carrying them out with the dash which befits a mounted leader. He is remarkable for the quickness of his decision—'can think at a gallop,' as an admirer expressed it. Such was the man, alert, resourceful, and determined, to whom was entrusted the holding back of the Colesberg Boers.

Although the main advance of the invaders was along the lines of the two railways, they ventured, as they realised how weak the forces were which opposed them, to break off both to the east and west, occupying Dordrecht on one side and Steynsberg on the other. Nothing of importance accrued from the possession of these points, and our attention may be concentrated upon the main line of action.

French's original force was a mere handful of men, scraped together from anywhere. Naauwpoort was his base, and thence he made a reconnaissance by rail on November 23rd towards Arundel, the next hamlet along the line, taking with him a company of the Black Watch, forty mounted infantry, and a troop of the New South Wales Lancers. Nothing resulted from the expedition save that the two forces came into touch with each other, a touch which was sustained for months under many vicissitudes, until the invaders were driven back once more over Norval's

Pont. Finding that Arundel was weakly held, French advanced up to it, and established his camp there towards the end of December, within six miles of the Boer lines at Rensburg, to the south of Colesberg. His mission—with his present forces—was to prevent the further advance of the enemy into the Colony, but he was not strong enough yet to make a serious attempt to drive them out.

Before the move to Arundel on December 13th his detachment had increased in size, and consisted largely of mounted men, so that it attained a mobility very unusual for a British force. On December 13th there was an attempt upon the part of the Boers to advance south, which was easily held by the British Cavalry and Horse Artillery. The country over which French was operating is dotted with those singular *kopjes* which the Boer loves—*kopjes* which are often so grotesque in shape that one feels as if they must be due to some error of refraction when one looks at them. But, on the other hand, between these hills there lie wide stretches of the green or russet *savannah*, the noblest field that a horseman or a horse gunner could wish. The riflemen clung to the hills, French's troopers circled warily upon the plain, gradually contracting the Boer position by threatening to cut off this or that outlying *kopje*, and so the enemy was slowly herded into Colesberg. The small but mobile British force covered a very large area, and hardly a day passed that one or other part of it did not come in contact with the enemy. With one regiment of infantry (the Berkshires) to hold the centre, his hard-riding Tasmanians, New Zealanders, and Australians, with the Scots Greys, the Inniskillings, and the Carabineers, formed an elastic but impenetrable screen to cover the Colony. They were aided by two batteries, O and R, of Horse Artillery. Every day General French rode out and made a close personal examination of the enemy's position, while his scouts and outposts were instructed to maintain the closest possible touch.

On December 30th the enemy abandoned Rensburg, which had been their advanced post, and concentrated at Colesberg, upon which French moved his force up and seized Rensburg. The very next day, December 31st, he began a vigorous and long-continued series of operations. At five o'clock on Sunday evening he moved out of Rensburg camp, with R and half of O batteries R.H.A., the 10th Hussars, the Inniskillings, and the Berkshires, to take up a position on the west of Colesberg. At the same time Colonel Porter, with the half-battery of O, his own regiment (the Carabineers), and the New Zealand Mounted Rifles, left camp at two on the Monday morning and took a position on the enemy's left flank. The Berkshires under Major McCracken seized the hill, driving a Boer picket off it, and the Horse enfiladed the enemy's right flank, and after a risky artillery duel succeeded in silencing his guns. Next morning, however

(January 2nd, 1900), it was found that the Boers, strongly reinforced, were back near their old positions, and French had to be content to hold them and to wait for more troops.

These were not long in coming, for the Suffolk Regiment had arrived, followed by the Composite Regiment (chosen from the Household Cavalry) and the 4th Battery R.F.A. The Boers, however, had also been reinforced, and showed great energy in their effort to break the cordon which was being drawn round them. Upon the 4th a determined effort was made by about a thousand of them under General Schoeman to turn the left flank of the British, and at dawn it was actually found that they had eluded the vigilance of the outposts and had established themselves upon a hill to the rear of the position. They were shelled off of it, however, by the guns of O Battery, and in their retreat across the plain they were pursued by the 10th Hussars and by one squadron of the Inniskillings, who cut off some of the fugitives. At the same time, De Lisle with his mounted infantry carried the position which they had originally held. In this successful and well-managed action the Boer loss was ninety, and we took in addition twenty-one prisoners. Our own casualties amounted only to six killed, including Major Harvey of the 10th, and to fifteen wounded.

Encouraged by this success an attempt was made by the Suffolk Regiment to carry a hill which formed the key of the enemy's position. The town of Colesberg lies in a basin surrounded by a ring of *kopjes*, and the possession by us of any one of them would have made the place untenable. The plan has been ascribed to Colonel Watson of the Suffolks, but it is time that some protest should be raised against this devolution of responsibility upon subordinates in the event of failure. When success has crowned our arms we have been delighted to honour our general; but when our efforts end in failure our attention is called to Colonel Watson, Colonel Long, or Colonel Thorneycroft. It is fairer to state that in this instance General French ordered Colonel Watson to make a night attack upon the hill.

The result was disastrous. At midnight four companies in canvas shoes or in their stocking feet set forth upon their venture, and just before dawn they found themselves upon the slope of the hill. They were in a formation of quarter column with files extended to two paces; H Company was leading. When half-way up a warm fire was opened upon them in the darkness. Colonel Watson gave the order to retire, intending, as it is believed, that the men should get under the shelter of the dead ground which they had just quitted, but his death immediately afterwards left matters in a confused condition. The night was black, the ground broken, a hail of bullets whizzing through the ranks. Companies got mixed in

161

the darkness and contradictory orders were issued. The leading company held its ground, though each of the officers, Brett, Carey, and Butler, was struck down. The other companies had retired, however, and the dawn found this fringe of men, most of them wounded, lying under the very rifles of the Boers. Even then they held out for some time, but they could neither advance, retire, or stay where they were without losing lives to no purpose, so the survivors were compelled to surrender. There is better evidence here than at Magersfontein that the enemy were warned and ready. Every one of the officers engaged, from the Colonel to the boy subaltern, was killed, wounded, or taken. Eleven officers and one hundred and fifty men were our losses in this unfortunate but not discreditable affair, which proves once more how much accuracy and how much secrecy is necessary for a successful night attack. Four companies of the regiment were sent down to Port Elizabeth to re-officer, but the arrival of the 1st Essex enabled French to fill the gap which had been made in his force.

In spite of this annoying check, French continued to pursue his original design of holding the enemy in front and working round him on the east. On January 9th, Porter, of the Carabineers, with his own regiment, two squadrons of Household Cavalry, the New Zealanders, the New South Wales Lancers, and four guns, took another step forward and, after a skirmish, occupied a position called Slingersfontein, still further to the north and east, so as to menace the main road of retreat to Norval's Pont. Some skirmishing followed, but the position was maintained. On the 15th the Boers, thinking that this long extension must have weakened us, made a spirited attack upon a position held by New Zealanders and a company of the 1st Yorkshires, this regiment having been sent up to reinforce French. The attempt was met by a volley and a bayonet charge. Captain Orr, of the Yorkshires, was struck down; but Captain Madocks, of the New Zealanders, who behaved with conspicuous gallantry at a critical instant, took command, and the enemy was heavily repulsed. Madocks engaged in a point-blank rifle duel with the frock-coated top-hatted Boer leader, and had the good fortune to kill his formidable opponent. Twenty-one Boer dead and many wounded left upon the field made a small set-off to the disaster of the Suffolks.

The next day, however (January 16th), the scales of fortune, which swung alternately one way and the other, were again tipped against us. It is difficult to give an intelligible account of the details of these operations, because they were carried out by thin fringes of men covering on both sides a very large area, each *kopje* occupied as a fort, and the intervening plains patrolled by cavalry.

As French extended to the east and north the Boers extended also to prevent him from outflanking them, and so the little armies stretched and stretched until they were two long mobile skirmishing lines. The actions therefore resolve themselves into the encounters of small bodies and the snapping up of exposed patrols—a game in which the Boer aptitude for guerrilla tactics gave them some advantage, though our own cavalry quickly adapted themselves to the new conditions. On this occasion a patrol of sixteen men from the South Australian Horse and New South Wales Lancers fell into an ambush, and eleven were captured. Of the remainder, three made their way back to camp, while one was killed and one was wounded.

The duel between French on the one side and Schoeman and Lambert on the other was from this onwards one of manoeuvring rather than of fighting. The dangerously extended line of the British at this period, over thirty miles long, was reinforced, as has been mentioned, by the 1st Yorkshire and later by the 2nd Wiltshire and a section of the 37th Howitzer Battery. There was probably no very great difference in numbers between the two little armies, but the Boers now, as always, were working upon internal lines. The monotony of the operations was broken by the remarkable feat of the Essex Regiment, which succeeded by hawsers and good-will in getting two 15-pounder guns of the 4th Field Battery on to the top of Coleskop, a hill which rises several hundred feet from the plain and is so precipitous that it is no small task for an unhampered man to climb it. From the summit a fire, which for some days could not be localised by the Boers, was opened upon their *laagers*, which had to be shifted in consequence. This energetic action upon the part of our gunners may be set off against those other examples where commanders of batteries have shown that they had not yet appreciated what strong tackle and stout arms can accomplish. The guns upon Coleskop not only dominated all the smaller *kopjes* for a range of 9000 yards, but completely commanded the town of Colesberg, which could not however, for humanitarian and political reasons, be shelled.

By gradual reinforcements the force under French had by the end of January attained the respectable figure of ten thousand men, strung over a large extent of country. His infantry consisted of the 2nd Berkshires, 1st Royal Irish, 2nd Wiltshires, 2nd Worcesters, 1st Essex, and 1st Yorkshires; his cavalry, of the 10th Hussars, the 6th Dragoon Guards, the Inniskillings, the New Zealanders, the N.S.W. Lancers, some Rimington Guides, and the composite Household Regiment; his artillery, the R and O batteries of R.H.A., the 4th R.F.A., and a section of the 37th Howitzer Battery. At the risk of tedium I have repeated the units of this force, because there are no operations during the war, with the exception perhaps of those of the Rhodesian Column, concerning which it is so difficult to get a clear impression. The fluctuating forces, the vast range of country covered, and the petty farms which give their names to positions, all tend to make the issue vague and the narrative obscure. The British still lay in a semicircle extending from Slingersfontein upon the right to Kloof Camp upon the left, and the general scheme of operations continued to be an enveloping movement upon the right. General Clements commanded this section of the forces, while the energetic Porter carried out the successive advances. The lines had gradually stretched until they were nearly fifty miles in length, and something of the obscurity in which the operations have been left is due to the impossibility of any single correspondent having a clear idea of what was occurring over so extended a front.

On January 25th French sent Stephenson and Brabazon to push a reconnaissance to the north of Colesberg, and found that the Boers were making a fresh position at Rietfontein, nine miles nearer their own border. A small action ensued, in which we lost ten or twelve of the Wiltshire Regiment, and gained some knowledge of the enemy's dispositions. For the remainder of the month the two forces remained in a state of equilibrium, each keenly on its guard, and neither strong enough to penetrate the lines of the other. General French descended to Cape Town to aid General Roberts in the elaboration of that plan which was soon to change the whole military situation in South Africa.

Reinforcements were still dribbling into the British force, Hoad's Australian Regiment, which had been changed from infantry to cavalry, and J battery R.H.A. from India, being the last arrivals. But very much stronger reinforcements had arrived for the Boers—so strong that they were able to take the offensive. De la Rey had left the Modder with three thousand men, and their presence infused new life into the defenders of Colesberg. At the moment, too, that the Modder Boers were coming to Colesberg, the British had begun to send cavalry reinforcements to the Modder in preparation for the march to Kimberley, so that Clements's Force (as it had now become) was depleted at the very instant when that of the enemy was largely increased. The result was that it was all they could do not merely to hold their own, but to avoid a very serious disaster.

The movements of De la Rey were directed towards turning the right of the position. On February 9th and 10th the mounted patrols, principally the Tasmanians, the Australians, and the Inniskillings, came in contact with the Boers, and some skirmishing ensued, with no heavy loss upon either side. A British patrol was surrounded and lost eleven prisoners, Tasmanians and Guides. On the 12th the Boer turning movement developed itself, and our position on the right at Slingersfontein was strongly attacked.

The key of the British position at this point was a *kopje* held by three companies of the 2nd Worcester Regiment. Upon this the Boers made a fierce onslaught, but were as fiercely repelled. They came up in the dark between the set of moon and rise of sun, as they had done at the great assault of Ladysmith, and the first dim light saw them in the advanced sangars. The Boer generals do not favour night attacks, but they are exceedingly fond of using darkness for taking up a good position and pushing onwards as soon as it is possible to see. This is what they did upon this occasion, and the first intimation which the outposts had of their presence was the rush of feet and loom of figures in the cold misty light of dawn. The occupants of the sangars were killed to a man, and the assailants rushed onwards. As the sun topped the line of the *veldt* half the *kopje* was in their possession. Shouting and firing, they pressed onwards.

But the Worcester men were steady old soldiers, and the battalion contained no less than four hundred and fifty marksmen in its ranks. Of these the companies upon the hill had their due proportion, and their fire was so accurate that the Boers found themselves unable to advance any further. Through the long day a desperate duel was maintained between the two lines of riflemen. Colonel Cuningham and Major Stubbs were killed while endeavouring to recover the ground which had been lost. Hovel and Bartholomew continued to encourage their men, and the British fire became so deadly that that of the Boers was dominated. Under the direction of Hacket Pain, who commanded the nearest post, guns of J battery were brought out into the open and shelled the portion of the *kopje* which was held by the Boers. The latter were reinforced, but could make no advance against the accurate rifle fire with which they were met. The Bisley champion of the battalion, with a bullet through his thigh, expended a hundred rounds before sinking from loss of blood. It was an excellent defence, and a pleasing exception to those too frequent cases where an isolated force has lost heart in face of a numerous and persistent foe. With the coming of darkness the Boers withdrew with a loss of over two hundred killed and wounded. Orders had come from Clements that the whole right wing should be drawn in, and in obedience to them the remains of the victorious companies were called in by Hacket Pain, who moved his force by night in the direction of Rensburg. The British loss in the action was twenty-eight killed and nearly a hundred wounded or missing, most of which was incurred when the sangars were rushed in the early morning.

While this action was fought upon the extreme right of the British position another as severe had occurred with much the same result upon the extreme left, where the 2nd Wiltshire Regiment was stationed. Some companies of this regiment were isolated upon a *kopje* and surrounded by the Boer riflemen when the pressure upon them was relieved by a desperate attack by about a hundred of the Victorian Rifles. The gallant Australians lost Major Eddy and six officers out of seven, with a large proportion of their men, but they proved once for all that amid all the scattered nations who came from the same home there is not one with a more fiery courage and a higher sense of martial duty than the men from the great island continent. It is the misfortune of the historian when dealing with these contingents that, as a rule, by their very nature they were employed in detached parties in fulfilling the duties which fall to the lot of scouts and light cavalry—duties which fill the casualty lists but not the pages of the chronicler. Be it said, however, once for all that throughout the whole African army there was nothing but the utmost admiration for the dash and spirit of the hard-riding, straight-shooting sons of Australia and New Zealand. In a host which held many brave men there were none braver than they.

It was evident from this time onwards that the turning movement had failed, and that the enemy had developed such strength that we were ourselves in imminent danger of being turned. The situation was a most serious one: for if Clements's force could be brushed aside there would be nothing to keep the enemy from cutting the communications of the army which Roberts had assembled for his march into the Free State. Clements drew in his wings hurriedly and concentrated his whole force at Rensburg. It was a difficult operation in the face of an aggressive enemy, but the movements were well timed and admirably carried out. There is always the possibility of a retreat degenerating into a panic, and a panic at that moment would have been a most serious matter. One misfortune occurred, through which two companies of the Wiltshire regiment were left without definite orders, and were cut off and captured after a resistance in which a third of their number was killed and wounded. No man in that trying time worked harder than Colonel Carter of the Wiltshires (the night of the retreat was the sixth which he had spent without sleep), and the loss of the two companies is to be set down to one of those accidents which may always occur in warfare. Some of the Inniskilling Dragoons and Victorian Mounted Rifles were also cut off in the retreat, but on the whole Clements was very fortunate in being able to concentrate his scattered army with so few mishaps. The withdrawal was heartbreaking to the soldiers who had worked so hard and so long in extending the lines, but it might be regarded with equanimity by the Generals, who understood that the greater strength the enemy developed at Colesberg the less they would have to oppose the critical movements which were about to be carried out in the west. Meanwhile Coleskop had also been abandoned, the guns removed, and the whole force on February 14th passed through

Rensburg and fell back upon Arundel, the spot from which six weeks earlier French had started upon this stirring series of operations. It would not be fair, however, to suppose that they had failed because they ended where they began. Their primary object had been to prevent the further advance of the Freestaters into the colony, and, during the most critical period of the war, this had been accomplished with much success and little loss. At last the pressure had become so severe that the enemy had to weaken the most essential part of their general position in order to relieve it. The object of the operations had really been attained when Clements found himself back at Arundel once more. French, the stormy petrel of the war, had flitted on from Cape Town to Modder River, where a larger prize than Colesberg awaited him. Clements continued to cover Naauwport, the important railway junction, until the advance of Roberts's army caused a complete reversal of the whole military situation.

CHAPTER 15

Spion Kop

Whilst Methuen and Gatacre were content to hold their own at the Modder and at Sterkstroom, and whilst the mobile and energetic French was herding the Boers into Colesberg, Sir Redvers Buller, the heavy, obdurate, inexplicable man, was gathering and organising his forces for another advance upon Ladysmith.

Nearly a month had elapsed since the evil day when his infantry had retired, and his ten guns had not, from the frontal attack upon Colenso. Since then Sir Charles Warren's division of infantry and a considerable reinforcement of artillery had come to him. And yet in view of the terrible nature of the ground in front of him, of the fighting power of the Boers, and of the fact that they were always acting upon internal lines, his force even now was, in the opinion of competent judges, too weak for the matter in hand.

There remained, however, several points in his favour. His excellent infantry were full of zeal and of confidence in their chief. It cannot be denied, however much we may criticise some incidents in his campaign, that he possessed the gift of impressing and encouraging his followers, and, in spite of Colenso, the sight of his square figure and heavy impassive face conveyed an assurance of ultimate victory to those around him. In artillery he was very much stronger than before, especially in weight of metal.

His cavalry was still weak in proportion to his other arms. When at last he moved out on January 10th to attempt to outflank the Boers, he took with him nineteen thousand infantry, three thousand cavalry, and sixty guns, which included six howitzers capable of throwing a 50-pound Lyddite shell, and ten long-range naval pieces. Barton's Brigade and other troops were left behind to hold the base and line of communications.

An analysis of Buller's force shows that its details were as follows:

Clery's Division

Hildyard's Brigade
    2nd West Surrey
    2nd Devonshire
    2nd West Yorkshire
    2nd East Surrey

Hart's Brigade
    1st Inniskilling Fusiliers
    1st Border Regiment
    1st Connaught Rangers
    2nd Dublin Fusiliers
    Field Artillery, three batteries, 19th, 28th, 63rd;
        one squadron 13th Hussars; Royal Engineers

Warren's Division

Lyttelton's Brigade
    2nd Cameronians
    3rd King's Royal Rifles
    1st Durham Light Infantry
    1st Rifle Brigade

Woodgate's Brigade
    2nd Royal Lancaster
    2nd Lancashire Fusiliers
    1st South Lancashire
    York and Lancasters
    Field Artillery, three batteries, 7th, 78th, 73rd;
        one squadron 13th Hussars

Corps Troops

Coke's Brigade
Imperial Light Infantry
    2nd Somersets
    2nd Dorsets
    2nd Middlesex
    61st Howitzer Battery; two 47 naval guns; eight naval
    12-pounder guns; one squadron 13th Hussars;
        Royal Engineers

Cavalry

1st Royal Dragoons
14th Hussars
Four squadrons South African Horse

One squadron Imperial Light Horse
Bethune's Mounted Infantry
Thorneycroft's Mounted Infantry
One squadron Natal Carabineers
One squadron Natal Police
One company King's Royal Rifles Mounted Infantry
Six machine guns

This is the force whose operations I shall attempt to describe.

About sixteen miles to the westward of Colenso there is a ford over the Tugela River which is called Potgieter's Drift. General Buller's apparent plan was to seize this, together with the ferry which runs at this point, and so to throw himself upon the right flank of the Colenso Boers. Once over the river there is one formidable line of hills to cross, but if this were passed there would be comparatively easy ground until the Ladysmith hills were reached. With high hopes Buller and his men sallied out upon their adventure.

Dundonald's cavalry force pushed rapidly forwards, crossed the Little Tugela, a tributary of the main river, at Springfield, and established themselves upon the hills which command the drift. Dundonald largely exceeded his instructions in going so far, and while we applaud his courage and judgment in doing so, we must remember and be charitable to those less fortunate officers whose private enterprise has ended in disaster and reproof. There can be no doubt that the enemy intended to hold all this tract, and that it was only the quickness of our initial movements which forestalled them. Early in the morning a small party of the South African Horse, under Lieutenant Carlisle, swam the broad river under fire and brought back the ferry boat, an enterprise which was fortunately bloodless, but which was most coolly planned and gallantly carried out. The way was now open to our advance, and could it have been carried out as rapidly as it had begun the Boers might conceivably have been scattered before they could concentrate. It was not the fault of the infantry that it was not so. They were trudging, mud-spattered and jovial, at the very heels of the horses, after a forced march which was one of the most trying of the whole campaign. But an army of 20,000 men cannot be conveyed over a river twenty miles from any base without elaborate preparations being made to feed them. The roads were in such a state that the wagons could hardly move, heavy rain had just fallen, and every stream was swollen into a river; bullocks might strain, and traction engines pant, and horses die, but by no human means could the stores be kept up if the advance guard were allowed to go at their own pace. And so, having ensured an ultimate crossing of the river by the seizure of Mount Alice, the high hill which commands the drift, the forces waited day after day, watching in the distance the swarms of strenuous dark figures who dug and hauled and worked upon the hillsides opposite, barring the road which they would have to take. Far away on the horizon a little shining point twinkled amid the purple haze, coming and going from morning to night. It was the heliograph of Ladysmith, explaining her troubles and calling for help, and from the heights of Mount Alice an answering star of hope glimmered and shone, soothing, encouraging, explaining, while the stern men of the *veldt* dug furiously at their trenches in between. 'We are coming! We are coming!' cried Mount Alice. 'Over our bodies,' said the men with the spades and mattocks.

On Thursday, January 12th, Dundonald seized the heights, on the 13th the ferry was taken and Lyttelton's Brigade came up to secure that which the cavalry had gained. On the 14th the heavy naval guns were brought up to cover the crossing. On the 15th Coke's Brigade and other infantry concentrated at the drift. On the 16th the four regiments of Lyttelton's Brigade went across, and then, and only then, it began to be apparent that Buller's plan was a more deeply laid one than had been thought, and that all this business of Potgieter's Drift was really a demonstration in order to cover the actual crossing which was to be effected at a ford named Trichard's Drift, five miles to the westward. Thus, while Lyttelton's and Coke's Brigades were ostentatiously attacking Potgieter's from in front, three other brigades (Hart's, Woodgate's, and Hildyard's) were marched rapidly on the night of the 16th to the real place of crossing, to which Dundonald's cavalry had already ridden. There, on the 17th, a pontoon bridge had been erected, and a strong force was thrown over in such a way as to turn the right of the trenches in front of Potgieter's. It was admirably planned and excellently carried out, certainly the most strategic movement, if there could be said to have been any strategic movement upon the British side, in the campaign up to that date. On the 18th the infantry, the cavalry, and most of the guns were safely across without loss of life. The Boers, however, still retained their formidable internal lines, and the only result of a change of position seemed to be to put them to the trouble of building a new series of those terrible entrenchments at which they had become such experts. After all the combinations the British were, it is true, upon the right side of the river, but they were considerably further from Ladysmith than when they started. There are times, however, when twenty miles are less than fourteen, and it was hoped that this might prove to be among them. But the first step was the most serious one, for right across their front lay the Boer position upon the edge of a lofty plateau, with the high peak of Spion Kop forming the left corner of it. If once that main ridge could be captured or commanded, it would carry them halfway to the goal. It was for that essential line of hills that two of the most dogged races upon earth were about to contend. An immediate advance might have secured the position at once, but, for some reason which is inexplicable, an aimless march to the left was followed by a retirement to the original position of Warren's division, and so two invaluable days were wasted. We have the positive assurance of Commandant Edwards, who was Chief of Staff to General Botha, that a vigorous turning movement upon the left would at this time have completely outflanked the Boer position and opened a way to Ladysmith.

A small success, the more welcome for its rarity, came to the British arms on this first day. Dundonald's men had been thrown out to cover the left of the infantry advance and to feel for the right of the Boer position. A strong Boer patrol, caught napping for once, rode into an ambuscade of the irregulars. Some escaped, some held out most gallantly in a *kopje*, but the final result was a surrender of twenty-four unwounded prisoners, and the finding of thirteen killed and wounded, including de Mentz, the field-cornet of Heilbron. Two killed and two wounded were the British losses in this well-managed affair. Dundonald's force then took its position upon the extreme left of Warren's advance.

The British were now moving upon the Boers in two separate bodies, the one which included Lyttelton's and Coke's Brigades from Potgieter's Drift, making what was really a frontal attack, while the main body under Warren, who had crossed at Trichard's Drift, was swinging round upon the Boer right. Midway between the two movements the formidable bastion of Spion Kop stood clearly outlined against the blue Natal sky. The heavy naval guns on Mount Alice (two 4.7's and eight twelve-pounders) were so placed as to support either advance, and the howitzer battery was given to Lyttelton to help the frontal attack. For two days the British pressed slowly but steadily on to the Boers under the cover of an incessant rain of shells. Dour and long-suffering the Boers made no reply, save with sporadic rifle-fire, and refused until the crisis should come to expose their great guns to the chance of injury.

On January 19th Warren's turning movement began to bring him into closer touch with the enemy, his thirty-six field guns and the six howitzers which had returned to him crushing down the opposition which faced him. The ground in front of him was pleated into long folds, and his advance meant the carrying of ridge after ridge. In the earlier stages of the war this would have entailed a murderous loss; but we had learned our lesson, and the infantry now, with intervals of ten paces, and every man choosing his own cover, went up in proper Boer form, carrying position after position, the enemy always retiring with dignity and decorum. There was no victory on one side or rout on the other—only a steady advance and an orderly retirement. That night the infantry slept in their fighting line, going on again at three in the morning, and light broke to find not only rifles, but the long-silent Boer guns all blazing at the British advance. Again, as at Colenso, the brunt of the fighting fell upon Hart's Irish Brigade, who upheld that immemorial tradition of valour with which that name, either in or out of the British service, has invariably been associated. Upon the Lancashire Fusiliers and the York and Lancasters came also a large share of the losses and the glory. Slowly but surely the inexorable line of the British lapped over the ground which the enemy had held. A gallant colonial, Tobin of the South African Horse, rode up one hill and signalled with his hat that it was clear. His comrades followed closely at his heels, and occupied the position with the loss of Childe, their Major. During this action Lyttelton had held the Boers in their trenches opposite to him by advancing to within 1500 yards of them, but the attack was not pushed further. On the evening of this day, January 20th, the British had gained some miles of ground, and the total losses had been about three hundred killed and wounded. The troops were in good heart, and all promised well for the future. Again the men lay where they had fought, and again the dawn heard the crash of the great guns and the rattle of the musketry.

The operations of this day began with a sustained cannonade from the field batteries and 61st Howitzer Battery, which was as fiercely answered by the enemy. About eleven the infantry began to go forward with an advance which would have astonished the martinets of Aldershot, an irregular fringe of crawlers, wrigglers, writhers, crouchers, all cool and deliberate, giving away no points in this grim game of death. Where now were the officers with their distinctive dresses and flashing swords, where the valiant rushes over the open, where the men who were too proud to lie down?—the tactics of three months ago seemed as obsolete as those of the Middle Ages. All day the line undulated forward, and by evening yet another strip of rock-strewn ground had been gained, and yet another train of ambulances was bearing a hundred of our wounded back to the base hospitals at Frere. It was on Hildyard's Brigade on the left that the fighting and the losses of this day principally fell. By the morning of January 22nd the regiments were clustering thickly all round the edges of the Boer main position, and the day was spent in resting the weary men, and in determining at what point the final assault should be delivered. On the right front, commanding the Boer lines on either side, towered the stark eminence of Spion Kop, so called because from its summit the Boer *voortrekkers* had first in 1835 gazed down upon the promised land of Natal. If that could only be seized and held! Buller and Warren swept its bald summit with their field-glasses. It was a venture. But all war is a venture; and the brave man is he who ventures most. One fiery rush and the master-key of all these locked doors might be in our keeping. That evening there came a telegram to London which left the whole Empire in a hush of anticipation. Spion Kop was to be attacked that night.

The troops which were selected for the task were eight companies of the 2nd Lancashire Fusiliers, six of the 2nd Royal Lancasters, two of the 1st South Lancashires, 180 of Thorneycroft's, and half a company of Sappers. It was to be a North of England job.

Under the friendly cover of a starless night the men, in Indian file, like a party of Iroquois braves upon the war trail, stole up the winding and ill-defined path which led to the summit. Woodgate, the Lancashire Brigadier, and Blomfield of the Fusiliers led the way. It was a severe climb of 2000 feet, coming after arduous work over broken ground, but the affair was well-timed, and it was at that blackest hour which precedes the dawn that the last steep ascent was reached. The Fusiliers crouched down among the rocks to recover their breath, and saw far down in the plain beneath them the placid lights which showed where their comrades were resting. A fine rain was falling, and rolling clouds hung low over their heads. The men with unloaded rifles and fixed bayonets stole on once more, their bodies bent, their eyes peering through the murk for the first sign of the enemy—that enemy whose first sign has usually been a shattering volley. Thorneycroft's men with their gallant leader had threaded their way up into the advance. Then the leading files found that they were walking on the level. The crest had been gained.

With slow steps and bated breath, the open line of skirmishers stole across it. Was it possible that it had been entirely abandoned? Suddenly a raucous shout of *'Wie da?'* came out of the darkness, then a shot, then a splutter of musketry and a yell, as the Fusiliers sprang onwards with their bayonets. The Boer post of Vryheid burghers clattered and scrambled away into the darkness, and a cheer that roused both the sleeping armies told that the surprise had been complete and the position won.

In the grey light of the breaking day the men advanced along the narrow undulating ridge, the prominent end of which they had captured. Another trench faced them, but it was weakly held and abandoned. Then the men, uncertain what remained beyond, halted and waited for full light to see where they were, and what the work was which lay before them—a fatal halt, as the result proved, and yet one so natural that it is hard to blame the officer who ordered it. Indeed, he might have seemed more culpable had he pushed blindly on, and so lost the advantage which had been already gained.

About eight o'clock, with the clearing of the mist, General Woodgate saw how matters stood. The ridge, one end of which he held, extended away, rising and falling for some miles. Had he the whole of the end plateau, and had he guns, he might hope to command the rest of the position. But he held only half the plateau, and at the further end of it the Boers were strongly entrenched. The Spion Kop mountain was really the salient or sharp angle of the Boer position, so that the British were exposed to a cross fire both from the left and right. Beyond were other eminences which sheltered strings of riflemen and several guns. The plateau which the British held was very much narrower than was usually represented in the press. In many places the possible front was not much more than a hundred yards wide, and the troops were compelled to bunch together, as there was not room for a single company to take an extended formation. The cover upon this plateau was scanty, far too scanty for the force upon it, and the shell fire—especially the fire of the pom-poms—soon became very murderous. To mass the troops under the cover of the edge of the plateau might naturally suggest itself, but with great tactical skill the Boer advanced line from Commandant Prinsloo's Heidelberg and Carolina commandos kept so aggressive an attitude that the British could not weaken the lines opposed to them. Their skirmishers were creeping round too in such a way that the fire was really coming from three separate points, left, centre, and right, and every corner of the position was searched by their bullets. Early in the action the gallant Woodgate and many of his Lancashire men were shot down. The others spread out and held on, firing occasionally at the whisk of a rifle-barrel or the glimpse of a broad-brimmed hat.

From morning to midday, the shell, Maxim, and rifle fire swept across the kop in a continual driving shower. The British guns in the plain below failed to localise the position of the enemy's, and they were able to vent their concentrated spite upon the exposed infantry. No blame attaches to the gunners for this, as a hill intervened to screen the Boer artillery, which consisted of five big guns and two pom-poms.

Upon the fall of Woodgate, Thorneycroft, who bore the reputation of a determined fighter, was placed at the suggestion of Buller in charge of the defence of the hill, and he was reinforced after noon by Coke's brigade, the Middlesex, the Dorsets, and the Somersets, together with the Imperial Light Infantry. The addition of this force to the defenders of the plateau tended to increase the casualty returns rather than the strength of the defence. Three thousand more rifles could do nothing to check the fire of the invisible cannon, and it was this which was the main source of the losses, while on the other hand the plateau had become so cumbered with troops that a shell could hardly fail to do damage. There was no cover to shelter them and no room for them to extend. The pressure was most severe upon the shallow trenches in the front, which had been abandoned by the Boers and were held by the Lancashire Fusiliers. They were enfiladed by rifle and cannon, and the dead and wounded outnumbered the hale. So close were the skirmishers that on at least one occasion Boer and Briton found themselves on each side of the same rock. Once a handful of men, tormented beyond endurance, sprang up as a sign that they had had enough, but Thorneycroft, a man of huge physique, rushed forward to the advancing Boers. 'You may go to hell!' he yelled. 'I command here, and allow no surrender. Go on with your firing.' Nothing could exceed the gallantry of Louis Botha's men in pushing the attack. Again and again they made their way up to the British firing line, exposing themselves with a recklessness which, with the exception of the grand attack upon Ladysmith, was unique in our experience of them. About two o'clock they rushed one trench occupied by the Fusiliers and secured the survivors of two companies as prisoners, but were subsequently driven out again. A detached group of the South Lancashires was summoned to surrender. 'When I surrender,' cried Colour-Sergeant Nolan, 'it will be my dead body!' Hour after hour of the unintermitting crash of the shells among the rocks and of the groans and screams of men torn and burst by the most horrible of all wounds had shaken the troops badly. Spectators from below who saw the shells pitching at the rate of seven a minute on to the crowded plateau marvelled at the endurance which held the devoted men to their post. Men were wounded and wounded and wounded yet again, and still went on fighting. Never since Inkerman had we had so grim a soldier's battle. The company officers were superb. Captain Muriel of the Middlesex was shot through the check while giving a cigarette to a wounded man, continued to lead his company, and was shot again through the brain. Scott Moncrieff of the same regiment was only disabled by the fourth bullet which hit him. Grenfell of Thorneycroft's was shot, and exclaimed, 'That's all right. It's not much.' A second wound made him remark, 'I can get on all right.' The third killed him. Ross of the Lancasters, who had crawled from a sickbed, was found dead upon the furthest crest. Young Murray of the Scottish Rifles, dripping from five wounds, still staggered about among his men. And the men were worthy of such officers. 'No retreat! No retreat!' they yelled when some of the front line were driven in. In all regiments there are weaklings and hang-backs, and many a man was wandering down the reverse slopes when he should have been facing death upon the top, but as a body British troops have never stood firm through a more fiery ordeal than on that fatal hill...

The position was so bad that no efforts of officers or men could do anything to mend it. They were in a murderous dilemma. If they fell back for cover the Boer riflemen would rush the position. If they held their ground this horrible shell fire must continue, which they had no means of answering. Down at Gun Hill in front of the Boer position we had no fewer than five batteries, the 78th, 7th, 73rd, 63rd, and 61st howitzer, but a ridge intervened between them and the Boer guns which were shelling Spion Kop, and this ridge was strongly entrenched. The naval guns from distant Mount Alice did what they could, but the range was very long, and the position of the Boer guns uncertain. The artillery, situated as it was, could not save the infantry from the horrible scourging which they were enduring.

There remains the debated question whether the British guns could have been taken to the top. Mr. Winston Churchill, the soundness of whose judgment has been frequently demonstrated during the war, asserts that it might have been done. Without venturing to contradict one who was personally present, I venture to think that there is strong evidence to show that it could not have been done without blasting and other measures, for which there was no possible time. Captain Hanwell of the 78th R.F.A., upon the day of the battle had the very utmost difficulty with the help of four horses in getting a light Maxim on to the top, and his opinion, with that of other artillery officers, is that the feat was an impossible one until the path had been prepared. When night fell Colonel Sim was despatched with a party of Sappers to clear the track and to prepare two emplacements upon the top, but in his advance he met the retiring infantry.

Throughout the day reinforcements had pushed up the hill, until two full brigades had been drawn into the fight. From the other side of the ridge Lyttelton sent up the Scottish Rifles, who reached the summit, and added their share to the shambles upon the top. As the shades of night closed in, and the glare of the bursting shells became more lurid, the men lay extended upon the rocky ground, parched and exhausted. They were hopelessly jumbled together, with the exception of the Dorsets, whose cohesion may have been due to superior discipline, less exposure, or to the fact that their khaki differed somewhat in colour from that of the others. Twelve hours of so terrible an experience had had a strange effect upon many of the men. Some were dazed and battle-struck, incapable of clear understanding. Some were as incoherent as drunkards. Some lay in an overpowering drowsiness. The most were doggedly patient and long-suffering, with a mighty longing for water obliterating every other emotion.

Before evening fell a most gallant and successful attempt had been made by the third battalion of the King's Royal Rifles from Lyttelton's Brigade to relieve the pressure upon their comrades on Spion Kop. In order to draw part of the Boer fire away they ascended from the northern side and carried the hills which formed a continuation of the same ridge. The movement was meant to be no more than a strong demonstration, but the riflemen pushed it until, breathless but victorious, they stood upon the very crest of the position, leaving nearly a hundred dead or dying to show the path which they had taken. Their advance being much further than was desired, they were recalled, and it was at the moment that Buchanan Riddell, their brave Colonel, stood up to read Lyttelton's note that he fell with a Boer bullet through his brain, making one more of those gallant leaders who died as they had lived, at the head of their regiments. Chisholm, Dick-Cunyngham, Downman, Wilford, Gunning, Sherston, Thackeray, Sitwell, MacCarthy O'Leary, Airlie—they have led their men up to and through the gates of death. It was a fine exploit of the 3rd Rifles. 'A finer bit of skirmishing, a finer bit of climbing, and a finer bit of fighting, I have never seen,' said their Brigadier. It is certain that if Lyttelton had not thrown his two regiments into the fight the pressure upon the hill-top might have become unendurable; and it seems also certain that if he had only held on to the position which the Rifles had gained, the Boers would never have reoccupied Spion Kop.

And now, under the shadow of night, but with the shells bursting thickly over the plateau, the much-tried Thorneycroft had to make up his mind whether he should hold on for another such day as he had endured, or whether now, in the friendly darkness, he should remove his shattered force. Could he have seen the discouragement of the Boers and the preparations which they had made for retirement, he would have held his ground. But this was hidden from him, while the horror of his own losses was but too apparent. Forty per cent of his men were down. Thirteen hundred dead and dying are a grim sight upon a wide-spread battle-field, but when this number is heaped upon a confined space, where from a single high rock the whole litter of broken and shattered bodies can be seen, and the groans of the stricken rise in one long droning chorus to the ear, then it is an iron mind indeed which can resist such evidence of disaster. In a harder age Wellington was able to survey four thousand bodies piled in the narrow compass of the breach of Badajos, but his resolution was sustained by the knowledge that the military end for which they fell had been accomplished. Had his task been unfinished it is doubtful whether even his steadfast soul would not have flinched from its completion. Thorneycroft saw the frightful havoc of one day, and he shrank from the thought of such another. 'Better six battalions safely down the hill than a mop up in the morning,' said he, and he gave the word to retire. One who had met the troops as they staggered down has told me how far they were from being routed. In mixed array, but steadily and in order, the long thin line trudged through the darkness. Their parched lips would not articulate, but they whispered 'Water! Where is water?' as they toiled upon their way. At the bottom of the hill they formed into regiments once more, and marched back to the camp. In the morning the blood-spattered hill-top, with its piles of dead and of wounded, were in the hands of Botha and his men, whose valour and perseverance deserved the victory which they had won. There is no doubt now that at 3 a.m. of that morning Botha, knowing that the Rifles had carried Burger's position, regarded the affair as hopeless, and that no one was more astonished than he when he found, on the report of two scouts, that it was a victory and not a defeat which had come to him.

How shall we sum up such an action save that it was a gallant attempt, gallantly carried out, and as gallantly met? On both sides the results of artillery fire during the war have been disappointing, but at Spion Kop beyond all question it was the Boer guns which won the action for them. So keen was the disappointment at home that there was a tendency to criticise the battle with some harshness, but it is difficult now, with the evidence at our command, to say what was left undone which could have altered the result. Had Thorneycroft known all that we know, he would have kept his grip upon the hill. On the face of it one finds it difficult to understand why so momentous a decision, upon which the whole operations depended, should have been left entirely to the judgment of one who in the morning had been a simple Lieutenant-Colonel. 'Where are the bosses?' cried a Fusilier, and the historian can only repeat the question. General Warren was at the bottom of the hill. Had he ascended and determined that the place should still be held, he might have sent down the wearied troops, brought up smaller numbers of fresh ones, ordered the Sappers to deepen the trenches, and tried to bring up water and guns. It was for the divisional commander to lay his hand upon the reins at so critical an instant, to relieve the weary man who had struggled so hard all day.

The subsequent publication of the official despatches has served little purpose, save to show that there was a want of harmony between Buller and Warren, and that the former lost all confidence in his subordinate during the course of the operations. In these papers General Buller expresses the opinion that had Warren's operations been more dashing, he would have found his turning movement upon the left a comparatively easy matter. In this judgment he would probably have the concurrence of most military critics. He adds, however, 'On the 19th, I ought to have assumed command myself. I saw that things were not going well—indeed, everyone saw that. I blame myself now for not having done so. I did not, because, if I did, I should discredit General Warren in the estimation of the troops, and, if I were shot, and he had to withdraw across the Tugela, and they had lost confidence in him, the consequences might be very serious. I must leave it to higher authority whether this argument was a sound one.' It needs no higher authority than common-sense to say that the argument is an absolutely unsound one. No consequences could be more serious than that the operations should miscarry and Ladysmith remain unrelieved, and such want of success must in any case discredit Warren in the eyes of his troops. Besides, a subordinate is not discredited because his chief steps in to conduct a critical operation. However, these personal controversies may be suffered to remain in that pigeon-hole from which they should never have been drawn.

On account of the crowding of four thousand troops into a space which might have afforded tolerable cover for five hundred the losses in the action were very heavy, not fewer than fifteen hundred being killed, wounded, or missing, the proportion of killed being, on account of the shell fire, abnormally high. The Lancashire Fusiliers were the heaviest sufferers, and their Colonel Blomfield was wounded and fell into the hands of the enemy. The Royal Lancasters also lost heavily. Thorneycroft's had 80 men hit out of 180 engaged. The Imperial Light Infantry, a raw corps of Rand refugees who were enduring their baptism of fire, lost 130 men. In officers the losses were particularly heavy, 60 being killed or wounded. The Boer returns show some 50 killed and 150 wounded, which may not be far from the truth. Without the shell fire the British losses might not have been much more.

General Buller had lost nearly two thousand men since he had crossed the Tugela, and his purpose was still unfulfilled. Should he risk the loss of a large part of his force in storming the ridges in front of him, or should he recross the river and try for an easier route elsewhere? To the surprise and disappointment both of the public and of the army, he chose the latter course, and by January 27th he had fallen back, unmolested by the Boers, to the other side of the Tugela. It must be confessed that his retreat was admirably conducted, and that it was a military feat to bring his men, his guns, and his stores in safety over a broad river in the face of a victorious enemy. Stolid and unmoved, his impenetrable demeanour restored serenity and confidence to the angry and disappointed troops. There might well be heavy hearts among both them and the public. After a fortnight's campaign, and the endurance of great losses and hardships, both Ladysmith and her relievers found themselves no better off than when they started. Buller still held the commanding position of Mount Alice, and this was all that he had to show for such sacrifices and such exertions. Once more there came a weary pause while Ladysmith, sick with hope deferred, waited gloomily upon half-rations of horse-flesh for the next movement from the South.

CHAPTER 16

Vaalkranz

Neither General Buller nor his troops appeared to be dismayed by the failure of their plans, or by the heavy losses which were entailed by the movement which culminated at Spion Kop. The soldiers grumbled, it is true, at not being let go, and swore that even if it cost them two-thirds of their number they could and would make their way through this labyrinth of hills with its fringe of death. So doubtless they might. But from first to last their General had shown a great—some said an exaggerated—respect for human life, and he had no intention of winning a path by mere slogging, if there were a chance of finding one by less bloody means. On the morrow of his return he astonished both his army and the Empire by announcing that he had found the key to the position and that he hoped to be in Ladysmith in a week. Some rejoiced in the assurance. Some shrugged their shoulders. Careless of friends or foes, the stolid Buller proceeded to work out his new combination.

In the next few days reinforcements trickled in which more than made up for the losses of the preceding week. A battery of horse artillery, two heavy guns, two squadrons of the 14th Hussars, and infantry drafts to the number of twelve or fourteen hundred men came to share the impending glory or disaster. On the morning of February 5th the army sallied forth once more to have another try to win a way to Ladysmith. It was known that enteric was rife in the town, that shell and bullet and typhoid germ had struck down a terrible proportion of the garrison, and that the rations of starved horse and commissariat mule were running low. With their comrades—in many cases their linked battalions—in such straits within fifteen miles of them, Buller's soldiers had high motives to brace them for a supreme effort.

The previous attempt had been upon the line immediately to the west of Spion Kop. If, however, one were to follow to the east of Spion Kop, one would come upon a high mountain called Doornkloof. Between these two peaks, there lies a low ridge, called Brakfontein, and a small detached hill named Vaalkranz. Buller's idea was that if he could seize this small Vaalkranz, it would enable him to avoid the high ground altogether and pass his troops through on to the plateau beyond. He still held the Ford at Potgieter's and commanded the country beyond with heavy guns on Mount Alice and at Swartz Kop, so that he could pass troops over at his will. He would make a noisy demonstration against Brakfontein, then suddenly seize Vaalkranz, and so, as he hoped, hold the outer door which opened on to the passage to Ladysmith.

The getting of the guns up Swartz Kop was a preliminary which was as necessary as it was difficult. A road was cut, sailors, engineers, and gunners worked with a will under the general direction of Majors Findlay and Apsley Smith. A mountain battery, two field guns, and six naval 12-pounders were slung up by steel hawsers, the sailors *yeo-hoing* on the halliards. The ammunition was taken up by hand. At six o'clock on the morning of the 5th the other guns opened a furious and probably harmless fire upon Brakfontein, Spion Kop, and all the Boer positions opposite to them. Shortly afterwards the feigned attack upon Brakfontein was commenced and was sustained with much fuss and appearance of energy until all was ready for the development of the true one. Wynne's Brigade, which had been Woodgate's, recovered already from its Spion Kop experience, carried out this part of the plan, supported by six batteries of field artillery, one howitzer battery, and two 4.7 naval guns. Three hours later a telegram was on its way to Pretoria to tell how triumphantly the burghers had driven back an attack which was never meant to go forward. The infantry retired first, then the artillery in alternate batteries, preserving a beautiful order and decorum. The last battery, the 78th, remained to receive the concentrated fire of the Boer guns, and was so enveloped in the dust of the exploding shells that spectators could only see a gun here or a limber there. Out of this whirl of death it quietly walked, without a bucket out of its place, the gunners drawing one wagon, the horses of which had perished, and so effected a leisurely and contemptuous withdrawal. The gallantry of the gunners has been one of the most striking features of the war, but it has never been more conspicuous than in this feint at Brakfontein.

While the attention of the Boers was being concentrated upon the Lancashire men, a pontoon bridge was suddenly thrown across the river at a place called Munger's Drift, some miles to the eastward. Three infantry brigades, those of Hart, Lyttelton, and Hildyard, had been massed all ready to be let slip when the false attack was sufficiently absorbing. The artillery fire (the Swartz Kop guns, and also the batteries which had been withdrawn from the Brakfontein demonstration) was then turned suddenly, with the crashing effect of seventy pieces, upon the real object of attack, the isolated Vaalkranz. It is doubtful whether any position has ever been subjected to so terrific a bombardment, for the weight of metal thrown by single guns was greater than that of a whole German battery in the days of their last great war. The 4-pounders and 6-pounders of which Prince Kraft discourses would have seemed toys beside these mighty howitzers and 4.7's. Yet though the hillside was sharded off in great flakes, it is doubtful if this terrific fire inflicted much injury upon the cunning and invisible riflemen with whom we had to contend.

About midday the infantry began to stream across the bridge, which had been most gallantly and efficiently constructed under a warm fire, by a party of sappers, under the command of Major Irvine. The attack was led by the Durham Light Infantry of Lyttelton's Brigade, followed by the 1st Rifle Brigade, with the Scottish and 3rd Rifles in support. Never did the old Light Division of Peninsular fame go up a Spanish hillside with greater spirit and dash than these, their descendants, facing the slope of Vaalkranz. In open order they moved across the plain, with a superb disregard of the crash and patter of the shrapnel, and then up they went, the flitting figures, springing from cover to cover, stooping, darting, crouching, running, until with their glasses the spectators on Swartz Kop could see the gleam of the bayonets and the strain of furious rushing men upon the summit, as the last Boers were driven from their trenches. The position was gained, but little else. Seven officers and seventy men were lying killed and wounded among the boulders. A few stricken Boers, five unwounded prisoners, and a string of Basuto ponies were the poor fruits of victory—those and the arid hill from which so much had been hoped, and so little was to be gained.

It was during this advance that an incident occurred of a more pictur-esque character than is usual in modern warfare. The invisibility of com-batants and guns, and the absorption of the individual in the mass, have robbed the battle-field of those episodes which adorned, if they did not justify it. On this occasion, a Boer gun, cut off by the British advance, flew out suddenly from behind its cover, like a hare from its tussock, and raced for safety across the plain. Here and there it wound, the horses stretched to their utmost, the drivers stooping and lashing, the little gun bounding behind. To right to left, behind and before, the British shells burst, Lyd-dite and shrapnel, crashing and riving. Over the lip of a hollow, the gallant gun vanished, and within a few minutes was banging away once more at the British advance. With cheers and shouts and laughter, the British infantrymen watched the race for shelter, their sporting spirit rising high above all racial hatred, and hailing with a 'gone to ground' whoop the final disappearance of the gun.

The Durhams had cleared the path, but the other regiments of Lyttelton's Brigade followed hard at their heels, and before night they had firmly established themselves upon the hill. But the fatal slowness which had marred General Buller's previous operations again prevented him from completing his success. Twice at least in the course of these operations there is evidence of sudden impulse to drop his tools in the midst of his task and to do no more for the day. So it was at Colenso, where an order was given at an early hour for the whole force to retire, and the guns which might have been covered by infantry fire and withdrawn after nightfall were abandoned. So it was also at a critical moment at this action at Vaalkranz. In the original scheme of operations it had been planned that an adjoining hill, called the Green Hill, which partly commanded Vaalkranz, should be carried also. The two together made a complete position, while singly each was a very bad neighbour to the other. On the *aide-de-camp* riding up, however, to inquire from General Buller whether the time had come for this advance, he replied, 'We have done enough for the day,' and left out this essential portion of his original scheme, with the result that all miscarried.

Speed was the most essential quality for carrying out his plan successfully. So it must always be with the attack. The defence does not know where the blow is coming, and has to distribute men and guns to cover miles of ground. The attacker knows where he will hit, and behind a screen of outposts he can mass his force and throw his whole strength against a mere fraction of that of his enemy. But in order to do so he must be quick. One tiger spring must tear the centre out of the line before the flanks can come to its assistance. If time is given, if the long line can concentrate, if the scattered guns can mass, if lines of defence can be reduplicated behind, then the one great advantage which the attack possesses is thrown away. Both at the second and at the third attempts of Buller the British movements were so slow that had the enemy been the slowest instead of the most mobile of armies, they could still always have made any dispositions which they chose. Warren's dawdling in the first days of the movement which ended at Spion Kop might with an effort be condoned on account of possible difficulties of supply, but it would strain the ingenuity of the most charitable critic to find a sufficient reason for the lethargy of Vaalkranz. Though daylight comes a little after four, the operations were not commenced before seven. Lyttelton's Brigade had stormed the hill at two, and nothing more was done during the long evening, while officers chafed and soldiers swore, and the busy Boers worked furiously to bring up their guns and to bar the path which we must take. General Buller remarked a day or two later that the way was not quite so easy as it had been. One might have deduced the fact without the aid of a balloon.

The brigade then occupied Vaalkranz and erected sangars and dug trenches. On the morning of the 6th, the position of the British force was not dissimilar to that of Spion Kop. Again they had some thousands of men upon a hill-top, exposed to shell fire from several directions and without any guns upon the hill to support them. In one or two points the situation was modified in their favour, and hence their escape from loss and disaster. A more extended position enabled the infantry to avoid bunching, but in other respects the situation was parallel to that in which they had found themselves a fortnight before.

The original plan was that the taking of Vaalkranz should be the first step towards the outflanking of Brakfontein and the rolling up of the whole Boer position. But after the first move the British attitude became one of defence rather than of attack. Whatever the general and ultimate effect of these operations may have been, it is beyond question that their contemplation was annoying and bewildering in the extreme to those who were present. The position on February 6th was this. Over the river upon the hill was a single British brigade, exposed to the fire of one enormous gun—a 96-pound Creusot, the longest of all Long Toms—which was stationed upon Doornkloof, and of several smaller guns and pom-poms which spat at them from nooks and crevices of the hills. On our side were seventy-two guns, large and small, all very noisy and impotent. It is not too much to say, as it appears to me, that the Boers have in some ways revolutionised our ideas in regard to the use of artillery, by bringing a fresh and healthy common-sense to bear upon a subject which had been unduly fettered by pedantic rules. The Boer system is the single stealthy gun crouching where none can see it. The British system is the six brave guns coming into action in line of full interval, and spreading out into accurate dressing visible to all men. 'Always remember,' says one of our artillery maxims, 'that one gun is no gun.' Which is prettier on a field-day, is obvious, but which is business—let the many duels between six Boer guns and sixty British declare. With black powder it was useless to hide the gun, as its smoke must betray it. With smokeless powder the guns are so invisible that it was only by the detection with powerful glasses of the dust from the trail on the recoil that the officers were ever able to localise the guns against which they were fighting. But if the Boers had had six guns in line, instead of one behind that *kopje*, and another between those distant rocks, it would not have been so difficult to say where they were. Again, British traditions are all in favour of planting guns close together. At this very action of Vaalkranz the two largest guns were so placed that a single shell bursting between them would have disabled them both. The officer who placed them there, and so disregarded in a vital matter the most obvious dictates of common-sense, would probably have been shocked by any want of technical smartness, or irregularity in the routine drill. An over-elaboration of trifles, and a want of grip of common-sense, and of adaptation to new ideas, is the most serious and damaging criticism which can be levelled against our army. That the function of infantry is to shoot, and not to act like spearmen in the Middle Ages; that the first duty of artillery is so far as is possible to be invisible—these are two of the lessons which have been driven home so often during the war, that even our hidebound conservatism can hardly resist them.

Lyttelton's Brigade, then, held Vaalkranz; and from three parts of the compass there came big shells and little shells, with a constant shower of long-range rifle bullets. Behind them, and as useful as if it had been on Woolwich Common, there was drawn up an imposing mass of men, two infantry divisions, and two brigades of cavalry, all straining at the leash, prepared to shed their blood until the *spruits* ran red with it, if only they could win their way to where their half-starved comrades waited for them. But nothing happened. Hours passed and nothing happened. An occasional shell from the big gun plumped among them. One, through some freak of gunnery, lobbed slowly through a division, and the men whooped and threw their caps at it as it passed. The guns on Swartz Kop, at a range of nearly five miles, tossed shells at the monster on Doornkloof, and finally blew up his powder magazine amid the applause of the infantry. For the army it was a picnic and a spectacle.

But it was otherwise with the men up on Vaalkranz. In spite of sangar and trench, that cross fire was finding them out; and no feint or demonstration on either side came to draw the concentrated fire from their position. Once there was a sudden alarm at the western end of the hill, and stooping bearded figures with slouch hats and bandoliers were right up on the ridge before they could be stopped, so cleverly had their advance been conducted. But a fiery rush of Durhams and Rifles cleared the crest again, and it was proved once more how much stronger is the defence than the attack. Nightfall found the position unchanged, save that another pontoon bridge had been constructed during the day. Over this Hildyard's Brigade marched to relieve Lyttelton's, who came back for a rest under the cover of the Swartz Kop guns. Their losses in the two days had been under two hundred and fifty, a trifle if any aim were to be gained, but excessive for a mere demonstration.

That night Hildyard's men supplemented the defences made by Lyttelton, and tightened their hold upon the hill. One futile night attack caused them for an instant to change the spade for the rifle. When in the morning it was found that the Boers had, as they naturally would, brought up their outlying guns, the tired soldiers did not regret their labours of the night. It was again demonstrated how innocuous a thing is a severe shell fire, if the position be an extended one with chances of cover. A total of forty killed and wounded out of a strong brigade was the result of a long day under an incessant cannonade. And then at nightfall came the conclusion that the guns were too many, that the way was too hard, and down came all their high hopes with the order to withdraw once more across that accursed river. Vaalkranz was abandoned, and Hildyard's Brigade, seething with indignation, was ordered back once more to its camp.

CHAPTER 17

Buller's Final Advance

The heroic moment of the siege of Ladysmith was that which witnessed the repulse of the great attack. The epic should have ended at that dramatic instant. But instead of doing so the story falls back to an anticlimax of crowded hospitals, slaughtered horses, and sporadic shell fire. For another six weeks of inactivity the brave garrison endured all the sordid evils which had steadily grown from inconvenience to misfortune and from misfortune to misery. Away in the south they heard the thunder of Buller's guns, and from the hills round the town they watched with pale faces and bated breath the tragedy of Spion Kop, preserving a firm conviction that a very little more would have transformed it into their salvation. Their hearts sank with the sinking of the cannonade, and rose again with the roar of Vaalkranz. But Vaalkranz also failed them, and they waited on in the majesty of their hunger and their weakness for the help which was to come.

It has been already narrated how General Buller had made his three attempts for the relief of the city. The General who was inclined to despair was now stimulated by despatches from Lord Roberts, while his army, who were by no means inclined to despair, were immensely cheered by the good news from the Kimberley side. Both General and army prepared for a last supreme effort. This time, at least, the soldiers hoped that they would be permitted to burst their way to the help of their starving comrades or leave their bones among the hills which had faced them so long. All they asked was a fight to a finish, and now they were about to have one. General Buller had tried the Boers' centre, he had tried their extreme right, and now he was about to try their extreme left. There were some obvious advantages on this side which make it surprising that it was not the first to be attempted. In the first place, the enemy's main position upon that flank was at Hlangwane mountain, which is to the south of the Tugela, so that in case of defeat the river ran behind them. In the second, Hlangwane mountain was the one point from which the Boer position at

Colenso could be certainly enfiladed, and therefore the fruits of victory would be greater on that flank than on the other. Finally, the operations could be conducted at no great distance from the railhead, and the force would be exposed to little danger of having its flank attacked or its communications cut, as was the case in the Spion Kop advance. Against these potent considerations there is only to be put the single fact that the turning of the Boer right would threaten the Freestaters' line of retreat. On the whole, the balance of advantage lay entirely with the new attempt, and the whole army advanced to it with a premonition of success. Of all the examples which the war has given of the enduring qualities of the British troops there is none more striking than the absolute confidence and whole hearted delight with which, after three bloody repulses, they set forth upon another venture.

On February 9th the movements were started which transferred the greater part of the force from the extreme left to the centre and right. By the 11th Lyttelton's (formerly Clery's) second division and Warren's fifth division had come eastward, leaving Burn Murdoch's cavalry brigade to guard the Western side. On the 12th Lord Dundonald, with all the colonial cavalry, two battalions of infantry, and a battery, made a strong reconnaissance towards Hussar Hill, which is the nearest of the several hills which would have to be occupied in order to turn the position. The hill was taken, but was abandoned again by General Buller after he had used it for some hours as an observatory. A long-range action between the retiring cavalry and the Boers ended in a few losses upon each side.

What Buller had seen during the hour or two which he had spent with his telescope upon Hussar Hill had evidently confirmed him in his views, for two days later (February 14th) the whole army set forth for this point. By the morning of the 15th twenty thousand men were concentrated upon the sides and spurs of this eminence. On the 16th the heavy guns were in position, and all was ready for the advance.

Facing them now were the formidable Boer lines of Hlangwane Hill and Green Hill, which would certainly cost several thousands of men if they were to take them by direct storm. Beyond them, upon the Boer flank, were the hills of Monte Christo and Cingolo, which appeared to be the extreme outside of the Boer position. The plan was to engage the attention of the trenches in front by a terrific artillery fire and the threat of an assault, while at the same time sending the true flank attack far round to carry the Cingolo ridge, which must be taken before any other hill could be approached.

On the 17th, in the early morning, with the first tinge of violet in the east, the irregular cavalry and the second division (Lyttelton's) with Wynne's Brigade started upon their widely curving flanking march. The country through which they passed was so broken that the troopers led their horses in single file, and would have found themselves helpless in face of any resistance. Fortunately, Cingolo Hill was very weakly held, and by evening both our horsemen and our infantry had a firm grip upon it, thus turning the extreme left flank of the Boer position. For once their mountainous fortresses were against them, for a mounted Boer force is so mobile that in an open position, such as faced Methuen, it is very hard and requires great celerity of movement ever to find a flank at all. On a succession of hills, however, it was evident that some one hill must mark the extreme end of their line, and Buller had found it at Cingolo. Their answer to this movement was to throw their flank back so as to face the new position.

Even now, however, the Boer leaders had apparently not realised that this was the main attack, or it is possible that the intervention of the river made it difficult for them to send reinforcements. However that may be, it is certain that the task which the British found awaiting them on the 18th proved to be far easier than they had dared to hope. The honours of the day rested with Hildyard's English Brigade (East Surrey, West Surrey, West Yorkshires, and 2nd Devons). In open order and with a rapid advance, taking every advantage of the cover—which was better than is usual in South African warfare—they gained the edge of the Monte Christo ridge, and then swiftly cleared the crest. One at least of the regiments engaged, the Devons, was nerved by the thought that their own first battalion was waiting for them at Ladysmith. The capture of the hill made the line of trenches which faced Buller untenable, and he was at once able to advance with Barton's Fusilier Brigade and to take possession of the whole Boer position of Hlangwane and Green Hill. It was not a great tactical victory, for they had no trophies to show save the worthless debris of the Boer camps. But it was a very great strategical victory, for it not only gave them the whole south side of the Tugela, but also the means of commanding with their guns a great deal of the north side, including those Colenso trenches which had blocked the way so long. A hundred and seventy killed and wounded (of whom only fourteen were killed) was a trivial price for such a result. At last from the captured ridges the exultant troops could see far away the haze which lay over the roofs of Ladysmith, and the besieged, with hearts beating high with hope, turned their glasses upon the distant mottled patches which told them that their comrades were approaching.

By February 20th the British had firmly established themselves along the whole south bank of the river, Hart's brigade had occupied Colenso, and the heavy guns had been pushed up to more advanced positions. The crossing of the river was the next operation, and the question arose where it should be crossed. The wisdom which comes with experience shows us now that it would have been infinitely better to have crossed on their extreme left flank, as by an advance upon this line we should have turned their strong Pieters position just as we had already turned their Colenso one. With an absolutely master card in our hand we refused to play it, and won the game by a more tedious and perilous process. The assumption seems to have been made (on no other hypothesis can one understand the facts) that the enemy were demoralised and that the positions would not be strongly held. Our flanking advantage was abandoned and a direct advance was ordered from Colenso, involving a frontal attack upon the Pieters position.

On February 21st Buller threw his pontoon bridge over the river near Colenso, and the same evening his army began to cross. It was at once evident that the Boer resistance had by no means collapsed. Wynne's Lancashire Brigade were the first across, and found themselves hotly engaged before nightfall. The low *kopjes* in front of them were blazing with musketry fire. The brigade held its own, but lost the Brigadier (the second in a month) and 150 rank and file. Next morning the main body of the infantry was passed across, and the army was absolutely committed to the formidable and unnecessary enterprise of fighting its way straight to Ladysmith.

The force in front had weakened, however, both in numbers and in morale. Some thousands of the Freestaters had left in order to defend their own country from the advance of Roberts, while the rest were depressed by as much of the news as was allowed by their leaders to reach them. But the Boer is a tenacious fighter, and many a brave man was still to fall before Buller and White should shake hands in the High Street of Ladysmith.

The first obstacle which faced the army, after crossing the river, was a belt of low rolling ground, which was gradually cleared by the advance of our infantry. As night closed in the advance lines of Boers and British were so close to each other that incessant rifle fire was maintained until morning, and at more than one point small bodies of desperate riflemen charged right up to the bayonets of our infantry. The morning found us still holding our positions all along the line, and as more and more of our infantry came up and gun after gun roared into action we began to push our stubborn enemy northwards. On the 21st the Dorsets, Middlesex, and Somersets had borne the heat of the day. On the 22nd it was the Royal Lancasters, followed by the South Lancashires, who took up the running. It would take the patience and also the space of a Kinglake in this scrambling broken fight to trace the doings of those groups of men who strove and struggled through the rifle fire.

All day a steady advance was maintained over the low *kopjes*, until by evening we were faced by the more serious line of the Pieter's Hills. The operations had been carried out with a monotony of gallantry. Always the same extended advance, always the same rattle of Mausers and clatter of pom-poms from a ridge, always the same victorious soldiers on the barren crest, with a few crippled Boers before them and many crippled comrades behind. They were expensive triumphs, and yet every one brought them nearer to their goal. And now, like an advancing tide, they lapped along the base of Pieter's Hill. Could they gather volume enough to carry themselves over? The issue of the long-drawn battle and the fate of Ladysmith hung upon the question.

Brigadier Fitzroy Hart, to whom the assault was entrusted, is in some ways as singular and picturesque a type as has been evolved in the war. A dandy soldier, always the picture of neatness from the top of his helmet to the heels of his well-polished brown boots, he brings to military matters the same precision which he affects in dress. Pedantic in his accuracy, he actually at the battle of Colenso drilled the Irish Brigade for half an hour before leading them into action, and threw out markers under a deadly fire in order that his change from close to extended formation might be academically correct. The heavy loss of the Brigade at this action was to some extent ascribed to him and affected his popularity; but as his men came to know him better, his romantic bravery, his whimsical soldierly humour, their dislike changed into admiration. His personal disregard for danger was notorious and reprehensible. 'Where is General Hart?' asked some one in action. 'I have not seen him, but I know where you will find him. Go ahead of the skirmish line and you will see him standing on a rock,' was the answer. He bore a charmed life. It was a danger to be near him. 'Whom are you going to?' 'General Hart,' said the *aide-de-camp*. 'Then goodbye!' cried his fellows. A grim humour ran through his nature. It is gravely recorded and widely believed that he lined up a regiment on a hill-top in order to teach them not to shrink from fire. Amid the laughter of his Irishmen, he walked through the open files of his firing line holding a laggard by the ear. This was the man who had put such a spirit into the Irish Brigade that amid that army of valiant men there were none who held such a record. 'Their rushes were the quickest, their rushes were the longest, and they stayed the shortest time under cover,' said a shrewd military observer. To Hart and his brigade was given the task of clearing the way to Ladysmith.

The regiments which he took with him on his perilous enterprise were the 1st Inniskilling Fusiliers, the 2nd Dublin Fusiliers, the 1st Connaught Rangers, and the Imperial Light Infantry, the whole forming the famous 5th Brigade. They were already in the extreme British advance, and now, as they moved forwards, the Durham Light Infantry and the 1st Rifle Brigade from Lyttelton's Brigade came up to take their place. The hill to be taken lay on the right, and the soldiers were compelled to pass in single file under a heavy fire for more than a mile until they reached the spot which seemed best for their enterprise. There, short already of sixty of their comrades, they assembled and began a cautious advance upon the lines of trenches and sangars which seamed the brown slope above them.

For a time they were able to keep some cover, and the casualties were comparatively few. But now at last, as the evening sun threw a long shadow from the hills, the leading regiment, the Inniskillings, found themselves at the utmost fringe of boulders with a clear slope between them and the main trench of the enemy. Up there where the shrapnel was spurting and the great Lyddite shells crashing they could dimly see a line of bearded faces and the black dots of the slouch hats. With a yell the Inniskillings sprang out, carried with a rush the first trench, and charged desperately onwards for the second one. It was a supremely dashing attack against a supremely steady resistance, for among all their gallant deeds the Boers have never fought better than on that February evening. Amid such a smashing shell fire as living mortals have never yet endured they stood doggedly, these hardy men of the *veldt*, and fired fast and true into the fiery ranks of the Irishmen. The yell of the stormers was answered by the remorseless roar of the Mausers and the deep-chested shouts of the farmers. Up and up surged the infantry, falling, rising, dashing bull-headed at the crackling line of the trench. But still the bearded faces glared at them over the edge, and still the sheet of lead pelted through their ranks. The regiment staggered, came on, staggered again, was overtaken by supporting companies of the Dublins and the Connaughts, came on, staggered once more, and finally dissolved into shreds, who ran swiftly back for cover, threading their way among their stricken comrades. Never on this earth was there a retreat of which the survivors had less reason to be ashamed. They had held on to the utmost capacity of human endurance. Their Colonel, ten officers, and more than half the regiment were lying on the fatal hill. Honour to them, and honour also to the gallant Dutchmen who, rooted in the trenches, had faced the rush and fury of such an onslaught! Today to them, tomorrow to us—but it is for a soldier to thank the God of battles for worthy foes.

It is one thing, however, to repulse the British soldier and it is another to rout him. Within a few hundred yards of their horrible ordeal at Magersfontein the Highlanders reformed into a military body. So now the Irishmen fell back no further than the nearest cover, and there held grimly on to the ground which they had won. If you would know the advantage which the defence has over the attack, then do you come and assault this line of tenacious men, now in your hour of victory and exultation, friend Boer! Friend Boer did attempt it, and skilfully too, moving a flanking party to sweep the position with their fire. But the brigade, though sorely hurt, held them off without difficulty, and was found on the morning of the 24th to be still lying upon the ground which they had won.

Our losses had been very heavy, Colonel Thackeray of the Inniskillings, Colonel Sitwell of the Dublins, three majors, twenty officers, and a total of about six hundred out of 1200 actually engaged. To take such punishment and to remain undemoralised is the supreme test to which troops can be put. Could the loss have been avoided? By following the original line of advance from Monte Christo, perhaps, when we should have turned the enemy's left. But otherwise no. The hill was in the way and had to be taken. In the war game you cannot play without a stake. You lose and you pay forfeit, and where the game is fair the best player is he who pays with the best grace. The attack was well prepared, well delivered, and only miscarried on account of the excellence of the defence. We proved once more what we had proved so often before, that all valour and all discipline will not avail in a frontal attack against brave coolheaded men armed with quick-firing rifles.

While the Irish Brigade assaulted Railway Hill an attack had been made upon the left, which was probably meant as a demonstration to keep the Boers from reinforcing their comrades rather than as an actual attempt upon their lines. Such as it was, however, it cost the life of at least one brave soldier, for Colonel Thorold, of the Welsh Fusiliers, was among the fallen. Thorold, Thackeray, and Sitwell in one evening. Who can say that British colonels have not given their men a lead?

The army was now at a deadlock. Railway Hill barred the way, and if Hart's men could not carry it by assault it was hard to say who could. The 24th found the two armies facing each other at this critical point, the Irishmen still clinging to the slopes of the hill and the Boers lining the top. Fierce rifle firing broke out between them during the day, but each side was well covered and lay low. The troops in support suffered somewhat, however, from a random shell fire. Mr. Winston Churchill has left it upon record that within his own observation three of their shrapnel shells fired at a venture on to the reverse slope of a hill accounted for nineteen men and four horses. The enemy can never have known how hard those three shells had hit us, and so we may also believe that our artillery fire has often been less futile than it appeared.

General Buller had now realised that it was no mere rearguard action which the Boers were fighting, but that their army was standing doggedly at bay; so he reverted to that flanking movement which, as events showed, should never have been abandoned. Hart's Irish Brigade was at present almost the right of the army. His new plan—a masterly one—was to keep Hart pinning the Boers at that point, and to move his centre and left across the river, and then back to envelope the left wing of the enemy. By this manoeuvre Hart became the extreme left instead of the extreme right, and the Irish Brigade would be the hinge upon which the whole army should turn. It was a large conception, finely carried out. The 24th was a day of futile shell fire—and of plans for the future. The heavy guns were got across once more to the Monte Christo ridge and to Hlangwane, and preparations made to throw the army from the west to the east. The enemy still snarled and occasionally snapped in front of Hart's men, but with four companies of the 2nd Rifle Brigade to protect their flanks their position remained secure.

In the meantime, through a contretemps between our outposts and the Boers, no leave had been given to us to withdraw our wounded, and the unfortunate fellows, some hundreds of them, had lain between the lines in agonies of thirst for thirty-six hours—one of the most painful incidents of the campaign. Now, upon the 25th, an armistice was proclaimed, and the crying needs of the survivors were attended to. On the same day the hearts of our soldiers sank within them as they saw the stream of our wagons and guns crossing the river once more. What, were they foiled again? Was the blood of these brave men to be shed in vain? They ground their teeth at the thought. The higher strategy was not for them, but back was back and forward was forward, and they knew which way their proud hearts wished to go.

The 26th was occupied by the large movements of troops which so complete a reversal of tactics necessitated. Under the screen of a heavy artillery fire, the British right became the left and the left the right. A second pontoon bridge was thrown across near the old Boer bridge at Hlangwane, and over it was passed a large force of infantry, Barton's Fusilier Brigade, Kitchener's (vice Wynne's, vice Woodgate's) Lancashire Brigade, and two battalions of Norcott's (formerly Lyttelton's) Brigade. Coke's Brigade was left at Colenso to prevent a counter attack upon our left flank and communications. In this way, while Hart with the Durhams and the 1st Rifle Brigade held the Boers in front, the main body of the army was rapidly swung round on to their left flank. By the morning of the 27th all were in place for the new attack.

Opposite the point where the troops had been massed were three Boer hills; one, the nearest, may for convenience sake be called Barton's Hill. As the army had formerly been situated the assault upon this hill would have been a matter of extreme difficulty; but now, with the heavy guns restored to their commanding position, from which they could sweep its sides and summits, it had recovered its initial advantage. In the morning sunlight Barton's Fusiliers crossed the river, and advanced to the attack under a screaming canopy of shells. Up they went and up, darting and crouching, until their gleaming bayonets sparkled upon the summit. The masterful artillery had done its work, and the first long step taken in this last stage of the relief of Ladysmith. The loss had been slight and the advantage enormous. After they had gained the summit the Fusiliers were stung and stung again by clouds of skirmishers who clung to the flanks of the hill, but their grip was firm and grew firmer with every hour.

Of the three Boer hills which had to be taken the nearest (or eastern one) was now in the hands of the British. The furthest (or western one) was that on which the Irish Brigade was still crouching, ready at any moment for a final spring which would take them over the few hundred yards which separated them from the trenches. Between the two intervened a central hill, as yet untouched. Could we carry this the whole position would be ours. Now for the final effort! Turn every gun upon it, the guns of Monte Christo, the guns of Hlangwane! Turn every rifle upon it—the rifles of Barton's men, the rifles of Hart's men, the carbines of the distant cavalry! Scalp its crown with the machine-gun fire! And now up with you, Lancashire men, Norcott's men! The summit or a glorious death, for beyond that hill your suffering comrades are awaiting you! Put every bullet and every man and all of fire and spirit that you are worth into this last hour; for if you fail now you have failed for ever, and if you win, then when your hairs are white your blood will still run warm when you think of that morning's work. The long drama had drawn to an end, and one short day's work is to show what that end was to be.

But there was never a doubt of it. Hardly for one instant did the advance waver at any point of its extended line. It was the supreme instant of the Natal campaign, as, wave after wave, the long lines of infantry went shimmering up the hill. On the left the Lancasters, the Lancashire Fusiliers, the South Lancashires, the York and Lancasters, with a burr of north country oaths, went racing for the summit. Spion Kop and a thousand comrades were calling for vengeance. 'Remember, men, the eyes of Lancashire are watching you,' cried the gallant MacCarthy O'Leary. The old 40th swept on, but his dead body marked the way which they had taken. On the right the East Surrey, the Cameronians, the 3rd Rifles, the 1st Rifle Brigade, the Durhams, and the gallant Irishmen, so sorely stricken and yet so eager, were all pressing upwards and onwards. The Boer fire lulls, it ceases—they are running! Wild hat-waving men upon the Hlangwane uplands see the silhouette of the active figures of the stormers along the sky-line and know that the position is theirs. Exultant soldiers dance and

cheer upon the ridge. The sun is setting in glory over the great Drakensberg mountains, and so also that night set for ever the hopes of the Boer
invaders of Natal. Out of doubt and chaos, blood and labour, had come at
last the judgment that the lower should not swallow the higher, that the
world is for the man of the twentieth and not of the seventeenth century.
After a fortnight of fighting the weary troops threw themselves down that
night with the assurance that at last the door was ajar and the light breaking through. One more effort and it would be open before them.

Behind the line of hills which had been taken there extended a great
plain as far as Bulwana—that evil neighbour who had wrought such harm
upon Ladysmith. More than half of the Pieters position had fallen into
Buller's hands on the 27th, and the remainder had become untenable. The
Boers had lost some five hundred in killed, wounded, and prisoners.[1] It
seemed to the British General and his men that one more action would
bring them safely into Ladysmith.

But here they miscalculated, and so often have we miscalculated on
the optimistic side in this campaign that it is pleasing to find for once
that our hopes were less than the reality. The Boers had been beaten—
fairly beaten and disheartened. It will always be a subject for conjecture
whether they were so entirely on the strength of the Natal campaign,
or whether the news of the Cronje disaster from the western side had
warned them that they must draw in upon the east. For my own part I
believe that the honour lies with the gallant men of Natal, and that, moving on these lines, they would, Cronje or no Cronje, have forced their
way in triumph to Ladysmith.

And now the long-drawn story draws to a swift close. Cautiously
feeling their way with a fringe of horse, the British pushed over the great
plain, delayed here and there by the crackle of musketry, but finding always that the obstacle gave way and vanished as they approached it. At last
it seemed clear to Dundonald that there really was no barrier between
his horsemen and the beleaguered city. With a squadron of Imperial Light
Horse and a squadron of Natal Carabineers he rode on until, in the gathering twilight, the Ladysmith picket challenged the approaching cavalry,
and the gallant town was saved.

It is hard to say which had shown the greater endurance, the rescued
or their rescuers. The town, indefensible, lurking in a hollow under
commanding hills, had held out for 118 days. They had endured two
assaults and an incessant bombardment, to which, towards the end, owing to the failure of heavy ammunition, they were unable to make any

1. Accurate figures will probably never be obtained, but a well-known Boer in Pretoria informed me that Pieters was the most expensive fight to them of the whole
war.

adequate reply. It was calculated that 16,000 shells had fallen within the town. In two successful sorties they had destroyed three of the enemy's heavy guns. They had been pressed by hunger, horseflesh was already running short, and they had been decimated by disease. More than 2000 cases of enteric and dysentery had been in hospital at one time, and the total number of admissions had been nearly as great as the total number of the garrison. One-tenth of the men had actually died of wounds or disease. Ragged, bootless, and emaciated, there still lurked in the gaunt soldiers the martial spirit of warriors. On the day after their relief 2000 of them set forth to pursue the Boers. One who helped to lead them has left it on record that the most piteous sight that he has ever seen was these wasted men, stooping under their rifles and gasping with the pressure of their accoutrements, as they staggered after their retreating enemy. A Verestschagen might find a subject these 2000 indomitable men with their emaciated horses pursuing a formidable foe. It is God's mercy they failed to overtake them.

If the record of the besieged force was great, that of the relieving army was no less so. Through the blackest depths of despondency and failure they had struggled to absolute success. At Colenso they had lost 1200 men, at Spion Kop 1700, at Vaalkranz 400, and now, in this last long-drawn effort, 1600 more. Their total losses were over 5000 men, more than 20 per cent of the whole army. Some particular regiments had suffered horribly. The Dublin and Inniskilling Fusiliers headed the roll of honour with only five officers and 40 per cent of the men left standing. Next to them the Lancashire Fusiliers and the Royal Lancasters had been the hardest hit. It speaks well for Buller's power of winning and holding the confidence of his men that in the face of repulse after repulse the soldiers still went into battle as steadily as ever under his command.

On March 3rd Buller's force entered Ladysmith in state between the lines of the defenders. For their heroism the Dublin Fusiliers were put in the van of the procession, and it is told how, as the soldiers who lined the streets saw the five officers and small clump of men, the remains of what had been a strong battalion, realising, for the first time perhaps, what their relief had cost, many sobbed like children. With cheer after cheer the stream of brave men flowed for hours between banks formed by men as brave. But for the purposes of war the garrison was useless. A month of rest and food would be necessary before they could be ready to take the field once more.

So the riddle of the Tugela had at last been solved. Even now, with all the light which has been shed upon the matter, it is hard to apportion praise and blame. To the cheerful optimism of Symons must be laid some of the blame of the original entanglement; but man is mortal, and he laid down his life for his mistake. White, who had been but a week in the country, could not, if he would, alter the main facts of the military situation. He did his best, committed one or two errors, did brilliantly on one or two points, and finally conducted the defence with a tenacity and a gallantry which are above all praise. It did not, fortunately, develop into an absolutely desperate affair, like Massena's defence of Genoa, but a few more weeks would have made it a military tragedy. He was fortunate in the troops whom he commanded—half of them old soldiers from India[2]—and exceedingly fortunate in his officers, French (in the operations before the siege), Archibald Hunter, Ian Hamilton, Hedworth Lambton, Dick-Cunyngham, Knox, De Courcy Hamilton, and all the other good men and true who stood (as long as they could stand) by his side. Above all, he was fortunate in his commissariat officers, and it was in the offices of Colonels Ward and Stoneman as much as in the trenches and sangars of Caesar's Camp that the siege was won.

Buller, like White, had to take the situation as he found it. It is well known that his own belief was that the line of the Tugela was the true defence of Natal. When he reached Africa, Ladysmith was already beleaguered, and he, with his troops, had to abandon the scheme of direct invasion and to hurry to extricate White's division. Whether they might not have been more rapidly extricated by keeping to the original plan is a question which will long furnish an excellent subject for military debate. Had Buller in November known that Ladysmith was capable of holding out until March, is it conceivable that he, with his whole army corps and as many more troops as he cared to summon from England, would not have made such an advance in four months through the Free State as would necessitate the abandonment of the sieges both of Kimberley and of Ladysmith? If the Boers persisted in these sieges they could not possibly place more than 20,000 men on the Orange River to face 60, 000 whom Buller could have had there by the first week in December. Methuen's force, French's force, Gatacre's force, and the Natal force, with the exception of garrisons for Pietermaritzburg and Durban, would have assembled, with a reserve of another sixty thousand men in the colony or on the sea ready to fill the gaps in his advance. Moving over a flat country with plenty of flanking room, it is probable that he would have been in Bloemfontein by Christmas and at the Vaal River late in January. What could the Boers do then? They might remain before Ladysmith, and learn that their capital and their gold mines

---

2. Footnote: An officer in high command in Ladysmith has told me, as an illustration of the nerve and discipline of the troops, that though false alarms in the Boer trenches were matters of continual occurrence from the beginning to the end of the siege, there was not one single occasion when the British outposts made a mistake.

had been taken in their absence. Or they might abandon the siege and trek back to defend their own homes. This, as it appears to a civilian critic, would have been the least expensive means of fighting them; but after all the strain had to come somewhere, and the long struggle of Ladysmith may have meant a more certain and complete collapse in the future. At least, by the plan actually adopted we saved Natal from total devastation, and that must count against a great deal.

Having taken his line, Buller set about his task in a slow, deliberate, but pertinacious fashion. It cannot be denied, however, that the pertinacity was largely due to the stiffening counsel of Roberts and the soldierly firmness of White who refused to acquiesce in the suggestion of surrender. Let it be acknowledged that Buller's was the hardest problem of the war, and that he solved it. The mere acknowledgment goes far to soften criticism. But the singular thing is that in his proceedings he showed qualities which had not been generally attributed to him, and was wanting in those very points which the public had imagined to be characteristic of him. He had gone out with the reputation of a downright John Bull fighter, who would take punishment or give it, but slog his way through without wincing. There was no reason for attributing any particular strategical ability to him. But as a matter of fact, setting the Colenso attempt aside, the crossing for the Spion Kop enterprise, the withdrawal of the compromised army, the Vaalkranz crossing with the clever feint upon Brakfontein, the final operations, and especially the complete change of front after the third day of Pieters, were strategical movements largely conceived and admirably carried out. On the other hand, a hesitation in pushing onwards, and a disinclination to take a risk or to endure heavy punishment, even in the case of temporary failure, were consistent characteristics of his generalship. The Vaalkranz operations are particularly difficult to defend from the charge of having been needlessly slow and half-hearted. This 'saturnine fighter,' as he had been called, proved to be exceedingly sensitive about the lives of his men—an admirable quality in itself, but there are occasions when to spare them today is to needlessly imperil them tomorrow. The victory was his, and yet in the very moment of it he displayed the qualities which marred him. With two cavalry brigades in hand he did not push the pursuit of the routed Boers with their guns and endless streams of wagons. It is true that he might have lost heavily, but it is true also that a success might have ended the Boer invasion of Natal, and the lives of our troopers would be well spent in such a venture. If cavalry is not to be used in pursuing a retiring enemy encumbered with much baggage, then its day is indeed past.

The relief of Ladysmith stirred the people of the Empire as nothing, save perhaps the subsequent relief of Mafeking, has done during our generation. Even sober unemotional London found its soul for once and fluttered with joy. Men, women, and children, rich and poor, clubman and cabman, joined in the universal delight. The thought of our garrison, of their privations, of our impotence to relieve them, of the impending humiliation to them and to us, had lain dark for many months across our spirits. It had weighed upon us, until the subject, though ever present in our thoughts, was too painful for general talk. And now, in an instant, the shadow was lifted. The outburst of rejoicing was not a triumph over the gallant Boers. But it was our own escape from humiliation, the knowledge that the blood of our sons had not been shed in vain, above all the conviction that the darkest hour had now passed and that the light of peace was dimly breaking far away—that was why London rang with joy bells that March morning, and why those bells echoed back from every town and hamlet, in tropical sun and in Arctic snow, over which the flag of Britain waved.

Chapter 18

The Siege and Relief of Kimberley

It has already been narrated how, upon the arrival of the army corps from England, the greater part was drafted to Natal, while some went to the western side, and started under Lord Methuen upon the perilous enterprise of the relief of Kimberley. It has also been shown how, after three expensive victories, Lord Methuen's force met with a paralysing reverse, and was compelled to remain inactive within twenty miles of the town which they had come to succour. Before I describe how that succour did eventually arrive, some attention must be paid to the incidents which had occurred within the city.

> I am directed to assure you that there is no reason for apprehending that Kimberley or any part of the colony either is, or in any contemplated event will be, in danger of attack. Mr. Schreiner is of opinion that your fears are groundless and your anticipations in the matter entirely without foundation.

Such is the official reply to the remonstrance of the inhabitants, when, with the shadow of war dark upon them, they appealed for help. It is fortunate, however, that a progressive British town has usually the capacity for doing things for itself without the intervention of officials. Kimberley was particularly lucky in being the centre of the wealthy and alert De Beers Company, which had laid in sufficient ammunition and supplies to prevent the town from being helpless in the presence of the enemy. But the cannon were popguns, firing a 7-pound shell for a short range, and the garrison contained only seven hundred regulars, while the remainder were mostly untrained miners and artisans. Among them, however, there was a sprinkling of dangerous men from the northern wars, and all were nerved by a knowledge that the ground which they defended was essential to the Empire. Ladysmith was no more than any other strategic position, but Kimberley was unique, the centre of the richest tract of ground for its size in the whole world. Its loss would have been a heavy blow to the British cause, and an enormous encouragement to the Boers.

On October 12th, several hours after the expiration of Kruger's ultimatum, Cecil Rhodes threw himself into Kimberley. This remarkable man, who stood for the future of South Africa as clearly as the Dopper Boer stood for its past, had, both in features and in character, some traits which may, without extravagance, be called Napoleonic. The restless energy, the fertility of resource, the attention to detail, the wide sweep of mind, the power of terse comment—all these recall the great emperor. So did the simplicity of private life in the midst of excessive wealth. And so finally did a want of scruple where an ambition was to be furthered, shown, for example, in that enormous donation to the Irish party by which he made a bid for their parliamentary support, and in the story of the Jameson raid. A certain cynicism of mind and a grim humour complete the parallel. But Rhodes was a Napoleon of peace. The consolidation of South Africa under the freest and most progressive form of government was the large object on which he had expended his energies and his fortune but the development of the country in every conceivable respect, from the building of a railway to the importation of a pedigree bull, engaged his unremitting attention.

It was on October 15th that the fifty thousand inhabitants of Kimberley first heard the voice of war. It rose and fell in a succession of horrible screams and groans which travelled far over the *veldt*, and the outlying farmers marvelled at the dreadful clamour from the sirens and the hooters of the great mines. Those who have endured all—the rifle, the cannon, and the hunger—have said that those wild whoops from the sirens were what had tried their nerve the most.

The Boers in scattered bands of horsemen were thick around the town, and had blocked the railroad. They raided cattle upon the outskirts, but made no attempt to rush the defence. The garrison, who, civilian and military, approached four thousand in number, lay close in rifle pit and redoubt waiting for an attack which never came. The perimeter to be defended was about eight miles, but the heaps of tailings made admirable fortifications, and the town had none of those inconvenient heights around it which had been such bad neighbours to Ladysmith. Picturesque surroundings are not favourable to defence.

On October 24th the garrison, finding that no attack was made, determined upon a reconnaissance. The mounted force, upon which most of the work and of the loss fell, consisted of the Diamond Fields Horse, a small number of Cape Police, a company of Mounted Infantry, and a body called the Kimberley Light Horse. With two hundred and seventy volunteers from this force Major Scott-Turner, a redoubtable fighter, felt his way to the north until he came in touch with the Boers. The latter, who were much superior in numbers, manoeuvred to cut him off, but the arrival of two companies of the North Lancashire Regiment turned the scale in our favour. We lost three killed and twenty-one wounded in the skirmish. The Boer loss is unknown, but their commander Botha was slain.

On November 4th Commandant Wessels formally summoned the town, and it is asserted that he gave Colonel Kekewich leave to send out the women and children. That officer has been blamed for not taking advantage of the permission—or at the least for not communicating it to the civil authorities. As a matter of fact the charge rests upon a misapprehension. In Wessels' letter a distinction is made between Africander and English women, the former being offered an asylum in his camp. This offer was made known, and half a dozen persons took advantage of it. The suggestion, however, in the case of the English carried with it no promise that they would be conveyed to Orange River, and a compliance with it would have put them as helpless hostages into the hands of the enemy. As to not publishing the message it is not usual to publish such official documents, but the offer was shown to Mr. Rhodes, who concurred in the impossibility of accepting it.

It is difficult to allude to this subject without touching upon the painful but notorious fact that there existed during the siege considerable friction between the military authorities and a section of the civilians, of whom Mr. Rhodes was chief. Among other characteristics Rhodes bore any form of restraint very badly, and chafed mightily when unable to do a thing in the exact way which he considered best. He may have been a Napoleon of peace, but his warmest friends could never describe him as a Napoleon of war, for his military forecasts have been erroneous, and the management of the Jameson fiasco certainly inspired no confidence in the judgment of any one concerned. That his intentions were of the best, and that he had the good of the Empire at heart, may be freely granted; but that these motives should lead him to cabal against, and even to threaten, the military governor, or that he should attempt to force Lord Roberts's hand in a military operation, was most deplorable. Every credit may be given to him for all his aid to the military—he gave with a good grace what the garrison would otherwise have had to commandeer—but it is a fact that the town would have been more united, and therefore stronger, without his presence. Colonel Kekewich and his chief staff officer, Major O'Meara, were as much plagued by intrigue within as by the Boers without.

On November 7th the bombardment of the town commenced from nine 9-pounder guns to which the artillery of the garrison could give no adequate reply. The result, however, of a fortnight's fire, during which seven hundred shells were discharged, was the loss of two non-combatants. The question of food was recognised as being of more importance than the enemy's fire. An early relief appeared probable, however, as the advance of Methuen's force was already known. One pound of bread, two ounces of sugar, and half a pound of meat were allowed per head. It was only on the small children that the scarcity of milk told with tragic effect. At Ladysmith, at Mafeking, and at Kimberley hundreds of these innocents were sacrificed.

November 25th was a red-letter day with the garrison, who made a sortie under the impression that Methuen was not far off, and that they were assisting his operations. The attack was made upon one of the Boer positions by a force consisting of a detachment of the Light Horse and of the Cape Police, and their work was brilliantly successful. The actual storming of the redoubt was carried out by some forty men, of whom but four were killed. They brought back thirty-three prisoners as a proof of their victory, but the Boer gun, as usual, escaped us. In this brilliant affair Scott-Turner was wounded, which did not prevent him, only three days later, from leading another sortie, which was as disastrous as the first had been successful. Save under very exceptional circumstances it is in modern warfare long odds always upon the defence, and the garrison would probably have been better advised had they refrained from attacking the fortifications of their enemy—a truth which Baden-Powell learned also at Game Tree Hill. As it was, after a temporary success the British were blown back by the fierce Mauser fire, and lost the indomitable Scott-Turner, with twenty-one of his brave companions killed and twenty-eight wounded, all belonging to the colonial corps. The Empire may reflect with pride that the people in whose cause mainly they fought showed themselves by their gallantry and their devotion worthy of any sacrifice which has been made.

Again the siege settled down to a monotonous record of decreasing rations and of expectation. On December 10 there came a sign of hope from the outside world. Far on the southern horizon a little golden speck shimmered against the blue African sky. It was Methuen's balloon gleaming in the sunshine. Next morning the low grumble of distant cannon was the sweetest of music to the listening citizens. But days passed without further news, and it was not for more than a week that they learned of the bloody repulse of Magersfontein, and that help was once more indefinitely postponed. Heliographic communication had been opened with the relieving army, and it is on record that the first message flashed through from the south was a question about the number of a horse. With inconceivable stupidity this has been cited as an example of military levity and incapacity. Of course the object of the question was a test as to whether they were really in communication with the garrison. It must be confessed that the town seems to have contained some very querulous and unreasonable people.

The New Year found the beleaguered city reduced to a quarter of a pound of meat per head, while the health of the inhabitants began to break down under their confinement. Their interest, however, was keenly aroused by the attempt made in the De Beers workshops to build a gun which might reach their opponents. This remarkable piece of ordnance, constructed by an American named Labram by the help of tools manufactured for the purpose and of books found in the town, took the shape eventually of a 28 lb. rifled gun, which proved to be a most efficient piece of artillery. With grim humour, Mr. Rhodes's compliments had been inscribed upon the shells—a fair retort in view of the openly expressed threat of the enemy that in case of his capture they would carry him in a cage to Pretoria.

The Boers, though held off for a time by this unexpected piece of ordnance, prepared a terrible answer to it. On February 7th an enormous gun, throwing a 96 lb. shell, opened from Kamfersdam, which is four miles from the centre of the town. The shells, following the evil precedent of the Germans in 1870, were fired not at the forts, but into the thickly populated city. Day and night these huge missiles exploded, shattering the houses and occasionally killing or maiming the occupants. Some thousands of the women and children were conveyed down the mines, where, in the electric-lighted tunnels, they lay in comfort and safety. One surprising revenge the Boers had, for by an extraordinary chance one of the few men killed by their gun was the ingenious Labram who had constructed the 28-pounder. By an even more singular chance, Leon, who was responsible for bringing the big Boer gun, was struck immediately afterwards by a long-range rifle-shot from the garrison.

The historian must be content to give a tame account of the siege of Kimberley, for the thing itself was tame. Indeed 'siege' is a misnomer, for it was rather an investment or a blockade. Such as it was, however, the inhabitants became very restless under it, and though there were never any prospects of surrender the utmost impatience began to be manifested at the protracted delay on the part of the relief force. It was not till later that it was understood how cunningly Kimberley had been used as a bait to hold the enemy until final preparations had been made for his destruction.

And at last the great day came. It is on record how dramatic was the meeting between the mounted outposts of the defenders and the advance guard of the relievers, whose advent seems to have been equally unexpected by friend and foe. A skirmish was in progress on February 15th between a party of the Kimberley Light Horse and of the Boers, when a new body of horsemen, unrecognised by either side, appeared upon the plain and opened fire upon the enemy. One of the strangers rode up to the patrol. 'What the dickens does K.L.H. mean on your shoulder-strap?' he asked. 'It means Kimberley Light Horse. Who are you?' 'I am one of the New Zealanders.' Macaulay in his wildest dream of the future of the much-quoted New Zealander never pictured him as heading a rescue force for the relief of a British town in the heart of Africa.

The population had assembled to watch the mighty cloud of dust which rolled along the south-eastern horizon. What was it which swept westwards within its reddish heart? Hopeful and yet fearful they saw the huge bank draw nearer and nearer. An assault from the whole of Cronje's army was the thought which passed through many a mind. And then the dust-cloud thinned, a mighty host of horsemen spurred out from it, and in the extended far-flung ranks the glint of spearheads and the gleam of scabbards told of the Hussars and Lancers, while denser banks on either flank marked the position of the whirling guns. Wearied and spent with a hundred miles' ride the dusty riders and the panting, dripping horses took fresh heart as they saw the broad city before them, and swept with martial rattle and jingle towards the cheering crowds. Amid shouts and tears French rode into Kimberley while his troopers encamped outside the town.

To know how this bolt was prepared and how launched, the narrative must go back to the beginning of the month. At that period Methuen and his men were still faced by Cronje and his entrenched forces, who, in spite of occasional bombardments, held their position between Kimberley and the relieving army. French, having handed over the operations at Colesberg to Clements, had gone down to Cape Town to confer with Roberts and Kitchener. Thence they all three made their way to the Modder River, which was evidently about to be the base of a more largely conceived series of operations than any which had yet been undertaken.

In order to draw the Boer attention away from the thunderbolt which was about to fall upon their left flank, a strong demonstration ending in a brisk action was made early in February upon the extreme right of Cronje's position. The force, consisting of the Highland Brigade, two squadrons of the 9th Lancers, No. 7 Co. Royal Engineers, and the 62nd Battery, was under the command of the famous Hector Macdonald. 'Fighting Mac' as he was called by his men, had joined his regiment as a private, and had worked through the grades of corporal, sergeant, captain, major, and colonel, until now, still in the prime of his manhood, he found himself riding at the head of a brigade. A bony, craggy Scotsman, with a square fighting head and a bulldog jaw, he had conquered the exclusiveness and routine of the British service by the same dogged qualities which made him formidable to Dervish and to Boer. With a cool brain, a steady nerve, and a proud heart, he is an ideal leader of infantry, and those who saw him manoeuvre his brigade in the crisis of the battle of Omdurman speak of it as the one great memory which they carried back from the engagement. On the field of battle he turns to the speech of his childhood, the jagged, rasping, homely words which brace the nerves of the northern soldier. This was the man who had come from India to take the place of poor Wauchope, and to put fresh heart into the gallant but sorely stricken brigade.

The four regiments which composed the infantry of the force—the Black Watch, the Argyll and Sutherlands, the Seaforths, and the Highland Light Infantry—left Lord Methuen's camp on Saturday, February 3rd, and halted at Fraser's Drift, passing on next day to Koodoosberg. The day was very hot, and the going very heavy, and many men fell out, some never to return. The drift (or ford) was found, however, to be undefended, and was seized by Macdonald, who, after pitching camp on the south side of the river, sent out strong parties across the drift to seize and entrench the Koodoosberg and some adjacent *kopjes* which, lying some three-quarters of a mile to the north-west of the drift formed the key of the position. A few Boer scouts were seen hurrying with the news of his coming to the head *laager*.

The effect of these messages was evident by Tuesday (February 6th), when the Boers were seen to be assembling upon the north bank. By next morning they were there in considerable numbers, and began an attack upon a crest held by the Seaforths. Macdonald threw two companies of the Black Watch and two of the Highland Light Infantry into the fight. The Boers made excellent practice with a 7-pounder mountain gun, and their rifle fire, considering the good cover which our men had, was very deadly. Poor Tait, of the Black Watch, good sportsman and gallant soldier, with one wound hardly healed upon his person, was hit again. 'They've got me this time,' were his dying words. Blair, of the Seaforths, had his carotid cut by a shrapnel bullet, and lay for hours while the men of his company took turns to squeeze the artery. But our artillery silenced the Boer gun, and our infantry easily held their riflemen. Babington with the cavalry brigade arrived from the camp about 1.30, moving along the north bank of the river. In spite of the fact that men and horses were weary from a tiring march, it was hoped by Macdonald's force that they would work round the Boers and make an attempt to capture either them or their gun. But the horsemen seem not to have realised the position of the parties, or that possibility of bringing off a considerable coup, so the action came to a tame conclusion, the Boers retiring unpursued from their attack. On Thursday, February 8th, they were found to have withdrawn, and on the same evening our own force was recalled, to the surprise and disappointment of the public at home, who had not realised that in directing their attention to their right flank the column had already produced the effect upon the enemy for which they had been sent. They could not be left there, as they were needed for those great operations which were pending. It was on the 9th that the brigade returned; on the 10th they were congratulated by Lord Roberts in person; and on the 11th those new dispositions were made which were destined not only to relieve Kimberley, but to inflict a blow upon the Boer cause from which it was never able to recover.

Small, brown, and wrinkled, with puckered eyes and alert manner, Lord Roberts in spite of his sixty-seven years preserves the figure and energy of youth. The active open-air life of India keeps men fit for the saddle when in England they would only sit their club armchairs, and it is hard for any one who sees the wiry figure and brisk step of Lord Roberts to realise that he has spent forty-one years of soldiering in what used to be regarded as an unhealthy climate. He had carried into late life the habit of martial exercise, and a Russian traveller has left it on record that the sight which surprised him most in India was to see the veteran commander of the army ride forth with his spear and carry off the peg with the skill of a practised trooper. In his early youth he had shown in the Mutiny that he possessed the fighting energy of the soldier to a remarkable degree, but it was only in the Afghan War of 1880 that he had an opportunity of proving that he had rarer and more valuable gifts, the power of swift resolution and determined execution. At the crisis of the war he and his army disappeared entirely from the public ken only to emerge dramatically as victors at a point three hundred miles distant from where they had vanished.

It is not only as a soldier, but as a man, that Lord Roberts possesses some remarkable characteristics. He has in a supreme degree that magnetic quality which draws not merely the respect but the love of those who know him. In Chaucer's phrase, he is a very perfect gentle knight. Soldiers and regimental officers have for him a feeling of personal affection such as the unemotional British Army has never had for any leader in the course of our history. His chivalrous courtesy, his unerring tact, his kindly nature, his unselfish and untiring devotion to their interests have all endeared him to those rough loyal natures, who would follow him with as much confidence and devotion as the *grognards* of the Guard had in the case of the Great Emperor. There were some who feared that in Roberts's case, as in so many more, the *donga* and *kopje* of South Africa might form the grave and headstone of a military reputation, but far from this being so he consistently showed a wide sweep of strategy and a power of conceiving the effect of scattered movements over a great extent of country which have surprised his warmest admirers. In the second week of February his dispositions were ready, and there followed the swift series of blows which brought the Boers upon their knees. Of these we shall only describe here the exploits of the fine force of cavalry which, after a ride of a hundred miles, broke out of the heart of that reddish dust cloud and swept the Boer besiegers away from hard-pressed Kimberley.

In order to strike unexpectedly, Lord Roberts had not only made a strong demonstration at Koodoosdrift, at the other end of the Boer line, but he had withdrawn his main force some forty miles south, taking them down by rail to Belmont and Enslin with such secrecy that even commanding officers had no idea whither the troops were going. The cavalry which had come from French's command at Colesberg had already reached the rendezvous, travelling by road to Naauwpoort, and thence by train. This force consisted of the Carabineers, New South Wales Lancers, Inniskillings, composite regiment of Household Cavalry, 10th Hussars, with some mounted infantry and two batteries of Horse Artillery, making a force of nearly three thousand sabres. To this were added the 9th and 12th Lancers from Modder River, the 16th Lancers from India, the Scots Greys, which had been patrolling Orange River from the beginning of the war, Rimington's Scouts, and two brigades of mounted infantry under Colonels Ridley and Hannay. The force under this latter officer had a severe skirmish on its way to the rendezvous and lost fifty or sixty in killed, wounded, and missing. Five other batteries of Horse Artillery were added to the force, making seven in all, with a pontoon section of Royal Engineers. The total number of men was about five thousand. By the night of Sunday, February 11th, this formidable force had concentrated at Ramdam, twenty miles north-east of Belmont, and was ready to advance. At two in the morning of Monday, February 12th, the start was made, and the long sinuous line of night-riders moved off over the shadowy *veldt*, the beat of twenty thousand hoofs, the clank of steel, and the rumble of gun wheels and *tumbrels* swelling into a deep low roar like the surge upon the shingle.

Two rivers, the Riet and the Modder, intervened between French and Kimberley. By daylight on the 12th the head of his force had reached Waterval Drift, which was found to be defended by a body of Boers with a gun. Leaving a small detachment to hold them, French passed his men over Dekiel's Drift, higher up the stream, and swept the enemy out of his position. This considerable force of Boers had come from Jacobsdal, and were just too late to get into position to resist the crossing. Had we been ten minutes later, the matter would have been much more serious.

At the cost of a very small loss he held both sides of the ford, but it was not until midnight that the whole long column was brought across, and bivouacked upon the northern bank. In the morning the strength of the force was enormously increased by the arrival of one more horseman. It was Roberts himself, who had ridden over to give the men a send-off, and the sight of his wiry erect figure and mahogany face sent them full of fire and confidence upon their way.

But the march of this second day (February 13th) was a military operation of some difficulty. Thirty long waterless miles had to be done before they could reach the Modder, and it was possible that even then they might have to fight an action before winning the drift. The weather was very hot, and through the long day the sun beat down from an unclouded sky, while the soldiers were only shaded by the dust-bank in which they rode. A broad arid plain, swelling into stony hills, surrounded them on every side. Here and there in the extreme distance, mounted figures moved over the vast expanse—Boer scouts who marked in amazement the advance of this great array. Once or twice these men gathered together, and a sputter of rifle fire broke out upon our left flank, but the great tide swept on and carried them with it. Often in this desolate land the herds of mottled springbok and of grey rekbok could be seen sweeping over the plain, or stopping with that curiosity upon which the hunter trades, to stare at the unwonted spectacle.

So all day they rode, hussars, dragoons, and lancers, over the withered *veldt*, until men and horses drooped with the heat and the exertion. A front of nearly two miles was kept, the regiments moving two abreast in open order; and the sight of this magnificent cloud of horsemen sweeping over the great barren plain was a glorious one. The *veldt* had caught fire upon the right, and a black cloud of smoke with a lurid heart to it covered the flank. The beat of the sun from above and the swelter of dust from below were overpowering. Gun horses fell in the traces and died of pure exhaustion. The men, parched and silent, but cheerful, strained their eyes to pierce the continual mirage which played over the horizon, and to catch the first glimpse of the Modder. At last, as the sun began to slope down to the west, a thin line of green was discerned, the bushes which skirt the banks of that ill-favoured stream. With renewed heart the cavalry pushed on and made for the drift, while Major Rimington, to whom the onerous duty of guiding the force had been entrusted, gave a sigh of relief as he saw that he had indeed struck the very point at which he had aimed.

The essential thing in the movements had been speed—to reach each point before the enemy could concentrate to oppose them. Upon this it depended whether they would find five hundred or five thousand waiting on the further bank. It must have been with anxious eyes that French watched his first regiment ride down to Klip Drift. If the Boers should have had notice of his coming and have transferred some of their 40-pounders, he might lose heavily before he forced the stream. But this time, at last, he had completely outmanoeuvred them. He came with the news of his coming, and Broadwood with the 12th Lancers rushed the drift. The small Boer force saved itself by flight, and the camp, the wagons, and the supplies remained with the victors. On the night of the 13th he had secured the passage of the Modder, and up to the early morning the horses and the guns were splashing through its coffee-coloured waters.

French's force had now come level to the main position of the Boers, but had struck it upon the extreme left wing. The extreme right wing, thanks to the Koodoosdrift demonstration, was fifty miles off, and this line was naturally very thinly held, save only at the central position of Magersfontein. Cronje could not denude this central position, for he saw Methuen still waiting in front of him, and in any case Klip Drift is twenty-five miles from Magersfontein. But the Boer left wing, though scattered, gathered into some sort of cohesion on Wednesday (February 14th), and made an effort to check the victorious progress of the cavalry. It was necessary on this day to rest at Klip Drift, until Kelly-Kenny should come up with the infantry to hold what had been gained. All day the small bodies of Boers came riding in and taking up positions between the column and its objective.

Next morning the advance was resumed, the column being still forty miles from Kimberley with the enemy in unknown force between. Some four miles out French came upon their position, two hills with a long low *nek* between, from which came a brisk rifle fire supported by artillery. But French was not only not to be stopped, but could not even be retarded. Disregarding the Boer fire completely the cavalry swept in wave after wave over the low *nek*, and so round the base of the hills. The Boer riflemen upon the *kopjes* must have seen a magnificent military spectacle as regiment after regiment, the 9th Lancers leading, all in very open order, swept across the plain at a gallop, and so passed over the *nek*. A few score horses and half as many men were left behind them, but forty or fifty Boers were cut down in the pursuit. It appears to have been one of the very few occasions during the campaign when that obsolete and absurd weapon the sword was anything but a dead weight to its bearer.

And now the force had a straight run in before it, for it had outpaced any further force of Boers which may have been advancing from the direction of Magersfontein. The horses, which had come a hundred miles in four days with insufficient food and water, were so done that it was no uncommon sight to see the trooper not only walking to ease his horse, but carrying part of his monstrous weight of saddle gear. But in spite of fatigue the force pressed on until in the afternoon a distant view was seen, across the reddish plain, of the brick houses and corrugated roofs of Kimberley. The Boer besiegers cleared off in front of it, and that night (February 15th) the relieving column camped on the plain two miles away, while French and his staff rode in to the rescued city.

The war was a cruel one for the cavalry, who were handicapped throughout by the nature of the country and by the tactics of the enemy. They are certainly the branch of the service which had least opportunity for distinction. The work of scouting and patrolling is the most dangerous which a soldier can undertake, and yet from its very nature it can find no chronicler. The war correspondent, like Providence, is always with the big battalions, and there never was a campaign in which there was more unrecorded heroism, the heroism of the picket and of the vedette which finds its way into no newspaper paragraph. But in the larger operations of the war it is difficult to say that cavalry, as cavalry, have justified their existence. In the opinion of many the tendency of the future will be to convert the whole force into mounted infantry. How little is required to turn our troopers into excellent foot soldiers was shown at Magersfontein, where the 12th Lancers, dismounted by the command of their colonel, Lord Airlie, held back the threatened flank attack all the morning. A little training in taking cover, leggings instead of boots, and a rifle instead of a carbine would give us a formidable force of twenty thousand men who could do all that our cavalry does, and a great deal more besides. It is undoubtedly possible on many occasions in this war, at Colesberg, at Diamond Hill, to say 'Here our cavalry did well.' They are brave men on good horses, and they may be expected to do well. But the champion of the cavalry cause must point out the occasions where the cavalry did something which could not have been done by the same number of equally brave and equally well-mounted infantry. Only then will the existence of the cavalry be justified. The lesson both of the South African and of the American civil war is that the light horseman who is trained to fight on foot is the type of the future.

A few more words as a sequel to this short sketch of the siege and relief of Kimberley. Considerable surprise has been expressed that the great gun at Kamfersdam, a piece which must have weighed many tons and could not have been moved by bullock teams at a rate of more than two or three miles an hour, should have eluded our cavalry. It is indeed a surprising circumstance, and yet it was due to no inertia on the part of our leaders, but rather to one of the finest examples of Boer tenacity in the whole course of the war. The instant that Kekewich was sure of relief he mustered every available man and sent him out to endeavour to get the gun. It had already been removed, and its retreat was covered by the strong position of Dronfield, which was held both by riflemen and by light artillery. Finding himself unable to force it, Murray, the commander of the detachment, remained in front of it. Next morning (Friday) at three o'clock the weary men and horses of two of French's brigades were afoot with the same object. But still the Boers were obstinately holding on to Dronfield, and still their position was too strong to force, and too extended to get round with exhausted horses. It was not until the night after that the Boers abandoned their excellent rearguard action, leaving one light gun in the hands of the Cape Police, but having gained such a start for their heavy one that French, who had other and more important objects in view, could not attempt to follow it.

CHAPTER 19

Paardeberg

Lord Roberts's operations, prepared with admirable secrecy and carried out with extreme energy, aimed at two different results, each of which he was fortunate enough to attain. The first was that an overpowering force of cavalry should ride round the Boer position and raise the siege of Kimberley: the fate of this expedition has already been described. The second was that the infantry, following hard on the heels of the cavalry, and holding all that they had gained, should establish itself upon Cronje's left flank and cut his connection with Bloemfontein. It is this portion of the operations which has now to be described. The infantry force which General Roberts had assembled was a very formidable one. The Guards he had left under Methuen in front of the lines of Magersfontein to contain the Boer force. With them he had also left those regiments which had fought in the 9th Brigade in all Methuen's actions. These, as will be remembered, were the 1st Northumberland Fusiliers, the 2nd Yorkshire Light Infantry, the 2nd Northamptons, and one wing of the Loyal North Lancashire Regiment. These stayed to hold Cronje in his position.

There remained three divisions of infantry, one of which, the ninth, was made up on the spot. These were constituted in this way:

Sixth Division (Kelly-Kenny)

12th Brigade (Knox)
  Oxford Light Infantry
  Gloucesters (2nd)
  West Riding
  Buffs

18th Brigade (Stephenson)
  Essex
  Welsh
  Warwicks
  Yorks

Seventh Division (Tucker)

14th Brigade (Chermside)
> Scots Borderers
> Lincolns
> Hampshires
> Norfolks

15th Brigade (Wavell)
> North Staffords
> Cheshires
> S Wales Borderers
> East Lancashires

Ninth Division (Colvile)

Highland Brigade (Macdonald)
> Black Watch
> Argyll and Sutherlands
> Seaforths
> Highland Light Infantry

19th Brigade (Smith-Dorrien)
> Gordons
> Canadians
> Shropshire Light Infantry
> Cornwall Light Infantry

With these were two brigade divisions of artillery under General Marshall, the first containing the 18th, 62nd, and 75th batteries (Colonel Hall), the other the 76th, 81st, and 82nd (Colonel McDonnell). Besides these there were a howitzer battery, a naval contingent of four 4.7 guns and four 12-pounders under Captain Bearcroft of the 'Philomel.' The force was soon increased by the transfer of the Guards and the arrival of more artillery; but the numbers which started on Monday, February 12th, amounted roughly to twenty-five thousand foot and eight thousand horse with 98 guns—a considerable army to handle in a foodless and almost waterless country. Seven hundred wagons drawn by eleven thousand mules and oxen, all collected by the genius for preparation and organisation which characterises Lord Kitchener, groaned and creaked behind the columns.

Both arms had concentrated at Ramdam, the cavalry going down by road, and the infantry by rail as far as Belmont or Enslin. On Monday, February 12th, the cavalry had started, and on Tuesday the infantry were pressing hard after them. The first thing was to secure a position upon

Cronje's flank, and for that purpose the 6th Division and the 9th (Kelly-Kenny's and Colvile's) pushed swiftly on and arrived on Thursday, February 15th, at Klip Drift on the Modder, which had only been left by the cavalry that same morning. It was obviously impossible to leave Jacobsdal in the hands of the enemy on our left flank, so the 7th Division (Tucker's) turned aside to attack the town. Wavell's brigade carried the place after a sharp skirmish, chiefly remarkable for the fact that the City Imperial Volunteers found themselves under fire for the first time and bore themselves with the gallantry of the old train-bands whose descendants they are. Our loss was two killed and twenty wounded, and we found ourselves for the first time firmly established in one of the enemy's towns. In the excellent German hospital were thirty or forty of our wounded.

On the afternoon of Thursday, February 15th, our cavalry, having left Klip Drift in the morning, were pushing hard for Kimberley. At Klip Drift was Kelly-Kenny's 6th Division. South of Klip Drift at Wegdraai was Colvile's 9th Division, while the 7th Division was approaching Jacobsdal. Altogether the British forces were extended over a line of forty miles. The same evening saw the relief of Kimberley and the taking of Jacobsdal, but it also saw the capture of one of our convoys by the Boers, a dashing exploit which struck us upon what was undoubtedly our vulnerable point.

It has never been cleared up whence the force of Boers came which appeared upon our rear on that occasion. It seems to have been the same body which had already had a skirmish with Hannay's Mounted Infantry as they went up from Orange River to join the rendezvous at Ramdam. The balance of evidence is that they had not come from Colesberg or any distant point, but that they were a force under the command of Piet De Wet, the younger of two famous brothers. Descending to Waterval Drift, the ford over the Riet, they occupied a line of *kopjes*, which ought, one would have imagined, to have been carefully guarded by us, and opened a brisk fire from rifles and guns upon the convoy as it ascended the northern bank of the river. Numbers of bullocks were soon shot down, and the removal of the hundred and eighty wagons made impossible. The convoy, which contained forage and provisions, had no guard of its own, but the drift was held by Colonel Ridley with one company of Gordons and one hundred and fifty mounted infantry without artillery, which certainly seems an inadequate force to secure the most vital and vulnerable spot in the line of communications of an army of forty thousand men. The Boers numbered at the first some five or six hundred men, but their position was such that they could not be attacked. On the other hand they were not strong enough to leave their shelter in order to drive in the British guard, who, lying in extended order between the wagons and the assailants, were keeping up a steady and effective fire. Captain Head, of the

East Lancashire Regiment, a fine natural soldier, commanded the British firing line, and neither he nor any of his men doubted that they could hold off the enemy for an indefinite time. In the course of the afternoon reinforcements arrived for the Boers, but Kitchener's Horse and a field battery came back and restored the balance of power. In the evening the latter swayed altogether in favour of the British, as Tucker appeared upon the scene with the whole of the 14th Brigade; but as the question of an assault was being debated a positive order arrived from Lord Roberts that the convoy should be abandoned and the force return.

If Lord Roberts needed justification for this decision, the future course of events will furnish it. One of Napoleon's maxims in war was to concentrate all one's energies upon one thing at one time. Roberts's aim was to outflank and possibly to capture Cronje's army. If he allowed a brigade to be involved in a rearguard action, his whole swift-moving plan of campaign might be dislocated. It was very annoying to lose a hundred and eighty wagons, but it only meant a temporary inconvenience. The plan of campaign was the essential thing. Therefore he sacrificed his convoy and hurried his troops upon their original mission. It was with heavy hearts and bitter words that those who had fought so long abandoned their charge, but now at least there are probably few of them who do not agree in the wisdom of the sacrifice. Our loss in this affair was between fifty and sixty killed and wounded. The Boers were unable to get rid of the stores, and they were eventually distributed among the local farmers and recovered again as the British forces flowed over the country. Another small disaster occurred to us on the preceding day in the loss of fifty men of E company of Kitchener's Horse, which had been left as a guard to a well in the desert.

But great events were coming to obscure those small checks which are incidental to a war carried out over immense distances against a mobile and enterprising enemy. Cronje had suddenly become aware of the net which was closing round him. To the dark fierce man who had striven so hard to make his line of *kopjes* impregnable it must have been a bitter thing to abandon his trenches and his rifle pits. But he was crafty as well as tenacious, and he had the Boer horror of being cut off—an hereditary instinct from fathers who had fought on horseback against enemies on foot. If at any time during the last ten weeks Methuen had contained him in front with a thin line of riflemen with machine guns, and had thrown the rest of his force on Jacobsdal and the east, he would probably have attained the same result. Now at the rumour of English upon his flank Cronje instantly abandoned his position and his plans, in order to restore those communications with Bloemfontein upon which he depended for his supplies. With furious speed he drew in his right wing, and then, one huge mass of horsemen, guns, and wagons, he swept through the gap between the rear of the British cavalry bound for Kimberley and the head of the British infantry at Klip Drift. There was just room to pass, and at it he dashed with the furious energy of a wild beast rushing from a trap. A portion of his force with his heavy guns had gone north round Kimberley to Warrenton; many of the Freestaters also had slipped away and returned to their farms. The remainder, numbering about six thousand men, the majority of whom were Transvaalers, swept through between the British forces.

This movement was carried out on the night of February 15th, and had it been a little quicker it might have been concluded before we were aware of it. But the lumbering wagons impeded it, and on the Friday morning, February 16th, a huge rolling cloud of dust on the northern *veldt*, moving from west to east, told our outposts at Klip Drift that Cronje's army had almost slipped through our fingers. Lord Kitchener, who was in command at Klip Drift at the moment, instantly unleashed his mounted infantry in direct pursuit, while Knox's brigade sped along the northern bank of the river to cling on to the right haunch of the retreating column. Cronje's men had made a night march of thirty miles from Magersfontein, and the wagon bullocks were exhausted. It was impossible, without an absolute abandonment of his guns and stores, for him to get away from his pursuers.

This was no deer which they were chasing, however, but rather a grim old Transvaal wolf, with his teeth flashing ever over his shoulder. The sight of those distant white-tilted wagons fired the blood of every mounted infantryman, and sent the Oxfords, the Buffs, the West Ridings, and the Gloucesters racing along the river bank in the glorious virile air of an African morning. But there were *kopjes* ahead, sown with fierce Dopper Boers, and those tempting wagons were only to be reached over their bodies. The broad plain across which the English were hurrying was suddenly swept with a storm of bullets. The long infantry line extended yet further and lapped round the flank of the Boer position, and once more the terrible duet of the Mauser and the Lee-Metford was sung while the 81st field battery hurried up in time to add its deep roar to their higher chorus. With fine judgment Cronje held on to the last moment of safety, and then with a swift movement to the rear seized a further line two miles off, and again snapped back at his eager pursuers. All day the grim and weary rearguard stalled off the fiery advance of the infantry, and at nightfall the wagons were still untaken. The pursuing force to the north of the river was, it must be remembered, numerically inferior to the pursued, so that in simply retarding the advance of the enemy and in giving other British troops time to come up, Knox's brigade was doing splendid work. Had Cronje been well advised or well informed, he would have left his guns and wagons in the hope that by a swift dash over the Modder he might still bring his army away in safety. He seems to have underrated both the British numbers and the British activity.

On the night then of Friday, February 16th, Cronje lay upon the northern bank of the Modder, with his stores and guns still intact, and no enemy in front of him, though Knox's brigade and Hannay's Mounted Infantry were behind. It was necessary for Cronje to cross the river in order to be on the line for Bloemfontein. As the river tended to the north the sooner he could cross the better. On the south side of the river, however, were considerable British forces, and the obvious strategy was to hurry them forward and to block every drift at which he could get over. The river runs between very deep banks, so steep that one might almost describe them as small cliffs, and there was no chance of a horseman, far less a wagon, crossing at any point save those where the convenience of traffic and the use of years had worn sloping paths down to the shallows. The British knew exactly therefore what the places were which had to be blocked. On the use made of the next few hours the success or failure of the whole operation must depend.

The nearest drift to Cronje was only a mile or two distant, Klipkraal the name; next to that the Paardeberg Drift; next to that the Wolveskraal Drift, each about seven miles from the other. Had Cronje pushed on instantly after the action, he might have got across at Klipkraal. But men, horses, and bullocks were equally exhausted after a long twenty-four hours' marching and fighting. He gave his weary soldiers some hours' rest, and then, abandoning seventy-eight of his wagons, he pushed on before daylight for the farthest off of the three fords (Wolveskraal Drift). Could he reach and cross it before his enemies, he was safe. The Klipkraal Drift had in the meanwhile been secured by the Buffs, the West Ridings, and the Oxfordshire Light Infantry after a spirited little action which, in the rapid rush of events, attracted less attention than it deserved. The brunt of the fighting fell upon the Oxfords, who lost ten killed and thirty-nine wounded. It was not a waste of life, however, for the action, though small and hardly recorded, was really a very essential one in the campaign.

But Lord Roberts's energy had infused itself into his divisional commanders, his brigadiers, his colonels, and so down to the humblest Tommy who tramped and stumbled through the darkness with a devout faith that 'Bobs' was going to catch 'old Cronje' this time. The mounted infantry had galloped round from the north to the south of the river, crossing at Klip Drift and securing the southern end of Klipkraal. Thither also came Stephenson's brigade from Kelly-Kenny's Division, while Knox, finding in the morning that Cronje was gone, marched along the northern bank to the same spot. As Klipkraal was safe, the mounted infantry pushed on at once and secured the southern end of the Paardeberg Drift, whither they were followed the same evening by Stephenson and Knox. There remained only the Wolveskraal Drift to block, and this had already been done by as smart a piece of work as any in the war. Wherever French has gone he has done well, but his crowning glory was the movement from Kimberley to head off Cronje's retreat.

The exertions which the mounted men had made in the relief of Kimberley have been already recorded. They arrived there on Thursday with their horses dead beat. They were afoot at three o'clock on Friday morning, and two brigades out of three were hard at work all day in an endeavour to capture the Dronfield position. Yet when on the same evening an order came that French should start again instantly from Kimberley and endeavour to head Cronje's army off, he did not plead inability, as many a commander might, but taking every man whose horse was still fit to carry him (something under two thousand out of a column which had been at least five thousand strong), he started within a few hours and pushed on through the whole night. Horses died under their riders, but still the column marched over the shadowy *veldt* under the brilliant stars. By happy chance or splendid calculation they were heading straight for the one drift which was still open to Cronje. It was a close thing. At midday on Saturday the Boer advance guard was already near to the *kopjes* which command it. But French's men, still full of fight after their march of thirty miles, threw themselves in front and seized the position before their very eyes. The last of the drifts was closed. If Cronje was to get across now, he must crawl out of his trench and fight under Roberts's conditions, or he might remain under his own conditions until Roberts's forces closed round him. With him lay the alternative. In the meantime, still ignorant of the forces about him, but finding himself headed off by French, he made his way down to the river and occupied a long stretch of it between Paardeberg Drift and Wolveskraal Drift, hoping to force his way across. This was the situation on the night of Saturday, February 17th.

In the course of that night the British brigades, staggering with fatigue but indomitably resolute to crush their evasive enemy, were converging upon Paardeberg. The Highland Brigade, exhausted by a heavy march over soft sand from Jacobsdal to Klip Drift, were nerved to fresh exertions by the word 'Magersfontein,' which flew from lip to lip along the ranks, and pushed on for another twelve miles to Paardeberg. Close at their heels came Smith-Dorrien's 19th Brigade, comprising the Shropshires, the Cornwalls, the Gordons, and the Canadians, probably the very finest brigade in the whole army. They pushed across the river and took up their position upon the north bank. The old wolf was now fairly surrounded. On the west the Highlanders were south of the river, and Smith-Dorrien on the north. On the east Kelly-Kenny's Division was to the south of the river, and French with his cavalry and mounted infantry were to the north of it. Never was a general in a more hopeless plight. Do what he would, there was no possible loophole for escape.

There was only one thing which apparently should not have been done, and that was to attack him. His position was a formidable one. Not only were the banks of the river fringed with his riflemen under excellent cover, but from these banks there extended on each side a number of *dongas*, which made admirable natural trenches. The only possible attack from either side must be across a level plain at least a thousand or fifteen hundred yards in width, where our numbers would only swell our losses. It must be a bold soldier and a far bolder civilian, who would venture to question an operation carried out under the immediate personal direction of Lord Kitchener; but the general consensus of opinion among critics may justify that which might be temerity in the individual. Had Cronje not been tightly surrounded, the action with its heavy losses might have been justified as an attempt to hold him until his investment should be complete. There seems, however, to be no doubt that he was already entirely surrounded, and that, as experience proved, we had only to sit round him to insure his surrender. It is not given to the greatest man to have every soldierly gift equally developed, and it may be said without offence that Lord Kitchener's cool judgment upon the actual field of battle has not yet been proved as conclusively as his longheaded power of organisation and his iron determination.

Putting aside the question of responsibility, what happened on the morning of Sunday, February 18th, was that from every quarter an assault was urged across the level plains, to the north and to the south, upon the lines of desperate and invisible men who lay in the *dongas* and behind the banks of the river. Everywhere there was a terrible monotony about the experiences of the various regiments which learned once again the grim lessons of Colenso and Modder River. We surely did not need to prove once more what had already been so amply proved, that bravery can be of no avail against concealed riflemen well entrenched, and that the more hardy is the attack the heavier must be the repulse. Over the long circle of our attack Knox's brigade, Stephenson's brigade, the Highland brigade, Smith-Dorrien's brigade all fared alike. In each case there was the advance until they were within the thousand-yard fire zone, then the resistless sleet of bullets which compelled them to get down and to keep down. Had they even then recognised that they were attempting the impossible, no great harm might have been done, but with generous emulation the men of the various regiments made little rushes, company by company, towards the river bed, and found themselves ever exposed to a more withering fire. On the northern bank Smith-Dorrien's brigade, and especially the Canadian regiment, distinguished themselves by the magnificent tenacity with which they persevered in their attack. The Cornwalls of the same brigade swept up almost to the river bank in a charge which was the admiration of all who saw it. If the miners of Johannesburg had given the impression that the Cornishman is not a fighter, the record of the county regiment in the war has for ever exploded the calumny. Men who were not fighters could have found no place in Smith-Dorrien's brigade or in the charge of Paardeberg.

While the infantry had been severely handled by the Boer riflemen, our guns, the 76th, 81st, and 82nd field batteries, with the 65th howitzer battery, had been shelling the river bed, though our artillery fire proved as usual to have little effect against scattered and hidden riflemen. At least, however, it distracted their attention, and made their fire upon the exposed infantry in front of them less deadly. Now, as in Napoleon's time, the effect of the guns is moral rather than material. About midday French's horse-artillery guns came into action from the north. Smoke and flames from the *dongas* told that some of our shells had fallen among the wagons and their combustible stores.

The Boer line had proved itself to be unshakable on each face, but at its ends the result of the action was to push them up, and to shorten the stretch of the river which was held by them. On the north bank Smith-Dorrien's brigade gained a considerable amount of ground. At the other end of the position the Welsh, Yorkshire, and Essex regiments of Stephenson's brigade did some splendid work, and pushed the Boers for some distance down the river bank. A most gallant but impossible charge was made by Colonel Hannay and a number of mounted infantry against the northern bank. He was shot with the majority of his followers. General Knox of the 12th Brigade and General Macdonald of the Highlanders were among the wounded. Colonel Aldworth of the Cornwalls died at the head of his men. A bullet struck him dead as he whooped his West Countrymen on to the charge. Eleven hundred killed and wounded testified to the fire of our attack and the grimness of the Boer resistance. The distribution of the losses among the various battalions—eighty among the Canadians, ninety in the West Riding Regiment, one hundred and twenty in the Seaforths, ninety in the Yorkshires, seventy-six in the Argyll and Sutherlands, ninety-six in the Black Watch, thirty-one in the Oxfordshires, fifty-six in the Cornwalls, forty-six in the Shropshires—shows how universal was the gallantry, and especially how well the Highland Brigade carried itself. It is to be feared that they had to face, not only the fire of the enemy, but also that of their own comrades on the further side of the river. A great military authority has stated that it takes many years for a regiment to recover its spirit and steadiness if it has been heavily punished, and yet within two months of Magersfontein we find the indomitable Highlanders taking without flinching the very bloodiest share of this bloody day—and this after a march of thirty miles with no pause before going into action. A repulse it may have been, but they hear no name of which they may be more proud upon the victory scroll of their colours.

What had we got in return for our eleven hundred casualties? We had contracted the Boer position from about three miles to less than two. So much was to the good, as the closer they lay the more effective our artillery fire might be expected to be. But it is probable that our shrapnel alone, without any loss of life, might have effected the same thing. It is easy to be wise after the event, but it does certainly appear that with our present knowledge the action at Paardeberg was as unnecessary as it was expensive. The sun descended on Sunday, February 18th, upon a bloody field and crowded field hospitals, but also upon an unbroken circle of British troops still hemming in the desperate men who lurked among the willows and mimosas which drape the brown steep banks of the Modder.

There was evidence during the action of the presence of an active Boer force to the south of us, probably the same well-handled and enterprising body which had captured our convoy at Waterval. A small party of Kitchener's Horse was surprised by this body, and thirty men with four officers were taken prisoners. Much has been said of the superiority of South African scouting to that of the British regulars, but it must be confessed that a good many instances might be quoted in which the colonials, though second to none in gallantry, have been defective in that very quality in which they were expected to excel.

This surprise of our cavalry post had more serious consequences than can be measured by the loss of men, for by it the Boers obtained possession of a strong *kopje* called Kitchener's Hill, lying about two miles distant on the south-east of our position. The movement was an admirable one strategically upon their part, for it gave their beleaguered comrades a first station on the line of their retreat. Could they only win their way to that *kopje*, a rearguard action might be fought from there which would cover the escape of at least a portion of the force. De Wet, if he was indeed responsible for the manoeuvres of these Southern Boers, certainly handled his small force with a discreet audacity which marks him as the born leader which he afterwards proved himself to be.

If the position of the Boers was desperate on Sunday, it was hopeless on Monday, for in the course of the morning Lord Roberts came up, closely followed by the whole of Tucker's Division (7th) from Jacobsdal. Our artillery also was strongly reinforced. The 18th, 62nd, and 75th field batteries came up with three naval 4.7 guns and two naval 12-pounders. Thirty-five thousand men with sixty guns were gathered round the little Boer army. It is a poor spirit which will not applaud the supreme resolution with which the gallant farmers held out, and award to Cronje the title of one of the most grimly resolute leaders of whom we have any record in modern history.

For a moment it seemed as if his courage was giving way. On Monday morning a message was transmitted by him to Lord Kitchener asking for a twenty-four hours' armistice. The answer was of course a curt refusal. To this he replied that if we were so inhuman as to prevent him from burying his dead there was nothing for him save surrender. An answer was given that a messenger with power to treat should be sent out, but in the interval Cronje had changed his mind, and disappeared with a snarl of contempt into his burrows. It had become known that women and children were in the *laager*, and a message was sent offering them a place of safety, but even to this a refusal was given. The reasons for this last decision are inconceivable.

Lord Roberts's dispositions were simple, efficacious, and above all bloodless. Smith-Dorrien's brigade, who were winning in the Western army something of the reputation which Hart's Irishmen had won in Natal, were placed astride of the river to the west, with orders to push gradually up, as occasion served, using trenches for their approach. Chermside's brigade occupied the same position on the east. Two other divisions and the cavalry stood round, alert and eager, like terriers round a rat-hole, while all day the pitiless guns crashed their common shell, their shrapnel, and their Lyddite into the river-bed. Already down there, amid slaughtered oxen and dead horses under a burning sun, a horrible pest-hole had been formed which sent its mephitic vapours over the country-side. Occasionally the sentries down the river saw amid the brown eddies of the rushing water the floating body of a Boer which had been washed away from the Golgotha above. Dark Cronje, betrayer of Potchefstroom, iron-handed ruler of natives, reviler of the British, stern victor of Magersfontein, at last there has come a day of reckoning for you!

On Wednesday, the 21st, the British, being now sure of their grip of Cronje, turned upon the Boer force which had occupied the hill to the south-east of the drift. It was clear that this force, unless driven away, would be the vanguard of the relieving army which might be expected to assemble from Ladysmith, Bloemfontein, Colesberg, or wherever else the Boers could detach men. Already it was known that reinforcements who had left Natal whenever they heard that the Free State was invaded were drawing near. It was necessary to crush the force upon the hill before it became too powerful. For this purpose the cavalry set forth, Broadwood with the 10th Hussars, 12th Lancers, and two batteries going round on one side, while French with the 9th and 16th Lancers, the Household Cavalry, and two other batteries skirted the other. A force of Boers was met and defeated, while the defenders of the hill were driven off with considerable loss. In this well-managed affair the enemy lost at least a hundred, of whom fifty were prisoners. On Friday, February 23rd, another attempt at rescue was made from the south, but again it ended disastrously for the Boers. A party attacked a *kopje* held by the Yorkshire regiment and were blown back by a volley, upon which they made for a second *kopje*, where the Buffs gave them an even rougher reception. Eighty prisoners were marched in. Meantime hardly a night passed that some of the Boers did not escape from their *laager* and give themselves up to our pickets. At the end of the week we had taken six hundred in all.

In the meantime the cordon was being drawn ever tighter, and the fire became heavier and more deadly, while the conditions of life in that fearful place were such that the stench alone might have compelled surrender. Amid the crash of tropical thunderstorms, the glare of lightning, and the furious thrashing of rain there was no relaxation of British vigilance. A balloon floating overhead directed the fire, which from day to day became more furious, culminating on the 26th with the arrival of four 5-inch howitzers. But still there came no sign from the fierce Boer and his gallant followers. Buried deep within burrows in the river bank the greater part of them lay safe from the shells, but the rattle of their musketry when the outposts moved showed that the trenches were as alert as ever. The thing could only have one end, however, and Lord Roberts, with admirable judgment and patience, refused to hurry it at the expense of the lives of his soldiers.

The two brigades at either end of the Boer lines had lost no chance of pushing in, and now they had come within striking distance. On the night of February 26th it was determined that Smith-Dorrien's men should try their luck. The front trenches of the British were at that time seven hundred yards from the Boer lines. They were held by the Gordons and by the Canadians, the latter being the nearer to the river. It is worth while entering into details as to the arrangement of the attack, as the success of the campaign was at least accelerated by it. The orders were that the Canadians were to advance, the Gordons to support, and the Shropshires to take such a position on the left as would outflank any counter attack upon the part of the Boers. The Canadians advanced in the darkness of the early morning before the rise of the moon. The front rank held their rifles in the left hand and each extended right hand grasped the sleeve of the man next it. The rear rank had their rifles slung and carried spades. Nearest the river bank were two companies (G and H.) who were followed by the 7th company of Royal Engineers carrying picks and empty sand bags. The long line stole through a pitchy darkness, knowing that at any instant a blaze of fire such as flamed before the Highlanders at Magersfontein might crash out in front of them. A hundred, two, three, four, five hundred paces were taken. They knew that they must be close upon the trenches. If they could only creep silently enough, they might spring upon the defenders unannounced. On and on they stole, step by step, praying for silence. Would the gentle shuffle of feet be heard by the men who lay within stone-throw of them? Their hopes had begun to rise when there broke upon the silence of the night a resonant metallic rattle, the thud of a falling man, an empty clatter! They had walked into a line of meat-cans slung upon a wire. By measurement it was only ninety yards from the trench. At that instant a single rifle sounded, and the Canadians hurled themselves down upon the ground. Their bodies had hardly touched it when from a line six hundred yards long there came one furious glare of rifle fire, with a hiss like water on a red-hot plate, of speeding bullets. In that terrible red light the men as they lay and scraped desperately for cover could see the heads of the Boers pop up and down, and the fringe of rifle barrels quiver and gleam. How the regiment, lying helpless under this fire, escaped destruction is extraordinary. To rush the trench in the face of such a continuous blast of lead seemed impossible, and it was equally impossible to remain where they were. In a short time the moon would be up, and they would be picked off to a man. The outer companies upon the plain were ordered to retire. Breaking up into loose order, they made their way back with surprisingly little loss; but a strange contretemps occurred, for, leaping suddenly into a trench held by the Gordons, they transfixed themselves upon the bayonets of the men. A subaltern and twelve men received bayonet thrusts—none of them fortunately of a very serious nature.

While these events had been taking place upon the left of the line, the right was hardly in better plight. All firing had ceased for the moment—the Boers being evidently under the impression that the whole attack had recoiled. Uncertain whether the front of the small party on the right of the second line (now consisting of some sixty-five Sappers and Canadians lying in one mingled line) was clear for firing should the Boers leave their trenches, Captain Boileau, of the Sappers, crawled forward along the bank of the river, and discovered Captain Stairs and ten men of the Canadians, the survivors of the firing line, firmly ensconced in a crevice of the river bank overlooking the *laager*, quite happy on being reassured as to the proximity of support. This brought the total number of the dar-

227

ing band up to seventy-five rifles. Meanwhile, the Gordons, somewhat perplexed by the flying phantoms who had been flitting into and over their trenches for the past few minutes, sent a messenger along the river bank to ascertain, in their turn, if their own front was clear to fire, and if not, what state the survivors were in. To this message Colonel Kincaid, R.E., now in command of the remains of the assaulting party, replied that his men would be well entrenched by daylight. The little party had been distributed for digging as well as the darkness and their ignorance of their exact position to the Boers would permit. Twice the sound of the picks brought angry volleys from the darkness, but the work was never stopped, and in the early dawn the workers found not only that they were secure themselves, but that they were in a position to enfilade over half a mile of Boer trenches. Before daybreak the British crouched low in their shelter, so that with the morning light the Boers did not realise the change which the night had wrought. It was only when a burgher was shot as he filled his pannikin at the river that they understood how their position was overlooked. For half an hour a brisk fire was maintained, at the end of which time a white flag went up from the trench. Kincaid stood up on his parapet, and a single haggard figure emerged from the Boer warren. 'The burghers have had enough; what are they to do?' said he. As he spoke his comrades scrambled out behind him and came walking and running over to the British lines. It was not a moment likely to be forgotten by the parched and grimy warriors who stood up and cheered until the cry came crashing back to them again from the distant British camps. No doubt Cronje had already realised that the extreme limit of his resistance was come, but it was to that handful of Sappers and Canadians that the credit is immediately due for that white flag which fluttered on the morning of Majuba Day over the lines of Paardeberg.

It was six o'clock in the morning when General Pretyman rode up to Lord Roberts's headquarters. Behind him upon a white horse was a dark-bearded man, with the quick, restless eyes of a hunter, middle-sized, thickly built, with grizzled hair flowing from under a tall brown felt hat. He wore the black broadcloth of the burgher with a green summer overcoat, and carried a small whip in his hands. His appearance was that of a respectable London vestryman rather than of a most redoubtable soldier with a particularly sinister career behind him.

The Generals shook hands, and it was briefly intimated to Cronje that his surrender must be unconditional, to which, after a short silence, he agreed. His only stipulations were personal, that his wife, his grandson, his secretary, his adjutant, and his servant might accompany him. The same evening he was despatched to Cape Town, receiving those honourable attentions which were due to his valour rather than to his character. His men, a pallid ragged crew, emerged from their holes and burrows, and delivered up their rifles. It is pleasant to add that, with much in their memories to exasperate them, the British privates treated their enemies with as large-hearted a courtesy as Lord Roberts had shown to their leader. Our total capture numbered some three thousand of the Transvaal and eleven hundred of the Free State. That the latter were not far more numerous was due to the fact that many had already shredded off to their farms. Besides Cronje, Wolverans of the Transvaal, and the German artillerist Albrecht, with forty-four other field-cornets and commandants, fell into our hands. Six small guns were also secured. The same afternoon saw the long column of the prisoners on its way to Modder River, there to be entrained for Cape Town, the most singular lot of people to be seen at that moment upon earth—ragged, patched, grotesque, some with galoshes, some with umbrellas, coffee-pots, and Bibles, their favourite baggage. So they passed out of their ten days of glorious history.

A visit to the *laager* showed that the horrible smells which had been carried across to the British lines, and the swollen carcasses which had swirled down the muddy river were true portents of its condition. Strong-nerved men came back white and sick from a contemplation of the place in which women and children had for ten days been living. From end to end it was a festering mass of corruption, overshadowed by incredible swarms of flies. Yet the engineer who could face evil sights and nauseous smells was repaid by an inspection of the deep narrow trenches in which a rifleman could crouch with the minimum danger from shells, and the caves in which the non-combatants remained in absolute safety. Of their dead we have no accurate knowledge, but two hundred wounded in a *donga* represented their losses, not only during a bombardment of ten days, but also in that Paardeberg engagement which had cost us eleven hundred casualties. No more convincing example could be adduced both of the advantage of the defence over the attack, and of the harmlessness of the fiercest shell fire if those who are exposed to it have space and time to make preparations.

A fortnight had elapsed since Lord Roberts had launched his forces from Ramdam, and that fortnight had wrought a complete revolution in the campaign. It is hard to recall any instance in the history of war where a single movement has created such a change over so many different operations. On February 14th Kimberley was in danger of capture, a victorious Boer army was facing Methuen, the lines of Magersfontein appeared impregnable, Clements was being pressed at Colesberg, Gatacre was stopped at Stormberg, Buller could not pass the Tugela, and Ladysmith was in a perilous condition. On the 28th Kimberley had been relieved, the Boer army was scattered or taken, the lines of Magersfontein were in our possession, Clements found his assailants retiring before him, Gatacre was able to advance at Stormberg, Buller had a weakening army in front of him, and Ladysmith was on the eve of relief. And all this had been done at the cost of a very moderate loss of life, for most of which Lord Roberts was in no sense answerable. Here at last was a reputation so well founded that even South African warfare could only confirm and increase it. A single master hand had in an instant turned England's night to day, and had brought us out of that nightmare of miscalculation and disaster which had weighed so long upon our spirits. His was the master hand, but there were others at his side without whom that hand might have been paralysed: Kitchener the organiser, French the cavalry leader—to these two men, second only to their chief, are the results of the operations due. Henderson, the most capable head of Intelligence, and Richardson, who under all difficulties fed the army, may each claim his share in the success.

CHAPTER 20

Roberts's Advance on Bloemfontein

The surrender of Cronje had taken place on February 27th, obliterating for ever the triumphant memories which the Boers had for twenty years associated with that date. A halt was necessary to provide food for the hungry troops, and above all to enable the cavalry horses to pick up. The supply of forage had been most inadequate, and the beasts had not yet learned to find a living from the dry withered herbage of the *veldt*.[1] In addition to this, they had been worked most desperately during the fortnight which had elapsed. Lord Roberts waited therefore at Osfontein, which is a farmhouse close to Paardeberg, until his cavalry were fit for an advance. On March 6th he began his march for Bloemfontein.

The force which had been hovering to the south and east of him during the Paardeberg operations had meanwhile been reinforced from Colesberg and from Ladysmith until it had attained considerable proportions. This army, under the leadership of De Wet, had taken up a strong position a few miles to the east, covering a considerable range of *kopjes*. On March 3rd a reconnaissance was made of it, in which some of our guns were engaged; but it was not until three days later that the army advanced with the intention of turning or forcing it. In the meantime reinforcements had been arriving in the British camp, derived partly from the regiments which had been employed at other points during these operations, and partly from newcomers from the outer Empire. The Guards came up from Klip Drift, the City Imperial Volunteers, the Australian Mounted Infantry, the Burmese Mounted Infantry and a detachment of light horse from Ceylon helped to form this strange invading army which was drawn from five continents and yet had no alien in its ranks.

The position which the enemy had taken up at Poplars Grove (so

---

1. A battery which turned out its horses to graze found that the puzzled creatures simply galloped about the plain, and could only be reassembled by blowing the call which they associated with feeding, when they rushed back and waited in lines for their nosebags to be put on.

called from a group of poplars round a farmhouse in the centre of their position) extended across the Modder River and was buttressed on either side by well-marked hills, with intermittent *kopjes* between. With guns, trenches, rifle pits, and barbed wire a bull-headed general might have found it another Magersfontein. But it is only just to Lord Roberts's predecessors in command to say that it is easy to do things with three cavalry brigades which it is difficult to do with two regiments. The ultimate blame does not rest with the man who failed with the two regiments, but with those who gave him inadequate means for the work which he had to do. And in this estimate of means our military authorities, our politicians, and our public were all in the first instance equally mistaken.

Lord Roberts's plan was absolutely simple, and yet, had it been carried out as conceived, absolutely effective. It was not his intention to go near any of that entanglement of ditch and wire which had been so carefully erected for his undoing. The weaker party, if it be wise, atones for its weakness by entrenchments. The stronger party, if it be wise, leaves the entrenchments alone and uses its strength to go round them. Lord Roberts meant to go round. With his immense preponderance of men and guns the capture or dispersal of the enemy's army might be reduced to a certainty. Once surrounded, they must either come out into the open or they must surrender.

On March 6th the cavalry were brought across the river, and in the early morning of March 7th they were sent off in the darkness to sweep round the left wing of the Boers and to establish themselves on the line of their retreat. Kelly-Kenny's Division (6th) had orders to follow and support this movement. Meanwhile Tucker was to push straight along the southern bank of the river, though we may surmise that his instructions were, in case of resistance, not to push his attack home. Colvile's 9th Division, with part of the naval brigade, were north of the river, the latter to shell the drifts in case the Boers tried to cross, and the infantry to execute a turning movement which would correspond with that of the cavalry on the other flank.

The plan of action was based, however, upon one supposition which proved to be fallacious. It was that after having prepared so elaborate a position the enemy would stop at least a little time to defend it. Nothing of the sort occurred, however, and on the instant that they realised that the cavalry was on their flank they made off. The infantry did not fire a shot.

The result of this very decisive flight was to derange all calculations entirely. The cavalry was not yet in its place when the Boer army streamed off between the *kopjes*. One would have thought, however, that they would have had a dash for the wagons and the guns, even if they were past them. It is unfair to criticise a movement until one is certain as to the positive orders which the leader may have received; but on the face of it it is clear that the sweep of our cavalry was not wide enough, and that they erred by edging to the left instead of to the right, so leaving the flying enemies always to the outside of them.

As it was, however, there seemed every possibility of their getting the guns, but De Wet very cleverly covered them by his skirmishers. Taking possession of a farmhouse on the right flank they kept up a spirited fire upon the 16th Lancers and upon P battery R.H.A. When at last the latter drove them out of their shelter, they again formed upon a low *kopje* and poured so galling a fire upon the right wing that the whole movement was interrupted until we had driven this little body of fifty men from their position. When, after a delay of an hour, the cavalry at last succeeded in dislodging them—or possibly it may be fairer to say when, having accomplished their purpose, they retired—the guns and wagons were out of reach, and, what is more important, the two Presidents, both Steyn and Kruger, who had come to stiffen the resistance of the burghers, had escaped.

Making every allowance for the weary state of the horses, it is impossible to say that our cavalry were handled with energy or judgment on this occasion. That such a force of men and guns should be held off from an object of such importance by so small a resistance reflects no credit upon us. It would have been better to repeat the Kimberley tactics and to sweep the regiments in extended order past the obstacle if we could not pass over it. At the other side of that little ill-defended *kopje* lay a possible termination of the war, and our crack cavalry regiments manoeuvred for hours and let it pass out of their reach. However, as Lord Roberts good-humouredly remarked at the end of the action, 'In war you can't expect everything to come out right.' General French can afford to shed one leaf from his laurel wreath. On the other hand, no words can be too high for the gallant little band of Boers who had the courage to face that overwhelming mass of horsemen, and to bluff them into regarding this handful as a force fighting a serious rearguard action. When the stories of the war are told round the fires in the lonely *veldt* farmhouses, as they will be for a century to come, this one deserves an honoured place.

The victory, if such a word can apply to such an action, had cost some fifty or sixty of the cavalry killed and wounded, while it is doubtful if the Boers lost as many. The finest military display on the British side had been the magnificent marching of Kelly-Kenny's 6th Division, who had gone for ten hours with hardly a halt. One 9-pound Krupp gun was the only trophy. On the other hand, Roberts had turned them out of their strong position, had gained twelve or fifteen miles on he road to Bloemfontein, and for the first time shown how helpless a Boer army was in country which gave our numbers a chance. From now onwards it was only in surprise and ambuscade that they could hope for a success. We had learned and they had learned that they could not stand in the open field.

The action of Poplars Grove was fought on March 7th. On the 9th the army was again on its way, and on the 10th it attacked the new position which the Boers had occupied at a place called Driefontein, or Abram's Kraal. They covered a front of some seven miles in such a formation that their wings were protected, the northern by the river and the southern by flanking bastions of hill extending for some distance to the rear. If the position had been defended as well as it had been chosen, the task would have been a severe one.

Since the Modder covered the enemy's right the turning movement could only be developed on their left, and Tucker's Division was thrown out very wide on that side for the purpose. But in the meanwhile a contretemps had occurred which threw out and seriously hampered the whole British line of battle. General French was in command of the left wing, which included Kelly-Kenny's Division, the first cavalry brigade, and Alderson's Mounted Infantry. His orders had been to keep in touch with the centre, and to avoid pushing his attack home. In endeavouring to carry out these instructions French moved his men more and more to the right, until he had really squeezed in between the Boers and Lord Roberts's central column, and so masked the latter. The essence of the whole operation was that the frontal attack should not be delivered until Tucker had worked round to the rear of the position. It is for military critics to decide whether it was that the flankers were too slow or the frontal assailants were too fast, but it is certain that Kelly-Kenny's Division attacked before the cavalry and the 7th Division were in their place. Kelly-Kenny was informed that the position in front of him had been abandoned, and four regiments, the Buffs, the Essex, the Welsh, and the Yorkshires, were advanced against it. They were passing over the open when the crash of the Mauser fire burst out in front of them, and the bullets hissed and thudded among the ranks. The ordeal was a very severe one. The Yorkshires were swung round wide upon the right, but the rest of the brigade, the Welsh Regiment leading, made a frontal attack upon the ridge. It was done coolly and deliberately, the men taking advantage of every possible cover. Boers could be seen leaving their position in small bodies as the crackling, swaying line of the British surged ever higher upon the hillside. At last, with a cheer, the Welshmen with their Kent and Essex comrades swept over the crest into the ranks of that cosmopolitan crew of sturdy adventurers who are known as the Johannesburg Police. For once the loss of the defence was greater than that of the attack. These mercenaries had not the instinct which teaches the Boer the right instant for flight, and they held their position too long to get away. The British had left four hundred men on the track of that gallant advance, but the vast majority of them were wounded—too often by those explosive or expansive missiles which make war more hideous. Of the Boers we actually buried over a hundred on the ridge, and their total casualties must have been considerably in excess of ours.

The action was strategically well conceived; all that Lord Roberts could do for complete success had been done; but tactically it was a poor affair, considering his enormous preponderance in men and guns. There was no glory in it, save for the four regiments who set their faces against that sleet of lead. The artillery did not do well, and were browbeaten by guns which they should have smothered under their fire. The cavalry cannot be said to have done well either. And yet, when all is said, the action is an important one, for the enemy were badly shaken by the result. The Johannesburg Police, who had been among their *corps d'elite*, had been badly mauled, and the burghers were impressed by one more example of the impossibility of standing in anything approaching to open country against disciplined troops, Roberts had not captured the guns, but the road had been cleared for him to Bloemfontein and, what is more singular, to Pretoria; for though hundreds of miles intervene between the field of Driefontein and the Transvaal capital, he never again met a force which was willing to look his infantry in the eyes in a pitched battle. Surprises and skirmishes were many, but it was the last time, save only at Doornkop, that a chosen position was ever held for an effective rifle fire—to say nothing of the push of bayonet.

And now the army flowed swiftly onwards to the capital. The indefatigable 6th Division, which had done march after march, one more brilliant than another, since they had crossed the Riet River, reached Asvogel Kop on the evening of Sunday, March 11th, the day after the battle. On Monday the army was still pressing onwards, disregarding all else and striking straight for the heart as Blucher struck at Paris in 1814. At midday they halted at the farm of Gregorowski, he who had tried the Reform prisoners after the Raid. The cavalry pushed on down Kaal Spruit, and in the evening crossed the Southern railway line which connects Bloemfontein with the colony, cutting it at a point some five miles from the town. In spite of some not very strenuous opposition from a Boer force a hill was seized by a squadron of Greys with some mounted infantry and Rimington's Guides, aided by U battery R.H.A., and was held by them all that night.

On the same evening Major Hunter-Weston, an officer who had already performed at least one brilliant feat in the war, was sent with Lieutenant Charles and a handful of Mounted Sappers and Hussars to cut the line to the north. After a difficult journey on a very dark night he reached his object and succeeded in finding and blowing up a culvert. There is a Victoria Cross gallantry which leads to nothing save personal decoration, and there is another and far higher gallantry of calculation, which springs from a cool brain as well as a hot heart, and it is from the men who possess this rare quality that great warriors arise. Such feats as the cutting of this railway or the subsequent saving of the Bethulie Bridge by Grant and Popham are of more service to the country than any degree of mere valour untempered by judgment. Among other results the cutting of the line secured for us twenty-eight locomotives, two hundred and fifty trucks, and one thousand tons of coal, all of which were standing ready to leave Bloemfontein station. The gallant little band were nearly cut off on their return, but fought their way through with the loss of two horses, and so got back in triumph.

The action of Driefontein was fought on the 10th. The advance began on the morning of the 11th. On the morning of the 13th the British were practically masters of Bloemfontein. The distance is forty miles. No one can say that Lord Roberts cannot follow a victory up as well as win it.

Some trenches had been dug and sangars erected to the north-west of the town; but Lord Roberts, with his usual perverseness, took the wrong turning and appeared upon the broad open plain to the south, where resistance would have been absurd. Already Steyn and the irreconcilables had fled from the town, and the General was met by a deputation of the Mayor, the Landdrost, and Mr. Fraser to tender the submission of the capital. Fraser, a sturdy clear-headed Highlander, had been the one politician in the Free State who combined a perfect loyalty to his adopted country with a just appreciation of what a quarrel á l'outrance with the British Empire would mean. Had Fraser's views prevailed, the Orange Free State would still exist as a happy and independent State. As it is, he may help her to happiness and prosperity as the prime minister of the Orange River Colony.

It was at half-past one on Tuesday, March 13th, that General Roberts and his troops entered Bloemfontein, amid the acclamations of many of the inhabitants, who, either to propitiate the victor, or as a sign of their real sympathies, had hoisted union jacks upon their houses. Spectators have left it upon record how from all that interminable column of yellow-clad weary men, worn with half rations and whole-day marches, there came never one jeer, never one taunting or exultant word, as they tramped into the capital of their enemies. The bearing of the troops was chivalrous in its gentleness, and not the least astonishing sight to the inhabitants was the passing of the Guards, the dandy troops of England, the body-servants of the great Queen. Black with sun and dust, staggering after a march of thirty-eight miles, gaunt and haggard, with their clothes in such a state that decency demanded that some of the men should be discreetly packed away in the heart of the dense column, they still swung into the town with the aspect of Kentish hop-pickers and the bearing of heroes. She, the venerable mother, could remember the bearded ranks who marched past her when they came with sadly thinned files back from the Crimean winter; even those gallant men could not have endured more sturdily, nor have served her more loyally, than these their worthy descendants.

It was just a month after the start from Ramdam that Lord Roberts and his army rode into the enemy's capital. Up to that period we had in Africa Generals who were hampered for want of troops, and troops who were hampered for want of Generals. Only when the commander-in-chief took over the main army had we soldiers enough, and a man who knew how to handle them. The result was one which has not only solved the question of the future of South Africa, but has given an illustration of strategy which will become classical to the military student. How brisk was the course of events, how incessant the marching and fighting, may be shown by a brief recapitulation. On February 13th cavalry and in-fantry were marching to the utmost capacity of men and horses. On the 14th the cavalry were halted, but the infantry were marching hard. On the 15th the cavalry covered forty miles, fought an action, and relieved Kimberley. On the 16th the cavalry were in pursuit of the Boer guns all day, and were off on a thirty-mile march to the Modder at night, while the infantry were fighting Cronje's rearguard action, and closing up all day. On the 17th the infantry were marching hard. On the 18th was the battle of Paardeberg. From the 19th to the 27th was incessant fighting with Cronje inside the *laager* and with De Wet outside. From the 28th to March 6th was rest. On March 7th was the action of Poplars Grove with heavy marching; on March 10th the battle of Driefontein. On the 11th and 12th the infantry covered forty miles, and on the 13th were in Bloemfontein. All this was accomplished by men on half-rations, with horses which could hardly be urged beyond a walk, in a land where water is scarce and the sun semi-tropical, each infantryman carrying a weight of nearly forty pounds. There are few more brilliant achievements in the history of British arms. The tactics were occasionally faulty, and the bat-tle of Paardeberg was a blot upon the operations; but the strategy of the General and the spirit of the soldier were alike admirable.

CHAPTER 21

Strategic Effects of
Lord Roberts's March

From the moment that Lord Roberts with his army advanced from Ramdam all the other British forces in South Africa, the Colesberg force, the Stormberg force, Brabant's force, and the Natal force, had the pressure relieved in front of them, a tendency which increased with every fresh success of the main body. A short chapter must be devoted to following rapidly the fortunes of these various armies, and tracing the effect of Lord Roberts's strategy upon their movements. They may be taken in turn from west to east.

The force under General Clements (formerly French's) had, as has already been told, been denuded of nearly all its cavalry and horse artillery, and so left in the presence of a very superior body of the enemy. Under these circumstances Clements had to withdraw his immensely extended line, and to concentrate at Arundel, closely followed by the elated enemy. The situation was a more critical one than has been appreciated by the public, for if the force had been defeated the Boers would have been in a position to cut Lord Roberts's line of communications, and the main army would have been in the air. Much credit is due, not only to General Clements, but to Carter of the Wiltshires, Hacket Pain of the Worcesters, Butcher of the 4th R.F.A., the admirable Australians, and all the other good men and true who did their best to hold the gap for the Empire.

The Boer idea of a strong attack upon this point was strategically admirable, but tactically there was not sufficient energy in pushing home the advance. The British wings succeeded in withdrawing, and the concentrated force at Arundel was too strong for attack Yet there was a time of suspense, a time when every man had become of such importance that even fifty Indian *syces* were for the first and last time in the war, to their own supreme gratification, permitted for twenty-four hours to play their natural part as soldiers.[1] But then with the rapid strokes in front the hour of danger passed, and the Boer advance became first a halt and then a retreat.

On February 27th, Major Butcher, supported by the Inniskillings and Australians, attacked Rensburg and shelled the enemy out of it. Next morning Clements's whole force had advanced from Arundel and took up its old position. The same afternoon it was clear that the Boers were retiring, and the British, following them up, marched into Colesberg, around which they had manoeuvred so long. A telegram from Steyn to De Wet found in the town told the whole story of the retirement: 'As long as you are able to hold the positions you are in with the men you have, do so. If not, come here as quickly as circumstances will allow, as matters here are taking a serious turn.' The whole force passed over the Orange River unimpeded, and blew up the Norval's Pont railway bridge behind it. Clements's brigade followed on March 4th, and succeeded in the course of a week in throwing a pontoon bridge over the river and crossing into the Orange Free State. Roberts having in the meanwhile seized Bloemfontein, communication was restored by railway between the forces, and Clements was despatched to Phillipolis, Fauresmith, and the other towns in the south-west to receive the submission of the inhabitants and to enforce their disarmament. In the meantime the Engineers worked furiously at the restoration of the railway bridge over the Orange River, which was not, however, accomplished until some weeks later.

During the long period which had elapsed since the repulse at Stormberg, General Gatacre had held his own at Sterkstroom, under orders not to attack the enemy, repulsing them easily upon the only occasion when they ventured to attack him. Now it was his turn also to profit by the success which Lord Roberts had won. On February 23rd he re-occupied Molteno, and on the same day sent out a force to reconnoitre the enemy's position at Stormberg. The incident is memorable as having been the cause of the death of Captain de Montmorency,[2]

---

1. Footnote: There was something piteous in the chagrin of these fine Sikhs at being held back from their natural work as soldiers. A deputation of them waited upon Lord Roberts at Bloemfontein to ask, with many salaams, whether 'his children were not to see one little fight before they returned.'
2. Footnote: De Montmorency had established a remarkable influence over his rough followers. To the end of the war they could not speak of him without tears in their eyes. When I asked Sergeant Howe why his captain went almost alone up the hill, his answer was, 'Because the captain knew no fear.' Byrne, his soldier servant (an Omdurman V.C. like his master), galloped madly off next morning with a saddled horse to bring back his captain alive or dead, and had to be forcibly seized and restrained by our cavalry.

one of the most promising of the younger officers of the British army. He had formed a corps of scouts, consisting originally of four men, but soon expanding to seventy or eighty. At the head of these men he confirmed the reputation for desperate valour which he had won in the Soudan, and added to it proofs of the enterprise and judgment which go to make a leader of light cavalry. In the course of the reconnaissance he ascended a small *kopje* accompanied by three companions, Colonel Hoskier, a London Volunteer soldier, Vice, a civilian, and Sergeant Howe. 'They are right on the top of us,' he cried to his comrades, as he reached the summit, and dropped next instant with a bullet through his heart. Hoskier was shot in five places, and Vice was mortally wounded, only Howe escaping. The rest of the scouts, being farther back, were able to get cover and to keep up a fight until they were extricated by the remainder of the force. Altogether our loss was formidable rather in quality than in quantity, for not more than a dozen were hit, while the Boers suffered considerably from the fire of our guns.

On March 5th General Gatacre found that the Boers were retreating in front of him—in response, no doubt, to messages similar to those which had already been received at Colesberg. Moving forward he occupied the position which had confronted him so long. Thence, having spent some days in drawing in his scattered detachments and in mending the railway, he pushed forward on March 12th to Burghersdorp, and thence on the 13th to Olive Siding, to the south of the Bethulie Bridge.

There are two bridges which span the broad muddy Orange River, thick with the washings of the Basutoland mountains. One of these is the magnificent high railway bridge, already blown to ruins by the retreating Boers. Dead men or shattered horses do not give a more vivid impression of the unrelenting brutality of war than the sight of a structure, so graceful and so essential, blown into a huge heap of twisted girders and broken piers. Half a mile to the west is the road bridge, broad and old-fashioned. The only hope of preserving some mode of crossing the difficult river lay in the chance that the troops might anticipate the Boers who were about to destroy this bridge.

In this they were singularly favoured by fortune. On the arrival of a small party of scouts and of the Cape Police under Major Nolan-Neylan at the end of the bridge it was found that all was ready to blow it up, the mine sunk, the detonator fixed, and the wire laid. Only the connection between the wire and the charge had not been made. To make sure, the Boers had also laid several boxes of dynamite under the last span, in case the mine should fail in its effect. The advance guard of the Police, only six in number, with Nolan-Neylan at their head, threw themselves into a building which commanded the approaches of the bridge, and this handful of men opened so spirited and well-aimed a fire that the Boers were unable to approach it. As fresh scouts and policemen came up they were thrown into the firing line, and for a whole long day they kept the destroyers from the bridge. Had the enemy known how weak they were and how far from supports, they could have easily destroyed them, but the game of bluff was admirably played, and a fire kept up which held the enemy to their rifle pits.

The Boers were in a trench commanding the bridge, and their brisk fire made it impossible to cross. On the other hand, our rifle fire commanded the mine and prevented any one from exploding it. But at the approach of darkness it was certain that this would be done. The situation was saved by the gallantry of young Popham of the Derbyshires, who crept across with two men and removed the detonators. There still remained the dynamite under the further span, and this also they removed, carrying it off across the bridge under a heavy fire. The work was made absolutely complete a little later by the exploit of Captain Grant of the Sappers, who drew the charges from the holes in which they had been sunk, and dropped them into the river, thus avoiding the chance that they might be exploded next morning by shell fire. The feat of Popham and of Grant was not only most gallant but of extraordinary service to the country; but the highest credit belongs to Nolan-Neylan, of the Police, for the great promptitude and gallantry of his attack, and to McNeill for his support. On that road bridge and on the pontoon bridge at Norval's Pont Lord Roberts's army was for a whole month dependent for their supplies.

On March 15th Gatacre's force passed over into the Orange Free State, took possession of Bethulie, and sent on the cavalry to Springfontein, which is the junction where the railways from Cape Town and from East London meet. Here they came in contact with two battalions of Guards under Pole-Carew, who had been sent down by train from Lord Roberts's force in the north. With Roberts at Bloemfontein, Gatacre at Springfontein, Clements in the south-west, and Brabant at Aliwal, the pacification of the southern portion of the Free State appeared to be complete. Warlike operations seemed for the moment to be at an end, and scattered parties traversed the country, 'bill-sticking,' as the troops called it—that is, carrying Lord Roberts's proclamation to the lonely farmhouses and outlying villages.

In the meantime the colonial division of that fine old African fighter, General Brabant, had begun to play its part in the campaign. Among the many judicious arrangements which Lord Roberts made immediately after his arrival at the Cape was the assembling of the greater part of the scattered colonial bands into one division, and placing over it a General of their own, a man who had defended the cause of the Empire both in the legislative assembly and the field. To this force was entrusted the defence of the country lying to the east of Gatacre's position, and on February 15th they advanced from Penhoek upon Dordrecht. Their Imperial troops consisted of the Royal Scots and a section of the 79th R.F.A., the Colonial of Brabant's Horse, the Kaffrarian Mounted Rifles, the Cape Mounted Rifles and Cape Police, with Queenstown and East London Volunteers. The force moved upon Dordrecht, and on February 18th occupied the town after a spirited action, in which Brabant's Horse played a distinguished part. On March 4th the division advanced once more with the object of attacking the Boer position at Labuschagne's Nek, some miles to the north.

Aided by the accurate fire of the 79th R.F.A., the colonials succeeded, after a long day of desultory fighting, in driving the enemy from his position. Leaving a garrison in Dordrecht Brabant followed up his victory and pushed forward with two thousand men and eight guns (six of them light 7-pounders) to occupy Jamestown, which was done without resistance. On March 10th the colonial force approached Aliwal, the frontier town, and so rapid was the advance of Major Henderson with Brabant's Horse that the bridge at Aliwal was seized before the enemy could blow it up. At the other side of the bridge there was a strong stand made by the enemy, who had several Krupp guns in position; but the light horse, in spite of a loss of some twenty-five men killed and wounded, held on to the heights which command the river. A week or ten days were spent in pacifying the large north-eastern portion of Cape Colony, to which Aliwal acts as a centre. Barkly East, Herschel, Lady Grey, and other villages were visited by small detachments of the colonial horsemen, who pushed forward also into the south-eastern portion of the Free State, passing through Rouxville, and so along the Basutoland border as far as Wepener. The rebellion in the Colony was now absolutely dead in the north-east, while in the north-west in the Prieska and Carnarvon districts it was only kept alive by the fact that the distances were so great and the rebel forces so scattered that it was very difficult for our flying columns to reach them. Lord Kitchener had returned from Paardeberg to attend to this danger upon our line of communications, and by his exertions all chance of its becoming serious soon passed. With a considerable force of Yeomanry and Cavalry he passed swiftly over the country, stamping out the smouldering embers.

So much for the movements into the Free State of Clements, of Gatacre, and of Brabant. It only remains to trace the not very eventful history of the Natal campaign after the relief of Ladysmith.

General Buller made no attempt to harass the retreat of the Boers, although in two days no fewer than two thousand wagons were counted upon the roads to Newcastle and Dundee. The guns had been removed by train, the railway being afterwards destroyed. Across the north of Natal lies the chain of the Biggarsberg mountains, and to this the Transvaal Boers had retired, while the Freestaters had hurried through the passes of the Drakensberg in time to make the fruitless opposition to Roberts's march upon their capital. No accurate information had come in as to the strength of the Transvaalers, the estimates ranging from five to ten thousand, but it was known that their position was formidable and their guns mounted in such a way as to command the Dundee and Newcastle roads.

General Lyttelton's Division had camped as far out as Elandslaagte with Burn Murdoch's cavalry, while Dundonald's brigade covered the space between Burn Murdoch's western outposts and the Drakensberg passes. Few Boers were seen, but it was known that the passes were held in some strength. Meanwhile the line was being restored in the rear, and on March 9th the gallant White was enabled to take train for Durban, though it was not until ten days later that the Colenso bridge was restored. The Ladysmith garrison had been sent down to Colenso to recruit their health. There they were formed into a new division, the 4th, the brigades being given to Howard and Knox, and the command to Lyttelton, who had returned his former division, the second, to Clery. The 5th and 6th brigades were also formed into one division, the 10th, which was placed under the capable command of Hunter, who had confirmed in the south the reputation which he had won in the north of Africa. In the first week of April Hunter's Division was sent down to Durban and transferred to the western side, where they were moved up to Kimberley, whence they advanced northwards. The man on the horse has had in this war an immense advantage over the man on foot, but there have been times when the man on the ship has restored the balance. Captain Mahan might find some fresh texts in the transference of Hunter's Division, or in the subsequent expedition to Beira.

On April 10th the Boers descended from their mountains and woke up our sleepy army corps by a brisk artillery fire. Our own guns silenced it, and the troops instantly relapsed into their slumber. There was no movement for a fortnight afterwards upon either side, save that of Sir Charles Warren, who left the army in order to take up the governorship of British Bechuanaland, a district which was still in a disturbed state, and in which his presence had a peculiar significance, since he had rescued portions of it from Boer domination in the early days of the Transvaal Republic. Hildyard took over the command of the 5th Division. In this state of inertia the Natal force remained until Lord Roberts, after a six weeks' halt in Bloemfontein, necessitated by the insecurity of his railway communication and his want of every sort of military supply, more especially horses for his cavalry and boots for his infantry, was at last able on May 2nd to start upon his famous march to Pretoria. Before accompanying him, however, upon this victorious progress, it is necessary to devote a chapter to the series of incidents and operations which had taken place to the east and south-east of Bloemfontein during this period of compulsory inactivity.

One incident must be recorded in this place, though it was political rather than military. This was the interchange of notes concerning peace between Paul Kruger and Lord Salisbury. There is an old English jingle about 'the fault of the Dutch, giving too little and asking too much,' but surely there was never a more singular example of it than this. The united Presidents prepare for war for years, spring an insulting ultimatum upon us, invade our unfortunate Colonies, solemnly annex all the portions invaded, and then, when at last driven back, propose a peace which shall secure for them the whole point originally at issue. It is difficult to believe that the proposals could have been seriously meant, but more probable that the plan may have been to strengthen the hands of the Peace deputation who were being sent to endeavour to secure European intervention. Could they point to a proposal from the Transvaal and a refusal from England, it might, if not too curiously examined, excite the sympathy of those who follow emotions rather than facts.

The documents were as follow:

The Presidents of the Orange Free State and of the South African Republic to the Marques of Salisbury
Bloemfontein March 5th, 1900

The blood and the tears of the thousands who have suffered by this war, and the prospect of all the moral and economic ruin with which South Africa is now threatened, make it necessary for both belligerents to ask themselves dispassionately and as in the sight of the Triune God for what they are fighting and whether the aim of each justifies all this appalling misery and devastation.

With this object, and in view of the assertions of various British statesmen to the effect that this war was begun and is carried on with the set purpose of undermining Her Majesty's authority in South Africa, and of setting up an administration over all South Africa independent of Her Majesty's Government, we consider it our duty to solemnly declare that this war was undertaken solely as a defensive measure to safeguard the threatened independence of the South African Republic, and is only continued in order to secure and safeguard the incontestable independence of both Republics as sovereign international States, and to obtain the assurance that those of Her Majesty's subjects who have taken part with us in this war shall suffer no harm whatsoever in person or property.

On these conditions, but on these conditions alone, are we now as in the past desirous of seeing peace re-established in South Africa, and of putting an end to the evils now reigning over South Africa; while, if Her Majesty's Government is determined to destroy the independence of the Republics, there is nothing left to us and to our people but to persevere to the end in the course already begun, in spite of the overwhelming pre-eminence of the British Empire, conscious that that God who lighted the inextinguishable fire of the love of freedom in our hearts and those of our fathers will not forsake us, but will accomplish His work in us and in our descendants.

We hesitated to make this declaration earlier to your Excellency as we feared that, as long as the advantage was always on our side, and as long as our forces held defensive positions far in Her Majesty's Colonies, such a declaration might hurt the feelings of honour of the British people. But now that the prestige of the British Empire may be considered to be assured by the capture of one of our forces, and that we are thereby forced to evacuate other positions which we had occupied, that difficulty is over and we can no longer hesitate to inform your Government and people in the sight of the whole civilised world why we are fighting and on what conditions we are ready to restore peace.

Such was the message, deep in its simplicity and cunning in its candour, which was sent by the old President, for it is Kruger's style which we read in every line of it. One has to get back to facts after reading it, to the enormous war preparations of the Republics, to the unprepared state of the British Colonies, to the ultimatum, to the annexations, to the stirring up of rebellion, to the silence about peace in the days of success, to the fact that by 'inextinguishable love of freedom' is meant inextinguishable determination to hold other white men as helots—only then can we form a just opinion of the worth of his message. One must remember also, behind the homely and pious phraseology, that one is dealing with a man who has been too cunning for us again and again—a man who is as wily as the savages with whom he has treated and fought. This Paul Kruger with the simple words of peace is the same Paul Kruger who with gentle sayings insured the disarmament of Johannesburg, and then instantly arrested his enemies—the man whose name was a by-word for 'slimness' (craftiness) throughout South Africa. With such a man the best weapon is absolute naked truth with which Lord Salisbury confronted him in his reply:

Foreign Office
March 11th
I have the honour to acknowledge your Honours' telegram dated March 5th from Bloemfontein, of which the purport was principally to demand that Her Majesty's Government shall recognise the "incontestable independence" of the South African Republic and Orange Free State as "sovereign international States," and to offer on those terms to bring the war to a conclusion.

In the beginning of October last peace existed between Her Majesty and the two Republics under the conventions which then were in existence. A discussion had been proceeding for some months between Her Majesty's Government and the South African Republic, of which the object was to obtain redress for certain very serious grievances under which British residents in the Republic were suffering. In the course of those negotiations the Republic had, to the knowledge of Her Majesty's Government, made considerable armaments, and the latter had consequently taken steps to provide corresponding reinforcements to the British garrisons of Cape Town and Natal. No infringement of the rights guaranteed by the conventions had up to that time taken place on the British side. Suddenly, at two days' notice, the South African Republic, after issuing an insulting ultimatum, declared war, and the Orange Free State with whom there had not even been any discussion, took a similar step. Her Majesty's dominions were immediately invaded by the two Republics, siege was laid to three towns within the British frontier, a large portion of the two Colonies was overrun with great destruction to property and life, and the Republics claimed to treat the inhabitants as if those dominions had been annexed to one or other of them. In anticipation of these operations the South African Republic had been accumulating for many years past military stores upon an enormous scale, which by their character could only have been intended for use against Great Britain.

Your Honours make some observations of a negative character upon the object with which these preparations were made. I do not think it necessary to discuss the questions which you have raised. But the result of these preparations, carried on with great secrecy, has been that the British Empire has been compelled to confront an invasion which has entailed a costly war and the loss of thousands of precious lives. This great calamity has been the penalty which Great Britain has suffered for having in recent years acquiesced in the existence of the two Republics.

In view of the use to which the two Republics have put the position which was given to them, and the calamities which their unprovoked attack has inflicted upon Her Majesty's dominions, Her Majesty's Government can only answer your Honours' telegram by saying that they are not prepared to assent to the independence either of the South African Republic or of the Orange Free State.

With this frank and uncompromising reply the Empire, with the exception of a small party of dupes and doctrinaires, heartily agreed. The pens were dropped, and the Mauser and the Lee-Metford once more took up the debate.

CHAPTER 22

The Halt at Bloemfontein

On March 13th Lord Roberts occupied the capital of the Orange
Free State. On May 1st, more than six weeks later, the advance was
resumed. This long delay was absolutely necessary in order to supply
the place of the ten thousand horses and mules which are said to have
been used up in the severe work of the preceding month. It was not
merely that a large number of the cavalry chargers had died or been
abandoned, but it was that of those which remained the majority were
in a state which made them useless for immediate service. How far
this might have been avoided is open to question, for it is notorious
that General French's reputation as a horse-master does not stand so
high as his fame as a cavalry leader. But besides the horses there was
urgent need of every sort of supply, from boots to hospitals, and the
only way by which they could come was by two single-line railways
which unite into one single-line railway, with the alternative of passing
over a precarious pontoon bridge at Norval's Pont, or truck by truck
over the road bridge at Bethulie. To support an army of fifty thousand
men under these circumstances, eight hundred miles from a base, is no
light matter, and a premature advance which could not be thrust home
would be the greatest of misfortunes. The public at home and the army
in Africa became restless under the inaction, but it was one more example of the absolute soundness of Lord Roberts's judgment and the
quiet resolution with which he adheres to it. He issued a proclamation
to the inhabitants of the Free State promising protection to all who
should bring in their arms and settle down upon their farms. The most
stringent orders were issued against looting or personal violence, but
nothing could exceed the gentleness and good humour of the troops.
Indeed there seemed more need for an order which should protect
them against the extortion of their conquered enemies. It is strange to
think that we are separated by only ninety years from the savage sol-
diery of Badajoz and San Sebastian.

248

The streets of the little Dutch town formed during this interval a curious object-lesson in the resources of the Empire. All the scattered Anglo-Celtic races had sent their best blood to fight for the common cause. Peace is the great solvent, as war is the powerful unifier. For the British as for the German Empire much virtue had come from the stress and strain of battle. To stand in the market square of Bloemfontein and to see the warrior types around you was to be assured of the future of the race. The middle-sized, square-set, weather-tanned, straw-bearded British regulars crowded the footpaths. There also one might see the hard-faced Canadians, the loose-limbed dashing Australians, fire-blooded and keen, the dark New Zealanders, with a Maori touch here and there in their features, the gallant men of Tasmania, the gentlemen troopers of India and Ceylon, and everywhere the wild South African irregulars with their bandoliers and unkempt wiry horses, Rimington's men with the racoon bands, Roberts's Horse with the black plumes, some with pink *puggarees*, some with birdseye, but all of the same type, hard, rugged, and alert. The man who could look at these splendid soldiers, and, remembering the sacrifices of time, money, and comfort which most of them had made before they found themselves fighting in the heart of Africa, doubt that the spirit of the race burned now as brightly as ever, must be devoid of judgment and sympathy. The real glories of the British race lie in the future, not in the past. The Empire walks, and may still walk, with an uncertain step, but with every year its tread will be firmer, for its weakness is that of waxing youth and not of waning age.

The greatest misfortune of the campaign, one which it was obviously impolitic to insist upon at the time, began with the occupation of Bloemfontein. This was the great outbreak of enteric among the troops. For more than two months the hospitals were choked with sick. One general hospital with five hundred beds held seventeen hundred sick, nearly all enterics. A half field hospital with fifty beds held three hundred and seventy cases. The total number of cases could not have been less than six or seven thousand—and this not of an evanescent and easily treated complaint, but of the most persistent and debilitating of continued fevers, the one too which requires the most assiduous attention and careful nursing. How great was the strain only those who had to meet it can tell. The exertions of the military hospitals and of those others which were fitted out by private benevolence sufficed, after a long struggle, to meet the crisis. At Bloemfontein alone, as many as fifty men died in one day, and more than 1000 new graves in the cemetery testify to the severity of the epidemic. No men in the campaign served their country more truly than the officers and men of the medical service, nor can any one who went through the epidemic forget the bravery and unselfishness of those admirable nursing sisters who set the men around them a higher standard of devotion to duty.

Enteric fever is always endemic in the country, and especially at Bloemfontein, but there can be no doubt that this severe outbreak had its origin in the Paardeberg water. All through the campaign, while the machinery for curing disease was excellent, that for preventing it was elementary or absent. If bad water can cost us more than all the bullets of the enemy, then surely it is worth our while to make the drinking of unboiled water a stringent military offence, and to attach to every company and squadron the most rapid and efficient means for boiling it—for filtering alone is useless. An incessant trouble it would be, but it would have saved a division for the army. It is heartrending for the medical man who has emerged from a hospital full of water-born pestilence to see a regimental water-cart being filled, without protest, at some polluted wayside pool. With precautions and with inoculation all those lives might have been saved. The fever died down with the advance of the troops and the coming of the colder weather.

To return to the military operations: these, although they were stagnant so far as the main army was concerned, were exceedingly and inconveniently active in other quarters. Three small actions, two of which were disastrous to our arms, and one successful defence marked the period of the pause at Bloemfontein.

To the north of the town, some twelve miles distant lies the ubiquitous Modder River, which is crossed by a railway bridge at a place named Glen. The saving of the bridge was of considerable importance, and might by the universal testimony of the farmers of that district have been effected any time within the first few days of our occupation. We appear, however, to have imperfectly appreciated how great was the demoralisation of the Boers. In a week or so they took heart, returned, and blew up the bridge. Roving parties of the enemy, composed mainly of the redoubtable Johannesburg police, reappeared even to the south of the river. Young Lygon was killed, and Colonels Crabbe and Codrington with Captain Trotter, all of the Guards, were severely wounded by such a body, whom they gallantly but injudiciously attempted to arrest when armed only with revolvers.

These wandering patrols who kept the country unsettled, and harassed the farmers who had taken advantage of Lord Roberts's proclamation, were found to have their centre at a point some six miles to the north of Glen, named Karee. At Karee a formidable line of hills cut the British advance, and these had been occupied by a strong body of the enemy with guns. Lord Roberts determined to drive them off, and on March 28th Tucker's 7th Division, consisting of Chermside's brigade (Lincolns, Norfolks, Hampshires, and Scottish Borderers), and Wavell's brigade (Cheshires, East Lancashires, North Staffords, and South Wales Borderers), were assembled at Glen. The artillery consisted of the veteran 18th, 62nd, and 75th R.F.A. Three attenuated cavalry brigades with some mounted infantry completed the force.

The movement was to be upon the old model, and in result it proved to be only too truly so. French's cavalry were to get round one flank, Le Gallais's mounted infantry round the other, and Tucker's Division to attack in front. Nothing could be more perfect in theory and nothing apparently more defective in practice. Since on this as on other occasions the mere fact that the cavalry were demonstrating in the rear caused the complete abandonment of the position, it is difficult to see what the object of the infantry attack could be. The ground was irregular and unexplored, and it was late before the horsemen on their weary steeds found themselves behind the flank of the enemy. Some of them, Le Gallais's mounted infantry and Davidson's guns, had come from Bloemfontein during the night, and the horses were exhausted by the long march, and by the absurd weight which the British troop-horse is asked to carry. Tucker advanced his infantry exactly as Kelly-Kenny had done at Driefontein, and with a precisely similar result. The eight regiments going forward in echelon of battalions imagined from the silence of the enemy that the position had been abandoned. They were undeceived by a cruel fire which beat upon two companies of the Scottish Borderers from a range of two hundred yards. They were driven back, but reformed in a *donga*. About half-past two a Boer gun burst shrapnel over the Lincolnshires and Scottish Borderers with some effect, for a single shell killed five of the latter regiment. Chermside's brigade was now all involved in the fight, and Wavell's came up in support, but the ground was too open and the position too strong to push the attack home. Fortunately, about four o'clock, the horse batteries with French began to make their presence felt from behind, and the Boers instantly quitted their position and made off through the broad gap which still remained between French and Le Gallais. The Brandfort plain appears to be ideal ground for cavalry, but in spite of that the enemy with his guns got safely away. The loss of the infantry amounted to one hundred and sixty killed and wounded, the larger share of the casualties and of the honour falling to the Scottish Borderers and the East Lancashires. The infantry was not well handled, the cavalry was slow, and the guns were inefficient—altogether an inglorious day. Yet strategically it was of importance, for the ridge captured was the last before one came to the great plain which stretched, with a few intermissions, to the north. From March 29th until May 2nd Karee remained the advanced post.

In the meanwhile there had been a series of operations in the east which had ended in a serious disaster. Immediately after the occupation of Bloemfontein (on March 18th) Lord Roberts despatched to the east a small column consisting of the 10th Hussars, the composite regiment, two batteries (Q and U) of the Horse Artillery, some mounted infantry, Roberts's Horse, and Rimington's Guides. On the eastern horizon forty miles from the capital, but in that clear atmosphere looking only half the distance, there stands the impressive mountain named Thabanchu (the black mountain). To all Boers it is an historical spot, for it was at its base that the wagons of the *Voortrekkers*, coming by devious ways from various parts, assembled. On the further side of Thabanchu, to the north and east of it, lies the richest grain-growing portion of the Free State, the centre of which is Ladybrand. The forty miles which intervene between Bloemfontein and Thabanchu are intersected midway by the Modder River. At this point are the waterworks, erected recently with modern machinery, to take the place of the insanitary wells on which the town had been dependent. The force met with no resistance, and the small town of Thabanchu was occupied.

Colonel Pilcher, the leader of the Douglas raid, was inclined to explore a little further, and with three squadrons of mounted men he rode on to the eastward. Two commandos, supposed to be Grobler's and Olivier's, were seen by them, moving on a line which suggested that they were going to join Steyn, who was known to be rallying his forces at Kroonstad, his new seat of government in the north of the Free State. Pilcher, with great daring, pushed onwards until with his little band on their tired horses he found himself in Ladybrand, thirty miles from his nearest supports. Entering the town he seized the *landdrost* and the field-cornet, but found that strong bodies of the enemy were moving upon him and that it was impossible for him to hold the place. He retired, therefore, holding grimly on to his prisoners, and got back with small loss to the place from which he started. It was a dashing piece of bluff, and, when taken with the Douglas exploit, leads one to hope that Pilcher may have a chance of showing what he can do with larger means at his disposal. Finding that the enemy was following him in force, he pushed on the same night for Thabanchu. His horsemen must have covered between fifty and sixty miles in the twenty-four hours.

Apparently the effect of Pilcher's exploit was to halt the march of those commandos which had been seen trekking to the north-west, and to cause them to swing round upon Thabanchu. Broadwood, a young cavalry commander who had won a name in Egypt, considered that his position was unnecessarily exposed and fell back upon Bloemfontein. He halted on the first night near the waterworks, halfway upon his journey.

The Boers are great masters in the ambuscade. Never has any race shown such aptitude for this form of warfare—a legacy from a long succession of contests with cunning savages. But never also have they done anything so clever and so audacious as De Wet's dispositions in this action. One cannot go over the ground without being amazed at the ingenuity of their attack, and also at the luck which favoured them, for the trap which they had laid for others might easily have proved an absolutely fatal one for themselves.

The position beside the Modder at which the British camped had numerous broken hills to the north and east of it. A force of Boers, supposed to number about two thousand men, came down in the night, bringing with them several heavy guns, and with the early morning opened a brisk fire upon the camp. The surprise was complete. But the refinement of the Boer tactics lay in the fact that they had a surprise within a surprise—and it was the second which was the more deadly.

The force which Broadwood had with him consisted of the 10th Hussars and the composite regiment, Rimington's Scouts, Roberts's Horse, the New Zealand and Burmah Mounted Infantry, with Q and U batteries of Horse Artillery. With such a force, consisting entirely of mounted men, he could not storm the hills upon which the Boer guns were placed, and his twelve-pounders were unable to reach the heavier cannon of the enemy. His best game was obviously to continue his march to Bloemfontein. He sent on the considerable convoy of wagons and the guns, while he with the cavalry covered the rear, upon which the long-range pieces of the enemy kept up the usual well-directed but harmless fire.

Broadwood's retreating column now found itself on a huge plain which stretches all the way to Bloemfontein, broken only by two hills, both of which were known to be in our possession. The plain was one which was continually traversed from end to end by our troops and convoys, so that once out upon its surface all danger seemed at an end. Broadwood had additional reasons for feeling secure, for he knew that, in answer to his own wise request, Colvile's Division had been sent out before daybreak that morning from Bloemfontein to meet him. In a very few miles their vanguard and his must come together. There were obviously no Boers upon the plain, but if there were they would find themselves between two fires. He gave no thought to his front therefore, but rode behind, where the Boer guns were roaring, and whence the Boer riflemen might ride.

But in spite of the obvious there *were* Boers upon the plain, so placed that they must either bring off a remarkable surprise or be themselves cut off to a man. Across the *veldt*, some miles from the waterworks, there runs a deep *donga* or watercourse—one of many, but the largest. It cuts the rough road at right angles. Its depth and breadth are such that a wagon would dip down the incline, and disappear for about two minutes before it would become visible again at the crown of the other side. In appearance it was a huge curving ditch with a stagnant stream at the bottom. The sloping sides of the ditch were fringed with Boers, who had ridden thither before dawn and were now waiting for the unsuspecting column. There were not more than three hundred of them, and four times their number were approaching; but no odds can represent the difference between the concealed man with the magazine rifle and the man upon the plain.

There were two dangers, however, which the Boers ran, and, skilful as their dispositions were, their luck was equally great, for the risks were enormous. One was that a force coming the other way (Colvile's was only a few miles off) would arrive, and that they would be ground between the upper and the lower millstone. The other was that for once the British scouts might give the alarm and that Broadwood's mounted men would wheel swiftly to right and left and secure the ends of the long *donga*. Should that happen, not a man of them could possibly escape. But they took their chances like brave men, and fortune was their friend. The wagons came on without any scouts. Behind them was U battery, then Q, with Roberts's Horse abreast of them and the rest of the cavalry behind.

As the wagons, occupied for the most part only by unarmed sick soldiers and black transport drivers, came down into the drift, the Boers quickly but quietly took possession of them, and drove them on up the further slope. Thus the troops behind saw their wagons dip down, reappear, and continue on their course. The idea of an ambush could not suggest itself. Only one thing could avert an absolute catastrophe, and that was the appearance of a hero who would accept certain death in order to warn his comrades. Such a man rode by the wagons—though, unhappily, in the stress and rush of the moment there is no certainty as to his name or rank. We only know that one was found brave enough to fire his revolver in the face of certain death. The outburst of firing which answered his shot was the sequel which saved the column. Not often is it given to a man to die so choice a death as that of this nameless soldier.

But the detachment was already so placed that nothing could save it from heavy loss. The wagons had all passed but nine, and the leading battery of artillery was at the very edge of the *donga*. Nothing is so helpless as a limbered-up battery. In an instant the teams were shot down and the gunners were made prisoners. A terrific fire burst at the same instant upon Roberts's Horse, who were abreast of the guns. 'Files a bout! gallop!' yelled Colonel Dawson, and by his exertions and those of Major Pack-Beresford the corps was extricated and reformed some hundreds of yards further off. But the loss of horses and men was heavy. Major Pack-Beresford and other officers were shot down, and every unhorsed man remained necessarily as a prisoner under the very muzzles of the riflemen in the *donga*.

As Roberts's Horse turned and galloped for dear life across the flat, four out of the six guns[1] of Q battery and one gun (the rearmost) of U battery swung round and dashed frantically for a place of safety. At the same instant every Boer along the line of the *donga* sprang up and emptied his magazine into the mass of rushing, shouting soldiers, plunging horses, and screaming Kaffirs. It was for a few moments *a sauve-qui-peut*. Sergeant-Major Martin of U, with a single driver on a wheeler, got away the last gun of his battery. The four guns which were extricated of Q, under Major Phipps-Hornby, whirled across the plain, pulled up, unlimbered, and opened a brisk fire of shrapnel from about a thousand yards upon the *donga*. Had the battery gone on for double the distance, its action would have been more effective, for it would have been under a less deadly rifle fire, but in any case its sudden change from flight to discipline and order steadied the whole force. Roberts's men sprang from their horses, and with the Burmese and New Zealanders flung themselves down in a skirmish line. The cavalry moved to the left to find some drift by which the *donga* could be passed, and out of chaos there came in a few minutes calm and a settled purpose.

It was for Q battery to cover the retreat of the force, and most nobly it did it. A fortnight later a pile of horses, visible many hundreds of yards off across the plain, showed where the guns had stood. It was the Colenso of the horse gunners. In a devilish sleet of lead they stood to their work, loading and firing while a man was left. Some of the guns were left with two men to work them, one was loaded and fired by a single officer. When at last the order for retirement came, only ten men, several of them wounded, were left upon their feet. With scratch teams from the limbers, driven by single gunners, the twelve-pounders staggered out of action, and the skirmish line of mounted infantry sprang to their feet amid the hail of bullets to cheer them as they passed.

It was no slight task to extricate that sorely stricken force from the close contact of an exultant enemy, and to lead it across that terrible *donga*. Yet, thanks to the coolness of Broadwood and the steadiness of his rearguard, the thing was done. A practicable passage had been found two

---

1. Of the other two one overturned and could not be righted, the other had the wheelers shot and could not be extricated from the tumult. It was officially stated that the guns of Q battery were halted a thousand yards off the donga, but my impression was, from examining the ground, that it was not more than six hundred.

miles to the south by Captain Chester-Master of Rimington's. This corps, with Roberts's, the New Zealanders, and the 3rd Mounted Infantry, covered the withdrawal in turn. It was one of those actions in which the horseman who is trained to fight upon foot did very much better than the regular cavalry. In two hours' time the drift had been passed and the survivors of the force found themselves in safety.

The losses in this disastrous but not dishonourable engagement were severe. About thirty officers and five hundred men were killed, wounded, or missing. The prisoners came to more than three hundred. They lost a hundred wagons, a considerable quantity of stores, and seven twelve-pounder guns—five from U battery and two from Q. Of U battery only Major Taylor and Sergeant-Major Martin seem to have escaped, the rest being captured en bloc. Of Q battery nearly every man was killed or wounded. Roberts's Horse, the New Zealanders, and the mounted infantry were the other corps which suffered most heavily. Among many brave men who died, none was a greater loss to the service than Major Booth of the Northumberland Fusiliers, serving in the mounted infantry. With four comrades he held a position to cover the retreat, and refused to leave it. Such men are inspired by the traditions of the past, and pass on the story of their own deaths to inspire fresh heroes in the future.

Broadwood, the instant that he had disentangled himself, faced about, and brought his guns into action. He was not strong enough, however, nor were his men in a condition, to seriously attack the enemy. Martyr's mounted infantry had come up, led by the Queenslanders, and at the cost of some loss to themselves helped to extricate the disordered force. Colvile's Division was behind Bushman's Kop, only a few miles off, and there were hopes that it might push on and prevent the guns and wagons from being removed. Colvile did make an advance, but slowly and in a flanking direction instead of dashing swiftly forward to retrieve the situation. It must be acknowledged, however, that the problem which faced this General was one of great difficulty. It was almost certain that before he could throw his men into the action the captured guns would be beyond his reach, and it was possible that he might swell the disaster. With all charity, however, one cannot but feel that his return next morning, after a reinforcement during the night, without any attempt to force the Boer position, was lacking in enterprise.[2] The victory left the Boers in possession of the waterworks, and Bloemfontein had to fall back upon

---

2. It may be urged in General Colvile's defence that his division had already done a long march from Bloemfontein. A division, however, which contains two such brigades as Macdonald's and Smith-Dorrien's may safely be called upon for any exertions. The gunner officers in Colvile's division heard their comrades' guns in 'section—fire' and knew it to be the sign of a desperate situation.

her wells—a change which reacted most disastrously upon the enteric which was already decimating the troops.

The effect of the Sanna's Post defeat was increased by the fact that only four days later (on April 4th) a second even more deplorable disaster befell our troops. This was the surrender of five companies of infantry, two of them mounted, at Reddersberg. So many surrenders of small bodies of troops had occurred during the course of the war that the public, remembering how seldom the word 'surrender' had ever been heard in our endless succession of European wars, had become very restive upon the subject, and were sometimes inclined to question whether this new and humiliating fact did not imply some deterioration of our spirit. The fear was natural, and yet nothing could be more unjust to this the most splendid army which has ever marched under the red-crossed flag. The fact was new because the conditions were new, and it was inherent in those conditions. In that country of huge distances small bodies must be detached, for the amount of space covered by the large bodies was not sufficient for all military purposes. In reconnoitring, in distributing proclamations, in collecting arms, in overawing outlying districts, weak columns must be used. Very often these columns must contain infantry soldiers, as the demands upon the cavalry were excessive. Such bodies, moving through a hilly country with which they were unfamiliar, were always liable to be surrounded by a mobile enemy. Once surrounded the length of their resistance was limited by three things: their cartridges, their water, and their food. When they had all three, as at Wepener or Mafeking, they could hold out indefinitely. When one or other was wanting, as at Reddersberg or Nicholson's Nek, their position was impossible. They could not break away, for how can men on foot break away from horsemen? Hence those repeated humiliations, which did little or nothing to impede the course of the war, and which were really to be accepted as one of the inevitable prices which we had to pay for the conditions under which the war was fought. Numbers, discipline, and resources were with us. Mobility, distances, nature of the country, insecurity of supplies, were with them. We need not take it to heart therefore if it happened, with all these forces acting against them, that our soldiers found themselves sometimes in a position whence neither wisdom nor valour could rescue them. To travel through that country, fashioned above all others for defensive warfare, with trench and fort of superhuman size and strength, barring every path, one marvels how it was that such incidents were not more frequent and more serious. It is deplorable that the white flag should ever have waved over a company of British troops, but the man who is censorious upon the subject has never travelled in South Africa.

In the disaster at Reddersberg three of the companies were of the Irish Rifles, and two of the 2nd Northumberland Fusiliers—the same unfortunate regiments which had already been cut up at Stormberg. They had been detached from Gatacre's 3rd Division, the headquarters of which was at Springfontein. On the abandonment of Thabanchu and the disaster of Sanna's Post, it was obvious that we should draw in our detached parties to the east; so the five companies were ordered to leave Dewetsdorp, which they were garrisoning, and to get back to the railway line. Either the order was issued too late, or they were too slow in obeying it, for they were only halfway upon their journey, near the town of Reddersberg, when the enemy came down upon them with five guns. Without artillery they were powerless, but, having seized a *kopje*, they took such shelter as they could find, and waited in the hope of succour. Their assailants seem to have been detached from De Wet's force in the north, and contained among them many of the victors of Sanna's Post. The attack began at 11 a.m. of April 3rd, and all day the men lay among the stones, subjected to the pelt of shell and bullet. The cover was good, however, and the casualties were not heavy. The total losses were under fifty killed and wounded. More serious than the enemy's fire was the absence of water, save a very limited supply in a cart. A message was passed through of the dire straits in which they found themselves, and by the late afternoon the news had reached headquarters. Lord Roberts instantly despatched the Camerons, just arrived from Egypt, to Bethany, which is the nearest point upon the line, and telegraphed to Gatacre at Springfontein to take measures to save his compromised detachment. The telegram should have reached Gatacre early on the evening of the 3rd, and he had collected a force of fifteen hundred men, entrained it, journeyed forty miles up the line, detrained it, and reached Reddersberg, which is ten or twelve miles from the line, by 10.30 next morning. Already, however, it was too late, and the besieged force, unable to face a second day without water under that burning sun, had laid down their arms. No doubt the stress of thirst was dreadful, and yet one cannot say that the defence rose to the highest point of resolution. Knowing that help could not be far off, the garrison should have held on while they could lift a rifle. If the ammunition was running low, it was bad management which caused it to be shot away too fast. Captain McWhinnie, who was in command, behaved with the utmost personal gallantry. Not only the troops but General Gatacre also was involved in the disaster. Blame may have attached to him for leaving a detachment at Dewetsdorp, and not having a supporting body at Reddersberg upon which it might fall back; but it must be remembered that his total force was small and that he had to cover a long stretch of the lines of communication.

As to General Gatacre's energy and gallantry it is a by-word in the army; but coming after the Stormberg disaster this fresh mishap to his force made the continuance of his command impossible. Much sympathy was felt with him in the army, where he was universally liked and respected by officers and men. He returned to England, and his division was taken over by General Chermside.

In a single week, at a time when the back of the war had seemed to be broken, we had lost nearly twelve hundred men with seven guns. The men of the Free State—for the fighting was mainly done by commandos from the Ladybrand, Winburg, Bethlehem, and Harrismith districts—deserve great credit for this fine effort, and their leader De Wet confirmed the reputation which he had already gained as a dashing and indefatigable leader. His force was so weak that when Lord Roberts was able to really direct his own against it, he brushed it away before him; but the manner in which De Wet took advantage of Roberts's enforced immobility, and dared to get behind so mighty an enemy, was a fine exhibition of courage and enterprise. The public at home chafed at this sudden and unexpected turn of affairs; but the General, constant to his own fixed purpose, did not permit his strength to be wasted, and his cavalry to be again disorganised, by flying excursions, but waited grimly until he should be strong enough to strike straight at Pretoria.

In this short period of depression there came one gleam of light from the west. This was the capture of a commando of sixty Boers, or rather of sixty foreigners fighting for the Boers, and the death of the gallant Frenchman, De Villebois-Mareuil, who appears to have had the ambition of playing Lafayette in South Africa to Kruger's Washington. From the time that Kimberley had been reoccupied the British had been accumulating their force there so as to make a strong movement which should coincide with that of Roberts from Bloemfontein. Hunter's Division from Natal was being moved round to Kimberley, and Methuen already commanded a considerable body of troops, which included a number of the newly arrived Imperial Yeomanry. With these Methuen pacified the surrounding country, and extended his outposts to Barkly West on the one side, to Boshof on the other, and to Warrenton upon the Vaal River in the centre. On April 4th news reached Boshof that a Boer commando had been seen some ten miles to the east of the town, and a force, consisting of Yeomanry, Kimberley Light Horse, and half of Butcher's veteran 4th battery, was sent to attack them. They were found to have taken up their position upon a *kopje* which, contrary to all Boer custom, had no other *kopjes* to support it. French generalship was certainly not so astute as Boer cunning. The *kopje* was instantly surrounded, and the small force upon the summit being without artillery in the face of our guns found itself in exactly the same position which our men had been in twenty-four hours before at Reddersberg. Again was shown the advantage which the mounted rifleman has over the cavalry, for the Yeomanry and Light Horsemen left their horses and ascended the hill with the bayonet. In three hours all was over and the Boers had laid down their arms. Villebois was shot with seven of his companions, and there were nearly sixty prisoners. It speaks well for the skirmishing of the Yeomanry and the way in which they were handled by Lord Chesham that though they worked their way up the hill under fire they only lost four killed and a few wounded. The affair was a small one, but it was complete, and it came at a time when a success was very welcome. One bustling week had seen the expensive victory of Karee, the disasters of Sanna's Post and Reddersberg, and the successful skirmish of Boshof. Another chapter must be devoted to the movement towards the south of the Boer forces and the dispositions which Lord Roberts made to meet it.

CHAPTER 23

The Clearing of the South-East

Lord Roberts never showed his self-command and fixed purpose more clearly than during his six weeks' halt at Bloemfontein. De Wet, the most enterprising and aggressive of the Boer commanders, was attacking his eastern posts and menacing his line of communications. A fussy or nervous general would have harassed his men and worn out his horses by endeavouring to pursue a number of will-of-the-wisp commandos. Roberts contented himself by building up his strength at the capital, and by spreading nearly twenty thousand men along his line of rail from Bloemfontein to Bethulie. When the time came he would strike, but until then he rested. His army was not only being rehorsed and reshod, but in some respects was being reorganised. One powerful weapon which was forged during those weeks was the collection of the mounted infantry of the central army into one division, which was placed under the command of Ian Hamilton, with Hutton and Ridley as brigadiers. Hutton's brigade contained the Canadians, New South Wales men, West Australians, Queenslanders, New Zealanders, Victorians, South Australians, and Tasmanians, with four battalions of Imperial Mounted Infantry, and several light batteries. Ridley's brigade contained the South African irregular regiments of cavalry, with some imperial troops. The strength of the whole division came to over ten thousand rifles, and in its ranks there rode the hardiest and best from every corner of the earth over which the old flag is flying.

A word as to the general distribution of the troops at this instant while Roberts was gathering himself for his spring. Eleven divisions of infantry were in the field. Of these the 1st (Methuen's) and half the 10th (Hunter's) were at Kimberley, forming really the hundred-mile-distant left wing of Lord Roberts's army. On that side also was a considerable force of Yeomanry, as General Villebois discovered. In the centre with Roberts was the 6th division (Kelly-Kenny's) at Bloemfontein, the 7th (Tucker's) at Karee, twenty miles north, the 9th (Colvile's) and the 11th

261

(Pole-Carew's) near Bloemfontein. French's cavalry division was also in the centre. As one descended the line towards the Cape one came on the 3rd division (Chermside's, late Gatacre's), which had now moved up to Reddersberg, and then, further south, the 8th (Rundle's), near Rouxville. To the south and east was the other half of Hunter's division (Hart's brigade), and Brabant's Colonial division, half of which was shut up in Wepener and the rest at Aliwal. These were the troops operating in the Free State, with the addition of the division of mounted infantry in process of formation.

There remained the three divisions in Natal, the 2nd (Clery's), the 4th (Lyttelton's), and the 5th (Hildyard's, late Warren's), with the cavalry brigades of Burn-Murdoch, Dundonald, and Brocklehurst. These, with numerous militia and unbrigaded regiments along the lines of communi- cation, formed the British army in South Africa. At Mafeking some 900 irregulars stood at bay, with another force about as large under Plumer a little to the north, endeavouring to relieve them. At Beira, a Portuguese port through which we have treaty rights by which we may pass troops, a curious mixed force of Australians, New Zealanders and others was being disembarked and pushed through to Rhodesia, so as to cut off any trek which the Boers might make in that direction. Carrington, a fierce old soldier with a large experience of South African warfare, was in command of this picturesque force, which moved amid tropical forests over croc- odile-haunted streams, while their comrades were shivering in the cold southerly winds of a Cape winter. Neither our Government, our people, nor the world understood at the beginning of this campaign how grave was the task which we had undertaken, but, having once realised it, it must be acknowledged that it was carried through in no half-hearted way. So vast was the scene of operations that the Canadian might almost find his native climate at one end of it and the Queenslander at the other.

To follow in close detail the movements of the Boers and the counter movements of the British in the southeast portion of the Free State dur- ing this period would tax the industry of the historian and the patience of the reader. Let it be told with as much general truth and as little geographical detail as possible. The narrative which is interrupted by an eternal reference to the map is a narrative spoiled.

The main force of the Freestaters had assembled in the north-eastern corner of their State, and from this they made their sally southwards, at- tacking or avoiding at their pleasure the eastern line of British outposts. Their first engagement, that of Sanna's Post, was a great and deserved success. Three days later they secured the five companies at Reddersberg. Warned in time, the other small British bodies closed in upon their sup- ports, and the railway line, that nourishing artery which was necessary for the very existence of the army, was held too strongly for attack. The Bethulie Bridge was a particularly important point; but though the Boers approached it, and even went the length of announcing officially that they had destroyed it, it was not actually attacked. At Wepener, however, on the Basutoland border, they found an isolated force, and proceeded at once, according to their custom, to hem it in and to bombard it, until one of their three great allies, want of food, want of water, or want of cartridges, should compel a surrender.

On this occasion, however, the Boers had undertaken a task which was beyond their strength. The troops at Wepener were one thousand seven hundred in number, and formidable in quality. The place had been occupied by part of Brabant's Colonial division, consisting of hardy irregulars, men of the stuff of the defenders of Mafeking. Such men are too shrewd to be herded into an untenable position and too valiant to surrender a tenable one. The force was commanded by a dashing soldier, Colonel Dalgety, of the Cape Mounted Rifles, as tough a fighter as his famous namesake. There were with him nearly a thousand men of Brabant's Horse, four hundred of the Cape Mounted Rifles, four hundred Kaffrarian Horse, with some scouts, and one hundred regulars, including twenty invaluable Sappers. They were strong in guns—two seven-pounders, two naval twelve-pounders, two fifteen-pounders and several machine guns. The position which they had taken up, Jammersberg, three miles north of Wepener, was a very strong one, and it would have taken a larger force than De Wet had at his disposal to turn them out of it. The defence had been arranged by Major Cedric Maxwell, of the Sappers; and though the huge perimeter, nearly eight miles, made its defence by so small a force a most difficult matter, the result proved how good his dispositions were.

At the same time, the Boers came on with every confidence of victory, for they had a superiority in guns and an immense superiority in men. But after a day or two of fierce struggle their attack dwindled down into a mere blockade. On April 9th they attacked furiously, both by day and by night, and on the 10th the pressure was equally severe. In these two days occurred the vast majority of the casualties. But the defenders took cover in a way to which British regulars have not yet attained, and they outshot their opponents both with their rifles and their cannon. Captain Lukin's management of the artillery was particularly skilful. The weather was vile and the hastily dug trenches turned into ditches half full of water, but neither discomfort nor danger shook the courage of the gallant colonials. Assault after assault was repulsed, and the scourging of the cannon was met with stolid endurance. The Boers excelled all their previous feats in the handling of artillery by dragging two guns up to the summit of the lofty Jammersberg, whence they fired down upon the camp. Nearly all the horses were killed and three hundred of the troopers were hit, a number which is double that of the official return, for the simple reason that the spirit of the force was so high that only those who were very severely wounded reported themselves as wounded at all. None but the serious cases ever reached the hands of Dr. Faskally, who did admirable work with very slender resources. How many the enemy lost can never be certainly known, but as they pushed home several attacks it is impossible to imagine that their losses were less than those of the victorious defenders. At the end of seventeen days of mud and blood the brave irregulars saw an empty *laager* and abandoned trenches. Their own resistance and the advance of Brabant to their rescue had caused a hasty retreat of the enemy. Wepener, Mafeking, Kimberley, the taking of the first guns at Ladysmith, the deeds of the Imperial Light Horse—it cannot be denied that our irregular South African forces have a brilliant record for the war. They are associated with many successes and with few disasters. Their fine record cannot, I think, be fairly ascribed to any greater hardihood which one portion of our race has when compared with another, for a South African must admit that in the best colonial corps at least half the men were Britons of Britain. In the Imperial Light Horse the proportion was very much higher. But what may fairly be argued is that their exploits have proved, what the American war proved long ago, that the German conception of discipline is an obsolete fetish, and that the spirit of free men, whose individualism has been encouraged rather than crushed, is equal to any feat of arms. The clerks and miners and engineers who went up Elandslaagte Hill without bayonets, shoulder to shoulder with the Gordons, and who, according to Sir George White, saved Ladysmith on January 6th, have shown for ever that with men of our race it is the spirit within, and not the drill or the discipline, that makes a formidable soldier. An intelligent appreciation of the fact might in the course of the next few years save us as much money as would go far to pay for the war.

It may well be asked how for so long a period as seventeen days the British could tolerate a force to the rear of them when with their great superiority of numbers they could have readily sent an army to drive it away. The answer must be that Lord Roberts had despatched his trusty lieutenant, Kitchener, to Aliwal, whence he had been in heliographic communication with Wepener, that he was sure that the place could hold out, and that he was using it, as he did Kimberley, to hold the enemy while he was making his plans for their destruction. This was the bait to tempt them to their ruin. Had the trap not been a little slow in closing, the war in the Free State might have ended then and there. From the 9th to the 25th the Boers were held in front of Wepener. Let us trace the movements of the other British detachments during that time.

Brabant's force, with Hart's brigade, which had been diverted on its way to Kimberley, where it was to form part of Hunter's division, was moving on the south towards Wepener, advancing through Rouxville, but going slowly for fear of scaring the Boers away before they were sufficiently compromised. Chermside's 3rd division approached from the north-west, moving out from the railway at Bethany, and passing through Reddersberg towards Dewetsdorp, from which it would directly threaten the Boer line of retreat. The movement was made with reassuring slowness and gentleness, as when the curved hand approaches the unconscious fly. And then suddenly, on April 21st, Lord Roberts let everything go. Had the action of the agents been as swift and as energetic as the mind of the planner, De Wet could not have escaped us.

What held Lord Roberts's hand for some few days after he was ready to strike was the abominable weather. Rain was falling in sheets, and those who know South African roads, South African mud, and South African drifts will understand how impossible swift military movements are under those circumstances. But with the first clearing of the clouds the hills to the south and east of Bloemfontein were dotted with our scouts. Rundle with his 8th division was brought swiftly up from the south, united with Chermside to the east of Reddersberg, and the whole force, numbering 13,000 rifles with thirty guns, advanced upon Dewetsdorp, Rundle, as senior officer, being in command. As they marched the blue hills of Wepener lined the sky some twenty miles to the south, eloquent to every man of the aim and object of their march.

On April 20th, Rundle as he advanced found a force with artillery across his path to Dewetsdorp. It is always difficult to calculate the number of hidden men and lurking guns which go to make up a Boer army, but with some knowledge of their total at Wepener it was certain that the force opposed to him must be very inferior to his own. At Constantia Farm, where he found them in position, it is difficult to imagine that there were more than three thousand men. Their left flank was their weak point, as a movement on that side would cut them off from Wepener and drive them up towards our main force in the north. One would have thought that a containing force of three thousand men, and a flanking movement from eight thousand, would have turned them out, as it has turned them out so often before and since. Yet a long-range action began on Friday, April 20th, and lasted the whole of the 21st, the 22nd, and the 23rd, in which we sustained few losses, but made no impression upon the enemy. Thirty of the 1st Worcesters wandered at night into the wrong line, and were made prisoners, but with this exception the four days of noisy fighting does not appear to have cost either side fifty casualties. It is probable that the deliberation with which the operations were conducted was due to Rundle's instructions to wait until the other forces were in position. His subsequent movements showed that he was not a General who feared to strike.

On Sunday night (April 22nd) Pole-Carew sallied out from Bloemfontein on a line which would take him round the right flank of the Boers who were facing Rundle. The Boers had, however, occupied a strong position at Leeuw Kop, which barred his path, so that the Dewetsdorp Boers were covering the Wepener Boers, and being in turn covered by the Boers of Leeuw Kop. Before anything could be done, they must be swept out of the way. Pole-Carew is one of those finds which help to compensate us for the war. Handsome, dashing, debonair, he approaches a field of battle as a light-hearted schoolboy approaches a football field. On this occasion he acted with energy and discretion. His cavalry threatened the flanks of the enemy, and Stephenson's brigade carried the position in front at a small cost. On the same evening General French arrived and took over the force, which consisted now of Stephenson's and the Guards brigades (making up the 11th division), with two brigades of cavalry and one corps of mounted infantry. The next day, the 23rd, the advance was resumed, the cavalry bearing the brunt of the fighting. That gallant corps, Roberts's Horse, whose behaviour at Sanna's Post had been admirable, again distinguished itself, losing among others its Colonel, Brazier Creagh. On the 24th again it was to the horsemen that the honour and the casualties fell. The 9th Lancers, the regular cavalry regiment which bears away the honours of the war, lost several men and officers, and the 8th Hussars also suffered, but the Boers were driven from their position, and lost more heavily in this skirmish than in some of the larger battles of the campaign. The 'pom-poms,' which had been supplied to us by the belated energy of the Ordnance Department, were used with some effect in this engagement, and the Boers learned for the first time how unnerving are those noisy but not particularly deadly fireworks which they had so often crackled round the ears of our gunners.

On the Wednesday morning Rundle, with the addition of Pole-Carew's division, was strong enough for any attack, while French was in a position upon the flank. Every requisite for a great victory was there except the presence of an enemy. The Wepener siege had been raised and the force in front of Rundle had disappeared as only Boer armies can disappear. The combined movement was an admirable piece of work on the part of the enemy. Finding no force in front of them, the combined troops of French, Rundle, and Chermside occupied Dewetsdorp, where the latter remained, while the others pushed on to Thabanchu, the storm centre from which all our troubles had begun nearly a month before. All the way they knew that De Wet's retreating army was just in front of

them, and they knew also that a force had been sent out from Bloemfontein to Thabanchu to head off the Boers. Lord Roberts might naturally
suppose, when he had formed two cordons through which De Wet must
pass, that one or other must hold him. But with extraordinary skill and
mobility De Wet, aided by the fact that every inhabitant was a member
of his intelligence department, slipped through the double net which had
been laid for him. The first net was not in its place in time, and the second
was too small to hold him.

While Rundle and French had advanced on Dewetsdorp as described,
the other force which was intended to head off De Wet had gone direct
to Thabanchu. The advance began by a movement of Ian Hamilton on
April 22nd with eight hundred mounted infantry upon the waterworks.
The enemy, who held the hills beyond, allowed Hamilton's force to come
right down to the Modder before they opened fire from three guns. The
mounted infantry fell back, and encamped for the night out of range.[1]
Before morning they were reinforced by Smith-Dorrien's brigade (Gordons, Canadians, and Shropshires—the Cornwalls had been left behind)
and some more mounted Infantry. With daylight a fine advance was begun, the brigade moving up in very extended order and the mounted
men turning the right flank of the defence. By evening we had regained
the waterworks, a most important point for Bloemfontein, and we held all
the line of hills which command it. This strong position would not have
been gained so easily if it had not been for Pole-Carew's and French's actions two days before, on their way to join Rundle, which enabled them
to turn it from the south.

Ian Hamilton, who had already done good service in the war, having
commanded the infantry at Elandslaagte, and been one of the most prominent leaders in the defence of Ladysmith, takes from this time onwards a
more important and a more independent position. A thin, aquiline man,
of soft voice and gentle manners, he had already proved more than once
during his adventurous career that he not only possessed in a high degree
the courage of the soldier, but also the equanimity and decision of the
born leader. A languid elegance in his bearing covered a shrewd brain and
a soul of fire. A distorted and half-paralysed hand reminded the observer
that Hamilton, as a young lieutenant, had known at Majuba what it was
to face the Boer rifles. Now, in his forty-seventh year, he had returned,
matured and formidable, to reverse the results of that first deplorable
campaign. This was the man to whom Lord Roberts had entrusted the

---

1. This was a remarkable exhibition of the harmlessness of shell-fire against troops in
open formation. I myself saw at least forty shells, all of which burst, fall among the
ranks of the mounted infantry, who retired at a contemptuous walk. There were no
casualties.

command of that powerful flanking column which was eventually to form the right wing of his main advance. Being reinforced upon the morning after the capture of the Waterworks by the Highland Brigade, the Cornwalls, and two heavy naval guns, his whole force amounted to not less than seven thousand men. From these he detached a garrison for the Waterworks, and with the rest he continued his march over the hilly country which lies between them and Thabanchu.

One position, Israel's Poort, a *nek* between two hills, was held against them on April 25th, but was gained without much trouble, the Canadians losing one killed and two wounded. Colonel Otter, their gallant leader, was one of the latter, while Marshall's Horse, a colonial corps raised in Grahamstown, had no fewer than seven of their officers and several men killed or wounded. Next morning the town of Thabanchu was seized, and Hamilton found himself upon the direct line of the Boer retreat. He seized the pass which commands the road, and all next day he waited eagerly, and the hearts of his men beat high when at last they saw a long trail of dust winding up to them from the south. At last the wily De Wet had been headed off! Deep and earnest were the curses when out of the dust there emerged a khaki column of horsemen, and it was realised that this was French's pursuing force, closely followed by Rundle's infantry from Dewetsdorp. The Boers had slipped round and were already to the north of us.

It is impossible to withhold our admiration for the way in which the Boer force was manoeuvred throughout this portion of the campaign. The mixture of circumspection and audacity, the way in which French and Rundle were hindered until the Wepener force had disengaged itself, the manner in which these covering forces were then withdrawn, and finally the clever way in which they all slipped past Hamilton, make a brilliant bit of strategy. Louis Botha, the generalissimo, held all the strings in his hand, and the way in which he pulled them showed that his countrymen had chosen the right man for that high office, and that his was a master spirit even among those fine natural warriors who led the separate commandos.

Having got to the north of the British forces Botha made no effort to get away, and refused to be hustled by a reconnaissance developing into an attack, which French made upon April 27th. In a skirmish the night before Kitchener's Horse had lost fourteen men, and the action of the 27th cost us about as many casualties. It served to show that the Boer force was a compact body some six or seven thousand strong, which withdrew in a leisurely fashion, and took up a defensive position at Houtnek, some miles further on. French remained at Thabanchu, from which he afterwards joined Lord Roberts' advance, while Hamilton now assumed complete command of the flanking column, with which he proceeded to march north upon Winburg.

The Houtnek position is dominated upon the left of the advancing British force by Thoba Mountain, and it was this point which was the centre of Hamilton's attack. It was most gallantly seized by Kitchener's Horse, who were quickly supported by Smith-Dorrien's men. The mountain became the scene of a brisk action, and night fell before the crest was cleared. At dawn upon May 1st the fighting was resumed, and the position was carried by a determined advance of the Shropshires, the Canadians, and the Gordons: the Boers escaping down the reverse slope of the hill came under a heavy fire of our infantry, and fifty of them were wounded or taken. It was in this action, during the fighting on the hill, that Captain Towse, of the Gordons, though shot through the eyes and totally blind, encouraged his men to charge through a group of the enemy who had gathered round them. After this victory Hamilton's men, who had fought for seven days out of ten, halted for a rest at Jacobsrust, where they were joined by Broadwood's cavalry and Bruce Hamilton's infantry brigade. Ian Hamilton's column now contained two infantry brigades (Smith-Dorrien's and Bruce Hamilton's), Ridley's Mounted Infantry, Broadwood's Cavalry Brigade, five batteries of artillery, two heavy guns, altogether 13,000 men. With this force in constant touch with Botha's rearguard, Ian Hamilton pushed on once more on May 4th. On May 5th he fought a brisk cavalry skirmish, in which Kitchener's Horse and the 12th Lancers distinguished themselves, and on the same day he took possession of Winburg, thus covering the right of Lord Roberts's great advance.

The distribution of the troops on the eastern side of the Free State was, at the time of this the final advance of the main army, as follows—Ian Hamilton with his mounted infantry, Smith-Dorrien's brigade, Macdonald's brigade, Bruce Hamilton's brigade, and Broadwood's cavalry were at Winburg. Rundle was at Thabanchu, and Brabant's colonial division was moving up to the same point. Chermside was at Dewetsdorp, and had detached a force under Lord Castletown to garrison Wepener. Hart occupied Smithfield, whence he and his brigade were shortly to be transferred to the Kimberley force. Altogether there could not have been fewer than thirty thousand men engaged in clearing and holding down this part of the country. French's cavalry and Pole-Carew's division had returned to take part in the central advance.

Before entering upon a description of that great and decisive movement, one small action calls for comment. This was the cutting off of twenty men of Lumsden's Horse in a reconnaissance at Karee. The small post under Lieutenant Crane found themselves by some misunderstanding isolated in the midst of the enemy. Refusing to hoist the flag of shame, they fought their way out, losing half their number, while of the other half it is said that there was not one who could not show bullet marks upon his clothes or person. The men of this corps, volunteer Anglo-Indians, had abandoned the ease and even luxury of Eastern life for the hard fare and rough fighting of this most trying campaign. In coming they had set the whole empire an object-lesson in spirit, and now on their first field they set the army an example of military virtue. The proud traditions of Outram's Volunteers have been upheld by the men of Lumsden's Horse. Another minor action which cannot be ignored is the defence of a convoy on April 29th by the Derbyshire Yeomanry (Major Dugdale) and a company of the Scots Guards. The wagons were on their way to Rundle when they were attacked at a point about ten miles west of Thabanchu. The small guard beat off their assailants in the most gallant fashion, and held their own until relieved by Brabazon upon the following morning.

This phase of the war was marked by a certain change in the temper of the British. Nothing could have been milder than the original intentions and proclamations of Lord Roberts, and he was most ably seconded in his attempts at conciliation by General Pretyman, who had been made civil administrator of the State. There was evidence, however, that this kindness had been construed as weakness by some of the burghers, and during the Boer incursion to Wepener many who had surrendered a worthless firearm reappeared with the Mauser which had been concealed in some crafty hiding-place. Troops were fired at from farmhouses which flew the white flag, and the good housewife remained behind to charge the *rooinek* extortionate prices for milk and fodder while her husband shot at him from the hills. It was felt that the burghers might have peace or might have war, but could not have both simultaneously. Some examples were made therefore of offending farmhouses, and stock was confiscated where there was evidence of double dealing upon the part of the owner. In a country where property is a more serious thing than life, these measures, together with more stringent rules about the possession of horses and arms, did much to stamp out the chances of an insurrection in our rear. The worst sort of peace is an enforced peace, but if that can be established time and justice may do the rest.

The operations which have been here described may be finally summed up in one short paragraph. A Boer army came south of the British line and besieged a British garrison. Three British forces, those of French, Rundle, and Ian Hamilton, were despatched to cut it off. It successfully threaded its way among them and escaped. It was followed to the northward as far as the town of Winburg, which remained in the British possession. Lord Roberts had failed in his plan of cutting off De Wet's army, but, at the expense of many marches and skirmishes, the south-east of the State was cleared of the enemy.

CHAPTER 24

The Siege of Mafeking

This small place, which sprang in the course of a few weeks from obscurity to fame, is situated upon the long line of railway which connects Kimberley in the south with Rhodesia in the north. In character it resembles one of those western American townlets which possess small present assets but immense aspirations. In its litter of corrugated-iron roofs, and in the church and the racecourse, which are the first-fruits everywhere of Anglo-Celtic civilisation, one sees the seeds of the great city of the future. It is the obvious depot for the western Transvaal upon one side, and the starting-point for all attempts upon the Kalahari Desert upon the other. The Transvaal border runs within a few miles.

It is not clear why the imperial authorities should desire to hold this place, since it has no natural advantages to help the defence, but lies exposed in a widespread plain. A glance at the map must show that the railway line would surely be cut both to the north and south of the town, and the garrison isolated at a point some two hundred and fifty miles from any reinforcements. Considering that the Boers could throw any strength of men or guns against the place, it seemed certain that if they seriously desired to take possession of it they could do so. Under ordinary circumstances any force shut up there was doomed to capture. But what may have seemed short-sighted policy became the highest wisdom, owing to the extraordinary tenacity and resource of Baden-Powell, the officer in command. Through his exertions the town acted as a bait to the Boers, and occupied a considerable force in a useless siege at a time when their presence at other seats of war might have proved disastrous to the British cause.

Colonel Baden-Powell is a soldier of a type which is exceedingly popular with the British public. A skilled hunter and an expert at many games, there was always something of the sportsman in his keen appreciation of war. In the Matabele campaign he had out-scouted the savage scouts and found his pleasure in tracking them among their native mountains, often alone and at night, trusting to his skill in springing from rock to rock in his rubber-soled shoes to save him from their pursuit. There was a brain quality in his bravery which is rare among our officers. Full of *veldt* craft and resource, it was as difficult to outwit as it was to out-fight him. But there was another curious side to his complex nature. The French have said of one of their heroes, *'Il avait cette graine de folie dans sa bravoure que les Francais aiment,'* and the words might have been written of Powell. An impish humour broke out in him, and the mischievous schoolboy alternated with the warrior and the administrator. He met the Boer commandos with chaff and jokes which were as disconcerting as his wire entanglements and his rifle-pits. The amazing variety of his personal accomplishments was one of his most striking characteristics. From draw-ing caricatures with both hands simultaneously, or skirt dancing to lead-ing a forlorn hope, nothing came amiss to him; and he had that magnetic quality by which the leader imparts something of his virtues to his men. Such was the man who held Mafeking for the Queen.

In a very early stage, before the formal declaration of war, the enemy had massed several commandos upon the western border, the men being drawn from Zeerust, Rustenburg, and Lichtenburg. Baden-Powell, with the aid of an excellent group of special officers, who included Colonel Gould Adams, Lord Edward Cecil, the soldier son of England's Premier, and Colonel Hore, had done all that was possible to put the place into a state of defence. In this he had immense assistance from Benjamin Weil, a well known South African contractor, who had shown great energy in provisioning the town. On the other hand, the South African Govern-ment displayed the same stupidity or treason which had been exhibited in the case of Kimberley, and had met all demands for guns and reinforce-ments with foolish doubts as to the need of such precautions. In the en-deavour to supply these pressing wants the first small disaster of the cam-paign was encountered. On October 12th, the day after the declaration of war, an armoured train conveying two 7-pounders for the Mafeking defences was derailed and captured by a Boer raiding party at Kraaipan, a place forty miles south of their destination. The enemy shelled the shat-tered train until after five hours Captain Nesbitt, who was in command, and his men, some twenty in number, surrendered. It was a small affair, but it derived importance from being the first blood shed and the first tactical success of the war.

The garrison of the town, whose fame will certainly live in the history of South Africa, contained no regular soldiers at all with the exception of the small group of excellent officers. They consisted of irregular troops, three hundred and forty of the Protectorate Regiment, one hundred and seventy Police, and two hundred volunteers, made up of that singular mixture of adventurers, younger sons, broken gentlemen, and irresponsible sportsmen who have always been the *voortrekkers* of the British Empire. These men were of the same stamp as those other admirable bodies of natural fighters who did so well in Rhodesia, in Natal, and in the Cape. With them there was associated in the defence the Town Guard, who included the able-bodied shopkeepers, businessmen, and residents, the whole amounting to about nine hundred men. Their artillery was feeble in the extreme, two 7-pounder toy guns and six machine guns, but the spirit of the men and the resource of their leaders made up for every disadvantage. Colonel Vyvyan and Major Panzera planned the defences, and the little trading town soon began to take on the appearance of a fortress.

On October 13th the Boers appeared before Mafeking. On the same day Colonel Baden-Powell sent two truckloads of dynamite out of the place. They were fired into by the invaders, with the result that they exploded. On October 14th the pickets around the town were driven in by the Boers. On this the armoured train and a squadron of the Protectorate Regiment went out to support the pickets and drove the Boers before them. A body of the latter doubled back and interposed between the British and Mafeking, but two fresh troops with a 7-pounder throwing shrapnel drove them off. In this spirited little action the garrison lost two killed and fourteen wounded, but they inflicted considerable damage on the enemy. To Captain Williams, Captain FitzClarence, and Lord Charles Bentinck great credit is due for the way in which they handled their men; but the whole affair was ill advised, for if a disaster had occurred Mafeking must have fallen, being left without a garrison. No possible results which could come from such a sortie could justify the risk which was run.

On October 16th the siege began in earnest. On that date the Boers brought up two 12-pounder guns, and the first of that interminable flight of shells fell into the town. The enemy got possession of the water supply, but the garrison had already dug wells. Before October 20th five thousand Boers, under the formidable Cronje, had gathered round the town. 'Surrender to avoid bloodshed' was his message. 'When is the bloodshed going to begin?' asked Powell. When the Boers had been shelling the town for some weeks the light-hearted Colonel sent out to say that if they went on any longer he should be compelled to regard it as equivalent to a declaration of war. It is to be hoped that Cronje also possessed some sense of humour, or else he must have been as sorely puzzled by his eccentric opponent as the Spanish generals were by the vagaries of Lord Peterborough.

Among the many difficulties which had to be met by the defenders of the town the most serious was the fact that the position had a circumference of five or six miles to be held by about one thousand men against a force who at their own time and their own place could at any moment attempt to gain a footing. An ingenious system of small forts was devised to meet the situation. Each of these held from ten to forty riflemen, and was furnished with bomb-proofs and covered ways. The central bomb-proof was connected by telephone with all the outlying ones, so as to save the use of orderlies. A system of bells was arranged by which each quarter of the town was warned when a shell was coming in time to enable the inhabitants to scuttle off to shelter. Every detail showed the ingenuity of the controlling mind. The armoured train, painted green and tied round with scrub, stood unperceived among the clumps of bushes which surrounded the town.

On October 24th a savage bombardment commenced, which lasted with intermissions for seven months. The Boers had brought an enormous gun across from Pretoria, throwing a 96-pound shell, and this, with many smaller pieces, played upon the town. The result was as futile as our own artillery fire has so often been when directed against the Boers.

As the Mafeking guns were too weak to answer the enemy's fire, the only possible reply lay in a sortie, and upon this Colonel Powell decided. It was carried out with great gallantry on the evening of October 27th, when about a hundred men under Captain FitzClarence moved out against the Boer trenches with instructions to use the bayonet only. The position was carried with a rush, and many of the Boers bayoneted before they could disengage themselves from the tarpaulins which covered them. The trenches behind fired wildly in the darkness, and it is probable that as many of their own men as of ours were hit by their rifle fire. The total loss in this gallant affair was six killed, eleven wounded, and two prisoners. The loss of the enemy, though shrouded as usual in darkness, was certainly very much higher.

On October 31st the Boers ventured upon an attack on Cannon Kopje, which is a small fort and eminence to the south of the town. It was defended by Colonel Walford, of the British South African Police, with fifty-seven of his men and three small guns. The attack was repelled with heavy loss to the Boers. The British casualties were six killed and five wounded.

Their experience in this attack seems to have determined the Boers to make no further expensive attempts to rush the town, and for some weeks the siege degenerated into a blockade. Cronje had been recalled for more important work, and Commandant Snyman had taken over the uncompleted task. From time to time the great gun tossed its huge shells into the town, but boardwood walls and corrugated-iron roofs minimise the dangers of a bombardment. On November 3rd the garrison rushed the Brickfields, which had been held by the enemy's sharpshooters, and on the 7th another small sally kept the game going. On the 18th Powell sent a message to Snyman that he could not take the town by sitting and looking at it. At the same time he despatched a message to the Boer forces generally, advising them to return to their homes and their families. Some of the commandos had gone south to assist Cronje in his stand against Methuen, and the siege languished more and more, until it was woken up by a desperate sortie on December 26th, which caused the greatest loss which the garrison had sustained. Once more the lesson was to be enforced that with modern weapons and equality of forces it is always long odds on the defence.

On this date a vigorous attack was made upon one of the Boer forts on the north. There seems to be little doubt that the enemy had some inkling of our intention, as the fort was found to have been so strengthened as to be impregnable without scaling ladders. The attacking force consisted of two squadrons of the Protectorate Regiment and one of the Bechuanaland Rifles, backed up by three guns. So desperate was the onslaught that of the actual attacking party—a forlorn hope, if ever there was one—fifty-three out of eighty were killed and wounded, twenty-five of the former and twenty-eight of the latter. Several of that gallant band of officers who had been the soul of the defence were among the injured. Captain FitzClarence was wounded, Vernon, Sandford, and Paton were killed, all at the very muzzles of the enemy's guns. It must have been one of the bitterest moments of Baden-Powell's life when he shut his field-glass and said, 'Let the ambulance go out!'

Even this heavy blow did not damp the spirits nor diminish the energies of the defence, though it must have warned Baden-Powell that he could not afford to drain his small force by any more expensive attempts at the offensive, and that from then onwards he must content himself by holding grimly on until Plumer from the north or Methuen from the south should at last be able to stretch out to him a helping hand. Vigilant and indomitable, throwing away no possible point in the game which he was playing, the new year found him and his hardy garrison sternly determined to keep the flag flying.

January and February offer in their records that monotony of excitement which is the fate of every besieged town. On one day the shelling was a little more, on another a little less. Sometimes they escaped scatheless, sometimes the garrison found itself the poorer by the loss of Captain Girdwood or Trooper Webb or some other gallant soldier. Occasionally they had their little triumph when a too curious Dutchman, peering for an instant from his cover to see the effect of his shot, was carried back in the ambulance to the *laager*. On Sunday a truce was usually observed, and the snipers who had exchanged rifle-shots all the week met occasionally on that day with good-humoured chaff. Snyman, the Boer General, showed none of that chivalry at Mafeking which distinguished the gallant old Joubert at Ladysmith. Not only was there no neutral camp for women or sick, but it is beyond all doubt or question that the Boer guns were deliberately turned upon the women's quarters inside Mafeking in order to bring pressure upon the inhabitants. Many women and children were sacrificed to this brutal policy, which must in fairness be set to the account of the savage leader, and not of the rough but kindly folk with whom we were fighting. In every race there are individual ruffians, and it would be a political mistake to allow our action to be influenced or our feelings permanently embittered by their crimes. It is from the man himself, and not from his country, that an account should be exacted.

The garrison, in the face of increasing losses and decreasing food, lost none of the high spirits which it reflected from its commander. The programme of a single day of jubilee—Heaven only knows what they had to hold jubilee over—shows a cricket match in the morning, sports in the afternoon, a concert in the evening, and a dance, given by the bachelor officers, to wind up. Baden-Powell himself seems to have descended from the eyrie from which, like a captain on the bridge, he rang bells and telephoned orders, to bring the house down with a comic song and a humorous recitation. The ball went admirably, save that there was an interval to repel an attack which disarranged the programme. Sports were zealously cultivated, and the grimy inhabitants of casemates and trenches were pitted against each other at cricket or football.[1] The monotony was broken by the occasional visits of a postman, who appeared or vanished from the vast barren lands to the west of the town, which could not all be guarded by the besiegers. Sometimes a few words from home came to cheer the hearts of the exiles, and could be returned by the same uncertain and expensive means. The documents which found their way up were not always of an essential or even of a welcome character. At least one man received an unpaid bill from an angry tailor.

In one particular Mafeking had, with much smaller resources, rivalled Kimberley. An ordnance factory had been started, formed in the railway workshops, and conducted by Connely and Cloughlan, of the Locomotive Department. Daniels, of the police, supplemented their efforts by making both powder and fuses. The factory turned out shells, and eventually constructed a 5.5-inch smooth-bore gun, which threw a round shell with great accuracy to a considerable range. April found the garrison, in spite of all losses, as efficient and as resolute as it had been in

1. Sunday cricket so shocked Snyman that he threatened to fire upon it if it were continued.

October. So close were the advanced trenches upon either side that both parties had recourse to the old-fashioned hand grenades, thrown by the Boers, and cast on a fishing-line by ingenious Sergeant Page, of the Protectorate Regiment. Sometimes the besiegers and the number of guns diminished, forces being detached to prevent the advance of Plumer's relieving column from the north; but as those who remained held their forts, which it was beyond the power of the British to storm, the garrison was now much the better for the alleviation. Putting Mafeking for Ladysmith and Plumer for Buller, the situation was not unlike that which had existed in Natal.

At this point some account might be given of the doings of that northern force whose situation was so remote that even the ubiquitous correspondent hardly appears to have reached it. No doubt the book will eventually make up for the neglect of the journal, but some short facts may be given here of the Rhodesian column. Their action did not affect the course of the war, but they clung like bulldogs to a most difficult task, and eventually, when strengthened by the relieving column, made their way to Mafeking.

The force was originally raised for the purpose of defending Rhodesia, and it consisted of fine material pioneers, farmers, and miners from the great new land which had been added through the energy of Mr. Rhodes to the British Empire. Many of the men were veterans of the native wars, and all were imbued with a hardy and adventurous spirit. On the other hand, the men of the northern and western Transvaal, whom they were called upon to face the burghers of Watersberg and Zoutpansberg, were tough frontiersmen living in a land where a dinner was shot, not bought. Shaggy, hairy, half-savage men, handling a rifle as a mediaeval Englishman handled a bow, and skilled in every wile of *veldt* craft, they were as formidable opponents as the world could show.

On the war breaking out the first thought of the leaders in Rhodesia was to save as much of the line which was their connection through Mafeking with the south as was possible. For this purpose an armoured train was despatched only three days after the expiration of the ultimatum to the point four hundred miles south of Bulawayo, where the frontiers of the Transvaal and of Bechuanaland join. Colonel Holdsworth commanded the small British force. The Boers, a thousand or so in number, had descended upon the railway, and an action followed in which the train appears to have had better luck than has usually attended these ill-fated contrivances. The Boer commando was driven back and a number were killed. It was probably news of this affair, and not anything which had occurred at Mafeking, which caused those rumours of gloom at Pretoria very shortly after the outbreak of hostilities. An agency telegraphed that women were weeping in the streets of the Boer capital. We had not then realised how soon and how often we should see the same sight in Pall Mall.

The adventurous armoured train pressed on as far as Lobatsi, where it found the bridges destroyed; so it returned to its original position, having another brush with the Boer commandos, and again, in some marvellous way, escaping its obvious fate. From then until the new year the line was kept open by an admirable system of patrolling to within a hundred miles or so of Mafeking. An aggressive spirit and a power of dashing initiative were shown in the British operations at this side of the scene of war such as have too often been absent elsewhere. At Sekwani, on November 24th, a considerable success was gained by a surprise planned and carried out by Colonel Holdsworth. The Boer *laager* was approached and attacked in the early morning by a force of one hundred and twenty frontiersmen, and so effective was their fire that the Boers estimated their numbers at several thousand. Thirty Boers were killed or wounded, and the rest scattered.

While the railway line was held in this way there had been some skirmishing also on the northern frontier of the Transvaal. Shortly after the outbreak of the war the gallant Blackburn, scouting with six comrades in thick bush, found himself in the presence of a considerable commando. The British concealed themselves by the path, but Blackburn's foot was seen by a keen-eyed Kaffir, who pointed it out to his masters. A sudden volley riddled Blackburn with bullets; but his men stayed by him and drove off the enemy. Blackburn dictated an official report of the action, and then died.

In the same region a small force under Captain Hare was cut off by a body of Boers. Of the twenty men most got away, but the chaplain J.W. Leary, Lieutenant Haserick (who behaved with admirable gallantry), and six men were taken.[2] The commando which attacked this party, and on the same day Colonel Spreckley's force, was a powerful one, with several guns. No doubt it was organised because there were fears among the Boers that they would be invaded from the north. When it was understood that the British intended no large aggressive movement in that quarter, these burghers joined other commandos. Sarel Eloff, who was one of the leaders of this northern force, was afterwards taken at Mafeking.

Colonel Plumer had taken command of the small army which was now operating from the north along the railway line with Mafeking for its objective. Plumer is an officer of considerable experience in African warfare, a small, quiet, resolute man, with a knack of gently enforcing

2. Footnote: Mr. Leary was wounded in the foot by a shell. The German artillerist entered the hut in which he lay. 'Here's a bit of your work!' said Leary good-humouredly. 'I wish it had been worse,' said the amiable German gunner.

discipline upon the very rough material with which he had to deal. With his weak force—which never exceeded a thousand men, and was usually from six to seven hundred—he had to keep the long line behind him open, build up the ruined railway in front of him, and gradually creep onwards in face of a formidable and enterprising enemy. For a long time Gaberones, which is eighty miles north of Mafeking, remained his headquarters, and thence he kept up precarious communications with the besieged garrison. In the middle of March he advanced as far south as Lobatsi, which is less than fifty miles from Mafeking; but the enemy proved to be too strong, and Plumer had to drop back again with some loss to his original position at Gaberones. Sticking doggedly to his task, Plumer again came south, and this time made his way as far as Ramathlabama, within a day's march of Mafeking. He had with him, however, only three hundred and fifty men, and had he pushed through the effect might have been an addition of hungry men to the garrison. The relieving force was fiercely attacked, however, by the Boers and driven back on to their camp with a loss of twelve killed, twenty-six wounded, and fourteen missing. Some of the British were dismounted men, and it says much for Plumer's conduct of the fight that he was able to extricate these safely from the midst of an aggressive mounted enemy. Personally he set an admirable example, sending away his own horse, and walking with his rearmost soldiers. Captain Crewe Robertson and Lieutenant Milligan, the famous Yorkshire cricketer, were killed, and Rolt, Jarvis, Maclaren, and Plumer himself were wounded. The Rhodesian force withdrew again to near Lobatsi, and collected itself for yet another effort.

In the meantime Mafeking—abandoned, as it seemed, to its fate—was still as formidable as a wounded lion. Far from weakening in its defence it became more aggressive, and so persistent and skilful were its riflemen that the big Boer gun had again and again to be moved further from the town. Six months of trenches and rifle-pits had turned every inhabitant into a veteran. Now and then words of praise and encouragement came to them from without. Once it was a special message from the Queen, once a promise of relief from Lord Roberts. But the rails which led to England were overgrown with grass, and their brave hearts yearned for the sight of their countrymen and for the sound of their voices. 'How long, O Lord, how long?' was the cry which was wrung from them in their solitude. But the flag was still held high.

April was a trying month for the defence. They knew that Methuen, who had advanced as far as Fourteen Streams upon the Vaal River, had retired again upon Kimberley. They knew also that Plumer's force had been weakened by the repulse at Ramathlabama, and that many of his men were down with fever. Six weary months had this village withstood the pitiless pelt of rifle bullet and shell. Help seemed as far away from them as ever. But if troubles may be allayed by sympathy, then theirs should have lain lightly. The attention of the whole empire had centred upon them, and even the advance of Roberts's army became secondary to the fate of this gallant struggling handful of men who had upheld the flag so long. On the Continent also their resistance attracted the utmost interest, and the numerous journals there who find the imaginative writer cheaper than the war correspondent announced their capture periodically as they had once done that of Ladysmith. From a mere tin-roofed village Mafeking had become a prize of victory, a stake which should be the visible sign of the predominating manhood of one or other of the great white races of South Africa. Unconscious of the keenness of the emotions which they had aroused, the garrison manufactured brawn from horsehide, and captured locusts as a relish for their luncheons, while in the shot-torn billiard-room of the club an open tournament was started to fill in their hours off duty. But their vigilance, and that of the hawk-eyed man up in the Conning Tower, never relaxed. The besiegers had increased in number, and their guns were more numerous than before. A less acute man than Baden-Powell might have reasoned that at least one desperate effort would be made by them to carry the town before relief could come.

On Saturday, May 12th, the attack was made at the favourite hour of the Boer—the first grey of the morning. It was gallantly delivered by about three hundred volunteers under the command of Eloff, who had crept round to the west of the town—the side furthest from the lines of the besiegers. At the first rush they penetrated into the native quarter, which was at once set on fire by them. The first building of any size upon that side is the barracks of the Protectorate Regiment, which was held by Colonel Hore and about twenty of his officers and men. This was carried by the enemy, who sent an exultant message along the telephone to Baden-Powell to tell him that they had got it. Two other positions within the lines, one a stone *kraal* and the other a hill, were held by the Boers, but their supports were slow in coming on, and the movements of the defenders were so prompt and energetic that all three found themselves isolated and cut off from their own lines. They had penetrated the town, but they were as far as ever from having taken it. All day the British forces drew their cordon closer and closer round the Boer positions, making no attempt to rush them, but ringing them round in such a way that there could be no escape for them. A few burghers slipped away in twos and threes, but the main body found that they had rushed into a prison from which the only egress was swept with rifle fire. At seven o'clock in the evening they recognised that their position was hopeless, and Eloff with 117 men laid down their arms. Their losses had been ten killed and nineteen wounded. For some reason, either of lethargy, cowardice, or treachery, Snyman had not brought up the supports which might conceivably have altered the result. It was a gallant attack gallantly met, and for once the greater wiliness in fight was shown by the British. The end was characteristic. 'Good evening, Commandant,' said Powell to Eloff; 'won't you come in and have some dinner?' The prisoners—burghers, Hollanders, Germans, and Frenchmen—were treated to as good a supper as the destitute larders of the town could furnish.

So in a small blaze of glory ended the historic siege of Mafeking, for Eloff's attack was the last, though by no means the worst of the trials which the garrison had to face. Six killed and ten wounded were the British losses in this admirably managed affair. On May 17th, five days after the fight, the relieving force arrived, the besiegers were scattered, and the long-imprisoned garrison were free men once more. Many who had looked at their maps and saw this post isolated in the very heart of Africa had despaired of ever reaching their heroic fellow-countrymen, and now one universal outbreak of joy-bells and bonfires from Toronto to Melbourne proclaimed that there is no spot so inaccessible that the long arm of the empire cannot reach it when her children are in peril.

Colonel Mahon, a young Irish officer who had made his reputation as a cavalry leader in Egypt, had started early in May from Kimberley with a small but mobile force consisting of the Imperial Light Horse (brought round from Natal for the purpose), the Kimberley Mounted Corps, the Diamond Fields Horse, some Imperial Yeomanry, a detachment of the Cape Police, and 100 volunteers from the Fusilier brigade, with M battery R.H.A. and pom-poms, twelve hundred men in all. Whilst Hunter was fighting his action at Rooidam on May 4th, Mahon with his men struck round the western flank of the Boers and moved rapidly to the northwards. On May 11th they had left Vryburg, the halfway house, behind them, having done one hundred and twenty miles in five days. They pushed on, encountering no opposition save that of nature, though they knew that they were being closely watched by the enemy. At Koodoosrand it was found that a Boer force was in position in front, but Mahon avoided them by turning somewhat to the westward. His detour took him, however, into a bushy country, and here the enemy headed him off, opening fire at short range upon the ubiquitous Imperial Light Horse, who led the column. A short engagement ensued, in which the casualties amounted to thirty killed and wounded, but which ended in the defeat and dispersal of the Boers, whose force was certainly very much weaker than the British. On May 15th the relieving column arrived without further opposition at Masibi Stadt, twenty miles to the west of Mafeking.

In the meantime Plumer's force upon the north had been strengthened by the addition of C battery of four 12-pounder guns of the Canadian Artillery under Major Eudon and a body of Queenslanders. These forces had been part of the small army which had come with General Carrington through Beira, and after a detour of thousands of miles, through their own wonderful energy they had arrived in time to form portion of the relieving column. Foreign military critics, whose experience of warfare is to move troops across a frontier, should think of what the Empire has to do before her men go into battle. These contingents had been assembled by long railway journeys, conveyed across thousands of miles of ocean to Cape Town, brought round another two thousand or so to Beira, transferred by a narrow-gauge railway to Bamboo Creek, changed to a broader gauge to Marandellas, sent on in coaches for hundreds of miles to Bulawayo, transferred to trains for another four or five hundred miles to Ootsi, and had finally a forced march of a hundred miles, which brought them up a few hours before their presence was urgently needed upon the field. Their advance, which averaged twenty-five miles a day on foot for four consecutive days over deplorable roads, was one of the finest performances of the war. With these high-spirited reinforcements and with his own hardy Rhodesians Plumer pushed on, and the two columns reached the hamlet of Masibi Stadt within an hour of each other. Their united strength was far superior to anything which Snyman's force could place against them.

But the gallant and tenacious Boers would not abandon their prey without a last effort. As the little army advanced upon Mafeking they found the enemy waiting in a strong position. For some hours the Boers gallantly held their ground, and their artillery fire was, as usual, most accurate. But our own guns were more numerous and equally well served, and the position was soon made untenable. The Boers retired past Mafeking and took refuge in the trenches upon the eastern side, but Baden-Powell with his war-hardened garrison sallied out, and, supported by the artillery fire of the relieving column, drove them from their shelter. With their usual admirable tactics their larger guns had been removed, but one small cannon was secured as a souvenir by the townsfolk, together with a number of wagons and a considerable quantity of supplies. A long rolling trail of dust upon the eastern horizon told that the famous siege of Mafeking had at last come to an end.

So ended a singular incident, the defence of an open town which contained no regular soldiers and a most inadequate artillery against a numerous and enterprising enemy with very heavy guns. All honour to the towns folk who bore their trial so long and so bravely—and to the indomitable men who lined the trenches for seven weary months. Their constancy was of enormous value to the empire. In the all-important early month at least four or five thousand Boers were detained by them when their presence elsewhere would have been fatal. During all the rest of the war, two thousand men and eight guns (including one of the four big Creusots) had been held there. It prevented the invasion of Rhodesia, and it gave a rallying-point for loyal whites and natives in the huge stretch of country from Kimberley to Bulawayo. All this had, at a cost of two hundred lives, been done by this one devoted band of men, who killed, wounded, or took no fewer than one thousand of their opponents. Critics may say that the enthusiasm in the empire was excessive, but at least it was expended over worthy men and a fine deed of arms.

CHAPTER 25

The March on Pretoria

In the early days of May, when the season of the rains was past and the *veldt* was green, Lord Roberts's six weeks of enforced inaction came to an end. He had gathered himself once more for one of those tiger springs which should be as sure and as irresistible as that which had brought him from Belmont to Bloemfontein, or that other in olden days which had carried him from Cabul to Candahar. His army had been decimated by sickness, and eight thousand men had passed into the hospitals; but those who were with the colours were of high heart, longing eagerly for action. Any change which would carry them away from the pest-ridden, evil-smelling capital which had revenged itself so terribly upon the invader must be a change for the better. Therefore it was with glad faces and brisk feet that the centre column left Bloemfontein on May 1st, and streamed, with bands playing, along the northern road.

On May 3rd the main force was assembled at Karee, twenty miles upon their way. Two hundred and twenty separated them from Pretoria, but in little more than a month from the day of starting, in spite of broken railway, a succession of rivers, and the opposition of the enemy, this army was marching into the main street of the Transvaal capital. Had there been no enemy there at all, it would still have been a fine performance, the more so when one remembers that the army was moving upon a front of twenty miles or more, each part of which had to be co-ordinated to the rest. It is with the story of this great march that the present chapter deals.

Roberts had prepared the way by clearing out the south-eastern corner of the State, and at the moment of his advance his forces covered a semicircular front of about forty miles, the right under Ian Hamilton near Thabanchu, and the left at Karee. This was the broad net which was to be swept from south to north across the Free State, gradually narrowing as it went. The conception was admirable, and appears to have been an adoption of the Boers' own strategy, which had in turn been borrowed from the Zulus. The solid centre could hold any force which faced it, while the mobile flanks, Hutton upon the left and Hamilton upon the right, could lap round and pin it, as Cronje was pinned at Paardeberg. It seems admirably simple when done upon a small scale. But when the scale is one of forty miles, since your front must be broad enough to envelop the front which is opposed to it, and when the scattered wings have to be fed with no railway line to help, it takes such a master of administrative detail as Lord Kitchener to bring the operations to complete success.

On May 3rd, the day of the advance from our most northern post, Karee, the disposition of Lord Roberts's army was briefly as follows. On his left was Hutton, with his mixed force of mounted infantry drawn from every quarter of the empire. This formidable and mobile body, with some batteries of horse artillery and of pom-poms, kept a line a few miles to the west of the railroad, moving northwards parallel with it. Roberts's main column kept on the railroad, which was mended with extraordinary speed by the Railway Pioneer regiment and the Engineers, under Girouard and the ill-fated Seymour. It was amazing to note the shattered culverts as one passed, and yet to be overtaken by trains within a day. This main column consisted of Pole-Carew's 11th Division, which contained the Guards, and Stephenson's Brigade (Warwicks, Essex, Welsh, and Yorkshires). With them were the 83rd, 84th, and 85th R.F.A., with the heavy guns, and a small force of mounted infantry. Passing along the widespread British line one would then, after an interval of seven or eight miles, come upon Tucker's Division (the 7th), which consisted of Maxwell's Brigade (formerly Chermside's—the Norfolks, Lincolns, Hampshires, and Scottish Borderers) and Wavell's Brigade (North Staffords, Cheshires, East Lancashires, South Wales Borderers). To the right of these was Ridley's mounted infantry. Beyond them, extending over very many miles of country and with considerable spaces between, there came Broadwood's cavalry, Bruce Hamilton's Brigade (Derbyshires, Sussex, Camerons, and C.I.V.), and finally on the extreme right of all Ian Hamilton's force of Highlanders, Canadians, Shropshires, and Cornwalls, with cavalry and mounted infantry, starting forty miles from Lord Roberts, but edging westwards all the way, to merge with the troops next to it, and to occupy Winburg in the way already described. This was the army, between forty and fifty thousand strong, with which Lord Roberts advanced upon the Transvaal.

In the meantime he had anticipated that his mobile and enterprising opponents would work round and strike at our rear. Ample means had been provided for dealing with any attempt of the kind. Rundle with the 8th Division and Brabant's Colonial Division remained in rear of the right flank to confront any force which might turn it. At Bloemfontein were Kelly-Kenny's Division (the 6th) and Chermside's (the 3rd), with a force of cavalry and guns. Methuen, working from Kimberley towards

Boshof, formed the extreme left wing of the main advance, though distant a hundred miles from it. With excellent judgment Lord Roberts saw that it was on our right flank that danger was to be feared, and here it was that every precaution had been taken to meet it.

The objective of the first day's march was the little town of Brandfort, ten miles north of Karee. The head of the main column faced it, while the left arm swept round and drove the Boer force from their position. Tucker's Division upon the right encountered some opposition, but overbore it with artillery. May 4th was a day of rest for the infantry, but on the 5th they advanced, in the same order as before, for twenty miles, and found themselves to the south of the Vet River, where the enemy had prepared for an energetic resistance. A vigorous artillery duel ensued, the British guns in the open as usual against an invisible enemy. After three hours of a very hot fire the mounted infantry got across the river upon the left and turned the Boer flank, on which they hastily withdrew. The first lodgement was effected by two bodies of Canadians and New Zealanders, who were energetically supported by Captain Anley's 3rd Mounted Infantry. The rushing of a *kopje* by twenty-three West Australians was another gallant incident which marked this engagement, in which our losses were insignificant. A maxim and twenty or thirty prisoners were taken by Hutton's men. The next day (May 6th) the army moved across the difficult drift of the Vet River, and halted that night at Smaldeel, some five miles to the north of it. At the same time Ian Hamilton had been able to advance to Winburg, so that the army had contracted its front by about half, but had preserved its relative positions. Hamilton, after his junction with his reinforcements at Jacobsrust, had under him so powerful a force that he overbore all resistance. His actions between Thabanchu and Winburg had cost the Boers heavy loss, and in one action the German legion had been overthrown. The informal warfare which was made upon us by citizens of many nations without rebuke from their own Governments is a matter of which pride, and possibly policy, have forbidden us to complain, but it will be surprising if it does not prove that their laxity has established a very dangerous precedent, and they will find it difficult to object when, in the next little war in which either France or Germany is engaged, they find a few hundred British adventurers carrying a rifle against them.

The record of the army's advance is now rather geographical than military, for it rolled northwards with never a check save that which was caused by the construction of the railway diversions which atoned for the destruction of the larger bridges. The infantry now, as always in the campaign, marched excellently; for though twenty miles in the day may seem a moderate allowance to a healthy man upon an English road, it is a considerable performance under an African sun with a weight of between thirty and forty pounds to be carried. The good humour of the men was admirable, and they eagerly longed to close with the elusive enemy who flitted ever in front of them. Huge clouds of smoke veiled the northern sky, for the Boers had set fire to the dry grass, partly to cover their own retreat, and partly to show up our khaki upon the blackened surface. Far on the flanks the twinkling heliographs revealed the position of the wide-spread wings.

On May 10th Lord Roberts's force, which had halted for three days at Smaldeel, moved onwards to Welgelegen. French's cavalry had come up by road, and quickly strengthened the centre and left wing of the army. On the morning of the 10th the invaders found themselves confronted by a formidable position which the Boers had taken up on the northern bank of the Sand River. Their army extended over twenty miles of country, the two Bothas were in command, and everything pointed to a pitched battle. Had the position been rushed from the front, there was every material for a second Colenso, but the British had learned that it was by brains rather than by blood that such battles may be won. French's cavalry turned the Boers on one side, and Bruce Hamilton's infantry on the other. Theoretically we never passed the Boer flanks, but practically their line was so over-extended that we were able to pierce it at any point. There was never any severe fighting, but rather a steady advance upon the British side and a steady retirement upon that of the Boers. On the left the Sussex regiment distinguished itself by the dash with which it stormed an important *kopje*. The losses were slight, save among a detached body of cavalry which found itself suddenly cut off by a strong force of the enemy and lost Captain Elworthy killed, and Haig of the Inniskillings, Wilkinson of the Australian Horse, and twenty men prisoners. We also secured forty or fifty prisoners, and the enemy's casualties amounted to about as many more. The whole straggling action fought over a front as broad as from London to Woking cost the British at the most a couple of hundred casualties, and carried their army over the most formidable defensive position which they were to encounter. The war in its later phases certainly has the pleasing characteristic of being the most bloodless, considering the number of men engaged and the amount of powder burned, that has been known in history. It was at the expense of their boots and not of their lives that the infantry won their way.

On May 11th Lord Roberts's army advanced twenty miles to Geneva Siding, and every preparation was made for a battle next day, as it was thought certain that the Boers would defend their new capital, Kroonstad. It proved, however, that even here they would not make a stand, and on May 12th, at one o'clock, Lord Roberts rode into the town. Steyn, Botha, and De Wet escaped, and it was announced that the village of

Lindley had become the new seat of government. The British had now accomplished half their journey to Pretoria, and it was obvious that on the south side of the Vaal no serious resistance awaited them. Burghers were freely surrendering themselves with their arms, and returning to their farms. In the south-east Rundle and Brabant were slowly advancing, while the Boers who faced them fell back towards Lindley. On the west, Hunter had crossed the Vaal at Windsorton, and Barton's Fusilier Brigade had fought a sharp action at Rooidam, while Mahon's Mafeking relief column had slipped past their flank, escaping the observation of the British public, but certainly not that of the Boers. The casualties in the Rooidam action were nine killed and thirty wounded, but the advance of the Fusiliers was irresistible, and for once the Boer loss, as they were hustled from *kopje* to *kopje*, appears to have been greater than that of the British. The Yeomanry had an opportunity of showing once more that there are few more high-mettled troops in South Africa than these good sportsmen of the shires, who only showed a trace of their origin in their irresistible inclination to burst into a 'tally-ho!' when ordered to attack. The Boer forces fell back after the action along the line of the Vaal, making for Christiana and Bloemhof. Hunter entered into the Transvaal in pursuit of them, being the first to cross the border, with the exception of raiding Rhodesians early in the war. Methuen, in the meanwhile, was following a course parallel to Hunter but south of him, Hoopstad being his immediate objective. The little union jacks which were stuck in the war maps in so many British households were now moving swiftly upwards.

Buller's force was also sweeping northwards, and the time had come when the Ladysmith garrison, restored at last to health and strength, should have a chance of striking back at those who had tormented them so long. Many of the best troops had been drafted away to other portions of the seat of war. Hart's Brigade and Barton's Fusilier Brigade had gone with Hunter to form the 10th Division upon the Kimberley side, and the Imperial Light Horse had been brought over for the relief of Mafeking. There remained, however, a formidable force, the regiments in which had been strengthened by the addition of drafts and volunteers from home. Not less than twenty thousand sabres and bayonets were ready and eager for the passage of the Biggarsberg mountains.

This line of rugged hills is pierced by only three passes, each of which was held in strength by the enemy. Considerable losses must have ensued from any direct attempt to force them. Buller, however, with excellent judgment, demonstrated in front of them with Hildyard's men, while the rest of the army, marching round, outflanked the line of resistance, and on May 15th pounced upon Dundee. Much had happened since that October day when Penn Symons led his three gallant regiments up

Talana Hill, but now at last, after seven weary months, the ground was reoccupied which he had gained. His old soldiers visited his grave, and the national flag was raised over the remains of as gallant a man as ever died for the sake of it.

The Boers, whose force did not exceed a few thousands, were now rolled swiftly back through Northern Natal into their own country. The long strain at Ladysmith had told upon them, and the men whom we had to meet were very different from the warriors of Spion Kop and Nicholson's Nek. They had done magnificently, but there is a limit to human endurance, and no longer would these peasants face the bursting Lyddite and the bayonets of angry soldiers. There is little enough for us to boast of in this. Some pride might be taken in the campaign when at a disadvantage we were facing superior numbers, but now we could but deplore the situation in which these poor valiant burghers found themselves, the victims of a rotten government and of their own delusions. Hofer's Tyrolese, Charette's Vendeans, or Bruce's Scotchmen never fought a finer fight than these children of the *veldt*, but in each case they combated a real and not an imaginary tyrant. It is heart-sickening to think of the butchery, the misery, the irreparable losses, the blood of men, and the bitter tears of women, all of which might have been spared had one obstinate and ignorant man been persuaded to allow the State which he ruled to conform to the customs of every other civilised State upon the earth.

Buller was now moving with a rapidity and decision which contrast pleasantly with some of his earlier operations. Although Dundee was only occupied on May 15th, on May 18th his vanguard was in Newcastle, fifty miles to the north. In nine days he had covered 138 miles. On the 19th the army lay under the loom of that Majuba which had cast its sinister shadow for so long over South African politics. In front was the historical Laing's Nek, the pass which leads from Natal into the Transvaal, while through it runs the famous railway tunnel. Here the Boers had taken up that position which had proved nineteen years before to be too strong for British troops. The Rooineks had come back after many days to try again. A halt was called, for the ten days' supplies which had been taken with the troops were exhausted, and it was necessary to wait until the railway should be repaired. This gave time for Hildyard's 5th Division and Lyttelton's 4th Division to close up on Clery's 2nd Division, which with Dundonald's cavalry had formed our vanguard throughout. The only losses of any consequence during this fine march fell upon a single squadron of Bethune's mounted infantry, which being thrown out in the direction of Vryheid, in order to make sure that our flank was clear, fell into an ambuscade and was almost annihilated by a close-range fire. Sixty-six casualties, of which nearly half were killed, were the result of this action, which seems to have depended, like most of our reverses, upon defective scouting. Buller, having called up his two remaining divisions and having mended the railway behind him, proceeded now to manoeuvre the Boers out of Laing's Nek exactly as he had manoeuvred them out of the Biggarsberg. At the end of May Hildyard and Lyttelton were despatched in an eastern direction, as if there were an intention of turning the pass from Utrecht.

It was on May 12th that Lord Roberts occupied Kroonstad, and he halted there for eight days before he resumed his advance. At the end of that time his railway had been repaired, and enough supplies brought up to enable him to advance again without anxiety. The country through which he passed swarmed with herds and flocks, but, with as scrupulous a regard for the rights of property as Wellington showed in the south of France, no hungry soldier was allowed to take so much as a chicken as he passed. The punishment for looting was prompt and stern. It is true that farms were burned occasionally and the stock confiscated, but this was as a punishment for some particular offence and not part of a system. The limping Tommy looked askance at the fat geese which covered the dam by the roadside, but it was as much as his life was worth to allow his fingers to close round those tempting white necks. On foul water and bully beef he tramped through a land of plenty.

Lord Roberts's eight days' halt was spent in consolidating the general military situation. We have already shown how Buller had crept upwards to the Natal Border. On the west Methuen reached Hoopstad and Hunter Christiana, settling the country and collecting arms as they went. Rundle in the south-east took possession of the rich grain lands, and on May 21st entered Ladybrand. In front of him lay that difficult hilly country about Senekal, Ficksburg, and Bethlehem which was to delay him so long. Ian Hamilton was feeling his way northwards to the right of the railway line, and for the moment cleared the district between Lindley and Heilbron, passing through both towns and causing Steyn to again change his capital, which became Vrede, in the extreme north-east of the State. During these operations Hamilton had the two formidable De Wet brothers in front of him, and suffered nearly a hundred casualties in the continual skirmishing which accompanied his advance. His right flank and rear were continually attacked, and these signs of forces outside our direct line of advance were full of menace for the future.

On May 22nd the main army resumed its advance, moving forward fifteen miles to Honing's Spruit. On the 23rd another march of twenty miles over a fine rolling prairie brought them to Rhenoster River. The enemy had made some preparations for a stand, but Hamilton was near Heilbron upon their left and French was upon their right flank. The river was crossed without opposition. On the 24th the army was at Vredefort Road, and on the 26th the vanguard crossed the Vaal River at Viljoen's Drift, the whole army following on the 27th. Hamilton's force had been cleverly swung across from the right to the left flank of the British, so that the Boers were massed on the wrong side.

Preparations for resistance had been made on the line of the railway, but the wide turning movements on the flanks by the indefatigable French and Hamilton rendered all opposition of no avail. The British columns flowed over and onwards without a pause, tramping steadily northwards to their destination. The bulk of the Free State forces refused to leave their own country, and moved away to the eastern and northern portion of the State, where the British Generals thought—incorrectly, as the future was to prove—that no further harm would come from them. The State which they were in arms to defend had really ceased to exist, for already it had been publicly proclaimed at Bloemfontein in the Queen's name that the country had been annexed to the Empire, and that its style henceforth was that of 'The Orange River Colony.' Those who think this measure unduly harsh must remember that every mile of land which the Freestaters had conquered in the early part of the war had been solemnly annexed by them. At the same time, those Englishmen who knew the history of this State, which had once been the model of all that a State should be, were saddened by the thought that it should have deliberately committed suicide for the sake of one of the most corrupt governments which have ever been known. Had the Transvaal been governed as the Orange Free State was, such an event as the second Boer war could never have occurred.

Lord Roberts's tremendous march was now drawing to a close. On May 28th the troops advanced twenty miles, and passed Klip River without fighting. It was observed with surprise that the Transvaalers were very much more careful of their own property than they had been of that of their allies, and that the railway was not damaged at all by the retreating forces. The country had become more populous, and far away upon the low curves of the hills were seen high chimneys and gaunt iron pumps which struck the north of England soldier with a pang of homesickness. This long distant hill was the famous Rand, and under its faded grasses lay such riches as Solomon never took from Ophir. It was the prize of victory; and yet the prize is not to the victor, for the dust-grimed officers and men looked with little personal interest at this treasure-house of the world. Not one penny the richer would they be for the fact that their blood and their energy had brought justice and freedom to the gold fields. They had opened up an industry for the world, men of all nations would be the better for their labours, the miner and the financier or the trader would equally profit by them, but the men in khaki would tramp on, unrewarded and uncomplaining, to India, to China, to any spot where the needs of their worldwide empire called them.

The infantry, streaming up from the Vaal River to the famous ridge of gold, had met with no resistance upon the way, but great mist banks of cloud by day and huge twinkling areas of flame by night showed the handiwork of the enemy. Hamilton and French, moving upon the left flank, found Boers thick upon the hills, but cleared them off in a well-managed skirmish which cost us a dozen casualties. On May 29th, pushing swiftly along, French found the enemy posted very strongly with several guns at Doornkop, a point west of Klip River Berg. The cavalry leader had with him at this stage three horse batteries, four pom-poms, and 3000 mounted men. The position being too strong for him to force, Hamilton's infantry (19th and 21st Brigades) were called up, and the Boers were driven out. That splendid corps, the Gordons, lost nearly a hundred men in their advance over the open, and the C.I.V.s on the other flank fought like a regiment of veterans. There had been an inclination to smile at these citizen soldiers when they first came out, but no one smiled now save the General who felt that he had them at his back. Hamilton's attack was assisted by the menace rather than the pressure of French's turning movement on the Boer right, but the actual advance was as purely frontal as any of those which had been carried through at the beginning of the war. The open formation of the troops, the powerful artillery behind them, and perhaps also the lowered morale of the enemy combined to make such a movement less dangerous than of old. In any case it was inevitable, as the state of Hamilton's *commisariat* rendered it necessary that at all hazards he should force his way through.

Whilst this action of Doornkop was fought by the British left flank, Henry's mounted infantry in the centre moved straight upon the important junction of Germiston, which lies amid the huge white heaps of tailings from the mines. At this point, or near it, the lines from Johannesburg and from Natal join the line to Pretoria. Colonel Henry's advance was an extremely daring one, for the infantry were some distance behind; but after an irregular scrambling skirmish, in which the Boer snipers had to be driven off the mine heaps and from among the houses, the 8th mounted infantry got their grip of the railway and held it. The exploit was a very fine one, and stands out the more brilliantly as the conduct of the campaign cannot be said to afford many examples of that well-considered audacity which deliberately runs the risk of the minor loss for the sake of the greater gain. Henry was much assisted by J battery R.H.A., which was handled with energy and judgment.

French was now on the west of the town, Henry had cut the railway on the east, and Roberts was coming up from the south. His infantry had covered 130 miles in seven days, but the thought that every step brought them nearer to Pretoria was as exhilarating as their fifes and drums. On May 30th the victorious troops camped outside the city while Botha retired with his army, abandoning without a battle the treasure-house of his country. Inside the town were chaos and confusion. The richest mines in the world lay for a day or more at the mercy of a lawless rabble drawn from all nations. The Boer officials were themselves divided in opinion, Krause standing for law and order while Judge Koch advocated violence. A spark would have set the town blazing, and the worst was feared when a crowd of mercenaries assembled in front of the Robinson mine with threats of violence. By the firmness and tact of Mr. Tucker, the manager, and by the strong attitude of Commissioner Krause, the situation was saved and the danger passed. Upon May 31st, without violence to life or destruction to property, that great town which British hands have done so much to build found itself at last under the British flag. May it wave there so long as it covers just laws, honest officials, and clean-handed administrators—so long and no longer!

And now the last stage of the great journey had been reached. Two days were spent at Johannesburg while supplies were brought up, and then a move was made upon Pretoria thirty miles to the north. Here was the Boer capital, the seat of government, the home of Kruger, the centre of all that was anti-British, crouching amid its hills, with costly forts guarding every face of it. Surely at last the place had been found where that great battle should be fought which should decide for all time whether it was with the Briton or with the Dutchman that the future of South Africa lay.

On the last day of May two hundred Lancers under the command of Major Hunter Weston, with Charles of the Sappers and Burnham the scout, a man who has played the part of a hero throughout the campaign, struck off from the main army and endeavoured to descend upon the Pretoria to Delagoa railway line with the intention of blowing up a bridge and cutting the Boer line of retreat. It was a most dashing attempt; but the small party had the misfortune to come into contact with a strong Boer commando, who headed them off. After a skirmish they were compelled to make their way back with a loss of five killed and fourteen wounded.

The cavalry under French had waited for the issue of this enterprise at a point nine miles north of Johannesburg. On June 2nd it began its advance with orders to make a wide sweep round to the westward, and so skirt the capital, cutting the Pietersburg railway to the north of it. The country in the direct line between Johannesburg and Pretoria consists of a series of rolling downs which are admirably adapted for cavalry work, but the detour which French had to make carried him into the wild and broken district which lies to the north of the Little Crocodile River. Here he was fiercely attacked on ground where his troops could not deploy, but with extreme coolness and judgment beat off the enemy. To cover thirty-two miles in a day and fight a way out of an ambuscade in the evening is an ordeal for any leader and for any troops. Two killed and seven wounded were our trivial losses in a situation which might have been a serious one. The Boers appear to have been the escort of a strong convoy which had passed along the road some miles in front. Next morning both convoy and opposition had disappeared. The cavalry rode on amid a country of orange groves, the troopers standing up in their stirrups to pluck the golden fruit. There was no further fighting, and on June 4th French had established himself upon the north of the town, where he learned that all resistance had ceased.

Whilst the cavalry had performed this enveloping movement the main army had moved swiftly upon its objective, leaving one brigade behind to secure Johannesburg. Ian Hamilton advanced upon the left, while Lord Roberts's column kept the line of the railway, Colonel Henry's mounted infantry scouting in front. As the army topped the low curves of the *veldt* they saw in front of them two well-marked hills, each crowned by a low squat building. They were the famous southern forts of Pretoria. Between the hills was a narrow neck, and beyond the Boer capital.

For a time it appeared that the entry was to be an absolutely bloodless one, but the booming of cannon and the crash of Mauser fire soon showed that the enemy was in force upon the ridge. Botha had left a strong rearguard to hold off the British while his own stores and valuables were being withdrawn from the town. The silence of the forts showed that the guns had been removed and that no prolonged resistance was intended; but in the meanwhile fringes of determined riflemen, supported by cannon, held the approaches, and must be driven off before an entry could be effected. Each fresh corps as it came up reinforced the firing line. Henry's mounted infantrymen supported by the horse-guns of J battery and the guns of Tucker's division began the action. So hot was the answer, both from cannon and from rifle, that it seemed for a time as if a real battle were at last about to take place. The Guards' Brigade, Stephenson's Brigade, and Maxwell's Brigade streamed up and waited until Hamilton, who was on the enemy's right flank, should be able to make his presence felt. The heavy guns had also arrived, and a huge cloud of debris rising from the Pretorian forts told the accuracy of their fire.

But either the burghers were half-hearted or there was no real intention to make a stand. About half-past two their fire slackened and

Pole-Carew was directed to push on. That debonair soldier with his two veteran brigades obeyed the order with alacrity, and the infantry swept over the ridge, with some thirty or forty casualties, the majority of which fell to the Warwicks. The position was taken, and Hamilton, who came up late, was only able to send on De Lisle's mounted infantry, chiefly Australians, who ran down one of the Boer maxims in the open. The action had cost us altogether about seventy men. Among the injured was the Duke of Norfolk, who had shown a high sense of civic virtue in laying aside the duties and dignity of a Cabinet Minister in order to serve as a simple captain of volunteers. At the end of this one fight the capital lay at the mercy of Lord Roberts. Consider the fight which they made for their chief city, compare it with that which the British made for the village of Mafeking, and say on which side is that stern spirit of self-sacrifice and resolution which are the signs of the better cause.

In the early morning of June 5th, the Coldstream Guards were mounting the hills which commanded the town. Beneath them in the clear African air lay the famous city, embowered in green, the fine central buildings rising grandly out of the wide circle of villas. Through the Nek part of the Guards' Brigade and Maxwell's Brigade had passed, and had taken over the station, from which at least one train laden with horses had steamed that morning. Two others, both ready to start, were only just stopped in time.

The first thought was for the British prisoners, and a small party headed by the Duke of Marlborough rode to their rescue. Let it be said once for all that their treatment by the Boers was excellent and that their appearance would alone have proved it. One hundred and twenty-nine officers and thirty-nine soldiers were found in the Model Schools, which had been converted into a prison. A day later our cavalry arrived at Waterval, which is fourteen miles to the north of Pretoria. Here were confined three thousand soldiers, whose fare had certainly been of the scantiest, though in other respects they appear to have been well treated.[1] Nine hundred of their comrades had been removed by the Boers, but Porter's cavalry was in time to release the others, under a brisk shell fire from a Boer gun upon the ridge. Many pieces of good luck we had in the campaign, but this recovery of our prisoners, which left the enemy without a dangerous lever for exacting conditions of peace, was the most fortunate of all.

In the centre of the town there is a wide square decorated or disfigured by a bare pedestal upon which a statue of the President was to have been placed. Hard by is the bleak barnlike church in which he preached,

1. Further information unfortunately shows that in the case of the sick and of the Colonial prisoners the treatment was by no means good.

and on either side are the Government offices and the Law Courts, buildings which would grace any European capital. Here, at two o'clock on the afternoon of June 5th, Lord Roberts sat his horse and saw pass in front of him the men who had followed him so far and so faithfully— the Guards, the Essex, the Welsh, the Yorks, the Warwicks, the guns, the mounted infantry, the dashing irregulars, the Gordons, the Canadians, the Shropshires, the Cornwalls, the Camerons, the Derbys, the Sussex, and the London Volunteers. For over two hours the khaki waves with their crests of steel went sweeping by. High above their heads from the summit of the Raadsaal the broad Union Jack streamed for the first time. Through months of darkness we had struggled onwards to the light. Now at last the strange drama seemed to be drawing to its close. The God of battles had given the long-withheld verdict. But of all the hearts which throbbed high at that supreme moment there were few who felt one touch of bitterness towards the brave men who had been overborne. They had fought and died for their ideal. We had fought and died for ours. The hope for the future of South Africa is that they or their descendants may learn that that banner which has come to wave above Pretoria means no racial intolerance, no greed for gold, no paltering with injustice or corruption, but that it means one law for all and one freedom for all, as it does in every other continent in the whole broad earth. When that is learned it may happen that even they will come to date a happier life and a wider liberty from that 5th of June which saw the symbol of their nation pass for ever from among the ensigns of the world.

CHAPTER 26

Diamond Hill—Rundle's Operations

The military situation at the time of the occupation of Pretoria was roughly as follows. Lord Roberts with some thirty thousand men was in possession of the capital, but had left his long line of communications very imperfectly guarded behind him. On the flank of this line of communications, in the eastern and north-eastern corner of the Free State, was an energetic force of unconquered Freestaters who had rallied round President Steyn. They were some eight or ten thousand in number, well horsed, with a fair number of guns, under the able leadership of De Wet, Prinsloo, and Olivier. Above all, they had a splendid position, mountainous and broken, from which, as from a fortress, they could make excursions to the south or west. This army included the commandos of Ficksburg, Senekal, and Harrismith, with all the broken and desperate men from other districts who had left their farms and fled to the mountains. It was held in check as a united force by Rundle's Division and the Colonial Division on the south, while Colvile, and afterwards Methuen, endeavoured to pen them in on the west. The task was a hard one, however, and though Rundle succeeded in holding his line intact, it appeared to be impossible in that wide country to coop up altogether an enemy so mobile. A strange game of hide-and-seek ensued, in which De Wet, who led the Boer raids, was able again and again to strike our line of rails and to get back without serious loss. The story of these instructive and humiliating episodes will be told in their order. The energy and skill of the guerrilla chief challenge our admiration, and the score of his successes would be amusing were it not that the points of the game are marked by the lives of British soldiers.

General Buller had spent the latter half of May in making his way from Ladysmith to Laing's Nek, and the beginning of June found him with twenty thousand men in front of that difficult position. Some talk of a surrender had arisen, and Christian Botha, who commanded the Boers, succeeded in gaining several days' armistice, which ended in nothing.

The Transvaal forces at this point were not more than a few thousand in number, but their position was so formidable that it was a serious task to turn them out. Van Wyk's Hill, however, had been left unguarded, and as its possession would give the British the command of Botha's Pass, its unopposed capture by the South African Light Horse was an event of great importance. With guns upon this eminence the infantry were able, on June 8th, to attack and to carry with little loss the rest of the high ground, and so to get the Pass into their complete possession. Botha fired the grass behind him, and withdrew sullenly to the north. On the 9th and 10th the convoys were passed over the Pass, and on the 11th the main body of the army followed them.

The operations were now being conducted in that extremely acute angle of Natal which runs up between the Transvaal and the Orange Free State. In crossing Botha's Pass the army had really entered what was now the Orange River Colony. But it was only for a very short time, as the object of the movement was to turn the Laing's Nek position, and then come back into the Transvaal through Alleman's Pass. The gallant South African Light Horse led the way, and fought hard at one point to clear a path for the army, losing six killed and eight wounded in a sharp skirmish. On the morning of the 12th the flanking movement was far advanced, and it only remained for the army to force Alleman's Nek, which would place it to the rear of Laing's Nek, and close to the Transvaal town of Volksrust.

Had the Boers been the men of Colenso and of Spion Kop, this storming of Alleman's Nek would have been a bloody business. The position was strong, the cover was slight, and there was no way round. But the infantry came on with the old dash without the old stubborn resolution being opposed to them. The guns prepared the way, and then the Dorsets, the Dublins, the Middlesex, the Queen's, and the East Surrey did the rest. The door was open and the Transvaal lay before us. The next day Volksrust was in our hands.

The whole series of operations were excellently conceived and carried out. Putting Colenso on one side, it cannot be denied that General Buller showed considerable power of manoeuvring large bodies of troops. The withdrawal of the compromised army after Spion Kop, the change of the line of attack at Pieter's Hill, and the flanking marches in this campaign of Northern Natal, were all very workmanlike achievements. In this case a position which the Boers had been preparing for months, scored with trenches and topped by heavy artillery, had been rendered untenable by a clever flank movement, the total casualties in the whole affair being less than two hundred killed and wounded. Natal was cleared of the invader, Buller's foot was on the high plateau of the Transvaal, and Roberts could count on twenty thousand good men coming up to him from the south-east. More important than all, the Natal railway was being brought up, and soon the central British Army would depend upon Durban instead of Cape Town for its supplies—a saving of nearly two-thirds of the distance. The fugitive Boers made northwards in the Middelburg direction, while Buller advanced to Standerton, which town he continued to occupy until Lord Roberts could send a force down through Heidelberg to join hands with him. Such was the position of the Natal Field Force at the end of June. From the west and the south-west British forces were also converging upon the capital. The indomitable Baden-Powell sought for rest and change of scene after his prolonged trial by harrying the Boers out of Zeerust and Rustenburg. The forces of Hunter and of Mahon converged upon Potchefstroom, from which, after settling that district, they could be conveyed by rail to Krugersdorp and Johannesburg.

Before briefly recounting the series of events which took place upon the line of communications, the narrative must return to Lord Roberts at Pretoria, and describe the operations which followed his occupation of that city. In leaving the undefeated forces of the Free State behind him, the British General had unquestionably run a grave risk, and was well aware that his railway communication was in danger of being cut. By the rapidity of his movements he succeeded in gaining the enemy's capital before that which he had foreseen came to pass; but if Botha had held him at Pretoria while De Wet struck at him behind, the situation would have been a serious one. Having once attained his main object, Roberts could receive with equanimity the expected news that De Wet with a mobile force of less than two thousand men had, on June 7th, cut the line at Roodeval to the north of Kroonstad. Both rail and telegraph were destroyed, and for a few days the army was isolated. Fortunately there were enough supplies to go on with, and immediate steps were taken to drive away the intruder, though, like a mosquito, he was brushed from one place only to settle upon another.

Leaving others to restore his broken communications, Lord Roberts turned his attention once more to Botha, who still retained ten or fifteen thousand men under his command. The President had fled from Pretoria with a large sum of money, estimated at over two millions sterling, and was known to be living in a saloon railway carriage, which had been transformed into a seat of government even more mobile than that of President Steyn. From Waterval-Boven, a point beyond Middelburg, he was in a position either to continue his journey to Delagoa Bay, and so escape out of the country, or to travel north into that wild Lydenburg country which had always been proclaimed as the last ditch of the defence. Here he remained with his gold-bags waiting the turn of events.

Botha and his stalwarts had not gone far from the capital. Fifteen miles out to the east the railway line runs through a gap in the hills called Pien-aars Poort, and here was such a position as the Boer loves to hold. It was very strong in front, and it had widely spread formidable flanking hills to hamper those turning movements which had so often been fatal to the Boer generals. Behind was the uncut railway line along which the guns could in case of need be removed. The whole position was over fifteen miles from wing to wing, and it was well known to the Boer general that Lord Roberts had no longer that preponderance of force which would enable him to execute wide turning movements, as he had done in his advance from the south. His army had decreased seriously in numbers. The mounted men, the most essential branch of all, were so ill horsed that brigades were not larger than regiments. One brigade of infantry (the 14th) had been left to garrison Johannesburg, and another (the 18th) had been chosen for special duty in Pretoria. Smith-Dorrien's Brigade had been detached for duty upon the line of communications. With all these deductions and the wastage caused by wounds and disease, the force was in no state to assume a vigorous offensive. So hard pressed were they for men that the three thousand released prisoners from Waterval were hur-riedly armed with Boer weapons and sent down the line to help to guard the more vital points.

Had Botha withdrawn to a safe distance, Lord Roberts would certain-ly have halted, as he had done at Bloemfontein, and waited for remounts and reinforcements. But the war could not be allowed to languish when an active enemy lay only fifteen miles off, within striking distance of two cities and of the line of rail. Taking all the troops that he could muster, the British General moved out once more on Monday, June 11th, to drive Botha from his position. He had with him Pole-Carew's 11th Division, which numbered about six thousand men with twenty guns, Ian Hamil-ton's force, which included one infantry brigade (Bruce Hamilton's), one cavalry brigade, and a corps of mounted infantry, say, six thousand in all, with thirty guns. There remained French's Cavalry Division, with Hut-ton's Mounted Infantry, which could not have exceeded two thousand sabres and rifles. The total force was, therefore, not more than sixteen or seventeen thousand men, with about seventy guns. Their task was to carry a carefully prepared position held by at least ten thousand burghers with a strong artillery. Had the Boer of June been the Boer of December, the odds would have been against the British.

There had been some negotiations for peace between Lord Roberts and Botha, but the news of De Wet's success from the south had hardened the Boer general's heart, and on June 9th the cavalry had their orders to advance. Hamilton was to work round the left wing of the Boers, and French round their right, while the infantry came up in the centre. So wide was the scene of action that the attack and the resistance in each flank and in the centre constituted, on June 11th, three separate actions. Of these the latter was of least importance, as it merely entailed the advance of the infantry to a spot whence they could take advantage of the success of the flanking forces when they had made their presence felt. The centre did not on this as on several other occasions in the campaign make the mistake of advancing before the way had been prepared for it.

French with his attenuated force found so vigorous a resistance on Monday and Tuesday that he was hard put to it to hold his own. Fortunately he had with him three excellent Horse Artillery batteries, G, O, and T, who worked until, at the end of the engagement, they had only twenty rounds in their limbers. The country was an impossible one for cavalry, and the troopers fought dismounted, with intervals of twenty or thirty paces between the men. Exposed all day to rifle and shell fire, unable to advance and unwilling to retreat, it was only owing to their open formation that they escaped with about thirty casualties. With Boers on his front, his flank, and even on his rear, French held grimly on, realising that a retreat upon his part would mean a greater pressure at all other points of the British advance. At night his weary men slept upon the ground which they had held. All Monday and all Tuesday French kept his grip at Kameelsdrift, stolidly indifferent to the attempt of the enemy to cut his line of communications. On Wednesday, Hamilton, upon the other flank, had gained the upper hand, and the pressure was relaxed. French then pushed forward, but the horses were so utterly beaten that no effective pursuit was possible.

During the two days that French had been held up by the Boer right wing Hamilton had also been seriously engaged upon the left—so seriously that at one time the action appeared to have gone against him. The fight presented some distinctive features, which made it welcome to soldiers who were weary of the invisible man with his smokeless gun upon the eternal *kopje*. It is true that man, gun, and *kopje* were all present upon this occasion, but in the endeavours to drive him off some new developments took place, which formed for one brisk hour a reversion to picturesque warfare. Perceiving a gap in the enemy's line, Hamilton pushed up the famous Q battery—the guns which had plucked glory out of disaster at Sanna's Post. For the second time in one campaign they were exposed and in imminent danger of capture. A body of mounted Boers with great dash and hardihood galloped down within close range and opened fire. Instantly the 12th Lancers were let loose upon them. How they must have longed for their big-boned long-striding English troop horses as they strove to raise a gallop out of their spiritless overworked Argentines! For once, however, the lance meant more than five pounds dead weight and an encumbrance to the rider. The guns were saved, the Boers fled, and a dozen were left upon the ground. But a cavalry charge has to end in a re-formation, and that is the instant of danger if any unbroken enemy remains within range. Now a sleet of bullets hissed through their ranks as they retired, and the gallant Lord Airlie, as modest and brave a soldier as ever drew sword, was struck through the heart. 'Pray moderate your language!' was his last characteristic remark, made to a battle-drunken sergeant. Two officers, seventeen men, and thirty horses went down with their Colonel, the great majority only slightly injured. In the meantime the increasing pressure upon his right caused Broadwood to order a second charge, of the Life Guards this time, to drive off the assailants. The appearance rather than the swords of the Guards prevailed, and cavalry as cavalry had vindicated their existence more than they had ever done during the campaign. The guns were saved, the flank attack was rolled back, but one other danger had still to be met, for the Heidelberg commando—a *corps d'elite* of the Boers—had made its way outside Hamilton's flank and threatened to get past him. With cool judgment the British General detached a battalion and a section of a battery, which pushed the Boers back into a less menacing position. The rest of Bruce Hamilton's Brigade were ordered to advance upon the hills in front, and, aided by a heavy artillery fire, they had succeeded, before the closing in of the winter night, in getting possession of this first line of the enemy's defences. Night fell upon an undecided fight, which, after swaying this way and that, had finally inclined to the side of the British. The Sussex and the City Imperial Volunteers were clinging to the enemy's left flank, while the 11th Division were holding them in front. All promised well for the morrow.

By order of Lord Roberts the Guards were sent round early on Tuesday, the 12th, to support the flank attack of Bruce Hamilton's infantry. It was afternoon before all was ready for the advance, and then the Sussex, the London Volunteers, and the Derbyshires won a position upon the ridge, followed later by the three regiments of Guards. But the ridge was the edge of a considerable plateau, swept by Boer fire, and no advance could be made over its bare expanse save at a considerable loss. The infantry clung in a long fringe to the edge of the position, but for two hours no guns could be brought up to their support, as the steepness of the slope was insurmountable. It was all that the stormers could do to hold their ground, as they were enfiladed by a Vickers-Maxim, and exposed to showers of shrapnel as well as to an incessant rifle fire. Never were guns so welcome as those of the 82nd battery, brought by Major Connolly into the firing line. The enemy's riflemen were only a thousand yards away, and the action of the artillery might have seemed as foolhardy as that of

Long at Colenso. Ten horses went down on the instant, and a quarter of the gunners were hit; but the guns roared one by one into action, and their shrapnel soon decided the day. Undoubtedly it is with Connolly and his men that the honours lie.

At four o'clock, as the sun sank towards the west, the tide of fight had set in favour of the attack. Two more batteries had come up, every rifle was thrown into the firing line, and the Boer reply was decreasing in volume. The temptation to an assault was great, but even now it might mean heavy loss of life, and Hamilton shrank from the sacrifice. In the morning his judgment was justified, for Botha had abandoned the position, and his army was in full retreat. The mounted men followed as far as Elands River Station, which is twenty-five miles from Pretoria, but the enemy was not overtaken, save by a small party of De Lisle's Australians and Regular Mounted Infantry. This force, less than a hundred in number, gained a *kopje* which overlooked a portion of the Boer army. Had they been more numerous, the effect would have been incalculable. As it was, the Australians fired every cartridge which they possessed into the throng, and killed many horses and men. It would bear examination why it was that only this small corps was present at so vital a point, and why, if they could push the pursuit to such purpose, others should not be able to do the same. Time was bringing some curious revenges. Already Paardeberg had come upon Majuba Day. Buller's victorious soldiers had taken Laing's Nek. Now, the Spruit at which the retreating Boers were so mishandled by the Australians was that same Bronkers Spruit at which, nineteen years before, a regiment had been shot down. Many might have prophesied that the deed would be avenged; but who could ever have guessed the men who would avenge it?

Such was the battle of Diamond Hill, as it was called from the name of the ridge which was opposite to Hamilton's attack. The prolonged two days' struggle showed that there was still plenty of fight in the burghers. Lord Roberts had not routed them, nor had he captured their guns; but he had cleared the vicinity of the capital, he had inflicted a loss upon them which was certainly as great as his own, and he had again proved to them that it was vain for them to attempt to stand. A long pause followed at Pretoria, broken by occasional small alarms and excursions, which served no end save to keep the army from ennui. In spite of occasional breaks in his line of communications, horses and supplies were coming up rapidly, and, by the middle of July, Roberts was ready for the field again. At the same time Hunter had come up from Potchefstroom, and Hamilton had taken Heidelberg, and his force was about to join hands with Buller at Standerton. Sporadic warfare broke out here and there in the west, and in the course of it Snyman of Mafeking had reappeared, with two guns, which were promptly taken from him by the Canadian Mounted Rifles. On all sides it was felt that if the redoubtable De Wet could be captured there was every hope that the burghers might discontinue a struggle which was disagreeable to the British and fatal to themselves. As a point of honour it was impossible for Botha to give in while his ally held out. We will turn, therefore, to this famous guerrilla chief, and give some account of his exploits. To understand them some description must be given of the general military situation in the Free State.

When Lord Roberts had swept past to the north he had brushed aside the flower of the Orange Free State army, who occupied the considerable quadrilateral which is formed by the north-east of that State. The function of Rundle's 8th Division and of Brabant's Colonial Division was to separate the sheep from the goats by preventing the fighting burghers from coming south and disturbing those districts which had been settled. For this purpose Rundle formed a long line which should serve as a cordon. Moving up through Trommel and Clocolan, Ficksburg was occupied on May 25th by the Colonial Division, while Rundle seized Senekal, forty miles to the north-west. A small force of forty Yeomanry, who entered the town some time in advance of the main body, was suddenly attacked by the Boers, and the gallant Dalbiac, famous rider and sportsman, was killed, with four of his men. He was a victim, as so many have been in this campaign, to his own proud disregard of danger.

The Boers were in full retreat, but now, as always, they were dangerous. One cannot take them for granted, for the very moment of defeat is that at which they are capable of some surprising effort. Rundle, following them up from Senekal, found them in strong possession of the *kopjes* at Biddulphsberg, and received a check in his endeavour to drive them off. It was an action fought amid great grass fires, where the possible fate of the wounded was horrible to contemplate. The 2nd Grenadiers, the Scots Guards, the East Yorkshires, and the West Kents were all engaged, with the 2nd and 79th Field Batteries and a force of Yeomanry. Our losses incurred in the open from unseen rifles were thirty killed and 130 wounded, including Colonel Lloyd of the Grenadiers. Two days later Rundle, from Senekal, joined hands with Brabant from Ficksburg, and a defensive line was formed between those two places, which was held unbroken for two months, when the operations ended in the capture of the greater part of the force opposed to him. Clements's Brigade, consisting of the 1st Royal Irish, the 2nd Bedfords, the 2nd Worcesters, and the 2nd Wiltshires, had come to strengthen Rundle, and altogether he may have had as many as twelve thousand men under his orders. It was not a large force with which to hold a mobile adversary at least eight thousand strong, who might attack him at any point of his extended line. So well, however, did he select his positions that every attempt of the enemy, and there were many, ended in failure. Badly supplied with food, he and his half-starved men held bravely to their task, and no soldiers in all that great host deserve better of their country.

At the end of May, then, the Colonial Division, Rundle's Division, and Clements's Brigade held the Boers from Ficksburg on the Basuto border to Senekal. This prevented them from coming south. But what was there to prevent them from coming west, and falling upon the railway line? There was the weak point of the British position. Lord Methuen had been brought across from Boshof, and was available with six thousand men. Colvile was on that side also, with the Highland Brigade. A few details were scattered up and down the line, waiting to be gathered up by an enterprising enemy. Kroonstad was held by a single militia battalion; each separate force had to be nourished by convoys with weak escorts. Never was there such a field for a mobile and competent guerrilla leader. And, as luck would have it, such a man was at hand, ready to take full advantage of his opportunities.

CHAPTER 27

The Lines of Communication

Christian de Wet, the elder of two brothers of that name, was at this time in the prime of life, a little over forty years of age. He was a burly middle-sized bearded man, poorly educated, but endowed with much energy and common-sense. His military experience dated back to Majuba Hill, and he had a large share of that curious race hatred which is intelligible in the case of the Transvaal, but inexplicable in a Freestater who has received no injury from the British Empire. Some weakness of his sight compels the use of tinted spectacles, and he had now turned these, with a pair of particularly observant eyes behind them, upon the scattered British forces and the long exposed line of railway.

De Wet's force was an offshoot from the army of Freestaters under De Villiers, Olivier, and Prinsloo, which lay in the mountainous northeast of the State. To him were committed five guns, fifteen hundred men, and the best of the horses. Well armed, well mounted, and operating in a country which consisted of rolling plains with occasional fortress *kopjes*, his little force had everything in its favour. There were so many tempting objects of attack lying before him that he must have had some difficulty in knowing where to begin. The tinted spectacles were turned first upon the isolated town of Lindley.

Colvile with the Highland Brigade had come up from Ventersburg with instructions to move onward to Heilbron, pacifying the country as he passed. The country, however, refused to be pacified, and his march from Ventersburg to Lindley was harassed by snipers every mile of the way. Finding that De Wet and his men were close upon him, he did not linger at Lindley, but passed on to his destination, his entire march of 126 miles costing him sixty-three casualties, of which nine were fatal. It was a difficult and dangerous march, especially for the handful of Eastern Province Horse, upon whom fell all the mounted work. By evil fortune a force of five hundred Yeomanry, the 18th battalion, including the Duke of Cambridge's Own and the Irish companies, had been sent from Kroonstad to join Colvile at Lindley. Colonel Spragge was in command. On May 27th this body of horsemen reached their destination only to find that Colvile had already abandoned it. They appear to have determined to halt for a day in Lindley, and then follow Colvile to Heilbron. Within a few hours of their entering the town they were fiercely attacked by De Wet.

Colonel Spragge seems to have acted for the best. Under a heavy fire he caused his troopers to fall back upon his transport, which had been left at a point a few miles out upon the Kroonstad Road, where three defensible *kopjes* sheltered a valley in which the cattle and horses could be herded. A stream ran through it. There were all the materials there for a stand which would have brought glory to the British arms. The men were of peculiarly fine quality, many of them from the public schools and from the universities, and if any would fight to the death these with their sporting spirit and their high sense of honour might have been expected to do so.

They had the stronger motive for holding out, as they had taken steps to convey word of their difficulty to Colvile and to Methuen. The former continued his march to Heilbron, and it is hard to blame him for doing so, but Methuen on hearing the message, which was conveyed to him at great personal peril by Corporal Hankey of the Yeomanry, pushed on instantly with the utmost energy, though he arrived too late to prevent, or even to repair, a disaster. It must be remembered that Colvile was under orders to reach Heilbron on a certain date, that he was himself fighting his way, and that the force which he was asked to relieve was much more mobile than his own. His cavalry at that date consisted of 100 men of the Eastern Province Horse.

Colonel Spragge's men had held their own for the first three days of their investment, during which they had been simply exposed to a long-range rifle fire which inflicted no very serious loss upon them. Their principal defence consisted of a stone *kraal* about twenty yards square, which sheltered them from rifle bullets, but must obviously be a perfect death-trap in the not improbable event of the Boers sending for artillery. The spirit of the troopers was admirable. Several dashing sorties were carried out under the leadership of Captain Humby and Lord Longford. The latter was a particularly dashing business, ending in a bayonet charge which cleared a neighbouring ridge. Early in the siege the gallant Keith met his end. On the fourth day the Boers brought up five guns. One would have thought that during so long a time as three days it would have been possible for the officer in command to make such preparations against this obvious possibility as were so successfully taken at a later stage of the war by the handful who garrisoned Ladybrand. Surely in this period, even without engineers, it would not have been hard to construct such trenches as the Boers have again and again opposed to our own artillery. But the preparations which were made proved to be quite inadequate. One of the two smaller *kopjes* was carried, and the garrison fled to the other. This also was compelled to surrender, and finally the main *kopje* also hoisted the white flag. No blame can rest upon the men, for their presence there at all is a sufficient proof of their public spirit and their gallantry. But the lessons of the war seem to have been imperfectly learned, especially that very certain lesson that shell fire in a close formation is insupportable, while in an open formation with a little cover it can never compel surrender. The casualty lists (80 killed and wounded out of a force of 470) show that the Yeomanry took considerable punishment before surrendering, but do not permit us to call the defence desperate or heroic. It is only fair to add that Colonel Spragge was acquitted of all blame by a court of inquiry, which agreed, however, that the surrender was premature, and attributed it to the unauthorised hoisting of a white flag upon one of the detached *kopjes*. With regard to the subsequent controversy as to whether General Colvile might have returned to the relief of the Yeomanry, it is impossible to see how that General could have acted in any other way than he did.

Some explanation is needed of Lord Methuen's appearance upon the central scene of warfare, his division having, when last described, been at Boshof, not far from Kimberley, where early in April he fought the successful action which led to the death of Villebois. Thence he proceeded along the Vaal and then south to Kroonstad, arriving there on May 28th. He had with him the 9th Brigade (Douglas's), which contained the troops which had started with him for the relief of Kimberley six months before. These were the Northumberland Fusiliers, Loyal North Lancashires, Northamptons, and Yorkshire Light Infantry. With him also were the Munsters, Lord Chesham's Yeomanry (five companies), with the 4th and 37th batteries, two howitzers and two pom-poms. His total force was about 6000 men. On arriving at Kroonstad he was given the task of relieving Heilbron, where Colvile, with the Highland Brigade, some Colonial horse, Lovat's Scouts, two naval guns, and the 5th battery, were short of food and ammunition. The more urgent message from the Yeomen at Lindley, however, took him on a fruitless journey to that town on June 1st. So vigorous was the pursuit of the Yeomanry that the leading squadrons, consisting of South Notts Hussars and Sherwood Rangers, actually cut into the Boer convoy and might have rescued the prisoners had they been supported. As it was they were recalled, and had to fight their way back to Lindley with some loss, including Colonel Rolleston, the commander, who was badly wounded. A garrison was left under Paget, and the rest of the force pursued its original mission to Heilbron, arriving there on June 7th, when the Highlanders had been reduced to quarter rations. 'The Salvation Army' was the nickname by which they expressed their gratitude to the relieving force.

A previous convoy sent to the same destination had less good fortune. On June 1st fifty-five wagons started from the railway line to reach Heilbron. The escort consisted of one hundred and sixty details belonging to Highland regiments without any guns, Captain Corballis in command. But the gentleman with the tinted glasses was waiting on the way. 'I have twelve hundred men and five guns. Surrender at once!' Such was the message which reached the escort, and in their defenceless condition there was nothing for it but to comply. Thus one disaster leads to another, for, had the Yeomanry held out at Lindley, De Wet would not on June 4th have laid hands upon our wagons; and had he not recruited his supplies from our wagons it is doubtful if he could have made his attack upon Roodeval. This was the next point upon which he turned his attention.

Two miles beyond Roodeval station there is a well-marked *kopje* by the railway line, with other hills some distance to the right and the left. A militia regiment, the 4th Derbyshire, had been sent up to occupy this post. There were rumours of Boers on the line, and Major Haig, who with one thousand details of various regiments commanded at railhead, had been attacked on June 6th but had beaten off his assailants. De Wet, acting sometimes in company with, and sometimes independently of, his lieutenant Nel, passed down the line looking for some easier prey, and on the night of June 7th came upon the militia regiment, which was encamped in a position which could be completely commanded by artillery. It is not true that they had neglected to occupy the *kopje* under which they lay, for two companies had been posted upon it. But there seems to have been no thought of imminent danger, and the regiment had pitched its tents and gone very comfortably to sleep without a thought of the gentleman in the tinted glasses. In the middle of the night he was upon them with a hissing sleet of bullets. At the first dawn the guns opened and the shells began to burst among them. It was a horrible ordeal for raw troops. The men were miners and agricultural labourers, who had never seen more bloodshed than a cut finger in their lives. They had been four months in the country, but their life had been a picnic, as the luxury of their baggage shows. Now in an instant the picnic was ended, and in the grey cold dawn war was upon them—grim war with the whine of bullets, the screams of pain, the crash of shell, the horrible rending and riving of body and limb. In desperate straits, which would have tried the oldest soldiers, the brave miners did well. They never from the beginning had a chance save to show how gamely they could take punishment, but that at least they did. Bullets were coming from all sides at once and yet no enemy was visible. They lined one side of the embankment, and they were shot in the back. They lined the other, and were again shot in the back. Baird-Douglas, the Colonel, vowed to shoot the man who should raise the white flag, and he fell dead himself before he saw the hated emblem. But it had to come. A hundred and forty of the men were down, many of them suffering from the horrible wounds which shell inflicts. The place was a shambles. Then the flag went up and the Boers at last became visible. Outnumbered, out-generalled, and without guns, there is no shadow of stain upon the good name of the one militia regiment which was ever seriously engaged during the war. Their position was hopeless from the first, and they came out of it with death, mutilation, and honour.

Two miles south of the Rhenoster *kopje* stands Roodeval station, in which, on that June morning, there stood a train containing the mails for the army, a supply of great-coats, and a truck full of enormous shells. A number of details of various sorts, a hundred or more, had alighted from the train, twenty of them Post-office volunteers, some of the Pioneer Railway corps, a few Shropshires, and other waifs and strays. To them in the early morning came the gentleman with the tinted glasses, his hands still red with the blood of the Derbies. 'I have fourteen hundred men and four guns. Surrender!' said the messenger. But it is not in nature for a postman to give up his postbag without a struggle. 'Never!' cried the valiant postmen. But shell after shell battered the corrugated-iron buildings about their ears, and it was not possible for them to answer the guns which were smashing the life out of them. There was no help for it but to surrender. De Wet added samples of the British volunteer and of the British regular to his bag of militia. The station and train were burned down, the great-coats looted, the big shells exploded, and the mails burned. The latter was the one unsportsmanlike action which can up to that date be laid to De Wet's charge. Forty thousand men to the north of him could forego their coats and their food, but they yearned greatly for those home letters, charred fragments of which are still blowing about the *veld*.[1]

For three days De Wet held the line, and during all that time he worked his wicked will upon it. For miles and miles it was wrecked with most scientific completeness. The Rhenoster bridge was destroyed. So, for the second time, was the Roodeval bridge. The rails were blown upwards with dynamite until they looked like an unfinished line to heaven. De Wet's heavy hand was everywhere. Not a telegraph-post remained standing within ten miles. His headquarters continued to be the *kopje* at Roodeval.

---

1. Fragments continually met the eye which must have afforded curious reading for the victors. 'I hope you have killed all those Boers by now,' was the beginning of one letter which I could not help observing.

On June 10th two British forces were converging upon the point of danger. One was Methuen's, from Heilbron. The other was a small force consisting of the Shropshires, the South Wales Borderers, and a battery which had come south with Lord Kitchener. The energetic Chief of the Staff was always sent by Lord Roberts to the point where a strong man was needed, and it was seldom that he failed to justify his mission. Lord Methuen, however, was the first to arrive, and at once attacked De Wet, who moved swiftly away to the eastward. With a tendency to exaggeration, which has been too common during the war, the affair was described as a victory. It was really a strategic and almost bloodless move upon the part of the Boers. It is not the business of guerrillas to fight pitched battles. Methuen pushed for the south, having been informed that Kroonstad had been captured. Finding this to be untrue, he turned again to the eastward in search of De Wet.

That wily and indefatigable man was not long out of our ken. On June 14th he appeared once more at Rhenoster, where the construction trains, under the famous Girouard, were working furiously at the repair of the damage which he had already done. This time the guard was sufficient to beat him off, and he vanished again to the eastward. He succeeded, however, in doing some harm, and very nearly captured Lord Kitchener himself. A permanent post had been established at Rhenoster under the charge of Colonel Spens of the Shropshires, with his own regiment and several guns. Smith-Dorrien, one of the youngest and most energetic of the divisional commanders, had at the same time undertaken the supervision and patrolling of the line.

An attack had at this period been made by a commando of some hundred Boers at the Sand River to the south of Kroonstad, where there is a most important bridge. The attempt was frustrated by the Royal Lancaster regiment and the Railway Pioneer regiment, helped by some mounted infantry and Yeomanry. The fight was for a time a brisk one, and the Pioneers, upon whom the brunt of it fell, behaved with great steadiness. The skirmish is principally remarkable for the death of Major Seymour of the Pioneers, a noble American, who gave his services and at last his life for what, in the face of all slander and misrepresentation, he knew to be the cause of justice and of liberty.

It was hoped now, after all these precautions, that the last had been seen of the gentleman with the tinted glasses, but on June 21st he was back in his old haunts once more. Honing Spruit Station, about midway between Kroonstad and Roodeval, was the scene of his new raid. On that date his men appeared suddenly as a train waited in the station, and ripped up the rails on either side of it. There were no guns at this point, and the only available troops were three hundred of the prisoners from Pretoria, armed with Martini-Henry rifles and obsolete ammunition. A good man was in command, however—the same Colonel Bullock of the Devons who had distinguished himself at Colenso—and every tattered, half-starved wastrel was nerved by a recollection of the humiliations which he had already endured. For seven hours they lay helpless under the shell-fire, but their constancy was rewarded by the arrival of Colonel Brookfield with 300 Yeomanry and four guns of the 17th R.F.A., followed in the evening by a larger force from the south. The Boers fled, but left some of their number behind them; while of the British, Major Hobbs and four men were killed and nineteen wounded. This defence of three hundred half-armed men against seven hundred Boer riflemen, with three guns firing shell and shrapnel, was a very good performance. The same body of burghers immediately afterwards attacked a post held by Colonel Evans with two companies of the Shropshires and fifty Canadians. They were again beaten back with loss, the Canadians under Inglis especially distinguishing themselves by their desperate resistance in an exposed position.

All these attacks, irritating and destructive as they were, were not able to hinder the general progress of the war. After the battle of Diamond Hill the captured position was occupied by the mounted infantry, while the rest of the forces returned to their camps round Pretoria, there to await the much-needed remounts. At other parts of the seat of war the British cordon was being drawn more tightly round the Boer forces. Buller had come as far as Standerton, and Ian Hamilton, in the last week of June, had occupied Heidelberg. A week afterwards the two forces were able to join hands, and so to completely cut off the Free State from the Transvaal armies. Hamilton in these operations had the misfortune to break his collar-bone, and for a time the command of his division passed to Hunter—the one man, perhaps, whom the army would regard as an adequate successor.

It was evident now to the British commanders that there would be no peace and no safety for their communications while an undefeated army of seven or eight thousand men, under such leaders as De Wet and Olivier, was lurking amid the hills which flanked their railroad. A determined effort was made, therefore, to clear up that corner of the country. Having closed the only line of escape by the junction of Ian Hamilton and of Buller, the attention of six separate bodies of troops was concentrated upon the stalwart Freestaters. These were the divisions of Rundle and of Brabant from the south, the brigade of Clements on their extreme left, the garrison of Lindley under Paget, the garrison of Heilbron under Macdonald, and, most formidable of all, a detachment under Hunter which was moving from the north. A crisis was evidently approaching.

The nearest Free State town of importance still untaken was Bethlehem—a singular name to connect with the operations of war. The country on the south of it forbade an advance by Rundle or Brabant, but it was more accessible from the west. The first operation of the British consisted, therefore, in massing sufficient troops to be able to advance from this side. This was done by effecting a junction between Clements from Senekal, and Paget who commanded at Lindley, which was carried out upon July 1st near the latter place. Clements encountered some opposition, but besides his excellent infantry regiments, the Royal Irish, Worcesters, Wiltshires, and Bedfords, he had with him the 2nd Brabant's Horse, with yeomanry, mounted infantry, two 5-inch guns, and the 38th R.F.A. Aided by a demonstration on the part of Grenfell and of Brabant, he pushed his way through after three days of continual skirmish.

On getting into touch with Clements, Paget sallied out from Lindley, leaving the Buffs behind to garrison the town. He had with him Brookfield's mounted brigade one thousand strong, eight guns, and two fine battalions of infantry, the Munster Fusiliers and the Yorkshire Light Infantry. On July 3rd he found near Leeuw Kop a considerable force of Boers with three guns opposed to him, Clements being at that time too far off upon the flank to assist him. Four guns of the 38th R.F.A. (Major Oldfield) and two belonging to the City Volunteers came into action. The Royal Artillery guns appear to have been exposed to a very severe fire, and the losses were so heavy that for a time they could not be served. The escort was inadequate, insufficiently advanced, and badly handled, for the Boer riflemen were able, by creeping up a *donga*, to get right into the 38th battery, and the gallant major, with Lieutenant Belcher, was killed in the defence of the guns. Captain FitzGerald, the only other officer present, was wounded in two places, and twenty men were struck down, with nearly all the horses of one section. Captain Marks, who was brigade-major of Colonel Brookfield's Yeomanry, with the help of Lieutenant Keevil Davis and the 15th I.Y. came to the rescue of the disorganised and almost annihilated section. At the same time the C.I.V. guns were in imminent danger, but were energetically covered by Captain Budworth, adjutant of the battery. Soon, however, the infantry, Munster Fusiliers, and Yorkshire Light Infantry, which had been carrying out a turning movement, came into action, and the position was taken. The force moved onwards, and on July 6th they were in front of Bethlehem.

The place is surrounded by hills, and the enemy was found strongly posted. Clements's force was now on the left and Paget's on the right. From both sides an attempt was made to turn the Boer flanks, but they were found to be very wide and strong. All day a long-range action was kept up while Clements felt his way in the hope of coming upon some weak spot in the position, but in the evening a direct attack was made by Paget's two infantry regiments upon the right, which gave the British a footing on the Boer position. The Munster Fusiliers and the Yorkshire Light Infantry lost forty killed and wounded, including four officers, in this gallant affair, the heavier loss and the greater honour going to the men of Munster.

The centre of the position was still held, and on the morning of July 7th Clements gave instructions to the colonel of the Royal Irish to storm it if the occasion should seem favourable. Such an order to such a regiment means that the occasion will seem favourable. Up they went in three extended lines, dropping forty or fifty on the way, but arriving breathless and enthusiastic upon the crest of the ridge. Below them, upon the further side, lay the village of Bethlehem. On the slopes beyond hundreds of horsemen were retreating, and a gun was being hurriedly dragged into the town. For a moment it seemed as if nothing had been left as a trophy, but suddenly a keen-eyed sergeant raised a cheer, which was taken up again and again until it resounded over the *veldt*. Under the crest, lying on its side with a broken wheel, was a gun—one of the 15-pounders of Stormberg which it was a point of honour to regain once more. Many a time had the gunners been friends in need to the infantry. Now it was the turn of the infantry to do something in exchange. That evening Clements had occupied Bethlehem, and one more of their towns had passed out of the hands of the Freestaters.

A word now as to that force under General Hunter which was closing in from the north. The gallant and energetic Hamilton, lean, aquiline, and tireless, had, as already stated, broken his collar-bone at Heidelberg, and it was as his lieutenant that Hunter was leading these troops out of the Transvaal into the Orange River Colony. Most of his infantry was left behind at Heidelberg, but he took with him Broadwood's cavalry (two brigades) and Bruce Hamilton's 21st infantry brigade, with Ridley's mounted infantry, some seven thousand men in all. On the 2nd of July this force reached Frankfort in the north of the Free State without resistance, and on July 3rd they were joined there by Macdonald's force from Heilbron, so that Hunter found himself with over eleven thousand men under his command. Here was an instrument with which surely the *coup de grace* could be given to the dying State. Passing south, still without meeting serious resistance, Hunter occupied Reitz, and finally sent on Broadwood's cavalry to Bethlehem, where on July 8th they joined Paget and Clements.

The net was now in position, and about to be drawn tight, but at this last moment the biggest fish of all dashed furiously out from it. Leaving the main Free State force in a hopeless position behind him, De Wet, with fifteen hundred well-mounted men and five guns, broke through Slabbert's Nek between Bethlehem and Ficksburg, and made swiftly for the north-west, closely followed by Paget's and Broadwood's cavalry. It was on July 16th that he made his dash for freedom. On the 19th Little, with the 3rd Cavalry Brigade, had come into touch with him near Lindley. De Wet shook himself clear, and with splendid audacity cut the railway once more to the north of Honing Spruit, gathering up a train as he passed, and taking two hundred details prisoners. On July 22nd De Wet was at Vredefort, still closely followed by Broadwood, Ridley, and Little, who gleaned his wagons and his stragglers. Thence he threw himself into the hilly country some miles to the south of the Vaal River, where he lurked for a week or more while Lord Kitchener came south to direct the operations which would, as it was hoped, lead to a surrender.

Leaving the indomitable guerrilla in his hiding-place, the narrative must return to that drawing of the net which still continued in spite of the escape of this one important fish. On all sides the British forces had drawn closer, and they were both more numerous and more formidable in quality. It was evident now that by a rapid advance from Bethlehem in the direction of the Basuto border all Boers to the north of Ficksburg would be hemmed in. On July 22nd the columns were moving. On that date Paget moved out of Bethlehem, and Rundle took a step forward from Ficksburg. Bruce Hamilton had already, at the cost of twenty Cameron Highlanders, got a grip upon a bastion of that rocky country in which the enemy lurked. On the 23rd Hunter's force was held by the Boers at the strong pass of Retief's Nek, but on the 24th they were compelled to abandon it, as the capture of Slabbert's Nek by Clements threatened their rear. This latter pass was fortified most elaborately. It was attacked upon the 23rd by Brabant's Horse and the Royal Irish without success. Later in the day two companies of the Wiltshire Regiment were also brought to a standstill, but retained a position until nightfall within stone-throw of the Boer lines, though a single company had lost 17 killed and wounded. Part of the Royal Irish remained also close to the enemy's trenches. Under cover of darkness, Clements sent four companies of the Royal Irish and two of the Wiltshires under Colonel Guinness to make a flanking movement along the crest of the heights. These six companies completely surprised the enemy, and caused them to hurriedly evacuate the position. Their night march was performed under great difficulties, the men crawling on hands and knees along a rocky path with a drop of 400 feet upon one side. But their exertions were greatly rewarded. Upon the success of their turning movement depended the fall of Slabbert's Nek. Retief's Nek was untenable if we held Slabbert's Nek, and if both were in our hands the retreat of Prinsloo was cut off.

At every opening of the hills the British guns were thundering, and the heads of British columns were appearing on every height. The Highland Brigade had fairly established themselves over the Boer position, though not without hard fighting, in which a hundred men of the Highland Light Infantry had been killed and wounded. The Seaforths and the Sussex had also gripped the positions in front of them, and taken some punishment in doing so. The outworks of the great mountain fortress were all taken, and on July 26th the British columns were converging on Fouriesburg, while Naauwpoort on the line of retreat was held by Macdonald. It was only a matter of time now with the Boers.

On the 28th Clements was still advancing, and contracting still further the space which was occupied by our stubborn foe. He found himself faced by the stiff position of Slaapkrantz, and a hot little action was needed before the Boers could be dislodged. The fighting fell upon Brabant's Horse, the Royal Irish, and the Wiltshires. Three companies of the latter seized a farm upon the enemy's left, but lost ten men in doing so, while their gallant colonel, Carter, was severely wounded in two places. The Wiltshires, who were excellently handled by Captain Bolton, held on to the farm and were reinforced there by a handful of the Scots Guards. In the night the position was abandoned by the Boers, and the advance swept onwards. On all sides the pressure was becoming unendurable. The burghers in the valley below could see all day the twinkle of British heliographs from every hill, while at night the constant flash of signals told of the sleepless vigilance which hemmed them in. Upon July 29th, Prinsloo sent in a request for an armistice, which was refused. Later in the day he despatched a messenger with the white flag to Hunter, with an announcement of his unconditional surrender.

On July 30th the motley army which had held the British off so long emerged from among the mountains. But it soon became evident that in speaking for all Prinsloo had gone beyond his powers. Discipline was low and individualism high in the Boer army. Every man might repudiate the decision of his commandant, as every man might repudiate the white flag of his comrade. On the first day no more than eleven hundred men of the Ficksburg and Ladybrand commandos, with fifteen hundred horses and two guns, were surrendered. Next day seven hundred and fifty more men came in with eight hundred horses, and by August 6th the total of the prisoners had mounted to four thousand one hundred and fifty with three guns, two of which were our own. But Olivier, with fifteen hundred men and several guns, broke away from the captured force and escaped through the hills. Of this incident General Hunter, an honourable soldier, remarks in his official report: 'I regard it as a dishonourable breach of faith upon the part of General Olivier, for which I hold him personally responsible. He admitted that he knew that General Prinsloo had included him in the unconditional surrender.' It is strange that, on Olivier's capture shortly afterwards, he was not court-martialled for this breach of the rules of war, but that good-natured giant, the Empire, is quick—too quick, perhaps—to let bygones be bygones. On August 4th Harrismith surrendered to Macdonald, and thus was secured the opening of the Van Reenen's Pass and the end of the Natal system of railways. This was of the very first importance, as the utmost difficulty had been found in supplying so large a body of troops so far from the Cape base. In a day the base was shifted to Durban, and the distance shortened by two-thirds, while the army came to be on the railway instead of a hundred miles from it. This great success assured Lord Roberts's communications from serious attack, and was of the utmost importance in enabling him to consolidate his position at Pretoria.

CHAPTER 28

The Halt at Pretoria

Lord Roberts had now been six weeks in the capital, and British troops had overrun the greater part of the south and west of the Transvaal, but in spite of this there was continued Boer resistance, which flared suddenly up in places which had been nominally pacified and disarmed. It was found, as has often been shown in history, that it is easier to defeat a republican army than to conquer it. From Klerksdorp, from Ventersdorp, from Rustenburg, came news of risings against the newly imposed British authority. The concealed Mauser and the bandolier were dug up once more from the trampled corner of the cattle *kraal*, and the farmer was a warrior once again. Vague news of the exploits of De Wet stimulated the fighting burghers and shamed those who had submitted. A letter was intercepted from the guerrilla chief to Cronje's son, who had surrendered near Rustenburg. De Wet stated that he had gained two great victories and had fifteen hundred captured rifles with which to replace those which the burghers had given up. Not only were the outlying districts in a state of revolt, but even round Pretoria the Boers were inclined to take the offensive, while both that town and Johannesburg were filled with malcontents who were ready to fly to their arms once more.

Already at the end of June there were signs that the Boers realised how helpless Lord Roberts was until his remounts should arrive. The mosquitoes buzzed round the crippled lion. On June 29th there was an attack upon Springs near Johannesburg, which was easily beaten off by the Canadians. Early in July some of the cavalry and mounted infantry patrols were snapped up in the neighbourhood of the capital. Lord Roberts gave orders accordingly that Hutton and Mahon should sweep the Boers back upon his right, and push them as far as Bronkhorst Spruit. This was done on July 6th and 7th, the British advance meeting with considerable resistance from artillery as well as rifles. By this movement the pressure upon the right was relieved, which might have created a dangerous unrest in Johannesburg, and it was done at the moderate cost of thirty-four killed and wounded, half of whom belonged to the Imperial Light Horse. This famous corps, which had come across with Mahon from the relief of Mafeking, had, a few days before, ridden with mixed feelings through the streets of Johannesburg and past, in many instances, the deserted houses which had once been their homes. Many weary months were to pass before the survivors might occupy them. On July 9th the Boers again attacked, but were again pushed back to the eastward.

It is probable that all these demonstrations of the enemy upon the right of Lord Roberts's extended position were really feints in order to cover the far-reaching plans which Botha had in his mind. The disposition of the Boer forces at this time appears to have been as follows: Botha with his army occupied a position along Delagoa railway line, further east than Diamond Hill, whence he detached the bodies which attacked Hutton upon the extreme right of the British position to the south-east of Pretoria. To the north of Pretoria a second force was acting under Grobler, while a third under De la Rey had been despatched secretly across to the left wing of the British, north-west of Pretoria. While Botha engaged the attention of Lord Roberts by energetic demonstrations on his right, Grobler and De la Rey were to make a sudden attack upon his centre and his left, each point being twelve or fifteen miles from the other. It was well devised and very well carried out; but the inherent defect of it was that, when subdivided in this way, the Boer force was no longer strong enough to gain more than a mere success of outposts.

De la Rey's attack was delivered at break of day on July 11th at Uitval's Nek, a post some eighteen miles west of the capital. This position could not be said to be part of Lord Roberts's line, but rather to be a link to connect his army with Rustenburg. It was weakly held by three companies of the Lincolns with two others in support, one squadron of the Scots Greys, and two guns of O battery R.H.A. The attack came with the first grey light of dawn, and for many hours the small garrison bore up against a deadly fire, waiting for the help which never came. All day they held their assailants at bay, and it was not until evening that their ammunition ran short and they were forced to surrender. Nothing could have been better than the behaviour of the men, both infantry, cavalry, and gunners, but their position was a hopeless one. The casualties amounted to eighty killed and wounded. Nearly two hundred were made prisoners and the two guns were taken.

On the same day that De la Rey made his coup at Uitval's Nek, Grobler had shown his presence on the north side of the town by treating very roughly a couple of squadrons of the 7th Dragoon Guards which had attacked him. By the help of a section of the ubiquitous O battery and of the 14th Hussars, Colonel Lowe was able to disengage his cavalry from the trap into which they had fallen, but it was at the cost of between thirty and forty officers and men killed, wounded, or taken. The old 'Black Horse' sustained their historical reputation, and fought their way bravely out of an almost desperate situation, where they were exposed to the fire of a thousand riflemen and four guns.

On this same day of skirmishes, July 11th, the Gordons had seen some hot work twenty miles or so to the south of Uitval's Nek. Orders had been given to the 19th Brigade (Smith-Dorrien's) to proceed to Krugersdorp, and thence to make their way north. The Scottish Yeomanry and a section of the 78th R.F.A. accompanied them. The idea seems to have been that they would be able to drive north any Boers in that district, who would then find the garrison of Uitval's Nek at their rear. The advance was checked, however, at a place called Dolverkrantz, which was strongly held by Boer riflemen. The two guns were insufficiently protected, and the enemy got within short range of them, killing or wounding many of the gunners. The lieutenant in charge, Mr. A.J. Turner, the famous Essex cricketer, worked the gun with his own hands until he also fell wounded in three places. The situation was now very serious, and became more so when news was flashed of the disaster at Uitval's Nek, and they were ordered to retire. They could not retire and abandon the guns, yet the fire was so hot that it was impossible to remove them. Gallant attempts were made by volunteers from the Gordons—Captain Younger and other brave men throwing away their lives in the vain effort to reach and to limber up the guns. At last, under the cover of night, the teams were harnessed and the two field-pieces successfully removed, while the Boers who rushed in to seize them were scattered by a volley. The losses in the action were thirty-six and the gain nothing. Decidedly July 11th was not a lucky day for the British arms.

It was well known to Botha that every train from the south was bringing horses for Lord Roberts's army, and that it had become increasingly difficult for De Wet and his men to hinder their arrival. The last horse must win, and the Empire had the world on which to draw. Any movement which the Boers would make must be made at once, for already both the cavalry and the mounted infantry were rapidly coming back to their full strength once more. This consideration must have urged Botha to deliver an attack on July 16th, which had some success at first, but was afterwards beaten off with heavy loss to the enemy. The fighting fell principally upon Pole-Carew and Hutton, the corps chiefly engaged being the Royal Irish Fusiliers, the New Zealanders, the Shropshires, and the Canadian Mounted Infantry. The enemy tried repeatedly to assault the position, but were beaten back each time with a loss of nearly a hundred killed and wounded. The British loss was about sixty, and included two gallant young Canadian officers, Borden and Birch, the former being the only son of the minister of militia. So ended the last attempt made by Botha upon the British positions round Pretoria. The end of the war was not yet, but already its futility was abundantly evident. This had become more apparent since the junction of Hamilton and of Buller had cut off the Transvaal army from that of the Free State. Unable to send their prisoners away, and also unable to feed them, the Freestaters were compelled to deliver up in Natal the prisoners whom they had taken at Lindley and Roodeval. These men, a ragged and starving battalion, emerged at Ladysmith, having made their way through Van Reenen's Pass. It is a singular fact that no parole appears on these and similar occasions to have been exacted by the Boers.

Lord Roberts, having remounted a large part of his cavalry, was ready now to advance eastward and give Botha battle. The first town of any consequence along the Delagoa Railway is Middelburg, some seventy miles from the capital. This became the British objective, and the forces of Mahon and Hamilton on the north, of Pole-Carew in the centre, and of French and Hutton to the south, all converged upon it. There was no serious resistance, though the weather was abominable, and on July 27th the town was in the hands of the invaders. From that date until the final advance to the eastward French held this advanced post, while Pole-Carew guarded the railway line. Rumours of trouble in the west had convinced Roberts that it was not yet time to push his advantage to the east, and he recalled Ian Hamilton's force to act for a time upon the other side of the seat of the war. This excellent little army, consisting of Mahon's and Pilcher's mounted infantry, M battery R.H.A., the Elswick battery, two 5-inch and two 4.7 guns, with the Berkshires, the Border Regiment, the Argyle and Sutherlands, and the Scottish Borderers, put in as much hard work in marching and in fighting as any body of troops in the whole campaign.

The renewal of the war in the west had begun some weeks before, but was much accelerated by the transference of De la Rey and his burghers to that side. There is no district in the Transvaal which is better worth fighting for, for it is a fair country side, studded with farmhouses and green with orange-groves, with many clear streams running through it. The first sign of activity appears to have been on July 7th, when a commando with guns appeared upon the hills above Rustenburg. Hanbury Tracy, commandant of Rustenburg, was suddenly confronted with a summons to surrender. He had only 120 men and one gun, but he showed a bold front. Colonel Houldsworth, at the first whisper of danger, had started from Zeerust with a small force of Australian bushmen, and arrived at Rustenburg in time to drive the enemy away in a very spirited action. On the evening of July 8th Baden-Powell took over the command, the garrison being reinforced by Plumer's command.

The Boer commando was still in existence, however, and it was reinforced and reinvigorated by De la Rey's success at Uitval's Nek. On July 18th they began to close in upon Rustenburg again, and a small skirmish took place between them and the Australians. Methuen's division, which had been doing very arduous service in the north of the Free State during the last six weeks, now received orders to proceed into the Transvaal and to pass northwards through the disturbed districts en route for Rustenburg, which appeared to be the storm centre. The division was transported by train from Kroonstad to Krugersdorp, and advanced on the evening of July 18th upon its mission, through a bare and fire-blackened country. On the 19th Lord Methuen manoeuvred the Boers out of a strong position, with little loss to either side. On the 21st he forced his way through Olifant's Nek, in the Magaliesberg range, and so established communication with Baden-Powell, whose valiant bushmen, under Colonel Airey, had held their own in a severe conflict near Magato Pass, in which they lost six killed, nineteen wounded, and nearly two hundred horses. The fortunate arrival of Captain FitzClarence with the Protectorate Regiment helped on this occasion to avert a disaster. The force, only 300 strong, without guns, had walked into an ugly ambuscade, and only the tenacity and resource of the men enabled them ever to extricate themselves.

Although Methuen came within reach of Rustenburg, he did not actually join hands with Baden-Powell. No doubt he saw and heard enough to convince him that that astute soldier was very well able to take care of himself. Learning of the existence of a Boer force in his rear, Methuen turned, and on July 29th he was back at Frederickstad on the Potchefstroom to Krugersdorp railway. The sudden change in his plans was caused doubtless by the desire to head off De Wet in case he should cross the Vaal River. Lord Roberts was still anxious to clear the neighbourhood of Rustenburg entirely of the enemy; and he therefore, since Methuen was needed to complete the cordon round De Wet, recalled Hamilton's force from the east and despatched it, as already described, to the west of Pretoria.

Before going into the details of the great De Wet hunt, in which Methuen's force was to be engaged, I shall follow Hamilton's division across, and give some account of their services. On August 1st he set out from Pretoria for Rustenburg. On that day and on the next he had brisk skirmishes which brought him successfully through the Magaliesberg range with a loss of forty wounded, mostly of the Berkshires. On the 5th of August he had made his way to Rustenburg and drove off the investing force. A smaller siege had been going on to westward, where at Elands River another Mafeking man, Colonel Hore, had been held up by the burghers. For some days it was feared, and even officially announced, that the garrison had surrendered. It was known that an attempt by Carrington to relieve the place on August 5th had been beaten back, and that the state of the country appeared so threatening that he had been compelled, or had imagined himself to be compelled, to retreat as far as Mafeking, evacuating Zeerust and Otto's Hoop, abandoning the considerable stores which were collected at those places. In spite of all these sinister indications the garrison was still holding its own, and on August 16th it was relieved by Lord Kitchener.

This stand at Brakfontein on the Elands River appears to have been one of the very finest deeds of arms of the war. The Australians have been so split up during the campaign, that though their valour and efficiency were universally recognised, they had no single exploit which they could call their own. But now they can point to Elands River as proudly as the Canadians can to Paardeberg. They were 500 in number, Victorians, New South Welshmen, and Queenslanders, the latter the larger unit, with a corps of Rhodesians. Under Hore were Major Hopper of the Rhodesians, and Major Tonbridge of the Queenslanders. Two thousand five hundred Boers surrounded them, and most favourable terms of surrender were offered and scouted. Six guns were trained upon them, and during 11 days 1800 shells fell within their lines. The river was half a mile off, and every drop of water for man or beast had to come from there. Nearly all their horses and 75 of the men were killed or wounded. With extraordinary energy and ingenuity the little band dug shelters which are said to have exceeded in depth and efficiency any which the Boers have devised. Neither the repulse of Carrington, nor the jamming of their only gun, nor the death of the gallant Annett, was sufficient to dishearten them. They were sworn to die before the white flag should wave above them. And so fortune yielded, as fortune will when brave men set their teeth, and Broadwood's troopers, filled with wonder and admiration, rode into the lines of the reduced and emaciated but indomitable garrison. When the ballad-makers of Australia seek for a subject, let them turn to Elands River, for there was no finer resistance in the war. They will not grudge a place in their record to the 130 gallant Rhodesians who shared with them the honours and the dangers of the exploit.

On August 7th Ian Hamilton abandoned Rustenburg, taking Baden-Powell and his men with him. It was obviously unwise to scatter the British forces too widely by attempting to garrison every single town. For the instant the whole interest of the war centred upon De Wet and his dash into the Transvaal. One or two minor events, however, which cannot be fitted into any continuous narrative may be here introduced.

One of these was the action at Faber's Put, by which Sir Charles Warren crushed the rebellion in Griqualand. In that sparsely inhabited country of vast distances it was a most difficult task to bring the revolt to a decisive ending. This Sir Charles Warren, with his special local knowledge and interest, was able to do, and the success is doubly welcome as bringing additional honour to a man who, whatever view one may take of his action at Spion Kop, has grown grey in the service of the Empire. With a column consisting mainly of colonials and of yeomanry he had followed the rebels up to a point within twelve miles of Douglas. Here at the end of May they turned upon him and delivered a fierce night attack, so sudden and so strongly pressed that much credit is due both to General and to troops for having repelled it. The camp was attacked on all sides in the early dawn. The greater part of the horses were stampeded by the firing, and the enemy's riflemen were found to be at very close quarters. For an hour the action was warm, but at the end of that time the Boers fled, leaving a number of dead behind them. The troops engaged in this very creditable action, which might have tried the steadiness of veterans, were four hundred of the Duke of Edinburgh's volunteers, some of Paget's horse and of the 8th Regiment Imperial Yeomanry, four Canadian guns, and twenty-five of Warren's Scouts. Their losses were eighteen killed and thirty wounded. Colonel Spence, of the volunteers, died at the head of his regiment. A few days before, on May 27th, Colonel Adye had won a small engagement at Kheis, some distance to the westward, and the effect of the two actions was to put an end to open resistance. On June 20th De Villiers, the Boer leader, finally surrendered to Sir Charles Warren, handing over two hundred and twenty men with stores, rifles, and ammunition. The last sparks had for the time been stamped out in the colony.

There remain to be mentioned those attacks upon trains and upon the railway which had spread from the Free State to the Transvaal. On July 19th a train was wrecked on the way from Potchefstroom to Krugersdorp without serious injury to the passengers. On July 31st, however, the same thing occurred with more murderous effect, the train running at full speed off the metals. Thirteen of the Shropshires were killed and thirty-seven injured in this deplorable affair, which cost us more than many an important engagement. On August 2nd a train coming up from Bloemfontein was derailed by Sarel Theron and his gang some miles south of Kroonstad. Thirty-five trucks of stores were burned, and six of the passengers (unarmed convalescent soldiers) were killed or wounded. A body of mounted infantry followed up the Boers, who numbered eighty, and succeeded in killing and wounding several of them.

On July 21st the Boers made a determined attack upon the railhead at a point thirteen miles east of Heidelberg, where over a hundred Royal Engineers were engaged upon a bridge. They were protected by three hundred Dublin Fusiliers under Major English. For some hours the little party was hard pressed by the burghers, who had two field-pieces and a pom-pom. They could make no impression, however, upon the steady Irish infantry, and after some hours the arrival of General Hart with reinforcements scattered the assailants, who succeeded in getting their guns away in safety.

At the beginning of August it must be confessed that the general situation in the Transvaal was not reassuring. Springs near Johannesburg had in some inexplicable way, without fighting, fallen into the hands of the enemy. Klerksdorp, an important place in the south-west, had also been reoccupied, and a handful of men who garrisoned it had been made prisoners without resistance. Rustenburg was about to be abandoned, and the British were known to be falling back from Zeerust and Otto's Hoop, concentrating upon Mafeking. The sequel proved however, that there was no cause for uneasiness in all this. Lord Roberts was concentrating his strength upon those objects which were vital, and letting the others drift for a time. At present the two obviously important things were to hunt down De Wet and to scatter the main Boer army under Botha. The latter enterprise must wait upon the former, so for a fortnight all operations were in abeyance while the flying columns of the British endeavoured to run down their extremely active and energetic antagonist.

At the end of July De Wet had taken refuge in some exceedingly difficult country near Reitzburg, seven miles south of the Vaal River. The operations were proceeding vigorously at that time against the main army at Fouriesberg, and sufficient troops could not be spared to attack him, but he was closely observed by Kitchener and Broadwood with a force of cavalry and mounted infantry. With the surrender of Prinsloo a large army was disengaged, and it was obvious that if De Wet remained where he was he must soon be surrounded. On the other hand, there was no place of refuge to the south of him. With great audacity he determined to make a dash for the Transvaal, in the hope of joining hands with De la Rey's force, or else of making his way across the north of Pretoria, and so reaching Botha's army. President Steyn went with him, and a most singular experience it must have been for him to be harried like a mad dog through the country in which he had once been an honoured guest. De

Wet's force was exceedingly mobile, each man having a led horse, and the ammunition being carried in light Cape carts.

In the first week of August the British began to thicken round his lurking-place, and De Wet knew that it was time for him to go. He made a great show of fortifying a position, but it was only a ruse to deceive those who watched him. Travelling as lightly as possible, he made a dash on August 7th at the drift which bears his own name, and so won his way across the Vaal River, Kitchener thundering at his heels with his cavalry and mounted infantry. Methuen's force was at that time at Potchefstroom, and instant orders had been sent to him to block the drifts upon the northern side. It was found as he approached the river that the vanguard of the enemy was already across and that it was holding the spurs of the hills which would cover the crossing of their comrades. By the dash of the Royal Welsh Fusiliers and the exertions of the artillery ridge after ridge was carried, but before evening De Wet with supreme skill had got his convoy across, and had broken away, first to the eastward and then to the north. On the 9th Methuen was in touch with him again, and the two savage little armies, Methuen worrying at the haunch, and De Wet snapping back over his shoulder, swept northward over the huge plains. Wherever there was ridge or *kopje* the Boer riflemen staved off the eager pursuers. Where the ground lay flat and clear the British guns thundered onwards and fired into the lines of wagons. Mile after mile the running fight was sustained, but the other British columns, Broadwood's men and Kitchener's men, had for some reason not come up. Methuen alone was numerically inferior to the men he was chasing, but he held on with admirable energy and spirit. The Boers were hustled off the *kopjes* from which they tried to cover their rear. Twenty men of the Yorkshire Yeomanry carried one hill with the bayonet, though only twelve of them were left to reach the top.

De Wet trekked onwards during the night of the 9th, shedding wagons and stores as he went. He was able to replace some of his exhausted beasts from the farmhouses which he passed. Methuen on the morning of the 10th struck away to the west, sending messages back to Broadwood and Kitchener in the rear that they should bear to the east, and so nurse the Boer column between them. At the same time he sent on a messenger, who unfortunately never arrived, to warn Smith-Dorrien at Bank Station to throw himself across De Wet's path. On the 11th it was realised that De Wet had succeeded, in spite of great exertions upon the part of Smith-Dorrien's infantry, in crossing the railway line, and that he had left all his pursuers to the south of him. But across his front lay the Magaliesberg range. There are only three passes, the Magato Pass, Olifant's Nek, and Commando Nek. It was understood that all three were held by

British troops. It was obvious, therefore, that if Methuen could advance in such a way as to cut De Wet off from slipping through to the west he would be unable to get away. Broadwood and Kitchener would be behind him, and Pretoria, with the main British army, to the east.

Methuen continued to act with great energy and judgment. At three a.m. on the 12th he started from Fredericstadt, and by 5 p.m. on Tuesday he had done eighty miles in sixty hours. The force which accompanied him was all mounted, 1200 of the Colonial Division (1st Brabant's, Cape Mounted Rifles, Kaffrarian Rifles, and Border Horse), and the Yeomanry with ten guns. Douglas with the infantry was to follow behind, and these brave fellows covered sixty-six miles in seventy-six hours in their eagerness to be in time. No men could have made greater efforts than did those of Methuen, for there was not one who did not appreciate the importance of the issue and long to come to close quarters with the wily leader who had baffled us so long.

On the 12th Methuen's van again overtook De Wet's rear, and the old game of rearguard riflemen on one side, and a pushing artillery on the other, was once more resumed. All day the Boers streamed over the *veldt* with the guns and the horsemen at their heels. A shot from the 78th battery struck one of De Wet's guns, which was abandoned and captured. Many stores were taken and much more, with the wagons which contained them, burned by the Boers. Fighting incessantly, both armies traversed thirty-five miles of ground that day.

It was fully understood that Olifant's Nek was held by the British, so Methuen felt that if he could block the Magato Pass all would be well. He therefore left De Wet's direct track, knowing that other British forces were behind him, and he continued his swift advance until he had reached the desired position. It really appeared that at last the elusive raider was in a corner. But, alas for fallen hopes, and alas for the wasted efforts of gallant men! Olifant's Nek had been abandoned and De Wet had passed safely through it into the plains beyond, where De la Rey's force was still in possession. In vain Methuen's weary column forced the Magato Pass and descended into Rustenburg. The enemy was in a safe country once more. Whose the fault, or whether there was a fault at all, it is for the future to determine. At least unalloyed praise can be given to the Boer leader for the admirable way in which he had extricated himself from so many dangers. On the 17th., moving along the northern side of the mountains, he appeared at Commando Nek on the Little Crocodile River, where he summoned Baden-Powell to surrender, and received some chaff in reply from that light-hearted commander. Then, swinging to the eastward, he endeavoured to cross to the north of Pretoria. On the 19th he was heard of at Hebron. Baden-Powell and Paget had, however, already barred this path, and De Wet, having sent Steyn on with a small escort, turned back to the Free State. On the 22nd it was reported that, with only a handful of his followers, he had crossed the Magaliesberg range by a bridle path and was riding southwards. Lord Roberts was at last free to turn his undivided attention upon Botha.

Two Boer plots had been discovered during the first half of August, the one in Pretoria and the other in Johannesburg, each having for its object a rising against the British in the town. Of these the former, which was the more serious, involving as it did the kidnapping of Lord Roberts, was broken up by the arrest of the deviser, Hans Cordua, a German lieutenant in the Transvaal Artillery. On its merits it is unlikely that the crime would have been met by the extreme penalty, especially as it was a question whether the agent provocateur had not played a part. But the repeated breaches of parole, by which our prisoners of one day were in the field against us on the next, called imperatively for an example, and it was probably rather for his broken faith than for his hare-brained scheme that Cordua died. At the same time it is impossible not to feel sorrow for this idealist of twenty-three who died for a cause which was not his own. He was shot in the garden of Pretoria Gaol upon August 24th. A fresh and more stringent proclamation from Lord Roberts showed that the British Commander was losing his patience in the face of the wholesale return of paroled men to the field, and announced that such perfidy would in future be severely punished. It was notorious that the same men had been taken and released more than once. One man killed in action was found to have nine signed passes in his pocket. It was against such abuses that the extra severity of the British was aimed.

CHAPTER 29

The Advance to Komatipoort

The time had now come for the great combined movement which was to sweep the main Boer army off the line of the Delagoa railway, cut its source of supplies, and follow it into that remote and mountainous Lydenburg district which had always been proclaimed as the last refuge of the burghers. Before entering upon this most difficult of all his advances Lord Roberts waited until the cavalry and mounted infantry were well mounted again. Then, when all was ready, the first step in this last stage of the regular campaign was taken by General Buller, who moved his army of Natal veterans off the railway line and advanced to a position from which he could threaten the flank and rear of Botha if he held his ground against Lord Roberts. Buller's cavalry had been reinforced by the arrival of Strathcona's Horse, a fine body of Canadian troopers, whose services had been presented to the nation by the public-spirited nobleman whose name they bore. They were distinguished by their fine physique, and by the lassoes, cowboy stirrups, and large spurs of the North-Western plains.

It was in the first week of July that Clery joined hands with the Heidelberg garrison, while Coke with the 10th Brigade cleared the right flank of the railway by an expedition as far as Amersfoort. On July 6th the Natal communications were restored, and on the 7th Buller was able to come through to Pretoria and confer with the commander-in-chief. A Boer force with heavy guns still hung about the line, and several small skirmishes were fought between Vlakfontein and Greylingstad in order to drive it away. By the middle of July the immediate vicinity of the railway was clear save for some small marauding parties who endeavoured to tamper with the rails and the bridges. Up to the end of the month the whole of the Natal army remained strung along the line of communications from Heidelberg to Standerton, waiting for the collection of forage and transport to enable them to march north against Botha's position.

On August 8th Buller's troops advanced to the north-east from Paardekop, pushing a weak Boer force with five guns in front of them. At the cost of twenty-five wounded, principally of the 60th Rifles, the enemy was cleared off, and the town of Amersfoort was occupied. On the 13th, moving on the same line, and meeting with very slight opposition, Buller took possession of Ermelo. His advance was having a good effect upon the district, for on the 12th the Standerton commando, which numbered 182 men, surrendered to Clery. On the 15th, still skirmishing, Buller's men were at Twyfelaar, and had taken possession of Carolina. Here and there a distant horseman riding over the olive-coloured hills showed how closely and incessantly he was watched; but, save for a little sniping upon his flanks, there was no fighting. He was coming now within touch of French's cavalry, operating from Middelburg, and on the 14th heliographic communication was established with Gordon's Brigade.

Buller's column had come nearer to its friends, but it was also nearer to the main body of Boers who were waiting in that very rugged piece of country which lies between Belfast in the west and Machadodorp in the east. From this rocky stronghold they had thrown out mobile bodies to harass the British advance from the south, and every day brought Buller into closer touch with these advance guards of the enemy. On August 21st he had moved eight miles nearer to Belfast, French operating upon his left flank. Here he found the Boers in considerable numbers, but he pushed them northward with his cavalry, mounted infantry, and artillery, losing between thirty and forty killed and wounded, the greater part from the ranks of the 18th Hussars and the Gordon Highlanders. This march brought him within fifteen miles of Belfast, which lay due north of him. At the same time Pole-Carew with the central column of Lord Roberts's force had advanced along the railway line, and on August 24th he occupied Belfast with little resistance. He found, however, that the enemy were holding the formidable ridges which lie between that place and Dalmanutha, and that they showed every sign of giving battle, presenting a firm front to Buller on the south as well as to Roberts's army on the west.

On the 23rd some successes attended their efforts to check the advance from the south. During the day Buller had advanced steadily, though under incessant fire. The evening found him only six miles to the south of Dalmanutha, the centre of the Boer position. By some misfortune, however, after dark two companies of the Liverpool Regiment found themselves isolated from their comrades and exposed to a very heavy fire. They had pushed forward too far, and were very near to being surrounded and destroyed. There were fifty-six casualties in their ranks, and thirty-two, including their wounded captain, were taken. The total losses in the day were 121.

On August 25th it was evident that important events were at hand, for on that date Lord Roberts arrived at Belfast and held a conference with

Buller, French, and Pole-Carew. The general communicated his plans to his three lieutenants, and on the 26th and following days the fruits of the interview were seen in a succession of rapid manoeuvres which drove the Boers out of this, the strongest position which they had held since they left the banks of the Tugela.

The advance of Lord Roberts was made, as his wont is, with two widespread wings, and a central body to connect them. Such a movement leaves the enemy in doubt as to which flank will really be attacked, while if he denudes his centre in order to strengthen both flanks there is the chance of a frontal advance which might cut him in two. French with two cavalry brigades formed the left advance, Pole-Carew the centre, and Buller the right, the whole operations extending over thirty miles of infamous country. It is probable that Lord Roberts had reckoned that the Boer right was likely to be their strongest position, since if it were turned it would cut off their retreat upon Lydenburg, so his own main attack was directed upon their left. This was carried out by General Buller on August 26th and 27th.

On the first day the movement upon Buller's part consisted in a very deliberate reconnaissance of and closing in upon the enemy's position, his troops bivouacking upon the ground which they had won. On the second, finding that all further progress was barred by the strong ridge of Bergendal, he prepared his attack carefully with artillery and then let loose his infantry upon it. It was a gallant feat of arms upon either side. The Boer position was held by a detachment of the Johannesburg Police, who may have been bullies in peace, but were certainly heroes in war. The fire of sixty guns was concentrated for a couple of hours upon a position only a few hundred yards in diameter. In this infernal fire, which left the rocks yellow with Lyddite, the survivors still waited grimly for the advance of the infantry. No finer defence was made in the war. The attack was carried out across an open glacis by the 2nd Rifle Brigade and by the Inniskilling Fusiliers, the men of Pieter's Hill. Through a deadly fire the gallant infantry swept over the position, though Metcalfe, the brave colonel of the Rifles, with eight other officers, and seventy men were killed or wounded. Lysley, Steward, and Campbell were all killed in leading their companies, but they could not have met their deaths upon an occasion more honourable to their battalion. Great credit must also be given to A and B companies of the Inniskilling Fusiliers, who were actually the first over the Boer position. The cessation of the artillery fire was admirably timed. It was sustained up to the last possible instant. 'As it was,' said the captain of the leading company, 'a 94-pound shell burst about thirty yards in front of the right of our lot. The smell of the Lyddite was awful.' A pom-pom and twenty prisoners, including the commander of the police, were the trophies of the day. An outwork of the Boer position had been carried, and the rumour of defeat and disaster had already spread through their ranks. Braver men than the burghers have never lived, but they had reached the limits of human endurance, and a long experience of defeat in the field had weakened their nerve and lessened their morale. They were no longer men of the same fibre as those who had crept up to the trenches of Spion Kop, or faced the lean warriors of Ladysmith on that grim January morning at Caesar's Camp. Dutch tenacity would not allow them to surrender, and yet they realised how hopeless was the fight in which they were engaged. Nearly fifteen thousand of their best men were prisoners, ten thousand at the least had returned to their farms and taken the oath. Another ten had been killed, wounded, or incapacitated. Most of the European mercenaries had left; they held only the ultimate corner of their own country, they had lost their grip upon the railway line, and their supply of stores and of ammunition was dwindling. To such a pass had eleven months of war reduced that formidable army who had so confidently advanced to the conquest of South Africa.

While Buller had established himself firmly upon the left of the Boer position, Pole-Carew had moved forward to the north of the railway line, and French had advanced as far as Swart Kopjes upon the Boer right. These operations on August 26th and 27th were met with some resistance, and entailed a loss of forty or fifty killed and wounded; but it soon became evident that the punishment which they had received at Bergendal had taken the fight out of the Boers, and that this formidable position was to be abandoned as the others had been. On the 28th the burghers were retreating, and Machadodorp, where Kruger had sat so long in his railway carriage, protesting that he would eventually move west and not east, was occupied by Buller. French, moving on a more northerly route, entered Watervalonder with his cavalry upon the same date, driving a small Boer force before him. Amid rain and mist the British columns were pushing rapidly forwards, but still the burghers held together, and still their artillery was uncaptured. The retirement was swift, but it was not yet a rout.

On the 30th the British cavalry were within touch of Nooitgedacht, and saw a glad sight in a long trail of ragged men who were hurrying in their direction along the railway line. They were the British prisoners, eighteen hundred in number, half of whom had been brought from Waterval when Pretoria was captured, while the other half represented the men who had been sent from the south by De Wet, or from the west by De la Rey. Much allowance must be made for the treatment of prisoners by a belligerent who is himself short of food, but nothing can excuse the harshness which the Boers showed to the Colonials who fell into their power, or the callous neglect of the sick prisoners at Waterval. It is a humiliating but an interesting fact that from first to last no fewer than seven thousand of our men passed into their power, all of whom were now recovered save some sixty officers, who had been carried off by them in their flight.

On September 1st Lord Roberts showed his sense of the decisive nature of these recent operations by publishing the proclamation which had been issued as early as July 4th, by which the Transvaal became a portion of the British Empire. On the same day General Buller, who had ceased to advance to the east and retraced his steps as far as Helvetia, began his northerly movement in the direction of Lydenburg, which is nearly fifty miles to the north of the railway line. On that date his force made a march of fourteen miles, which brought them over the Crocodile River to Badfontein. Here, on September 2nd, Buller found that the indomitable Botha was still turning back upon him, for he was faced by so heavy a shell fire, coming from so formidable a position, that he had to be content to wait in front of it until some other column should outflank it. The days of unnecessary frontal attacks were for ever over, and his force, though ready for anything which might be asked of it, had gone through a good deal in the recent operations. Since August 21st they had been under fire almost every day, and their losses, though never great on any one occasion, amounted in the aggregate during that time to 365. They had crossed the Tugela, they had relieved Ladysmith, they had forced Laing's Nek, and now it was to them that the honour had fallen of following the enemy into this last fastness. Whatever criticism may be directed against some episodes in the Natal campaign, it must never be forgotten that to Buller and to his men have fallen some of the hardest tasks of the war, and that these tasks have always in the end been successfully carried out. The controversy about the unfortunate message to White, and the memory of the abandoned guns at Colenso, must not lead us to the injustice of ignoring all that is to be set to the credit account.

On September 3rd Lord Roberts, finding how strong a position faced Buller, despatched Ian Hamilton with a force to turn it upon the right. Brocklehurst's brigade of cavalry joined Hamilton in his advance. On the 4th he was within signalling distance of Buller, and on the right rear of the Boer position. The occupation of a mountain called Zwaggenhoek would establish Hamilton firmly, and the difficult task of seizing it at night was committed to Colonel Douglas and his fine regiment of Royal Scots. It was Spion Kop over again, but with a happier ending. At break of day the Boers discovered that their position had been rendered untenable and withdrew, leaving the road to Lydenburg clear to Buller. Hamilton and he occupied the town upon the 6th. The

Boers had split into two parties, the larger one with the guns falling back upon Kruger's Post, and the others retiring to Pilgrim's Rest. Amid cloud-girt peaks and hardly passable ravines the two long-enduring armies still wrestled for the final mastery.

To the north-east of Lydenburg, between that town and Spitzkop, there is a formidable ridge called the Mauchberg, and here again the enemy were found to be standing at bay. They were even better than their word, for they had always said that they would make their last stand at Lydenburg, and now they were making one beyond it. But the resistance was weakening. Even this fine position could not be held against the rush of the three regiments, the Devons, the Royal Irish, and the Royal Scots, who were let loose upon it. The artillery supported the attack admirably. 'They did nobly,' said one who led the advance. 'It is impossible to overrate the value of their support. They ceased also exactly at the right moment. One more shell would have hit us.' Mountain mists saved the defeated burghers from a close pursuit, but the hills were carried. The British losses on this day, September 8th, were thirteen killed and twenty-five wounded; but of these thirty-eight no less than half were accounted for by one of those strange malignant freaks which can neither be foreseen nor prevented. A shrapnel shell, fired at an incredible distance, burst right over the Volunteer Company of the Gordons who were marching in column. Nineteen men fell, but it is worth recording that, smitten so suddenly and so terribly, the gallant Volunteers continued to advance as steadily as before this misfortune befell them. On the 9th Buller was still pushing forward to Spitzkop, his guns and the 1st Rifles overpowering a weak rearguard resistance of the Boers. On the 10th he had reached Klipgat, which is halfway between the Mauchberg and Spitzkop. So close was the pursuit that the Boers, as they streamed through the passes, flung thirteen of their ammunition wagons over the cliffs to prevent them from falling into the hands of the British horsemen. At one period it looked as if the gallant Boer guns had waited too long in covering the retreat of the burghers. Strathcona's Horse pressed closely upon them. The situation was saved by the extreme coolness and audacity of the Boer gunners. 'When the cavalry were barely half a mile behind the rear gun' says an eye-witness 'and we regarded its capture as certain, the *leading* Long Tom deliberately turned to bay and opened with case shot at the pursuers streaming down the hill in single file over the head of his brother gun. It was a magnificent coup, and perfectly successful. The cavalry had to retire, leaving a few men wounded, and by the time our heavy guns had arrived both Long Toms had got clean away.' But the Boer riflemen would no longer stand. Demoralised after their magnificent struggle of eleven months the burghers were now a beaten and disorderly rabble flying wildly to the eastward, and only held together by the knowledge that in their desperate situation there was more comfort and safety in numbers. The war seemed to be swiftly approaching its close. On the 15th Buller occupied Spitzkop in the north, capturing a quantity of stores, while on the 14th French took Barberton in the south, releasing all the remaining British prisoners and taking possession of forty locomotives, which do not appear to have been injured by the enemy. Meanwhile Pole-Carew had worked along the railway line, and had occupied Kaapmuiden, which was the junction where the Barberton line joins that to Lourenco Marques. Ian Hamilton's force, after the taking of Lydenburg and the action which followed, turned back, leaving Buller to go his own way, and reached Komatipoort on September 24th, having marched since September 9th without a halt through a most difficult country.

On September 11th an incident had occurred which must have shown the most credulous believer in Boer prowess that their cause was indeed lost. On that date Paul Kruger, a refugee from the country which he had ruined, arrived at Lourenco Marques, abandoning his beaten commandos and his deluded burghers. How much had happened since those distant days when as a little herdsboy he had walked behind the bullocks on the great northward trek. How piteous this ending to all his strivings and his plottings! A life which might have closed amid the reverence of a nation and the admiration of the world was destined to finish in exile, impotent and undignified. Strange thoughts must have come to him during those hours of flight, memories of his virile and turbulent youth, of the first settlement of those great lands, of wild wars where his hand was heavy upon the natives, of the triumphant days of the war of independence, when England seemed to recoil from the rifles of the burghers. And then the years of prosperity, the years when the simple farmer found himself among the great ones of the earth, his name a household word in Europe, his State rich and powerful, his coffers filled with the spoil of the poor drudges who worked so hard and paid taxes so readily. Those were his great days, the days when he hardened his heart against their appeals for justice and looked beyond his own borders to his kinsmen in the hope of a South Africa which should be all his own. And now what had come of it all? A handful of faithful attendants, and a fugitive old man, clutching in his flight at his papers and his moneybags. The last of the old-world Puritans, he departed poring over his well-thumbed Bible, and proclaiming that the troubles of his country arose, not from his own narrow and corrupt administration, but from some departure on the part of his fellow burghers from the stricter tenets of the *dopper* sect. So Paul Kruger passed away from the country which he had loved and ruined.

Whilst the main army of Botha had been hustled out of their position at Machadodorp and scattered at Lydenburg and at Barberton, a number of other isolated events had occurred at different points of the seat of war, each of which deserves some mention. The chief of these was a sudden revival of the war in the Orange River Colony, where the band of Olivier was still wandering in the north-eastern districts. Hunter, moving northwards after the capitulation of Prinsloo at Fouriesburg, came into contact on August 15th with this force near Heilbron, and had forty casualties, mainly of the Highland Light Infantry, in a brisk engagement. For a time the British seemed to have completely lost touch with Olivier, who suddenly on August 24th struck at a small detachment consisting almost entirely of Queenstown Rifle Volunteers under Colonel Ridley, who were reconnoitring near Winburg. The Colonial troopers made a gallant defence. Throwing themselves into the farmhouse of Helpmakaar, and occupying every post of vantage around it, they held off more than a thousand assailants, in spite of the three guns which the latter brought to bear upon them. A hundred and thirty-two rounds were fired at the house, but the garrison still refused to surrender. Troopers who had been present at Wepener declared that the smaller action was the warmer of the two. Finally on the morning of the third day a relief force arrived upon the scene, and the enemy dispersed. The British losses were thirty-two killed and wounded. Nothing daunted by his failure, Olivier turned upon the town of Winburg and attempted to regain it, but was defeated again and scattered, he and his three sons being taken. The result was due to the gallantry and craft of a handful of the Queenstown Volunteers, who laid an ambuscade in a *donga*, and disarmed the Boers as they passed, after the pattern of Sanna's Post. By this action one of the most daring and resourceful of the Dutch leaders fell into the hands of the British. It is a pity that his record is stained by his dishonourable conduct in breaking the compact made on the occasion of the capture of Prinsloo. But for British magnanimity a drumhead court-martial should have taken the place of the hospitality of the Ceylon planters.

On September 2nd another commando of Free State Boers under Fourie emerged from the mountain country on the Basuto border, and fell upon Ladybrand, which was held by a feeble garrison consisting of one company of the Worcester regiment and forty-three men of the Wiltshire Yeomanry. The Boers, who had several guns with them, appear to have been the same force which had been repulsed at Winburg. Major White, a gallant marine, whose fighting qualities do not seem to have deteriorated with his distance from salt water, had arranged his defences upon a hill, after the Wepener model, and held his own most stoutly. So great was the disparity of the forces that for days acute anxiety was felt lest another of those humiliating surrenders should interrupt the record of victories, and encourage the Boers to further resistance. The point was distant, and it was some time before relief could reach them. But the dusky chiefs, who from their native mountains looked down on the military drama which was played so close to their frontier, were again, as on the Jammersberg, to see the Boer attack beaten back by the constancy of the British defence. The thin line of soldiers, 150 of them covering a mile and a half of ground, endured a heavy shell and rifle fire with unshaken resolution, repulsed every attempt of the burghers, and held the flag flying until relieved by the forces under White and Bruce Hamilton. In this march to the relief Hamilton's infantry covered eighty miles in four and a half days. Lean and hard, inured to warfare, and far from every temptation of wine or women, the British troops at this stage of the campaign were in such training, and marched so splendidly, that the infantry was often very little slower than the cavalry. Methuen's fine performance in pursuit of De Wet, where Douglas's infantry did sixty-six miles in seventy-five hours, the City Imperial Volunteers covering 224 miles in fourteen days, with a single forced march of thirty miles in seventeen hours, the Shropshires forty-three miles in thirty-two hours, the forty-five miles in twenty-five hours of the Essex Regiment, Bruce Hamilton's march recorded above, and many other fine efforts serve to show the spirit and endurance of the troops.

In spite of the defeat at Winburg and the repulse at Ladybrand, there still remained a fair number of broken and desperate men in the Free State who held out among the difficult country of the east. A party of these came across in the middle of September and endeavoured to cut the railway near Brandfort. They were pursued and broken up by Macdonald, who, much aided in his operations by the band of scouts which Lord Lovat had brought with him from Scotland, took several prisoners and a large number of wagons and of oxen. A party of these Boers attacked a small post of sixteen Yeomanry under Lieutenant Slater at Bultfontein, but were held at bay until relief came from Brandfort.

At two other points the Boer and British forces were in contact during these operations. One was to the immediate north of Pretoria, where Grobler's commando was faced by Paget's brigade. On August 18th the Boers were forced with some loss out of Hornies Nek, which is ten miles to the north of the capital. On the 22nd a more important skirmish took place at Pienaar's River, in the same direction, between Baden-Powell's men, who had come thither in pursuit of De Wet, and Grobler's band. The advance guards of the two forces galloped into each other, and for once Boer and Briton looked down the muzzles of each other's rifles. The gallant Rhodesian Regiment, which had done such splendid service during the war, suffered most heavily. Colonel Spreckley and four others were killed, and six or seven wounded. The Boers were broken, however, and fled, leaving twenty-five prisoners to the victors. Baden-Powell and Paget pushed forwards as far as Nylstroom, but finding themselves in wild and profitless country they returned towards Pretoria, and established the British northern posts at a place called Warm Baths. Here Paget commanded, while Baden-Powell shortly afterwards went down to Cape Town to make arrangements for taking over the police force of the conquered countries, and to receive the enthusiastic welcome of his colonial fellow-countrymen. Plumer, with a small force operating from Warm Baths, scattered a Boer commando on September 1st, capturing a few prisoners and a considerable quantity of munitions of war. On the 5th there was another skirmish in the same neighbourhood, during which the enemy attacked a *kopje* held by a company of Munster Fusiliers, and was driven off with loss. Many thousands of cattle were captured by the British in this part of the field of operations, and were sent into Pretoria, whence they helped to supply the army in the east.

There was still considerable effervescence in the western districts of the Transvaal, and a mounted detachment met with fierce opposition at the end of August on their journey from Zeerust to Krugersdorp. Methuen, after his unsuccessful chase of De Wet, had gone as far as Zeerust, and had then taken his force on to Mafeking to refit. Before leaving Zeerust, however, he had despatched Colonel Little to Pretoria with a column which consisted of his own third cavalry brigade, 1st Brabant's, the Kaffrarian Rifles, R battery of Horse Artillery, and four Colonial guns. They were acting as guard to a very large convoy of 'returned empties.' The district which they had to traverse is one of the most fertile in the Transvaal, a land of clear streams and of orange groves. But the farmers are numerous and aggressive, and the column, which was 900 strong, could clear all resistance from its front, but found it impossible to brush off the snipers upon its flanks and rear. Shortly after their start the column was deprived of the services of its gallant leader, Colonel Little, who was shot while riding with his advance scouts. Colonel Dalgety took over the command. Numerous desultory attacks culminated in a fierce skirmish at Quaggafontein on August 31st, in which the column had sixty casualties. The event might have been serious, as De la Rey's main force appears to have been concentrated upon the British detachment, the brunt of the action falling upon the Kaffrarian Rifles. By a rapid movement the column was able to extricate itself and win its way safely to Krugersdorp, but it narrowly escaped out of the wolf's jaws, and as it emerged into the open country De la Rey's guns were seen galloping for the pass which they had just come through. This force was sent south to Kroonstad to refit.

Lord Methuen's army, after its long marches and arduous work, arrived at Mafeking on August 28th for the purpose of refitting. Since his departure from Boshof on May 14th his men had been marching with hardly a rest, and he had during that time fought fourteen engagements. He was off upon the war-path once more, with fresh horses and renewed energy, on September 8th, and on the 9th, with the co-operation of General Douglas, he scattered a Boer force at Malopo, capturing thirty prisoners and a great quantity of stores. On the 14th he ran down a convoy and regained one of the Colenso guns and much ammunition. On the 20th he again made large captures. If in the early phases of the war the Boers had given Paul Methuen some evil hours, he was certainly getting his own back again. At the same time Clements was despatched from Pretoria with a small mobile force for the purpose of clearing the Rustenburg and Krugersdorp districts, which had always been storm centres. These two forces, of Methuen and of Clements, moved through the country, sweeping the scattered Boer bands before them, and hunting them down until they dispersed. At Kekepoort and at Hekspoort Clements fought successful skirmishes, losing at the latter action Lieutenant Stanley of the Yeomanry, the Somersetshire cricketer, who showed, as so many have done, how close is the connection between the good sportsman and the good soldier. On the 12th Douglas took thirty-nine prisoners near Lichtenburg. On the 18th Rundle captured a gun at Bronkhorstfontein. Hart at Potchefstroom, Hildyard in the Utrecht district, Macdonald in the Orange River Colony, everywhere the British Generals were busily stamping out the remaining embers of what had been so terrible a conflagration.

Much trouble but no great damage was inflicted upon the British during this last stage of the war by the incessant attacks upon the lines of railway by roving bands of Boers. The actual interruption of traffic was of little consequence, for the assiduous Sappers with their gangs of Basuto labourers were always at hand to repair the break. But the loss of stores, and occasionally of lives, was more serious. Hardly a day passed that the stokers and drivers were not made targets of by snipers among the *kopjes*, and occasionally a train was entirely destroyed.[1] Chief among these raiders was the wild Theron, who led a band which contained men of all nations—the same gang who had already, as narrated, held up a train in the Orange River Colony. On August 31st he derailed another at Flip River to the south of Johannesburg, blowing up the engine and burn-

---

1. It is to be earnestly hoped that those in authority will see that these men obtain the medal and any other reward which can mark our sense of their faithful service. One of them in the Orange River Colony, after narrating to me his many hairbreadth escapes, prophesied bitterly that the memory of his services would pass with the need for them.

ing thirteen trucks. Almost at the same time a train was captured near Kroonstad, which appeared to indicate that the great De Wet was back in his old hunting-grounds. On the same day the line was cut at Standerton. A few days later, however, the impunity with which these feats had been performed was broken, for in a similar venture near Krugersdorp the dashing Theron and several of his associates lost their lives.

Two other small actions performed at this period of the war demand a passing notice. One was a smart engagement near Kraai Railway Station, in which Major Broke of the Sappers with a hundred men attacked a superior Boer force upon a *kopje* and drove them off with loss—a feat which it is safe to say he could not have accomplished six months earlier. The other was the fine defence made by 125 of the Canadian Mounted Rifles, who, while guarding the railway, were attacked by a considerable Boer force with two guns. They proved once more, as Ladybrand and Elands River had shown, that with provisions, cartridges, and brains, the smallest force can successfully hold its own if it confines itself to the defensive.

And now the Boer cause appeared to be visibly tottering to its fall. The flight of the President had accelerated that process of disintegration which had already set in. Schalk Burger had assumed the office of Vice-President, and the notorious Ben Viljoen had become first lieutenant of Louis Botha in maintaining the struggle. Lord Roberts had issued an extremely judicious proclamation, in which he pointed out the uselessness of further resistance, declared that guerrilla warfare would be ruthlessly suppressed, and informed the burghers that no fewer than fifteen thousand of their fellow-countrymen were in his hands as prisoners, and that none of these could be released until the last rifle had been laid down. From all sides in the third week of September the British forces were converging on Komatipoort, the frontier town. Already wild figures, stained and tattered after nearly a year of warfare, were walking the streets of Lourenco Marques, gazed at with wonder and some distrust by the Portuguese inhabitants. The exiled burghers moodily pacing the streets saw their exiled President seated in his corner of the Governor's veranda, the well-known curved pipe still dangling from his mouth, the Bible by his chair. Day by day the number of these refugees increased. On September 17th special trains were arriving crammed with the homeless burghers, and with the mercenaries of many nations—French, German, Irish-American, and Russian—all anxious to make their way home. By the 19th no fewer than seven hundred had passed over.

At dawn on September 22nd a half-hearted attempt was made by the commando of Erasmus to attack Elands River Station, but it was beaten back by the garrison. While it was going on Paget fell upon the camp which Erasmus had left behind him, and captured his stores. From all over the country, from Plumer's Bushmen, from Barton at Krugersdorp, from the Colonials at Heilbron, from Clements on the west, came the same reports of dwindling resistance and of the abandoning of cattle, arms, and ammunition.

On September 24th came the last chapter in this phase of the campaign in the Eastern Transvaal, when at eight in the morning Pole-Carew and his Guardsmen occupied Komatipoort. They had made desperate marches, one of them through thick bush, where they went for nineteen miles without water, but nothing could shake the cheery gallantry of the men. To them fell the honour, an honour well deserved by their splendid work throughout the whole campaign, of entering and occupying the ultimate eastern point which the Boers could hold. Resistance had been threatened and prepared for, but the grim silent advance of that veteran infantry took the heart out of the defence. With hardly a shot fired the town was occupied. The bridge which would enable the troops to receive their supplies from Lourenco Marques was still intact. General Pienaar and the greater part of his force, amounting to over two thousand men, had crossed the frontier and had been taken down to Delagoa Bay, where they met the respect and attention which brave men in misfortune deserve. Small bands had slipped away to the north and the south, but they were insignificant in numbers and depressed in spirit. For the time it seemed that the campaign was over, but the result showed that there was greater vitality in the resistance of the burghers and less validity in their oaths than any one had imagined.

One find of the utmost importance was made at Komatipoort, and at Hector Spruit on the Crocodile River. That excellent artillery which had fought so gallant a fight against our own more numerous guns, was found destroyed and abandoned. Pole-Carew at Komatipoort got one Long Tom (96-pound) Creusot, and one smaller gun. Ian Hamilton at Hector Spruit found the remains of many guns, which included two of our horse artillery twelve-pounders, two large Creusot guns, two Krupps, one Vickers-Maxim quick firer, two pompoms and four mountain guns.

CHAPTER 30

The Campaign of De Wet

It had been hoped that the dispersal of the main Boer army, the capture of its guns and the expulsion of many both of the burghers and of the foreign mercenaries, would have marked the end of the war. These expectations were, however, disappointed, and South Africa was destined to be afflicted and the British Empire disturbed by a useless guerrilla campaign. After the great and dramatic events which characterised the earlier phases of the struggle between the Briton and the Boer for the mastery of South Africa it is somewhat of the nature of an anticlimax to turn one's attention to those scattered operations which prolonged the resistance for a turbulent year at the expense of the lives of many brave men on either side. These raids and skirmishes, which had their origin rather in the hope of vengeance than of victory, inflicted much loss and misery upon the country, but, although we may deplore the desperate resolution which bids brave men prefer death to subjugation, it is not for us, the countrymen of Hereward or Wallace, to condemn it.

In one important respect these numerous, though trivial, conflicts differed from the battles in the earlier stages of the war. The British had learned their lesson so thoroughly that they often turned the tables upon their instructors. Again and again the surprise was effected, not by the nation of hunters, but by those *rooineks* whose want of cunning and of *veldt*-craft had for so long been a subject of derision and merriment. A year of the *kopje* and the *donga* had altered all that. And in the proportion of casualties another very marked change had occurred. Time was when in battle after battle a tenth would have been a liberal estimate for the losses of the Boers compared with those of the Briton. So it was at Stormberg; so it was at Colenso; so it may have been at Magersfontein. But in this last stage of the war the balance was rather in favour of the British. It may have been because they were now frequently acting on the defensive, or it may have been from an improvement in their fire, or it may have come from the more desperate mood of the burghers, but

342

in any case the fact remains that every encounter diminished the small reserves of the Boers rather than the ample forces of their opponents.

One other change had come over the war, which caused more distress and searchings of conscience among some of the people of Great Britain than the darkest hours of their misfortunes. This lay in the increased bitterness of the struggle, and in those more strenuous measures which the British commanders felt themselves entitled and compelled to adopt. Nothing could exceed the lenity of Lord Roberts's early proclamations in the Free State. But, as the months went on and the struggle still continued, the war assumed a harsher aspect. Every farmhouse represented a possible fort, and a probable depot for the enemy. The extreme measure of burning them down was only carried out after a definite offence, such as affording cover for snipers, or as a deterrent to railway wreckers, but in either case it is evident that the women or children who were usually the sole occupants of the farm could not by their own unaided exertions prevent the line from being cut or the riflemen from firing. It is even probable that the Boers may have committed these deeds in the vicinity of houses the destruction of which they would least regret. Thus, on humanitarian grounds there were strong arguments against this policy of destruction being pushed too far, and the political reasons were even stronger, since a homeless man is necessarily the last man to settle down, and a burned-out family the last to become contented British citizens. On the other hand, the impatience of the army towards what they regarded as the abuses of lenity was very great, and they argued that the war would be endless if the women in the farm were allowed always to supply the sniper on the *kopje*. The irregular and brigand-like fashion in which the struggle was carried out had exasperated the soldiers, and though there were few cases of individual outrage or unauthorised destruction, the general orders were applied with some harshness, and repressive measures were taken which warfare may justify but which civilisation must deplore.

After the dispersal of the main army at Komatipoort there remained a considerable number of men in arms, some of them irreconcilable burghers, some of them foreign adventurers, and some of them Cape rebels, to whom British arms were less terrible than British law. These men, who were still well armed and well mounted, spread themselves over the country, and acted with such energy that they gave the impression of a large force. They made their way into the settled districts, and brought fresh hope and fresh disaster to many who had imagined that the war had passed for ever away from them. Under compulsion from their irreconcilable countrymen, a large number of the farmers broke their parole, mounted the horses which British leniency had left with them, and threw themselves once more into the struggle, adding their honour to the other sacrifices which they had made for their country. In any account of the continual brushes between these scattered bands and the British forces, there must be such a similarity in procedure and result, that it would be hard for the writer and intolerable for the reader if they were set forth in detail. As a general statement it may be said that during the months to come there was no British garrison in any one of the numerous posts in the Transvaal, and in that portion of the Orange River Colony which lies east of the railway, which was not surrounded by prowling riflemen, there was no convoy sent to supply those garrisons which was not liable to be attacked upon the road, and there was no train upon any one of the three lines which might not find a rail up and a hundred raiders covering it with their Mausers. With some two thousand miles of railroad to guard, so many garrisons to provide, and an escort to be furnished to every convoy, there remained out of the large body of British troops in the country only a moderate force who were available for actual operations. This force was distributed in different districts scattered over a wide extent of country, and it was evident that while each was strong enough to suppress local resistance, still at any moment a concentration of the Boer scattered forces upon a single British column might place the latter in a serious position. The distribution of the British in October and November was roughly as follows. Methuen was in the Rustenburg district, Barton at Krugersdorp and operating down the line to Klerksdorp, Settle was in the West, Paget at Pienaar's River, Clements in the Magaliesberg, Hart at Potchefstroom, Lyttelton at Middelburg, Smith-Dorrien at Belfast, W. Kitchener at Lydenburg, French in the Eastern Transvaal, Hunter, Rundle, Brabant, and Bruce Hamilton in the Orange River Colony. Each of these forces was occupied in the same sort of work, breaking up small bodies of the enemy, hunting for arms, bringing in refugees, collecting supplies, and rounding up cattle. Some, however, were confronted with organised resistance and some were not. A short account may be given in turn of each separate column.

I would treat first the operations of General Barton, because they form the best introduction to that narrative of the doings of Christian De Wet to which this chapter will be devoted.

The most severe operations during the month of October fell to the lot of this British General, who, with some of the faithful fusiliers whom he had led from the first days in Natal, was covering the line from Krugersdorp to Klerksdorp. It is a long stretch, and one which, as the result shows, is as much within striking distance of the Orange Free Staters as of the men of the Transvaal. Upon October 5th Barton left Krugersdorp with a force which consisted of the Scots and Welsh Fusiliers, five hundred mounted men, the 78th R.F.A., three pom-poms, and a 4.7 naval gun. For a fortnight, as the small army moved slowly down the line of the railroad, their progress was one continual skirmish. On October 6th they brushed the enemy aside in an action in which the volunteer company of the Scots Fusiliers gained the applause of their veteran comrades. On the 8th and 9th there was sharp skirmishing, the brunt of which on the latter date fell upon the Welsh Fusiliers, who had three officers and eleven men injured. The commandos of Douthwaite, Liebenberg, and Van der Merwe seem to have been occupied in harassing the column during their progress through the Gatsrand range. On the 15th the desultory sniping freshened again into a skirmish in which the honours and the victory belonged mainly to the Welshmen and to that very keen and efficient body, the Scottish Yeomanry. Six Boers were left dead upon the ground. On October 17th the column reached Frederickstad, where it halted. On that date six of Marshall's Horse were cut off while collecting supplies. The same evening three hundred of the Imperial Light Horse came in from Krugersdorp.

Up to this date the Boer forces which dogged the column had been annoying but not seriously aggressive. On the 19th, however, affairs took an unexpected turn. The British scouts rode in to report a huge dust cloud whirling swiftly northwards from the direction of the Vaal River— soon plainly visible to all, and showing as it drew nearer the hazy outline of a long column of mounted men. The dark coats of the riders, and possibly the speed of their advance, showed that they were Boers, and soon it was rumoured that it was no other than Christian De Wet with his merry men, who, with characteristic audacity, had ridden back into the Transvaal in the hope of overwhelming Barton's column.

It is some time since we have seen anything of this energetic gentleman with the tinted glasses, but as the narrative will be much occupied with him in the future a few words are needed to connect him with the past. It has been already told how he escaped through the net which caught so many of his countrymen at the time of the surrender of Prinsloo, and how he was chased at furious speed from the Vaal River to the mountains of Magaliesberg. Here he eluded his pursuers, separated from Steyn, who desired to go east to confer with Kruger, and by the end of August was back again in his favourite recruiting ground in the north of the Orange River Colony. Here for nearly two months he had lain very quiet, refitting and reassembling his scattered force, until now, ready for action once more, and fired by the hope of cutting off an isolated British force, he rode swiftly northwards with two thousand men under that rolling cloud which had been spied by the watchers of Frederickstad.

The problem before him was a more serious one, however, than any which he had ever undertaken, for this was no isolated regiment or ill-manned post, but a complete little field force very ready to do battle with him. De Wet's burghers, as they arrived, sprang from their ponies and went into action in their usual invisible but effective fashion, covered by the fire of several guns. The soldiers had thrown up lines of sangars, however, and were able, though exposed to a very heavy fire coming from several directions, to hold their own until nightfall, when the defences were made more secure. On the 20th, 21st, 22nd, 23rd, and 24th the cordon of the attack was drawn gradually closer, the Boers entirely surrounding the British force, and it was evident that they were feeling round for a point at which an assault might be delivered.

The position of the defenders upon the morning of October 25th was as follows. The Scots Fusiliers were holding a ridge to the south. General Barton with the rest of his forces occupied a hill some distance off. Between the two was a valley down which ran the line, and also the *spruit* upon which the British depended for their water supply. On each side of the line were ditches, and at dawn on this seventh day of the investment it was found that these had been occupied by snipers during the night, and that it was impossible to water the animals. One of two things must follow. Either the force must shift its position or it must drive these men out of their cover. No fire could do it, as they lay in perfect safety. They must be turned out at the point of the bayonet.

About noon several companies of Scots and Welsh Fusiliers advanced from different directions in very extended order upon the ditches. Captain Baillie's company of the former regiment first attracted the fire of the burghers. Wounded twice the brave officer staggered on until a third bullet struck him dead. Six of his men were found lying beside him. The other companies were exposed in their turn to a severe fire, but rushing onwards they closed rapidly in upon the ditches. There have been few finer infantry advances during the war, for the *veldt* was perfectly flat and the fire terrific. A mile of ground was crossed by the fusiliers. Three gallant officers—Dick, Elliot, and Best—went down; but the rush of the men was irresistible. At the edge of the ditches the supports overtook the firing line, and they all surged into the trenches together. Then it was seen how perilous was the situation of the Boer snipers. They had placed themselves between the upper and the nether millstone. There was no escape for them save across the open. It says much for their courage that they took that perilous choice rather than wave the white flag, which would have ensured their safety.

The scene which followed has not often been paralleled. About a hundred and fifty burghers rushed out of the ditches, streaming across the *veldt* upon foot to the spot where their horses had been secreted. Rifles, pom-poms, and shrapnel played upon them during this terrible race. 'A black running mob carrying coats, blankets, boots, rifles, &c., was seen to rise as if from nowhere and rush as fast as they could, dropping the various things they carried as they ran.' One of their survivors has described how awful was that wild blind flight, through a dust-cloud thrown up by the shells. For a mile the *veldt* was dotted with those who had fallen. Thirty-six were found dead, thirty were wounded, and thirty more gave themselves up as prisoners. Some were so demoralised that they rushed into the hospital and surrendered to the British doctor. The Imperial Light Horse were for some reason slow to charge. Had they done so at once, many eye-witnesses agree that not a fugitive should have escaped. On the other hand, the officer in command may have feared that in doing so he might mask the fire of the British guns.

One incident in the action caused some comment at the time. A small party of Imperial Light Horse, gallantly led by Captain Yockney of B Squadron, came to close quarters with a group of Boers. Five of the enemy having held up their hands Yockney passed them and pushed on against their comrades. On this the prisoners seized their rifles once more and fired upon their captors. A fierce fight ensued with only a few feet between the muzzles of the rifles. Three Boers were shot dead, five wounded, and eight taken. Of these eight three were shot next day by order of court-martial for having resumed their weapons after surrender, while two others were acquitted. The death of these men in cold blood is to be deplored, but it is difficult to see how any rules of civilised warfare can be maintained if a flagrant breach of them is not promptly and sternly punished.

On receiving this severe blow De Wet promptly raised the investment and hastened to regain his favourite haunts. Considerable reinforcements had reached Barton upon the same day, including the Dublins, the Essex, Strathcona's Horse, and the Elswick Battery, with some very welcome supplies of ammunition. As Barton had now more than a thousand mounted men of most excellent quality it is difficult to imagine why he did not pursue his defeated enemy. He seems to have underrated the effect which he had produced, for instead of instantly assuming the offensive he busied himself in strengthening his defences. Yet the British losses in the whole operations had not exceeded one hundred, so that there does not appear to have been any reason why the force should be crippled. As Barton was in direct and constant telegraphic communication with Pretoria, it is possible that he was acting under superior orders in the course which he adopted.

It was not destined, however, that De Wet should be allowed to escape with his usual impunity. On the 27th, two days after his retreat from Frederickstad he was overtaken—stumbled upon by pure chance apparently—by the mounted infantry and cavalry of Charles Knox and De Lisle. The Boers, a great disorganised cloud of horsemen, swept swiftly along the northern bank of the Vaal, seeking for a place to cross, while the British rode furiously after them, spraying them with shrapnel at every opportunity. Darkness and a violent storm gave De Wet his opportunity to cross, but the closeness of the pursuit compelled him to abandon two of his guns, one of them a Krupp and the other one of the British twelve-pounders of Sanna's Post, which, to the delight of the gunners, was regained by that very U battery to which it belonged.

Once across the river and back in his own country De Wet, having placed seventy miles between himself and his pursuers, took it for granted that he was out of their reach, and halted near the village of Bothaville to refit. But the British were hard upon his track, and for once they were able to catch this indefatigable man unawares. Yet their knowledge of his position seems to have been most hazy, and on the very day before that on which they found him, General Charles Knox, with the main body of the force, turned north, and was out of the subsequent action. De Lisle's mounted troops also turned north, but fortunately not entirely out of call. To the third and smallest body of mounted men, that under Le Gallais, fell the honour of the action which I am about to describe.

It is possible that the move northwards of Charles Knox and of De Lisle had the effect of a most elaborate stratagem, since it persuaded the Boer scouts that the British were retiring. So indeed they were, save only the small force of Le Gallais, which seems to have taken one last cast round to the south before giving up the pursuit. In the grey of the morning of November 6th, Major Lean with forty men of the 5th Mounted Infantry came upon three weary Boers sleeping upon the *veldt*. Having secured the men, and realising that they were an outpost, Lean pushed on, and topping a rise some hundreds of yards further, he and his men saw a remarkable scene. There before them stretched the camp of the Boers, the men sleeping, the horses grazing, the guns parked, and the wagons outspanned.

There was little time for consideration. The Kaffir drivers were already afoot and strolling out for their horses, or lighting the fires for their masters' coffee. With splendid decision, although he had but forty men to oppose to over a thousand, Lean sent back for reinforcements and opened fire upon the camp. In an instant it was buzzing like an overturned hive. Up sprang the sleepers, rushed for their horses, and galloped away across the *veldt*, leaving their guns and wagons behind. A few stalwarts remained, however, and their numbers were increased by those whose horses had stampeded, and who were, therefore, unable to get away. They occupied an enclosed *kraal* and a farmhouse in front of the British, whence they opened a sharp fire. At the same time a number of the Boers who had ridden away came back again, having realised how weak their assailants were, and worked round the British flanks upon either side.

Le Gallais, with his men, had come up, but the British force was still far inferior to that which it was attacking. A section of U battery was able to unlimber, and open fire at four hundred yards from the Boer position. The British made no attempt to attack, but contented themselves with holding on to the position from which they could prevent the Boer guns from being removed. The burghers tried desperately to drive off the stubborn fringe of riflemen. A small stone shed in the possession of the British was the centre of the Boer fire, and it was within its walls that Ross of the Durhams was horribly wounded by an explosive ball, and that the brave Jerseyman, Le Gallais, was killed. Before his fall he had despatched his staff officer, Major Hickie, to hurry up men from the rear.

On the fall of Ross and Le Gallais the command fell upon Major Taylor of U battery. The position at that time was sufficiently alarming. The Boers were working round each flank in considerable numbers, and they maintained a heavy fire from a stone enclosure in the centre. The British forces actually engaged were insignificant, consisting of forty men of the 5th Mounted Infantry, and two guns in the centre, forty-six men of the 17th and 18th Imperial Yeomanry upon the right, and 105 of the 8th Mounted Infantry on the left or 191 rifles in all. The flanks of this tiny force had to extend to half a mile to hold off the Boer flank attack, but they were heartened in their resistance by the knowledge that their comrades were hastening to their assistance. Taylor, realising that a great effort must be made to tide over the crisis, sent a messenger back with orders that the convoy should be parked, and every available man sent up to strengthen the right flank, which was the weakest. The enemy got close on to one of the guns, and swept down the whole detachment, but a handful of the Suffolk Mounted Infantry under Lieutenant Peebles most gallantly held them off from it. For an hour the pressure was extreme. Then two companies of the 7th Mounted Infantry came up, and were thrown on to each flank. Shortly afterwards Major Welch, with two more companies of the same corps, arrived, and the tide began slowly to turn. The Boers were themselves outflanked by the extension of the British line and were forced to fall back. At half-past eight De Lisle, whose force had trotted and galloped for twelve miles, arrived with several companies of Australians, and the success of the day was assured. The smoke of the Prussian guns at Waterloo was not a more welcome sight than the dust of De Lisle's horsemen. But the question now was whether the Boers, who were in the walled enclosure and farm which formed their centre, would manage to escape. The place was shelled, but here, as often before, it was found how useless a weapon is shrapnel against buildings. There was nothing for it but to storm it, and a grim little storming party of fifty men, half British, half Australian, was actually waiting with fixed bayonets for the whistle which was to be their signal, when the white flag flew out from the farm, and all was over. Warned by many a tragic experience the British still lay low in spite of the flag. 'Come out! come out!' they shouted. Eighty-two unwounded Boers filed out of the enclosure, and the total number of prisoners came to 114, while between twenty and thirty Boers were killed. Six guns, a pom-pom, and 1000 head of cattle were the prizes of the victors.

This excellent little action showed that the British mounted infantry had reached a point of efficiency at which they were quite able to match the Boers at their own game. For hours they held them with an inferior force, and finally, when the numbers became equal, were able to drive them off and capture their guns. The credit is largely due to Major Lean for his prompt initiative on discovering their *laager*, and to Major Taylor for his handling of the force during a very critical time. Above all, it was due to the dead leader, Le Gallais, who had infected every man under him with his own spirit of reckless daring. 'If I die, tell my mother that I die happy, as we got the guns,' said he, with his failing breath. The British total losses were twelve killed (four officers) and thirty-three wounded (seven officers). Major Welch, a soldier of great promise, much beloved by his men, was one of the slain. Following closely after the repulse at Frederickstad this action was a heavy blow to De Wet. At last, the British were beginning to take something off the score which they owed the bold raider, but there was to be many an item on either side before the long reckoning should be closed. The Boers, with De Wet, fled south, where it was not long before they showed that they were still a military force with which we had to reckon.

In defiance of chronology it may perhaps make a clearer narrative if I continue at once with the movements of De Wet from the time that he lost his guns at Bothaville, and then come back to the consideration of the campaign in the Transvaal, and to a short account of those scattered and disconnected actions which break the continuity of the story. Before following De Wet, however, it is necessary to say something of the general state of the Orange River Colony and of some military developments which had occurred there. Under the wise and conciliatory rule of General Pretyman the farmers in the south and west were settling down, and for the time it looked as if a large district was finally pacified. The mild taxation was cheerfully paid, schools were reopened, and a peace party made itself apparent, with Fraser and Piet de Wet, the brother of Christian, among its strongest advocates.

Apart from the operations of De Wet there appeared to be no large force in the field in the Orange River Colony, but early in October of 1900 a small but very mobile and efficient Boer force skirted the eastern outposts of the British, struck the southern line of communications, and then came up the western flank, attacking, where an attack was possible, each of the isolated and weakly garrisoned townlets to which it came, and recruiting its strength from a district which had been hardly touched by the ravages of war, and which by its prosperity alone might have proved the amenity of British military rule. This force seems to have skirted Wepener without attacking a place of such evil omen to their cause. Their subsequent movements are readily traced by a sequence of military events.

On October 1st Rouxville was threatened. On the 9th an outpost of the Cheshire Militia was taken and the railway cut for a few hours in the neighbourhood of Bethulie. A week later the Boer riders were dotting the country round Phillipolis, Springfontein and Jagersfontein, the latter town being occupied upon October 16th, while the garrison held out upon the nearest *kopje*. The town was retaken from the enemy by King Hall and his men, who were Seaforth Highlanders and police. There was fierce fighting in the streets, and from twenty to thirty of each side were killed or wounded. Fauresmith was attacked on October 19th, but was also in the very safe hands of the Seaforths, who held it against a severe assault. Phillipolis was continually attacked between the 18th and the 24th, but made a most notable defence, which was conducted by Gostling, the resident magistrate, with forty civilians. For a week this band of stalwarts held their own against 600 Boers, and were finally relieved by a force from the railway. All the operations were not, however, as successful as these three defences. On October 24th a party of cavalry details belonging to many regiments were snapped up in an ambuscade. On the next day Jacobsdal was attacked, with considerable loss to the British. The place was entered in the night, and the enemy occupied the houses which surrounded the square. The garrison, consisting of about sixty men of the Capetown Highlanders, had encamped in the square, and were helpless when fire was opened upon them in the morning. There was practically no resistance, and yet for hours a murderous fire was kept up upon the tents in which they cowered, so that the affair seems not to have been far removed from murder. Two-thirds of the little force were killed or wounded. The number of the assailants does not appear to have been great, and they vanished upon the appearance of a relieving force from Modder River.

After the disaster at Jacobsdal the enemy appeared on November 1st near Kimberley and captured a small convoy. The country round was disturbed, and Settle was sent south with a column to pacify it. In this way we can trace this small cyclone from its origin in the old storm centre in the north-east of the Orange River Colony, sweeping round the whole country, striking one post after another, and finally blowing out at the corresponding point upon the other side of the seat of war.

We have last seen De Wet upon November 6th, when he fled south from Bothaville, leaving his guns but not his courage behind him. Trekking across the line, and for a wonder gathering up no train as he passed, he made for that part of the eastern Orange River Colony which had been reoccupied by his countrymen. Here, in the neighbourhood of Thabanchu, he was able to join other forces, probably the commandos of Haasbroek and Fourie, which still retained some guns. At the head of a considerable force he attacked the British garrison of Dewetsdorp, a town some forty miles to the south-east of Bloemfontein.

It was on November 18th that De Wet assailed the place, and it fell upon the 24th, after a defence which appears to have been a very creditable one. Several small British columns were moving in the south-east of the Colony, but none of them arrived in time to avert the disaster, which is the more inexplicable as the town is within one day's ride of Bloemfontein. The place is a village hemmed in upon its western side by a semicircle of steep rocky hills broken in the centre by a gully. The position was a very extended one, and had the fatal weakness that the loss of any portion of it meant the loss of it all. The garrison consisted of one company of Highland Light Infantry on the southern horn of the semicircle, three companies of the 2nd Gloucester Regiment on the northern and central part, with two guns of the 68th battery. Some of the Royal Irish Mounted Infantry and a handful of police made up the total of the defenders to something over four hundred, Major Massy in command.

The attack developed at that end of the ridge which was held by the company of Highlanders. Every night the Boer riflemen drew in closer, and every morning found the position more desperate. On the 20th the water supply of the garrison was cut, though a little was still brought up by volunteers during the night. The thirst in the sultry trenches was terrible, but the garrison still, with black lips and parched tongues, held on to their lines. On the 22nd the attack had made such progress that the post had by the Highlanders became untenable, and had to be withdrawn. It was occupied next morning by the Boers, and the whole ridge was at their mercy. Out of eighteen men who served one of the British guns sixteen were killed or wounded, and the last rounds were fired by the sergeant-farrier, who carried, loaded, and fired all by himself. All day the soldiers held out, but the thirst was in itself enough to justify if not to compel a surrender. At half-past five the garrison laid down their arms, having lost about sixty killed or wounded. There does not, as far as one can learn, seem to have been any attempt to injure the two guns which fell into the hands of the enemy. De Wet himself was one of the first to ride into the British trenches, and the prisoners gazed with interest at the short strong figure, with the dark tail coat and the square-topped bowler hat, of the most famous of the Boer leaders.

British columns were converging, however, from several quarters, and De Wet had to be at once on the move. On the 26th Dewetsdorp was reoccupied by General Charles Knox with fifteen hundred men. De Wet had two days' start, but so swift was Knox that on the 27th he had run him down at Vaalbank, where he shelled his camp. De Wet broke away, however, and trekking south for eighteen hours without a halt, shook off the pursuit. He had with him at this time nearly 8000 men with several guns under Haasbroek, Fourie, Philip Botha, and Steyn. It was his declared intention to invade Cape Colony with his train of weary footsore prisoners, and the laurels of Dewetsdorp still green upon him. He was much aided in all his plans by that mistaken leniency which had refused to recognise that a horse is in that country as much a weapon as a rifle, and had left great numbers upon the farms with which he could replace his useless animals. So numerous were they that many of the Boers had two or three for their own use. It is not too much to say that our weak treatment of the question of horses will come to be recognised as the one great blot upon the conduct of the war, and that our undue and fantastic scruples have prolonged hostilities for months, and cost the country many lives and many millions of pounds.

De Wet's plan for the invasion of the Colony was not yet destined to be realised, for a tenacious man had set himself to frustrate it. Several small but mobile British columns, those of Pilcher, of Barker, and of Herbert, under the supreme direction of Charles Knox, were working desperately to head him off. In torrents of rain which turned every *spruit* into a river and every road into a quagmire, the British horsemen stuck manfully to their work. De Wet had hurried south, crossed the Caledon River, and made for Odendaal's Drift. But Knox, after the skirmish at Vaalbank, had trekked swiftly south to Bethulie, and was now ready with three mobile columns and a network of scouts and patrols to strike in any direction. For a few days he had lost touch, but his arrangements were such that he must recover it if the Boers either crossed the railroad or approached the river. On December 2nd he had authentic information that De Wet was crossing the Caledon, and in an instant the British columns were all off at full cry once more, sweeping over the country with a front of fifteen miles. On the 3rd and 4th, in spite of frightful weather, the two little armies of horsemen struggled on, fetlock-deep in mud, with the rain lashing their faces. At night without cover, drenched and bitterly cold, the troopers threw themselves down on the sodden *veldt* to snatch a few hours' sleep before renewing the interminable pursuit. The drift over the Caledon flowed deep and strong, but the Boer had passed and the Briton must pass also. Thirty guns took to the water, diving completely under the coffee-coloured surface, to reappear glistening upon the southern bank. Everywhere there were signs of the passage of the enemy. A litter of crippled or dying horses marked their track, and a Krupp gun was found abandoned by the drift. The Dewetsdorp prisoners, too, had been set loose, and began to stumble and stagger back to their countrymen, their boots worn off, and their *putties* wrapped round their bleeding feet. It is painful to add that they had been treated with a personal violence and a brutality in marked contrast to the elaborate hospitality shown by the British Government to its involuntary guests.

On December 6th De Wet had at last reached the Orange River a clear day in front of his pursuers. But it was only to find that his labours had been in vain. At Odendaal, where he had hoped to cross, the river was in spate, the British flag waved from a post upon the further side, and a strong force of expectant Guardsmen eagerly awaited him there. Instantly recognising that the game was up, the Boer leader doubled back for the north and safety. At Rouxville he hesitated as to whether he should snap up the small garrison, but the commandant, Rundle, showed a bold face, and De Wet passed on to the Coomassie Bridge over the Caledon. The small post there refused to be bluffed into a surrender, and the Boers, still dropping their horses fast, passed on, and got over the drift at Amsterdam, their rearguard being hardly across before Knox had also reached the river.

On the 10th the British were in touch again near Helvetia, where there was a rearguard skirmish. On the 11th both parties rode through Reddersberg, a few hours separating them. The Boers in their cross-country trekking go, as one of their prisoners observed, 'slap-bang at everything,' and as they are past-masters in the art of ox and mule driving, and have such a knowledge of the country that they can trek as well by night as by day, it says much for the energy of Knox and his men that he was able for a fortnight to keep in close touch with them.

It became evident now that there was not much chance of overtaking the main body of the burghers, and an attempt was therefore made to interpose a fresh force who might head them off. A line of posts existed between Thabanchu and Ladybrand, and Colonel Thorneycroft was stationed there with a movable column. It was Knox's plan therefore to prevent the Boers from breaking to the west and to head them towards the Basuto border. A small column under Parsons had been sent by Hunter from Bloemfontein, and pushed in upon the flank of De Wet, who had on the 12th got back to Dewetsdorp. Again the pursuit became warm, but

De Wet's time was not yet come. He headed for Springhaan Nek, about fifteen miles east of Thabanchu. This pass is about four miles broad, with a British fort upon either side of it. There was only one way to safety, for Knox's mounted infantrymen and lancers were already dotting the southern skyline. Without hesitation the whole Boer force, now some 2500 strong, galloped at full speed in open order through the Nek, braving the long range fire of riflemen and guns. The tactics were those of French in his ride to Kimberley, and the success was as complete. De Wet's force passed through the last barrier which had been held against him, and vanished into the mountainous country round Ficksburg, where it could safely rest and refit.

The result then of these bustling operations had been that De Wet and his force survived, but that he had failed in his purpose of invading the Colony, and had dropped some five hundred horses, two guns, and about a hundred of his men. Haasbroek's commando had been detached by De Wet to make a feint at another pass while he made his way through the Springhaan. Parsons's force followed Haasbroek up and engaged him, but under cover of night he was able to get away and to join his leader to the north of Thabanchu. On December 13th, this, the second great chase after De Wet, may be said to have closed.

CHAPTER 31

The Guerilla Warfare in the Transvaal: Nooitgedacht

Leaving De Wet in the Ficksburg mountains, where he lurked until after the opening of the New Year, the story of the scattered operations in the Transvaal may now be carried down to the same point—a story comprising many skirmishes and one considerable engagement, but so devoid of any central thread that it is difficult to know how to approach it. From Lichtenburg to Komati, a distance of four hundred miles, there was sporadic warfare everywhere, attacks upon scattered posts, usually beaten off but occasionally successful, attacks upon convoys, attacks upon railway trains, attacks upon anything and everything which could harass the invaders. Each General in his own district had his own work of repression to perform, and so we had best trace the doings of each up to the end of the year 1900.

Lord Methuen after his pursuit of De Wet in August had gone to Mafeking to refit. From that point, with a force which contained a large proportion of yeomanry and of Australian bushmen, he conducted a long series of operations in the difficult and important district which lies between Rustenburg, Lichtenburg, and Zeerust. Several strong and mobile Boer commandos with guns moved about in it, and an energetic though not very deadly warfare raged between Lemmer, Snyman, and De la Rey on the one side, and the troops of Methuen, Douglas, Broadwood, and Lord Errol upon the other. Methuen moved about incessantly through the broken country, winning small skirmishes and suffering the indignity of continual sniping. From time to time he captured stores, wagons, and small bodies of prisoners. Early in October he and Douglas had successes. On the 15th Broadwood was engaged. On the 20th there was a convoy action. On the 25th Methuen had a success and twenty-eight prisoners. On November 9th he surprised Snyman and took thirty prisoners. On the 10th he got a pom-pom. Early in this month Douglas separated from Methuen, and marched south from Zeerust through Ventersdorp to Klerksdorp, passing over a country which had been hardly touched before, and arriving at his goal with much cattle and some prisoners. Towards the end of the month a considerable stock of provisions were conveyed to Zeerust, and a garrison left to hold that town so as to release Methuen's column for service elsewhere.

Hart's sphere of action was originally round Potchefstroom. On September 9th he made a fine forced march to surprise this town, which had been left some time before with an entirely inadequate garrison to fall into the hands of the enemy. His infantry covered thirty-six and his cavalry fifty-four miles in fifteen hours. The operation was a complete success, the town with eighty Boers falling into his hands with little opposition. On September 30th Hart returned to Krugersdorp, where, save for one skirmish upon the Gatsrand on November 22nd, he appears to have had no actual fighting to do during the remainder of the year.

After the clearing of the eastern border of the Transvaal by the movement of Pole-Carew along the railway line, and of Buller aided by Ian Hamilton in the mountainous country to the north of it, there were no operations of importance in this district. A guard was kept upon the frontier to prevent the return of refugees and the smuggling of ammunition, while General Kitchener, the brother of the Sirdar, broke up a few small Boer *laagers* in the neighbourhood of Lydenburg. Smith-Dorrien guarded the line at Belfast, and on two occasions, November 1st and November 6th, he made aggressive movements against the enemy. The first, which was a surprise executed in concert with Colonel Spens of the Shropshires, was frustrated by a severe blizzard, which prevented the troops from pushing home their success. The second was a two days' expedition, which met with a spirited opposition, and demands a fuller notice.

This was made from Belfast, and the force, which consisted of about fourteen hundred men, advanced south to the Komati River. The infantry were Suffolks and Shropshires, the cavalry Canadians and 5th Lancers, with two Canadian guns and four of the 84th battery. All day the Boer snipers clung to the column, as they had done to French's cavalry in the same district. Mere route marches without a very definite and adequate objective appear to be rather exasperating than overawing, for so long as the column is moving onwards the most timid farmer may be tempted into long-range fire from the flanks or rear. The river was reached and the Boers driven from a position which they had taken up, but their signal fires brought mounted riflemen from every farm, and the retreat of the troops was pressed as they returned to Belfast. There was all the material for a South African Lexington. The most difficult of military operations, the covering of a detachment from a numerous and aggressive enemy, was admirably carried out by the Canadian gunners and dragoons under the command of Colonel Lessard. So severe was the pressure that sixteen of the latter were for a time in the hands of the enemy, who attempted something in the nature of a charge upon the steadfast rearguard. The movement was repulsed, and the total Boer loss would appear to have been considerable, since two of their leaders, Commandant Henry Prinsloo and General Joachim Fourie, were killed, while General Johann Grobler was wounded. If the rank and file suffered in proportion the losses must have been severe. The British casualties in the two days amounted to eight killed and thirty wounded, a small total when the arduous nature of the service is considered. The Canadians and the Shropshires seem to have borne off the honours of these trying operations.

In the second week of October, General French, with three brigades of cavalry (Dickson's, Gordon's, and Mahon's), started for a cross-country ride from Machadodorp. Three brigades may seem an imposing force, but the actual numbers did not exceed two strong regiments, or about 1500 sabres in all. A wing of the Suffolk Regiment went with them. On October 13th Mahon's brigade met with a sharp resistance, and lost ten killed and twenty-nine wounded. On the 14th the force entered Carolina. On the 16th they lost six killed and twenty wounded, and from the day that they started until they reached Heidelberg on the 27th there was never a day that they could shake themselves clear of their attendant snipers. The total losses of the force were about ninety killed and wounded, but they brought in sixty prisoners and a large quantity of cattle and stores. The march had at least the effect of making it clear that the passage of a column of troops encumbered with baggage through a hostile country is an inefficient means for quelling a popular resistance. Light and mobile parties acting from a central depot were in future to be employed, with greater hopes of success.

Some appreciable proportion of the British losses during this phase of the war arose from railway accidents caused by the persistent tampering with the lines. In the first ten days of October there were four such mishaps, in which two Sappers, twenty-three of the Guards (Coldstreams), and eighteen of the 66th battery were killed or wounded. On the last occasion, which occurred on October 10th near Vlakfontein, the reinforcements who came to aid the sufferers were themselves waylaid, and lost twenty, mostly of the Rifle Brigade, killed, wounded, or prisoners. Hardly a day elapsed that the line was not cut at some point. The bringing of supplies was complicated by the fact that the Boer women and children were coming more and more into refugee camps, where they had to be fed by the British, and the strange spectacle was frequently seen of Boer snipers killing or wounding the drivers and stokers of the very trains which were bringing up food upon which Boer families were dependent for their lives. Considering that these tactics were continued for over a year, and that they resulted in the death or mutilation of many hundreds of British officers and men, it is really inexplicable that the British authorities did not employ the means used by all armies under such circumstances— which is to place hostages upon the trains. A truckload of Boers behind every engine would have stopped the practice for ever. Again and again in this war the British have fought with the gloves when their opponents used their knuckles.

We will pass now to a consideration of the doings of General Paget, who was operating to the north and north-east of Pretoria with a force which consisted of two regiments of infantry, about a thousand horsemen, and twelve guns. His mounted men were under the command of Plumer. In the early part of November this force had been withdrawn from Warm Baths and had fallen back upon Pienaar's River, where it had continual skirmishes with the enemy. Towards the end of November, news having reached Pretoria that the enemy under Erasmus and Viljoen were present in force at a place called Rhenoster Kop, which is about twenty miles north of the Delagoa Railway line and fifty miles northeast of the capital, it was arranged that Paget should attack them from the south, while Lyttelton from Middelburg should endeavour to get behind them. The force with which Paget started upon this enterprise was not a very formidable one. He had for mounted troops some Queensland, South Australian, New Zealand, and Tasmanian Bushmen, together with the York, Montgomery, and Warwick Yeomanry. His infantry were the 1st West Riding regiment and four companies of the Munsters. His guns were the 7th and 38th batteries, with two naval quick-firing twelve-pounders and some smaller pieces. The total could not have exceeded some two thousand men. Here, as at other times, it is noticeable that in spite of the two hundred thousand soldiers whom the British kept in the field, the lines of communication absorbed so many that at the actual point of contact they were seldom superior and often inferior in numbers to the enemy. The opening of the Natal and Delagoa lines though valuable in many ways, had been an additional drain. Where every culvert needs its picket and every bridge its company, the guardianship of many hundreds of miles of rail is no light matter.

In the early morning of November 29th Paget's men came in contact with the enemy, who were in some force upon an admirable position. A ridge for their centre, a flanking *kopje* for their cross fire, and a grass glacis for the approach—it was an ideal Boer battlefield. The colonials and the yeomanry under Plumer on the left, and Hickman on the right, pushed in upon them, until it was evident that they meant to hold their ground. Their advance being checked by a very severe fire, the horsemen dismounted and took such cover as they could. Paget's original idea had been a turning movement, but the Boers were the more numerous body, and it was impossible for the smaller British force to find their flanks, for they extended over at least seven miles. The infantry were moved up into the centre, therefore, between the wings of dismounted horsemen, and the guns were brought up to cover the advance. The country was ill-suited, however, to the use of artillery, and it was only possible to use an indirect fire from under a curve of the grass land. The guns made good practice, however, one section of the 38th battery being in action all day within 800 yards of the Boer line, and putting themselves out of action after 300 rounds by the destruction of their own rifling. Once over the curve every yard of the *veldt* was commanded by the hidden riflemen. The infantry advanced, but could make no headway against the deadly fire which met them. By short rushes the attack managed to get within 300 yards of the enemy, and there it stuck. On the right the Munsters carried a detached *kopje* which was in front of them, but could do little to aid the main attack. Nothing could have exceeded the tenacity of the Yorkshiremen and the New Zealanders, who were immediately to their left. Though unable to advance they refused to retire, and indeed they were in a position from which a retirement would have been a serious operation. Colonel Lloyd of the West Ridings was hit in three places and killed. Five out of six officers of the New Zealand corps were struck down. There were no reserves to give a fresh impetus to the attack, and the thin scattered line, behind bullet-spotted stones or anthills, could but hold its own while the sun sank slowly upon a day which will not be forgotten by those who endured it. The Boers were reinforced in the afternoon, and the pressure became so severe that the field guns were retired with much difficulty. Many of the infantry had shot away all their cartridges and were helpless. Just one year before British soldiers had lain under similar circumstances on the plain which leads to Modder River, and now on a smaller scale the very same drama was being enacted. Gradually the violet haze of evening deepened into darkness, and the incessant rattle of the rifle fire died away on either side. Again, as at Modder River, the British infantry still lay in their position, determined to take no backward step, and again the Boers stole away in the night, leaving the ridge which they had defended so well. A hundred killed and wounded was the price paid by the British for that line of rock studded hills—a heavier proportion of losses than had befallen Lord Methuen in the corresponding action. Of the Boer losses there was as usual no means of judging, but several grave-mounds, newly dug, showed that they also had something to deplore. Their retreat, however, was not due to exhaustion, but to the demonstration which Lyttelton had been able to make in their rear. The gunners and the infantry had all done well in a most trying action, but by common consent it was with the men from New Zealand that the honours lay. It was no empty compliment when Sir Alfred Milner telegraphed to the Premier of New Zealand his congratulations upon the distinguished behaviour of his fellow countrymen.

From this time onwards there was nothing of importance in this part of the seat of war.

It is necessary now to turn from the north-east to the north-west of Pretoria, where the presence of De la Rey and the cover afforded by the Magaliesberg mountains had kept alive the Boer resistance. Very rugged lines of hill, alternating with fertile valleys, afforded a succession of forts and of granaries to the army which held them. To General Clements' column had been committed the task of clearing this difficult piece of country. His force fluctuated in numbers, but does not appear at any time to have consisted of more than three thousand men, which comprised the Border Regiment, the Yorkshire Light Infantry, the second Northumberland Fusiliers, mounted infantry, yeomanry, the 8th R.F.A., P battery R.H.A., and one heavy gun. With this small army he moved about the district, breaking up Boer bands, capturing supplies, and bringing in refugees. On November 13th he was at Krugersdorp, the southern extremity of his beat. On the 24th he was moving north again, and found himself as he approached the hills in the presence of a force of Boers with cannon. This was the redoubtable De la Rey, who sometimes operated in Methuen's country to the north of the Magaliesberg, and sometimes to the south. He had now apparently fixed upon Clements as his definite opponent. De la Rey was numerically inferior, and Clements had no difficulty in this first encounter in forcing him back with some loss. On November 26th Clements was back at Krugersdorp again with cattle and prisoners. In the early days of December he was moving northwards once more, where a serious disaster awaited him. Before narrating the circumstances connected with the Battle of Nooitgedacht there is one incident which occurred in this same region which should be recounted.

This consists of the determined attack made by a party of De la Rey's men, upon December 3rd, on a convoy which was proceeding from Pretoria to Rustenburg, and had got as far as Buffel's Hoek. The convoy was a very large one, consisting of 150 wagons, which covered about three miles upon the march. It was guarded by two companies of the West Yorkshires, two guns of the 75th battery, and a handful of the Victoria Mounted Rifles. The escort appears entirely inadequate when it is remembered that these stores, which were of great value, were being taken through a country which was known to be infested by the enemy. What might have been foreseen occurred. Five hundred Boers suddenly rode down upon the helpless line of wagons and took possession of them. The escort rallied, however, upon a *kopje*, and, though attacked all day, succeeded in holding their own until help arrived. They prevented the Boers from destroying or carrying off as much of the convoy as was under their guns, but the rest was looted and burned. The incident was a most unfortunate one, as it supplied the enemy with a large quantity of stores, of which they were badly in need. It was the more irritating as it was freely rumoured that a Boer attack was pending; and there is evidence that a remonstrance was addressed from the convoy before it left Rietfontein to the General of the district, pointing out the danger to which it was exposed. The result was the loss of 120 wagons and of more than half the escort. The severity of the little action and the hardihood of the defence are indicated by the fact that the small body who held the *kopje* lost fifteen killed and twenty-two wounded, the gunners losing nine out of fifteen. A relieving force appeared at the close of the action, but no vigorous pursuit was attempted, although the weather was wet and the Boers had actually carried away sixty loaded wagons, which could only go very slowly. It must be confessed that from its feckless start to its spiritless finish the story of the Buffel's Hoek convoy is not a pleasant one to tell.

Clements, having made his way once more to the Magaliesberg range, had pitched his camp at a place called Nooitgedacht—not to be confused with the post upon the Delagoa Railway at which the British prisoners had been confined. Here, in the very shadow of the mountain, he halted for five days, during which, with the usual insouciance of British commanders, he does not seem to have troubled himself with any entrenching. He knew, no doubt, that he was too strong for his opponent De la Rey, but what he did not know, but might have feared, was that a second Boer force might appear suddenly upon the scene and join with De la Rey in order to crush him. This second Boer force was that of Commandant Beyers from Warm Baths. By a sudden and skilful movement the two united, and fell like a thunderbolt upon the British column, which was weakened by the absence of the Border Regiment. The result was such a reverse as the British had not sustained since Sanna's Post—a reverse which showed that, though no regular Boer army might exist, still a sudden coalition of scattered bands could at any time produce a force which would be dangerous to any British column which might be taken at a disadvantage. We had thought that the days of battles in this war were over, but an action which showed a missing and casualty roll of 550 proved that in this, as in so many other things, we were mistaken.

As already stated, the camp of Clements lay under a precipitous cliff, upon the summit of which he had placed four companies of the 2nd

Northumberland Fusiliers. This strong post was a thousand feet higher than the camp. Below lay the main body of the force, two more companies of fusiliers, four of Yorkshire Light Infantry, the 2nd Mounted Infantry, Kitchener's Horse, yeomanry, and the artillery. The latter consisted of one heavy naval gun, four guns of the 8th R.F.A., and P battery R.H.A. The whole force amounted to about fifteen hundred men.

It was just at the first break of dawn—the hour of fate in South African warfare—that the battle began. The mounted infantry post between the camp and the mountains were aware of moving figures in front of them. In the dim light they could discern that they were clothed in grey, and that they wore the broad-brimmed hats and feathers of some of our own irregular corps. They challenged, and the answer was a shattering volley, instantly returned by the survivors of the picket. So hot was the Boer attack that before help could come every man save one of the picket was on the ground. The sole survivor, Daley of the Dublins, took no backward step, but continued to steadily load and fire until help came from the awakened camp. There followed a savage conflict at point blank-range. The mounted infantry men, rushing half clad to the support of their comrades, were confronted by an ever-thickening swarm of Boer riflemen, who had already, by working round on the flank, established their favourite cross fire. Legge, the leader of the mounted infantry, a hard little Egyptian veteran, was shot through the head, and his men lay thick around him. For some minutes it was as hot a corner as any in the war. But Clements himself had appeared upon the scene, and his cool gallantry turned the tide of fight. An extension of the line checked the cross fire, and gave the British in turn a flanking position. Gradually the Boer riflemen were pushed back, until at last they broke and fled for their horses in the rear. A small body were cut off, many of whom were killed and wounded, while a few were taken prisoners.

This stiff fight of an hour had ended in a complete repulse of the attack, though at a considerable cost. Both Boers and British had lost heavily. Nearly all the staff were killed or wounded, though General Clements had come through untouched. Fifty or sixty of both sides had fallen. But it was noted as an ominous fact that in spite of shell fire the Boers still lingered upon the western flank. Were they coming on again? They showed no signs of it. And yet they waited in groups, and looked up towards the beetling crags above them. What were they waiting for? The sudden crash of a murderous Mauser fire upon the summit, with the rolling volleys of the British infantry, supplied the answer.

Only now must it have been clear to Clements that he was not dealing merely with some spasmodic attack from his old enemy De la Rey, but that this was a largely conceived movement, in which a force at least double the strength of his own had suddenly been concentrated upon him. His camp was still menaced by the men whom he had repulsed, and he could not weaken it by sending reinforcements up the hill. But the roar of the musketry was rising louder and louder. It was becoming clearer that there was the main attack. It was a Majuba Hill action up yonder, a thick swarm of skirmishers closing in from many sides upon a central band of soldiers. But the fusiliers were hopelessly outnumbered, and this rock fighting is that above all others in which the Boer has an advantage over the regular. A helio on the hill cried for help. The losses were heavy, it said, and the assailants numerous. The Boers closed swiftly in upon the flanks, and the fusiliers were no match for their assailants. Till the very climax the helio still cried that they were being overpowered, and it is said that even while working it the soldier in charge was hurled over the cliff by the onrush of the victorious Boers.

The fight of the mounted infantry men had been at half-past four. At six the attack upon the hill had developed, and Clements in response to those frantic flashes of light had sent up a hundred men of the yeomanry, from the Fife and Devon squadrons, as a reinforcement. To climb a precipitous thousand feet with rifle, bandolier, and spurs, is no easy feat, yet that roar of battle above them heartened them upon their way. But in spite of all their efforts they were only in time to share the general disaster. The head of the line of hard-breathing yeomen reached the plateau just as the Boers, sweeping over the remnants of the Northumberland Fusiliers, reached the brink of the cliff. One by one the yeomen darted over the edge, and endeavoured to find some cover in the face of an infernal point-blank fire. Captain Mudie of the staff, who went first, was shot down. So was Purvis of the Fifes, who followed him. The others, springing over their bodies, rushed for a small trench, and tried to restore the fight. Lieutenant Campbell, a gallant young fellow, was shot dead as he rallied his men. Of twenty-seven of the Fifeshires upon the hill six were killed and eleven wounded. The statistics of the Devons are equally heroic. Those yeomen who had not yet reached the crest were in a perfectly impossible position, as the Boers were firing from complete cover right down upon them. There was no alternative for them but surrender. By seven o'clock every British soldier upon the hill, yeoman or fusilier, had been killed, wounded, or taken. It is not true that the supply of cartridges ran out, and the fusiliers, with the ill-luck which has pursued the 2nd battalion, were outnumbered and outfought by better skirmishers than themselves.

Seldom has a General found himself in a more trying position than Clements, or extricated himself more honourably. Not only had he lost nearly half his force, but his camp was no longer tenable, and his whole army was commanded by the fringe of deadly rifles upon the cliff. From the berg to the camp was from 800 to 1000 yards, and a sleet of bullets whistled down upon it. How severe was the fire may be gauged from the fact that the little pet monkey belonging to the yeomanry—a small enough object—was hit three times, though he lived to survive as a battle-scarred veteran. Those wounded in the early action found themselves in a terrible position, laid out in the open under a withering fire, 'like helpless Aunt Sallies,' as one of them described it. 'We must get a red flag up, or we shall be blown off the face of the earth,' says the same correspondent, a corporal of the Ceylon Mounted Infantry. 'We had a pillow-case, but no red paint. Then we saw what would do instead, so they made the upright with my blood, and the horizontal with Paul's.' It is pleasant to add that this grim flag was respected by the Boers. Bullocks and mules fell in heaps, and it was evident that the question was not whether the battle could be restored, but whether the guns could be saved. Leaving a fringe of yeomen, mounted infantry, and Kitchener's Horse to stave off the Boers, who were already descending by the same steep *kloof* up which the yeomen had climbed, the General bent all his efforts to getting the big naval gun out of danger. Only six oxen were left out of a team of forty, and so desperate did the situation appear that twice dynamite was placed beneath the gun to destroy it. Each time, however, the General intervened, and at last, under a stimulating rain of pom-pom shells, the great cannon lurched slowly forward, quickening its pace as the men pulled on the drag-ropes, and the six oxen broke into a wheezy canter. Its retreat was covered by the smaller guns which rained shrapnel upon the crest of the hill, and upon the Boers who were descending to the camp. Once the big gun was out of danger, the others limbered up and followed, their rear still covered by the staunch mounted infantry, with whom rest all the honours of the battle. Cookson and Brooks with 250 men stood for hours between Clements and absolute disaster. The camp was abandoned as it stood, and all the stores, four hundred picketed horses, and, most serious of all, two wagons of ammunition, fell into the hands of the victors. To have saved all his guns, however, after the destruction of half his force by an active enemy far superior to him in numbers and in mobility, was a feat which goes far to condone the disaster, and to increase rather than to impair the confidence which his troops feel in General Clements. Having retreated for a couple of miles he turned his big gun round upon the hill, which is called Yeomanry Hill, and opened fire upon the camp, which was being looted by swarms of Boers. So bold a face did he present that he was able to remain with his crippled force upon Yeomanry Hill from about nine until four in the afternoon, and no attack was pressed home, though he lay under both shell and rifle fire all day. At four in the afternoon he began his retreat, which did not cease till he had reached Rietfontein, twenty miles off, at six o'clock upon the following morning. His weary men had been working for twenty-six hours, and actually fighting for fourteen, but the bitterness of defeat was alleviated by the feeling that every man, from the General downwards, had done all that was possible, and that there was every prospect of their having a chance before long of getting their own back.

The British losses at the battle of Nooitgedacht amounted to 60 killed, 180 wounded, and 315 prisoners, all of whom were delivered up a few days later at Rustenburg. Of the Boer losses it is, as usual, impossible to speak with confidence, but all the evidence points to their actual casualties being as heavy as those of the British. There was the long struggle at the camp in which they were heavily punished, the fight on the mountain, where they exposed themselves with unusual recklessness, and the final shelling from shrapnel and from Lyddite. All accounts agree that their attack was more open than usual. 'They were mowed down in twenties that day, but it had no effect. They stood like fanatics,' says one who fought against them. From first to last their conduct was most gallant, and great credit is due to their leaders for the skilful sudden concentration by which they threw their whole strength upon the exposed force. Some eighty miles separate Warm Baths from Nooitgedacht, and it seems strange that our Intelligence Department should have remained in ignorance of so large a movement.

General Broadwood's 2nd Cavalry Brigade had been stationed to the north of Magaliesberg, some twelve miles westward of Clements, and formed the next link in the long chain of British forces. Broadwood does not appear, however, to have appreciated the importance of the engagement, and made no energetic movement to take part in it. If Colvile is open to the charge of having been slow to 'march upon the cannon' at Sanna's Post, it might be urged that Broadwood in turn showed some want of energy and judgment upon this occasion. On the morning of the 13th his force could hear the heavy firing to the eastward, and could even see the shells bursting on the top of the Magaliesberg. It was but ten or twelve miles distant, and, as his Elswick guns have a range of nearly five, a very small advance would have enabled him to make a demonstration against the flank of the Boers, and so to relieve the pressure upon Clements. It is true that his force was not large, but it was exceptionally mobile. Whatever the reasons, no effective advance was made by Broadwood. On hearing the result he fell back upon Rustenburg, the nearest British post, his small force being dangerously isolated.

Those who expected that General Clements would get his own back had not long to wait. In a few days he was in the field again. The remains of his former force had, however, been sent into Pretoria to re-fit, and nothing remained of it save the 8th R.F.A. and the indomitable cow-gun still pocked with the bullets of Nooitgedacht. He had also F battery R.H.A., the Inniskillings, the Border regiment, and a force of mounted infantry under Alderson. More important than all, however, was the co-operation of General French, who came out from Pretoria to assist in the operations. On the 19th, only six days after his defeat, Clements found himself on the very same spot fighting some at least of the very same men. This time, however, there was no element of surprise, and the British were able to approach the task with delibera-tion and method. The result was that both upon the 19th and 20th the Boers were shelled out of successive positions with considerable loss, and driven altogether away from that part of the Magaliesberg. Shortly afterwards General Clements was recalled to Pretoria, to take over the command of the 7th Division, General Tucker having been appointed to the military command of Bloemfontein in the place of the gallant Hunter, who, to the regret of the whole army, was invalided home. General Cunningham henceforward commanded the column which Clements had led back to the Magaliesberg.

Upon November 13th the first of a series of attacks was made upon the posts along the Delagoa Railway line. These were the work of Vil-joen's commando, who, moving swiftly from the north, threw themselves upon the small garrisons of Balmoral and of Wilge River, stations which are about six miles apart. At the former was a detachment of the Buffs, and at the latter of the Royal Fusiliers. The attack was well delivered, but in each instance was beaten back with heavy loss to the assailants. A picket of the Buffs was captured at the first rush, and the detachment lost six killed and nine wounded. No impression was made upon the posi-tion, however, and the double attack seems to have cost the Boers a large number of casualties.

Another incident calling for some mention was the determined at-tack made by the Boers upon the town of Vryheid, in the extreme south-east of the Transvaal near the Natal border. Throughout Novem-ber this district had been much disturbed, and the small British garrison had evacuated the town and taken up a position on the adjacent hills. Upon December 11th the Boers attempted to carry the trenches. The garrison of the town appears to have consisted of the 2nd Royal Lan-caster regiment, some five hundred strong, a party of the Lancashire Fu-siliers, 150 strong, and fifty men of the Royal Garrison Artillery, with a small body of mounted infantry. They held a hill about half a mile north of the town, and commanding it. The attack, which was a surprise in the middle of the night, broke upon the pickets of the British, who held their own in a way which may have been injudicious but was certainly heroic. Instead of falling back when seriously attacked, the young officers in charge of these outposts refused to move, and were speedily under such a fire that it was impossible to reinforce them. There were four outposts, under Woodgate, Theobald, Lippert, and Mangles. The attack at 2.15 on a cold dark morning began at the post held by Woodgate, the Boers coming hand-to-hand before they were detected. Woodgate, who was unarmed at the instant, seized a hammer, and rushed at the nearest Boer, but was struck by two bullets and killed. His post was dispersed or taken. Theobald and Lippert, warned by the firing, held on behind their sangars, and were ready for the storm which burst over them. Lippert was unhappily killed, and his ten men all hit or taken, but young Theobald held his own under a heavy fire for twelve hours. Mangles also, the gallant son of a gallant father, held his post all day with the utmost tenacity. The troops in the trenches behind were never seriously pressed, thanks to the desperate resistance of the outposts, but Colonel Gawne of the Lancasters was unfortunately killed. Towards evening the Boers abandoned the attack, leaving fourteen of their number dead upon the ground, from which it may be guessed that their total casualties were not less than a hundred. The British losses were three officers and five men killed, twenty-two men wounded, and thirty men with one officer missing—the latter being the survivors of those outposts which were overwhelmed by the Boer advance.

A few incidents stand out among the daily bulletins of snipings, skirmishes, and endless marchings which make the dull chronicle of these, the last months of the year 1900. These must be enumerated without any attempt at connecting them. The first is the long-drawn-out siege or investment of Schweizer-Renecke. This small village stands upon the Harts River, on the western border of the Transvaal. It is not easy to understand why the one party should desire to hold, or the other to attack, a position so insignificant. From August 19th onwards it was defended by a garrison of 250 men, under the very capable command of Colonel Chamier, who handled a small business in a way which marks him as a leader. The Boer force, which varied in numbers from five hundred to a thousand, never ventured to push home an attack, for Chamier, fresh from the experience of Kimberley, had taken such precautions that his defences were formidable, if not impregnable. Late in September a relieving force under Colonel Settle threw fresh supplies into the town, but when he passed on upon his endless march the enemy closed in once more, and the siege was renewed. It lasted for several months, until a column withdrew the garrison and abandoned the position.

Of all the British detachments, the two which worked hardest and marched furthest during this period of the war was the 21st Brigade (Derbyshires, Sussex, and Camerons) under General Bruce Hamilton, and the column under Settle, which operated down the western border of the Orange River Colony, and worked round and round with such pertinacity that it was familiarly known as Settle's Imperial Circus. Much hard and disagreeable work, far more repugnant to the soldier than the actual dangers of war, fell to the lot of Bruce Hamilton and his men. With Kroonstad as their centre they were continually working through the dangerous Lindley and Heilbron districts, returning to the railway line only to start again immediately upon a fresh quest. It was work for mounted police, not for infantry soldiers, but what they were given to do they did to the best of their ability. Settle's men had a similar thankless task. From the neighbourhood of Kimberley he marched in November with his small column down the border of the Orange River Colony, capturing supplies and bringing in refugees. He fought one brisk action with Hertzog's commando at Kloof, and then, making his way across the colony, struck the railway line again at Edenburg on December 7th, with a train of prisoners and cattle.

Rundle also had put in much hard work in his efforts to control the difficult district in the north-east of the Colony which had been committed to his care. He traversed in November from north to south the same country which he had already so painfully traversed from south to north. With occasional small actions he moved about from Vrede to Reitz, and so to Bethlehem and Harrismith. On him, as on all other commanders, the vicious system of placing small garrisons in the various towns imposed a constant responsibility lest they should be starved or overwhelmed.

The year and the century ended by a small reverse to the British arms in the Transvaal. This consisted in the capture of a post at Helvetia defended by a detachment of the Liverpool Regiment and by a 4.7 gun. Lydenburg, being seventy miles off the railway line, had a chain of posts connecting it with the junction at Machadodorp. These posts were seven in number, ten miles apart, each defended by 250 men. Of these Helvetia was the second. The key of the position was a strongly fortified hill about three-quarters of a mile from the headquarter camp, and commanding it. This post was held by Captain Kirke with forty garrison artillery to work the big gun, and seventy Liverpool infantry. In spite of the barbed-wire entanglements, the Boers most gallantly rushed this position, and their advance was so rapid, or the garrison so slow, that the place was carried with hardly a shot fired. Major Cotton, who commanded the main lines, found himself deprived in an instant of nearly half his force and fiercely attacked by a victorious and exultant enemy. His position was much too extended for the small force at his disposal, and the line of trenches was pierced and enfiladed at many points. It must be acknowledged that the defences were badly devised— little barbed wire, frail walls, large loopholes, and the outposts so near the trenches that the assailants could reach them as quickly as the supports. With the dawn Cotton's position was serious, if not desperate. He was not only surrounded, but was commanded from Gun Hill. Perhaps it would have been wiser if, after being wounded, he had handed over the command to Jones, his junior officer. A stricken man's judgement can never be so sound as that of the hale. However that may be, he came to the conclusion that the position was untenable, and that it was best to prevent further loss of life. Fifty of the Liverpools were killed and wounded, 200 taken. No ammunition of the gun was captured, but the Boers were able to get safely away with this humiliating evidence of their victory. One post, under Captain Wilkinson with forty men, held out with success, and harassed the enemy in their retreat. As at Dewetsdorp and at Nooitgedacht, the Boers were unable to retain their prisoners, so that the substantial fruits of their enterprise were small, but it forms none the less one more of those incidents which may cause us to respect our enemy and to be critical towards ourselves.[1]

In the last few months of the year some of those corps which had served their time or which were needed elsewhere were allowed to leave the seat of war. By the middle of November the three different corps of the City Imperial Volunteers, the two Canadian contingents, Lumsden's Horse, the Composite Regiment of Guards, six hundred Australians, A battery R.H.A., and the volunteer companies of the regular regiments, were all homeward bound. This loss of several thousand veteran troops before the war was over was to be deplored, and though unavoidable in the case of volunteer contingents, it is difficult to explain where regular troops are concerned. Early in the new year the Government was compelled to send out strong reinforcements to take their place.

Early in December Lord Roberts also left the country, to take over the duties of Commander-in-Chief. High as his reputation stood when, in January, he landed at Cape Town, it is safe to say that it had been immensely enhanced when, ten months later, he saw from the quarter-deck of the 'Canada' the Table Mountain growing dimmer in the distance. He found a series of disconnected operations, in which we were uniformly worsted. He speedily converted them into a series of

---

1. Considering that Major Stapelton Cotton was himself wounded in three places during the action (one of these wounds being in the head), he has had hard measure in being deprived of his commission by a court-martial which sat eight months after the event. It is to be earnestly hoped that there may be some revision of this severe sentence.

connected operations in which we were almost uniformly successful. Proceeding to the front at the beginning of February, within a fortnight he had relieved Kimberley, within a month he had destroyed Cronje's force, and within six weeks he was in Bloemfontein. Then, after a six weeks' halt which could not possibly have been shortened, he made another of his tiger leaps, and within a month had occupied Johannesburg and Pretoria. From that moment the issue of the campaign was finally settled, and though a third leap was needed, which carried him to Komatipoort, and though brave and obstinate men might still struggle against their destiny, he had done what was essential, and the rest, however difficult, was only the detail of the campaign. A kindly gentleman, as well as a great soldier, his nature revolted from all harshness, and a worse man might have been a better leader in the last hopeless phases of the war. He remembered, no doubt, how Grant had given Lee's army their horses, but Lee at the time had been thoroughly beaten, and his men had laid down their arms. A similar boon to the partially conquered Boers led to very different results, and the prolongation of the war is largely due to this act of clemency. At the same time political and military considerations were opposed to each other upon the point, and his moral position in the use of harsher measures is the stronger since a policy of conciliation had been tried and failed. Lord Roberts returned to London with the respect and love of his soldiers and of his fellow-countrymen. A passage from his farewell address to his troops may show the qualities which endeared him to them.

The service which the South African Force has performed is, I venture to think, unique in the annals of war, inasmuch as it has been absolutely almost incessant for a whole year, in some cases for more than a year. There has been no rest, no days off to recruit, no going into winter quarters, as in other campaigns which have extended over a long period. For months together, in fierce heat, in biting cold, in pouring rain, you, my comrades, have marched and fought without halt, and bivouacked without shelter from the elements. You frequently have had to continue marching with your clothes in rags and your boots without soles, time being of such consequence that it was impossible for you to remain long enough in one place to refit. When not engaged in actual battle you have been continually shot at from behind *kopjes* by invisible enemies to whom every inch of the country was familiar, and who, from the peculiar nature of the country, were able to inflict severe punishment while perfectly safe themselves. You have forced your way through dense jungles, over precipitous mountains, through and over which with infinite manual labour you have had to drag heavy guns and ox-wagons. You have covered with almost incredible speed enormous distances, and that often on very short supplies of food. You have endured the sufferings inevitable in war to sick and wounded men far from the base, without a murmur and even with cheerfulness.

The words reflect honour both upon the troops addressed and upon the man who addressed them. From the middle of December 1900 Lord Kitchener took over the control of the campaign.

CHAPTER 32

The Second Invasion of Cape Colony
(December 1900 to April 1901)

During the whole war the task of the British had been made very much more difficult by the openly expressed sympathy with the Boers from the political association known as the Afrikander Bond, which either inspired or represented the views which prevailed among the great majority of the Dutch inhabitants of Cape Colony. How strong was this rebel impulse may be gauged by the fact that in some of the border districts no less than ninety per cent of the voters joined the Boer invaders upon the occasion of their first entrance into the Colony. It is not pretended that these men suffered from any political grievances whatever, and their action is to be ascribed partly to a natural sympathy with their northern kinsmen, and partly to racial ambition and to personal dislike to their British neighbours. The liberal British policy towards the natives had especially alienated the Dutch, and had made as well-marked a line of cleavage in South Africa as the slave question had done in the States of the Union.

With the turn of the war the discontent in Cape Colony became less obtrusive, if not less acute, but in the later months of the year 1900 it increased to a degree which became dangerous. The fact of the farm-burning in the conquered countries, and the fiction of outrages by the British troops, raised a storm of indignation. The annexation of the Republics, meaning the final disappearance of any Dutch flag from South Africa, was a racial humiliation which was bitterly resented. The Dutch papers became very violent, and the farmers much excited. The agitation culminated in a conference at Worcester upon December 6th, at which some thousands of delegates were present. It is suggestive of the Imperial nature of the struggle that the assembly of Dutch Afrikanders was carried out under the muzzles of Canadian artillery, and closely watched by Australian cavalry. Had violent words transformed themselves into deeds, all was ready for the crisis.

Fortunately the good sense of the assembly prevailed, and the agitation, though bitter, remained within those wide limits which a British constitution permits. Three resolutions were passed, one asking that the war be ended, a second that the independence of the Republics be restored, and a third protesting against the actions of Sir Alfred Milner. A deputation which carried these to the Governor received a courteous but an uncompromising reply. Sir Alfred Milner pointed out that the Home Government, all the great Colonies, and half the Cape were unanimous in their policy, and that it was folly to imagine that it could be reversed on account of a local agitation. All were agreed in the desire to end the war, but the last way of bringing this about was by encouraging desperate men to go on fighting in a hopeless cause. Such was the general nature of the Governor's reply, which was, as might be expected, entirely endorsed by the British Government and people.

Had De Wet, in the operations which have already been described, evaded Charles Knox and crossed the Orange River, his entrance into the Colony would have been synchronous with the congress at Worcester, and the situation would have become more acute. This peril was fortunately averted. The agitation in the Colony suggested to the Boer leaders, however, that here was an untouched recruiting ground, and that small mobile invading parties might gather strength and become formidable. It was obvious, also, that by enlarging the field of operations the difficulties of the British Commander-in-chief would be very much increased, and the pressure upon the Boer guerrillas in the Republics relaxed. Therefore, in spite of De Wet's failure to penetrate the Colony, several smaller bands under less-known leaders were despatched over the Orange River. With the help of the information and the supplies furnished by the local farmers, these bands wandered for many months over the great expanse of the Colony, taking refuge, when hard pressed, among the mountain ranges. They moved swiftly about, obtaining remounts from their friends, and avoiding everything in the nature of an action, save when the odds were overwhelmingly in their favour. Numerous small posts or patrols cut off, many skirmishes, and one or two railway smashes were the fruits of this invasion, which lasted till the end of the war, and kept the Colony in an extreme state of unrest during that period. A short account must be given here of the movement and exploits of these hostile bands, avoiding, as far as possible, that catalogue of obscure *fonteins* and *kops* which mark their progress.

The invasion was conducted by two main bodies, which shed off numerous small raiding parties. Of these two, one operated on the western side of the Colony, reaching the sea-coast in the Clanwilliam district, and attaining a point which is less than a hundred miles from Cape Town.

The other penetrated even more deeply down the centre of the Colony, reaching almost to the sea in the Mossel Bay direction. Yet the incursion, although so far-reaching, had small effect, since the invaders held nothing save the ground on which they stood, and won their way, not by victory, but by the avoidance of danger. Some recruits were won to their cause, but they do not seem at that time to have been more than a few hundreds in number, and to have been drawn for the most part from the classes of the community which had least to lose and least to offer.

The Western Boers were commanded by Judge Hertzog of the Free State, having with him Brand, the son of the former president, and about twelve hundred well-mounted men. Crossing the Orange River at Sand Drift, north of Colesberg, upon December 16th, they paused at Kameel-fontein to gather up a small post of thirty yeomen and guardsmen under Lieutenant Fletcher, the well-known oar. Meeting with a stout resistance, and learning that British forces were already converging upon them, they abandoned the attack, and turning away from Colesberg they headed west, cutting the railway line twenty miles to the north of De Aar. On the 22nd they occupied Britstown, which is eighty miles inside the border, and on the same day they captured a small body of yeomanry who had been following them. These prisoners were released again some days later. Taking a sweep round towards Prieska and Strydenburg, they pushed south again. At the end of the year Hertzog's column was 150 miles deep in the Colony, sweeping through the barren and thinly-inhabited western lands, heading apparently for Fraserburg and Beaufort West.

The second column was commanded by Kritzinger, a burgher of Zastron, in the Orange River Colony. His force was about 800 strong. Crossing the border at Rhenoster Hoek upon December 16th, they pushed for Burghersdorp, but were headed off by a British column. Passing through Venterstad, they made for Steynsberg, fighting two indecisive skirmishes with small British forces. The end of the year saw them crossing the rail road at Sherburne, north of Rosmead Junction, where they captured a train as they passed, containing some Colonial troops. At this time they were a hundred miles inside the Colony, and nearly three hundred from Hertzog's western column.

In the meantime Lord Kitchener, who had descended for a few days to De Aar, had shown great energy in organising small mobile columns which should follow and, if possible, destroy the invaders. Martial law was proclaimed in the parts of the Colony affected, and as the invaders came further south the utmost enthusiasm was shown by the loyalists, who formed themselves everywhere into town guards. The existing Colonial regiments, such as Brabant's, the Imperial and South African Light Horse—Thorneycroft's, Rimington's, and the others—had already been brought up to strength again, and now two new regiments were added, Kitchener's Bodyguard and Kitchener's Fighting Scouts, the latter being raised by Johann Colenbrander, who had made a name for himself in the Rhodesian wars. At this period of the war between twenty and thirty thousand Cape colonists were under arms. Many of these were untrained levies, but they possessed the martial spirit of the race, and they set free more seasoned troops for other duties.

It will be most convenient and least obscure to follow the movements of the western force (Hertzog's), and afterwards to consider those of the eastern (Kritzinger's). The opening of the year saw the mobile column of Free Staters 150 miles over the border, pushing swiftly south over the barren surface of the Karoo. It is a country of scattered farms and scanty population; desolate plains curving upwards until they rise into still more desolate mountain ranges. Moving in a very loose formation over a wide front, the Boers swept southwards. On or about January 4th they took possession of the small town of Calvinia, which remained their headquarters for more than a month. From this point their roving bands made their way as far as the seacoast in the Clanwilliam direction, for they expected at Lambert's Bay to meet with a vessel with mercenaries and guns from Europe. They pushed their outposts also as far as Sutherland and Beaufort West in the south. On January 15th strange horsemen were seen hovering about the line at Touws River, and the citizens of Cape Town learned with amazement that the war had been carried to within a hundred miles of their own doors.

Whilst the Boers were making this daring raid a force consisting of several mobile columns was being organised by General Settle to arrest and finally to repel the western invasion. The larger body was under the command of Colonel De Lisle, an officer who brought to the operations of war the same energy and thoroughness with which he had made the polo team of an infantry regiment the champions of the whole British Army. His troops consisted of the 6th Mounted Infantry, the New South Wales Mounted Infantry, the Irish Yeomanry, a section of R battery R.H.A., and a pom-pom. With this small but mobile and hardy force he threw himself in front of Hertzog's line of advance. On January 13th he occupied Piquetburg, eighty miles south of the Boer headquarters. On the 23rd he was at Clanwilliam, fifty miles south-west of them. To his right were three other small British columns under Bethune, Thorneycroft, and Henniker, the latter resting upon the railway at Matjesfontein, and the whole line extending over 120 miles—barring the southern path to the invaders.

Though Hertzog at Calvinia and De Lisle at Clanwilliam were only fifty miles apart, the intervening country is among the most broken and mountainous in South Africa. Between the two points, and nearer to De Lisle than to Hertzog, flows the Doorn River. The Boers advancing from Calvinia came into touch with the British scouts at this point, and drove them in upon January 21st. On the 28th De Lisle, having been reinforced by Bethune's column, was able at last to take the initiative. Bethune's force consisted mainly of Colonials, and included Kitchener's Fighting Scouts, the Cape Mounted Police, Cape Mounted Rifles, Brabant's Horse, and the Diamond Field Horse. At the end of January the united forces of Bethune and of De Lisle advanced upon Calvinia. The difficulties lay rather in the impassable country than in the resistance of an enemy who was determined to refuse battle. On February 6th, after a fine march, De Lisle and his men took possession of Calvinia, which had been abandoned by the Boers. It is painful to add that during the month that they had held the town they appear to have behaved with great harshness, especially to the *kaffirs*. The flogging and shooting of a coloured man named Esan forms one more incident in the dark story of the Boer and his relations to the native.

The British were now sweeping north on a very extended front. Colenbrander had occupied Van Rhyns Dorp, to the east of Calvinia, while Bethune's force was operating to the west of it. De Lisle hardly halted at Calvinia, but pushed onwards to Williston, covering seventy-two miles of broken country in forty-eight hours, one of the most amazing performances of the war. Quick as he was, the Boers were quicker still, and during his northward march he does not appear to have actually come into contact with them. Their line of retreat lay through Carnarvon, and upon February 22nd they crossed the railway line to the north of De Aar, and joined upon February 26th the new invading force under De Wet, who had now crossed the Orange River. De Lisle, who had passed over five hundred miles of barren country since he advanced from Piquetburg, made for the railway at Victoria West, and was despatched from that place on February 22nd to the scene of action in the north. From all parts Boer and Briton were concentrating in their effort to aid or to repel the inroad of the famous guerrilla.

Before describing this attempt it would be well to trace the progress of the eastern invasion (Kritzinger's), a movement which may be treated rapidly, since it led to no particular military result at that time, though it lasted long after Hertzog's force had been finally dissipated. Several small columns, those of Williams, Byng, Grenfell, and Lowe, all under the direction of Haig, were organised to drive back these commandos; but so nimble were the invaders, so vast the distances and so broken the country, that it was seldom that the forces came into contact. The operations were conducted over a portion of the Colony which is strongly Dutch in sympathy, and the enemy, though they do not appear to have obtained any large number of recruits, were able to gather stores, horses, and information wherever they went.

When last mentioned Kritzinger's men had crossed the railway north of Rosmead on December 30th, and held up a train containing some Colonial troops. From then onwards a part of them remained in the Middelburg and Graaf-Reinet districts, while part moved towards the south. On January 11th there was a sharp skirmish near Murraysburg, in which Byng's column was engaged, at the cost of twenty casualties, all of Brabant's or the South African Light Horse. On the 16th a very rapid movement towards the south began. On that date Boers appeared at Aberdeen, and on the 18th at Willowmore, having covered seventy miles in two days. Their long, thin line was shredded out over 150 miles, and from Maraisburg, in the north, to Uniondale, which is only thirty miles from the coast, there was rumour of their presence. In this wild district and in that of Oudtshoorn the Boer vanguard flitted in and out of the hills, Haig's column striving hard to bring them to an action. So well-informed were the invaders that they were always able to avoid the British concentrations, while if a British outpost or patrol was left exposed it was fortunate if it escaped disaster. On February 6th a small body of twenty-five of the 7th King's Dragoon Guards and of the West Australians, under Captain Oliver, were overwhelmed at Klipplaat, after a very fine defence, in which they held their own against 200 Boers for eight hours, and lost nearly fifty per cent of their number. On the 12th a patrol of yeomanry was surprised and taken near Willowmore.

The coming of De Wet had evidently been the signal for all the Boer raiders to concentrate, for in the second week of February Kritzinger also began to fall back, as Hertzog had done in the west, followed closely by the British columns. He did not, however, actually join De Wet, and his evacuation of the country was never complete, as was the case with Hertzog's force. On the 19th Kritzinger was at Bethesda, with Gorringe and Lowe at his heels. On the 23rd an important railway bridge at Fish River, north of Cradock, was attacked, but the attempt was foiled by the resistance of a handful of Cape Police and Lancasters. On March 6th a party of Boers occupied the village of Pearston, capturing a few rifles and some ammunition. On the same date there was a skirmish between Colonel Parsons's column and a party of the enemy to the north of Aberdeen. The main body of the invading force appears to have been lurking in this neighbourhood, as they were able upon April 7th to cut off a strong British patrol, consisting of a hundred Lancers and Yeomanry, seventy-five of whom remained as temporary prisoners in the hands of the enemy. With this success we may for the time leave Kritzinger and his lieutenant, Scheepers, who commanded that portion of his force which had penetrated to the south of the Colony.

The two invasions which have been here described, that of Hertzog in the west and of Kritzinger in the midlands, would appear in themselves to be unimportant military operations, since they were carried out by small bodies of men whose policy was rather to avoid than to overcome resistance. Their importance, however, is due to the fact that they were really the forerunners of a more important incursion upon the part of De Wet. The object of these two bands of raiders was to spy out the land, so that on the arrival of the main body all might be ready for that general rising of their kinsmen in the Colony which was the last chance, not of winning, but of prolonging the war. It must be confessed that, however much their reason might approve of the Government under which they lived, the sentiment of the Cape Dutch had been cruelly, though unavoidably, hurt in the course of the war. The appearance of so popular a leader as De Wet with a few thousand veterans in the very heart of their country might have stretched their patience to the breaking-point. Inflamed, as they were, by that racial hatred which had always smouldered, and had now been fanned into a blaze by the speeches of their leaders and by the fictions of their newspapers, they were ripe for mischief, while they had before their eyes an object-lesson of the impotence of our military system in those small bands who had kept the country in a ferment for so long. All was propitious, therefore, for the attempt which Steyn and De Wet were about to make to carry the war into the enemy's country.

We last saw De Wet when, after a long chase, he had been headed back from the Orange River, and, winning clear from Knox's pursuit, had in the third week of December passed successfully through the British cordon between Thabanchu and Ladybrand. Thence he made his way to Senekal, and proceeded, in spite of the shaking which he had had, to recruit and recuperate in the amazing way which a Boer army has. There is no force so easy to drive and so difficult to destroy. The British columns still kept in touch with De Wet, but found it impossible to bring him to an action in the difficult district to which he had withdrawn. His force had split up into numerous smaller bodies, capable of reuniting at a signal from their leader. These scattered bodies, mobile as ever, vanished if seriously attacked, while keenly on the alert to pounce upon any British force which might be overpowered before assistance could arrive. Such an opportunity came to the commando led by Philip Botha, and the result was another petty reverse to the British arms.

Upon January 3rd Colonel White's small column was pushing north, in co-operation with those of Knox, Pilcher, and the others. Upon that date it had reached a point just north of Lindley, a district which has never been a fortunate one for the invaders. A patrol of Kitchener's newly raised bodyguard, under Colonel Laing, 120 strong, was sent forward to reconnoitre upon the road from Lindley to Reitz.

The scouting appears to have been negligently done, there being only two men out upon each flank. The little force walked into one of those horse-shoe positions which the Boers love, and learned by a sudden volley from a *kraal* upon their right that the enemy was present in strength. On attempting to withdraw it was instantly evident that the Boers were on all sides and in the rear with a force which numbered at least five to one. The camp of the main column was only four miles away, however, and the bodyguard, having sent messages of their precarious position, did all they could to make a defence until help could reach them. Colonel Laing had fallen, shot through the heart, but found a gallant successor in young Nairne, the adjutant. Part of the force had thrown themselves, under Nairne and Milne, into a *donga*, which gave some shelter from the sleet of bullets. The others, under Captain Butters, held on to a ruined *kraal*. The Boers pushed the attack very rapidly, however, and were soon able with their superior numbers to send a raking fire down the *donga*, which made it a perfect death-trap. Still hoping that the laggard reinforcements would come up, the survivors held desperately on; but both in the *kraal* and in the *donga* their numbers were from minute to minute diminishing. There was no formal surrender and no white flag, for, when fifty per cent of the British were down, the Boers closed in swiftly and rushed the position. Philip Botha, the brother of the commandant, who led the Boers, behaved with courtesy and humanity to the survivors; but many of the wounds were inflicted with those horrible explosive and expansive missiles, the use of which among civilised combatants should now and always be a capital offence. To disable one's adversary is a painful necessity of warfare, but nothing can excuse the wilful mutilation and torture which is inflicted by these brutal devices.

'How many of you are there?' asked Botha. 'A hundred,' said an officer. 'It is not true. There are one hundred and twenty. I counted you as you came along.' The answer of the Boer leader shows how carefully the small force had been nursed until it was in an impossible position. The margin was a narrow one, however, for within fifteen minutes of the disaster White's guns were at work. There may be some question as to whether the rescuing force could have come sooner, but there can be none as to the resistance of the bodyguard. They held out to the last cartridge. Colonel Laing and three officers with sixteen men were killed, four officers and twenty-two men were wounded. The high proportion of fatal casualties can only be explained by the deadly character of the Boer bullets. Hardly a single horse of the bodyguard was left unwounded, and the profit to the victors, since they were unable to carry away their prisoners, lay entirely in the captured rifles. It is worthy of record that the British wounded were despatched to Heilbron without guard through the Boer forces. That they arrived there unmolested is due to the forbearance of the enemy and to the tact and energy of Surgeon-Captain Porter, who commanded the convoy.

Encouraged by this small success, and stimulated by the news that Hertzog and Kritzinger had succeeded in penetrating the Colony without disaster, De Wet now prepared to follow them. British scouts to the north of Kroonstad reported horsemen riding south and east, sometimes alone, sometimes in small parties. They were recruits going to swell the forces of De Wet. On January 23rd five hundred men crossed the line, journeying in the same direction. Before the end of the month, having gathered together about 2500 men with fresh horses at the Doornberg, twenty miles north of Winburg, the Boer leader was ready for one of his lightning treks once more. On January 28th he broke south through the British net, which appears to have had more meshes than cord. Passing the Bloemfontein-Ladybrand line at Israel Poort he swept southwards, with British columns still wearily trailing behind him, like honest bull-dogs panting after a greyhound.

Before following him upon this new venture it is necessary to say a few words about that peace movement in the Boer States to which some allusion has already been made. On December 20th Lord Kitchener had issued a proclamation which was intended to have the effect of affording protection to those burghers who desired to cease fighting, but who were unable to do so without incurring the enmity of their irreconcilable brethren. 'It is hereby notified,' said the document, 'to all burghers that if after this date they voluntarily surrender they will be allowed to live with their families in Government *laagers* until such time as the guerrilla warfare now being carried on will admit of their returning safely to their homes. All stock and property brought in at the time of the surrender of such burghers will be respected and paid for if requisitioned.' This wise and liberal offer was sedulously concealed from their men by the leaders of the fighting commandos, but was largely taken advantage of by those Boers to whom it was conveyed. Boer refugee camps were formed at Pretoria, Johannesburg, Kroonstad, Bloemfontein, Warrenton; and other points, to which by degrees the whole civil population came to be transferred. It was the *reconcentrado* system of Cuba over again, with the essential difference that the guests of the British Government were well fed and well treated during their detention. Within a few months the camps had 50,000 inmates.

It was natural that some of these people, having experienced the amenity of British rule, and being convinced of the hopelessness of the struggle, should desire to convey their feelings to their friends and relations in the field. Both in the Transvaal and in the Orange River Colony Peace Committees were formed, which endeavoured to persuade their countrymen to bow to the inevitable. A remarkable letter was published from Piet de Wet, a man who had fought bravely for the Boer cause, to his brother, the famous general. 'Which is better for the Republics,' he asked, 'to continue the struggle and run the risk of total ruin as a nation, or to submit? Could we for a moment think of taking back the country if it were offered to us, with thousands of people to be supported by a Government which has not a farthing?... Put passionate feeling aside for a moment and use common-sense, and you will then agree with me that the best thing for the people and the country is to give in, to be loyal to the new government, and to get responsible government...Should the war continue a few months longer the nation will become so poor that they will be the working class in the country, and disappear as a nation in the future... The British are convinced that they have conquered the land and its people, and consider the matter ended, and they only try to treat magnanimously those who are continuing the struggle in order to prevent unnecessary bloodshed.'

Such were the sentiments of those of the burghers who were in favour of peace. Their eyes had been opened and their bitterness was transferred from the British Government to those individual Britons who, partly from idealism and partly from party passion, had encouraged them to their undoing. But their attempt to convey their feelings to their country-men in the field ended in tragedy. Two of their number, Morgendaal and Wessels, who had journeyed to De Wet's camp, were condemned to death by order of that leader. In the case of Morgendaal the execution actually took place, and seems to have been attended by brutal circumstances, the man having been thrashed with a *sjambok* before being put to death. The circumstances are still surrounded by such obscurity that it is impossible to say whether the message of the peace envoys was to the General himself or to the men under his command. In the former case the man was murdered. In the latter the Boer leader was within his rights, though the rights may have been harshly construed and brutally enforced.

On January 29th, in the act of breaking south, De Wet's force, or a portion of it, had a sharp brush with a small British column (Crewe's) at Tabaksberg, which lies about forty miles north-east of Bloemfontein; This small force, seven hundred strong, found itself suddenly in the presence of a very superior body of the enemy, and had some difficulty in extricating itself. A pom-pom was lost in this affair. Crewe fell back upon Knox, and the combined columns made for Bloemfontein, whence they could use the rails for their transport. De Wet meanwhile moved south as far as Smithfield, and then, detaching several small bodies to divert the attention of the British, he struck due west, and crossed the track between Springfontein and Jagersfontein road, capturing the usual supply train as he passed. On February 9th he had reached Phillipolis, well ahead of the British pursuit, and spent a day or two in making his final arrangements before carrying the war over the border. His force consisted at this time of nearly 8000 men, with two 15-pounders, one pom-pom, and one maxim. The garrisons of all the towns in the south-west of the Orange River Colony had been removed in accordance with the policy of concentration, so De Wet found himself for the moment in a friendly country.

The British, realising how serious a situation might arise should De Wet succeed in penetrating the Colony and in joining Hertzog and Kritzinger, made every effort both to head him off and to bar his return. General Lyttelton at Naauwpoort directed the operations, and the possession of the railway line enabled him to concentrate his columns rapidly at the point of danger. On February 11th De Wet forded the Orange River at Zand Drift, and found himself once more upon British territory. Lyttelton's plan of campaign appears to have been to allow De Wet to come some distance south, and then to hold him in front by De Lisle's force, while a number of small mobile columns under Plumer, Crabbe, Henniker, Bethune, Haig, and Thorneycroft should shepherd him behind. On crossing, De Wet at once moved westwards, where, upon February 12th, Plumer's column, consisting of the Queensland Mounted Infantry, the Imperial Bushmen, and part of the King's Dragoon Guards, came into touch with his rearguard. All day upon the 13th and 14th, amid terrific rain, Plumer's hardy troopers followed close upon the enemy, gleaning a few ammunition wagons, a maxim, and some prisoners. The invaders crossed the railway line near Houtnek, to the north of De Aar, in the early hours of the 15th, moving upon a front of six or eight miles. Two armoured trains from the north and the south closed in upon him as he passed, Plumer still thundered in his rear, and a small column under Crabbe came pressing from the south. This sturdy Colonel of Grenadiers had already been wounded four times in the war, so that he might be excused if he felt some personal as well as patriotic reasons for pushing a relentless pursuit. On crossing the railroad De Wet turned furiously upon his pursuers, and, taking an excellent position upon a line of *kopjes* rising out of the huge expanse of the Karoo, he fought a stubborn rearguard action in order to give time for his convoy to get ahead. He was hustled off the hills, however, the Australian Bushmen with great dash carrying the central *kopje*, and the guns driving the invaders to the westward. Leaving all his wagons and his reserve ammunition behind him, the guerrilla chief struck north-west, moving with great swiftness, but never succeeding in shaking off Plumer's pursuit. The weather continued, however, to be atrocious, rain and hail falling with such violence that the horses could hardly be induced to face it. For a week the two sodden, sleepless, mud-splashed little armies swept onwards over the Karoo. De Wet passed northwards through Strydenburg, past Hopetown, and so to the Orange River, which was found to be too swollen with the rains to permit of his crossing. Here upon the 23rd, after a march of forty-five miles on end, Plumer ran into him once more, and captured with very little fighting a fifteen-pounder, a pom-pom, and close on to a hundred prisoners. Slipping away to the east, De Wet upon February 24th crossed the railroad again between Krankuil and Orange River Station, with Thorneycroft's column hard upon his heels. The Boer leader was now more anxious to escape from the Colony than ever he had been to enter it, and he rushed distractedly from point to point, endeavouring to find a ford over the great turbid river which cut him off from his own country. Here he was joined by Hertzog's commando with a number of invaluable spare horses. It is said also that he had been able to get remounts in the Hopetown district, which had not been cleared—an omission for which, it is to be hoped, someone has been held responsible. The Boer ponies, used to the succulent grasses of the *veldt*, could make nothing of the rank Karoo, and had so fallen away that an enormous advantage should have rested with the pursuers had ill luck and bad management not combined to enable the invaders to renew their mobility at the very moment when Plumer's horses were dropping dead under their riders.

The Boer force was now so scattered that, in spite of the advent of Hertzog, De Wet had fewer men with him than when he entered the Colony. Several hundreds had been taken prisoners, many had deserted, and a few had been killed. It was hoped now that the whole force might be captured, and Thorneycroft's, Crabbe's, Henniker's, and other columns were closing swiftly in upon him, while the swollen river still barred his retreat. There was a sudden drop in the flood, however; one ford became passable, and over it, upon the last day of February, De Wet and his bedraggled, dispirited commando escaped to their own country. There was still a sting in his tail, however; for upon that very day a portion of his force succeeded in capturing sixty and killing or wounding twenty of Colenbrander's new regiment, Kitchener's Fighting Scouts. On the other hand, De Wet was finally relieved upon the same day of all care upon the score of his guns, as the last of them was most gallantly captured by Captain Dallimore and fifteen Victorians, who at the same time brought in thirty-three Boer prisoners. The net result of De Wet's invasion was that he gained nothing, and that he lost about four thousand horses, all his guns, all his convoy, and some three hundred of his men.

Once safely in his own country again, the guerrilla chief pursued his way northwards with his usual celerity and success. The moment that it was certain that De Wet had escaped, the indefatigable Plumer, wiry, tenacious man, had been sent off by train to Springfontein, while Bethune's column followed direct. This latter force crossed the Orange River bridge and marched upon Luckhoff and Fauresmith. At the latter town they overtook Plumer, who was again hard upon the heels of De Wet. Together they ran him across the Riet River and north to Petrusburg, until they gave it up as hopeless upon finding that, with only fifty followers, he had crossed the Modder River at Abram's Kraal. There they abandoned the chase and fell back upon Bloemfontein to refit and prepare for a fresh effort to run down their elusive enemy.

While Plumer and Bethune were following upon the track of De Wet until he left them behind at the Modder, Lyttelton was using the numerous columns which were ready to his hand in effecting a drive up the south-eastern section of the Orange River Colony. It was disheartening to remember that all this large stretch of country had from April to November been as peaceful and almost as prosperous as Kent or Yorkshire. Now the intrusion of the guerrilla bands, and the pressure put by them upon the farmers, had raised the whole country once again, and the work of pacification had to be set about once more, with harsher measures than before. A continuous barrier of barbed-wire fencing had been erected from Bloemfontein to the Basuto border, a distance of eighty miles, and this was now strongly held by British posts. From the south Bruce Hamilton, Hickman, Thorneycroft, and Haig swept upwards, stripping the country as they went in the same way that French had done in the Eastern Transvaal, while Pilcher's column waited to the north of the barbed-wire barrier. It was known that Fourie, with a considerable commando, was lurking in this district, but he and his men slipped at night between the British columns and escaped. Pilcher, Bethune, and Byng were able, however, to send in 200 prisoners and very great numbers of cattle. On April 10th Monro, with Bethune's Mounted Infantry, captured eighty fighting Boers near Dewetsdorp, and sixty more were taken by a night attack at Boschberg. There is no striking victory to record in these operations, but they were an important part of that process of attrition which was wearing the Boers out and helping to bring the war to an end. Terrible it is to see that barren countryside, and to think of the depths of misery to which the once flourishing and happy Orange Free State had fallen, through joining in a quarrel with a nation which bore it nothing but sincere friendship and goodwill. With nothing to gain and everything to lose, the part played by the Orange Free State in this South African drama is one of the most inconceivable things in history. Never has a nation so deliberately and so causelessly committed suicide.

CHAPTER 33

The Northern Operations

(January to April, 1901)

Three consecutive chapters have now given some account of the campaign of De Wet, of the operations in the Transvaal up to the end of the year 1900, and of the invasion of Cape Colony up to April 1901. The present chapter will deal with the events in the Transvaal from the beginning of the new century. The military operations in that country, though extending over a very large area, may be roughly divided into two categories: the attacks by the Boers upon British posts, and the aggressive sweeping movements of British columns. Under the first heading come the attacks on Belfast, on Zuurfontein, on Kaalfontein, on Zeerust, on Modderfontein, and on Lichtenburg, besides many minor affairs. The latter comprises the operations of Babington and of Cunningham to the west and south-west of Pretoria, those of Methuen still further to the south-west, and the large movement of French in the south-east. In no direction did the British forces in the field meet with much active resistance. So long as they moved the gnats did not settle; it was only when quiet that they buzzed about and occasionally stung.

The early days of January 1901 were not fortunate for the British arms, as the check in which Kitchener's Bodyguard was so roughly handled, near Lindley, was closely followed by a brisk action at Naauwpoort or Zandfontein, near the Magaliesberg, in which De la Rey left his mark upon the Imperial Light Horse. The Boer commandos, having been driven into the mountains by French and Clements in the latter part of December, were still on the look-out to strike a blow at any British force which might expose itself. Several mounted columns had been formed to scour the country, one under Kekewich, one under Gordon, and one under Babington. The two latter, meeting in a mist upon the morning of January 5th, actually turned their rifles upon each other, but fortunately without any casualties resulting. A more deadly *rencontre* was, however, awaiting them.

A force of Boers were observed, as the mist cleared, making for a ridge which would command the road along which the convoy and guns were moving. Two squadrons (B and C) of the Light Horse were instantly detached to seize the point. They do not appear to have realised that they were in the immediate presence of the enemy, and they imagined that the ground over which they were passing had been already reconnoitred by a troop of the 14th Hussars. It is true that four scouts were thrown forward, but as both squadrons were cantering there was no time for these to get ahead. Presently C squadron, which was behind, was ordered to close up upon the left of B squadron, and the 150 horsemen in one long line swept over a low grassy ridge. Some hundreds of De la Rey's men were lying in the long grass upon the further side, and their first volley, fired at a fifty-yard range, emptied a score of saddles. It would have been wiser, if less gallant, to retire at once in the presence of a numerous and invisible enemy, but the survivors were ordered to dismount and return the fire. This was done, but the hail of bullets was terrific and the casualties were numerous. Captain Norman, of C squadron, then retired his men, who withdrew in good order. B squadron having lost Yockney, its brave leader, heard no order, so they held their ground until few of them had escaped the driving sleet of lead. Many of the men were struck three and four times. There was no surrender, and the extermination of B company added another laurel, even at a moment of defeat, to the regiment whose reputation was so grimly upheld. The Boer victors walked in among the litter of stricken men and horses.

> Practically all of them were dressed in khaki and had the water-bottles and haversacks of our soldiers. One of them snatched a bayonet from a dead man, and was about to despatch one of our wounded when he was stopped in the nick of time by a man in a black suit, who, I afterwards heard, was De la Rey himself... The feature of the action was the incomparable heroism of our dear old Colonel Wools-Sampson.

So wrote a survivor of B company, himself shot through the body. It was four hours before a fresh British advance reoccupied the ridge, and by that time the Boers had disappeared. Some seventy killed and wounded, many of them terribly mutilated, were found on the scene of the disaster. It is certainly a singular coincidence that at distant points of the seat of war two of the crack irregular corps should have suffered so severely within three days of each other. In each case, however, their prestige was enhanced rather than lowered by the result. These incidents tend, however, to shake the belief that scouting is better performed in the Colonial than in the regular forces.

Of the Boer attacks upon British posts to which allusion has been made, that upon Belfast, in the early morning of January 7th, appears to have been very gallantly and even desperately pushed. On the same date a number of smaller attacks, which may have been meant simply as diversions, were made upon Wonderfontein, Nooitgedacht, Wildfontein, Pan, Dalmanutha, and Machadodorp. These seven separate attacks, occurring simultaneously over sixty miles, show that the Boer forces were still organised and under one effective control. The general object of the operations was undoubtedly to cut Lord Roberts's communications upon that side and to destroy a considerable section of the railway.

The town of Belfast was strongly held by Smith-Dorrien, with 1750 men, of which 1300 were infantry belonging to the Royal Irish, the Shropshires, and the Gordons. The perimeter of defence, however, was fifteen miles, and each little fort too far from its neighbour for mutual support, though connected with headquarters by telephone. It is probable that the leaders and burghers engaged in this very gallant attack were in part the same as those concerned in the successful attempt at Helvetia upon December 29th, for the assault was delivered in the same way, at the same hour, and apparently with the same primary object. This was to gain possession of the big 5-inch gun, which is as helpless by night as it is formidable by day. At Helvetia they attained their object and even succeeded not merely in destroying, but in removing their gigantic trophy. At Belfast they would have performed the same feat had it not been for the foresight of General Smith-Dorrien, who had the heavy gun trundled back into the town every night.

The attack broke first upon Monument Hill, a post held by Captain Fosbery with eighty-three Royal Irish. Chance or treason guided the Boers to the weak point of the wire entanglement and they surged into the fort, where the garrison fought desperately to hold its own. There was thick mist and driving rain; and the rush of vague and shadowy figures amid the gloom was the first warning of the onslaught. The Irishmen were overborne by a swarm of assailants, but they nobly upheld their traditional reputation. Fosbery met his death like a gallant gentleman, but not more heroically than Barry, the humble private, who, surrounded by Boers, thought neither of himself nor of them, but smashed at the maxim gun with a pickaxe until he fell riddled with bullets. Half the garrison were on the ground before the post was carried.

A second post upon the other side of the town was defended by Lieutenant Marshall with twenty men, mostly Shropshires. For an hour they held out until Marshall and nine out of his twelve Shropshires had been hit. Then this post also was carried.

The Gordon Highlanders held two posts to the southeast and to the south-west of the town, and these also were vigorously attacked. Here, however, the advance spent itself without result. In vain the Ermelo and Carolina commandos stormed up to the Gordon pickets. They were blown back by the steady fire of the infantry. One small post manned by twelve Highlanders was taken, but the rest defied all attack. Seeing therefore that his attempt at a *coup-de-main* was a failure, Viljoen withdrew his men before daybreak. The Boer casualties have not been ascertained, but twenty-four of their dead were actually picked up within the British lines. The British lost sixty killed and wounded, while about as many were taken prisoners. Altogether the action was a brisk and a gallant one, of which neither side has cause to be ashamed. The simultaneous attacks upon six other stations were none of them pressed home, and were demonstrations rather than assaults.

The attempts upon Kaalfontein and on Zuurfontein were both made in the early morning of January 12th. These two places are small stations upon the line between Johannesburg and Pretoria. It is clear that the Boers were very certain of their own superior mobility before they ventured to intrude into the very heart of the British position, and the result showed that they were right in supposing that even if their attempt were repulsed, they would still be able to make good their escape. Better horsed, better riders, with better intelligence and a better knowledge of the country, their ventures were always attended by a limited liability.

The attacks seem to have been delivered by a strong commando, said to have been under the command of Beyers, upon its way to join the Boer concentration in the Eastern Transvaal. They had not the satisfaction, however, of carrying the garrison of a British post with them, for at each point they were met by a stout resistance and beaten off. Kaalfontein was garrisoned by 120 men of Cheshire under Williams-Freeman, Zuurfontein by as many Norfolks and a small body of Lincolns under Cordeaux and Atkinson. For six hours the pressure was considerable, the assailants of Kaalfontein keeping up a brisk shell and rifle fire, while those of Zuurfontein were without artillery. At the end of that time two armoured trains came up with reinforcements and the enemy continued his trek to the eastward. Knox 's 2nd cavalry brigade followed them up, but without any very marked result.

Zeerust and Lichtenburg had each been garrisoned and provisioned by Lord Methuen before he carried his column away to the south-west, where much rough and useful work awaited him. The two towns were at once invested by the enemy, who made an attack upon each of them. That upon Zeerust, on January 7th, was a small matter and easily repulsed. A more formidable one was made on Lichtenburg, on March 3rd. The attack was delivered by De la Rey, Smuts, and Celliers, with 1500 men, who galloped up to the pickets in the early morning. The defenders were 600 in number, consisting of Paget's Horse and three companies of the 1st battalion of the Northumberland Fusiliers, a veteran regiment with a long record of foreign service, not to be confused with that 2nd battalion which was so severely handled upon several occasions. It was well that it was so, for less sturdy material might have been overborne by the vigour of the attack. As it was, the garrison were driven to their last trench, but held out under a very heavy fire all day, and next morning the Boers abandoned the attack. Their losses appear to have been over fifty in number, and included Commandant Celliers, who was badly wounded and afterwards taken prisoner at Warm Baths. The brave garrison lost fourteen killed, including two officers of the Northumberlands, and twenty wounded.

In each of these instances the attacks by the Boers upon British posts had ended in a repulse to themselves. They were more fortunate, however, in their attempt upon Modderfontein on the Gatsrand at the end of January. The post was held by 200 of the South Wales Borderers, reinforced by the 59th Imperial Yeomanry, who had come in as escort to a convoy from Krugersdorp. The attack, which lasted all day, was carried out by a commando of 2000 Boers under Smuts, who rushed the position upon the following morning. As usual, the Boers, who were unable to retain their prisoners, had little to show for their success. The British casualties, however, were between thirty and forty, mostly wounded.

On January 22nd General Cunninghame left Oliphant's Nek with a small force consisting of the Border and Worcester Regiments, the 6th Mounted Infantry, Kitchener's Horse, 7th Imperial Yeomanry, 8th R.F.A., and P battery R.H.A. It had instructions to move south upon the enemy known to be gathering there. By midday this force was warmly engaged, and found itself surrounded by considerable bodies of De la Rey's burghers. That night they camped at Middelfontein, and were strongly attacked in the early morning. So menacing was the Boer attitude, and so formidable the position, that the force was in some danger. Fortunately they were in heliographic communication with Oliphant's Nek, and learned upon the 23rd that Babington had been ordered to their relief. All day Cunninghame's men were under a long-range fire, but on the 24th Babington appeared, and the British force was successfully extricated, having seventy-five casualties. This action of Middelfontein is interesting as having been begun in Queen Victoria's reign, and ended in that of Edward VII.

Cunninghame's force moved on to Krugersdorp, and there, having heard of the fall of the Modderfontein post as already described, a part of his command moved out to the Gatsrand in pursuit of Smuts. It was found, however, that the Boers had taken up a strong defensive position, and the British were not numerous enough to push the attack. On February 3rd Cunninghame endeavoured to outflank the enemy with his small cavalry force while pushing his infantry up in front, but in neither attempt did he succeed, the cavalry failing to find the flank, while the infantry were met with a fire which made further advance impossible. One company of the Border Regiment found itself in such a position that the greater part of it was killed, wounded, or taken. This check constituted the action of Modderfontein. On the 4th, however, Cunningham, assisted by some of the South African Constabulary, made his way round the flank, and dislodged the enemy, who retreated to the south. A few days later some of Smuts's men made an attempt upon the railway near Bank, but were driven off with twenty-six casualties. It was after this that Smuts moved west and joined De la Rey's commando to make the attack already described upon Lichtenburg. These six attempts represent the chief aggressive movements which the Boers made against British posts in the Transvaal during these months. Attacks upon trains were still common, and every variety of sniping appears to have been rife, from the legitimate ambuscade to something little removed from murder.

It has been described in a previous chapter how Lord Kitchener made an offer to the burghers which amounted to an amnesty, and how a number of those Boers who had come under the influence of the British formed themselves into peace committees, and endeavoured to convey to the fighting commandos some information as to the hopelessness of the struggle, and the lenient mood of the British. Unfortunately these well-meant offers appear to have been mistaken for signs of weakness by the Boer leaders, and encouraged them to harden their hearts. Of the delegates who conveyed the terms to their fellow countrymen two at least were shot, several were condemned to death, and few returned without ill-usage. In no case did they bear back a favourable answer. The only result of the proclamation was to burden the British resources by an enormous crowd of women and children who were kept and fed in refugee camps, while their fathers and husbands continued in most cases to fight.

This allusion to the peace movement among the burghers may serve as an introduction to the attempt made by Lord Kitchener, at the end of February 1901, to bring the war to a close by negotiation. Throughout its course the fortitude of Great Britain and of the Empire had never for an instant weakened, but her conscience had always been sensitive at the sight of the ruin which had befallen so large a portion of South Africa, and any settlement would have been eagerly hailed which would insure that the work done had not been wasted, and would not need to be done again. A peace on any other terms would simply shift upon the shoulders of our descendants those burdens which we were not manly enough to bear ourselves. There had arisen, as has been said, a considerable peace movement among the burghers of the refugee camps and also among the prisoners of war. It was hoped that some reflection of this might be found among the leaders of the people. To find out if this were so Lord Kitchener, at the end of February, sent a verbal message to Louis Botha, and on the 27th of that month the Boer general rode with an escort of Hussars into Middelburg. 'Sunburned, with a pleasant, fattish face of a German type, and wearing an imperial,' says one who rode beside him. Judging from the sounds of mirth heard by those without, the two leaders seem to have soon got upon amiable terms, and there was hope that a definite settlement might spring from their interview. From the beginning Lord Kitchener explained that the continued independence of the two republics was an impossibility. But on every other point the British Government was prepared to go great lengths in order to satisfy and conciliate the burghers.

On March 7th Lord Kitchener wrote to Botha from Pretoria, recapitulating the points which he had advanced. The terms offered were certainly as far as, and indeed rather further than, the general sentiment of the Empire would have gone. If the Boers laid down their arms there was to be a complete amnesty, which was apparently to extend to rebels also so long as they did not return to Cape Colony or Natal. Self-government was promised after a necessary interval, during which the two States should be administered as Crown colonies. Law courts should be independent of the Executive from the beginning, and both languages be official. A million pounds of compensation would be paid to the burghers—a most remarkable example of a war indemnity being paid by the victors. Loans were promised to the farmers to restart them in business, and a pledge was made that farms should not be taxed. The Kaffirs were not to have the franchise, but were to have the protection of law. Such were the generous terms offered by the British Government. Public opinion at home, strongly supported by that of the colonies, and especially of the army, felt that the extreme step had been taken in the direction of conciliation, and that to do more would seem not to offer peace, but to implore it. Unfortunately, however, the one thing which the British could not offer was the one thing which the Boers would insist upon having, and the leniency of the proposals in all other directions may have suggested weakness to their minds. On March 15th an answer was returned by General Botha to the effect that nothing short of total independence would satisfy them, and the negotiations were accordingly broken off.

There was a disposition, however, upon the Boer side to renew them, and upon May 10th General Botha applied to Lord Kitchener for permission to cable to President Kruger, and to take his advice as to the making of peace. The stern old man at The Hague was still, however, in an unbending mood. His reply was to the effect that there were great hopes of a successful issue of the war, and that he had taken steps to make proper provision for the Boer prisoners and for the refugee women. These steps, and very efficient ones too, were to leave them entirely to the generosity of that Government which he was so fond of reviling.

On the same day upon which Botha applied for leave to use the British cable, a letter was written by Reitz, State Secretary of the Transvaal, to Steyn, in which the desperate condition of the Boers was clearly set forth. This document explained that the burghers were continually surrendering, that the ammunition was nearly exhausted, the food running low, and the nation in danger of extinction. 'The time has come to take the final step,' said the Secretary of State. Steyn wrote back a reply in which, like his brother president, he showed a dour resolution to continue the struggle, prompted by a fatalist conviction that some outside interference would reverse the result of his appeal to arms. His attitude and that of Kruger determined the Boer leaders to hold out for a few more months, a resolution which may have been injudicious, but was certainly heroic. 'It's a fight to a finish this time,' said the two combatants in the 'Punch' cartoon which marked the beginning of the war. It was indeed so, as far as the Boers were concerned. As the victors we can afford to acknowledge that no nation in history has ever made a more desperate and prolonged resistance against a vastly superior antagonist. A Briton may well pray that his own people may be as staunch when their hour of adversity comes round.

The British position at this stage of the war was strengthened by a greater centralisation. Garrisons of outlying towns were withdrawn so that fewer convoys became necessary. The population was removed also and placed near the railway lines, where they could be more easily fed. In this way the scene of action was cleared and the Boer and British forces left face to face. Convinced of the failure of the peace policy, and morally strengthened by having tried it, Lord Kitchener set himself to finish the war by a series of vigorous operations which should sweep the country from end to end. For this purpose mounted troops were essential, and an appeal from him for reinforcements was most nobly answered. Five thousand horsemen were despatched from the colonies, and twenty thousand cavalry, mounted infantry, and Yeomanry were sent from home. Ten thousand mounted men had already been raised in Great Britain, South Africa, and Canada for the Constabulary force which was being organised by Baden-Powell. Altogether the reinforcements of horsemen amounted to more than thirty-five thousand men, all of whom had arrived in South Africa before the end of April. With the remains of his old regiments Lord Kitchener had under him at this final period of the war between fifty and sixty thousand cavalry—such a force as no British General in his happiest dream had ever thought of commanding, and no British war minister in his darkest nightmare had ever imagined himself called upon to supply.

Long before his reinforcements had come to hand, while his Yeomanry was still gathering in long queues upon the London pavement to wait their turn at the recruiting office, Lord Kitchener had dealt the enemy several shrewd blows which materially weakened their resources in men and material. The chief of these was the great drive down the Eastern Transvaal undertaken by seven columns under the command of French. Before considering this, however, a few words must be devoted to the doings of Methuen in the south-west.

This hard-working General, having garrisoned Zeerust and Lichtenburg, had left his old district and journeyed with a force which consisted largely of Bushmen and Yeomanry to the disturbed parts of Bechuanaland which had been invaded by De Villiers. Here he cleared the country as far as Vryburg, which he had reached in the middle of January, working round to Kuruman and thence to Taungs. From Taungs his force crossed the Transvaal border and made for Klerksdorp, working through an area which had never been traversed and which contained the difficult Masakani hills. He left Taungs upon February 2nd, fighting skirmishes at Uitval's Kop, Paardefontein and Lilliefontein, in each of which the enemy was brushed aside. Passing through Wolmaranstad, Methuen turned to the north, where at Haartebeestefontein, on February 19th, he fought a brisk engagement with a considerable force of Boers under De Villiers and Liebenberg. On the day before the fight he successfully outwitted the Boers, for, learning that they had left their *laager* in order to take up a position for battle, he pounced upon the *laager* and captured 10,000 head of cattle, forty-three wagons, and forty prisoners. Stimulated by this success, he attacked the Boers next day, and after five hours of hard fighting forced the pass which they were holding against him. As Methuen had but 1500 men, and was attacking a force which was as large as his own in a formidable position, the success was a very creditable one. The Yeomanry all did well, especially the 5th and 10th battalions. So also did the Australians and the Loyal North Lancashires. The British casualties amounted to sixteen killed and thirty-four wounded, while the Boers left eighteen of their dead upon the position which they had abandoned. Lord Methuen's little force returned to Klerksdorp, having deserved right well of their country. From Klerksdorp Methuen struck back westwards to the south of his former route, and on March 14th he was reported at Warrenton. Here also in April came Erroll's small column, bringing with it the garrison and inhabitants of Hoopstad, a post which it had been determined, in accordance with Lord Kitchener's policy of centralisation, to abandon.

In the month of January, 1901, there had been a considerable concentration of the Transvaal Boers into that large triangle which is bounded by the Delagoa railway line upon the north, the Natal railway line upon the south, and the Swazi and Zulu frontiers upon the east. The bush-*veldt* is at this season of the year unhealthy both for man and beast, so that for the sake of their herds, their families, and themselves the burghers were constrained to descend into the open *veldt*. There seemed the less objection to their doing so since this tract of country, though traversed once both by Buller and by French, had still remained a stronghold of the Boers and a storehouse of supplies. Within its borders are to be found Carolina, Ermelo, Vryheid, and other storm centres. Its possession offers peculiar strategical advantages, as a force lying there can always attack either railway, and might even make, as was indeed intended, a descent into Natal. For these mingled reasons of health and of strategy a considerable number of burghers united in this district under the command of the Bothas and of Smuts.

Their concentration had not escaped the notice of the British military authorities, who welcomed any movement which might bring to a focus that resistance which had been so nebulous and elusive. Lord Kitchener having once seen the enemy fairly gathered into this huge cover, undertook the difficult task of driving it from end to end. For this enterprise General French was given the chief command, and had under his orders no fewer than seven columns, which started from different points of the Delagoa and of the Natal railway lines, keeping in touch with each other and all trending south and east. A glance at the map would show, however, that it was a very large field for seven guns, and that it would need all their alertness to prevent the driven game from breaking back. Three columns started from the Delagoa line, namely, Smith-Dorrien's from Wonderfontein (the most easterly), Campbell's from Middelburg, and Alderson's from Eerstefabrieken, close to Pretoria. Four columns came from the western railway line: General Knox's from Kaalfontein, Major Allenby's from Zuurfontein (both stations between Pretoria and Johannesburg), General Dartnell's from Springs, close to Johannesburg, and finally General Colville (not to be confused with Colvile) from Greylingstad in the south. The whole movement resembled a huge drag net, of which Wonderfontein and Greylingstad formed the ends, exactly one hundred miles apart. On January 27th the net began to be drawn. Some thousands of Boers with a considerable number of guns were known to be within the enclosure, and it was hoped that even if their own extreme mobility enabled them to escape it would be impossible for them to save their transport and their cannon.

Each of the British columns was about 2000 strong, making a total of 14,000 men with about fifty guns engaged in the operations. A front of not less than ten miles was to be maintained by each force. The first decided move was on the part of the extreme left wing, Smith-Dorrien's column, which moved south on Carolina, and thence on Bothwell near Lake Chrissie. The arduous duty of passing supplies down from the line fell mainly upon him, and his force was in consequence larger than the others, consisting of 8500 men with thirteen guns. On the arrival of Smith-Dorrien at Carolina the other columns started, their centre of advance being Ermelo. Over seventy miles of *veldt* the gleam of the helio by day and the flash of the signal lamps at night marked the steady flow of the British tide. Here and there the columns came in touch with the enemy and swept him before them. French had a skirmish at Wilge River at the end of January, and Campbell another south of Middelburg, in which he had twenty casualties. On February 4th Smith-Dorrien was at Lake Chrissie; French had passed through Bethel and the enemy was retiring on Amsterdam. The hundred-mile ends of the drag net were already contracted to a third of that distance, and the game was still known to be within it. On the 5th Ermelo was occupied, and the fresh deep ruts upon the *veldt* told the British horsemen of the huge Boer convoy that was ahead of them. For days enormous herds, endless flocks, and lines of wagons which stretched from horizon to horizon had been trekking eastward. Cavalry and mounted infantry were all hot upon the scent.

Botha, however, was a leader of spirit, not to be hustled with impunity. Having several thousand burghers with him, it was evident that if he threw himself suddenly upon any part of the British line he might hope for a time to make an equal fight, and possibly to overwhelm it. Were Smith-Dorrien out of the way there would be a clear road of escape for his whole convoy to the north, while a defeat of any of the other columns would not help him much. It was on Smith-Dorrien, therefore, that he threw himself with great impetuosity. That General's force was, however, formidable, consisting of the Suffolks, West Yorks and Camerons, 5th Lancers, 2nd Imperial Light Horse, and 3rd Mounted Infantry, with eight field guns and three heavy pieces. Such a force could hardly be defeated in the open, but no one can foresee the effect of a night surprise well pushed home, and such was the attack delivered by Botha at 3 a.m. upon February 6th, when his opponent was encamped at Bothwell Farm.

The night was favourable to the attempt, as it was dark and misty. Fortunately, however, the British commander had fortified himself and was ready for an assault. The Boer forlorn hope came on with a gallant dash, driving a troop of loose horses in upon the outposts, and charging forward into the camp. The West Yorkshires, however, who bore the brunt of the attack, were veterans of the Tugela, who were no more to be flurried at three in the morning than at three in the afternoon. The attack was blown backwards, and twenty dead Boers, with their brave leader Spruyt, were left within the British lines. The main body of the Boers contented themselves with a heavy fusillade out of the darkness, which was answered and crushed by the return fire of the infantry. In the morning no trace, save their dead, was to be seen of the enemy, but twenty killed and fifty wounded in Smith-Dorrien's column showed how heavy had been the fire which had swept through the sleeping camp. The Carolina attack, which was to have co-operated with that of the Heidelbergers, was never delivered, through difficulties of the ground, and considerable recriminations ensued among the Boers in consequence.

Beyond a series of skirmishes and rearguard actions this attack of Botha's was the one effort made to stay the course of French's columns. It did not succeed, however, in arresting them for an hour. From that day began a record of captures of men, herds, guns, and wagons, as the fugitives were rounded up from the north, the west, and the south. The operation was a very thorough one, for the towns and districts occupied were denuded of their inhabitants, who were sent into the refugee camps while the country was laid waste to prevent its furnishing the commandos with supplies in the future. Still moving south-east, General French's columns made their way to Piet Retief upon the Swazi frontier, pushing a disorganised array which he computed at 5000 in front of them. A party of the enemy, including the Carolina commando, had broken back in the middle of February and Louis Botha had got away at the same time, but so successful were his main operations that French was able to report his total results at the end of the month as being 292 Boers killed or wounded, 500 surrendered, 3 guns and one maxim taken, with 600 rifles, 4000 horses, 4500 trek oxen, 1300 wagons and carts, 24,000 cattle, and 165,000 sheep. The whole vast expanse of the eastern *veldt* was dotted with the broken and charred wagons of the enemy.

Tremendous rains were falling and the country was one huge quagmire, which crippled although it did not entirely prevent the further operations. All the columns continued to report captures. On March 3rd Dartnell got a maxim and 50 prisoners, while French reported 50 more, and Smith-Dorrien 80. On March 6th French captured two more guns, and on the 14th he reported 46 more Boer casualties and 146 surrenders, with 500 more wagons, and another great haul of sheep and oxen. By the end of March French had moved as far south as Vryheid, his troops having endured the greatest hardships from the continual heavy rains, and the difficulty of bringing up any supplies. On the 27th he reported seventeen more Boer casualties and 140 surrenders, while on the last day of the month he took another gun and two pom-poms. The enemy at that date were still retiring eastward, with Alderson and Dartnell pressing upon their rear. On April 4th French announced the capture of the last piece of artillery which the enemy possessed in that region. The rest of the Boer forces doubled back at night between the columns and escaped over the Zululand border, where 200 of them surrendered. The total trophies of French's drive down the Eastern Transvaal amounted to eleven hundred of the enemy killed, wounded, or taken, the largest number in any operation since the surrender of Prinsloo. There is no doubt that the movement would have been even more successful had the weather been less boisterous, but this considerable loss of men, together with the capture of all the guns in that region, and of such enormous quantities of wagons, munitions, and stock, inflicted a blow upon the Boers from which they never wholly recovered. On April 20th French was back in Johannesburg once more.

While French had run to earth the last Boer gun in the south-eastern corner of the Transvaal, De la Rey, upon the western side, had still managed to preserve a considerable artillery with which he flitted about the passes of the Magaliesberg or took refuge in the safe districts to the south-west of it. This part of the country had been several times traversed, but had never been subdued by British columns. The Boers, like their own *veldt* grass, need but a few sparks to be left behind to ensure a conflagration breaking out again. It was into this inflammable country that Babington moved in March with Klerksdorp for his base. On March 21st he had reached Haartebeestefontein, the scene not long before of a successful action by Methuen. Here he was joined by Shekleton's Mounted Infantry, and his whole force consisted of these, with the 1st Imperial Light Horse, the 6th Imperial Bushmen, the New Zealanders, a squadron of the 14th Hussars, a wing each of the Somerset Light Infantry and of the Welsh Fusiliers, with Carter's guns and four pom-poms. With this mobile and formidable little force Babington pushed on in search of Smuts and De la Rey, who were known to be in the immediate neighbourhood.

As a matter of fact the Boers were not only there, but were nearer and in greater force than had been anticipated. On the 22nd three squadrons of the Imperial Light Horse under Major Briggs rode into 1500 of them, and it was only by virtue of their steadiness and gallantry that they succeeded in withdrawing themselves and their pom-pom without a disaster. With Boers in their front and Boers on either flank they fought an admirable rearguard action. So hot was the fire that A squadron alone had twenty-two casualties. They faced it out, however, until their gun had reached a place of safety, when they made an orderly retirement towards Babington's camp, having inflicted as heavy a loss as they had sustained. With Elandslaagte, Wagon Hill, the relief of Mafeking, Naauwpoort, and Haartebeestefontein upon their standards, the Imperial Light Horse, should they take a permanent place in the Army List, will start with a record of which many older regiments might be proud.

If the Light Horse had a few bad hours on March 22nd at the hands of the Boers, they and their colonial comrades were soon able to return the same with interest. On March 23rd Babington moved forward through Kafir Kraal, the enemy falling back before him. Next morning the British again advanced, and as the New Zealanders and Bushmen, who formed the vanguard under Colonel Gray, emerged from a pass they saw upon the plain in front of them the Boer force with all its guns moving towards them. Whether this was done of set purpose or whether the Boers imagined that the British had turned and were intending to pursue them cannot now be determined, but whatever the cause it is certain that for almost the first time in the campaign a considerable force of each side found themselves in the open and face to face.

It was a glorious moment. Setting spurs to their horses, officers and men with a yell dashed forward at the enemy. One of the Boer guns unlimbered and attempted to open fire, but was overwhelmed by the wave of horsemen. The Boer riders broke and fled, leaving their artillery to escape as best it might. The guns dashed over the *veldt* in a mad gallop, but wilder still was the rush of the fiery cavalry behind them. For once the brave and cool-headed Dutchmen were fairly panic-stricken. Hardly a shot was fired at the pursuers, and the riflemen seem to have been only too happy to save their own skins. Two field guns, one pom-pom, six maxims, fifty-six wagons and 140 prisoners were the fruits of that one magnificent charge, while fifty-four stricken Boers were picked up after the action. The pursuit was reluctantly abandoned when the spent horses could go no farther.

While the vanguard had thus scattered the main body of the enemy a detachment of riflemen had ridden round to attack the British rear and convoy. A few volleys from the escort drove them off, however, with some loss. Altogether, what with the loss of nine guns and of at least 200 men, the rout of Haartebeestefontein was a severe blow to the Boer cause. A week or two later Sir H. Rawlinson's column, acting with Babington, rushed Smuts's *laager* at daylight and effected a further capture of two guns and thirty prisoners. Taken in conjunction with French's successes in the east and Plumer's in the north, these successive blows might have seemed fatal to the Boer cause, but the weary struggle was still destined to go on until it seemed that it must be annihilation rather than incorporation which would at last bring a tragic peace to those unhappy lands.

All over the country small British columns had been operating during these months—operations which were destined to increase in scope and energy as the cold weather drew in. The weekly tale of prisoners and captures, though small for any one column, gave the aggregate result of a considerable victory. In these scattered and obscure actions there was much good work which can have no reward save the knowledge of duty done. Among many successful raids and skirmishes may be mentioned two by Colonel Park from Lydenburg, which resulted between them in the capture of nearly 100 of the enemy, including Abel Erasmus of sinister reputation. Nor would any summary of these events be complete without a reference to the very gallant defence of Mahlabatini in Zululand, which was successfully held by a handful of police and civilians against an irruption of the Boers. With the advent of winter and of reinforcements the British operations became very energetic in every part of the country, and some account of them will now be added.

CHAPTER 34

The Winter Campaign

(April to September, 1901)

The African winter extends roughly from April to September, and as the grass during that period would be withered on the *veldt*, the mobility of the Boer commandos must be very much impaired. It was recognised therefore that if the British would avoid another year of war it could only be done by making good use of the months which lay before them. For this reason Lord Kitchener had called for the considerable reinforcements which have been already mentioned, but on the other hand he was forced to lose many thousands of his veteran Yeomanry, Australians, and Canadians, whose term of service was at an end. The volunteer companies of the infantry returned also to England, and so did nine militia battalions, whose place was taken however by an equal number of new-comers.

The British position was very much strengthened during the winter by the adoption of the block-house system. These were small square or hexagonal buildings, made of stone up to nine feet with corrugated iron above it. They were loopholed for musketry fire and held from six to thirty men. These little forts were dotted along the railways at points not more than 2000 yards apart, and when supplemented by a system of armoured trains they made it no easy matter for the Boers to tamper with or to cross the lines. So effective did these prove that their use was extended to the more dangerous portions of the country, and lines were pushed through the Magaliesberg district to form a chain of posts between Krugersdorp and Rustenburg. In the Orange River Colony and on the northern lines of the Cape Colony the same system was extensively applied. I will now attempt to describe the more important operations of the winter, beginning with the incursion of Plumer into the untrodden ground to the north.

At this period of the war the British forces had overrun, if they had not subdued, the whole of the Orange River Colony and every part of the Transvaal which is south of the Mafeking-Pretoria-Komati line. Through this great tract of country there was not a village and hardly a farmhouse which had not seen the invaders. But in the north there remained a vast district, two hundred miles long and three hundred broad, which had hardly been touched by the war. It is a wild country, scrub-covered, antelope-haunted plains rising into desolate hills, but there are many *kloofs* and valleys with rich water meadows and lush grazings, which formed natural granaries and depots for the enemy. Here the Boer government continued to exist, and here, screened by their mountains, they were able to organise the continuation of the struggle. It was evident that there could be no end to the war until these last centres of resistance had been broken up.

The British forces had advanced as far north as Rustenburg in the west, Pienaar in the centre, and Lydenburg in the east, but here they had halted, unwilling to go farther until their conquests had been made good behind them. A General might well pause before plunging his troops into that vast and rugged district, when an active foe and an exposed line of communication lay for many hundreds of miles to the south of them. But Lord Kitchener with characteristic patience waited for the right hour to come, and then with equally characteristic audacity played swiftly and boldly for his stake. De Wet, impotent for the moment, had been hunted back over the Orange River. French had harried the burghers in the South-east Transvaal, and the main force of the enemy was known to be on that side of the seat of war. The north was exposed, and with one long, straight lunge to the heart, Pietersburg might be transfixed.

There could only be one direction for the advance, and that must be along the Pretoria to Pietersburg railroad. This is the only line of rails which leads to the north, and as it was known to be in working order (the Boers were running a bi-weekly service from Pietersburg to Warm Baths), it was hoped that a swift advance might seize it before any extensive damage could be done. With this object a small but very mobile force rapidly assembled at the end of March at Pienaar River, which was the British rail-head forty miles north of Pretoria and a hundred and thirty from Pietersburg. This column consisted of the Bush-*veldt* Carabineers, the 4th Imperial Bushmen's Corps, and the 6th New Zealand contingent. With them were the 18th battery R.F.A., and three pom-poms. A detachment of the invaluable mounted Sappers rode with the force, and two infantry regiments, the 2nd Gordons and the Northamptons, were detached to garrison the more vulnerable places upon the line of advance.

Upon March 29th the untiring Plumer, called off from the chase of De Wet, was loosed upon this fresh line, and broke swiftly away to the north. The complete success of his undertaking has obscured our estimate of its danger, but it was no light task to advance so great a distance into a bitterly hostile country with a fighting force of 2000 rifles. As an enterprise it was in many ways not unlike Mahon's dash on Mafeking, but without any friendly force with which to join hands at the end. However from the beginning all went well. On the 30th the force had reached Warm Baths, where a great isolated hotel already marks the site of what will be a rich and fashionable spa. On April 1st the Australian scouts rode into Nylstroom, fifty more miles upon their way. There had been sufficient sniping to enliven the journey, but nothing which could be called an action. Gleaning up prisoners and refugees as they went, with the railway engineers working like bees behind them, the force still swept unchecked upon its way. On April 5th Piet Potgietersrust was entered, another fifty-mile stage, and on the morning of the 8th the British vanguard rode into Pietersburg. Kitchener's judgment and Plumer's energy had met with their reward.

The Boer commando had evacuated the town and no serious opposition was made to the British entry. The most effective resistance came from a single schoolmaster, who, in a moment of irrational frenzy or of patriotic exaltation, shot down three of the invaders before he met his own death. Some rolling stock, one small gun, and something under a hundred prisoners were the trophies of the capture, but the Boer arsenal and the printing press were destroyed, and the Government sped off in a couple of Cape carts in search of some new capital. Pietersburg was principally valuable as a base from which a sweeping movement might be made from the north at the same moment as one from the south-east. A glance at the map will show that a force moving from this point in conjunction with another from Lydenburg might form the two crooked claws of a crab to enclose a great space of country, in which smaller columns might collect whatever was to be found. Without an instant of unnecessary delay the dispositions were made, and no fewer than eight columns slipped upon the chase. It will be best to continue to follow the movements of Plumer's force, and then to give some account of the little armies which were operating from the south, with the results of their enterprise.

It was known that Viljoen and a number of Boers were within the district which lies north of the line in the Middelburg district. An impenetrable bush-*veldt* had offered them a shelter from which they made their constant sallies to wreck a train or to attack a post. This area was now to be systematically cleared up. The first thing was to stop the northern line of retreat. The Oliphant River forms a loop in that direction, and as it is a considerable stream, it would, if securely held, prevent any escape upon that side. With this object Plumer, on April 14th, the sixth day after his occupation of Pietersburg, struck east from that town and trekked over the *veldt*, through the formidable Chunies Pass, and so to the north bank of the Oliphant, picking up thirty or forty Boer prisoners upon the way. His route lay through a fertile country dotted with native *kraals*. Having reached the river which marked the line which he was to hold, Plumer, upon April 17th, spread his force over many miles, so as to block the principal drifts. The flashes of his helio were answered by flash after flash from many points upon the southern horizon. What these other forces were, and whence they came, must now be made clear to the reader.

General Bindon Blood, a successful soldier, had confirmed in the Transvaal a reputation which he had won on the northern frontier of India. He and General Elliot were two of the late comers who had been spared from the great Eastern dependency to take the places of some of those Generals who had returned to England for a well-earned rest. He had distinguished himself by his systematic and effective guardianship of the Delagoa railway line, and he was now selected for the supreme control of the columns which were to advance from the south and sweep the Roos-Senekal district. There were seven of them, which were arranged as follows:

Two columns started from Middelburg under Beatson and Benson, which might be called the left wings of the movement. The object of Beatson's column was to hold the drifts of the Crocodile River, while Benson's was to seize the neighbouring hills called the Bothasberg. This it was hoped would pin the Boers from the west, while Kitchener from Lydenburg advanced from the east in three separate columns. Pulteney and Douglas would move up from Belfast in the centre, with Dulstoom for their objective. It was the familiar drag net of French, but facing north instead of south.

On April 13th the southern columns were started, but already the British preparations had alarmed the Boers, and Botha, with his main commandos, had slipped south across the line into that very district from which he had been so recently driven. Viljoen's commando still remained to the north, and the British troops, pouring in from every side, converged rapidly upon it. The success of the operations was considerable, though not complete. The Tantesberg, which had been the rallying-point of the Boers, was occupied, and Roos-Senekal, their latest capital, was taken, with their State papers and treasure. Viljoen, with a number of followers, slipped through between the columns, but the greater part of the burghers, dashing furiously about like a shoal of fish when they become conscious of the net, were taken by one or other of the columns. A hundred of the Boksburg commando surrendered en masse, fifty more were taken at Roos-Senekal; forty-one of the formidable Zarps with Schroeder, their leader, were captured in the north by the gallantry and wit of a young Australian officer named Reid; sixty more were hunted down by the indefatigable Vialls, leader of the Bushmen. From all parts of the district came the same story of captures and surrenders.

Knowing, however, that Botha and Viljoen had slipped through to the south of the railway line, Lord Kitchener determined to rapidly transfer the scene of the operations to that side. At the end of April, after a fortnight's work, during which this large district was cropped, but by no means shaved, the troops turned south again. The results of the operation had been eleven hundred prisoners, almost the same number as French had taken in the south-east, together with a broken Krupp, a pom-pom, and the remains of the big naval gun taken from us at Helvetia.

It was determined that Plumer's advance upon Pietersburg should not be a mere raid, but that steps should be taken to secure all that he had gained, and to hold the lines of communication. With this object the 2nd Gordon Highlanders and the 2nd Wiltshires were pushed up along the railroad, followed by Kitchener's Fighting Scouts. These troops garrisoned Pietersburg and took possession of Chunies Poort, and other strategic positions. They also furnished escorts for the convoys which supplied Plumer on the Oliphant River, and they carried out some spirited operations themselves in the neighbourhood of Pietersburg. Grenfell, who commanded the force, broke up several *laagers*, and captured a number of prisoners, operations in which he was much assisted by Colenbrander and his men. Finally the last of the great Creusot guns, the formidable Long Toms, was found mounted near Haenertsburg. It was the same piece which had in succession scourged Mafeking and Kimberley. The huge gun, driven to bay, showed its powers by opening an effective fire at ten thousand yards. The British galloped in upon it, the Boer riflemen were driven off, and the gun was blown up by its faithful gunners. So by suicide died the last of that iron brood, the four sinister brothers who had wrought much mischief in South Africa. They and their lesson will live in the history of modern artillery.

The sweeping of the Roos-Senekal district being over, Plumer left his post upon the River of the Elephants, a name which, like Rhenoster, Zeekoe, Kameelfontein, Leeuw Kop, Tigerfontein, Elands River, and so many more, serves as a memorial to the great mammals which once covered the land. On April 28th the force turned south, and on May 4th they had reached the railroad at Eerstefabrieken close to Pretoria. They had come in touch with a small Boer force upon the way, and the indefatigable Vialls hounded them for eighty miles, and tore away the tail of their convoy with thirty prisoners. The main force had left Pretoria on horseback on March 28th, and found themselves back once again upon foot on May 5th. They had something to show, however, for the loss of their horses, since they had covered a circular march of 400 miles, had captured some hundreds of the enemy, and had broken up their last organised capital. From first to last it was a most useful and well-managed expedition.

It is the more to be regretted that General Blood was recalled from his northern trek before it had attained its full results, because those operations to which he turned did not offer him any great opportunities for success. Withdrawing from the north of the railway with his columns, he at once started upon a sweep of that portion of the country which forms an angle between the Delagoa line and the Swazi frontier—the Barberton district. But again the two big fish, Viljoen and Botha, had slipped away, and the usual collection of sprats was left in the net. The sprats count also, however, and every week now telegrams were reaching England from Lord Kitchener which showed that from three to five hundred more burghers had fallen into our hands. Although the public might begin to look upon the war as interminable, it had become evident to the thoughtful observer that it was now a mathematical question, and that a date could already be predicted by which the whole Boer population would have passed into the power of the British.

Among the numerous small British columns which were at work in different parts of the country, in the latter half of May, there was one under General Dixon which was operating in the neighbourhood of the Magaliesberg Range. This locality has never been a fortunate one for the British arms. The country is peculiarly mountainous and broken, and it was held by the veteran De la Rey and a numerous body of irreconcilable Boers. Here in July we had encountered a check at Uitval's Nek, in December Clements had met a more severe one at Nooitgedacht, while shortly afterwards Cunningham had been repulsed at Middelfontein, and the Light Horse cut up at Naauwpoort. After such experiences one would have thought that no column which was not of overmastering strength would have been sent into this dangerous region, but General Dixon had as a matter of fact by no means a strong force with him. With 1600 men and a battery he was despatched upon a quest after some hidden guns which were said to have been buried in those parts.

On May 26th Dixon's force, consisting of Derbyshires, King's Own Scottish Borderers, Imperial Yeomanry, Scottish Horse, and six guns (four of 8th R.F.A. and two of 28th R.F.A.), broke camp at Naauwpoort and moved to the west. On the 28th they found themselves at a place called Vlakfontein, immediately south of Oliphant's Nek. On that day there were indications that there were a good many Boers in the neighbourhood. Dixon left a guard over his camp and then sallied out in search of the buried guns. His force was divided into three parts, the left column under Major Chance consisting of two guns of the 28th R.F.A., 230 of the Yeomanry, and one company of the Derbys. The centre comprised two guns (8th R.F. A.), one howitzer, two companies of the Scottish Borderers and one of the Derbys; while the right was made up of two guns (8th R.F.A.), 200 Scottish Horse, and two companies of Borderers. Having ascertained that the guns were not there, the force about midday was returning to the camp, when the storm broke suddenly and fiercely upon the rearguard.

There had been some sniping during the whole morning, but no indications of the determined attack which was about to be delivered. The force in retiring upon the camp had become divided, and the rearguard consisted of the small column under Major Chance which had originally formed the left wing. A *veldt* fire was raging on one flank of this rearguard, and through the veil of smoke a body of five hundred Boers charged suddenly home with magnificent gallantry upon the guns. We have few records of a more dashing or of a more successful action in the whole course of the war. So rapid was it that hardly any time elapsed between the glimpse of the first dark figures galloping through the haze and the thunder of their hoofs as they dashed in among the gunners. The Yeomanry were driven back and many of them shot down. The charge of the mounted Boers was supported by a very heavy fire from a covering party, and the gun-detachments were killed or wounded almost to a man. The lieutenant in charge and the sergeant were both upon the ground. So far as it is possible to reconstruct the action from the confused accounts of excited eye-witnesses and from the exceedingly obscure official report of General Dixon, there was no longer any resistance round the guns, which were at once turned by their captors upon the nearest British detachment.

The company of infantry which had helped to escort the guns proved however to be worthy representatives of that historic branch of the British service. They were northerners, men of Derbyshire and Nottingham, the same counties which had furnished the brave militia who had taken their punishment so gamely at Roodeval. Though hustled and broken they re-formed and clung doggedly to their task, firing at the groups of Boers who surrounded the guns. At the same time word had been sent of their pressing need to the Scotch Borderers and the Scottish Horse, who came swarming across the valley to the succour of their comrades. Dixon had brought two guns and a howitzer into action, which subdued the fire of the two captured pieces, and the infantry, Derbys and Borderers, swept over the position, retaking the two guns and shooting down those of the enemy who tried to stand. The greater number vanished into the smoke, which veiled their retreat as it had their advance. Forty-one of them were left dead upon the ground. Six officers and fifty men killed with about a hundred and twenty wounded made up the British losses, to which two guns would certainly have been added but for the gallant counter-attack of the infantry. With Dargai and Vlakfontein to their credit the Derbys have green laurels upon their war-worn colours. They share them on this occasion with the Scottish Borderers, whose volunteer company carried itself as stoutly as the regulars.

How is such an action to be summed up? To Kemp, the young Boer leader, and his men belongs the credit of the capture of the guns; to the British that of their recapture and of the final possession of the field. The British loss was probably somewhat higher than that of the Boers, but upon the other hand there could be no question as to which side could afford loss the better. The Briton could be replaced, but there were no reserves behind the fighting line of the Boers.

There is one subject which cannot be ignored in discussing this battle, however repugnant it may be. That is the shooting of some of the British wounded who lay round the guns. There is no question at all about the fact, which is attested by many independent witnesses. There is reason to hope that some of the murderers paid for their crimes with their lives before the battle was over. It is pleasant to add that there is at least one witness to the fact that Boer officers interfered with threats to prevent some of these outrages. It is unfair to tarnish the whole Boer nation and cause on account of a few irresponsible villains, who would be disowned by their own decent comrades. Very many—too many—British soldiers have known by experience what it is to fall into the hands of the enemy, and it must be confessed that on the whole they have been dealt with in no ungenerous spirit, while the British treatment of the Boers has been unexampled in all military history for its generosity and humanity. That so fair a tale should be darkened by such ruffianly outrages is indeed deplorable, but the incident is too well authenticated to be left unrecorded in any detailed account of the campaign. General Dixon, finding the Boers very numerous all round him, and being hampered by his wounded, fell back upon Naauwpoort, which he reached on June 1st.

In May, Sir Bindon Blood, having returned to the line to refit, made yet another cast through that thrice-harried belt of country which contains Ermelo, Bethel, and Carolina, in which Botha, Viljoen, and the fighting Boers had now concentrated. Working over the blackened *veldt* he swung round in the Barberton direction, and afterwards made a westerly drive in conjunction with small columns commanded by Walter Kitchener, Douglas, and Campbell of the Rifles, while Colville, Garnett, and Bullock co-operated from the Natal line. Again the results were disappointing when compared with the power of the instrument employed. On July

5th he reached Springs, near Johannesburg, with a considerable amount of stock, but with no great number of prisoners. The elusive Botha had slipped away to the south and was reported upon the Zululand border, while Viljoen had succeeded in crossing the Delagoa line and winning back to his old lair in the district north of Middelburg, from which he had been evicted in April. The commandos were like those pertinacious flies which buzz upwards when a hand approaches them, but only to settle again in the same place. One could but try to make the place less attractive than before.

Before Viljoen's force made its way over the line it had its revenge for the long harrying it had undergone by a well-managed night attack, in which it surprised and defeated a portion of Colonel Beatson's column at a place called Wilmansrust, due south of Middelburg, and between that town and Bethel. Beatson had divided his force, and this section consisted of 850 of the 5th Victorian Mounted Rifles, with thirty gunners and two pom-poms, the whole under the command of Major Morris. Viljoen's force trekking north towards the line came upon this detachment upon June 12th. The British were aware of the presence of the enemy, but do not appear to have posted any extra outposts or taken any special precautions. Long months of commando chasing had imbued them too much with the idea that these were fugitive sheep, and not fierce and wily wolves, whom they were endeavouring to catch. It is said that 700 yards separated the four pickets. With that fine eye for detail which the Boer leaders possess, they had started a *veldt* fire upon the west of the camp and then attacked from the east, so that they were themselves invisible while their enemies were silhouetted against the light. Creeping up between the pickets, the Boers were not seen until they opened fire at point-blank range upon the sleeping men. The rifles were stacked—another noxious military tradition—and many of the troopers were shot down while they rushed for their weapons. Surprised out of their sleep and unable to distinguish their antagonists, the brave Australians did as well as any troops could have done who were placed in so impossible a position. Captain Watson, the officer in charge of the pom-poms, was shot down, and it proved to be impossible to bring the guns into action. Within five minutes the Victorians had lost twenty killed and forty wounded, when the survivors surrendered. It is pleasant to add that they were very well treated by the victors, but the high-spirited colonials felt their reverse most bitterly. 'It is the worst thing that ever happened to Australia!' says one in the letter in which he describes it. The actual number of Boers who rushed the camp was only 180, but 400 more had formed a cordon round it. To Viljoen and his lieutenant Muller great credit must be given for this well-managed affair, which gave them a fresh supply of stores and clothing at a time when they were hard pressed for both. These same Boer officers had led the attack upon Helvetia where the 4.7 gun was taken. The victors succeeded in getting away with all their trophies, and having temporarily taken one of the blockhouses on the railway near Brugspruit, they crossed the line in safety and returned, as already said, to their old quarters in the north, which had been harried but not denuded by the operations of General Blood.

It would take a volume to catalogue, and a library to entirely describe the movements and doings of the very large number of British columns which operated over the Transvaal and the Orange River Colony during this cold-weather campaign. If the same columns and the same leaders were consistently working in the same districts, some system of narrative might enable the reader to follow their fortunes, but they were, as a matter of fact, rapidly transferred from one side of the field of action to another in accordance with the concentrations of the enemy. The total number of columns amounted to at least sixty, which varied in number from two hundred to two thousand, and seldom hunted alone. Could their movements be marked in red upon a chart, the whole of that huge district would be criss-crossed, from Taungs to Komati and from Touws River to Pietersburg, with the track of our weary but indomitable soldiers.

Without attempting to enter into details which would be unbecoming to the modesty of a single volume, one may indicate what the other more important groupings were during the course of these months, and which were the columns that took part in them. Of French's drive in the south-east, and of Blood's incursion into the Roos-Senekal district some account has been given, and of his subsequent sweeping of the south. At the same period Babington, Dixon, and Rawlinson were co-operating in the Klerksdorp district, though the former officer transferred his services suddenly to Blood's combination, and afterwards to Elliot's column in the north of Orange River Colony. Williams and Fetherstonhaugh came later to strengthen this Klerksdorp district, in which, after the clearing of the Magaliesberg, De la Rey had united his forces to those of Smuts. This very important work of getting a firm hold upon the Magaliesberg was accomplished in July by Barton, Allenby, Kekewich, and Lord Basing, who penetrated into the wild country and established blockhouses and small forts in very much the same way as Cumberland and Wade in 1746 held down the Highlands. The British position was much strengthened by the firm grip obtained of this formidable stronghold of the enemy, which was dangerous not only on account of its extreme strength, but also of its proximity to the centres of population and of wealth.

De la Rey, as already stated, had gone down to the Klerksdorp district, whence, for a time at least, he seems to have passed over into the north of the Orange River Colony. The British pressure at Klerksdorp had become severe, and thither in May came the indefatigable Methuen, whom we last traced to Warrenton. From this point on May 1st he railed his troops to Mafeking, whence he trekked to Lichtenburg, and south as far as his old fighting ground of Haartebeestefontein, having one skirmish upon the way and capturing a Boer gun. Thence he returned to Mafeking, where he had to bid adieu to those veteran Yeomanry who had been his comrades on so many a weary march. It was not their fortune to be present at any of the larger battles of the war, but few bodies of troops have returned to England with a finer record of hard and useful service.

No sooner, however, had Methuen laid down one weapon than he snatched up another. Having refitted his men and collected some of the more efficient of the new Yeomanry, he was off once more for a three weeks' circular tour in the direction of Zeerust. It is difficult to believe that the oldest inhabitant could have known more of the western side of the Transvaal, for there was hardly a track which he had not traversed or a *kopje* from which he had not been sniped. Early in August he had made a fresh start from Mafeking, dividing his force into two columns, the command of the second being given to Von Donop. Having joined hands with Fetherstonhaugh, he moved through the south-west and finally halted at Klerksdorp. The harried Boers moved a hundred miles north to Rustenburg, followed by Methuen, Fetherstonhaugh, Hamilton, Kekewich, and Allenby, who found the commandos of De la Rey and Kemp to be scattering in front of them and hiding in the *kloofs* and *dongas*, whence in the early days of September no less than two hundred were extracted. On September 6th and 8th Methuen engaged the main body of De la Rey in the valley of the Great Marico River which lies to the north-west of Rustenburg. In these two actions he pushed the Boers in front of him with a loss of eighteen killed and forty-one prisoners, but the fighting was severe, and fifteen of his men were killed and thirty wounded before the position had been carried. The losses were almost entirely among the newly raised Yeomanry, who had already shown on several occasions that, having shed their weaker members and had some experience of the field, they were now worthy to take their place beside their veteran comrades.

The only other important operation undertaken by the British columns in the Transvaal during this period was in the north, where Beyers and his men were still harried by Grenfell, Colenbrander, and Wilson. A considerable proportion of the prisoners which figured in the weekly lists came from this quarter. On May 30th there was a notable action, the truth of which was much debated but finally established, in which Kitchener's Scouts under Wilson surprised and defeated a Boer force under

Pretorius, killing and wounding several, and taking forty prisoners. On July 1st Grenfell took nearly a hundred of Beyers' men with a considerable convoy. North, south, east, and west the tale was ever the same, but so long as Botha, De la Rey, Steyn, and De Wet remained uncaptured, the embers might still at any instant leap into a flame.

It only remains to complete this synopsis of the movements of columns within the Transvaal that I should add that after the conclusion of Blood's movement in July, several of his columns continued to clear the country and to harass Viljoen in the Lydenburg and Dulstroom districts. Park, Kitchener, Spens, Beatson, and Benson were all busy at this work, never succeeding in forcing more than a skirmish, but continually whittling away wagons, horses, and men from that nucleus of resistance which the Boer leaders still held together.

Though much hampered by the want of forage for their horses, the Boers were ever watchful for an opportunity to strike back, and the long list of minor successes gained by the British was occasionally interrupted by a petty reverse. Such a one befell the small body of South African Constabulary stationed near Vereeniging, who encountered upon July 13th a strong force of Boers supposed to be the main commando of De Wet. The Constabulary behaved with great gallantry but were hopelessly outnumbered, and lost their seven-pounder gun, four killed, six wounded, and twenty-four prisoners. Another small reverse occurred at a far distant point of the seat of war, for the irregular corps known as Steinacker's Horse was driven from its position at Bremersdorp in Swaziland upon July 24th, and had to fall back sixteen miles, with a loss of ten casualties and thirty prisoners. Thus in the heart of a native state the two great white races of South Africa were to be seen locked in a desperate conflict. However unavoidable, the sight was certainly one to be deplored.

To the Boer credit, or discredit, are also to be placed those repeated train wreckings, which cost the British during this campaign the lives and limbs of many brave soldiers who were worthy of some less ignoble fate. It is true that the laws of war sanction such enterprises, but there is something indiscriminate in the results which is repellent to humanity, and which appears to justify the most energetic measures to prevent them. Women, children, and sick must all travel by these trains and are exposed to a common danger, while the assailants enjoy a safety which renders their exploit a peculiarly inglorious one. Two Boers, Trichardt and Hindon, the one a youth of twenty-two, the other a man of British birth, distinguished, or disgraced, themselves by this unsavoury work upon the Delagoa line, but with the extension of the blockhouse system the attempts became less successful. There was one, however, upon the northern line near Naboomspruit which cost the lives of Lieutenant Best and eight Gordon Highlanders, while ten were wounded. The party of Gordons continued to resist after the smash, and were killed or wounded to a man. The painful incident is brightened by such an example of military virtue, and by the naive reply of the last survivor, who on being questioned why he continued to fight until he was shot down, answered with fine simplicity, 'Because I am a Gordon Highlander.'

Another train disaster of an even more tragic character occurred near Waterval, fifteen miles north of Pretoria, upon the last day of August. The explosion of a mine wrecked the train, and a hundred Boers who lined the banks of the cutting opened fire upon the derailed carriages. Colonel Vandeleur, an officer of great promise, was killed and twenty men, chiefly of the West Riding regiment, were shot. Nurse Page was also among the wounded. It was after this fatal affair that the regulation of carrying Boer hostages upon the trains was at last carried out.

It has been already stated that part of Lord Kitchener's policy of concentration lay in his scheme for gathering the civil population into camps along the lines of communication. The reasons for this, both military and humanitarian, were overwhelming. Experience had proved that the men if left at liberty were liable to be persuaded or coerced by the fighting Boers into breaking their parole and rejoining the commandos. As to the women and children, they could not be left upon the farms in a denuded country. That the Boers in the field had no doubts as to the good treatment of these people was shown by the fact that they repeatedly left their families in the way of the columns so that they might be conveyed to the camps. Some consternation was caused in England by a report of Miss Hobhouse, which called public attention to the very high rate of mortality in some of these camps, but examination showed that this was not due to anything insanitary in their situation or arrangement, but to a severe epidemic of measles which had swept away a large number of the children. A fund was started in London to give additional comforts to these people, though there is reason to believe that their general condition was superior to that of the Uitlander refugees, who still waited permission to return to their homes. By the end of July there were no fewer than sixty thousand inmates of the camps in the Transvaal alone, and half as many in the Orange River Colony. So great was the difficulty in providing the supplies for so large a number that it became more and more evident that some at least of the camps must be moved down to the sea coast.

Passing to the Orange River Colony we find that during this winter period the same British tactics had been met by the same constant evasions on the part of the dwindling commandos. The Colony had been divided into four military districts: that of Bloemfontein, which was given to Charles Knox, that of Lyttelton at Springfontein, that of Rundle at Harrismith, and that of Elliot in the north. The latter was infinitely the most important, and Elliot, the warden of the northern marches, had under him during the greater part of the winter a mobile force of about 6000 men, commanded by such experienced officers as Broadwood, De Lisle, and Bethune. Later in the year Spens, Bullock, Plumer, and Rimington were all sent into the Orange River Colony to help to stamp out the resistance. Numerous skirmishes and snipings were reported from all parts of the country, but a constant stream of prisoners and of surrenders assured the soldiers that, in spite of the difficulty of the country and the obstinacy of the enemy, the term of their labours was rapidly approaching.

In all the petty and yet necessary operations of these columns, two incidents demand more than a mere mention. The first was a hard-fought skirmish in which some of Elliot's horsemen were engaged upon June 6th. His column had trekked during the month of May from Kroonstad to Harrismith, and then turning north found itself upon that date near the hamlet of Reitz. Major Sladen with 200 Mounted Infantry, when detached from the main body, came upon the track of a Boer convoy and ran it down. Over a hundred vehicles with forty-five prisoners were the fruits of their enterprise. Well satisfied with his morning's work, the British leader despatched a party of his men to convey the news to De Lisle, who was behind, while he established himself with his loot and his prisoners in a convenient *kraal*. Thence they had an excellent view of a large body of horsemen approaching them with scouts, flankers, and all military precautions. One warm-hearted officer seems actually to have sallied out to meet his comrades, and it was not till his greeting of them took the extreme form of handing over his rifle that the suspicion of danger entered the heads of his companions. But if there was some lack of wit there was none of heart in Sladen and his men. With forty-five Boers to hold down, and 500 under Fourie, De Wet, and De la Rey around them, the little band made rapid preparation for a desperate resistance: the prisoners were laid upon their faces, the men knocked loopholes in the mud walls of the *kraal*, and a blunt soldierly answer was returned to the demand for surrender.

But it was a desperate business. The attackers were five to one, and the five were soldiers of De Wet, the hard-bitten veterans of a hundred encounters. The captured wagons in a long double row stretched out over the plain, and under this cover the Dutchmen swarmed up to the *kraal*. But the men who faced them were veterans also, and the defence made up for the disparity of numbers. With fine courage the Boers made their way up to the village, and established themselves in the outlying huts, but the Mounted Infantry clung desperately to their position. Out of the few officers present Findlay was shot through the head, Moir and Cameron through the heart, and Strong through the stomach. It was a Wagon Hill upon a small scale, two dour lines of skirmishers emptying their rifles into each other at point-blank range. Once more, as at Bothaville, the British Mounted Infantry proved that when it came to a dogged pelting match they could stand punishment longer than their enemy. They suffered terribly. Fifty-one out of the little force were on the ground, and the survivors were not much more numerous than their prisoners. To the 1st Gordons, the 2nd Bedfords, the South Australians, and the New South Welsh men belongs the honour of this magnificent defence. For four hours the fierce battle raged, until at last the parched and powder-stained survivors breathed a prayer of thanks as they saw on the southern horizon the vanguard of De Lisle riding furiously to the rescue. For the last hour, since they had despaired of carrying the *kraal*, the Boers had busied themselves in removing their convoy; but now, for the second time in one day, the drivers found British rifles pointed at their heads, and the oxen were turned once more and brought back to those who had fought so hard to hold them. Twenty-eight killed and twenty-six wounded were the losses in this desperate affair. Of the Boers seventeen were left dead in front of the *kraal*, and the forty-five had not escaped from the bulldog grip which held them. There seems for some reason to have been no effective pursuit of the Boers, and the British column held on its way to Kroonstad.

The second incident which stands out amid the dreary chronicle of hustlings and snipings is the surprise visit paid by Broadwood with a small British column to the town of Reitz upon July 11th, which resulted in the capture of nearly every member of the late government of the Free State, save only the one man whom they particularly wanted. The column consisted of 200 yeomen, 200 of the 7th Dragoon Guards, and two guns. Starting at 11 p.m., the raiders rode hard all night and broke with the dawn upon the sleeping village. Racing into the main street, they secured the startled Boers as they rushed from the houses. It is easy to criticise such an operation from a distance, and to overlook the practical difficulties in the way, but on the face of it it seems a pity that the holes had not been stopped before the ferret was sent in. A picket at the farther end of the street would have barred Steyn's escape. As it was, he flung himself upon his horse and galloped half-clad out of the town. Sergeant Cobb of the Dragoons snapped a rifle at close quarters upon him, but the cold of the night had frozen the oil on the striker and the cartridge hung fire. On such trifles do the large events of history turn! Two Boer generals, two commandants, Steyn's brother, his secretary, and several other officials were among the nine-and-twenty prisoners. The treasury was also captured, but it is feared that the Yeomen and Dragoons will not be much the richer from their share of the contents.

Save these two incidents, the fight at Reitz and the capture of a portion of Steyn's government at the same place, the winter's campaign furnished little which was of importance, though a great deal of very hard and very useful work was done by the various columns under the direction of the governors of the four military districts. In the south General Bruce Hamilton made two sweeps, one from the railway line to the western frontier, and the second from the south and east in the direction of Petrusburg. The result of the two operations was about 300 prisoners. At the same time Monro and Hickman re-cleared the already twice-cleared districts of Rouxville and Smithfield. The country in the east of the Colony was verging now upon the state which Grant described in the Shenandoah Valley: 'A crow,' said he, 'must carry his own rations when he flies across it.'

In the middle district General Charles Knox, with the columns of Pine-Coffin, Thorneycroft, Pilcher, and Henry, were engaged in the same sort of work with the same sort of results.

The most vigorous operations fell to the lot of General Elliot, who worked over the northern and north-eastern district, which still contained a large number of fighting burghers. In May and June Elliot moved across to Vrede and afterwards down the eastern frontier of the Colony, joining hands at last with Rundle at Harrismith. He then worked his way back to Kroonstad through Reitz and Lindley. It was on this journey that Sladen's Mounted Infantry had the sharp experience which has been already narrated. Western's column, working independently, co-operated with Elliot in this clearing of the north-east. In August there were very large captures by Broadwood's force, which had attained considerable mobility, ninety miles being covered by it on one occasion in two days.

Of General Rundle there is little to be said, as he was kept busy in exploring the rough country in his own district—the same district which had been the scene of the operations against Prinsloo and the Fouriesburg surrender. Into this district Kritzinger and his men trekked after they were driven from the Colony in July, and many small skirmishes and snipings among the mountains showed that the Boer resistance was still alive.

July and August were occupied in the Orange River Colony by energetic operations of Spens' and Rimington's columns in the midland districts, and by a considerable drive to the north-eastern corner, which was shared by three columns under Elliot and two under Plumer, with one under Henry and several smaller bodies. A considerable number of prisoners and a large amount of stock were the result of the movement, but it was very evident that there was a waste of energy in the employment of such forces for such an end. The time appeared to be approaching when a strong force of military police stationed permanently in each district

416

might prove a more efficient instrument. One interesting development of this phase of the war was the enrolment of a burgher police among the Boers who had surrendered. These men—well paid, well mounted, and well armed—were an efficient addition to the British forces. The movement spread until before the end of the war there were several thousand burghers under such well-known officers as Celliers, Villonel, and young Cronje, fighting against their own guerrilla countrymen. Who, in 1899, could have prophesied such a phenomenon as that!

Lord Kitchener's proclamation issued upon August 9th marked one more turn in the screw upon the part of the British authorities. By it the burghers were warned that those who had not laid down their arms by September 15th would in the case of the leaders be banished, and in the case of the burghers be compelled to support their families in the refugee camps. As many of the fighting burghers were men of no substance, the latter threat did not affect them much, but the other, though it had little result at the time, may be useful for the exclusion of firebrands during the period of reconstruction. Some increase was noticeable in the number of surrenders after the proclamation, but on the whole it had not the result which was expected, and its expediency is very open to question. This date may be said to mark the conclusion of the winter campaign and the opening of a new phase in the struggle.

CHAPTER 35

The Guerilla Operations in Cape Colony

In the account which has been given in a preceding chapter of the invasion of Cape Colony by the Boer forces, it was shown that the Western bands were almost entirely expelled, or at least that they withdrew, at the time when De Wet was driven across the Orange River. This was at the beginning of March 1901. It was also mentioned that though the Boers evacuated the barren and unprofitable desert of the Karoo, the Eastern bands which had come with Kritzinger did not follow the same course, but continued to infest the mountainous districts of the Central Colony, whence they struck again and again at the railway lines, the small towns, British patrols, or any other quarry which was within their reach and strength. From the surrounding country they gathered a fair number of recruits, and they were able through the sympathy and help of the Dutch farmers to keep themselves well mounted and supplied. In small wandering bands they spread themselves over a vast extent of country, and there were few isolated farmhouses from the Orange River to the Oudtshoorn Mountains, and from the Cape Town railroad in the west to the Fish River in the east, which were not visited by their active and enterprising scouts. The object of the whole movement was, no doubt, to stimulate a general revolt in the Colony; and it must be acknowledged that if the powder did not all explode it was not for want of the match being thoroughly applied.

It might at first sight seem the simplest of military operations to hunt down these scattered and insignificant bands; but as a matter of fact nothing could be more difficult. Operating in a country which was both vast and difficult, with excellent horses, the best of information and supplies ready for them everywhere, it was impossible for the slow-moving British columns with their guns and their wagons to overtake them. Formidable even in flight, the Boers were always ready to turn upon any force which exposed itself too rashly to retaliation, and so amid the mountain passes the British chiefs had to use an amount of caution which was incompatible with extreme speed. Only when a commando was exactly localised so that two or three converging British forces could be brought to bear upon it, was there a reasonable chance of forcing a fight. Still, with all these heavy odds against them, the various little columns continued month after month to play hide-and-seek with the commandos, and the game was by no means always on the one side. The varied fortunes of this scrambling campaign can only be briefly indicated in these pages.

It has already been shown that Kritzinger's original force broke into many bands, which were recruited partly from the Cape rebels and partly from fresh bodies which passed over from the Orange River Colony. The more severe the pressure in the north, the greater reason was there for a trek to this land of plenty. The total number of Boers who were wandering over the eastern and midland districts may have been about two thousand, who were divided into bands which varied from fifty to three hundred. The chief leaders of separate commandos were Kritzinger, Scheepers, Malan, Myburgh, Fouche, Lotter, Smuts, Van Reenen, Lategan, Maritz, and Conroy, the two latter operating on the western side of the country. To hunt down these numerous and active bodies the British were compelled to put many similar detachments into the field, known as the columns of Gorringe, Crabbe, Henniker, Scobell, Doran, Kavanagh, Alexander, and others. These two sets of miniature armies performed an intricate devil's dance over the Colony, the main lines of which are indicated by the red lines upon the map. The Zuurberg mountains to the north of Steynsburg, the Sneeuwberg range to the south of Middelburg, the Oudtshoorn Mountains in the south, the Cradock district, the Murraysburg district, and the Graaf-Reinet district—these were the chief centres of Boer activity.

In April Kritzinger made his way north to the Orange River Colony, for the purpose of consulting with De Wet, but he returned with a following of 200 men about the end of May. Continual brushes occurred during this month between the various columns, and much hard marching was done upon either side, but there was nothing which could be claimed as a positive success.

Early in May two passengers sailed for Europe, the journey of each being in its way historical. The first was the weary and overworked Pro-Consul who had the foresight to distinguish the danger and the courage to meet it. Milner's worn face and prematurely grizzled hair told of the crushing weight which had rested upon him during three eventful years. A gentle scholar, he might have seemed more fitted for a life of academic calm than for the stormy part which the discernment of Mr. Chamberlain had assigned to him. The fine flower of an English university, low-voiced and urbane, it was difficult to imagine what impression he would produce upon those rugged types of which South Africa is so peculiarly prolific. But behind the reserve of a gentleman there lay within him a lofty sense of duty, a singular clearness of vision, and a moral courage which would brace him to follow whither his reason pointed. His visit to England for three months' rest was the occasion for a striking manifestation of loyalty and regard from his fellow-countrymen. He returned in August as Lord Milner to the scene of his labours, with the construction of a united and loyal commonwealth of South Africa as the task of his life.

The second traveller who sailed within a few days of the Governor was Mrs. Botha, the wife of the Boer General, who visited Europe for private as well as political reasons. She bore to Kruger an exact account of the state of the country and of the desperate condition of the burghers. Her mission had no immediate or visible effect, and the weary war, exhausting for the British but fatal for the Boers, went steadily on.

To continue the survey of the operations in the Cape, the first point scored was by the invaders, for Malan's commando succeeded upon May 13th in overwhelming a strong patrol of the Midland Mounted Rifles, the local colonial corps, to the south of Maraisburg. Six killed, eleven wounded, and forty-one prisoners were the fruits of his little victory, which furnished him also with a fresh supply of rifles and ammunition. On May 21st Crabbe's column was in touch with Lotter and with Lategan, but no very positive result came from the skirmish.

The end of May showed considerable Boer activity in the Cape Colony, that date corresponding with the return of Kritzinger from the north. Haig had for the moment driven Scheepers back from the extreme southerly point which he had reached, and he was now in the Graaf-Reinet district; but on the other side of the colony Conroy had appeared near Kenhart, and upon May 23rd he fought a sharp skirmish with a party of Border Scouts. The main Boer force under Kritzinger was in the midlands, however, and had concentrated to such an extent in the Cradock district that it was clear that some larger enterprise was on foot. This soon took shape, for on June 2nd, after a long and rapid march, the Boer leader threw himself upon Jamestown, overwhelmed the sixty townsmen who formed the guard, and looted the town, from which he drew some welcome supplies and 100 horses. British columns were full cry upon his heels, however, and the Boers after a few hours left the gutted town and vanished into the hills once more. On June 6th the British had a little luck at last, for on that date Scobell and Lukin in the Barkly East district surprised a *laager* and took twenty prisoners, 166 horses, and much of the Jamestown loot. On the same day Windham treated Van Reenen in a similar rough fashion near Steynsburg, and took twenty-two prisoners.

On June 8th the supreme command of the operations in Cape Colony was undertaken by General French, who from this time forward manoeuvred his numerous columns upon a connected plan with the main idea of pushing the enemy northwards. It was some time, however, before his disposition bore fruit, for the commandos were still better mounted and lighter than their pursuers. On June 13th the youthful and dashing Scheepers, who commanded his own little force at an age when he would have been a junior lieutenant of the British army, raided Murraysburg and captured a patrol. On June 17th Monro with Lovat's Scouts and Bethune's Mounted Infantry had some slight success near Tarkastad, but three days later the ill-fated Midland Mounted Rifles were surprised in the early morning by Kritzinger at Waterkloof, which is thirty miles west of Cradock, and were badly mauled by him. They lost ten killed, eleven wounded, and sixty-six prisoners in this unfortunate affair. Again the myth that colonial alertness is greater than that of regular troops seems to have been exposed.

At the end of June, Fouche, one of the most enterprising of the guerrilla chiefs, made a dash from Barkly East into the native reserves of the Transkei in order to obtain horses and supplies. It was a desperate measure, as it was vain to suppose that the warlike Kaffirs would permit their property to be looted without resistance, and if once the assegais were reddened no man could say how far the mischief might go. With great loyalty the British Government, even in the darkest days, had held back those martial races—Zulus, Swazis, and Basutos—who all had old grudges against the Amaboon. Fouche's raid was stopped, however, before it led to serious trouble. A handful of Griqualand Mounted Rifles held it in front, while Dalgety and his colonial veterans moving very swiftly drove him back northwards.

Though baulked, Fouche was still formidable, and on July 14th he made a strong attack in the neighbourhood of Jamestown upon a column of Connaught Rangers who were escorting a convoy. Major Moore offered a determined resistance, and eventually after some hours of fighting drove the enemy away and captured their *laager*. Seven killed and seventeen wounded were the British losses in this spirited engagement.

On July 10th General French, surveying from a lofty mountain peak the vast expanse of the field of operations, with his heliograph calling up responsive twinkles over one hundred miles of country, gave the order for the convergence of four columns upon the valley in which he knew Scheepers to be lurking. We have it from one of his own letters that his commando at the time consisted of 240 men, of whom forty were Free Staters and the rest colonial rebels. Crewe, Windham, Doran, and Scobell each answered to the call, but the young leader was a man of resource, and a long *kloof* up the precipitous side of the hill gave him a road to safety. Yet the operations showed a new mobility in the British columns, which shed their guns and their baggage in order to travel faster. The main commando escaped, but twenty-five laggards were taken. The action took place among the hills thirty miles to the west of Graaf-Reinet.

On July 21st Crabbe and Kritzinger had a skirmish in the mountains near Cradock, in which the Boers were strong enough to hold their own; but on the same date near Murraysburg, Lukin, the gallant colonial gunner, with ninety men rode into 150 of Lategan's band and captured ten of them, with a hundred horses. On July 27th a small party of twenty-one Imperial Yeomanry was captured, after a gallant resistance, by a large force of Boers at the Doorn River on the other side of the Colony. The Kaffir scouts of the British were shot dead in cold blood by their captors after the action. There seems to be no possible excuse for the repeated murders of coloured men by the Boers, as they had themselves from the beginning of the war used their Kaffirs for every purpose short of actually fighting. The war had lost much of the good humour which marked its outset. A fiercer feeling had been engendered on both sides by the long strain, but the execution of rebels by the British, though much to be deplored, is still recognised as one of the rights of a belligerent. When one remembers the condonation upon the part of the British of the use of their own uniforms by the Boers, of the wholesale breaking of paroles, of the continual use of expansive bullets, of the abuse of the pass system and of the red cross, it is impossible to blame them for showing some severity in the stamping out of armed rebellion within their own Colony. If stern measures were eventually adopted it was only after extreme leniency had been tried and failed. The loss of five years' franchise as a penalty for firing upon their own flag is surely the most gentle correction which an Empire ever laid upon a rebellious people.

At the beginning of August the connected systematic work of French's columns began to tell. In a huge semicircle the British were pushing north, driving the guerrillas in front of them. Scheepers in his usual wayward fashion had broken away to the south, but the others had been unable to penetrate the cordon and were herded over the Stormberg to Naauwport line. The main body of the Boers was hustled swiftly along from August 7th to August 10th, from Graaf-Reinet to Thebus, and thrust over the railway line at that point with some loss of men and a great shedding of horses. It was hoped that the blockhouses on the railroad would have held the enemy, but they slipped across by night and got into the

Steynsburg district, where Gorringe's colonials took up the running. On August 18th he followed the commandos from Steynsburg to Venterstad, killing twenty of them and taking several prisoners. On the 15th, Kritzinger with the main body of the invaders passed the Orange River near Bethulie, and made his way to the Wepener district of the Orange River Colony. Scheepers, Lotter, Lategan, and a few small wandering bands were the only Boers left in the Colony, and to these the British columns now turned their attention, with the result that Lategan, towards the end of the month, was also driven over the river. For the time, at least, the situation seemed to have very much improved, but there was a drift of Boers over the north-western frontier, and the long-continued warfare at their own doors was undoubtedly having a dangerous effect upon the Dutch farmers. Small successes from time to time, such as the taking of sixty of French's Scouts by Theron's commando on August 10th, served to keep them from despair. Of the guerrilla bands which remained, the most important was that of Scheepers, which now numbered 300 men, well mounted and supplied. He had broken back through the cordon, and made for his old haunts in the south-west. Theron, with a smaller band, was also in the Uniondale and Willowmore district, approaching close to the sea in the Mossel Bay direction, but being headed off by Kavanagh. Scheepers turned in the direction of Cape Town, but swerved aside at Montagu, and moved northwards towards Touws River.

So far the British had succeeded in driving and injuring, but never in destroying, the Boer bands. It was a new departure therefore when, upon September 4th, the commando of Lotter was entirely destroyed by the column of Scobell. This column consisted of some of the Cape Mounted Rifles and of the indefatigable 9th Lancers. It marked the enemy down in a valley to the west of Cradock and attacked them in the morning, after having secured all the approaches. The result was a complete success. The Boers threw themselves into a building and held out valiantly, but their position was impossible, and after enduring considerable punishment they were forced to hoist the white flag. Eleven had been killed, forty-six wounded, and fifty-six surrendered—figures which are in themselves a proof of the tenacity of their defence. Lotter was among the prisoners, 260 horses were taken, and a good supply of ammunition, with some dynamite. A few days later, on September 10th, a similar blow, less final in its character, was dealt by Colonel Crabbe to the commando of Van der Merve, which was an offshoot of that of Scheepers. The action was fought near Laingsburg, which is on the main line, just north of Matjesfontein, and it ended in the scattering of the Boer band, the death of their boy leader (he was only eighteen years of age), and the capture of thirty-seven prisoners. Seventy of the Beers escaped by a hidden road. To Colonials and Yeomanry belongs the honour of the action, which cost the British force seven casualties. Colonel Crabbe pushed on after the success, and on September 14th he was in touch with Scheepers's commando near Ladismith (not to be confused with the historical town of Natal), and endured and inflicted some losses. On the 17th a patrol of Grenadier Guards was captured in the north of the Colony, Rebow, the young lieutenant in charge of them, meeting with a soldier's death.

On the same day a more serious engagement occurred near Tarkastad, a place which lies to the east of Cradock, a notorious centre of disaffection in the midland district. Smuts's commando, some hundreds strong, was marked down in this part, and several forces converged upon it. One of the outlets, Elands River Poort, was guarded by a single squadron of the 17th Lancers. Upon this the Boers made a sudden and very fierce attack, their approach being facilitated partly by the mist and partly by the use of khaki, a trick which seems never to have grown too stale for successful use. The result was that they were able to ride up to the British camp before any preparations had been made for resistance, and to shoot down a number of the Lancers before they could reach their horses. So terrible was the fire that the single squadron lost thirty-four killed and thirty-six wounded. But the regiment may console itself for the disaster by the fact that the sorely stricken detachment remained true to the spirited motto of the corps, and that no prisoners appear to have been lost.

After this one sharp engagement there ensued several weeks during which the absence of historical events, or the presence of the military censor, caused a singular lull in the account of the operations. With so many small commandos and so many pursuing columns it is extraordinary that there should not have been a constant succession of actions. That there was not must indicate a sluggishness upon the part of the pursuers, and this sluggishness can only be explained by the condition of their horses. Every train of thought brings the critic back always to the great horse question, and encourages the conclusion that there, at all seasons of the war and in all scenes of it, is to be found the most damning indictment against British foresight, common-sense, and power of organisation. That the third year of the war should dawn without the British forces having yet got the legs of the Boers, after having penetrated every portion of their country and having the horses of the world on which to draw, is the most amazingly inexplicable point in the whole of this strange campaign. From the telegram 'Infantry preferred' addressed to a nation of rough-riders, down to the failure to secure the excellent horses on the spot, while importing them unfit for use from the ends of the earth, there has been nothing but one long series of blunders in this, the most vital question of all. Even up to the end, in the Colony the obvious lesson had not yet been learnt that it is better to give 1000 men two horses each, and to let them reach the enemy, than give 2000 men one horse each, with which they can never attain their object. The chase during two years of the man with two horses by the man with one horse, has been a sight painful to ourselves and ludicrous to others.

In connection with this account of operations within the Colony, there is one episode which occurred in the extreme north-west which will not fit in with this connected narrative, but which will justify the distraction of the reader's intelligence, for few finer deeds of arms are recorded in the war. This was the heroic defence of a convoy by the 14th Company of Irish Imperial Yeomanry. The convoy was taking food to Griquatown, on the Kimberley side of the seat of war. The town had been long invested by Conroy, and the inhabitants were in such straits that it was highly necessary to relieve them. To this end a convoy, two miles long, was despatched under Major Humby of the Irish Yeomanry. The escort consisted of seventy-five Northumberland Fusiliers, twenty-four local troops, and 100 of the 74th Irish Yeomanry. Fifteen miles from Griquatown, at a place called Rooikopjes, the convoy was attacked by the enemy several hundred in number. Two companies of the Irishmen seized the ridge, however, which commanded the wagons, and held it until they were almost exterminated. The position was covered with bush, and the two parties came to the closest of quarters, the Yeomen refusing to take a backward step, though it was clear that they were vastly outnumbered. Encouraged by the example of Madan and Ford, their gallant young leaders, they deliberately sacrificed their lives in order to give time for the guns to come up and for the convoy to pass. Oliffe, Bonynge, and Maclean, who had been children together, were shot side by side on the ridge, and afterwards buried in one grave. Of forty-three men in action, fourteen were killed and twenty severely wounded. Their sacrifice was not in vain, however. The Boers were beaten back, and the convoy, as well as Griquatown, was saved. Some thirty or forty Boers were killed or wounded in the skirmish, and Conroy, their leader, declared that it was the stiffest fight of his life.

In the autumn and winter of 1901 General French had steadily pursued the system of clearing certain districts, one at a time, and endeavouring by his blockhouses and by the arrangement of his forces to hold in strict quarantine those sections of the country which were still infested by the commandos. In this manner he succeeded by the November of this year in confining the active forces of the enemy to the extreme north-east and to the south-west of the peninsula. It is doubtful if the whole Boer force, three-quarters of whom were colonial rebels, amounted to more than fifteen hundred men. When we learn that at this period of the war they were indifferently armed, and that many of them were mounted upon donkeys, it is impossible, after making every allowance for the passive assistance of the farmers, and the difficulties of the country, to believe that the pursuit was always pushed with the spirit and vigour which was needful.

In the north-east, Myburgh, Wessels, and the truculent Fouche were allowed almost a free hand for some months, while the roving bands were rounded up in the midlands and driven along until they were west of the main railroad. Here, in the Calvinia district, several commandos united in October 1901 under Maritz, Louw, Smit, and Theron. Their united bands rode down into the rich grain-growing country round Piquetberg and Malmesbury, pushing south until it seemed as if their academic supporters at Paarl were actually to have a sight of the rebellion which they had fanned to a flame. At one period their patrols were within forty miles of Cape Town. The movement was checked, however, by a small force of Lancers and district troops, and towards the end of October, Maritz, who was chief in this quarter, turned northwards, and on the 29th captured a small British convoy which crossed his line of march. Early in November he doubled back and attacked Piquetberg, but was beaten off with some loss. From that time a steady pressure from the south and east drove these bands farther and farther into the great barren lands of the west, until, in the following April, they had got as far as Namaqualand, many hundred miles away.

Upon October 9th, the second anniversary of the Ultimatum, the hands of the military were strengthened by the proclamation of Cape Town and all the seaport towns as being in a state of martial law. By this means a possible source of supplies and recruits for the enemy was effectually blocked. That it had not been done two years before is a proof of how far local political considerations can be allowed to over-ride the essentials of Imperial policy. Meanwhile treason courts were sitting, and sentences, increasing rapidly from the most trivial to the most tragic, were teaching the rebel that his danger did not end upon the field of battle. The execution of Lotter and his lieutenants was a sign that the patience of a long-suffering Empire had at last reached an end.

The young Boer leader, Scheepers, had long been a thorn in the side of the British. He had infested the southern districts for some months, and he had distinguished himself both by the activity of his movements and by the ruthless vigour of some of his actions. Early in October a serious illness and consequent confinement to his bed brought him at last within the range of British mobility. On his recovery he was tried for repeated breaches of the laws of war, including the murder of several natives. He was condemned to death, and was executed in December. Much sympathy was excited by his gallantry and his youth—he was only twenty-three. On the other hand, our word was pledged to protect the natives, and if he whose hand had been so heavy upon them escaped, all confidence would have been lost in our promises and our justice. That British vengeance was not indiscriminate was shown soon afterwards in the case of a more important commander, Kritzinger, who was the chief leader of the Boers within Cape Colony. Kritzinger was wounded and captured while endeavouring to cross the line near Hanover Road upon December 15th. He was put upon his trial, and his fate turned upon how far he was responsible for the misdeeds of some of his subordinates. It was clearly shown that he had endeavoured to hold them within the bounds of civilised warfare, and with congratulations and hand-shakings he was acquitted by the military court.

In the last two months of the year 1901, a new system was introduced into the Cape Colony campaign by placing the Colonial and district troops immediately under the command of Colonial officers and of the Colonial Government. It had long been felt that some devolution was necessary, and the change was justified by the result. Without any dramatic incident, an inexorable process of attrition, caused by continual pursuit and hardship, wore out the commandos. Large bands had become small ones, and small ones had vanished. Only by the union of several bodies could any enterprise higher than the looting of a farmhouse be successfully attempted.

Such a union occurred, however, in the early days of February 1902, when Smuts, Malan, and several other Boer leaders showed great activity in the country round Calvinia. Their commandos seem to have included a proportion of veteran Republicans from the north, who were more formidable fighting material than the raw Colonial rebels. It happened that several dangerously weak British columns were operating within reach at that time, and it was only owing to the really admirable conduct of the troops that a serious disaster was averted. Two separate actions, each of them severe, were fought on the same date, and in each case the Boers were able to bring very superior numbers into the field.

The first of these was the fight in which Colonel Doran's column extricated itself with severe loss from a most perilous plight. The whole force under Doran consisted of 350 men with two guns, and this handful was divided by an expedition which he, with 150 men, undertook in order to search a distant farm. The remaining two hundred men, under Captain Saunders, were left upon February 5th with the guns and the convoy at a place called Middlepost, which lies about fifty miles south-west of Calvinia. These men were of the 11th, 23rd, and 24th Imperial Yeomanry, with a troop of Cape Police. The Boer Intelligence was excellent, as might be expected in a country which is dotted with farms. The weakened force at Middlepost was instantly attacked by Smuts's commando. Saunders evacuated the camp and abandoned the convoy, which was the only thing he could do, but he concentrated all his efforts upon preserving his guns. The night was illuminated by the blazing wagons, and made hideous by the whoops of the drunken rebels who caroused among the captured stores. With the first light of dawn the small British force was fiercely assailed on all sides, but held its own in a manner which would have done credit to any troops. The much criticised Yeomen fought like veterans. A considerable position had to be covered, and only a handful of men were available at the most important points. One ridge, from which the guns would be enfiladed, was committed to the charge of Lieutenants Tabor and Chichester with eleven men of the 11th Imperial Yeomanry, their instructions being 'to hold it to the death.' The order was obeyed with the utmost heroism. After a desperate defence the ridge was only taken by the Boers when both officers had been killed and nine out of eleven men were on the ground. In spite of the loss of this position the fight was still sustained until shortly after midday, when Doran with the patrol returned. The position was still most dangerous, the losses had been severe, and the Boers were increasing in strength. An immediate retreat was ordered, and the small column, after ten days of hardship and anxiety, reached the railway line in safety. The wounded were left to the care of Smuts, who behaved with chivalry and humanity.

At about the same date a convoy proceeding from Beaufort West to Fraserburg was attacked by Malan's commando. The escort, which consisted of sixty Colonial Mounted Rifles and 100 of the West Yorkshire militia, was overwhelmed after a good defence, in which Major Crofton, their commander, was killed. The wagons were destroyed, but the Boers were driven off by the arrival of Crabbe's column, followed by those of Capper and Lund. The total losses of the British in these two actions amounted to twenty-three killed and sixty-five wounded.

The re-establishment of settled law and order was becoming more marked every week in those south-western districts, which had long been most disturbed. Colonel Crewe in this region, and Colonel Lukin upon the other side of the line, acting entirely with Colonial troops, were pushing back the rebels, and holding, by a well-devised system of district defence, all that they had gained. By the end of February there were none of the enemy south of the Beaufort West and Clanwilliam line. These results were not obtained without much hard marching and a little hard fighting. Small columns under Crabbe, Capper, Wyndham, Nickall, and Lund, were continually on the move, with little to show for it save an ever-widening area of settled country in their rear. In a skirmish on February 20th Judge Hugo, a well-known Boer leader, was killed, and Vanheerden, a notorious rebel, was captured. At the end of this month Fouche's tranquil occupation of the north-east was at last disturbed, and he was driven out of it into the midlands, where he took refuge with the remains of his commando in the Camdeboo Mountains. Malan's men had already sought shelter in the same natural fortress. Malan was wounded and taken in a skirmish near Somerset East a few days before the general Boer surrender. Fouche gave himself up at Cradock on June 2nd.

The last incident of this scattered, scrambling, unsatisfactory campaign in the Cape peninsula was the raid made by Smuts, the Transvaal leader, into the Port Nolloth district of Namaqualand, best known for its copper mines. A small railroad has been constructed from the coast at this point, the terminus being the township of Ookiep. The length of the line is about seventy miles. It is difficult to imagine what the Boers expected to gain in this remote corner of the seat of war, unless they had conceived the idea that they might actually obtain possession of Port Nolloth itself, and so restore the communications with their sympathisers and allies. At the end of March the Boer horsemen appeared suddenly out of the desert, drove in the British outposts, and summoned Ookiep to surrender. Colonel Shelton, who commanded the small garrison, sent an uncompromising reply, but he was unable to protect the railway in his rear, which was wrecked, together with some of the blockhouses which had been erected to guard it. The loyal population of the surrounding country had flocked into Ookiep, and the Commandant found himself burdened with the care of six thousand people. The enemy had succeeded in taking the small post of Springbok, and Concordia, the mining centre, was surrendered into their hands without resistance, giving them welcome supplies of arms, ammunition, and dynamite. The latter was used by the Boers in the shape of hand-bombs, and proved to be a very efficient weapon when employed against blockhouses. Several of the British defences were wrecked by them, with considerable loss to the garrison; but in the course of a month's siege, in spite of several attacks, the Boers were never able to carry the frail works which guarded the town. Once more, at the end of the war as at the beginning of it, there was shown the impotence of the Dutch riflemen against a British defence. A relief column, under Colonel Cooper, was quickly organised at Port Nolloth, and advanced along the railway line, forcing Smuts to raise the siege in the first week of May. Immediately afterwards came the news of the negotiations for peace, and the Boer general presented himself at Port Nolloth, whence he was conveyed by ship to Cape Town, and so north again to take part in the deliberations of his fellow-countrymen. Throughout the war he had played a manly and honourable part. It may be hoped that with youth and remarkable experience, both of diplomacy and of war, he may now find a long and brilliant career awaiting him in a wider arena than that for which he strove.

CHAPTER 36

The Spring Campaign
(September to December, 1901)

The history of the war during the African winter of 1901 has now been sketched, and some account given of the course of events in the Transvaal, the Orange River Colony, and the Cape Colony. The hope of the British that they might stamp out resistance before the grass should restore mobility to the larger bodies of Boers was destined to be disappointed. By the middle of September the *veldt* had turned from drab to green, and the great drama was fated to last for one more act, however anxious all the British and the majority of the Boers might be to ring down the curtain. Exasperating as this senseless prolongation of a hopeless struggle might be, there was still some consolation in the reflection that those who drank this bitter cup to the very lees would be less likely to thirst for it again.

September 15th was the date which brought into force the British Proclamation announcing the banishment of those Boer leaders who continued in arms. It must be confessed that this step may appear harsh and unchivalrous to the impartial observer, so long as those leaders were guilty of no practices which are foreign to the laws of civilised warfare. The imposition of personal penalties upon the officers of an opposing army is a step for which it is difficult to quote a precedent, nor is it wise to officially rule your enemy outside the pale of ordinary warfare, since it is equally open to him to take the same step against you. The only justification for such a course would be its complete success, as this would suggest that the Intelligence Department were aware that the leaders desired some strong excuse for coming in—such an excuse as the Proclamation would afford. The result proved that nothing of the kind was needed, and the whole proceeding must appear to be injudicious and high-handed. In honourable war you conquer your adversary by superior courage, strength, or wit, but you do not terrorise him by particular penalties aimed at individuals. The burghers of the Transvaal and of the late Orange Free State were legitimate belligerents, and to be treated as such—a statement which does not, of course, extend to the Afrikander rebels who were their allies.

The tendency of the British had been to treat their antagonists as a broken and disorganised banditti, but with the breaking of the spring they were sharply reminded that the burghers were still capable of a formidable and coherent effort. The very date which put them beyond the pale as belligerents was that which they seem to have chosen in order to prove what active and valiant soldiers they still remained. A quick succession of encounters occurred at various parts of the seat of war, the general tendency of which was not entirely in favour of the British arms, though the weekly export of prisoners reassured all who noted it as to the sapping and decay of the Boer strength. These incidents must now be set down in the order of their occurrence, with their relation to each other so far as it is possible to trace it.

General Louis Botha, with the double intention of making an offensive move and of distracting the wavering burghers from a close examination of Lord Kitchener's proclamation, assembled his forces in the second week of September in the Ermelo district. Thence he moved them rapidly towards Natal, with the result that the volunteers of that colony had once more to grasp their rifles and hasten to the frontier. The whole situation bore for an instant an absurd resemblance to that of two years before—Botha playing the part of Joubert, and Lyttelton, who commanded on the frontier, that of White. It only remained, to make the parallel complete, that some one should represent Penn Symons, and this perilous role fell to a gallant officer, Major Gough, commanding a detached force which thought itself strong enough to hold its own, and only learned by actual experiment that it was not.

This officer, with a small force consisting of three companies of Mounted Infantry with two guns of the 69th R.F.A., was operating in the neighbourhood of Utrecht in the south-eastern corner of the Transvaal, on the very path along which Botha must descend. On September 17th he had crossed De Jagers Drift on the Blood River, not very far from Dundee, when he found himself in touch with the enemy. His mission was to open a path for an empty convoy returning from Vryheid, and in order to do so it was necessary that Blood River Poort, where the Boers were now seen, should be cleared. With admirable zeal Gough pushed rapidly forward, supported by a force of 350 Johannesburg Mounted Rifles under Stewart. Such a proceeding must have seemed natural to any British officer at this stage of the war, when a swift advance was the only chance of closing with the small bodies of Boers; but it is strange that the

Intelligence Department had not warned the patrols upon the frontier that a considerable force was coming down upon them, and that they should be careful to avoid action against impossible odds. If Gough had known that Botha's main commando was coming down upon him, it is inconceivable that he would have pushed his advance until he could neither extricate his men nor his guns. A small body of the enemy, said to have been the personal escort of Louis Botha, led him on, until a large force was able to ride down upon him from the flank and rear. Surrounded at Scheepers Nek by many hundreds of riflemen in a difficult country, there was no alternative but a surrender, and so sharp and sudden was the Boer advance that the whole action was over in a very short time. The new tactics of the Boers, already used at Vlakfontein, and afterwards to be successful at Brakenlaagte and at Tweebosch, were put in force. A large body of mounted men, galloping swiftly in open order and firing from the saddle, rode into and over the British. Such temerity should in theory have met with severe punishment, but as a matter of fact the losses of the enemy seem to have been very small. The soldiers were not able to return an effective fire from their horses, and had no time to dismount. The sights and breech-blocks of the two guns are said to have been destroyed, but the former statement seems more credible than the latter. A Colt gun was also captured. Of the small force twenty were killed, forty wounded, and over two hundred taken. Stewart's force was able to extricate itself with some difficulty, and to fall back on the Drift. Gough managed to escape that night and to report that it was Botha himself, with over a thousand men, who had eaten up his detachment. The prisoners and wounded were sent in a few days later to Vryheid, a town which appeared to be in some danger of capture had not Walter Kitchener hastened to carry reinforcements to the garrison. Bruce Hamilton was at the same time despatched to head Botha off, and every step taken to prevent his southern advance. So many columns from all parts converged upon the danger spot that Lyttelton, who commanded upon the Natal frontier, had over 20,000 men under his orders.

Botha's plans appear to have been to work through Zululand and then strike at Natal, an operation which would be the more easy as it would be conducted a considerable distance from the railway line. Pushing on a few days after his successful action with Gough, he crossed the Zulu frontier, and had in front of him an almost unimpeded march as far as the Tugela. Crossing this far from the British base of power, his force could raid the Greytown district and raise recruits among the Dutch farmers, laying waste one of the few spots in South Africa which had been untouched by the blight of war. All this lay before him, and in his path nothing save only two small British posts which might be either disregarded or gathered up as he passed. In an evil moment for himself, tempted by the thought of the supplies which they might contain, he stopped to gather them up, and the force of the wave of invasion broke itself as upon two granite rocks.

These two so-called forts were posts of very modest strength, a chain of which had been erected at the time of the old Zulu war. Fort Itala, the larger, was garrisoned by 300 men of the 5th Mounted Infantry, drawn from the Dublin Fusiliers, Middlesex, Dorsets, South Lancashires, and Lancashire Fusiliers—most of them old soldiers of many battles. They had two guns of the 69th R.F.A., the same battery which had lost a section the week before. Major Chapman, of the Dublins, was in command.

Upon September 25th the small garrison heard that the main force of the Boers was sweeping towards them, and prepared to give them a soldiers' welcome. The fort is situated upon the flank of a hill, on the summit of which, a mile from the main trenches, a strong outpost was stationed. It was upon this that the first force of the attack broke at midnight of September 25th. The garrison, eighty strong, was fiercely beset by several hundred Boers, and the post was eventually carried after a sharp and bloody contest. Kane, of the South Lancashires, died with the words 'No surrender' upon his lips, and Potgieter, a Boer leader, was pistolled by Kane's fellow officer, Lefroy. Twenty of the small garrison fell, and the remainder were overpowered and taken.

With this vantage-ground in their possession the Boers settled down to the task of overwhelming the main position. They attacked upon three sides, and until morning the force was raked from end to end by unseen riflemen. The two British guns were put out of action and the maxim was made unserviceable by a bullet. At dawn there was a pause in the attack, but it recommenced and continued without intermission until sunset. The span betwixt the rising of the sun and its last red glow in the west is a long one for the man who spends it at his ease, but how never-ending must have seemed the hours to this handful of men, outnumbered, surrounded, pelted by bullets, parched with thirst, torn with anxiety, holding desperately on with dwindling numbers to their frail defences! To them it may have seemed a hard thing to endure so much for a tiny fort in a savage land. The larger view of its vital importance could have scarcely come to console the regimental officer, far less the private. But duty carried them through, and they wrought better than they knew, for the brave Dutchmen, exasperated by so disproportionate a resistance, stormed up to the very trenches and suffered as they had not suffered for many a long month. There have been battles with 10,000 British troops hotly engaged in which the Boer losses have not been so great as in this obscure conflict against an isolated post. When at last, baffled and disheartened, they drew off with the waning light, it is said that no fewer than a hundred of their dead and two hundred of their wounded attested the severity of the fight. So strange are the conditions of South African warfare that this loss, which would have hardly made a skirmish memorable in the slogging days of the Peninsula, was one of the most severe blows which the burghers had sustained in the course of a two years' warfare against a large and aggressive army. There is a conflict of evidence as to the exact figures, but at least they were sufficient to beat the Boer army back and to change their plan of campaign.

Whilst this prolonged contest had raged round Fort Itala, a similar attack upon a smaller scale was being made upon Fort Prospect, some fifteen miles to the eastward. This small post was held by a handful of Durham Artillery Militia and of Dorsets. The attack was delivered by Grobler with several hundred burghers, but it made no advance although it was pushed with great vigour, and repeated many times in the course of the day. Captain Rowley, who was in command, handled his men with such judgment that one killed and eight wounded represented his casualties during a long day's fighting. Here again the Boer losses were in proportion to the resolution of their attack, and are said to have amounted to sixty killed and wounded. Considering the impossibility of replacing the men, and the fruitless waste of valuable ammunition, September 26th was an evil day for the Boer cause. The British casualties amounted to seventy-three.

The water of the garrison of Fort Itala had been cut off early in the attack, and their ammunition had run low by evening. Chapman withdrew his men and his guns therefore to Nkandhla, where the survivors of his gallant garrison received the special thanks of Lord Kitchener. The country around was still swarming with Boers, and on the last day of September a convoy from Melmoth fell into their hands and provided them with some badly needed supplies.

But the check which he had received was sufficient to prevent any important advance upon the part of Botha, while the swollen state of the rivers put an additional obstacle in his way. Already the British commanders, delighted to have at last discovered a definite objective, were hurrying to the scene of action. Bruce Hamilton had reached Fort Itala upon September 28th and Walter Kitchener had been despatched to Vryheid. Two British forces, aided by smaller columns, were endeavouring to surround the Boer leader. On October 6th Botha had fallen back to the north-east of Vryheid, whither the British forces had followed him. Like De Wet's invasion of the Cape, Botha's advance upon Natal had ended in placing himself and his army in a critical position. On October 9th he had succeeded in crossing the Privaan River, a branch of the Pongolo, and was pushing north in the direction of Piet Retief, much helped by misty weather and incessant rain. Some of his force escaped between the British columns, and some remained in the *kloofs* and forests of that difficult country.

Walter Kitchener, who had followed up the Boer retreat, had a brisk engagement with the rearguard upon October 6th. The Boers shook themselves clear with some loss, both to themselves and to their pursuers. On the 10th those of the burghers who held together had reached Luneburg, and shortly afterwards they had got completely away from the British columns. The weather was atrocious, and the lumbering wagons, axle-deep in mud, made it impossible for troops who were attached to them to keep in touch with the light riders who sped before them. For some weeks there was no word of the main Boer force, but at the end of that time they reappeared in a manner which showed that both in numbers and in spirit they were still a formidable body.

Of all the sixty odd British columns which were traversing the Boer states there was not one which had a better record than that commanded by Colonel Benson. During seven months of continuous service this small force, consisting at that time of the Argyle and Sutherland Highlanders, the 2nd Scottish Horse, the 18th and 19th Mounted Infantry, and two guns, had acted with great energy, and had reduced its work to a complete and highly effective system. Leaving the infantry as a camp guard, Benson operated with mounted troops alone, and no Boer *laager* within fifty miles was safe from his nocturnal visits. So skilful had he and his men become at these night attacks in a strange, and often difficult country, that out of twenty-eight attempts twenty-one resulted in complete success. In each case the rule was simply to gallop headlong into the Boer *laager*, and to go on chasing as far as the horses could go. The furious and reckless pace may be judged by the fact that the casualties of the force were far greater from falls than from bullets. In seven months forty-seven Boers were killed and six hundred captured, to say nothing of enormous quantities of munitions and stock. The success of these operations was due, not only to the energy of Benson and his men, but to the untiring exertions of Colonel Wools-Sampson, who acted as intelligence officer. If, during his long persecution by President Kruger, Wools-Sampson in the bitterness of his heart had vowed a feud against the Boer cause, it must be acknowledged that he has most amply fulfilled it, for it would be difficult to point to any single man who has from first to last done them greater harm.

In October Colonel Benson's force was reorganised, and it then consisted of the 2nd Buffs, the 2nd Scottish Horse, the 3rd and 25th Mounted Infantry, and four guns of the 84th battery. With this force, numbering nineteen hundred men, he left Middelburg upon the Delagoa line on October 20th and proceeded south, crossing the course along which the Boers, who were retiring from their abortive raid into Natal, might be expected to come. For several days the column performed its familiar work, and gathered up forty or fifty prisoners. On the 26th came news that the Boer commandos under Grobler were concentrating against it, and that an attack in force might be expected. For two days there was continuous sniping, and the column as it moved through the country saw Boer horsemen keeping pace with it on the far flanks and in the rear. The weather had been very bad, and it was in a deluge of cold driving rain that the British set forth upon October 30th, moving towards Brakenlaagte, which is a point about forty miles due south of Middelburg. It was Benson's intention to return to his base.

About midday the column, still escorted by large bodies of aggressive Boers, came to a difficult *spruit* swollen by the rain. Here the wagons stuck, and it took some hours to get them all across. The Boer fire was continually becoming more severe, and had broken out at the head of the column as well as the rear. The situation was rendered more difficult by the violence of the rain, which raised a thick steam from the ground and made it impossible to see for any distance. Major Anley, in command of the rearguard, peering back, saw through a rift of the clouds a large body of horsemen in extended order sweeping after them. 'There's miles of them, begob!' cried an excited Irish trooper. Next instant the curtain had closed once more, but all who had caught a glimpse of that vision knew that a stern struggle was at hand.

At this moment two guns of the 84th battery under Major Guinness were in action against Boer riflemen. As a rear screen on the farther side of the guns was a body of the Scottish Horse and of the Yorkshire Mounted Infantry. Near the guns themselves were thirty men of the Buffs. The rest of the Buffs and of the Mounted Infantry were out upon the flanks or else were with the advance guard, which was now engaged, under the direction of Colonel Wools-Sampson, in parking the convoy and in forming the camp. These troops played a small part in the day's fighting, the whole force of which broke with irresistible violence upon the few hundred men who were in front of or around the rear guns. Colonel Benson seems to have just ridden back to the danger point when the Boers delivered their furious attack.

Louis Botha with his commando is said to have ridden sixty miles in order to join the forces of Grobler and Oppermann, and overwhelm the British column. It may have been the presence of their commander or a desire to have vengeance for the harrying which they had undergone upon the Natal border, but whatever the reason, the Boer attack was made with a spirit and dash which earned the enthusiastic applause of every soldier who survived to describe it. With the low roar of a great torrent, several hundred horsemen burst through the curtain of mist, riding at a furious pace for the British guns. The rear screen of Mounted Infantry fell back before this terrific rush, and the two bodies of horsemen came pell-mell down upon the handful of Buffs and the guns. The infantry were ridden into and surrounded by the Boers, who found nothing to stop them from galloping on to the low ridge upon which the guns were stationed. This ridge was held by eighty of the Scottish Horse and forty of the Yorkshire M.I., with a few riflemen from the 25th Mounted Infantry. The latter were the escort of the guns, but the former were the rear screen who had fallen back rapidly because it was the game to do so, but who were in no way shaken, and who instantly dismounted and formed when they reached a defensive position.

These men had hardly time to take up their ground when the Boers were on them. With that extraordinary quickness to adapt their tactics to circumstances which is the chief military virtue of the Boers, the horsemen did not gallop over the crest, but lined the edge of it, and poured a withering fire on to the guns and the men beside them. The heroic nature of the defence can be best shown by the plain figures of the casualties. No rhetoric is needed to adorn that simple record. There were thirty-two gunners round the guns, and twenty-nine fell where they stood. Major Guinness was mortally wounded while endeavouring with his own hands to fire a round of case. There were sixty-two casualties out of eighty among the Scottish Horse, and the Yorkshires were practically annihilated. Altogether 123 men fell, out of about 160 on the ridge. 'Hard pounding, gentlemen,' as Wellington remarked at Waterloo, and British troops seemed as ready as ever to endure it.

The gunners were, as usual, magnificent. Of the two little bullet-pelted groups of men around the guns there was not one who did not stand to his duty without flinching. Corporal Atkin was shot down with all his comrades, but still endeavoured with his failing strength to twist the breech-block out of the gun. Another bullet passed through his upraised hands as he did it. Sergeant Hayes, badly wounded, and the last survivor of the crew, seized the lanyard, crawled up the trail, and fired a last round before he fainted. Sergeant Mathews, with three bullets through him, kept steadily to his duty. Five drivers tried to bring up a limber and remove the gun, but all of them, with all the horses, were hit. There have been incidents in this war which have not increased our military reputation, but you might search the classical records of valour and fail to find anything finer than the consistent conduct of the British artillery.

Colonel Benson was hit in the knee and again in the stomach, but wounded as he was he despatched a message back to Wools-Sampson, asking him to burst shrapnel over the ridge so as to prevent the Boers from carrying off the guns. The burghers had ridden in among the litter of dead and wounded men which marked the British position, and some of the baser of them, much against the will of their commanders, handled the injured soldiers with great brutality. The shell-fire drove them back, however, and the two guns were left standing alone, with no one near them save their prostrate gunners and escort.

There has been some misunderstanding as to the part played by the Buffs in this action, and words have been used which seem to imply that they had in some way failed their mounted companions. It is due to the honour of one of the finest regiments in the British army to clear this up. As a matter of fact, the greater part of the regiment under Major Dauglish was engaged in defending the camp. Near the guns there were four separate small bodies of Buffs, none of which appears to have been detailed as an escort. One of these parties, consisting of thirty men under Lieutenant Greatwood, was ridden over by the horsemen, and the same fate befell a party of twenty who were far out upon the flank. Another small body under Lieutenant Lynch was over taken by the same charge, and was practically destroyed, losing nineteen killed and wounded out of thirty. In the rear of the guns was a larger body of Buffs, 130 in number, under Major Eales. When the guns were taken this handful attempted a counter-attack, but Eales soon saw that it was a hopeless effort, and he lost thirty of his men before he could extricate himself. Had these men been with the others on the gun ridge they might have restored the fight, but they had not reached it when the position was taken, and to persevere in the attempt to retake it would have led to certain disaster. The only just criticism to which the regiment is open is that, having just come off blockhouse duty, they were much out of condition, which caused the men to straggle and the movements to be unduly slow.

It was fortunate that the command of the column devolved upon so experienced and cool-headed a soldier as Wools-Sampson. To attempt a counter-attack for the purpose of recapturing the guns would, in case of disaster, have risked the camp and the convoy. The latter was the prize which the Boers had particularly in view, and to expose it would be to play their game. Very wisely, therefore, Wools-Sampson held the attacking Boers off with his guns and his riflemen, while every spare pair of hands was set to work entrenching the position and making it impregnable against attack. Outposts were stationed upon all those sur-rounding points which might command the camp, and a summons to surrender from the Boer leader was treated with contempt. All day a long-range fire, occasionally very severe, rained upon the camp. Colonel

Benson was brought in by the ambulance, and used his dying breath in exhorting his subordinate to hold out. 'No more night marches' are said to have been the last words spoken by this gallant soldier as he passed away in the early morning after the action. On October 31st the force remained on the defensive, but early on November 1st the gleaming of two heliographs, one to the north-east and one to the south-west, told that two British columns, those of De Lisle and of Barter, were hastening to the rescue. But the Boers had passed as the storm does, and nothing but their swathe of destruction was left to show where they had been. They had taken away the guns during the night, and were already beyond the reach of pursuit.

Such was the action at Brakenlaagte, which cost the British sixty men killed and 170 wounded, together with two guns. Colonel Benson, Colonel Guinness, Captain Eyre Lloyd of the Guards, Major Murray and Captain Lindsay of the Scottish Horse, with seven other officers were among the dead, while sixteen officers were wounded. The net result of the action was that the British rear-guard had been annihilated, but that the main body and the convoy, which was the chief object of the attack, was saved. The Boer loss was considerable, being about one hundred and fifty. In spite of the Boer success nothing could suit the British better than hard fighting of the sort, since whatever the immediate result of it might be, it must necessarily cause a wastage among the enemy which could never be replaced. The gallantry of the Boer charge was only equalled by that of the resistance offered round the guns, and it is an action to which both sides can look back without shame or regret. It was feared that the captured guns would soon be used to break the blockhouse line, but nothing of the kind was attempted, and within a few weeks they were both recovered by British columns.

In order to make a consecutive and intelligible narrative, I will continue with an account of the operations in this south-eastern portion of the Transvaal from the action of Brakenlaagte down to the end of the year 1901. These were placed in the early part of November, under the supreme command of General Bruce Hamilton, and that energetic commander set in motion a number of small columns, which effected numerous captures. He was much helped in his work by the new lines of blockhouses, one of which extended from Standerton to Ermelo, while another connected Brugspruit with Greylingstad. The huge country was thus cut into manageable districts, and the fruits were soon seen by the large returns of prisoners which came from this part of the seat of war.

Upon December 3rd Bruce Hamilton, who had the valuable assistance of Wools-Sampson to direct his intelligence, struck swiftly out from Ermelo and fell upon a Boer *laager* in the early morning, capturing ninety-six prisoners. On the 10th he overwhelmed the Bethel commando by a similar march, killing seven and capturing 131. Williams and Wing commanded separate columns in this operation, and their energy may be judged from the fact that they covered fifty-one miles during the twenty-four hours. On the 12th Hamilton's columns were on the war-path once more, and another commando was wiped out. Sixteen killed and seventy prisoners were the fruits of this expedition. For the second time in a week the columns had done their fifty miles a day, and it was no surprise to hear from their commander that they were in need of a rest. Nearly four hundred prisoners had been taken from the most warlike portion of the Transvaal in ten days by one energetic commander, with a list of twenty-five casualties to ourselves. The thanks of the Secretary of War were specially sent to him for his brilliant work. From then until the end of the year 1901, numbers of smaller captures continued to be reported from the same region, where Plumer, Spens, Mackenzie, Rawlinson, and others were working. On the other hand there was one small setback which occurred to a body of two hundred Mounted Infantry under Major Bridgford, who had been detached from Spens's column to search some farmhouses at a place called Holland, to the south of Ermelo. The expedition set forth upon the night of December 19th, and next morning surrounded and examined the farms.

The British force became divided in doing this work, and were suddenly attacked by several hundred of Britz's commando, who came to close quarters through their khaki dress, which enabled them to pass as Plumer's vanguard. The brunt of the fight fell upon an outlying body of fifty men, nearly all of whom were killed, wounded or taken. A second body of fifty men were overpowered in the same way, after a creditable defence. Fifteen of the British were killed and thirty wounded, while Bridgford the commander was also taken. Spens came up shortly afterwards with the column, and the Boers were driven off. There seems every reason to think that upon this occasion the plans of the British had leaked out, and that a deliberate ambush had been laid for them round the farms, but in such operations these are chances against which it is not always possible to guard. Considering the number of the Boers, and the cleverness of their dispositions, the British were fortunate in being able to extricate their force without greater loss, a feat which was largely due to the leading of Lieutenant Sterling.

Leaving the Eastern Transvaal, the narrative must now return to several incidents of importance which had occurred at various points of the seat of war during the latter months of 1901.

On September 19th, two days after Gough's disaster, a misfortune occurred near Bloemfontein by which two guns and a hundred and forty men fell temporarily into the hands of the enemy. These guns, belonging to U battery, were moving south under an escort of Mounted Infantry, from that very Sanna's Post which had been so fatal to the same battery eighteen months before. When fifteen miles south of the Waterworks, at a place called Vlakfontein (another Vlakfontein from that of General Dixon's engagement), the small force was surrounded and captured by Ackermann's commando. The gunner officer, Lieutenant Barry, died beside his guns in the way that gunner officers have. Guns and men were taken, however, the latter to be released, and the former to be recovered a week or two later by the British columns. It is certainly a credit to the Boers that the spring campaign should have opened by four British guns falling into their hands, and it is impossible to withhold our admiration for those gallant farmers who, after two years of exhausting warfare, were still able to turn upon a formidable and victorious enemy, and to renovate their supplies at his expense.

Two days later, hard on the heels of Gough's mishap, of the Vlakfontein incident, and of the annihilation of the squadron of Lancers in the Cape, there was a serious affair at Elands Kloof, near Zastron, in the extreme south of the Orange River Colony. In this a detachment of the Highland Scouts raised by the public spirit of Lord Lovat was surprised at night and very severely handled by Kritzinger's commando. The loss of Colonel Murray, their commander, of the adjutant of the same name, and of forty-two out of eighty of the Scouts, shows how fell was the attack, which broke as sudden and as strong as a South African thunderstorm upon the unconscious camp. The Boers appear to have eluded the outposts and crept right among the sleeping troops, as they did in the case of the Victorians at Wilmansrust. Twelve gunners were also hit, and the only field gun taken. The retiring Boers were swiftly followed up by Thorneycroft's column, however, and the gun was retaken, together with twenty of Kritzinger's men. It must be confessed that there seems some irony in the fact that, within five days of the British ruling by which the Boers were no longer a military force, these non-belligerents had inflicted a loss of nearly six hundred men killed, wounded, or taken. Two small commandos, that of Koch in the Orange River Colony, and that of Carolina, had been captured by Williams and Benson. Combined they only numbered a hundred and nine men, but here, as always, they were men who could never be replaced.

Those who had followed the war with care, and had speculated upon the future, were prepared on hearing of Botha's movement upon Natal to learn that De la Rey had also made some energetic attack in the western quarter of the Transvaal. Those who had formed this expectation were not disappointed, for upon the last day of September the Boer chief struck fiercely at Kekewich's column in a vigorous night attack, which led to as stern an encounter as any in the campaign. This was the action at Moedwill, near Magato Nek, in the Magaliesberg.

When last mentioned De la Rey was in the Marico district, near Zeerust, where he fought two actions with Methuen in the early part of September. Thence he made his way to Rustenburg and into the Magaliesberg country, where he joined Kemp. The Boer force was followed up by two British columns under Kekewich and Fetherstonhaugh. The former commander had camped upon the night of Sunday, September 30th, at the farm of Moedwill, in a strong position within a triangle formed by the Selous River on the west, a *donga* on the east, and the Zeerust-Rustenburg road as a base. The apex of the triangle pointed north, with a ridge on the farther side of the river.

The men with Kekewich were for the most part the same as those who had fought in the Vlakfontein engagement—the Derbys, the 1st Scottish Horse, the Yeomanry, and the 28th R.F.A. Every precaution appears to have been taken by the leader, and his pickets were thrown out so far that ample warning was assured of an attack. The Boer onslaught came so suddenly and fiercely, however, in the early morning, that the posts upon the river bank were driven in or destroyed and the riflemen from the ridge on the farther side were able to sweep the camp with their fire. In numbers the two forces were not unequal, but the Boers had already obtained the tactical advantage, and were playing a game in which they are the schoolmasters of the world. Never has the British spirit flamed up more fiercely, and from the commander to the latest yeoman recruit there was not a man who flinched from a difficult and almost a desperate task. The Boers must at all hazard be driven from the position which enabled them to command the camp. No retreat was possible without such an abandonment of stores as would amount to a disaster. In the confusion and the uncertain light of early dawn there was no chance of a concerted movement, though Kekewich made such dispositions as were possible with admirable coolness and promptness. Squadrons and companies closed in upon the river bank with the one thought of coming to close quarters and driving the enemy from their commanding position. Already more than half the horses and a very large number of officers and men had gone down before the pelting bullets. Scottish Horse, Yeomanry, and Derbys pushed on, the young soldiers of the two former corps keeping pace with the veteran regiment. 'All the men behaved simply splendidly,' said a spectator, 'taking what little cover there was and advancing yard by yard. An order was given to try and saddle up a squadron, with the idea of getting round their flank. I had the saddle almost on one of my ponies when he was hit in two places. Two men trying to saddle alongside of me were both shot dead, and Lieutenant Wortley was shot through the knee. I ran back to where I had been firing from and found the Colonel slightly hit, the Adjutant wounded and dying, and men dead and wounded all round.' But the counter-attack soon began to make way. At first the advance was slow, but soon it quickened into a magnificent rush, the wounded Kekewich whooping on his men, and the guns coming into action as the enemy began to fall back before the fierce charge of the British riflemen. At six o'clock De la Rey's burghers had seen that their attempt was hopeless, and were in full retreat—a retreat which could not be harassed by the victors, whose cavalry had been converted by that hail of bullets into footmen. The repulse had been absolute and complete, for not a man or a cartridge had been taken from the British, but the price paid in killed and wounded was a heavy one. No fewer than 161 had been hit, including the gallant leader, whose hurt did not prevent him from resuming his duties within a few days. The heaviest losses fell upon the Scottish Horse, and upon the Derbys; but the Yeomanry also proved on this, as on some other occasions, how ungenerous were the criticisms to which they had been exposed. There are few actions in the war which appear to have been more creditable to the troops engaged.

Though repulsed at Moedwill, De la Rey, the grim, long-bearded fighting man, was by no means discouraged. From the earliest days of the campaign, when he first faced Methuen upon the road to Kimberley, he had shown that he was a most dangerous antagonist, tenacious, ingenious, and indomitable. With him were a body of irreconcilable burghers, who were the veterans of many engagements, and in Kemp he had an excellent fighting subordinate. His command extended over a wide stretch of populous country, and at any time he could bring considerable reinforcements to his aid, who would separate again to their farms and hiding-places when their venture was accomplished. For some weeks after the fight at Moedwill the Boer forces remained quiet in that district. Two British columns had left Zeerust on October 17th, under Methuen and Von Donop, in order to sweep the surrounding country, the one working in the direction of Elands River and the other in that of Rustenburg. They returned to Zeerust twelve days later, after a successful foray, which had been attended with much sniping and skirmishing, but only one action which is worthy of record.

This was fought on October 24th at a spot near Kleinfontein, upon the Great Marico River, which runs to the north-east of Zeerust. Von Donop's column was straggling through very broken and bush-covered country when it was furiously charged in the flank and rear by two separate bodies of burghers. Kemp, who commanded the flank attack, cut into the line of wagons and destroyed eight of them, killing many of the Kaffir drivers, before he could be driven off. De la Rey and Steenkamp, who rushed the rear-guard, had a more desperate contest. The Boer horsemen got among the two guns of the 4th R.F.A., and held temporary possession of them, but the small escort were veterans of the 'Fighting Fifth,' who lived up to the traditions of their famous north-country regiment. Of the gun crews of the section, amounting to about twenty-six men, the young officer, Hill, and sixteen men were hit. Of the escort of Northumberland Fusiliers hardly a man was left standing, and forty-one of the supporting Yeomanry were killed and wounded. It was for some little time a fierce and concentrated struggle at the shortest of ranges. The British horsemen came galloping to the rescue, however, and the attack was finally driven back into that broken country from which it had come. Forty dead Boers upon the ground, with their brave chieftain, Ouisterhuisen, amongst them, showed how manfully the attack had been driven home. The British losses were twenty-eight killed and fifty-six wounded. Somewhat mauled, and with eight missing wagons, the small column made its way back to Zeerust.

From this incident until the end of the year nothing of importance occurred in this part of the seat of war, save for a sharp and well-managed action at Beestekraal upon October 29th, in which seventy-nine Boers were surrounded and captured by Kekewich's horsemen. The process of attrition went very steadily forwards, and each of the British columns returned its constant tale of prisoners. The blockhouse system had now been extended to such an extent that the Magaliesberg was securely held, and a line had been pushed through from Klerksdorp and Fredericstad to Ventersdorp. One of Colonel Hickie's Yeomanry patrols was roughly handled near Brakspruit upon November 13th, but with this exception the points scored were all upon one side. Methuen and Kekewich came across early in November from Zeerust to Klerksdorp, and operated from the railway line. The end of the year saw them both in the Wolmaranstad district, where they were gathering up prisoners and clearing the country.

Of the events in the other parts of the Transvaal, during the last three months of the year 1901, there is not much to be said. In all parts the lines of blockhouses and of constabulary posts were neutralising the Boer mobility, and bringing them more and more within reach of the British. The only fighting forces left in the Transvaal were those under Botha in the south-east and those under De la Rey in the west. The others attempted nothing save to escape from their pursuers, and when overtaken they usually gave in without serious opposition. Among the larger hauls may be mentioned that of Dawkins in the Nylstrom district (seventy-six prisoners), Kekewich (seventy-eight), Colenbrander in the north (fifty-seven), Dawkins and Colenbrander (104), Colenbrander (sixty-two); but the great majority of the captures were in smaller bodies, gleaned from the caves, the *kloofs*, and the farmhouses.

Only two small actions during these months appear to call for any separate notice. The first was an attack made by Buys' commando, upon November 20th, on the Railway Pioneers when at work near Villiersdorp, in the extreme north-east of the Orange River Colony. This corps, consisting mainly of miners from Johannesburg, had done invaluable service during the war. On this occasion a working party of them was suddenly attacked, and most of them taken prisoners. Major Fisher, who commanded the pioneers, was killed, and three other officers with several men were wounded. Colonel Rimington's column appeared upon the scene, however, and drove off the Boers, who left their leader, Buys, a wounded prisoner in our hands.

The second action was a sharp attack delivered by Muller's Boers upon Colonel Park's column on the night of December 19th, at Elandspruit. The fight was sharp while it lasted, but it ended in the repulse of the assailants. The British casualties were six killed and twenty-four wounded. The Boers, who left eight dead behind them, suffered probably to about the same extent.

Already the most striking and pleasing feature in the Transvaal was the tranquillity of its central provinces, and the way in which the population was settling down to its old avocations. Pretoria had resumed its normal quiet life, while its larger and more energetic neighbour was rapidly recovering from its two years of paralysis. Every week more stamps were dropped in the mines, and from month to month a steady increase in the output showed that the great staple industry of the place would soon be as vigorous as ever. Most pleasing of all was the restoration of safety upon the railway lines, which, save for some precautions at night, had resumed their normal traffic. When the observer took his eyes from the dark clouds which shadowed every horizon, he could not but rejoice at the ever-widening central stretch of peaceful blue which told that the storm was nearing its end.

Having now dealt with the campaign in the Transvaal down to the end of 1901, it only remains to bring the chronicle of the events in the Orange River Colony down to the same date. Reference has already been made to two small British reverses which occurred in September, the loss of two guns to the south of the Waterworks near Bloemfontein, and the surprise of the camp of Lord Lovat's Scouts. There were some indications at this time that a movement had been planned through the passes of the Drakensberg by a small Free State force which should aid Louis Botha's invasion of Natal. The main movement was checked, however, and the demonstration in aid of it came to nothing.

The blockhouse system had been developed to a very complete extent in the Orange River Colony, and the small bands of Boers found it increasingly difficult to escape from the British columns who were for ever at their heels. The southern portion of the country had been cut off from the northern by a line which extended through Bloemfontein on the east to the Basuto frontier, and on the west to Jacobsdal. To the south of this line the Boer resistance had practically ceased, although several columns moved continually through it, and gleaned up the broken fragments of the commandos. The north-west had also settled down to a large extent, and during the last three months of 1901 no action of importance occurred in that region. Even in the turbulent north-east, which had always been the centre of resistance, there was little opposition to the British columns, which continued every week to send in their tale of prisoners. Of the column commanders, Williams, Damant, Du Moulin, Lowry Cole, and Wilson were the most successful. In their operations they were much aided by the South African Constabulary. One young officer of this force, Major Pack-Beresford, especially distinguished himself by his gallantry and ability. His premature death from enteric was a grave loss to the British army. Save for one skirmish of Colonel Wilson's early in October, and another of Byng's on November 14th, there can hardly be said to have been any actual fighting until the events late in December which I am about to describe.

In the meanwhile the peaceful organisation of the country was being pushed forward as rapidly as in the Transvaal, although here the problems presented were of a different order, and the population an exclusively Dutch one. The schools already showed a higher attendance than in the days before the war, while a continual stream of burghers presented themselves to take the oath of allegiance, and even to join the ranks against their own irreconcilable countrymen, whom they looked upon with justice as the real authors of their troubles.

Towards the end of November there were signs that the word had gone forth for a fresh concentration of the fighting Boers in their old haunts in the Heilbron district, and early in December it was known that the indefatigable De Wet was again in the field. He had remained quiet so long that there had been persistent rumours of his injury and even of his death, but he was soon to show that he was as alive as ever. President Steyn was ill of a most serious complaint, caused possibly by the mental and physical sufferings which he had undergone; but with an indomitable resolution which makes one forget and forgive the fatuous policy which brought him and his State to such a pass, he still appeared in his Cape cart at the *laager* of the faithful remnant of his commandos. To those who remembered how widespread was our conviction of the half-heartedness of the Free Staters at the outbreak of the war, it was indeed a revelation to see them after two years still making a stand against the forces which had crushed them.

It had been long evident that the present British tactics of scouring the country and capturing the isolated burghers must in time bring the war to a conclusion. From the Boer point of view the only hope, or at least the only glory, lay in reassembling once more in larger bodies and trying conclusions with some of the British columns. It was with this purpose that De Wet early in December assembled Wessels, Manie Botha, and others of his lieutenants, together with a force of about two thousand men, in the Heilbron district. Small as this force was, it was admirably mobile, and every man in it was a veteran, toughened and seasoned by two years of constant fighting. De Wet's first operations were directed against an isolated column of Colonel Wilson's, which was surrounded within twenty miles of Heilbron. Rimington, in response to a heliographic call for assistance, hurried with admirable promptitude to the scene of action, and joined hands with Wilson. De Wet's men were as numerous, however, as the two columns combined, and they harassed the return march into Heilbron. A determined attack was made on the convoy and on the rearguard, but it was beaten off. That night Rimington's camp was fired into by a large body of Boers, but he had cleverly moved his men away from the fires, so that no harm was done. The losses in these operations were small, but with troops which had not been trained in this method of fighting the situation would have been a serious one. For a fortnight or more after this the burghers contented themselves by skirmishing with British columns and avoiding a drive which Elliot's forces made against them. On December 18th they took the offensive, however, and within a week fought three actions, two of which ended in their favour.

News had come to British headquarters that Kaffir's Kop, to the north-west of Bethlehem, was a centre of Boer activity. Three columns were therefore turned in that direction, Elliot's, Barker's, and Dartnell's. Some desultory skirmishing ensued, which was only remarkable for the death of Haasbroek, a well-known Boer leader. As the columns separated again, unable to find an objective, De Wet suddenly showed one of them that their failure was not due to his absence. Dartnell had retraced his steps nearly as far as Eland's River Bridge, when the Boer leader sprang out of his lair in the Langberg and threw himself upon him. The burghers attempted to ride in, as they had successfully done at Brakenlaagte, but they were opposed by the steady old troopers of the two regiments of Imperial Horse, and by a General who was familiar with every Boer ruse. The horsemen never got nearer than 150 yards to the British line, and were beaten back by the steady fire which met them. Finding that he made no headway, and learning that Campbell's column was coming up from Bethlehem, De Wet withdrew his men after four hours' fighting. Fifteen were hit upon the British side, and the Boer loss seems to have been certainly as great or greater.

De Wet's general aim in his operations seems to have been to check the British blockhouse building. With his main force in the Langberg he could threaten the line which was now being erected between Bethlehem and Harrismith, a line against which his main commando was destined, only two months later, to beat itself in vain. Sixty miles to the north a second line was being run across country from Frankfort to Standerton, and had reached a place called Tafelkop. A covering party of East Lancashires and Yeomanry watched over the workers, but De Wet had left a portion of his force in that neighbourhood, and they harassed the blockhouse builders to such an extent that General Hamilton, who was in command, found it necessary to send in to Frankfort for support. The British columns there had just returned exhausted from a drive, but three bodies under Damant, Rimington, and Wilson were at once despatched to clear away the enemy.

The weather was so atrocious that the *veldt* resembled an inland sea, with the *kopjes* as islands rising out of it. By this stage of the war the troops were hardened to all weathers, and they pushed swiftly on to the scene of action. As they approached the spot where the Boers had been reported, the line had been extended over many miles, with the result that it had become very attenuated and dangerously weak in the centre. At this point Colonel Damant and his small staff were alone with the two guns and the maxim, save for a handful of Imperial Yeomanry (91st), who acted as escort to the guns. Across the face of this small force there rode a body of men in khaki uniforms, keeping British formation, and actually firing bogus volleys from time to time in the direction of some distant Boers. Damant and his staff seem to have taken it for granted that these were Rimington's men, and the clever ruse succeeded to perfection. Nearer and nearer came the strangers, and suddenly throwing off all disguise, they made a dash for the guns. Four rounds of case failed to stop them, and in a few minutes they were over the *kopje* on which the guns stood and had ridden among the gunners, supported in their attack by a flank fire from a number of dismounted riflemen.

The instant that the danger was realised Damant, his staff, and the forty Yeomen who formed the escort dashed for the crest in the hope of anticipating the Boers. So rapid was the charge of the others that they had overwhelmed the gunners before the supports could reach the hill, and the latter found themselves under the deadly fire of the Boer rifles from above. Damant was hit in four places, all of his staff were wounded, and hardly a man of the small body of Yeomanry was left standing. Nothing could exceed their gallantry. Gaussen their captain fell at their head.

On the ridge the men about the guns were nearly all killed or wounded. Of the gun detachment only two men remained, both of them hit, and Jeffcoat their dying captain bequeathed them fifty pounds each in a will drawn upon the spot. In half an hour the centre of the British line had been absolutely annihilated. Modern warfare is on the whole much less bloody than of old, but when one party has gained the tactical mastery it is a choice between speedy surrender and total destruction.

The wide-spread British wings had begun to understand that there was something amiss, and to ride in towards the centre. An officer on the far right peering through his glasses saw those tell-tale puffs at the very muzzles of the British guns, which showed that they were firing case at close quarters. He turned his squadron inwards and soon gathered up Scott's squadron of Damant's Horse, and both rode for the *kopje*. Rimington's men were appearing on the other side, and the Boers rode off. They were unable to remove the guns which they had taken, because all the horses had perished. 'I actually thought,' says one officer who saw them ride away, 'that I had made a mistake and been fighting our own men. They were dressed in our uniforms and some of them wore the tiger-skin, the badge of Damant's Horse, round their hats.' The same officer gives an account of the scene on the gun-*kopje*. 'The result when we got to the guns was this, gunners all killed except two (both wounded), pom-pom officers and men all killed, maxim all killed, 91st (the gun escort) one officer and one man not hit, all the rest killed or wounded; staff, every officer hit.' That is what it means to those who are caught in the vortex of the cyclone. The total loss was about seventy-five.

In this action the Boers, who were under the command of Wessels, delivered their attack with a cleverness and dash which deserved success. Their stratagem, however, depending as it did upon the use of British uniforms and methods, was illegitimate by all the laws of war, and one can but marvel at the long-suffering patience of officers and men who endured such things without any attempt at retaliation. There is too much reason to believe also, that considerable brutality was shown by those Boers who carried the *kopje*, and the very high proportion of killed to wounded among the British who lay there corroborates the statement of the survivors that several were shot at close quarters after all resistance had ceased.

This rough encounter of Tafelkop was followed only four days later by a very much more serious one at Tweefontein, which proved that even after two years of experience we had not yet sufficiently understood the courage and the cunning of our antagonist. The blockhouse line was being gradually extended from Harrismith to Bethlehem, so as to hold down this turbulent portion of the country. The Harrismith section had been pushed as far as Tweefontein, which is nine miles west of Elands River Bridge, and here a small force was stationed to cover the workers. This column consisted of four squadrons of the 4th Imperial Yeomanry, one gun of the 79th battery, and one pom-pom, the whole under the temporary command of Major Williams of the South Staffords, Colonel Firmin being absent.

Knowing that De Wet and his men were in the neighbourhood, the camp of the Yeomen had been pitched in a position which seemed to secure it against attack. A solitary *kopje* presented a long slope to the north, while the southern end was precipitous. The outposts were pushed well out upon the plain, and a line of sentries was placed along the crest. The only precaution which seems to have been neglected was to have other outposts at the base of the southern declivity. It appears to have been taken for granted, however, that no attack was to be apprehended from that side, and that in any case it would be impossible to evade the vigilance of the sentries upon the top.

Of all the daring and skilful attacks delivered by the Boers during the war there is certainly none more remarkable than this one. At two o'clock in the morning of a moonlight night De Wet's forlorn hope assembled at the base of the hill and clambered up to the summit. The fact that it was Christmas Eve may conceivably have had something to do with the want of vigilance upon the part of the sentries. In a season of good will and conviviality the rigour of military discipline may insensibly relax. Little did the sleeping Yeomen in the tents, or the drowsy outposts upon the crest, think of the terrible Christmas visitors who were creeping on to them, or of the grim morning gift which Santa Claus was bearing.

The Boers, stealing up in their stockinged feet, poured under the crest until they were numerous enough to make a rush. It is almost inconceivable how they could have got so far without their presence being suspected by the sentries—but so it was. At last, feeling strong enough to advance, they sprang over the crest and fired into the pickets, and past them into the sleeping camp. The top of the hill being once gained, there was nothing to prevent their comrades from swarming up, and in a very few minutes nearly a thousand Boers were in a position to command the camp. The British were not only completely outnumbered, but were hurried from their sleep into the fight without any clear idea as to the danger or how to meet it, while the hissing sleet of bullets struck many of them down as they rushed out of their tents. Considering how terrible the ordeal was to which they were exposed, these untried Yeomen seem to have behaved very well. 'Some brave gentlemen ran away at the first shot, but I am thankful to say they were not many,' says one of their number. The most veteran troops would have been tried very high had they been placed in such a position. 'The noise and the clamour,' says one spectator, 'were awful. The yells of the Dutch, the screams and shrieks of dying men and horses, the cries of natives, howls of dogs, the firing, the galloping of horses, the whistling of bullets, and the whirr volleys make in the air, made up such a compound of awful and diabolical sounds as I never heard before nor hope to hear again. In the confusion some of the men killed each other and some killed themselves. Two Boers who put on helmets were killed by their own people. The men were given no time to rally or to collect their thoughts, for the gallant Boers barged right into them, shooting them down, and occasionally being shot down, at a range of a few yards. Harwich and Watney, who had charge of the maxim, died nobly with all the men of their gun section round them. Reed, the sergeant-major, rushed at the enemy with his clubbed rifle, but was riddled with bullets. Major Williams, the commander, was shot through the stomach as he rallied his men. The gunners had time to fire two rounds before they were overpowered and shot down to a man. For half an hour the resistance was maintained, but at the end of that time the Boers had the whole camp in their possession, and were already hastening to get their prisoners away before the morning should bring a rescue.

The casualties are in themselves enough to show how creditable was the resistance of the Yeomanry. Out of a force of under four hundred men they had six officers and fifty-one men killed, eight officers and eighty men wounded. There have been very few surrenders during the war in which there has been such evidence as this of a determined stand. Nor was it a bloodless victory upon the part of the Boers, for there was evidence that their losses, though less than those of the British, were still severe.

The prisoners, over two hundred in number, were hurried away by the Boers, who seemed under the immediate eye of De Wet to have behaved with exemplary humanity to the wounded. The captives were taken by forced marches to the Basuto border, where they were turned adrift, half clad and without food. By devious ways and after many adventures, they all made their way back again to the British lines. It was well for De Wet that he had shown such promptness in getting away, for within three hours of the end of the action the two regiments of Imperial Horse appeared upon the scene, having travelled seventeen miles in the time. Already, however, the rearguard of the Boers was disappearing into the fastness of the Langberg, where all pursuit was vain.

Such was the short but vigorous campaign of De Wet in the last part of December of the year 1901. It had been a brilliant one, but none the less his bolt was shot, and Tweefontein was the last encounter in which British troops should feel his heavy hand. His operations, bold as they had been, had not delayed by a day the building of that iron cage which was gradually enclosing him. Already it was nearly completed, and in a few more weeks he was destined to find himself and his commando struggling against bars.

CHAPTER 37

The Campaign of January to April, 1902

At the opening of the year 1902 it was evident to every observer that the Boer resistance, spirited as it was, must be nearing its close. By a long succession of captures their forces were much reduced in numbers. They were isolated from the world, and had no means save precarious smuggling of renewing their supplies of ammunition. It was known also that their mobility, which had been their great strength, was decreasing, and that in spite of their admirable horsemastership their supply of remounts was becoming exhausted. An increasing number of the burghers were volunteering for service against their own people, and it was found that all fears as to this delicate experiment were misplaced, and that in the whole army there were no keener and more loyal soldiers.

The chief factor, however, in bringing the Boers to their knees was the elaborate and wonderful blockhouse system, which had been strung across the whole of the enemy's country. The original blockhouses had been far apart, and were a hindrance and an annoyance rather than an absolute barrier to the burghers. The new models, however, were only six hundred yards apart, and were connected by such impenetrable strands of wire that a Boer pithily described it by saying that if one's hat blew over the line anywhere between Ermelo and Standerton one had to walk round Ermelo to fetch it. Use was made of such barriers by the Spaniards in Cuba, but an application of them on such a scale over such an enormous tract of country is one of the curiosities of warfare, and will remain one of several novelties which will make the South African campaign for ever interesting to students of military history.

The spines of this great system were always the railway lines, which were guarded on either side, and down which, as down a road, went flocks, herds, pedestrians, and everything which wished to travel in safety. From these long central cords the lines branched out to right and left, cutting up

454

the great country into manageable districts. A category of them would but weary the reader, but suffice it that by the beginning of the year the south-east of the Transvaal and the north-east of the Orange River Colony, the haunts of Botha and De Wet, had been so intersected that it was obvious that the situation must soon be impossible for both of them. Only on the west of the Transvaal was there a clear run for De la Rey and Kemp. Hence it was expected, as actually occurred, that in this quarter the most stirring events of the close of the campaign would happen.

General Bruce Hamilton in the Eastern Transvaal had continued the energetic tactics which had given such good results in the past. With the new year his number of prisoners fell, but he had taken so many, and had hustled the remainder to such an extent, that the fight seemed to have gone out of the Boers in this district. On January 1st he presented the first-fruits of the year in the shape of twenty-two of Grobler's burghers. On the 3rd he captured forty-nine, while Wing, co-operating with him, took twenty more. Among these was General Erasmus, who had helped, or failed to help, General Lucas Meyer at Talana Hill. On the 10th Colonel Wing's column, which was part of Hamilton's force, struck out again and took forty-two prisoners, including the two Wolmarans. Only two days later Hamilton returned to the same spot, and was rewarded with thirty-two more captures. On the 18th he took twenty-seven, on the 24th twelve, and on the 26th no fewer than ninety. So severe were these blows, and so difficult was it for the Boers to know how to get away from an antagonist who was ready to ride thirty miles in a night in order to fall upon their *laager*, that the enemy became much scattered and too de-moralised for offensive operations. Finding that they had grown too shy in this much shot over district, Hamilton moved farther south, and early in March took a cast round the Vryheid district, where he made some captures, notably General Cherry Emmett, a descendant of the famous Irish rebel, and brother-in-law of Louis Botha. For all these repeated suc-cesses it was to the Intelligence Department, so admirably controlled by Colonel Wools-Sampson, that thanks are mainly due.

Whilst Bruce Hamilton was operating so successfully in the Ermelo district, several British columns under Plumer, Spens, and Colville were stationed some fifty miles south to prevent the fugitives from getting away into the mountainous country which lies to the north of Wakker-stroom. On January 3rd a small force of Plumer's New Zealanders had a brisk skirmish with a party of Boers, whose cattle they captured, though at some loss to themselves. These Boers were strongly reinforced, how-ever, and when on the following day Major Vallentin pursued them with fifty men he found himself at Onverwacht in the presence of several hundred of the enemy, led by Oppermann and Christian Botha. Vallentin was killed and almost all of his small force were hit before British reinforcements, under Colonel Pulteney, drove the Boers off. Nineteen killed and twenty-three wounded were our losses in this most sanguinary little skirmish. Nine dead Boers, with Oppermann himself, were left upon the field of battle. His loss was a serious one to the enemy, as he was one of their most experienced Generals.

From that time until the end these columns, together with Mackenzie's column to the north of Ermelo, continued to break up all combinations, and to send in their share of prisoners to swell Lord Kitchener's weekly list. A final drive, organised on April 11th against the Standerton line, resulted in 134 prisoners.

In spite of the very large army in South Africa, so many men were absorbed by the huge lines of communications and the blockhouse system that the number available for active operations was never more than forty or fifty thousand men. With another fifty thousand there is no doubt that at least six months would have been taken from the duration of the war. On account of this short handedness Lord Kitchener had to leave certain districts alone, while he directed his attention to those which were more essential. Thus to the north of the Delagoa Railway line there was only one town, Lydenburg, which was occupied by the British. They had, however, an energetic commander in Park of the Devons. This leader, striking out from his stronghold among the mountains, and aided by Urmston from Belfast, kept the commando of Ben Viljoen and the peripatetic Government of Schalk Burger continually upon the move. As already narrated, Park fought a sharp night action upon December 19th, after which, in combination with Urmston, he occupied Dulstroom, only missing the government by a few hours. In January Park and Urmston were again upon the war-path, though the incessant winds, fogs, and rains of that most inclement portion of the Transvaal seriously hampered their operations. Several skirmishes with the commandos of Muller and Trichardt gave no very decisive result, but a piece of luck befell the British on January 25th in the capture of General Viljoen by an ambuscade cleverly arranged by Major Orr in the neighbourhood of Lydenburg. Though a great firebrand before the war, Viljoen had fought bravely and honourably throughout the contest, and he had won the respect and esteem of his enemy.

Colonel Park had had no great success in his last two expeditions, but on February 20th he made an admirable march, and fell upon a Boer *laager* which lay in placid security in the heart of the hills. One hundred and sixty-four prisoners, including many Boer officers, were the fruits of this success, in which the National Scouts, or 'tame Boers,' as they were familiarly called, played a prominent part. This commando was that of

Middelburg, which was acting as escort to the government, who again escaped dissolution. Early in March Park was again out on trek, upon one occasion covering seventy miles in a single day. Nothing further of importance came from this portion of the seat of war until March 23rd, when the news reached England that Schalk Burger, Reitz, Lucas Meyer, and others of the Transvaal Government had come into Middelburg, and that they were anxious to proceed to Pretoria to treat. On the Eastern horizon had appeared the first golden gleam of the dawning peace.

Having indicated the course of events in the Eastern Transvaal, north and south of the railway line, I will now treat one or two incidents which occurred in the more central and northern portions of the country. I will then give some account of De Wet's doings in the Orange River Colony, and finally describe that brilliant effort of De la Rey's in the west which shed a last glory upon the Boer arms.

In the latter days of December, Colenbrander and Dawkins operating together had put in a great deal of useful work in the northern district, and from Nylstrom to Pietersburg the burghers were continually harried by the activity of these leaders. Late in the month Dawkins was sent down into the Orange River Colony in order to reinforce the troops who were opposed to De Wet. Colenbrander alone, with his hardy colonial forces, swept through the Magaliesburg, and had the double satisfaction of capturing a number of the enemy and of heading off and sending back a war party of Linchwe's Kaffirs who, incensed by a cattle raid of Kemp's, were moving down in a direction which would have brought them dangerously near to the Dutch women and children. This instance and several similar ones in the campaign show how vile are the lies which have been told of the use, save under certain well-defined conditions, of armed natives by the British during the war. It would have been a perfectly easy thing at any time for the Government to have raised all the fighting native races of South Africa, but it is not probable that we, who held back our admirable and highly disciplined Sikhs and Ghoorkas, would break our self-imposed restrictions in order to enrol the inferior but more savage races of Africa. Yet no charge has been more often repeated and has caused more piteous protests among the soft-hearted and soft-headed editors of Continental journals.

The absence of Colenbrander in the Rustenburg country gave Beyers a chance of which he was not slow to avail himself. On January 24th, in the early morning, he delivered an attack upon Pietersburg itself, but he was easily driven off by the small garrison. It is probable, however, that the attack was a mere feint in order to enable a number of the inmates of the refugee camp to escape. About a hundred and fifty made off, and rejoined the commandos. There were three thousand Boers in all in this camp, which was shortly afterwards moved down to Natal in order to avoid the recurrence of such an incident.

Colenbrander, having returned to Pietersburg once more, determined to return Beyers's visit, and upon April 8th he moved out with a small force to surprise the Boer *laager*. The Inniskilling Fusiliers seized the ground which commanded the enemy's position. The latter retreated, but were followed up, and altogether about one hundred and fifty were killed, wounded, and taken. On May 3rd a fresh operation against Beyers was undertaken, and resulted in about the same loss to the Boers. On the other hand, the Boers had a small success against Kitchener's Scouts, killing eighteen and taking thirty prisoners.

There is one incident, however, in connection with the war in this region which one would desire to pass over in silence if such a course were permissible. Some eighty miles to the east of Pietersburg is a wild part of the country called the Spelonken. In this region an irregular corps, named the Bush-*veldt* Carabineers, had been operating. It was raised in South Africa, but contained both Colonials and British in its ranks. Its wild duties, its mixed composition, and its isolated situation must have all militated against discipline and restraint, and it appears to have degenerated into a band not unlike those Southern 'bush-whackers' in the American war to whom the Federals showed little mercy. They had given short shrift to the Boer prisoners who had fallen into their hands, the excuse offered for their barbarous conduct being that an officer who had served in the corps had himself been murdered by the Boers. Such a reason, even if it were true, could of course offer no justification for indiscriminate revenge. The crimes were committed in July and August 1901, but it was not until January 1902 that five of the officers were put upon their trial and were found to be guilty as principals or accessories of twelve murders. The corps was disbanded, and three of the accused officers, Handcock, Wilton, and Morant, were sentenced to death, while another, Picton, was cashiered. Handcock and Morant were actually executed. This stern measure shows more clearly than volumes of argument could do how high was the standard of discipline in the British Army, and how heavy was the punishment, and how vain all excuses, where it had been infringed. In the face of this actual outrage and its prompt punishment how absurd becomes that crusade against imaginary outrages preached by an ignorant press abroad, and by renegade Englishmen at home.

To the south of Johannesburg, half-way between that town and the frontier, there is a range of hills called the Zuikerboschrand, which extends across from one railway system to the other. A number of Boers were known to have sought refuge in this country, so upon February 12th a small British force left Klip River Post in order to clear them out. There were 320 men in all, composing the 28th Mounted Infantry, drawn from the Lancashire Fusiliers, Warwicks, and Derbys, most of whom had just arrived from Malta, which one would certainly imagine to be the last place where mounted infantry could be effectively trained. Major Dowell was in command. An advance was made into the hilly country, but it was found that the enemy was in much greater force than had been imagined. The familiar Boer tactics were used with the customary success. The British line was held by a sharp fire in front, while strong flanking parties galloped round each of the wings. It was with great difficulty that any of the British extricated themselves from their perilous position, and the safety of a portion of the force was only secured by the devotion of a handful of officers and men, who gave their lives in order to gain time for their comrades to get away. Twelve killed and fifty wounded were our losses in this unfortunate skirmish, and about one hundred prisoners supplied the victors with a useful addition to their rifles and ammunition. A stronger British force came up next day, and the enemy were driven out of the hills.

A week later, upon February 18th, there occurred another skirmish at Klippan, near Springs, between a squadron of the Scots Greys and a party of Boers who had broken into this central reserve which Lord Kitchener had long kept clear of the enemy. In this action the cavalry were treated as roughly as the mounted infantry had been the week before, losing three officers killed, eight men killed or wounded, and forty-six taken. They had formed a flanking party to General Gilbert Hamilton's column, but were attacked and overwhelmed so rapidly that the blow had fallen before their comrades could come to their assistance.

One of the consequences of the successful drives about to be described in the Orange River Colony was that a number of the Free Staters came north of the Vaal in order to get away from the extreme pressure upon the south. At the end of March a considerable number had reinforced the local commandos in that district to the east of Springs, no very great distance from Johannesburg, which had always been a storm centre. A cavalry force was stationed at this spot which consisted at that time of the 2nd Queen's Bays, the 7th Hussars, and some National Scouts, all under Colonel Lawley of the Hussars. After a series of minor engagements east of Springs, Lawley had possessed himself of Boschman's Kop, eighteen miles from that town, close to the district which was the chief scene of Boer activity. From this base he despatched upon the morning of April 1st three squadrons of the Bays under Colonel Fanshawe, for the purpose of surprising a small force of the enemy which was reported at one of the farms. Fanshawe's strength was about three hundred men.

The British cavalry found themselves, however, in the position of the hunter who, when he is out for a snipe, puts up a tiger. All went well with the expedition as far as Holspruit, the farm which they had started to search. Commandant Pretorius, to whom it belonged, was taken by the energy of Major Vaughan, who pursued and overtook his Cape cart. It was found, however, that Alberts's commando was camped at the farm, and that the Bays were in the presence of a very superior force of the enemy. The night was dark, and when firing began it was almost muzzle to muzzle, with the greatest possible difficulty in telling friend from foe. The three squadrons fell back upon some rising ground, keeping admirable order under most difficult circumstances. In spite of the darkness the attack was pressed fiercely home, and with their favourite tactics the burghers rapidly outflanked the position taken up by the cavalry. The British moved by alternate squadrons on to a higher rocky *kopje* on the east, which could be vaguely distinguished looming in the darkness against the skyline. B squadron, the last to retire, was actually charged and ridden through by the brave assailants, firing from their saddles as they broke through the ranks. The British had hardly time to reach the *kopje* and to dismount and line its edge when the Boers, yelling loudly, charged with their horses up the steep flanks. Twice they were beaten back, but the third time they seized one corner of the hill and opened a hot fire upon the rear of the line of men who were defending the other side. Dawn was now breaking, and the situation most serious, for the Boers were in very superior numbers and were pushing their pursuit with the utmost vigour and determination. A small party of officers and men whose horses had been shot covered the retreat of their comrades, and continued to fire until all of them, two officers and twenty-three men, were killed or wounded, the whole of their desperate defence being conducted within from thirty to fifty yards of the enemy. The remainder of the regiment was now retired to successive ridges, each of which was rapidly outflanked by the Boers, whose whole method of conducting their attack was extraordinarily skilful. Nothing but the excellent discipline of the overmatched troopers prevented the retreat from becoming a rout. Fortunately, before the pressure became intolerable the 7th Hussars with some artillery came to the rescue, and turned the tide. The Hussars galloped in with such dash that some of them actually got among the Boers with their swords, but the enemy rapidly fell back and disappeared.

In this very sharp and sanguinary cavalry skirmish the Bays lost eighty killed and wounded out of a total force of 270. To stand such losses under such circumstances, and to preserve absolute discipline and order, is a fine test of soldierly virtue. The adjutant, the squadron leaders, and six out of ten officers were killed or wounded. The Boers lost equally heavily. Two Prinsloos, one of them a commandant, and three field-cornets were among the slain, with seventy other casualties. The force under General Alberts was a considerable one, not fewer than six hundred rifles, so that the action at Holspruit is one which adds another name of honour to the battle-roll of the Bays. It is pleasing to add that in this and the other actions which were fought at the end of the war our wounded met with kindness and consideration from the enemy.

We may now descend to the Orange River Colony and trace the course of those operations which were destined to break the power of De Wet's commando. On these we may concentrate our attention, for the marchings and gleanings and snipings of the numerous small columns in the other portions of the colony, although they involved much arduous and useful work, do not claim a particular account.

After the heavy blow which he dealt Firmin's Yeomanry, De Wet retired, as has been told, into the Langberg, whence he afterwards retreated towards Reitz. There he was energetically pushed by Elliot's columns, which had attained such mobility that 150 miles were performed in three days within a single week. Our rough schoolmasters had taught us our lesson, and the soldiering which accomplished the marches of Bruce Hamilton, Elliot, Rimington, and the other leaders of the end of the war was very far removed from that which is associated with oxwagons and harmoniums.

Moving rapidly, and covering himself by a succession of rearguard skirmishes, De Wet danced like a will-o'-the-wisp in front of and round the British columns. De Lisle, Fanshawe, Byng, Rimington, Dawkins, and Rawlinson were all snatching at him and finding him just beyond their finger-tips. The master-mind at Pretoria had, however, thought out a scheme which was worthy of De Wet himself in its ingenuity. A glance at the map will show that the little branch from Heilbron to Wolvehoek forms an acute angle with the main line. Both these railways were strongly blockhoused and barbed-wired, so that any force which was driven into the angle, and held in it by a force behind it, would be in a perilous position. To attempt to round De Wet's mobile burghers into this obvious pen would have been to show one's hand too clearly. In vain is the net laid in sight of the bird. The drive was therefore made away from this point, with the confident expectation that the guerrilla chief would break back through the columns, and that they might then pivot round upon him and hustle him so rapidly into the desired position that he would not realise his danger until it was too late. Byng's column was left behind the driving line to be ready for the expected backward break. All came off exactly as expected. De Wet doubled back through the columns, and one of his commandos stumbled upon Byng's men, who were waiting on the Vlei River to the west of Reitz. The Boers seem to have taken it for granted that, having passed the British driving line, they were out of danger, and for once it was they who were surprised. The South African Light Horse, the New Zealanders, and the Queensland Bushmen all rode in upon them. A fifteen-pounder, the one taken at Tweefontein, and two pom-poms were captured, with thirty prisoners and a considerable quantity of stores.

This successful skirmish was a small matter, however, compared to the importance of being in close touch with De Wet and having a definite objective for the drive. The columns behind expanded suddenly into a spray of mounted men forming a continuous line for over sixty miles. On February 5th the line was advancing, and on the 6th it was known that De Wet was actually within the angle, the mouth of which was spanned by the British line. Hope ran high in Pretoria. The space into which the burgher chief had been driven was bounded by sixty-six miles of block-house and wire on one side and thirty on the other, while the third side of the triangle was crossed by fifty-five miles of British horsemen, flanked by a blockhouse line between Kroonstad and Lindley. The tension along the lines of defence was extreme. Infantry guarded every yard of them, and armoured trains patrolled them, while at night searchlights at regular intervals shed their vivid rays over the black expanse of the *veldt* and il-luminated the mounted figures who flitted from time to time across their narrow belts of light.

On the 6th De Wet realised his position, and with characteristic audacity and promptness he took means to clear the formidable toils which had been woven round him. The greater part of his command scattered, with orders to make their way as best they might out of the danger. Working in their own country, where every crease and fold of the ground was familiar to them, it is not surprising that most of them managed to make their way through gaps in the attenuated line of horsemen behind them. A few were killed, and a considerable number taken, 270 being the respectable total of the prisoners. Three or four slipped through, however, for every one who stuck in the meshes. De Wet himself was reported to have made his escape by driving cattle against the wire fences which enclosed him. It seems, however, to have been nothing more romantic than a wire-cutter which cleared his path, though cattle no doubt made their way through the gap which he left. With a loss of only three of his immediate followers be Wet won his way out of the most dangerous position which even his adventurous career had ever known. Lord Kitchener had descended to Wolvehoek to be present at the climax of the operations, but it was not fated that he was to receive the submission of the most energetic of his opponents, and he returned to Pretoria to weave a fresh mesh around him.

This was not hard to do, as the Boer General had simply escaped from one pen into another, though a larger one. After a short rest to restore the columns, the whole pack were full cry upon his heels once more. An acute angle is formed by the Wilge River on one side and the line of blockhouses between Harrismith and Van Reenen upon the other. This was strongly manned by troops and five columns; those of Rawlinson, Nixon, Byng, Rimington, and Keir herded the broken commandos into the trap. From February 20th the troops swept in an enormous skirmish line across the country, ascending hills, exploring *kloofs*, searching river banks, and always keeping the enemy in front of them. At last, when the pressure was severely felt, there came the usual break-back, which took the form of a most determined night attack upon the British line. This was delivered shortly after midnight on February 23rd. It struck the British cordon at the point of juncture between Byng's column and that of Rimington. So huge were the distances which had to be covered, and so attenuated was the force which covered them, that the historical thin red line was a massive formation compared to its khaki equivalent. The chain was frail and the links were not all carefully joined, but each particular link was good metal, and the Boer impact came upon one of the best. This was the 7th New Zealand Contingent, who proved themselves to be worthy comrades to their six gallant predecessors. Their patrols were broken by the rush of wild, yelling, firing horsemen, but the troopers made a most gallant resistance. Having pierced the line the Boers, who were led in their fiery rush by Manie Botha, turned to their flank, and, charging down the line of weak patrols, overwhelmed one after another and threatened to roll up the whole line. They had cleared a gap of half a mile, and it seemed as if the whole Boer force would certainly escape through so long a gap in the defences. The desperate defence of the New Zealanders gave time, however, for the further patrols, which consisted of Cox's New South Wales Mounted Infantry, to fall back almost at right angles so as to present a fresh face to the attack. The pivot of the resistance was a maxim gun, most gallantly handled by Captain Begbie and his men. The fight at this point was almost muzzle to muzzle, fifty or sixty New Zealanders and Australians with the British gunners holding off a force of several hundred of the best fighting men of the Boer forces. In this desperate duel many dropped on both sides. Begbie died beside his gun, which fired eighty rounds before it jammed. It was run back by its crew in order to save it from capture. But reinforcements were coming up, and the Boer attack was beaten back. A number of them had escaped, however, through the opening which they had cleared, and it was conjectured that the wonderful De Wet was among them. How fierce was the storm which had broken on the New Zealanders may be shown by their roll of twenty killed and forty wounded, while thirty dead Boers were picked up in front of their picket line. Of eight New Zealand officers seven are reported to have been hit, an even higher proportion than that which the same gallant race endured at the battle of Rhenoster Kop more than a year before.

It was feared at first that the greater part of the Boers might have escaped upon this night of the 23rd, when Manie Botha's storming party burst through the ranks of the New Zealanders. It was soon discovered that this was not so, and the columns as they closed in had evidence from the numerous horsemen who scampered aimlessly over the hills in front of them that the main body of the enemy was still in the toils. The advance was in tempestuous weather and over rugged country, but the men were filled with eagerness, and no precaution was neglected to keep the line intact.

This time their efforts were crowned with considerable success. A second attempt was made by the corralled burghers to break out on the night of February 26th, but it was easily repulsed by Nixon. The task of the troopers as the cordon drew south was more and more difficult, and there were places traversed upon the Natal border where an alpen stock would have been a more useful adjunct than a horse. At six o'clock on the morning of the 27th came the end. Two Boers appeared in front of the advancing line of the Imperial Light Horse and held up a flag. They proved to be Truter and De Jager, ready to make terms for their commando. The only terms offered were absolute surrender within the hour. The Boers had been swept into a very confined space, which was closely hemmed in by troops, so that any resistance must have ended in a tragedy. Fortunately there was no reason for desperate councils in their case, since they did not fight as Lotter had done, with the shadow of judgment hanging over him. The burghers piled arms, and all was over.

The total number captured in this important drive was 780 men, including several leaders, one of whom was De Wet's own son. It was found that De Wet himself had been among those who had got away through the picket lines on the night of the 23rd. Most of the commando were Transvaalers, and it was typical of the wide sweep of the net that many of them were the men who had been engaged against the 28th Mounted Infantry in the district south of Johannesburg upon the 12th of the same month. The loss of 2000 horses and 50,000 cartridges meant as much as that of the men to the Boer army. It was evident that a few more such blows would clear the Orange River Colony altogether.

The wearied troopers were allowed little rest, for in a couple of days after their rendezvous at Harrismith they were sweeping back again to pick up all that they had missed. This drive, which was over the same ground, but sweeping backwards towards the Heilbron to Wolvehoek line, ended in the total capture of 147 of the enemy, who were picked out of holes, retrieved from amid the reeds of the river, called down out of trees, or otherwise collected. So thorough were the operations that it is recorded that the angle which formed the apex of the drive was one drove of game upon the last day, all the many types of antelope, which form one of the characteristics and charms of the country, having been herded into it.

More important even than the results of the drive was the discovery of one of De Wet's arsenals in a cave in the Vrede district. Half-way down a precipitous *krantz*, with its mouth covered by creepers, no writer of romance could have imagined a more fitting headquarters for a guerrilla chief. The find was made by Ross's Canadian Scouts, who celebrated Dominion Day by this most useful achievement. Forty wagon-loads of ammunition and supplies were taken out of the cave. De Wet was known to have left the north-east district, and to have got across the railway, travelling towards the Vaal as if it were his intention to join De la Rey in the Transvaal. The Boer resistance had suddenly become exceedingly energetic in that part, and several important actions had been fought, to which we will presently turn.

Before doing so it would be as well to bring the chronicle of events in the Orange River Colony down to the conclusion of peace. There were still a great number of wandering Boers in the northern districts and in the frontier mountains, who were assiduously, but not always success-fully, hunted down by the British troops. Much arduous and useful work was done by several small columns, the Colonial Horse and the Artillery Mounted Rifles especially distinguishing themselves. The latter corps, formed from the gunners whose field-pieces were no longer needed, proved themselves to be a most useful body of men; and the British gun-ner, when he took to carrying his gun, vindicated the reputation which he had won when his gun had carried him.

From the 1st to the 4th of May a successful drive was conducted by many columns in the often harried but never deserted Lindley to Kroon-stad district. The result was propitious, as no fewer than 321 prisoners were brought in. Of these, 150 under Mentz were captured in one body as they attempted to break through the encircling cordon.

Amid many small drives and many skirmishes, one stands out for its severity. It is remarkable as being the last action of any importance in the campaign. This was the fight at Moolman's Spruit, near Ficksburg, upon April 20th, 1902. A force of about one hundred Yeomanry and forty

Mounted Infantry (South Staffords) was despatched by night to attack an isolated farm in which a small body of Boers was supposed to be sleeping. Colonel Perceval was in command. The farm was reached after a difficult march, but the enemy were found to have been forewarned, and to be in much greater strength than was anticipated. A furious fire was opened on the advancing troops, who were clearly visible in the light of a full moon. Sir Thomas Fowler was killed and several men of the Yeomanry were hit. The British charged up to the very walls, but were unable to effect an entrance, as the place was barricaded and loopholed. Captain Blackwood, of the Staffords, was killed in the attack. Finding that the place was impregnable, and that the enemy outnumbered him, Colonel Perceval gave the order to retire, a movement which was only successfully carried out because the greater part of the Boer horses had been shot. By morning the small British force had extricated itself, from its perilous position with a total loss of six killed, nineteen wounded, and six missing. The whole affair was undoubtedly a cleverly planned Boer ambush, and the small force was most fortunate in escaping destruction.

One other isolated incident may be mentioned here, though it occurred far away in the Vryheid district of the Transvaal. This was the unfortunate encounter between Zulus and Boers by which the latter lost over fifty of their numbers under deplorable circumstances. This portion of the Transvaal has only recently been annexed, and is inhabited by warlike Zulus, who are very different from the debased Kaffirs of the rest of the country. These men had a blood-feud against the Boers, which was embittered by the fact that they had lost heavily through Boer depredations. Knowing that a party of fifty-nine men were sleeping in a farmhouse, the Zulus crept on to it and slaughtered every man of the inmates. Such an incident is much to be regretted, and yet, looking back upon the long course of the war, and remembering the turbulent tribes who surrounded the combatants—Swazis, Basutos, and Zulus—we may well congratulate ourselves that we have been able to restrain those black warriors, and to escape the brutalities and the bitter memories of a barbarian invasion.

CHAPTER 38

De La Rey's Campaign of 1902

It will be remembered that at the close of 1901 Lord Methuen and Colonel Kekewich had both come across to the eastern side of their district and made their base at the railway line in the Klerksdorp section. Their position was strengthened by the fact that a blockhouse cordon now ran from Klerksdorp to Ventersdorp, and from Ventersdorp to Potchefstroom, so that this triangle could be effectively controlled. There remained, however, a huge tract of difficult country which was practically in the occupation of the enemy. Several thousand stalwarts were known to be riding with De la Rey and his energetic lieutenant Kemp. The strenuous operations of the British in the Eastern Transvaal and in the Orange River Colony had caused this district to be comparatively neglected, and so everything was in favour of an aggressive movement of the Boers. There was a long lull after the unsuccessful attack upon Kekewich's camp at Moedwill, but close observers of the war distrusted this ominous calm and expected a storm to follow.

The new year found the British connecting Ventersdorp with Tafelkop by a blockhouse line. The latter place had been a centre of Boer activity. Colonel Hickie's column covered this operation. Meanwhile Methuen had struck across through Wolmaranstad as far as Vryburg. In these operations, which resulted in constant small captures, he was assisted by a column under Major Paris working from Kimberley. From Vryburg Lord Methuen made his way in the middle of January to Lichtenburg, meeting with a small rebuff in the neighbourhood of that town, for a detachment of Yeomanry was overwhelmed by General Celliers, who killed eight, wounded fifteen, and captured forty. From Lichtenburg Lord Methuen continued his enormous trek, and arrived on February 1st at Klerksdorp once more. Little rest was given to his hard-worked troops, and they were sent off again within the week under the command of Von Donop, with the result that on February 8th, near Wolmaranstad, they captured Potgieter's *laager* with forty Boer prisoners. Von Donop remained at Wolmaranstad until late in February; On the 23rd he despatched an empty convoy back to Klerksdorp, the fate of which will be afterwards narrated.

Kekewich and Hickie had combined their forces at the beginning of February. On February 4th an attempt was made by them to surprise General De la Rey. The mounted troops who were despatched under Major Leader failed in this enterprise, but they found and overwhelmed the *laager* of Sarel Alberts, capturing 132 prisoners. By stampeding the horses the Boer retreat was cut off, and the attack was so furiously driven home, especially by the admirable Scottish Horse, that few of the enemy got away. Alberts himself with all his officers were among the prisoners. From this time until the end of February this column was not seriously engaged.

It has been stated above that on February 23rd Von Donop sent in an empty convoy from Wolmaranstad to Klerksdorp, a distance of about fifty miles. Nothing had been heard for some time of De la Rey, but he had called together his men and was waiting to bring off some coup. The convoy gave him the very opportunity for which he sought.

The escort of the convoy consisted of the 5th Imperial Yeomanry, sixty of Paget's Horse, three companies of the ubiquitous Northumberland Fusiliers, two guns of the 4th R.F.A., and a pom-pom, amounting in all to 630 men. Colonel Anderson was in command. On the morning of Tuesday, February 25th, the convoy was within ten miles of its destination, and the sentries on the *kopjes* round the town could see the gleam of the long line of white-tilted wagons. Their hazardous voyage was nearly over, and yet they were destined to most complete and fatal wreck within sight of port. So confident were they that the detachment of Paget's Horse was permitted to ride on the night before into the town. It was as well, for such a handful would have shared and could not have averted the disaster.

The night had been dark and wet, and the Boers under cover of it had crept between the sleeping convoy and the town. Some bushes which afford excellent cover lie within a few hundred yards of the road, and here the main ambush was laid. In the first grey of the morning the long line of the convoy, 130 wagons in all, came trailing past—guns and Yeomanry in front, Fusiliers upon the flanks and rear. Suddenly the black bank of scrub was outlined in flame, and a furious rifle fire was opened upon the head of the column. The troops behaved admirably under most difficult circumstances. A counter-attack by the Fusiliers and some of the Yeomanry, under cover of shrapnel from the guns, drove the enemy out of the scrub and silenced his fire at this point. It was evident, however, that he was present in force, for firing soon broke out along the whole left flank, and the rearguard found itself as warmly attacked as the van. Again, however, the assailants were driven off. It was now broad daylight, and the wagons, which had got into great confusion in the first turmoil of battle, had been remarshalled and arranged. It was Colonel Anderson's hope that he might be able to send them on into safety while he with the escort covered their retreat. His plan was certainly the best one, and if it did not succeed it was due to nothing which he could avert, but to the nature of the ground and the gallantry of the enemy.

The physical obstacle consisted in a very deep and difficult *spruit*, the Jagd Spruit, which forms an ugly passage in times of peace, but which when crowded and choked with stampeding mules and splintering wagons, under their terrified conductors, soon became impassable. Here the head of the column was clubbed and the whole line came to a stand. Meanwhile the enemy, adopting their new tactics, came galloping in on the left flank and on the rear. The first attack was repelled by the steady fire of the Fusiliers, but on the second occasion the horsemen got up to the wagons, and galloping down them were able to overwhelm in detail the little knots of soldiers who were scattered along the flank. The British, who were outnumbered by at least three to one, made a stout resistance, and it was not until seven o'clock that the last shot was fired. The result was a complete success to the burghers, but one which leaves no shadow of discredit on any officer or man among those who were engaged. Eleven officers and 176 men fell out of about 550 actually engaged. The two guns were taken. The convoy was no use to the Boers, so the teams were shot and the wagons burned before they withdrew. The prisoners too, they were unable to retain, and their sole permanent trophies consisted of the two guns, the rifles, and the ammunition. Their own losses amounted to about fifty killed and wounded.

A small force sallied out from Klerksdorp in the hope of helping Anderson, but on reaching the Jagd Drift it was found that the fighting was over and that the field was in possession of the Boers. De la Rey was seen in person among the burghers, and it is pleasant to add that he made himself conspicuous by his humanity to the wounded. His force drew off in the course of the morning, and was soon out of reach of immediate pursuit, though this was attempted by Kekewich, Von Donop, and Grenfell. It was important to regain the guns if possible, as they were always a menace to the blockhouse system, and for this purpose Grenfell with sixteen hundred horsemen was despatched to a point south of Lichtenburg, which was conjectured to be upon the Boer line of retreat. At the same time Lord Methuen was ordered up from Vryburg in order to cooperate in this movement, and to join his forces to those of Grenfell. It was obvious that with an energetic and resolute adversary like De la Rey there was great danger of these two forces being taken in detail, but it was hoped that each was strong enough to hold its own until the other could come to its aid. The result was to show that the danger was real and the hope fallacious.

It was on March 2nd that Methuen left Vryburg. The column was not his old one, consisting of veterans of the trek, but was the Kimberley column under Major Paris, a body of men who had seen much less service and were in every way less reliable. It included a curious mixture of units, the most solid of which were four guns (two of the 4th, and two of the 38th R.F.A.), 200 Northumberland Fusiliers, and 100 Loyal North Lancashires. The mounted men included 5th Imperial Yeomanry (184), Cape Police (233), Cullinan's Horse (64), 86th Imperial Yeomanry (110), Diamond Fields Horse (92), Dennison's Scouts (58), Ashburner's Horse (126), and British South African Police (24). Such a collection of samples would be more in place, one would imagine, in a London procession than in an operation which called for discipline and cohesion. In warfare the half is often greater than the whole, and the presence of a proportion of half-hearted and inexperienced men may be a positive danger to their more capable companions.

Upon March 6th Methuen, marching east towards Lichtenburg, came in touch near Leeuwspruit with Van Zyl's commando, and learned in the small skirmish which ensued that some of his Yeomanry were unreliable and ill-instructed. Having driven the enemy off by his artillery fire, Methuen moved to Tweebosch, where he *laagered* until next morning. At 3 a.m. of the 7th the ox-convoy was sent on, under escort of half of his little force. The other half followed at 4. 20, so as to give the slow-moving oxen a chance of keeping ahead. It was evident, however, immediately after the column had got started that the enemy were all round in great numbers, and that an attack in force was to be expected. Lord Methuen gave orders therefore that the ox-wagons should be halted and that the mule-transport should close upon them so as to form one solid block, instead of a straggling line. At the same time he reinforced his rearguard with mounted men and with two guns, for it was in that quarter that the enemy appeared to be most numerous and aggressive. An attack was also developing upon the right flank, which was held off by the infantry and by the second section of the guns.

It has been said that Methuen's horsemen were for the most part inexperienced irregulars. Such men become in time excellent soldiers, as all this campaign bears witness, but it is too much to expose them to a severe ordeal in the open field when they are still raw and untrained. As it happened, this particular ordeal was exceedingly severe, but nothing can excuse the absolute failure of the troops concerned to rise to the occasion. Had Methuen's rearguard consisted of Imperial Light Horse, or Scottish Horse, it is safe to say that the battle of Tweebosch would have had a very different ending.

What happened was that a large body of Boers formed up in five lines and charged straight home at the rear screen and rearguard, firing from their saddles as they had done at Brakenlaagte. The sight of those wide-flung lines of determined men galloping over the plain seems to have been too much for the nerves of the unseasoned troopers. A panic spread through their ranks, and in an instant they had turned their horses' heads and were thundering to their rear, leaving the two guns uncovered and streaming in wild confusion past the left flank of the jeering infantry who were lying round the wagons. The limit of their flight seems to have been the wind of their horses, and most of them never drew rein until they had placed many miles between themselves and the comrades whom they had deserted. 'It was pitiable,' says an eye-witness, 'to see the grand old General begging them to stop, but they would not; a large body of them arrived in Kraaipan without firing a shot.' It was a South African 'Battle of the Spurs.'

By this defection of the greater portion of the force the handful of brave men who remained were left in a hopeless position. The two guns of the 38th battery were overwhelmed and ridden over by the Boer horsemen, every man being killed or wounded, including Lieutenant Nesham, who acted up to the highest traditions of his corps.

The battle, however, was not yet over. The infantry were few in number, but they were experienced troops, and they maintained the struggle for some hours in the face of overwhelming numbers. Two hundred of the Northumberland Fusiliers lay round the wagons and held the Boers off from their prey. With them were the two remaining guns, which were a mark for a thousand Boer riflemen. It was while encouraging by his presence and example the much-tried gunners of this section that the gallant Methuen was wounded by a bullet which broke the bone of his thigh. Lieutenant Venning and all the detachment fell with their General round the guns.

An attempt had been made to rally some of the flying troopers at a neighbouring *kraal*, and a small body of Cape Police and Yeomanry under the command of Major Paris held out there for some hours. A hundred of the Lancashire Infantry aided them in their stout defence. But the guns taken by the Boers from Von Donop's convoy had free play now that the British guns were out of action, and they were brought to bear with crushing effect upon both the *kraal* and the wagons. Further resistance meant a useless slaughter, and orders were given for a surrender. Convoy, ammunition, guns, horses—nothing was saved except the honour of the infantry and the gunners. The losses, 68 killed and 121 wounded, fell chiefly upon these two branches of the service. There were 205 unwounded prisoners.

This, the last Boer victory in the war, reflected equal credit upon their valour and humanity, qualities which had not always gone hand in hand in our experience of them. Courtesy and attention were extended to the British wounded, and Lord Methuen was sent under charge of his chief medical officer, Colonel Townsend (the doctor as severely wounded as the patient), into Klerksdorp. In De la Rey we have always found an opponent who was as chivalrous as he was formidable. The remainder of the force reached the Kimberley to Mafeking railway line in the direction of Kraaipan, the spot where the first bloodshed of the war had occurred some twenty-nine months before.

On Lord Methuen himself no blame can rest for this unsuccessful action. If the workman's tool snaps in his hand he cannot be held responsible for the failure of his task. The troops who misbehaved were none of his training. 'If you hear anyone slang him,' says one of his men, 'you are to tell them that he is the finest General and the truest gentleman that ever fought in this war.' Such was the tone of his own troopers, and such also that of the spokesmen of the nation when they commented upon the disaster in the Houses of Parliament. It was a fine example of British justice and sense of fair play, even in that bitter moment, that to hear his eulogy one would have thought that the occasion had been one when thanks were being returned for a victory. It is a generous public with fine instincts, and Paul Methuen, wounded and broken, still remained in their eyes the heroic soldier and the chivalrous man of honour.

The De Wet country had been pretty well cleared by the series of drives which have already been described, and Louis Botha's force in the Eastern Transvaal had been much diminished by the tactics of Bruce Hamilton and Wools-Sampson. Lord Kitchener was able, therefore, to concentrate his troops and his attention upon that wide-spread western area in which General De la Rey had dealt two such shrewd blows within a few weeks of each other. Troops were rapidly concentrated at Klerksdorp. Kekewich, Walter Kitchener, Rawlinson, and Rochfort, with a number of small columns, were ready in the third week of March to endeavour to avenge Lord Methuen.

The problem with which Lord Kitchener was confronted was a very difficult one, and he has never shown more originality and audacity than in the fashion in which he handled it. De la Rey's force was scattered over a long tract of country, capable of rapidly concentrating for a blow, but otherwise as intangible and elusive as a phantom army. Were Lord Kitchener simply to launch ten thousand horsemen at him, the result would be a weary ride over illimitable plains without sight of a Boer, unless it were a distant scout upon the extreme horizon. De la Rey and his men would have slipped away to his northern hiding-places beyond the Marico River. There was no solid obstacle here, as in the Orange River Colony, against which the flying enemy could be rounded up. One line of blockhouses there was, it is true—the one called the Schoonspruit cordon, which flanked the De la Rey country. It flanked it, however, upon the same side as that on which the troops were assembled. If the troops were only on the other side, and De la Rey was between them and the blockhouse line, then, indeed, something might be done. But to place the troops there, and then bring them instantly back again, was to put such a strain upon men and horses as had never yet been done upon a large scale in the course of the war. Yet Lord Kitchener knew the mettle of the men whom he commanded, and he was aware that there were no exertions of which the human frame is capable which he might not confidently demand.

The precise location of the Boer *laagers* does not appear to have been known, but it was certain that a considerable number of them were scattered about thirty miles or so to the west of Klerksdorp and the Schoonspruit line. The plan was to march a British force right through them, then spread out into a wide line and come straight back, driving the burghers on to the cordon of blockhouses, which had been strengthened by the arrival of three regiments of Highlanders. But to get to the other side of the Boers it was necessary to march the columns through by night. It was a hazardous operation, but the secret was well kept, and the movement was so well carried out that the enemy had no time to check it. On the night of Sunday, March 23rd, the British horsemen passed stealthily in column through the De la Rey country, and then, spreading out into a line, which from the left wing at Lichtenburg to the right wing at Commando Drift measured a good eighty miles, they proceeded to sweep back upon their traces. In order to reach their positions the columns had, of course, started at different points of the British blockhouse line, and some had a good deal farther to go than others, while the southern extension of the line was formed by Rochfort's troops, who had moved up from the Vaal. Above him from south to north came Walter Kitchener, Rawlinson, and Kekewich in the order named.

On the morning of Monday, March 24th, a line of eighty miles of horsemen, without guns or transport, was sweeping back towards the blockhouses, while the country between was filled with scattered parties of Boers who were seeking for gaps by which to escape. It was soon learned from the first prisoners that De la Rey was not within the cordon. His *laager* had been some distance farther west. But the sight of fugitive horsemen rising and dipping over the rolling *veldt* assured the British that they had something within their net. The catch was, however, by no means as complete as might have been desired. Three hundred men in khaki slipped through between the two columns in the early morning. Another large party escaped to the southwards. Some of the Boers adopted extraordinary devices in order to escape from the ever-narrowing cordon. 'Three, in charge of some cattle, buried themselves, and left a small hole to breathe through with a tube. Some men began to probe with bayonets in the new-turned earth and got immediate and vociferous subterranean yells. Another man tried the same game and a horse stepped on him. He writhed and reared the horse, and practically the horse found the prisoner for us.' But the operations achieved one result, which must have lifted a load of anxiety from Lord Kitchener's mind. Three fifteen-pounders, two pom-poms, and a large amount of ammunition were taken. To Kekewich and the Scottish Horse fell the honour of the capture, Colonel Wools-Sampson and Captain Rice heading the charge and pursuit. By this means the constant menace to the blockhouses was lessened, if not entirely removed. One hundred and seventy-five Boers were disposed of, nearly all as prisoners, and a considerable quantity of transport was captured. In this operation the troops had averaged from seventy to eighty miles in twenty-six hours without change of horses. To such a point had the slow-moving ponderous British Army attained after two years' training of that stern drill-master, necessity.

The operations had attained some success, but nothing commensurate with the daring of the plan or the exertions of the soldiers. Without an instant's delay, however, Lord Kitchener struck a second blow at his enemy. Before the end of March Kekewich, Rawlinson, and Walter Kitchener were all upon the trek once more. Their operations were pushed farther to the west than in the last drive, since it was known that on that occasion De la Rey and his main commando had been outside the cordon.

It was to one of Walter Kitchener's lieutenants that the honour fell to come in direct contact with the main force of the burghers. This General had moved out to a point about forty miles west of Klerksdorp. Forming his *laager* there, he despatched Cookson on March 30th with seventeen hundred men to work further westward in the direction of the Harts River. Under Cookson's immediate command were the 2nd Canadian Mounted Infantry, Damant's Horse, and four guns of the 7th R.F.A. His lieutenant, Keir, commanded the 28th Mounted Infantry, the Artillery Mounted Rifles, and 2nd Kitchener's Fighting Scouts. The force was well mounted, and carried the minimum of baggage.

It was not long before this mobile force found itself within touch of the enemy. The broad weal made by the passing of a convoy set them off at full cry, and they were soon encouraged by the distant cloud of dust which shrouded the Boer wagons. The advance guard of the column galloped at the top of their speed for eight miles, and closed in upon the convoy, but found themselves faced by an escort of five hundred Boers, who fought a clever rearguard action, and covered their charge with great skill. At the same time Cookson closed in upon his mounted infantry, while on the other side De la Rey's main force fell back in order to reinforce the escort. British and Boers were both riding furiously to help their own comrades. The two forces were fairly face to face.

Perceiving that he was in front of the whole Boer army, and knowing that he might expect reinforcements, Cookson decided to act upon the defensive. A position was rapidly taken up along the Brakspruit, and preparations made to resist the impending attack. The line of defence was roughly the line of the *spruit*, but for some reason, probably to establish a cross fire, one advanced position was occupied upon either flank. On the left flank was a farmhouse, which was held by two hundred men of the Artillery Rifles. On the extreme right was another outpost of twenty-four Canadians and forty-five Mounted Infantry. They occupied no defensible position, and their situation was evidently a most dangerous one, only to be justified by some strong military reason which is not explained by any account of the action.

The Boer guns had opened fire, and considerable bodies of the enemy appeared upon the flanks and in front. Their first efforts were devoted towards getting possession of the farmhouse, which would give them a *point d'appui* from which they could turn the whole line. Some five hundred of them charged on horseback, but were met by a very steady fire from the Artillery Rifles, while the guns raked them with shrapnel. They reached a point within five hundred yards of the building, but the fire was too hot, and they wheeled round in rapid retreat. Dismounting in a *mealie*-patch they skirmished up towards the farmhouse once more, but they were again checked by the fire of the defenders and by a pom-pom which Colonel Keir had brought up. No progress whatever was made by the attack in this quarter.

In the meantime the fate which might have been foretold had befallen the isolated detachment of Canadians and 28th Mounted Infantry upon the extreme right. Bruce Carruthers, the Canadian officer in command, behaved with the utmost gallantry, and was splendidly seconded by his men. Overwhelmed by vastly superior numbers, amid a perfect hail of bullets they fought like heroes to the end. 'There have been few finer instances of heroism in the course of the campaign,' says the reticent Kitchener in his official despatch. Of the Canadians eighteen were hit out of twenty-one, and the Mounted Infantry hard by lost thirty out of forty-five before they surrendered.

This advantage gained upon the right flank was of no assistance to the Boers in breaking the British line. The fact that it was so makes it the more difficult to understand why this outpost was so exposed. The burghers had practically surrounded Cookson's force, and De la Rey and Kemp urged on the attack; but their artillery fire was dominated by the British guns, and no weak point could be found in the defence. At 1 o'clock the attack had been begun, and at 5.30 it was finally abandoned, and De la Rey was in full retreat. That he was in no sense routed is shown by the fact that Cookson did not attempt to follow him up or to capture his guns; but at least he had failed in his purpose, and had lost more heavily than in any engagement which he had yet fought. The moral effect of his previous victories had also been weakened, and his burghers had learned, if they had illusions upon the subject, that the men who fled at Tweebosch were not typical troopers of the British Army. Altogether, it was a well-fought and useful action, though it cost the British force some two hundred casualties, of which thirty-five were fatal. Cookson's force stood to arms all night until the arrival of Walter Kitchener's men in the morning.

General Ian Hamilton, who had acted for some time as Chief of the Staff to Lord Kitchener, had arrived on April 8th at Klerksdorp to take supreme command of the whole operations against De la Rey. Early in April the three main British columns had made a rapid cast round without success. To the very end the better intelligence and the higher mobility seem to have remained upon the side of the Boers, who could always force a fight when they wished and escape when they wished. Occasionally, however, they forced one at the wrong time, as in the instance which I am about to describe.

Hamilton had planned a drive to cover the southern portion of De la Rey's country, and for this purpose, with Hartebeestefontein for his centre, he was manoeuvring his columns so as to swing them into line and then sweep back towards Klerksdorp. Kekewich, Rawlinson, and Walter Kitchener were all manoeuvring for this purpose. The Boers, however, game to the last, although they were aware that their leaders had gone in to treat, and that peace was probably due within a few days, determined to have one last gallant fall with a British column. The forces of Kekewich were the farthest to the westward, and also, as the burghers thought, the most isolated, and it was upon them, accordingly, that the attack was made. In the morning of April 11th, at a place called Rooiwal, the enemy, who had moved up from Wolmaranstad, nineteen hundred strong, under Kemp and Vermaas, fell with the utmost impetuosity upon the British column. There was no preliminary skirmishing, and a single gallant charge by 1500 Boers both opened and ended the engagement. 'I was just saying to the staff officer that there were no Boers within twenty miles,' says one who was present, 'when we heard a roar of musketry and saw a lot of men galloping down on us.' The British were surprised but not shaken by this unexpected apparition. 'I never saw a more splendid attack. They kept a distinct line,' says the eye-witness. Another spectator says, 'They came on in one long line four deep and knee to knee.' It was an old-fashioned cavalry charge, and the fact that it got as far as it did shows that we have over rated the stopping power of modern rifles. They came for a good five hundred yards under direct fire, and were only turned within a hundred of the British line. The Yeomanry, the Scottish Horse, and the Constabulary poured a steady fire upon the advancing wave of horsemen, and the guns opened with case at two hundred yards. The Boers were stopped, staggered, and turned. Their fire, or rather the covering fire of those who had not joined in the charge, had caused some fifty casualties, but their own losses were very much more severe. The fierce Potgieter fell just in front of the British guns. 'Thank goodness he is dead!' cried one of his wounded burghers, 'for he *sjamboked* me into the firing line this morning.' Fifty dead and a great number of wounded were left upon the field of battle. Rawlinson's column came up on Kekewich's left, and the Boer flight became a rout, for they were chased for twenty miles, and their two guns were captured. It was a brisk and decisive little engagement, and it closed the Western campaign, leaving the last trick, as well as the game, to the credit of the British. From this time until the end there was a gleaning of prisoners but little fighting in De la Rey's country, the most noteworthy event being a surprise visit to Schweizer-Renecke by Rochfort, by which some sixty prisoners were taken, and afterwards the drive of Ian Hamilton's forces against the Mafeking railway line by which no fewer than 364 prisoners were secured. In this difficult and well-managed operation the gaps between the British columns were concealed by the lighting of long *veldt*-fires and the discharge of rifles by scattered scouts. The newly arrived Australian Commonwealth Regiments gave a brilliant start to the military history of their united country by the energy of their marching and the thoroughness of their entrenching.

Upon May 29th, only two days before the final declaration of peace, a raid was made by a few Boers upon the native cattle reserves near Fredericstad. A handful of horsemen pursued them, and were ambushed by a considerable body of the enemy in some hilly country ten miles from the British lines. Most of the pursuers got away in safety, but young Sutherland, second lieutenant of the Seaforths, and only a few months from Eton, found himself separated from his horse and in a hopeless position. Scorning to surrender, the lad actually fought his way upon foot for over a mile before he was shot down by the horsemen who circled round him. Well might the Boer commander declare that in the whole course of the war he had seen no finer example of British courage. It is indeed sad that at this last instant a young life should be thrown away, but Sutherland died in a noble fashion for a noble cause, and many inglorious years would be a poor substitute for the example and tradition which such a death will leave behind.

CHAPTER 39

The End

It only remains in one short chapter to narrate the progress of the peace negotiations, the ultimate settlement, and the final consequences of this long-drawn war. However disheartening the successive incidents may have been in which the Boers were able to inflict heavy losses upon us and to renew their supplies of arms and ammunition, it was none the less certain that their numbers were waning and that the inevitable end was steadily approaching. With mathematical precision the scientific soldier in Pretoria, with his web of barbed wire radiating out over the whole country, was week by week wearing them steadily down. And yet after the recent victory of De la Rey and various *braggadocio* pronouncements from the refugees at The Hague, it was somewhat of a surprise to the British public when it was announced upon March 22nd that the acting Government of the Transvaal, consisting of Messrs. Schalk Burger, Lucas Meyer, Reitz, Jacoby, Krogh, and Van Velden had come into Middelburg and requested to be forwarded by train to Pretoria for the purpose of discussing terms of peace with Lord Kitchener. A thrill of hope ran through the Empire at the news, but so doubtful did the issue seem that none of the preparations were relaxed which would ensure a vigorous campaign in the immediate future. In the South African as in the Peninsular and in the Crimean wars, it may truly be said that Great Britain was never so ready to fight as at the dawning of peace. At least two years of failure and experience are needed to turn a civilian and commercial nation into a military power.

In spite of the optimistic pronouncements of Mr. Fischer and the absurd forecasts of Dr. Leyds the power of the Boers was really broken, and they had come in with the genuine intention of surrender. In a race with such individuality it was not enough that the government should form its conclusion. It was necessary for them to persuade their burghers that the game was really up, and that they had no choice but to throw down their well-worn rifles and their ill-filled bandoliers. For this purpose a long series of negotiations had to be entered into which put a strain upon the complacency of the authorities in South Africa and upon the patience of the attentive public at home. Their ultimate success shows that this complacency and this patience were eminently the right attitude to adopt.

On March 23rd the Transvaal representatives were despatched to Kroonstad for the purpose of opening up the matter with Steyn and De Wet. Messengers were sent to communicate with these two leaders, but had they been British columns instead of fellow-countrymen they could not have found greater difficulty in running them to earth. At last, however, at the end of the month the message was conveyed, and resulted in the appearance of De Wet, De la Rey, and Steyn at the British outposts at Klerksdorp. The other delegates had come north again from Kroonstad, and all were united in the same small town, which, by a whimsical fate, had suddenly become the centre both for the making of peace and for the prosecution of the war, with the eyes of the whole world fixed upon its insignificant litter of houses. On April 11th, after repeated conferences, both parties moved on to Pretoria, and the most sceptical observers began to confess that there was something in the negotiations after all. After conferring with Lord Kitchener the Boer leaders upon April 18th left Pretoria again and rode out to the commandos to explain the situation to them. The result of this mission was that two delegates were chosen from each body in the field, who assembled at Vereeniging upon May 15th for the purpose of settling the question by vote. Never was a high matter of state decided in so democratic a fashion.

Up to that period the Boer leaders had made a succession of tentative suggestions, each of which had been put aside by the British Government. Their first had been that they should merely concede those points which had been at issue at the beginning of the war. This was set aside. The second was that they should be allowed to consult their friends in Europe. This also was refused. The next was that an armistice should be granted, but again Lord Kitchener was obdurate. A definite period was suggested within which the burghers should make their final choice between surrender and a war which must finally exterminate them as a people. It was tacitly understood, if not definitely promised, that the conditions which the British Government would be prepared to grant would not differ much in essentials from those which had been refused by the Boers a twelvemonth before, after the Middelburg interview.

On May 15th the Boer conference opened at Vereeniging. Sixty-four delegates from the commandos met with the military and political chiefs of the late republics, the whole amounting to 150 persons. A more singular gathering has not met in our time. There was Botha, the young lawyer, who had found himself by a strange turn of fate commanding a victorious army in a great war. De Wet was there, with his grim mouth and sun-browned face; De la Rey, also, with the grizzled beard and the strong aquiline features. There, too, were the politicians, the grey-bearded, genial Reitz, a little graver than when he looked upon 'the whole matter as an immense joke,' and the unfortunate Steyn, stumbling and groping, a broken and ruined man. The burly Lucas Meyer, smart young Smuts fresh from the siege of Ookiep, Beyers from the north, Kemp the dashing cavalry leader, Muller the hero of many fights—all these with many others of their sun-blackened, gaunt, hard-featured comrades were grouped within the great tent of Vereeniging. The discussions were heated and prolonged. But the logic of facts was inexorable, and the cold still voice of common-sense had more power than all the ravings of enthusiasts. The vote showed that the great majority of the delegates were in favour of surrender upon the terms offered by the British Government. On May 31st this resolution was notified to Lord Kitchener, and at half-past ten of the same night the delegates arrived at Pretoria and set their names to the treaty of peace. After two years seven and a half months of hostilities the Dutch republics had acquiesced in their own destruction, and the whole of South Africa, from Cape Town to the Zambezi, had been added to the British Empire. The great struggle had cost us twenty thousand lives and a hundred thousand stricken men, with two hundred millions of money; but, apart from a peaceful South Africa, it had won for us a national resuscitation of spirit and a closer union with our great Colonies which could in no other way have been attained. We had hoped that we were a solid empire when we engaged in the struggle, but we knew that we were when we emerged from it. In that change lies an ample recompense for all the blood and treasure spent.

The following were in brief the terms of surrender:—

1. That the burghers lay down their arms and acknowledge themselves subjects of Edward VII.

2. That all prisoners taking the oath of allegiance be returned.

3. That their liberty and property be inviolate.

4. That an amnesty be granted—save in special cases.

5. That the Dutch language be allowed in schools and law-courts.

6. That rifles be allowed if registered.

7. That self-government be granted as soon as possible.

8. That no franchise be granted for natives until after self-government.

9. That no special land tax be levied.

10. That the people be helped to reoccupy the farms.

11. That 3,000,000 pounds be given to help the farmers.

12. That the rebels be disfranchised and their leaders tried, on condition that no death penalty be inflicted.

These terms were practically the same as those which had been refused by Botha in March 1901. Thirteen months of useless warfare had left the situation as it was.

It had been a war of surprises, but the surprises have unhappily been hitherto invariably unpleasant ones. Now at last the balance swung the other way, for in all the long paradoxical history of South African strife there is nothing more wonderful than the way in which these two sturdy and unemotional races clasped hands the instant that the fight was done. The fact is in itself a final answer to the ill-natured critics of the Continent. Men do not so easily grasp a hand which is reddened with the blood of women and children. From all parts as the commandos came in there was welcome news of the fraternisation between them and the soldiers; while the Boer leaders, as loyal to their new ties as they had been to their old ones, exerted themselves to promote good feeling among their people. A few weeks seemed to do more to lessen racial bitterness than some of us had hoped for in as many years. One can but pray that it will last.

The surrenders amounted in all to twenty thousand men, and showed that in all parts of the seat of war the enemy had more men in the field than we had imagined, a fact which may take the sting out of several of our later mishaps. About twelve thousand surrendered in the Transvaal, six thousand in the Orange River Colony, and about two thousand in the Cape Colony, showing that the movement in the rebel districts had always been more vexatious than formidable. A computation of the prisoners of war, the surrenders, the mercenaries, and the casualties, shows that the total forces to which we were opposed were certainly not fewer than seventy-five thousand well-armed mounted men, while they may have considerably exceeded that number. No wonder that the Boer leaders showed great confidence at the outset of the war.

That the heavy losses caused us by the war were borne without a murmur is surely evidence enough how deep was the conviction of the nation that the war was not only just but essential—that the possession of South Africa and the unity of the Empire were at stake. Could it be shown, or were it even remotely possible, that ministers had incurred so immense a responsibility and entailed such tremendous sacrifices upon their people without adequate cause, is it not certain that, the task once done, an explosion of rage from the deceived and the bereaved would have driven them for ever from public life? Among high and low, in England, in Scotland, in Ireland, in the great Colonies, how many high hopes had been crushed, how often the soldier son had gone forth and never returned, or come back maimed and stricken in the pride of his youth. Everywhere was the voice of pity and sorrow, but nowhere that of reproach. The deepest instincts of the nation told it that it must fight and win, or for ever abdicate its position in the world. Through dark days which brought out the virtues of our race as nothing has done in our generation, we struggled grimly on until the light had fully broken once again. And of all gifts that God has given to Britain there is none to compare with those days of sorrow, for it was in them that the nation was assured of its unity, and learned for all time that blood is stronger to bind than salt water is to part. The only difference in the point of view of the Briton from Britain and the Briton from the ends of the earth, was that the latter with the energy of youth was more whole-souled in the Imperial cause. Who has seen that Army and can forget it—its spirit, its picturesqueness—above all, what it stands for in the future history of the world? Cowboys from the vast plains of the North-West, gentlemen who ride hard with the Quorn or the Belvoir, gillies from the Sutherland deer-forests, bushmen from the back blocks of Australia, exquisites of the Raleigh Club or the Bachelor's, hard men from Ontario, dandy sportsmen from India and Ceylon, the horsemen of New Zealand, the wiry South African irregulars—these are the Reserves whose existence was chronicled in no Blue-book, and whose appearance came as a shock to the pedant soldiers of the Continent who had sneered so long at our little Army, since long years of peace have caused them to forget its exploits. On the plains of South Africa, in common danger and in common privation, the blood brotherhood of the Empire was sealed.

So much for the Empire. But what of South Africa? There in the end we must reap as we sew. If we are worthy of the trust, it will be left to us. If we are unworthy of it, it will be taken away. Kruger's downfall should teach us that it is not rifles but Justice which is the title-deed of a nation. The British flag under our best administrators will mean clean government, honest laws, liberty and equality to all men. So long as it continues to do so, we shall hold South Africa. When, out of fear or out or greed, we fall from that ideal, we may know that we are stricken with that disease which has killed every great empire before us.

Appendix

OFFICIAL TABLE OF CASUALTIES

CASUALTIES IN THE FIELD FORCE, SOUTH AFRICA, REPORTED DURING THE WEEK ENDED SEPTEMBER 8, 1900, AND TOTAL CASUALTIES REPORTED SINCE THE BEGINNING OF THE WAR, UP TO AND INCLUDING THE WEEK.

CASUALTIES IN ACTION	Killed		Wounded		Died of Wounds in South Africa (included in wound'd)		Missing and prisoners		Total killed, wounded, missing, and prisoners	
	Officers	N.C.O.'s and men	Officers	N.C.O.'s and men	Officers	N.C.O.'s and men	Officers	N.C.O.'s and men	Officers	N.C.O.'s and men
Casualties reported during the week .	—	28	21	118	2	21	2	42	23	188
Total casualties reported up to and including the week—										
Belmont, Nov. 23 .	3	50	25	220	1	21	—	—	28	270
Colenso, Dec. 15 .	7	129	43	719	2	20	21	207	71	1,055
Driefontein, Mar. 10 .	5	58	19	342	1	18	—	2	24	402
Dundee, Oct. 20 .	8	42	11	84	8	—	25	306	44	432
Elandslaagte, Oct. 21 .	5	50	30	169	—	6	—	4	35	228
Enslin (Graspan), Nov. 25 . . .	8	14	6	162	1	4		9	9	185
Farquhar's Farm and Nicholson's Nek, Oct. 30 . .	6	58	9	244		10	43	925	58	1,227
Johannesburg and Pretoria, capture of .	8	20	34	180	1	8	5	88	42	188
Karee, near Brandfort, March 29 .	1	20	9	152	1	11		—	10	172
Ladysmith, Relief of, Feb. 19 to 27 .	22	241	91	1,530	3	76	1	11	114	1,782
Magersfontein, Dec. 11 . . .	23	149	45	646	3	35	—	108	68	903
Monte Christo (Colenso), &c., Feb. 15 to 18 . .	1	13	8	180	—	3	—	4	9	197
Modder River, Nov. 28 . . .	4	66	20	393	—	31	—	2	24	461
Paardeberg, Feb. 16 to 27 . .	17	239	74	1,136	6	66	7	62	98	1,437
Potgeiter's Drift, Feb. 5 to 7 .	2	23	18	326	—	8	—	5	20	354
Pretoria, east of, June 11 and 12 .	8	6	16	128	1	8	1	8	25	137
Reddersburg, April 3 and 4 . . .	2	10	2	33	1	1	8	397	12	440

Casualties in Action	Killed		Wounded		Died of Wounds in South Africa (Included in wound'd)		Missing and prisoners		Total killed, wounded, missing, and prisoners	
	Officers	N.C.O.'s and men	Officers	N.C.O.'s and men	Officers	N.C.O.'s and men	Officers	N.C.O.'s and men	Officers	N.C.O.'s and men
Rietfontein, Oct. 24 .	1	11	6	98	—	4	—	2	7	111
Sanna's Post, Mar. 31	3	15	16	121	2	7	18	408	37	544
Senekal, May 29 .	—	88	7	127	1	5	—	12	7	177
Spion Kop, &c., Jan. 17 to 24 . .	27	250	53	1,050	6	40	7	347	87	1,847
Stormberg, Dec. 10 .	—	31	7	51	—	1	13	620	20	702
Uitval's Nek, July 11	3	16	3	53	—	3	4	186	10	255
Willow Grange, Nov. 23 . . .	—	11	1	66	—	2	1	8	2	85
At Ladysmith during Investment—										
Battle of Jan. 6 .	14	164	33	287	4	25	—	2	47	453
Other casualties .	6	60	36	280	8	29	—	12	42	352
At Kimberley during Investment . .	2	36	15	124	—	4	1	3	18	163
At Mafeking during Investment . .	5	64	10	152	—	9	1	41	16	257
Other casualties .	102	799	417	8,865	45	329	127	3,606	646	8,270
Total casualties in action reported up to September 8 .	283	2,683	1,064	12,868	85	779	283*	7,830*	1,690	22,881

* Of these, 240 officers and 6,299 men have been released or have escaped, and three officers and 86 men have died in captivity.

Other Casualties	Officers	N.C.O.'s and men
Reported during the week—		
Died of disease in South Africa	1	140
Accidental deaths in South Africa . . .	—	6
Invalids sent home	6	—
Total up to and including the week—		
Died of disease in South Africa	149	5,472
Accidental deaths in South Africa . . .	3	101
Invalids sent home—		
Wounded	1,219 {	3,061
Sick		22,896
Not specified which		1,080
Abstract of losses in the Field Force, South Africa, excluding sick and wounded men still in British hospitals in South Africa.		
Reported during the week—		
Killed in action	—	28
Died of wounds in South Africa	2	21
Missing and prisoners	2	42
Died of disease in South Africa	1	140
Accidental deaths in South Africa	—	6

488

OTHER CASUALTIES	Officers	N.C.O.'s and men
Invalids sent home—		
Wounded		8,061
Sick	1,219	22,896
Not specified which		1,080
Abstract of losses in the Field Force, South Africa, excluding sick and wounded men still in British hospitals in South Africa.		
Reported during the week—		
Killed in action	—	28
Died of wounds in South Africa	2	21
Missing and prisoners	2	42
Died of disease in South Africa . . .	1	140
Accidental deaths in South Africa. . . .	—	6
Sent home as invalids	6	—
Total	11	237
Total losses reported up to and including the week—		
Killed in action	283	2,688
Died of wounds	85	779
Missing and prisoners (excluding those who have been recovered or have died in captivity) . . .	40	945†
Prisoners who have died in captivity . . .	3	86
Died of disease	149	5,472
Accidental deaths	3	101
Sent home as invalids	1,219	27,987‡
Total	1,782	38,003
Total losses reported (exclusive of sick and wounded men now in British hospitals in South Africa) . .	39,785	

† This total probably includes a large number of men reported 'missing' who subsequently rejoined, but whose return was not notified.

‡ Of these, 178 have died, 740 have been discharged from the Service as unfit, and 920 are in hospital.

Maps

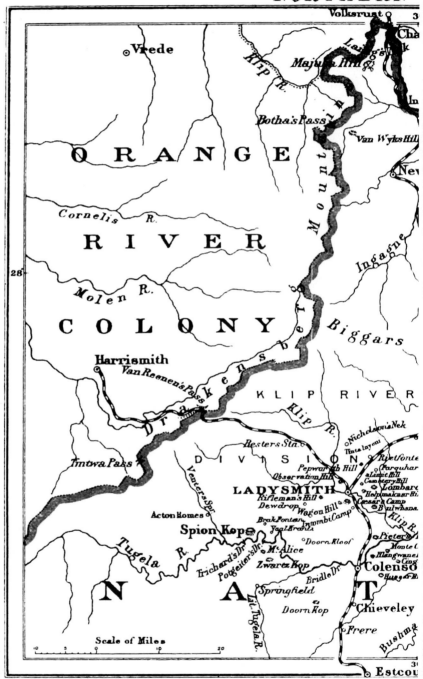

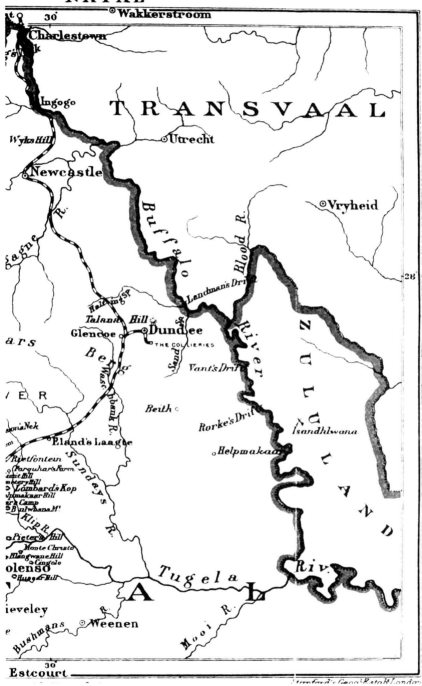

493

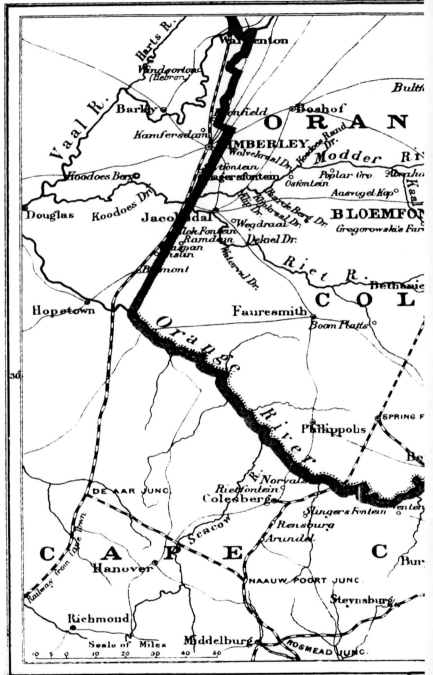

26

Sand R.

Vet R.

Ventersburg

Welgelegen

Smaldeel

Bultfontein

Somehel

Winburg

ANGE RIVER

Brandfort

Trommel

dder River

Karree

Jacobsrust

Clocoland

ar Gro

Abrahamskraal

Coten

Houtnek

asvegel Kop

Leeuw Kop

WATERWORKS

Israel's Poort

Ladybrand

BLOEMFONTEIN

Sannas Post

Spr.

Thabanchu

Gregorowski's Farm

Leeuw Kop

Bethanie

De Wet's Dorp

Constantia Farm

OLONY

Redersburg

BASUTO

Platts

Edenburg

Commereberg

Caledon R.

Wepener

LAND

Smithfield

SPRING FONTEIN JUNC.

pols

Rouxville

R.

Bethulie

Orange R.

Olivenhout

Herschel

Aliwal North

Lady Grey

rs Fontein

enterstad

Kraai

ALBERT JUNC.

COLONY

Berkly
East

UNC.

Burghersdorp

Jamestown

evnsburg

Labuscagne's Nek

STORMBERG JUNC.

Dordrecht

Allemans Nek

R.

Molteno

Stormberg Range

Indwe

UNC.

Sterkstroom

26

ORANGE RIVER

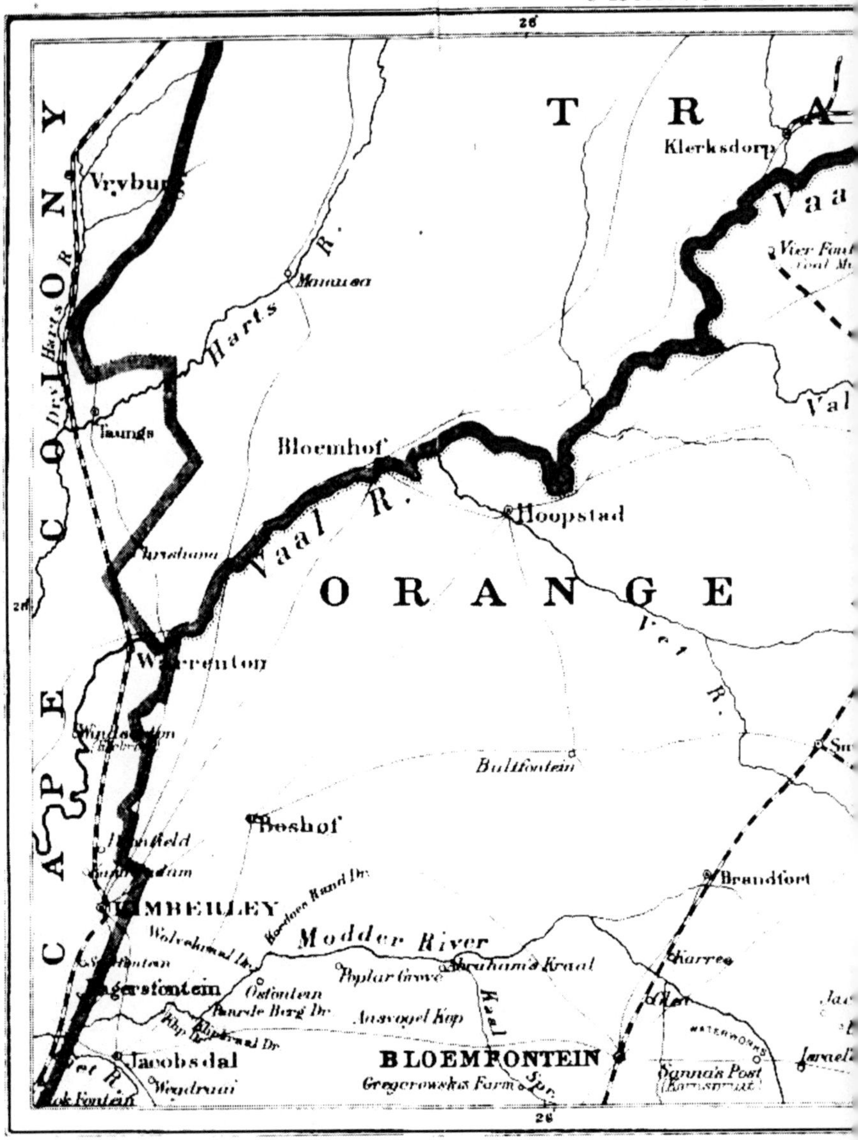

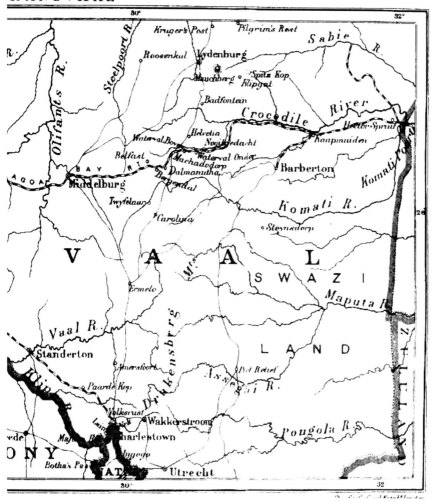

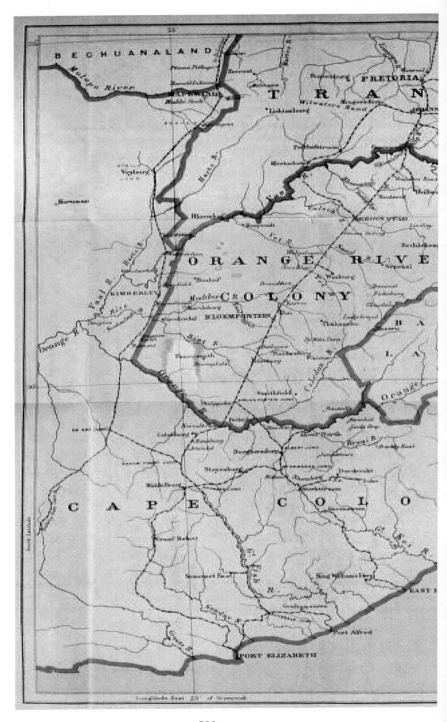

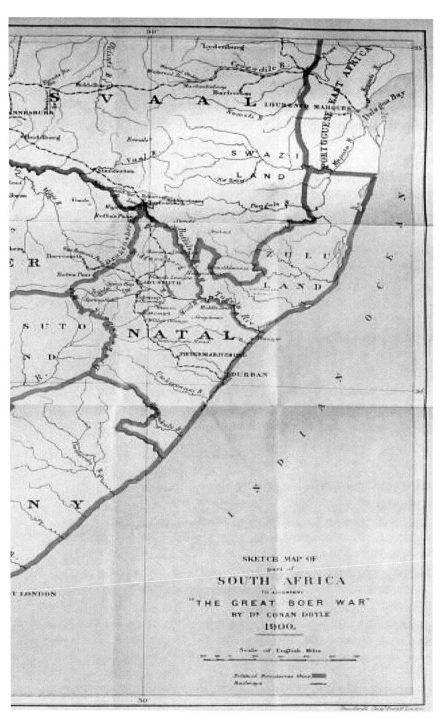

SKETCH MAP OF
part of
SOUTH AFRICA
TO ACCOMPANY
"THE GREAT BOER WAR"
BY DR CONAN DOYLE
1900.

Scale of English Miles

501

LEONAUR

ALSO FROM LEONAUR
AVAILABLE IN SOFTCOVER OR HARDCOVER WITH DUST JACKET

BUGEAUD: A PACK WITH A BATON *by Thomas Robert Bugeaud*—The Early Campaigns of a Soldier of Napoleon's Army Who Would Become a Marshal of France.

WATERLOO RECOLLECTIONS *by Frederick Llewellyn*—Rare First Hand Accounts, Letters, Reports and Retellings from the Campaign of 1815.

SERGEANT NICOL *by Daniel Nicol*—The Experiences of a Gordon Highlander During the Napoleonic Wars in Egypt, the Peninsula and France.

THE JENA CAMPAIGN: 1806 *by F. N. Maude*—The Twin Battles of Jena & Auerstadt Between Napoleon's French and the Prussian Army.

PRIVATE O'NEIL *by Charles O'Neil*—The recollections of an Irish Rogue of H. M. 28th Regt.—The Slashers—during the Peninsula & Waterloo campaigns of the Napoleonic war.

ROYAL HIGHLANDER *by James Anton*—A soldier of H.M 42nd (Royal) Highlanders during the Peninsular, South of France & Waterloo Campaigns of the Napoleonic Wars.

CAPTAIN BLAZE *by Elzéar Blaze*—Life in Napoleons Army.

LEJEUNE VOLUME 1 *by Louis-François Lejeune*—The Napoleonic Wars through the Experiences of an Officer on Berthier's Staff.

LEJEUNE VOLUME 2 *by Louis-François Lejeune*—The Napoleonic Wars through the Experiences of an Officer on Berthier's Staff.

CAPTAIN COIGNET *by Jean-Roch Coignet*—A Soldier of Napoleon's Imperial Guard from the Italian Campaign to Russia and Waterloo.

FUSILIER COOPER *by John S. Cooper*—Experiences in the 7th (Royal) Fusiliers During the Peninsular Campaign of the Napoleonic Wars and the American Campaign to New Orleans.

FIGHTING NAPOLEON'S EMPIRE *by Joseph Anderson*—The Campaigns of a British Infantryman in Italy, Egypt, the Peninsular & the West Indies During the Napoleonic Wars.

CHASSEUR BARRES *by Jean-Baptiste Barres*—The experiences of a French Infantryman of the Imperial Guard at Austerlitz, Jena, Eylau, Friedland, in the Peninsular, Lutzen, Bautzen, Zinnwald and Hanau during the Napoleonic Wars.

LEONAUR

ALSO FROM LEONAUR
AVAILABLE IN SOFTCOVER OR HARDCOVER WITH DUST JACKET

CAPTAIN COIGNET *by Jean-Roch Coignet*—A Soldier of Napoleon's Imperial Guard from the Italian Campaign to Russia and Waterloo.

HUSSAR ROCCA *by Albert Jean Michel de Rocca*—A French cavalry officer's experiences of the Napoleonic Wars and his views on the Peninsular Campaigns against the Spanish, British And Guerilla Armies.

MARINES TO 95TH (RIFLES) *by Thomas Fernyhough*—The military experiences of Robert Fernyhough during the Napoleonic Wars.

LIGHT BOB *by Robert Blakeney*—The experiences of a young officer in H.M 28th & 36th regiments of the British Infantry during the Peninsular Campaign of the Napoleonic Wars 1804 - 1814.

WITH WELLINGTON'S LIGHT CAVALRY *by William Tomkinson*—The Experiences of an officer of the 16th Light Dragoons in the Peninsular and Waterloo campaigns of the Napoleonic Wars.

SERGEANT BOURGOGNE *by Adrien Bourgogne*—With Napoleon's Imperial Guard in the Russian Campaign and on the Retreat from Moscow 1812 - 13.

SURTEES OF THE 95TH (RIFLES) *by William Surtees*—A Soldier of the 95th (Rifles) in the Peninsular campaign of the Napoleonic Wars.

SWORDS OF HONOUR *by Henry Newbolt & Stanley L. Wood*—The Careers of Six Outstanding Officers from the Napoleonic Wars, the Wars for India and the American Civil War.

ENSIGN BELL IN THE PENINSULAR WAR *by George Bell*—The Experiences of a young British Soldier of the 34th Regiment 'The Cumberland Gentlemen' in the Napoleonic wars.

HUSSAR IN WINTER *by Alexander Gordon*—A British Cavalry Officer during the retreat to Corunna in the Peninsular campaign of the Napoleonic Wars.

THE COMPLEAT RIFLEMAN HARRIS *by Benjamin Harris as told to and transcribed by Captain Henry Curling, 52nd Regt. of Foot*—The adventures of a soldier of the 95th (Rifles) during the Peninsular Campaign of the Napoleonic Wars.

THE ADVENTURES OF A LIGHT DRAGOON *by George Farmer & G.R. Gleig*—A cavalryman during the Peninsular & Waterloo Campaigns, in captivity & at the siege of Bhurtpore, India.

LEONAUR

ALSO FROM LEONAUR

AVAILABLE IN SOFTCOVER OR HARDCOVER WITH DUST JACKET

THE LIFE OF THE REAL BRIGADIER GERARD VOLUME 1—THE YOUNG HUSSAR 1782-1807 *by Jean-Baptiste De Marbot*—A French Cavalryman Of the Napoleonic Wars at Marengo, Austerlitz, Jena, Eylau & Friedland.

THE LIFE OF THE REAL BRIGADIER GERARD VOLUME 2—IMPERIAL AIDE-DE-CAMP 1807-1811 *by Jean-Baptiste De Marbot*—A French Cavalryman of the Napoleonic Wars at Saragossa, Landshut, Eckmuhl, Ratisbon, Aspern-Essling, Wagram, Busaco & Torres Vedras.

THE LIFE OF THE REAL BRIGADIER GERARD VOLUME 3—COLONEL OF CHASSEURS 1811-1815 *by Jean-Baptiste De Marbot*—A French Cavalryman in the retreat from Moscow, Lutzen, Bautzen, Katzbach, Leipzig, Hanau & Waterloo.

THE INDIAN WAR OF 1864 *by Eugene Ware*—The Experiences of a Young Officer of the 7th Iowa Cavalry on the Western Frontier During the Civil War.

THE MARCH OF DESTINY *by Charles E. Young & V. Devinny*—Dangers of the Trail in 1865 by Charles E. Young & The Story of a Pioneer by V. Devinny, two Accounts of Early Emigrants to Colorado.

CROSSING THE PLAINS *by William Audley Maxwell*—A First Hand Narrative of the Early Pioneer Trail to California in 1857.

CHIEF OF SCOUTS *by William F. Drannan*—A Pilot to Emigrant and Government Trains, Across the Plains of the Western Frontier.

THIRTY-ONE YEARS ON THE PLAINS AND IN THE MOUNTAINS *by William F. Drannan*—William Drannan was born to be a pioneer, hunter, trapper and wagon train guide during the momentous days of the Great American West.

THE INDIAN WARS VOLUNTEER *by William Thompson*—Recollections of the Conflict Against the Snakes, Shoshone, Bannocks, Modocs and Other Native Tribes of the American North West.

THE 4TH TENNESSEE CAVALRY *by George B. Guild*—The Services of Smith's Regiment of Confederate Cavalry by One of its Officers.

COLONEL WORTHINGTON'S SHILOH *by T. Worthington*—The Tennessee Campaign, 1862, by an Officer of the Ohio Volunteers.

FOUR YEARS IN THE SADDLE *by W. L. Curry*—The History of the First Regiment Ohio Volunteer Cavalry in the American Civil War.

LEONAUR

ALSO FROM LEONAUR

AVAILABLE IN SOFTCOVER OR HARDCOVER WITH DUST JACKET

THE RELUCTANT REBEL *by William G. Stevenson*—A young Kentuckian's experiences in the Confederate Infantry & Cavalry during the American Civil War..

BOOTS AND SADDLES *by Elizabeth B. Custer*—The experiences of General Custer's Wife on the Western Plains.

FANNIE BEERS' CIVIL WAR *by Fannie A. Beers*—A Confederate Lady's Experiences of Nursing During the Campaigns & Battles of the American Civil War.

LADY SALE'S AFGHANISTAN *by Florentia Sale*—An Indomitable Victorian Lady's Account of the Retreat from Kabul During the First Afghan War.

THE TWO WARS OF MRS DUBERLY *by Frances Isabella Duberly*—An Intrepid Victorian Lady's Experience of the Crimea and Indian Mutiny.

THE REBELLIOUS DUCHESS *by Paul F. S. Dermoncourt*—The Adventures of the Duchess of Berri and Her Attempt to Overthrow French Monarchy.

LADIES OF WATERLOO *by Charlotte A. Eaton, Magdalene de Lancey & Juana Smith*—The Experiences of Three Women During the Campaign of 1815: Waterloo Days by Charlotte A. Eaton, A Week at Waterloo by Magdalene de Lancey & Juana's Story by Juana Smith.

TWO YEARS BEFORE THE MAST *by Richard Henry Dana. Jr.*—The account of one young man's experiences serving on board a sailing brig—the Penelope—bound for California, between the years 1834-36.

A SAILOR OF KING GEORGE *by Frederick Hoffman*—From Midshipman to Captain—Recollections of War at Sea in the Napoleonic Age 1793-1815.

LORDS OF THE SEA *by A. T. Mahan*—Great Captains of the Royal Navy During the Age of Sail.

COGGESHALL'S VOYAGES: VOLUME 1 *by George Coggeshall*—The Recollections of an American Schooner Captain.

COGGESHALL'S VOYAGES: VOLUME 2 *by George Coggeshall*—The Recollections of an American Schooner Captain.

TWILIGHT OF EMPIRE *by Sir Thomas Ussher & Sir George Cockburn*—Two accounts of Napoleon's Journeys in Exile to Elba and St. Helena: Narrative of Events by Sir Thomas Ussher & Napoleon's Last Voyage: Extract of a diary by Sir George Cockburn.

LEONAUR

ALSO FROM LEONAUR
AVAILABLE IN SOFTCOVER OR HARDCOVER WITH DUST JACKET

ESCAPE FROM THE FRENCH *by Edward Boys*—A Young Royal Navy Midshipman's Adventures During the Napoleonic War.

THE VOYAGE OF H.M.S. PANDORA *by Edward Edwards R. N. & George Hamilton, edited by Basil Thomson*—In Pursuit of the Mutineers of the Bounty in the South Seas—1790-1791.

MEDUSA *by J. B. Henry Savigny and Alexander Correard and Charlotte-Adélaïde Dard* —Narrative of a Voyage to Senegal in 1816 & The Sufferings of the Picard Family After the Shipwreck of the Medusa.

THE SEA WAR OF 1812 VOLUME 1 *by A. T. Mahan*—A History of the Maritime Conflict.

THE SEA WAR OF 1812 VOLUME 2 *by A. T. Mahan*—A History of the Maritime Conflict.

WETHERELL OF H. M. S. HUSSAR *by John Wetherell*—The Recollections of an Ordinary Seaman of the Royal Navy During the Napoleonic Wars.

THE NAVAL BRIGADE IN NATAL *by C. R. N. Burne*—With the Guns of H. M. S. Terrible & H. M. S. Tartar during the Boer War 1899-1900.

THE VOYAGE OF H. M. S. BOUNTY *by William Bligh*—The True Story of an 18th Century Voyage of Exploration and Mutiny.

SHIPWRECK! *by William Gilly*—The Royal Navy's Disasters at Sea 1793-1849.

KING'S CUTTERS AND SMUGGLERS: 1700-1855 *by E. Keble Chatterton*—A unique period of maritime history-from the beginning of the eighteenth to the middle of the nineteenth century when British seamen risked all to smuggle valuable goods from wool to tea and spirits from and to the Continent.

CONFEDERATE BLOCKADE RUNNER *by John Wilkinson*—The Personal Recollections of an Officer of the Confederate Navy.

NAVAL BATTLES OF THE NAPOLEONIC WARS *by W. H. Fitchett*—Cape St. Vincent, the Nile, Cadiz, Copenhagen, Trafalgar & Others.

PRISONERS OF THE RED DESERT *by R. S. Gwatkin-Williams*—The Adventures of the Crew of the Tara During the First World War.

U-BOAT WAR 1914-1918 *by James B. Connolly/Karl von Schenk*—Two Contrasting Accounts from Both Sides of the Conflict at Sea D uring the Great War.

LEONAUR

ALSO FROM LEONAUR

AVAILABLE IN SOFTCOVER OR HARDCOVER WITH DUST JACKET

IRON TIMES WITH THE GUARDS *by An O. E. (G. P. A. Fildes)*—The Experiences of an Officer of the Coldstream Guards on the Western Front During the First World War.

THE GREAT WAR IN THE MIDDLE EAST: 1 *by W. T. Massey*—The Desert Campaigns & How Jerusalem Was Won---two classic accounts in one volume.

THE GREAT WAR IN THE MIDDLE EAST: 2 *by W. T. Massey*—Allenby's Final Triumph.

SMITH-DORRIEN *by Horace Smith-Dorrien*—Isandlwhana to the Great War.

1914 *by Sir John French*—The Early Campaigns of the Great War by the British Commander.

GRENADIER *by E. R. M. Fryer*—The Recollections of an Officer of the Grenadier Guards throughout the Great War on the Western Front.

BATTLE, CAPTURE & ESCAPE *by George Pearson*—The Experiences of a Canadian Light Infantryman During the Great War.

DIGGERS AT WAR *by R. Hugh Knyvett & G. P. Cuttriss*—"Over There" With the Australians by R. Hugh Knyvett and Over the Top With the Third Australian Division by G. P. Cuttriss. Accounts of Australians During the Great War in the Middle East, at Gallipoli and on the Western Front.

HEAVY FIGHTING BEFORE US *by George Brenton Laurie*—The Letters of an Officer of the Royal Irish Rifles on the Western Front During the Great War.

THE CAMELIERS *by Oliver Hogue*—A Classic Account of the Australians of the Imperial Camel Corps During the First World War in the Middle East.

RED DUST *by Donald Black*—A Classic Account of Australian Light Horsemen in Palestine During the First World War.

THE LEAN, BROWN MEN *by Angus Buchanan*—Experiences in East Africa During the Great War with the 25th Royal Fusiliers—the Legion of Frontiersmen.

THE NIGERIAN REGIMENT IN EAST AFRICA *by W. D. Downes*—On Campaign During the Great War 1916-1918.

THE 'DIE-HARDS' IN SIBERIA *by John Ward*—With the Middlesex Regiment Against the Bolsheviks 1918-19.

LEONAUR

ALSO FROM LEONAUR
AVAILABLE IN SOFTCOVER OR HARDCOVER WITH DUST JACKET

FARAWAY CAMPAIGN *by F. James*—Experiences of an Indian Army Cavalry Officer in Persia & Russia During the Great War.

REVOLT IN THE DESERT *by T. E. Lawrence*—An account of the experiences of one remarkable British officer's war from his own perspective.

MACHINE-GUN SQUADRON *by A. M. G.*—The 20th Machine Gunners from British Yeomanry Regiments in the Middle East Campaign of the First World War.

A GUNNER'S CRUSADE *by Antony Bluett*—The Campaign in the Desert, Palestine & Syria as Experienced by the Honourable Artillery Company During the Great War .

DESPATCH RIDER *by W. H. L. Watson*—The Experiences of a British Army Motorcycle Despatch Rider During the Opening Battles of the Great War in Europe.

TIGERS ALONG THE TIGRIS *by E. J. Thompson*—The Leicestershire Regiment in Mesopotamia During the First World War.

HEARTS & DRAGONS *by Charles R. M. F. Crutwell*—The 4th Royal Berkshire Regiment in France and Italy During the Great War, 1914-1918.

INFANTRY BRIGADE: 1914 *by John Ward*—The Diary of a Commander of the 15th Infantry Brigade, 5th Division, British Army, During the Retreat from Mons.

DOING OUR 'BIT' *by Ian Hay*—Two Classic Accounts of the Men of Kitchener's 'New Army' During the Great War including *The First 100,000 & All In It.*

AN EYE IN THE STORM *by Arthur Ruhl*—An American War Correspondent's Experiences of the First World War from the Western Front to Gallipoli-and Beyond.

STAND & FALL *by Joe Cassells*—With the Middlesex Regiment Against the Bolsheviks 1918-19.

RIFLEMAN MACGILL'S WAR *by Patrick MacGill*—A Soldier of the London Irish During the Great War in Europe including *The Amateur Army, The Red Horizon & The Great Push.*

WITH THE GUNS *by C. A. Rose & Hugh Dalton*—Two First Hand Accounts of British Gunners at War in Europe During World War 1- Three Years in France with the Guns and With the British Guns in Italy.

THE BUSH WAR DOCTOR *by Robert V. Dolbey*—The Experiences of a British Army Doctor During the East African Campaign of the First World War.

Lightning Source UK Ltd.
Milton Keynes UK
UKOW041828131212

203596UK00002B/11/P